READINGS FROM THE
ROOTS OF WISDOM

Third Edition

Helen Buss Mitchell
Howard Community College

WADSWORTH
™
THOMSON LEARNING

Australia • Canada • Mexico • Singapore • Spain • United Kingdom • United States

Philosophy Editor: Peter Adams
Assistant Editor: Kara Kindstrom
Editorial Assistant: Chalida Anusasananan
Marketing Manager: Dave Garrison
Print Buyer: April Vanderbilt
Permissions Editor: Bob Kauser

Production Service: Forbes Mill Press
Copy Editor: Robin Gold
Cover Designer: Laurie Anderson
Cover Illustrator: Amy Kolman
Compositor: Wolf Creek Press
Printer: Webcom, Ltd.

Printed in Canada

3 4 5 6 7 05 04

For more information, contact
Wadsworth/Thomson Learning
10 Davis Drive
Belmont, CA 94002-3098
USA

For more information about our products, contact us:
Thomson Learning Academic Resource Center
1-800-423-0563
http://www.wadsworth.com

International Headquarters
Thomson Learning
International Division
290 Harbor Drive, 2nd Floor
Stamford, CT 06902-7477
USA

UK/Europe/Middle East/South Africa
Thomson Learning
Berkshire House
168-173 High Holborn
London WC1V 7AA
United Kingdom

Asia
Thomson Learning
60 Albert Complex, #15-01
Singapore 189969

Canada
Nelson Thomson Learning
1120 Birchmount Road
Toronto, Ontario M1K 5G4
Canada

Library of Congress Cataloging-in-Publication Data

Mitchell, Helen Buss.
    Readings from the roots of wisdom / Helen Buss Mitchell. -- 3rd ed.
        p.cm.
    Includes bibliographical references.
    ISBN 0-534-56111-X
    1. Philosophy--Introductions. 2. Philosophy, Comparative. I. Title.

BD21 .M47 2001
100--dc21   00-054987

This book is printed on acid-free recycled paper.

In memory of Ruth and Joe who launched me

For Joe and Jason who sustained me

To the philosophers—women and men—who inspired me

Contents

Descriptive Contents

CHAPTER 1: WHY PHILOSOPHY?

1.1: *Republic* **by Plato:** This famous allegory depicts what Plato thinks is our position—as prisoners in the world of the senses, thinking shadows to be reality, and unaware of the world outside the cave where the sun of enlightenment reveals the perfect prototypes for everything that exists. Making your way out of the cave is what "doing" philosophy is all about.

1.2: *Clouds* **by Aristophanes:** In this play Socrates runs a Think-shop in which he teaches students to make the weaker argument appear the stronger. Laws appear to exist for reasons of expediency only; when no longer expedient, laws may be revised. Aristophanes wished to lampoon the Sophists, and he chose the best-known philosopher in Athens as his target.

1.3: *Is There an African Philosophy?* **by Innocent Onyewuenyi:** Philosophy is a universal human enterprise in which each culture creates its own unity and meaning out of some basic themes, using its particular conception of life. Professor Onyewuenyi describes African ontology (being is dynamic rather than static); epistemology (knowledge or wisdom consists in understanding the forces of being, their cohesion and interaction, rather than book learning); and ethics (an ontological and communal understanding of morality leads to objective and universal standards according to which injustice means loss in "joy of life" rather than material damage).

1.4: *I, Rigoberta Menchú* **by Rigoberta Menchú:** This description of the welcoming of a new baby into the Maya-Quiché community reveals a blend of Indian and Roman Catholic traditions. Present events can be explained only in the context of a living past, as ritual blends worship and work into a seamless fabric of meaning. Rigoberta Menchú won the 1992 Nobel Peace Prize for her work in organizing the peasant people of Guatemala. She learned Spanish so she could understand the worldview of the landowners whose economic and social system she saw as oppressing her people.

1.5: *The Tao Te Ching:* These selections from the classic Taoist text of 2500 years ago reveal the timeless wisdom found in nature and within the human person. Balance is the key. Know when to work and when to rest. Be like the *Tao* and learn to operate with effortless efficiency. As the source of everything, the *Tao* cannot be described without compromising its original wholeness, but we can see it at work—taking no credit, demanding no loyalty, yet moving the natural system from winter to spring

CHAPTER 2: REALITY AND BEING

2.1: *The Leviathan* **by Thomas Hobbes:** Our only point of contact with the world, according to Hobbes, is through our senses of seeing, hearing, touching, tasting, smelling. What they reveal is that all reality is matter in motion. Machines are matter, but so are thoughts and emotions. Ideas in your mind began as sense impressions. Matter, in short, explains everything.

2.2: *Flatland* **by Edwin Abbot:** When a sphere arrives in Flatland to preach the Gospel of the Three Dimensions, Flatlanders resist this heresy mightily. Abbot's 1882 classic captures our own reaction to living in a four-dimensional world, only three of which are perceptible to us. When the sphere pulls an intellectual square out of Flatland to demonstrate "reality," the enlightened square begins asking difficult questions about the next dimension.

2.3: *The African Philosophical Tradition* **by Lancinay Keita:** Professor Keita argues in this selection that ancient Egyptian cosmology was a complementarity of empiricism and metaphysics—the first providing facts about the world, the second explaining them. The Greeks, by accepting the empiricism of the Egyptians but being less enthusiastic about their metaphysics, broke the easy union that had existed. European philosophy derives from a Greek worldview in which the material world is perceived as opposed to the metaphysical world, rather than in harmony with it as had been the case in Egypt.

2.4: *Alice's Adventures in Wonderland* **by Lewis Carroll:** When a little English girl falls down a rabbit hole, much of what she thought she knew in the above ground world seems quite useless. The underground world seems to operate on entirely different principles. As she keeps reminding herself of what she knows, Alice becomes less and less sure of who she is. Perhaps she has changed into another child, who has a completely different base of knowledge, or perhaps reality itself has changed.

2.5: *Lives of the Buddha* **from Buddhist Scriptures:** What does a *bodhisattva* do in the presence of a starving tigress who is too exhausted and weak from giving birth to feed herself or her kittens? He sacrifices himself to feed them, crossing the ocean of birth and death and, in the process, revealing the deep compassion that this view of what is entails. This story and the tale of the Buddha's death underscore the Buddhist notion of the interconnectedness of all things.

CHAPTER 3: HUMAN NATURE

3.1: *Existentialism as a Humanism* **by Jean-Paul Sartre:** If there is no God, there is no law giver, no one to tell me who or what I am. For atheistic existentialists such as Sartre this is a liberating realization. The task of a human lifetime is to face life's uncertainties with existential courage and, in choosing and being accountable for your choices, to make a self for yourself.

3.2: *Genesis,* **Chapters 1 and 2 from the Bible:** These separate and complete accounts of the creation, from two different oral traditions, offer contrasting views of the creation of woman and man. In Chapter One, which begins "In the beginning, when God created the heavens and the earth . . . ," creation occurs hierarchically from simple to complex; woman and man are created together last and jointly given dominion over the earth. Chapter Two tells the story of Adam, created first and lonely, being shown (and naming) other created things until finally God takes one of Adam's ribs to create Eve.

3.3: *Aristotle and the Politicization of the Soul* **by Elizabeth V. Spelman:** Aristotle's political argument that men are by nature the rulers of women is said to rest on his metaphysical claim that the rational part of the soul must rule over the irrational part. In her examination of Aristotle's logic, Spelman finds that each of these claims is used to justify the other—in other words, the argument seems to be circular and, therefore, invalid.

3.4: *Person and Community in Traditional African Thought* **by Ifeanyi A. Menkiti:** In contrast with the Western world, African traditional thought emphasizes the communal over the individual. As a result, Professor Menkiti says, the community defines the person as person, rather than as some isolated static quality of rationality, will, or memory. Personhood must be attained in a kind of ontological progression throughout one's life, achieved under the instruction of the organically constituted community.

3.5: *Code of the Lifemaker* **by James P. Hogan:** Playing with the idea of AI, or artificial intelligence, Hogan tells the story of a robot race established by an alien civilization more than a million years ago. Through a series of environmental and mechanical catastrophes, the robots achieve genetic variability and recombination, competition, selection, and adaptation—all the essentials for continuing evolution. Are they a life form?

and political turmoil involving Christians, Jews, and Muslims as well as among sects within Islam, this commentary is intended as a guide for seeking and finding religious truth. Too much knowledge, Maimonides reminds us, like too much honey, can be harmful to our health and wellbeing.

5.5: *Beyond Consciousness* by Shunryu Suzuki: In this selection Shunryu Suzuki describes *zazen,* the Zen Buddhist practice of sitting meditation. Our true nature, he says, is beyond our conscious experience and must be the foundation for both the practice of Zen and for enlightenment. Seeking enlightenment as if seeking a bright star in the sky, one may be tempted to think the bright star is enlightenment. This, however, is the way of self and object. Emptiness of mind, or beginner's mind, is a state of absolute calmness and emptiness that understands that one thing flows into another and cannot be grasped.

Chapter 6: The Search for Truth

6.1: *Dialogues Concerning Natural Religion* by David Hume: If we want to know the truth about religion, Hume suggests we go no further than our reasoning can logically take us. In this parody of the teleological or design argument for the existence of God, Hume suggests the evidence found in the world might indicate its creation by an inept craftsman or even a committee.

6.2: *Zen and the Art of Motorcycle Maintenance* by Robert Pirsig: Phaedrus, the protagonist of this novel, explains that pursuit of scientific truth caused his mental breakdown. Coining a law: "The number of rational hypotheses that can explain any given phenomenon is infinite," Phaedrus realizes its implications. If the number of hypotheses grows faster than the experimental method can test and eliminate them, the results of any experiment must be inconclusive and the goal of scientific knowledge can never be reached.

6.3: *On Indian-White Relations: A Point of View* by N. Scott Momaday: Does the sun live in the sky or in the earth? If he answers as the white world has taught him, Pulitzer Prize winner N. Scott Momaday will reply that the sun lives in the sky. But, if he remembers the Kiowa sun-watcher who prays the sun out of the ground, he must answer that the sun lives in the earth. Each of these widely diverging worldviews represents a truth. The question is: How can people who hold these differing views learn to speak the truth to each other?

6.4: *African Logical Heritage and Contemporary Life* by S. A. Mwanahewa: Many of the world's people are illiterate. This does not, however, mean that they have no way to test for truth. Professor Mwanahewa argues that the scientific approach of logic and the artistic approach of orature (oral literature) can benefit from and complement one another. Whereas logic uses rules, the illiterate community uses the structure of language to convey truth in proverbs, riddles, sayings, and songs.

6.5: *Letters to Bernard of Clairvaux and the Mainz Prelates* by Hildegard of Bingen: Like other mystics, Hildegard of Bingen experienced personal revelation from God in the form of visions. She is one of several medieval women who asserted truth claims, using God as the guarantor. In the first letter, she explains her lifelong "gift of vision," and in her second letter she defends her decision to disobey a direct order from her clerical superiors. Knowing the truth from God, she felt compelled to ignore earthly authority.

Chapter 7: Aesthetic Experience

7.1: *Republic* by Plato: Is art two steps removed from what is real and, therefore, more likely to confuse and mislead us? According to Plato, the answer is yes. If the purpose of art is *mimesis* or representation, we must admit that art is very far from the perfect Forms; the best art can do is copy the copies of the Forms found in this imperfect world—not very inspiring.

7.2: *Poetics* **by Aristotle:** Like all excellent students, Aristotle learned from his mentor Plato and then went on to become an original thinker. Agreeing that art is imitation, Aristotle finds art to be, like philosophy, concerned with universals rather than with particulars. The tragic playwrights, he believes, can imitate life in such a way that we explore the consequences of our actions vicariously and are cleansed of the negative emotions that can destroy our happiness and the stability of our communities.

7.3: *Zen in the Art of Archery* **by Eugen Herrigel:** Like all the great arts of Japan— painting, flower arranging, calligraphy—archery is a door to the "Great Doctrine." Herrigel's experiences with a master reveal to him that the art of archery can be practiced only in a state of emptiness and detachment. Concentrating deeply, the archer bows to the target, offering the bow and arrow "like consecrated gifts," releases the arrow, and slowly expels his breath before lowering his arm.

7.4: *Arrow of God* **by Chinua Achebe:** This gifted Nigerian writer describes a similar process to the one described in selection 7.3. Edogo, eldest son of Ezeulu, is carving a mask for the Festival of Pumpkin Leaves while his father, Chief Priest of Ulu, god of the six Ibo villages, struggles against the new ways of the West. In this selection, we see Edogo finishing a mask through which a new ancestral spirit will appear to humans. Like Herrigel, Edogo enters a sacred space, the spirit-house that faces the forest, empties himself, and allows the art to emerge.

7.5: *The Cultural Importance of Art* **by Susanne K. Langer:** Is art a cultural frill that should fall to the budget ax during harsh economic times? American philosopher Susanne Langer argues that art is essential to human life and even civilization because art makes sense of the inner experience of emotions in the same way language makes sense of outer experience. Art stabilizes culture by helping us understand

and manage what we are feeling. Without it, we learn how to feel from those forces that shape popular culture—for better or worse.

CHAPTER 8: POLITICAL PHILOSOPHY

8.1: *Treatise of Civil Government* **by John Locke:** Are we capable of ruling ourselves with only minimal government direction? That is the conclusion of political theorist John Locke, who describes people in the state of nature as possessing "natural rights" to life, liberty, and property. Because these rights are God-given, the job of government is to preserve them.

8.2: *Declaration of Sentiments, Seneca Falls* **by Elizabeth Cady Stanton:** Using the Declaration of Independence as a model, Elizabeth Cady Stanton drafted this document for the first Women's Rights Convention held in America in July of 1848. "We hold these truths to be self-evident:" it states, "that all men and women are created equal." Taking revolutionary rhetoric seriously, Stanton catalogues the "injuries and usurpations on the part of men toward women" as a parallel to the grievances of the colonists against King George III of England.

8.3: *The Fuzzy Social Contract* **by Bart Kosko:** Outside the world of A and not-A we need "fuzzy thinking." Our air conditioners use it, running at full blast when the room is hot and then gradually slowing down as the air cools. Far beyond "on" and "off," they operate according to the rules of fuzzy logic. Applying this principle to the social contract, Kosko describes the fuzzy agreement the individual actually makes with the government of the United States by virtue of being a citizen.

8.4: *The Speeches of Malcolm X at Harvard* **by Malcolm X:** Speaking at Harvard in 1964, Malcolm X describes how both the North and the South as well as both political parties deny real political power to African Americans. Black Nationalism, as a political philosophy, an economic philosophy, and a social philosophy, when combined with the religion of Islam, provides all that is needed to solve what Malcolm calls the problems in the "so-called Negro community."

8.5: *The End of the Golden Road* **by Nicholas D. Kristof:** Kristof traces waning enthusiasm for communism in China in part to belief among ordinary Chinese that their leaders are no longer "worthy of the mandate of heaven." In the twelfth century B.C.E., the Duke of Zhou had described the political legitimacy of divine right in terms of the mandate of heaven. If the leaders are virtuous and the people content, a regime endures; but, as the Duke of Zhou had advised, "the mandate of heaven is not easily preserved." Mao Zedong had won it because of a public perception of virtue. Today that perception is changing and the idea of the mandate is again threatened.

CHAPTER 9: SOCIAL PHILOSOPHY

9.1: *Utilitarianism* **by John Stuart Mill:** How can we be sure justice is done? One method, proposed by Jeremy Bentham and John Stuart Mill, is to ask ourselves what will produce the greatest good in the world at large—and then do that. Called utilitarianism, this philosophy is based on utility, or social usefulness. Advocates of this philosophy suggest that, no matter what high-sounding words we use to describe our aims, they all come down to increasing pleasure, decreasing pain or both.

9.2: *Human Rights in a Divided Society* **by Ignacio Ellacuría, S.J.:** Thomas Aquinas's medieval theories of the common good and human rights can still speak to the modern world. We must simply historicize them: that is, apply them in a living, historical context. Taking El Salvador as his laboratory, Ellacuría rejects utilitarian arguments that balance the sufferings of some against the greater benefits of others. The higher pleasures of the elite can never compensate for denying the masses education and the basic tools of survival. In his view, the common

good can never be divided, and those who prefer their own private good to the common good cannot call themselves ethical.

9.3: *A Vindication of the Rights of Women* **by Mary Wollstonecraft:** Published in 1792, this book seems strangely topical two hundred years later. In it Wollstonecraft responds to a proposal by Talleyrand that French girls be educated in school only until the age of eight, at which time they be returned to their homes to learn the vital skills that will make them pleasing to a man. If woman is not educated to be the companion of man, Wollstonecraft asserts, knowledge and virtue will not progress and children cannot be expected to become patriots. Justice for women is, in Wollstonecraft's view, necessary to the stability and success of the nation.

9.4: *Age, Race, Class, and Sex: Women Redefining the Difference* **by Audre Lorde:** The so-called "first wave" of feminism (which Mary Wollstonecraft represents) insisted that women were inherently as rational as men. Its arguments, and the conditions of women's lives it described, reflected a white, middle-class world. In the "second wave" of feminism (which Audre Lorde represents), feminists have been challenged to acknowledge differences among women. For women of color, Mary Wollstonecraft's arguments might not address the most significant aspects of oppression.

9.5: *Ender's Game* **by Orson Scott Card:** Ender Wiggin is selected by the state, taken from his family and home planet, and brutally trained in the art of high-tech, computer-managed war. At the age of eleven, he is put through the rigors of Command School and, after passing the final exam, learns that the battles were not simulations. He was the unwitting commander, and now the enemy is destroyed. Proclaimed a hero, he becomes instead a SPEAKER FOR THE DEAD, telling the enemy's story and looking for a place to safely deposit the cocoon of its next generation. Is there such a thing as a "just war"?

CHAPTER 10: ETHICS

10.1: *Foundations for the Metaphysics of Morals* **by Immanuel Kant:** As a deontologist, Kant believes morality lies in doing one's duty, regardless of the consequences. If you want to know what is the right thing to do in any situation, Kant suggests, ask yourself whether you would want everyone who encounters the same situation to act as you are about to act. If you would wish this, you are about to do the right thing; if you would not, what you propose to do is wrong. This position offers a clear contrast to John Stuart Mill's utilitarianism (in the last chapter).

10.2: *Borderlands/La Frontera* **by Gloria Anzaldúa:** If we want to stop treating people and nations as the "other," Gloria Anzaldúa argues, we must adopt a new consciousness that leads to altered behavior. Living on the borderlands, the mestiza understands the dynamics of shifting identity. Mestiza consciousness may help all of us break down dichotomies of race and gender and transcend their destructive consequences: rape, violence, and war. Majority people and cultures must take back what Jungian psychology calls their "shadow" and overcome the subject/object dualism that creates the "other."

10.3: *Speaking from the Heart* **by Rita Manning:** The ancient Greeks had offered an alternative to deontology and utilitarianism, known as virtue ethics. Rather than focusing on what to do, the goal was the development of a virtuous character. For philosophers such as Aristotle, the highest human quality or the source of our human "virtuosity" was our reason. Modern virtue theorists, such as Rita Manning, substitute the ideal of a caring self for the older ideal of a rational self. After all, they observe, we have reasoned our way into war, slavery, and other immoral actions. But a caring self, rooted in relationships, will be more likely to lead us to virtue.

10.4: *The Moral Foundations of an African Culture* **by Kwasi Wiredu:** Professor Wiredu sets forth an Akan ethic rooted in a strong sense of communal belonging and, at the same time, a sense of the irreducibility of human dignity. However socially inept a person may be, he or she is still a direct gift of God and a product of the intimacy between a man and a woman. Foreigners have traditionally benefited from this Akan communalism because they have been seen first as fellow human beings and second as cut off from kinship supports and in need of hospitality.

10.5: *The Te of Piglet* **by Benjamin Hoff:** Taoism, a way of living in harmony with the *Tao* or Way of the Universe, had its origins in a time before what Hoff calls The Great Separation of humans from the rest of nature. Its chief principles are Natural Simplicity, Effortless Action, Spontaneity, and Compassion. Hoff contrasts Taoism with Confucianism and its principles of Propriety, Benevolence, Loyalty, Good Faith, Duty, and Justice. Following Taoist principles could lead us to ethical concern for other animals, and even for the environment itself.

Preface

Those who take the multicultural challenge seriously are sometimes overwhelmed by the array of possible readings and unclear about how to blend them with the Western discourse. A smorgasbord of selections can effectively convey the message that philosophy is not an exclusively European/American enterprise, and yet both teacher and student may be hard pressed to find any thematic unity. *Readings from the Roots of Wisdom* chooses a middle path that blends new readings with traditional Western ones, setting the unfamiliar in the context of the familiar and enriching both in the juxtaposition.

Keyed to the structure of *Roots of Wisdom, Readings from the Roots of Wisdom* would be an appropriate adjunct for any introductory philosophy course. Like the text, *Readings from the Roots of Wisdom* introduces the student to a multicultural world, one in which philosophical ideas emerge from Asia and Africa as well as from Europe and the Americas, and one in which women as well as men are philosophers. As in life, wisdom appears in many forms—ancient Taoist wisdom and contemporary science fiction, medieval Jewish and Islamic philosophy, and African versions of natural theology.

Each chapter begins with classic Western ideas and includes Buddhist, Taoist, African, and often Spanish-language and indigenous variations, the voices of women, and philosophical fiction. Section introductions define the parameters of metaphysics, epistemology, and axiology, and each chapter—as well as each reading—is framed with context-building and summary material. Specialized vocabulary appears in boldface in the text and is defined in a glossary. Explaining the worldview of an African artist or a Buddhist monk can be daunting, but a short story or novel with this as its theme can be much more accessible.

Fiction brings philosophy from the abstract to the concrete by placing ideas in actual historical and "real life" situations. *Readings from the Roots of Wisdom* introduces students to more lengthy primary source material than they meet in most texts, and it balances these nonfiction readings with philosophical fiction. This feature encourages students to look for philosophy in life as well as in textbooks and to find its issues on the evening news, in the newspaper, at the movies, on TV, and in their own lives. It also provides rich source material for student papers, group discussions, individual analysis, and reflection.

The overall theme of the text and reader is the universality of the search for wisdom and the cross-cultural commonality of issues as well as the richness that unique cultural and gender perspectives provide. Students are invited to see their problems as neither unique to themselves nor peculiar to the beginning of a new millennium and to consider the responses of intelligent and wise women and men from many times and places to universal human questions.

Topics are the traditional ones: (1) Why Philosophy? (2) Reality and Being, (3) Human Nature, (4) Philosophy and God, (5) Knowledge and the Mind, (6) The Search for Truth, (7) Aesthetic Experience, (8) Political Philosophy, (9) Social Philosophy, and (10) Ethics. The first four address metaphysics, the next three epistemology, and the final three axiology; they move through time from the age of Socrates, the Buddha, and Lao-tzu to the present.

New to This Edition

In this third edition, I have responded to requests from my own students and from formal and informal reviewers who have requested shorter and more readable translations. Wherever possible, I abridged to present and showcase the heart of the argument. My guiding principles have been clarity of thought and freshness of language. The selection from Hobbes has been modernized for grammar and spelling. Others have been put into the kind of direct speaking that students respond to. My assumption has been that, during their own times and writing for their own peers, these philosophers achieved similar goals. In some cases, however, what once counted as elegant and erudite writing has become cumbersome and unclear.

There are also several new selections. Six short chapters from the Taoist classic *Tao Te Ching* in the first chapter bring that tradition into this mix of thinkers and thought systems for the first time. New to Chapter 4 is a key section of Augustine's *City of God,* giving him the anchor position for this chapter on Philosophy and God. And, Aristotle joins Plato in Chapter 7 for a debate on the role of art as imitation and its relative value in this role.

For those who use this reader with its accompanying text *Roots of Wisdom,* connections between the two have been strengthened. Each continues to stand alone, of course, but together they are better partners.

Each chapter begins by defining the issue and setting up the basic questions to be addressed by all five of the readings. The length of the selections—from one to nineteen pages—yields a chapter of about thirty pages. The readings form a unity, so any or all of them may be used. Next follows a general preview of all the readings to underscore the focus of the chapter, provide a context for student reading, and explain how this chapter follows the previous one and links with its ideas.

Each individual reading is preceded by a brief introductory section (Preparing to Read), highlighting some questions to keep in mind, and followed by an afterword (Continuing to Think), specifically related to that selection. Each chapter concludes with a summary of all five readings, indicating their thematic unity, and some general questions, inviting comparison and perhaps contrast between and among the various selections. Summary questions also point toward the next chapter.

Organization and Features

The diversity of the readings provides a unique opportunity for critical thinking as students consider how much we are alike as human beings and to what extent gender, culture, historical circumstances, and social class influence how particular individuals, groups, and societies see the world and their place within it. Questions offer bridges to popular culture and help students see the philosophical enterprise as a universal one and as significant in their own lives.

Plato's Cave Allegory in Chapter 1 appears with excerpts from *Clouds* by the comic playwright Aristophanes, a contemporary of Plato and Socrates. In the play, which he attended, Socrates is depicted (unfairly) as a Sophist—one who charges money to teach the skillful manipulation of words and arguments. Indeed the charges later brought against him seem to resonate against this caricature. And, the Cave Allegory comes from *Republic,* Plato's utopia, which can be compared with Charlotte Perkins Gilman's *Herland,* written more than 2,000 years later.

I have found philosophical science fiction novels, like *Ender's Game* and *Code of the Lifemaker,* valuable because they raise questions about ethics, God, and human nature just as effectively as traditional readings do, and students are more open to a genre they might already read for pleasure. These works and more traditional fiction, like *Siddhārtha* and *Arrow of God,* can also provide the basis for a reflective paper that analyzes a literary theme in philosophical terms.

By collecting and grouping less-well-known non-Western and women thinkers under traditional topics, this reader offers the philosophy teacher an effective way to enlarge the canon without neglecting the Western tradition. Students who read Benjamin Ewuku Oguah's article in Chapter 4, for instance, will encounter not only an African thinker but also scholastic natural theology, which Oguah finds in the language of the Fantis of Ghana. And Elizabeth Cady Stanton's *Declaration of Sentiments* from Chapter 8 throws new light on natural rights arguments by asserting that "all men and women are created equal." Finally, in Chapter 9 Ignacio Ellacuría, S.J. reflects on traditional theories of justice and ethics in contemporary El Salvador.

There is the very modern in Bart Kosko's *Fuzzy Social Contract,* which applies the fuzzy logic of air conditioners to the relationship between the individual and the state; in Nicholas Kristof's *The End of the Golden Road,* which lays part of the blame for the failure of communism in China on the people's belief that their leaders have lost the Mandate of Heaven—the traditional divine right justification; in Gloria Anzaldúa's *Borderlands/La Frontera;* in Audre Lorde's *Age, Race, Class, and Sex;* in Benjamin Hoff's *The Te of Piglet;* and in Rigoberta Menchú's memoir of her life as an Indian woman in Guatemala. And, there is the very ancient in traditional Buddhist and Zen Buddhist texts, some of which date back 2,500 years.

Juxtaposed as they are in this reader, the very old and the very new speak across centuries to what may seem like uniquely contemporary problems. Students are always pleased, and sometimes astounded, to discover that people in other times and places have faced problems similar to their own. Sor Juana Inés de la Cruz and Hildegard of Bingen sound oddly modern as they insist they know what is right and are determined to do it—no matter what the cost. Edwin Abbot's 1882 classic *Flatland* shows us that we are no less parochial than the square who refuses to believe there is a third dimension.

I have followed four major cultural lines—the European, the African, the Asian (using Buddhism and Taoism) and Peoples of the Americas—Spanish-language and indigenous thinkers. Meeting these four cultures in each section, students can begin to form some concept of the basic worldviews of each as they move through the reader. It would be possible to assign some students to follow the African line, others the Asian line, and still others the European line or Peoples of the Americas line throughout the semester or quarter and structure small group activities around their observations.

Another variation might involve assigning some students fiction selections and others nonfiction readings, inviting discussion about which is the more effective way to present the key ideas of each chapter. Women students might particularly relish reading those of their own gender, but male students could also provide an interesting perspective after reading women philosophers. One additional possibility is comparing the old with the new, the ancient with the modern, looking for commonalities as well as points of departure.

Acknowledgments

When I took my first philosophy course at Hood College, it was love at first sight. Paul Mehl showed me how easy it is to fall in love with wisdom and what a thrilling ride it offers. Tom Scheye and Frank Cunningham from Loyola College opened my eyes to the possibilities that emerge when literature and philosophy meet, and Frank Haig, S.J. helped me see the philosophical implications of modern physics. Kimpei Munei introduced me to the thought systems of Africa while he was an AFS exchange student in our home. From my colleagues at Howard Community College—especially Dawn Barnes, Valerie Costantini, Yifei Gan, Ron Roberson, and Jane Winer—I have learned how art illuminates the philosophical quest. Marc Edwards recommended *Code of the Lifemaker.* And, Susan Myers, of the Howard Community College library, found several hard-to-find books and located on the Internet the original version of *Herland* from Gilman's 1915 magazine.

Bruce Casteel keeps the beginner's mind that makes life always fresh; Heffer, Edna Brandt, Dianne Connelly, Dee Weir, Betty Caldwell, and Julia Vanek live the creative synthesis between east and west; Rich' Walter makes the complex clear when he speaks about Zen or the brain; Victor Young lives the harmony of Native American culture; Jason Mitchell and Shannon Tenney remind me how twenty-somethings see the world; Doc Costantini, Sam Berkowitz, and Mike Giuliano keep me connected with classic and modern foreign films; the HCC and First Thursday book clubs help me remember how much literature in general and the voices of women in particular have to teach us; and Sara Baum, Marge Cangiano, JoAnn Hawkins, Marla Schreck, Janis Cripe, Amy Hannon, Marie Siracusa, and Mary Young inspire me with their deep spirituality. To all these wisdom keepers from my past and present, I offer my gratitude.

Joe and Jason Mitchell have welcomed this book and its older sibling, *Roots of Wisdom,* into the family and graciously made space for them. My parents, Ruth and Joe Buss, who started me on the search for wisdom, embodied it throughout their own, rich lives. Tammy Goldfeld was wise enough to see that a text and reader would complement each other well, and Peter Adams has encouraged their further evolution into new editions, demonstrating how critical a strong philosophy editor is to the entire process and offering unfailing support along with wit and wisdom when I needed them most. Bob Kauser cheerfully helped me chase down permissions. Robin Gold, as she did with the text, made the production process efficient and smooth and the creation of a polished product a pleasure. Finally, Joe Mitchell kept our lives going while I was tethered to my computer, inspiring me with his love of opera and history; Jason Mitchell brought books and movies to my attention that I might otherwise have missed; and Shannon Tenney used her eagle eye to catch many small but significant errors during the final proofreading.

My reviewers provided sage guidance on the choice of selections and eloquently described their own classroom needs: Sara Goering, University of Colorado; Greg Weis, University of South Carolina, Aiken; John King, University of North Carolina, Greensboro; Marina Oshana, California State University, Sacramento; Mathhias Schulte, Montgomery College; and Philip Ruge-Jones, Texas Lutheran University. This essential input shaped the book throughout its development. And, John Hernandez and Jose Lopez-Gonzalez made many valuable suggestions, pointing me toward indigenous and Spanish-language thinkers, through whom some of our students might find a more familiar path to the world's wisdom. Finally, it is always our students who let us know when we have hit the mark and when we have not. The Rouse Scholars—Jeff, Lindsey, Phil, Carrie, Chiara, Laura, Kelly, Dave, Posido, and Bruce in 1998 and Sarah, Laura, Meghan, Jen, Kelley, Kristina, Ila, Josh, Shaun, Jason, Jenny, Liana, Mike, Melissa, Justine, Jonathan, Amy, Jon, Matt, Adam, and Nina in 1999 tested the second edition in their lively seminars. To all those in my families of birth and choice, the professionals at Wadsworth, and the wisdom seekers in philosophy and women's studies courses at Howard Community College, my deepest and most heartfelt thanks.

Student Introduction

You might not think so, but you have already seen and heard a lot of philosophy. It's in the books you read, the movies you watch, the songs you listen to, the conversations you have with your friends, even in your own thoughts and dreams. That's because philosophy is about life and the heart-stopping questions it raises. Why is this happening to me? Who am I anyway? Where did the world come from? Is there a God? How do I know you're telling the truth? What's the right thing to do?

Because philosophy addresses basic, human questions, it exists in every culture. People everywhere have the same concerns and the same needs. After food, clothing, and shelter are taken care of, they yearn to be happy, to enjoy their lives to the fullest, to be the best they can be, to figure out their places in the world and in the community of other human beings.

That's what this book is about—the search for a fully human existence and the desire to figure things out. Some of what you will read is formal—essays written by philosophers or fiction (excerpts from novels, plays, or short stories) and some is a little more informal—a "fuzzy" social contract from the Internet, letters from a medieval woman mystic, a speech given by Malcolm X at Harvard.

Some of it comes from Europe and North America (the traditional sources of the Western philosophical tradition), but some makes its way from Central and South America, ancient China and Japan, the Arab and Jewish world of the Middle Ages, and modern Africa. The roots of wisdom have gone deep into every culture, and women as well as men are wisdom speakers in what you are about to read. You might be surprised to find that a German abbess, a Greek comic playwright, people living in Ghana, a contempory Guatemalan woman, and a Japanese Zen Master share many of your present-day concerns.

Part of the richness of philosophy is also its diversity. Universal human problems, like breath blown into a bottle, have varying sounds, depending on what they strike. Different cultural containers create unique voices and invite us to hear a symphony of responses. Just as travel changes the way we see new places and the home we've left behind, this philosophical tour can open our minds to new possibilities—variations on familiar themes.

I have taken the Western philosophical tradition as my starting point and organized the readings around its usual structure and categories, choosing selections from other cultures that speak its language. This helps all of us comfortable with Western culture hear these "foreign" voices more clearly. But we must always keep in mind that, in most cases, the writers and speakers did not have the Western tradition in mind. Their philosophical musings, like ours, arise out of and speak to specific social and historical contexts. We need to take them on their own terms as well as on ours.

The organizational structure of the book is also a typically Western one. If you are using a textbook in addition to this reader, chances are it follows this standard sequence. Although we in the West have found this order useful, it is certainly not the only possible one and not necessarily the best one in all situations. It begins with **metaphysics,** an investigation into what is real, in the world and in the human person, moves to **epistemology,** the study of what we know and how we think we know, and concludes with **axiology,** an exploration of what we value and why.

These three major divisions are all interrelated. Particularly in the West, it is almost impossible to talk about what is real without, at the same time, deciding what means of knowing we will use to find out. If we decide knowing is a matter of reason and rational processes, one model of reality emerges; if we insist knowing depends entirely on sense experience, the picture of reality we construct may look quite different. In a similar way, how we decide the morally right thing to do (an axiology question) depends quite a bit on who qualifies as a person. If only humans count, I may treat other animals and artificial life forms any way I choose. Only if I value all three must I take them into account in deciding how to act.

Other considerations include spiritual values (if God gave humans a unique status and value, my actions must reflect that), political views (in the West we place a very high value on individualism, but this is not universally the case), aesthetic considerations (does art have intrinsic value or only extrinsic worth as we decide what's good and what's not—and who decides?), and there are special issues depending on one's age, race, gender, ethnic background, sexual orientation, social class, religion, and so forth.

To extend our musical metaphor, the score and the conductor are Western but the musicians retain their individuality. Women, who have often been excluded from or marginally included in philosophy, add a distinct tone or style in some passages. This composition is not the only one that could be written around the theme of "philosophy"; still, it will give each player a chance to play a solo and to contribute to the beauty and power of the symphony.

Part I

Metaphysics

Metaphysics is sometimes called "first philosophy" because it asks the first or most fundamental question: What is real in the cosmos (**cosmology**) and in being (**ontology**)? In this section we take up four considerations. First, why do philosophy at all? What does it have to offer us as we take on the problems and challenges of life as well as its rich gifts?

Next, we zero in on the issue of reality itself. Is reality primarily matter, immaterial entities, or some combination of the two? In philosophy, these views are known respectively as *materialism, idealism,* and *dualism.* The West has tended to be dualistic—dividing mind from matter and considering mind the superior substance—but African and Asian views tend to blur this sharp distinction and see the material and the immaterial as less clearly different. Another view, called *pragmatism,* avoids this debate altogether by asking: What works?

A related issue is human nature. Is there an essence or central core that makes us who we are and are we born with it? Or, is human nature ours for the making after we find ourselves existing? Does human nature come from God? Can we create it in a robotics laboratory or through cloning? How much of who we are comes from the culture in which we live? Do we stand alone or is community an integral part of our identity? Which is better? By elevating the mind and devaluing the body in the West, have we created eating disorders as well as technological marvels?

Finally, are we on our own to define ourselves and reality, or is there a divine being to do both for us? And, do we make our own place in the cosmos or stand in a long line of ancestors?

1   Why Philosophy?

Defining the Issue

Why study philosophy at all? What does it have to offer us, as we struggle to understand ourselves and our world, that cannot be found in the so-called hard sciences, in "soft" sciences such as psychology and sociology, or in political theory? As we explore the roots of wisdom in many cultures, we find some common threads—a search for what is real, what is worth living and perhaps dying for; a willingness to question the apparent and the seemingly obvious in pursuit of something more clearly certain; the attempt to define what we value and what has worth. These are the concerns of philosophy.

It is possible, of course, to lead an unreflective life—eating, drinking, sleeping, going to work or school, watching TV—and not ever wondering if any deeper meaning exists. You are free to do this, but philosophers think that living what Socrates called an "unexamined life" is hardly worth the effort involved. To be human is to be capable of more.

And even the most unreflective of us can be jolted into awareness by life's unexpected twists and turns. A federal office building in Oklahoma is bombed, someone you love gets AIDS, you win the lottery, someone wonderful loves you, a relationship ends in betrayal—these are the times when the questions of philosophy insist on being addressed. Who am I? Does anything really matter? What am I doing here? How can I be happy?

Philosophy (literally the "love of wisdom") can help us thread our way through life's minefields, drawing on the wisdom of the past and the present, following its roots deeply into many cultures, and learning what people at other times and in other places have thought and done when confronted with the same puzzles and possibilities.

Previewing the Readings

Two of our readings come from the ancient Greeks—Plato's essay on distinguishing reality from mere shadows and Aristophanes the comic playwright's ridiculing of Socrates as a stand-in for his real target, the Sophists. Contemporary African and Guatemalan thinkers offer alternatives to traditional Western philosophy, and the final selection describes Taoism's timeless wisdom.

Both Aristophanes and Plato lived during a politically turbulent time not unlike the 1960s. Athens fought a lengthy and divisive war with its traditional rival, Sparta, from 431–404 B.C.E. (before the common or present era) and lost. The war was costly in both human life and treasure and was marked by atrocities. "Clouds" was performed near the beginning of this so-called Peloponnesian War in 423 B.C.E. when Aristophanes was in his twenties. Plato wrote the *Republic,* his vision of a perfect society, during the 390s, in the aftermath of this war and following the execution of his mentor and teacher Socrates in 399 B.C.E. on charges of "corrupting the youth" and "irreligion." Like Aristophanes, Plato blamed the **Sophists** for the breakdown of a core of common values that weakened the Athenian democracy. As in the 1960s, people were anxious about the future and unsure of what they could believe in with confidence.

Innocent Onyewuenyi is a college professor, reflecting on the Western philosophical tradition from the present and faulting it for divorcing "thought from life." Rigoberta Menchú, who won the 1992 Nobel Peace Prize for her work in organizing the peasants of Guatemala, describes the communal life into which a new baby is welcomed—facing more duties than rights, responsible to the ancestors and the entire community. Our final selection, from the Taoist classic *Tao Te Ching,* dates from the sixth century B.C.E. Attributed to the Chinese master Lao Tzu, it reflects the view that what we call "reality" may be best discerned by observing the Tao, engaged in its perfectly efficient and ego-free work in the natural world.

In this first chapter we begin exploring the roots of our Western tradition as well as considering some alternatives to it. You may be surprised to find that the questions have remained substantially the same over thousands of years and over thousands of miles. People everywhere seem to be concerned about what they can rely on, how they can make sense out of the predictable and unpredictable experiences of human life.

People in modern Europe and the Americas have sometimes assumed that our approach (rooted primarily in the Greek culture) was the only valuable one, that our assumptions were the only valid ones to make, and that if people weren't doing philosophy our way they weren't doing philosophy at all. Recently we have started taking another look at our neighbors in a shrinking, multicultural world and finding that we can learn from them as well as share our wisdom with them.

This chapter previews the variety of sources we will be exploring. Ancient Greece, Medieval and Early Modern Europe, Africa, Asia, and the Americas make their contributions to the search for wisdom. Women as well as men blend their voices in the dialogue. Many of our wisdom sources will be philosophical essays, but some will be fictional. Novels, short stories, and plays can help us raise and answer fundamental questions about what is real, how we know, and what we value.

1.1   *Republic*

PLATO

Preparing to Read

The Cave Allegory, which appears in book VII of Plato's utopian essay *Republic,* is probably the best known story in Western philosophy. Plato asks us to imagine prisoners, bound hand and foot in a cave, who see only shadows cast on the wall by fire-lit images, and mistake them for reality. This story has much to say about reality, about how we know, and about what is worth valuing. Not surprisingly, philosophers in the Western world have found it very rich in meaning, and you will find its echoes throughout this book. For now, we want to look at what it has to say about our chapter title: Why Philosophy?

People who have spent their lives in a cave, unable to see even their fellow prisoners because their heads are fixed forward, will naturally be convinced they know everything worth knowing about reality. They will be confident, maybe even arrogant, about the correctness of their views. When we read about the prisoners, we chuckle at their expense. We know what they don't know—that they see only shadows of objects and that the objects themselves are copies of real things that exist in the world outside the cave. With our bird's eye view, we can see how limited the cave dwellers are and how blind they are to their own limitations.

Any one of them, who was released and dragged out of the cave, would leave unwillingly and, once outside, would be blinded by the sunlight and painfully disoriented. If that person could endure the pain and wait for his or her eyes to adjust, a whole new world would reveal itself—a world of real objects, the true objects of knowledge. But the process would be difficult.

Beyond the world we can apprehend using our senses (the cave world in this analogy), Plato asserted another realm containing perfect **Forms**—the perfect circle, true justice, and, above all of them, the Idea or perfect Form of the Good from which an accurate understanding of reality and the moral life must derive. We cannot reach these Forms or Ideas using our senses; they are only accessible to reason, and yet they exist independent of us in their own perfect world. Plato offers us this choice: Stay in the cave and remain ignorant or make the rough ascent to the world of true knowledge. The choice is ours.

Republic, Book VII
The Cave Allegory

IF YOU WOULD LIKE an allegory of the human condition, with special attention to the question of education and ignorance, then imagine people living in a cave. They have been there since birth, forced by the chains that bind them to sit in a fixed position and stare straight ahead. At the far end of the cave is an opening to the outside world but, of course, the prisoners are unaware of this. Above and behind the prisoners a fire blazes, and between the fire and the prisoners is a path running beside a low wall. People pass by this wall, carrying human statues and figures of animals and plants crafted from wood or stone, and speaking to one another from time to time. The firelight casts shadows of these images on the wall the prisoners face and these shadows, accompanied by the intermittent sounds of voices, are the only reality the prisoners know. For as long as anyone can remember this has constituted the entire truth about the world.

Now, imagine that one of the prisoners is abruptly freed and forced to stand up and turn to face the firelight. How disoriented that person would feel! And how skeptical that person would be if told that the statues and figures being carried past the low wall were closer to reality than the much more familiar shadows on the far wall. Would this freed prisoner even be able to correctly name the objects that had previously appeared only as shadows? In fact, wouldn't the person be much more likely to insist that the shadows were real?

Suppose further that this person were dragged to the mouth of the cave and, finally, out into the bright light of the sun. The pain of its brightness would surely be overwhelming. Who among us would blame the prisoner for feeling angry and confused. It would take a long time, but with patience and perseverance, the prisoner might gradually be able to look at reflections of objects in the water or at the world bathed in moonlight. Eventually, the former prisoner would even be able to gaze at the sun directly and, using reason, connect the sun with the seasons and with all of life in the visible world. With this fuller understanding, the freed prisoner would surely pity the inhabitants of the cave and realize how distorted and incomplete their vision of reality actually was.

If the former prisoner were to return to the cave, there would be another period of disorientation, another adjustment—this time from light into darkness. Surely this would tempt the cave dwellers to laugh and agree that (just as they had always supposed) leaving the cave ruins one's eyesight. They would likely be even more resistant than ever to anyone's urging them to explore beyond the shadows and they might even feel threatened enough to kill the person who tried to free them.

This whole allegory depicts the human condition. The cave is the world revealed to us by our senses, dimly lit by firelight and filled with shadows we mistake for reality. The climb out of the cave and into the sunlight represents the ascent of the soul into the intellectual life—the life of the mind and the path of reason. By applying the tools of the intellect, one will come, finally, to the idea of The Good, which is the source of all that is beautiful and right. In truth, it is the only reliable ground for moral conduct as well.

Those who have seen things as they really are, using the full powers of the mind, will understandably be reluctant to return to the mundane world of human exchanges. Such a person might even seem a fool amid the shadows of the law courts and the hypocrisy of everyday life. We would do well to remember that those who seem disoriented are as likely to be moving from light to darkness as from darkness to light. And, we should be very careful whom we laugh at lest we find ourselves in the position of the happy prisoners who cling fiercely to their ignorance and mock what they do not understand.

From this allegory, we must also conclude that much of our educational system is misguided. Schools and colleges sometimes imagine that they are pouring knowledge into empty, waiting vessels. But, we have seen that the ability to learn is already present in all of us. We are not putting sight into blind eyes but rather turning those eyes (speaking metaphorically) from the world of becoming, available to our senses, toward the world of being, crowned by the idea of The Good, that is accessible only to our minds.

The process of freeing ourselves from reliance on the sensual world must begin in childhood. And, we must be vigilant over the course of our lives to keep our attention fixed always on what is good and true. Otherwise, we are in danger of becoming clever but shallow or, even worse, master criminals unwittingly serving evil ends.

Continuing to Think

If you have ever met someone whose view of the world was very different from your own, the Cave Allegory may be especially interesting to you. Is the other person's view closer to or further from "the way things are" than your own? It is tempting to write off or ignore anyone who makes us question our certainties. Like the people in the cave, we probably associate mainly with people who see things the same way we do; someone with a different version of reality represents a threat.

What Plato means us to wonder about is whether the person seems wrong because he or she is more ignorant than we are or because he or she is more enlightened. Both variations will seem strange to us. At the very least, Plato wants us not to reject new ideas sight unseen. But, if we are to evaluate them, what standard shall we use? And, are all versions of reality equally valid?

Plato doesn't think they are. In fact, he has designed the Cave Allegory in such a way that only one interpretation is possible: A living tree is one step closer to reality than an image of a tree and two steps closer than a shadow cast by that image. Plato is not a relativist, someone who thinks everything is of equal value or correctness; instead, he thinks there are absolutes, things that are always true because there is an objective order, a "way things are."

Philosophy is the way out of the cave. For Plato, when we use our reason rather than our unreliable senses, we have the power to discover the truth about what is real and what has worth. The problem is that philosophy, in the hands of the unscrupulous, can be misused. People who care less about truth and more about making money can use the method of philosophy—its logic—to distort and confuse the unsuspecting. This is exactly what happens in our next reading.

1.2   *Clouds*

ARISTOPHANES

Preparing to Read

Plato blamed the Sophists for creating a climate of relativism by teaching people to make the weaker argument appear the stronger. If you've ever been out-talked by someone good at misleading and confusing, you may appreciate the problem raised in this reading. Although sound reasoning is essential for arriving at the truth, its methods can also be misused. The Sophists were convinced there was no way to be certain about anything because opposite opinions could both be supported. That being the case, there was, in their view, no point in trying to do the impossible (separate truth from falsity). The sensible thing to do would be to teach people how to become successful and make a lot of money.

In this play, written in the fifth century B.C.E., Aristophanes is making fun of the Sophists, but he puts their ideas into the mouth of Socrates, the most famous philosopher in Athens. As the proprietor of a Think-shop, Socrates teaches his willing students to make the weaker argument appear the stronger by the skillful use of a warped kind of logic. Although Socrates was in the audience at the play's premier and took the ribbing with good humor, he was eventually put to death for corrupting the youth and denying the gods, the very charges leveled against the fictional Socrates in the play. Plato never forgave the Sophists for the death of his teacher and friend Socrates.

Notice in this selection how Strepsiades, who has sent his son Pheidippides to Socrates's Think-shop to learn arguments for justifying refusal to repay debts, ends up being beaten by his son—who has learned solid "logic" for supporting what he is doing.

Clouds
Perils of the New Logic

(Socrates emerges from the Think-shop and Strepsiades from his own house with his son Pheidippides)

SOCRATES. Well, what's your decision? Shall I teach your son rhetoric or not?
STREPSIADES. By all means, teach him well. Beat some sense into him while you're at it. But, don't forget to sharpen his tongue for legal duplicity.

SOCRATES. Put your mind at ease. When I've finished with him, he'll be able to out-argue even the sophists.
STREPSIADES. I want him back looking pale from study and thoroughly unprincipled.
CHORUS. (As Socrates leads Pheidippides into the Think-shop and Strepsiades heads home)
You're not the first nor will you be the last
To taste regret for playing loose and fast
With logic and traditions of the past

ACT TWO

SOCRATES. Good day, Strepsiades.

STREPSIADES. And to you, Socrates. Tell me, has my son learned how to make the weaker argument appear to be the stronger?

SOCRATES. Indeed he has. He was a splendid pupil.

STREPSIADES. Goddess be praised—we're golden now!

SOCRATES. You can certainly avoid any lawsuit.

STREPSIADES. Even if there were witnesses when I borrowed the money?

SOCRATES. Even a thousand witnesses won't get in your way.

STREPSIADES.

Sing and shout; let's celebrate
Creditors I've learned to hate
Now I'll stop you in your tracks
Show you to be greedy hacks
Ah, my son, your tongue is honed
All those nights when I have moaned
are vanished now, my prayers are heard.
Come Pheidippides, my word
I give, we two will celebrate!
Come, join me now. Don't make me wait.

SOCRATES. Here he comes.

STREPSIADES. My wonderful son!

SOCRATES. Take him and go.

STREPSIADES. (to Pheidippides) Ah yes, I see you've learned duplicity well. Your pale complexion and that sly, cynical look—so thoroughly Athenian. Come! Teach me what you've learned. Your playboy ways have gotten me into debt. Now it's time for your sophistry to save us both. (both exit)

(Later, Strepsiades is outside his house. Amynias enters with torn clothing and his head covered in blood, having just had a chariot accident.)

AMYNIAS. O goddess, why do you test me so—first my fortune and now my chariot? Ah, Strepsiades, just the man I've been looking for. Please tell your son I'm here to collect the money he owes me. I've had some financial reversals and need to reclaim what is mine.

STREPSIADES. I don't know what you're talking about. Maybe the accident has confused your brain. Why don't you just go home and rest.

AMYNIAS. Don't try to shuffle me off like that. I'm here for what is owed me and I'll see you in court if you refuse to pay me.

STREPSIADES. Tell me, Amynias, what's your opinion about rainfall? Does Zeus send new rain every time or is the same rain drawn up to the clouds and re-circulated?

AMYNIAS. I have no opinion and absolutely no interest!

STREPSIADES. How dare you threaten me and demand money when you don't know the most basic scientific facts?

AMYNIAS. Look, my head's starting to hurt. If you're short on cash right now, just pay me the interest.

STREPSIADES. Interest? What's that?

AMYNIAS. My dear sir, as everybody knows, when you don't repay a debt, it keeps on growing, little by little, as time passes.

STREPSIADES. Oh, I see. Well then, I suppose you also believe the ocean is larger this year than it was last year.

AMYNIAS. No, of course not. The ocean has a fixed size—it can't grow larger or smaller. We'd all be shocked if it did.

STREPSIADES. Ah, I rest my case. If the mighty ocean, with rivers rushing to join it all the time, stays the same size, what right have you to expect your money to grow? Such arrogance! Get out of here before I take this crop to you. (Strepsiades flicks the riding crop in Amynias's direction)

AMYNIAS. Help! Witnesses! Assault! Help!

STREPSIADES. (flicks the crop again, closer this time and more threateningly) Go on! Giddyup! Get a move on!

AMYNIAS. Not funny! I'll have you in court. (Strepsiades touches him with the crop) Ouch! Stop! (Amynias retreats)

STREPSIADES. Leaving so soon? Good riddance and don't come back or I'll give you more of the same. (Exit Amynias. Strepsiades enters his house for a celebratory feast with his son Pheidippides)

CLOUDS.
What a hollow victory
Wars of words with crops as judges
Soon Strepsiades will see
That his son has saved some grudges
When the sophistry is turned
And the trick returns to him
What Pheidippides has learned
Will fill his pain cup to the brim

(Later. Strepsiades rushes out followed by Pheidippides, still beating him)

STREPSIADES. Ouch! Help! Friends and neighbors, anybody, can't you see he's beating me. Ouch!

(to Pheidippides) You thug! Hitting your own father?

PHEIDIPPIDES. Quite right!

STREPSIADES. See, he doesn't even bother denying it.

PHEIDIPPIDES. Why should I? I have very good reasons for doing so and logic from the Think-shop to back them up.

STREPSIADES. You've gone too far. There's no justification for a son to hit his father. None!

PHEIDIPPIDES. Shall I prove it to you? Choose either the old logic or the new.

STREPSIADES. Hmmmmmm! I did send you to the Think-shop to learn how to counter just claims, but I never expected this. Is this the result of your education?

CHORUS.
Beware, Strepsiades, Beware!
Your keen request has now been granted
Pheidippedes has ceased to care
For virtues that you thought you planted
He's taken up your logic dare
Now watch your viewpoint get supplanted

STREPSIADES. (to the Chorus of Clouds) It all started out innocently enough. We had a great dinner together, but then my son refused my very polite request that he take up his lyre and sing. All right then, I said, how about a little Aeschylus? He turned up his nose at that, too. So, through clenched teeth, I asked for something modern. He responded with a disgusting speech from Euripides about, of all things, a man committing incest with his sister. Well, I'd had enough and I told him off. Words led to blows and the result is what you've just seen.

PHEIDIPPIDES. What did you expect—insulting a genius like Euripides?

STREPSIADES. A genius? Oh, come on. (Pheidippides raises his stick) You ungrateful little brat! Why, when you were a baby, I anticipated your every need. You had only to reach out your little hand and I understood what you wanted to eat or drink. And, at the first grunt, I whisked you right outside to do your business. And, how do you repay my kindnesses? As if it weren't bad enough that you were choking me, you ignored my pleas to let me go outside because I was losing control over my bowels. You just kept yelling at me . . . and then it was too late.

CHORUS.
Youth awaits the lad's reply
For, if he shows
That all those blows
Were justified—oh my!

PHEIDIPPIDES. How happy I am that my father sent me to learn the modern way of looking at things and how to thumb my nose at tradition and convention. Believe it or not, I used to spend all my time with horses and I couldn't string three intelligible words together, unless they were, "And, they're off!" But, Socrates and my father have changed all that. I've learned to argue any point-of-view and can easily prove I was justified in beating my father.

STREPSIADES. Oh, please, go back to the horses. That only put me in debt, this is much more serious. What kind of monster have I created?

PHEIDIPPIDES. Too late for that. Now then, did you beat me when I was a boy?

STREPSIADES. Of course I did, but it was for your own good. I did it out of love.

PHEIDIPPIDES. Then, I claim the same right—to beat you for your own good, out of love for you. Why should you be exempt from this prescription when I wasn't? Am I not, like you, a free-born Athenian and not a slave? And don't forget that old age is a second childhood, except that we expect better behavior from old men than we do from boys because of their life experiences. If anything, we sons would be justified in beating our fathers more severely than they beat us.

STREPSIADES. I challenge you to name one city where the law permits this!

PHEIDIPPIDES. Thanks to you, I've learned that laws are mere expediencies, passed when someone convinces enough people to agree with him. What's to stop me from starting a campaign for a law permitting sons to beat their fathers? In fact, on behalf of the boys, I'll generously renounce our claims to compensation for all whippings received before the new law's passage. Convinced I'm right? If not, look to the barnyard for further proof. Roosters have a merciless pecking order that pits fathers against sons and sons against fathers—laws are completely unnecessary as well as irrelevant.

STREPSIADES. Well, we're not roosters, now are we? Look, why don't you just wait until you have a son and get even on him? Leave me out of it!

PHEIDIPPIDES. Suppose I have no son. Then, I'll be shortchanged and you'll be one-up on me when you die with a smirk on your face.

STREPSIADES. (to the audience) I'm afraid he's got us there. Speaking on behalf of the fathers, I admit defeat. The boy's got logic on his side as well as that stick.

PHEIDIPPIDES. One more point.

STREPSIADES. Enough! Any more points and I might bleed to death!

PHEIDIPPIDES. This one might comfort you and make you feel less alone.

STREPSIADES. I'm all ears.

PHEIDIPPIDES. Very well then, using the same logic I'll go right in the house and beat Mother, too.

STREPSIADES. Hold on now! This has gone far enough. Take your warped logic and Socrates along with it and all of you go to the devil! (to the Chorus) Clouds, this is all your fault. I never should have trusted you in the first place. Why didn't you warn me? You know I'm an old man, only recently come from the countryside into the city. Why play me for a fool?

CHORUS.
Oh, we're just clouds
You brought your greed to us
And then, in fear,
Began to make a fuss

Remember, clouds we are
Your life is still your own
And apples don't fall far
From where the tree has grown

STREPSIADES. Ouch! Your judgment's harsh but accurate. I should never have tried to cheat my creditors. Look at the mess I got myself into in the process!

Continuing to Think

At first glance, Pheidippides's logic makes a certain kind of sense. On closer examination, however, there seems to be something wrong with arguing that a son has the duty as well as the right to beat his father. If you have ever been left with your head spinning by a fast-talking salesperson or a practiced politician, you may find yourself with some sympathy for Strepsiades. If nothing is any truer than anything else, then any conclusion can be supported.

Suppose I argue that people who repeatedly break the law should receive the death penalty and then catch you cheating on your taxes three years in a row and demand capital punishment. On what grounds will you argue that your life should be spared? Is life merely a verbal fencing match in which the person with the greater skill wins? Or, are there standards by which we ought to decide what to do?

The Sophists argued the former position and Plato supported the latter. In the hands of the Sophists, philosophy was vulnerable to becoming one cheap trick among many others. Like any valuable tool, philosophy can be misused. So, we are left with two cautions. From this selection, we are warned against being tricked by slick but shallow logic. From the Cave Allegory, we are warned against being happy in our ignorance. There is a middle ground between being too easily swayed by those who would dazzle us with words and being too closed to new ideas from someone who has climbed outside the cave and into the sunshine. Philosophy can help us find that middle ground.

1.3   *Is There an African Philosophy?*

INNOCENT ONYEWUENYI

Preparing to Read

It is tempting to take the norms of our own culture as norms for all of existence. Especially for those of us who live in the Western world—the so-called first world—there is a strong temptation to assume that our economic and military prominence guarantee the superiority of our ideas and our worldview. It has been easy for us to dismiss the cultures and thought systems of Asia and Africa as "primitive" and to assume that our philosophy would be as welcome as our technology in these "backward" regions of the world.

We have been shocked when writers, even from the so-called third world, have dared to criticize the West and to suggest the superiority of their own ways of doing and being. Suppose I define higher order thinking as the ability to demonstrate extrasensory perception and declare that since you lack this ability you clearly have no possibility of becoming a philosopher? You would have several options open to you. You could accept my judgment and your implied deficiency, or you could question my definition and attempt to broaden it.

This is precisely what Professor Onyewuenyi does in the next reading. Calling Western philosophy a disease that "divorced thought from life," he creates a broader definition for philosophy and demonstrates how the African version of it operates.

IN CONVERSATION WITH professors and students in America who knew I was teaching African philosophy, the question always put to me was: Are there African philosophers and what have they written? I have not heard or read of any. In other words, if there are no known academic philosophers in Africa, then there is no African philosophy.

Remember that I am in no way conceding that there are no academic philosophers in Africa. There are several of them, but their accounts were purposely withheld from history of philosophy books. . . . When they are mentioned they are grouped with Greco-Oriental philosophers. Little do some of us know that Plotinus, who wrote works on philosophy and opened a school in Rome, was from Lycon in Egypt. He made an attempt to travel to Persia and India to study their philosophies, but the expedition failed. Little do some of us know that the first woman philosopher, Hypatia, was from Alexandria and was murdered by Christians. Names like St. Augustine, Origen, Cyril, and Tertulian are not unfamiliar; they are black Africans. More pertinent to our subject is the fact that what today we call Greek or Western philosophy is copied from indigenous African philosophy of the "Mystery System." All the values of the mystery system were adopted by the Greeks and Ionians who came to Egypt to study; or studied elsewhere under Egyptian-trained teachers. These included Herodotus, Socrates, Hypocrates, Anaxagoras, Plato, Aristotle, and others. Are we not taught that Socrates is the first man to say "Man know thyself?" Yet, this expression was found commonly inscribed on Egyptian temple doors centuries before Socrates was born. Aristotle not only received his education in Africa, but he took over an entire library of works belonging to the Egyptian mystery system when he entered Egypt with Alexander the Great, after which we hear of the Corpus Aristotelium. Plato's alleged Theory of Ideas is borrowed from Egypt. Parmenides's references to "charioteers" and "winged steeds" were already dramatized in the *Judgement Scene* of the Egyptian *Book of the Dead*.

One would have to read *The Stolen Legacy* by George G. M. James to get some idea of the apprenticeship of the so-called Greek philosophers under Egyptian Mystery Priests. From his reading of Herodotus, Pliny, Diogenes Laertius, and early historians of philosophy, James noted about Pythagoras: "We are also further informed through Herodotus and Pliny, that after severe trials, including circumcision, had been imposed upon him by Egyptian priests, he was finally initiated into all their secrets. That he learnt the doctrine of metempsychosis, of which there was no trace before in the Greek religion; that his knowledge of medicine and strict system of diethetics rules, distinguished him as a product of Egypt . . . and that his attainment in geometry corresponded with the ascertained fact that Egypt was the birth place of that science."[1]

A contemporary African author, Willie E. Abraham, in his *Mind of Africa,* gives an account of a Ghanaian philosopher by the name Amo Anton, born near Axim about the year 1700. He went to Holland, entered the University of Thalle and in 1729 publicly defended his dissertation. He moved on to Wittenberg, and while Kant was still a boy, became Master of Philosophy there. In 1734 he defended a work in which he argued that sensation was not a mental faculty. (Amo was a rationalist philosopher after Leibniz, whom as a boy he met at the Duke of Brunswick's.) His performance was greatly praised. And the chairman and faculty members described him as a most noble and renowned man from Africa, extraordinarily honest, diligent, and so erudite that he stood above his mates. In 1738 he produced his magnum opus, a book on logic, theory of knowledge and metaphysics.[2]

From *African Philosophy: The Essential Readings,* Wright. Courtesy of Paragon House.

There were philosophers in the university towns of Timbucktu and Jene in West Africa who wrote works on the subject. Basil Davidson quotes the historian Leo Africanus, who wrote around 1520 concerning African scholars in the Mali and Songhai empires, "By the sixteenth century, West African writers were at work on historical, legal, moral and religious subjects."[3] Alexis Kagame has written on the concept of being among the Ruanda-Urundis. Adesany Adebayo has written on Yoruba metaphysical thinking. Placide Tempels sketched the worldview and ethics of the Congo. Joseph B. Danquah in Ghana did extensive work on the concept of God among the Akans.

Philosophizing: A Universal Experience

Be that as it may, my contention is that the philosophy of a people has little or nothing to do with the academic exponents of that philosophy. Philosophizing is a universal experience. Every culture has its own worldview. If you study the history of philosophy, you will find there is no agreement on the definition of philosophy. Some say it is the love of wisdom, others, the search for truth, and still others, the sense of wonder. What is generally agreed about philosophy is that it seeks to establish order among the various phenomena of the surrounding world, and it traces their unity by reducing them to their simplest elements. What are these various phenomena? They are things, facts, events, an intelligible world, an ethical world, and a metaphysical world.

These various phenomena of the surrounding world are the same in all cultures and societies. The themes dealt with in philosophy are universal. How each culture traces the unity of these themes, synthesizes, or organizes them into a totality is based on each culture's concept of life, namely the interrelationship between objects and persons and between persons and persons themselves. Hence it is that the order or

unity the people of a culture establish is their own order relative to their own conception of life in which everything around them becomes meaningful. No culture has *the* order or *the* last word. Hence the establishment of various truths of a spontaneous, logical, ethical, aesthetical, and metaphysical nature, not one of them being of absolute or universal validity.

This is the basis for calling a philosophy European, Asian, Indian, or American. If what we have said is true, we can and should talk of African philosophy, because the African culture has its own way of establishing order. It has its own view of life. And "life" according to Dilthey, is the starting point of philosophy. Georg Misch, summarizes him thus: "Dilthey regarded 'life' as the starting-point of philosophy; life as actually lived and embodied or 'objectified' in the spiritual world we live in. Life, according to Dilthey, is a subject for scientific investigation insofar as history and moral philosophy or the human sciences deal with it; but our knowledge of life is, above all, contained in certain cultural or personal views of the world—which plays a prominent part in philosophy as well as in religion and poetry."[4]

Hegel underscored the cultural and relative aspect of philosophy when he said: "But men do not at certain epochs merely philosophize in general. For there is a definite philosophy which arises among a people and the definite character which permeates all the other historical sides of the Spirit of the people, which is most intimately related to them, and which constitutes their foundation. The particular form of a philosophy is thus contemporaneous with a particular constitution of the people amongst whom it makes its appearance, with their institutions and forms of government, their morality, their social life and their capabilities, customs and enjoyments of the same."[5] The notion of philosophy itself for Hegel, as can be deduced from his words, is a factor in the life history of the human experience of the individual mind and is subject to the conditions of race, culture, and civilization. A further support to the issue of philosophical relativity was given by Victor Uchendu in his monograph *The Igbo of Southeast Nigeria*. He said, "To know how a people view the world around them is to understand how they evaluate life, and a people's evaluation of life, both temporal and non-temporal, provides them with a 'charter' of action, a guide to Behaviour." [6]

The African has an unwritten timeless code of behavior and attitudes which have persisted for centuries. The condition for the possibility of this, its explanation, lies in the presence of a corpus of coordinated mental or intellectual concepts. Placide Tempels puts it better: "Behaviour can be neither universal nor permanent unless it is based upon a concatenation of ideas, a logical system of thought, a complete positive philosophy of the universe, of man and of the things which surround him, of existence, life, death and the life beyond." [7]

Having shown that there can be and there certainly is an African philosophy, I now expose the content of this philosophy as briefly as possible. We are going to treat the core areas of philosophy, any philosophy—namely, metaphysics or ontology, epistemology, and ethics.

African Metaphysics or Ontology

Henry Alpern in his *March of Philosophy* said: "Metaphysics by the very definition that it is a study of reality, of that which does not appear to our senses, of truth in the absolute sense, is the groundwork of any theory concerning all phases of human behavior. David Hume, whom no one can charge of shutting his eyes to experience, said that metaphysics is necessary for art, morality, religion, economics, sociology; for the abstract sciences, as well as for every branch of human endeavour considered from the practical angle. It is the foundation upon which one builds one's career consciously and unconsciously; it is the guide; the author of the human interests; upon its truth or falsity depends what type of man you may develop into." [8]

The ideas from this quotation explain adequately the singular and unique importance of African ontology in the overall treatment and understanding of African philosophy. In recent decades, studies that were made of the scientific, religious, and practical human endeavor of Africans have accepted their foundation as consisting in ancestor worship, animism, totemism, and magic. These are only vague ideas, because no well-founded definitions of animism, totemism, and magic have been laid down, and the roots of these conceptions have not been explored. The root is in the fundamental concept of African ontology. When we understand this ontology, the concepts of magic, ancestor worship, totemism, and sorcery, as ethnologists apply them to Africa, become ridiculous if not foolish.

What then is ontology? It is the science of "being as such," "the reality that is." The metaphysics of Western philosophy has generally been based upon a static conception of being. In the African philosophical thought, being is dynamic. Existence-in-relation sums up the African conception of life and reality. The African does not separate being from force as its attribute. Rather "the Africans speak, act, live, as if for them beings were forces. . . . Force, for them, is the nature of being, force is being, being is force." When you say, in terms of Western philosophy, that beings are differentiated by their essences or nature; Africans say that forces differ in their essences or nature. There is the divine force, terrestrial or celestial forces, human forces, and vegetable and even mineral forces. [9] When Western metaphysics defines "being" as "that which is" or "the thing insofar as it is," the African definition reads: "that which is force," or "an existent force." God of course is the Great Force. There is a hierarchy of forces starting from God, spirits, founding fathers, the dead, according to the order of primogeniture; then the living according to their rank in terms of seniority. After living men come animals, vegetables, and minerals, which are in turn categorized on their relative importance in their own classes.

The Interaction Forces:
One Being Influences Another

The concept of separate beings, of substances, to use a scholastic term, which exist side by side, independent one of another, is foreign to African thought.[10] I might add parenthetically that I am not so sure that this concept of separate substances might not be the ontological basis for so much individualism and personal freedom in the Western world. The African thought holds that created beings preserve a bond one with another, an intimate ontological relationship. There is interaction of being with being, that is to say of force with force. This is more so among rational beings known as *Muntu,* a term which includes the living and the dead, Orishas, and God. *Muntu* is a force endowed with intelligence, a force which has control over irrational creatures known as *bintu.* Because of this ontological relationship among beings, the African knows and feels himself to be in intimate and personal relationship with other forces acting above or below him in the hierarchy of forces. "The human being, apart from the ontological hierarchy and interaction of forces, has no existence in the conception of the Bantu."[11] So much for the ontology—sketchy though it may be.

African Epistemology
or Theory of Knowledge

Theory of knowledge follows closely upon ontology. The view adopted by the African theory of knowledge is consonant with its metaphysics. Knowledge or wisdom for the African consists in how deeply he understands the nature of forces and their interaction. "True wisdom," Tempels tells us, "lies in ontological knowledge; it is the intelligence of forces, of their hierarchy, their cohesion and their interaction."[12] We said earlier that God is Force; God is also wisdom in that He knows all forces, their ordering, their dependence, their potential, and their mutual interaction. A person is said to

know or have wisdom inasmuch as he approaches divine wisdom. One approaches divine knowledge when one's flesh becomes less fleshy, to use Leopold Senghor's expression, that is, the older a person gets, the more wisdom he has. The same note of hierarchy comes into play here. The ancestors have more wisdom, followed by the elders, dead or living.

Distinction must be made here of the two levels of human intelligence. Intelligence can be either *practical* or *habitual.* Practical intelligence is cleverness, slyness in dealing with the contingent aspects of forces. Habitual intelligence is active knowledge of the nature of forces, their relationship. And this includes how man, the being with intelligence, makes use of things and activates the forces asleep in them. This kind of wisdom is different from book knowledge, which is not regarded as wisdom in the strict traditional sense. "Study and personal search for knowledge does not give wisdom. One can learn to read, to write; but all that has nothing in common with 'wisdom.' It gives no ontological knowledge of the nature of beings. There are many talents and clever skills that remain far short of wisdom."[13] Having a college degree does not qualify an African as a wise person in the community. This in part explains why there has been confusion in Africa since the colonial era, because the colonial administrators regarded the educated as the wise people, and consequently and arbitrarily appointed them legislators and leaders in the community, contrary to African political philosophy, which took the eldest of the community, to be, by divine law, the repository of wisdom and the link between God, the ancestors, and the living. He is divine. Swailem Sidhom in his article, "The Theological Estimate of Man" lamented the state of things when he said: "Power is conceived by the African as something pertaining to the divine. Hence it cannot be placed into unexercised hands. But the hands are rarely exercised nowadays. Scheduled education has replaced experience and has toppled the accepted standards. Seniority of age does not mean much anymore, and a father may now be instructed by the child of his bowels. Nevertheless, power is dangerous and it kills. Like a live coal from upon the very altar of God, it can only be cared for by those who have been graduated into maturity."[14] This despair is understandable if you grasp the African's conception of existence and his philosophy of vital forces.

African Ethical Theory

Some foreign observers of the African scene have declared that the African has no sense of sin. An example is Edwin Smith, who said in his *African Ideas of God:* "It would seem that in general Africans are not conscious of any direct relation between their theism and their ethic of dynamism."[15] Others maintain that Africans have but a vague idea of the Supreme Being, that he always keeps his distance and does not associate himself with the daily lives of men. All these and more are mere prejudices. The Nigerian writer, E. Adeolu Adegbola, said about African morality: "Everywhere African morality is hinged on many sanctions. But the most fundamental sanction is the fact that God's all-seeing eyes scan the total area of human behaviour and personal relationships. God is spoken of as having eyes all over like a sieve."[16] Placide Tempels, who questioned Africans closely on this point, informs us that, "the influence of God in the daily life of man is recognized in many African proverbs and sayings. . . ."[17] He says that such authors, as I mentioned above, are speaking under the influence of Western moral theory, according to which the social order is mere conformity with conventionalized behavior. On the contrary, African morality and moral law are filled with fixed beliefs, unshakable principles held from conviction. They surely know the distinction between good and evil. They refer to moral evil as "stinking"; they feel it deeply in their spirit.

The norms of good and evil are objective and of universal validity; no room for subjectivism or solipsism and situation ethics. African ethical truths are not relative. Except for cases of ignorance, there are little or no mitigating circumstances.

The root of their knowledge of good and evil is bound up with their philosophy. The Africans see a relationship between morality and the ontological order. Everything is associated and coordinated under the all-embracing unity of "vital force." In his judgment of his conduct the African takes into consideration the fact that he is not alone; that he is a cog in a wheel of interacting forces. He knows that the most important thing in his action is not how it affects him personally, but how it affects the world order, the spiritual republic, outside of which he does not exist as a *Muntu,* outside of which he is a planet off its orbit, meaningless and nonexisting. His life is not his own in a selfish manner. It belongs to God. The strengthening of this life and its preservation are in the hands of his ancestors and elders. In the life of the community each person has his place and each has his right to well-being and happiness. Therefore, what to do and what to avoid in order to preserve, increase, and strengthen vital force in himself and others of his clan constitute morality. "Objective morality to the Bantu is ontological, immanent and intrinsic morality. Bantu moral standards depend essentially on things ontologically understood."[18]

It follows that an act will be accounted ethically good if it can be judged ontologically good and by deduction be assessed as juridically just. The same idea is introduced by Plato in the *Republic.* The individual Greek citizen is to interpret an action good or evil, not in reference to selfish interests, but in reference to the community of which he is a part. The African ethical theory is what I would like to call metaphysical ethics in one sense and ethical communalism in another sense—where an individual takes into consideration the community of vital forces in deciding the goodness or evil of his proper actions.

Human positive or customary laws are made in reference to the growth or preservation of *Muntu*'s vital force; otherwise they are meaningless. All customary law that is worthy of the name is inspired, animated, and justified from the African's point of view, by the philosophy of living forces, or growth, of influence, and of the vital hierarchy The validity and strength of the customary law of indigenous peoples reside in its foundation in their philosophy. This is why we say in African ethical theory that an act which is characterized as ontologically good "will therefore be accounted *ethically good;* and at length, be assessed as *juridically just*."[19] "In contrast to the European sense of justice, which measures liability by material damage, it is according to African philosophy the loss in force, in joy of life that is evaluated, independently of material considerations."[20]

Conclusion

The rediscovery of African philosophy has influenced African scholars in writing about African personality or what the French-speaking Africans call Negritude. Kwame Nkrumah, Julius Nyerere, Léopold Senghor, Aimé Césaire, Nnamdi Azikiwe, and Chinua Achebe have written prose and verse to celebrate this philosophy—a philosophy of unity and complete encounter of all things and beings, which by reason of the dynamic character of African ontology, has surfaced on the communal structure of our society based on the division of labor and rights; in which man attains growth and recognition by how well he fulfills a function for the overall well-being of the community. We Africans have not yet yielded to the subtlety (and I pray we shall never) which would allow our traditional lawmakers and judges to design customary laws

divorced from our philosophy, from the nature of beings, as we understand them, and from our view of the world.

NOTES

1. James, *The Stolen Legacy* (New York, 1954), p. 43.
2. Abraham, *The Mind of Africa* (Chicago, 1966), p. 129.
3. Davidson, *A History of West Africa* (New York, 1966), p. 166.
4. Misch, *The Dawn of Philosophy* (London, 1950), p. 47.
5. Hegel, *Lectures on the History of Philosophy* (London, 1968), 1: 53.
6. Uchendu, *The Igbo of Southeast Nigeria* (New York, 1965), p. 12.
7. Tempels, *Bantu Philosophy* (Paris: *Présence Africaine,* 1969), p. 19.
8. Alpern, *The March of Philosophy* (New York, 1934), p. 99.
9. Tempels, *Bantu Philosophy,* pp. 51 and 52.
10. Ibid., p. 58.
11. Ibid., p. 104.
12. Ibid., p. 73.
13. Ibid., p. 74.
14. Sidhom, "The Theological Estimate of Man," in *Biblical Revelation and African Beliefs,* ed. Kwesi Dickinson (London, 1969), p. 115.
15. Smith, *African Ideas of God* (London, 1950), p. 22.
16. Dickinson, *Biblical Revelation,* p. 116.
17. Tempels, *Bantu Philosophy,* p. 117.
18. Ibid., p. 121.
19. Ibid.
20. Janheinz Jahn, *Muntu: An Outline of the New African Culture* (New York, 1961), p. 117.

Continuing to Think

Does Onyewuenyi make a convincing case for expanding the definition of philosophy? Does restricting the term "philosophy" to formal, academic philosophy narrow and distort its meaning? Putting Western labels on the worldviews of non-Western cultures allows us to discuss them using words we understand, but is anything distorted in the process?

A larger question, and the real purpose of writing the essay, asks: Is there an African philosophy? It is interesting that the argument uses the traditional, Western categories or divisions—metaphysics or ontology, epistemology, and axiology or **ethics.** Going back to the preceding example (from Preparing to Read), if you expand the definition of extrasensory perception to "knowing" when someone you love is in trouble, being able to "predict" how someone will react in a given hypothetical situation, and "sensing" who is on the phone before you pick it up, you may successfully include yourself in my definition. And, at the same time, you may demonstrate the unfair narrowness of my original definition.

This is somewhat the position Professor Onyewuenyi has taken. By demonstrating the existence of an African ontology, epistemology, and ethics, he establishes the existence of an African philosophy. Even if the African version differs from traditional, Western ones (being is dynamic rather than static, knowledge or wisdom involves understanding the forces of being rather than book learning, and injustice means loss in "joy of life" rather than material damage), this is no reason to disqualify it.

The last category is particularly intriguing. Suppose it was considered as unjust to take away my "joy in life" as it currently is to take away my property? Would anyone seriously argue that property is more valuable than "joy in life"? And, yet, our laws fail to take this more devastating stealing into account.

1.4 *I, Rigoberta Menchú: An Indian Woman in Guatemala*

RIGOBERTA MENCHÚ

Preparing to Read

Each culture has its own worldview—a way of conceptualizing reality that places the individual within the cosmos. The Greeks saw rational minds unlocking the mysteries of a predictable universe. Many Africans have a more dynamic and communal worldview than the Greeks do. In this spirit, among the indigenous peoples of Central America, each new person is reminded from birth of his or her place in nature, in a long line of ancestors, and in a community.

Reading this account of welcoming a baby into the Maya-Quiché community, we enter a world in which present events can be understood and explained only in terms of a living past. Ritual is the way of integration that weaves past, present, and future into one seamless fabric of meaning. There is no separation between what we might label sacred and profane; worship and work are indistinguishable.

As the baby's candle is lighted and placed among those representing the entire cosmos—earth, water, sun, moon, the incense pom, and the sacred lime—a new life enters the web of generations that stretches back to the beginning of time and forward into a limitless future. The new baby belongs, not just to the parents, but to the entire community. And, while the community welcomes its youngest member with joy, it also initiates the baby into a life of suffering.

Rigoberta Menchú, winner of the 1992 Nobel Peace Prize for her work in organizing the peasant people of Guatemala, learned Spanish so she could understand the worldview of the landowners whose economic and social system she understood as oppressing her people.

II: Birth Ceremonies

Whoever may ask where we are, tell them what you know of us and nothing more.

—*Popol Vuh*

Learn to protect yourselves, by keeping our secret.

—*Popol Vuh*

IN OUR COMMUNITY there is an elected representative, someone who is highly respected. He's not a king but someone whom the community looks up to like a father. In our village, my father and mother were the representatives. Well, then the whole community becomes the children of the woman who's elected. So, a mother, on her first day of pregnancy goes with her husband to tell these elected leaders that she's going to have a child, because the child will not only belong to them but to the whole community, and must follow as far as he can our ancestors' traditions. The leaders then pledge the support of the community and say: "We will help you, we will be the child's second parents." They are known as *abuelos,* "grandparents" or "forefathers." The parents then ask the "grandparents" to help them find the child some godparents, so that if he's orphaned, he shouldn't be tempted by any of the bad habits our people sometimes fall into. So the "grandparents" and the parents choose the godparents together. It's also the custom for the pregnant mother's neighbours to visit her every day and take her little

things, no matter how simple. They stay and talk to her, and she'll tell them all her problems.

Later, when she's in her seventh month, the mother introduces her baby to the natural world, as our customs tell her to. She goes out in the fields or walks over the hills. She also has to show her baby the kind of life she leads, so that if she gets up at three in the morning, does her chores and tends the animals, she does it all the more so when she's pregnant, conscious that the child is taking all this in. She talks to the child continuously from the first moment he's in her stomach, telling him how hard his life will be. It's as if the mother were a guide explaining things to a tourist. She'll say, for instance; "You must never abuse nature and you must live your life as honestly as I do." As she works in the fields, she tells her child all the little things about her work. It's a duty to her child that a mother must fulfil. And then, she also has to think of a way of hiding the baby's birth from her other children.

When her baby is born, the mother mustn't have her other children round her. The people present should be the husband, the village leaders, and the couple's parents. Three couples. The parents are often away in other places, so if they can't be there, the husband's father and the wife's mother can perhaps make up one pair. If one of the village leaders can't come, one of them should be there to make up a couple with one of the parents. If none of the parents can come, some aunts and uncles should come to represent

---

the family on both sides, because the child is to be part of the community. The birth of a new member is very significant for the community, as it belongs to the community not just to the parents, and that's why three couples (but not just anybody) must be there to receive it. They explain that this child is the fruit of communal love. If the village leader is not a midwife as well, another midwife is called (it might be a grandmother) to receive the child. Our customs don't allow single women to see a birth. But it does happen in times of need. For instance, I was with my sister when she went into labour. Nobody else was at home. This was when we were being heavily persecuted. Well, I didn't exactly see, but I was there when the baby was born.

My mother was a midwife from when she was sixteen right up to her death at forty-three. She used to say that a woman hadn't the strength to push the baby out when she's lying down. So what she did with my sister was to hang a rope from the roof and pull her up, because my brother wasn't there to lift her up. My mother helped the baby out with my sister in that position. It's a scandal if an Indian woman goes to hospital and gives birth there. None of our women would agree to that. Our ancestors would be shocked at many of the things which go on today. Family planning, for example. It's an insult to our culture and a way of swindling the people, to get money out of them.

This is part of the reserve that we've maintained to defend our customs and our culture. Indians have been very careful not to disclose any details of their communities, and the community does not allow them to talk about Indian things. I too must abide by this. This is because many religious people have come among us and drawn a false impression of the Indian world. We also find a *ladino* using Indian clothes very offensive. All this has meant that we keep a lot of things to ourselves and the community doesn't like us telling its secrets. This applies to all our customs. When the Catholic Action[1] arrived, for instance, everyone started going to mass, and praying, but it's not their only religion, not the only way they

have of expressing themselves. Anyway, when a baby is born, he's always baptized within the community before he's taken to church. Our people have taken Catholicism as just another channel of expression, not our one and only belief. Our people do the same with other religions. The priests, monks and nuns haven't gained the people's confidence because so many of their things contradict our own customs. For instance, they say; "You have too much trust in your elected leaders." But the village elects them *because* they trust them, don't they? The priests say; "The trouble is you follow those sorcerers," and speak badly of them. But for our people this is like speaking ill of their own fathers, and they lose faith in the priests. They say; "Well, they're not from here, they can't understand our world." So there's not much hope of winning our people's hearts.

To come back to the children, they aren't to know how the baby is born. He's born somewhere hidden away and only the parents know about it. They are told that a baby has arrived and that they can't see their mother for eight days. Later on, the baby's companion, the placenta that is, has to be burned at a special time. If the baby is born at night, the placenta is burned at eight in the morning, and if he's born in the afternoon, it'll be burned at five o'clock. This is out of respect for both the baby and his companion. The placenta is not buried, because the earth is the mother and the father of the child and mustn't be abused by having the placenta buried in it. All these reasons are very important for us. Either the placenta is burned on a log and the ashes left there, or else it is put in the *temascal*. This is a stove which our people use to make vapour baths. It's a small hut made of adobe and inside this hut is another one made of stone, and when we want to have a bath, we light a fire to heat the stones, close the door, and throw water on the stones to produce steam. Well, when the woman is about four months pregnant, she starts taking these baths infused with evergreens, pure natural aromas. There are many plants the community uses for pregnant women, colds, headaches, and things like that. So the pregnant mother takes baths with plants prescribed for her by the midwife or the village leader. The fields are full of plants whose names I don't know in Spanish. Pregnant women use orange and peach leaves a lot for bathing and there's another one we call Saint Mary's leaf which they use. The mother needs these leaves and herbs to relax because she won't be able to rest while she's pregnant since our women go on working just as hard in the fields. So, after work, she takes this calming bath so that she can sleep well, and the baby won't be harmed by her working hard. She's given medicines to take as well. And leaves to feed the child. I believe that in practice (even if this isn't a scientific recommendation) these leaves work very well, because many of them contain vitamins. How else would women who endure hunger and hard work give birth to healthy babies? I think that these plants have helped our people survive.

The purity with which the child comes into the world is protected for eight days. Our customs say that the new-born baby should be alone with his mother in a special place for eight days, without any of her other children. Her only visitors are the people who bring her food. This is the baby's period of integration into the family; he very slowly becomes a member of it. When the child is born, they kill a sheep and there's a little fiesta just for the family. Then the neighbours start coming to visit, and bring presents. They either bring food for the mother, or something for the baby. The mother has to taste all the food her neighbours bring to show her appreciation for their kindness. After the eight days are over, the family counts up how many visitors the mother had, and how many presents were received; things like eggs or food apart from what was brought for the mother, or clothing, small animals, and wood for the fire, or services like carrying water and chopping wood. If, during the eight days, most of the community has called, this is very important, because it means that this child will

have a lot of responsibility towards his community when he grows up. The community takes over all the household expenses for these eight days and the family spends nothing.

After eight days everything has been received, and another animal is killed as recognition that the child's right to be alone with his mother is over. All the mother's clothes, bedclothes, and everything she used during the birth, are taken away by our elected leader and washed. She can't wash them in the well, so no matter how far away the river is, they must be carried and washed there. The baby's purity is washed away and he's ready to learn the ways of humanity. The mother's bed is moved to a part of the house which has first been washed with water and lime. Lime is sacred. It strengthens the child's bones. I believe this really is true. It gives a child strength to face the world. The mother has a bath in the *temascal* and puts on clean clothes. Then, the whole house is cleaned. The child is also washed and dressed and put into the new bed. Four candles are placed on the corners of the bed to represent the four corners of the house and show him that this will be his home. They symbolize the respect the child must have for his community, and the responsibility he must feel towards it as a member of a household. The candles are lit and give off an incense which incorporates the child into the world he must live in. When the baby is born, his hands and feet are bound to show him that they are sacred and must only be used to work or do whatever nature meant them to do. They must never steal or abuse the natural world, or show disrespect for any living thing.

After the eight days, his hands and feet are untied and he's now with his mother in the new bed. This means he opens the doors to the other members of the community, because neither the family or the community know him yet. Or rather, they weren't shown the baby when he was born. Now they can all come and kiss him. The neighbours bring another animal, and there's a big lunch in the new baby's house for all the community. This is to celebrate his integration "in the universe," as our parents used to say. Candles will be lit for him and his candle becomes part of the candle of the whole community, which now has one more person, one more member. The whole community is at the ceremony, or at least, if not all of it, then some of it. Candles are lit to represent all the things which belong to the universe—earth, water, sun, and man—and the child's candle is put with them, together with incense (what we call *pom*) and lime—our sacred lime. Then, the parents tell the baby of the suffering of the family he will be joining. With great feeling, they express their sorrow at bringing a child into the world to suffer. To us, suffering is our fate, and the child must be introduced to the sorrows and hardship, but he must learn that despite his suffering, he will be respectful and live through his pain. The child is then entrusted with the responsibility for his community and told to abide by its rules. After the ceremony comes the lunch, and then the neighbours go home. Now, there is only the baptism to come.

When the baby is born, he's given a little bag with a garlic, a bit of lime, salt, and tobacco in it, to hang round his neck. Tobacco is important because it is a sacred plant for Indians. This all means that the child can ward off all the evil things in life. For us, bad things are like spirits, which exist only in our imagination. Something bad, for instance, would be if the child were to turn out to be a gossip—not sincere, truthful, and respectful, as a child should be. It also helps him collect together and preserve all our ancestors' things. That's more or less the idea of the bag—to keep him pure. The bag is put inside the four candles as well, and this represents the promise of the child when he grows up.

When the child is forty days old, there are more speeches, more promises on his behalf, and he becomes a full member of the community. This is his baptism. All the important people of the village are invited and they speak. The parents make a commitment. They promise to teach the child to keep the secrets of our people, so that our culture and customs will be preserved. The village leaders come and offer their experience, their example, and their knowledge of our ancestors. They explain how to preserve our traditions. Then, they promise to be responsible for the child, teach him as he grows up, and see that he follows in their ways. It's also something of a criticism of humanity, and of the many people who have forsaken their traditions. They say almost a prayer, asking that our traditions again enter the spirits of those who have forsaken them. Then, they evoke the names of our ancestors, like Tecun Umán and others who form part of the ceremony, as a kind of chant. They must be remembered as heroes of the Indian peoples. And then they say (I analyse all this later); "Let no landowner extinguish all this, nor any rich man wipe out our customs. Let our children, be they workers or servants, respect and keep their secrets." The child is present for all of this, although he's all wrapped up and can scarcely be seen. He is told that he will eat maize and that, naturally, he is already made of maize because his mother ate it while he was forming in her stomach. He must respect the maize; even the grain of maize which has been thrown away, he must pick up. The child will multiply our race, he will replace all those who have died. From this moment, he takes on this responsibility, and is told to live as his "grandparents" have lived. The parents then reply that their child promises to accomplish all this. So, the village leaders and the parents both make promises on behalf of the child. It's his initiation into the community.

The ceremony is very important. It is also when the child is considered a child of God, our one father. We don't actually have the word God but that is what it is, because the one father is the only one we have. To reach this one father, the child must love beans, maize, the earth. The one father is the heart of the sky, that is, the sun, The sun is the father and our mother is the moon. She is a gentle mother. And she lights our way. Our people have many notions about the moon, and about the sun. They are the pillars of the universe.

When children reach ten years old, that's the moment when their parents and the village leaders talk to them again. They tell them that they will be young men and women and that one day they will be fathers and mothers. This is actually when they tell the child that he must never abuse his dignity, in the same way his ancestors never abused their dignity. It's also when they remind them that our ancestors were dishonoured by the White Man, by colonization. But they don't tell them the way that it's written down in books, because the majority of Indians can't read or write, and don't even know that they have their own texts. No, they learn it through oral recommendations, the way it has been handed down through the generations. They are told that the Spaniards dishonoured our ancestors' finest sons, and the most humble of them. And it is to honour these humble people that we must keep our secrets. And no-one except we Indians must know. They talk a lot about our ancestors. And the ten-years ceremony is also when our children are reminded that they must respect their elders, even though

this is something their parents have been telling them ever since they were little. . . .

. . . The elected fathers of the community explain to us that all these things come down to us from our grandfathers and we must conserve them. Nearly everything we do today is based on what our ancestors did. This is the main purpose of our elected leader—to embody all the values handed down from our ancestors. He is the leader of the community, a father to all our children, and he must lead an exemplary life. Above all, he has a commitment to the whole community. Everything that is done today, is done in memory of those who have passed on.

NOTE

1. Association created in 1945 by Monsignor Rafael Gonzalez, to try and control the Indian fraternities of the *Altiplano*.

Continuing to Think

How does this worldview differ from your own? Raised in a culture that prizes individualism and views history in terms of progress, many Westerners find this more traditional way of looking at reality puzzling at best. Taught to rely on our own resources and learn independence, we may bristle at the thought of making every decision in a communal context or having every decision pre-ordained by a living past, peopled with ancestors who must be honored.

As an oppressed people, the Maya-Quiché have taken comfort in ritualizing and sacrilizing daily life. Lacking access to political and economic power, they find meaning in the integrity of everyday life. Being born into this community means learning as your first lesson: Never forget your place in the cosmos. Your obligations to your ancestors, to the community, and to those who will come after you supersede any plans you might think of making for yourself. The strongest ethical principle is: Don't abuse nature or your own dignity.

In contrast with the orderly cosmos described by Plato, Menchú suggests a present that is out of control and filled with suffering; at the same time, this present is embedded in a much longer span of time, informed by both the distant past and the future on the horizon. With a bag of sacred substances for protection—garlic, lime, salt, and tobacco—the new baby is instructed in the community's rules and given a share in responsibility for its protection.

1.5   *The Tao Te Ching*

Preparing to Read

What if we are not merely culture bound but totally wrong about the nature of what is? The first four readings have introduced us to diversity and even disagreement, but all have shared a respect for reason or at least honored the value of thinking. These assumptions are dramatically challenged by our last reading from the Taoist classic *Tao Te Ching*. If "The Tao we can speak of has already lost its wholeness," our usual reliance on words and concepts may be more of a hindrance than a help. By observing the Tao, at play in the natural world, we can see that it produces everything, yet takes no credit and demands no loyalty.

Our senses and our powers of direct observation—the very things that Plato disparaged in our first selection—are the keys to a wisdom deeper than words. Words and reasoning may be the way to knowledge, but wisdom is reached through simplicity and ego-free action. This classic, written (according to legend) as Lao-tzu was leaving the city in disgust for a life as a hermit, offers the Way of wisdom and happiness.

Tao Te Ching

CHAPTER ONE

The Tao we can speak of
  has already lost its wholeness.
The name we can name
  is no longer the everlasting Way.
How can we give a name
  to the source of heaven and earth?
The mother or matrix of all
  is beyond naming.
Free yourself from desire
  and live within the mystery of creation.
Caught in desire, you will see
  only its manifestations.
And yet, at a deeper level,
  the source and its expression are one.
Meditate on this profound pairing —
  it opens the way to all wisdom

CHAPTER SEVENTEEN

With ego-free leadership
  only the Tao is visible.
Leaders who are loved, feared,
  or (worst of all) despised
  proclaim with increasing intensity
  how much of themselves
  they place
  between the Way and the people.
Lack of faith breeds unfaithfulness.
The best leaders know
  the Tao accomplishes everything anyway.
They smile when the people say,
  "Look what we did!"

CHAPTER TWENTY-TWO

The way of Nature is clear
  to anyone who looks.

Bend with the wind
    if you wish to remain rooted and upright.
Empty yourself and expect to be filled.
What wears out is continually renewed.
Don't be foolish enough
    to try to improve upon Nature
    or to set yourself against
    its immutable ways.
Instead, learn from Nature
    how to lead your own life.
Let others discover how clever you are
    and how much you've accomplished.
Those who don't compete
    meet the least resistance
    and reach their goals unopposed.
The wise have always understood this.
Bend with the wind
    if you wish to remain rooted and upright.

CHAPTER THIRTY-FOUR

The Tao moves the stars
    and rests in the heart of the atom.
All things arise from it
    yet it takes no credit,
    demands no loyalty,
    asserts itself over nothing.
Since it is the invisible force within everything,
    we might think of it as humble.
Because all things return to it, pulled like the
    waves, we recognize its power.
The Tao has no need to make claims.
All of nature acclaims it.

CHAPTER FORTY-EIGHT

When we pursue knowledge,
    acquiring more is the goal.
When we pursue wisdom,
    simplicity is the path.
Less and less doing is required until,
    ultimately, we reach perfect efficiency.
Without striving, everything is accomplished
    effortlessly.
We have simply gained the wisdom
    to let everything follow its own nature
This is the path of pure mastery.

CHAPTER SEVENTY-NINE

In any decision,
    the world sees
    winners and losers
This sows the seeds
    of future conflict.
If you find yourself
    declared a winner,
    win graciously.
Be scrupulous in monitoring
    your own conduct.
Remember that the Tao
    remains impartial
    and recognizes
    neither winners
    nor losers.

Continuing to Think

What if everything we needed to know about what is was right in front of us? This is the claim of Taoist wisdom. We don't need to spend our lives lost in wisdom texts, or spend years apprenticed to a master. All we really need to do is to pay attention to the world around and within us—and, the further claim is—they are the same.

Just as the trees are wise enough and practical enough to bend in a windstorm and, therefore, live to remain straight and tall; we would be wise to know when to bend and when to insist on standing firm. Nature doesn't deplete herself by being active all the time. Even the sun takes a rest for part of each day-night cycle. Why would we be foolish enough to burn ourselves out in a burst of energy that permits no rest? Seasons change throughout the year, reminding us that there is a time for planning, for joy, for thoughtfulness, for grieving, and for deep wisdom—in every day as well as in every year.

What an astounding claim! The key to understanding the mystery of all that is, and the way to happiness and a life well lived, are right outside our windows and right inside ourselves. The wisdom text we seek is all around us and within us—what could be simpler?

Summing Up the Readings

Why philosophy? All five answers in this chapter seem to be negative ones. If you don't pursue philosophy, Plato warns, you can never leave the cave of sense experience and crowd psychology. Aristophanes agrees: If philosophy is misused, the weaker argument will appear the stronger and you may get more than you bargained for. Draw too narrow a definition of philosophy, Professor Onyewuenyi asserts, and you wrongfully exclude those who differ from you in minor ways but who are your partners in the search for wisdom and truth. If you don't know and understand your place in the cosmos, Rigoberta Menchú explains, how will you honor your ancestors and fulfill the duties your community expects? Finally, Lao-tzu gently urges us to let go of our frantic search for wisdom and happiness and open our eyes to what is everywhere to be seen.

All these readings agree that an unreflective life is a waste of time, less than we are capable of, and may be downright dangerous. Philosophy, like many valuable things, must be handled carefully, protected from abuse, and kept out of the hands of those who don't know what to do with it. Used with respect, it is the royal road to wisdom and its roots lie deep in every culture. Our task in this book will be to discover those roots and follow them to their sources.

Continuing to Question

1. What is there about the philosophy of the Sophists that was so repulsive to Plato? Do you agree with his criticisms of them? Why or why not?

2. Are you convinced that there is an African philosophy? Does fitting into the thought and logic patterns of the Western world constitute the only path to philosophical legitimacy? From what you know of Western philosophy at this point, is it "divorced from real life"?

3. Where does your own worldview place you? Do you think of yourself only as an autonomous individual with rights that must be protected, or do you also see yourself as having duties that complement those rights?

4. Of the things you are pretty sure are "real," how many seem real because you can reason their existence, how many are accessible to your senses, and how many seem real for reasons other than reason or sense experience?

5. What are the penalties for living an "unexamined life"? Are there things one misses? Is it possible to be fully human while living a totally unreflective life?

Suggestions for Further Exploration

Achebe, Chinua, *Things Fall Apart*—London: Heinemann, 1983. Also by the same author: *No Longer At Ease*. London, Heinemann, 1962. Both these novels by a Nigerian writer deal with the clash between traditional values and the influence of the technological West. In the first, the setting is the traditional culture; in the second, a young man goes to the big city and is corrupted.

Aristophanes, "The Clouds"—In *The Complete Plays of Aristophanes,* ed. Moses Hadas. New York: Bantam, 1988. In this play by ancient Greece's most famous comic playwright, Socrates is lampooned as a Sophist who tries to persuade his students that "wrong things are right" and "make the weaker argument appear the stronger" (according to critics within the play). Socrates felt that these charges were what some people had in mind in bringing him to trial. Since the play was quite a success, it is worth speculating about how entertainment influences opinion. You might think about today's debate on television violence and its possible effects on human behavior.

Bianco, Margery Williams, *The Velveteen Rabbit*—New York: Avon Books, 1960. This is a children's book that is really a philosophical musing on what it means to be "real" and how one goes about achieving it, as well as some of the costs involved.

Carroll, Lewis, *Alice in Wonderland*—New York: Norton, 1971. When a little English girl falls down a rabbit hole, she discovers a world in which nothing she has learned to do in the aboveground world works. Does the world ever seem that way to you? What is Carroll saying about metaphysics, about epistemology, and about axiology through the medium of this story?

Hesse, Hermann, *Siddhārtha*—trans. Hilda Rosner. New York: Bantam, 1974. This book is a kind of retelling of the life of the Buddha (whose first name was Siddhārtha), a kind of explanation of Buddhism, and an entertaining story of one person (also named Siddhārtha) and his search for wisdom.

Little Buddha—In this film, director Bernardo Bertolucci gives an introduction to Buddhism by exploring the claim of some Tibetan monks that a young Caucasian boy in Seattle may be a Buddhist master reborn.

2   Reality and Being

Defining the Issue

Have you ever wondered what is really real? A powerfully vivid dream can make you wonder because it seems totally real while it is occurring and seems dreamlike only after you "wake up." So can optical illusions. Our senses seem fully reliable until we realize how easy it is to fool them. **Virtual reality** is the ultimate mind bender, taking us inside a computer program so that what we experience seems as real to us as our ordinary lives. Philosophers want to know how we determine what is real and how we can distinguish it from the only apparently real.

In metaphysics, the quest for the real, there are four basic interpretations—**idealism, materialism,** a dualism that blends materialism with idealism, and **pragmatism**—that appear in cultures around the world and throughout history. Idealism asserts that reality is essentially ideas or other immaterial entities; materialism insists that reality is essentially matter; and pragmatism is the belief that what is real is what works and what helps us predict what will happen next.

Before reading how some philosophers have answered the basic question of metaphysics—what is real and how will I know when I encounter the real thing?—try thinking of something you are sure is real. It might be the book or pencil in your hand, the idea of representative government, the love of someone, or the belief that if you hit a tennis ball against the wall it will rebound to you. You might ask yourself what makes you sure it is real. In other words, what is the basis for your certainty? A related question is: What could happen to me or to the world to shatter or at least cast doubt on that certainty?

Previewing the Readings

Three of our readings approach the question of reality as we have traditionally done in the West. One examines the African philosophical tradition by looking to metaphysics in ancient Egypt, and the last reading steps inside Buddhism to ask how we should act based on what we believe about what is.

Our first reading, from Thomas Hobbes's *The Leviathan,* asserts a straightforward, materialist interpretation of reality. Having lived through the Thirty Years War, an ugly European conflict that lasted from 1618 to 1648 and left thousands homeless and hopeless, as well as civil war in England, Thomas Hobbes knew firsthand the brutality and mindless cruelty humans were capable of inflicting on each other. His most famous book, *The Leviathan,* asserts that we need a strong state and a virtual dictator to protect us from the worst in our human nature. *The Leviathan* also puts forth a materialist philosophy. All of reality, it states, is matter in motion. The other two Western readings—*Flatland* and *Alice's Adventures in Wonderland*—take a fictional look at what happens when the world itself changes before our eyes, when things we were certain about are no longer true. What if, instead of the two dimensions that have framed your world all your life, there were really three? What would it take to convince you? Or, suppose you fell down a rabbit hole and nothing that seemed real and certain aboveground could be counted on below?

Our two fictional selections date from the nineteenth century. Lewis Carroll's *Alice's Adventures in Wonderland* (1865) and Edwin Abbot's *Flatland* (1882) both raise philosophical questions about the nature of reality and especially about our certainty that the world as we imagine it to be matches the world as it actually is. Alice, who finds herself in Wonderland, and the mathematically inclined square in Flatland are jolted out of their complacency when new experiences change their assumptions about reality.

Our third reading, about thought systems in ancient Egypt, is historical. It looks at what happened when the Greeks borrowed part of the Egyptian worldview but not all of it. What had been a unity in Egypt became a duality in Greece. The question of unity emerges again in the Buddhist story of the enlightened being and the hungry tigress. A lot depends on whether we judge all of what is to be one, or dual, or multiple. The West has traditionally placed great emphasis on the separateness and independence of the individual. Neither African nor Asian philosophy makes this assumption.

Two of our readings have their roots in antiquity. Both the Egyptian philosophical tradition of 3,500 years ago, discussed by contemporary philosopher Lancinay Keita, and stories about the Buddha, dating from at least 400 years before the common era, continue to influence the modern world. The Hermetic tradition from ancient Egypt fascinated Renaissance thinkers in the West, and Buddhism remains a vibrant force throughout the world even in the present. Both these traditions help us focus on where the Western tradition touches them as well as where significant points of departure occur.

2.1   *The Leviathan*

THOMAS HOBBES

Preparing to Read

How did your thoughts become your thoughts? Were any of them there at birth? Have they arisen spontaneously within your mind? Philosophers are concerned about the relation (if any) between our ideas about reality and reality itself. In the West it is nearly impossible to ask the question of metaphysics (what is real) without, at the same time, asking the question of epistemology (how do we know?).

If my version of the world bears no resemblance to the world as it actually is, then my version is of no value. Only if some connection can be made between the way the world seems to me and the way the world is are my thoughts about it useful. Thomas Hobbes's version of materialism, one of the four views of reality we discussed earlier, asserts: What exists is matter (bodies) in motion. Trees are matter in motion; machines are matter in motion; even your thoughts and emotions are matter in motion.

According to Hobbes, there is nothing in your mind that was not first impressed on your sense organs (through seeing, hearing, touching, tasting, smelling). This is an epistemological assertion—an assertion about how we know. The corresponding metaphysical assertion is that the movement of matter (the only reality) outside you causes a related movement within you—what Hobbes calls *perception*. Everything you think and feel is the result either of an original perception or of something derived from that original perception—recombinations or different sequences. In short, matter alone explains everything.

Part I.—Of *Man*

CHAP. I: *OF* SENSE

CONCERNING THE THOUGHTS of man, I will consider them first singly, and afterwards in sequence, or dependence upon one another. Singly, they are every one a representation or appearance of some quality or other accident of a body outside us, which is commonly called an object. By working on the eyes, ears, and other parts of a person's body in a variety of ways, objects produce a variety of appearances.

The original of them all is that which we call sense (for there is no conception in a person's mind which has not first, either totally or by parts, been produced upon the organs of sense). The rest are derived from that original . . .

The cause of sense is the external body or object which presses the organ proper to each sense, either immediately, as in taste and touch, or mediately, as in seeing, hearing, and smelling, in which the mediation of nerves and other membranes of the body, continued inward to the brain and heart, causes there a resistance or counter pressure, or endeavor of the heart to deliver itself. Because this endeavor is outward, it seems to be some outside matter. And this seeming or fancy is what people call sense; it consists for the eye in a light or color, for the ear in a sound, for the nostril in an odor, for the tongue and palate in a savor, and for the rest of the body in heat, cold, hardness, softness, and such other qualities as we discern by feeling. All qualities called sensible are in the object that causes them and, by motion, the matter presses our sense organs in various ways. Sensible qualities in us are nothing else but diverse motions (for motion produces nothing but motion.) Their appearance to us is fancy and it is the same whether waking or dreaming . . . and, though at some distance the actual object seems invested with the fancy it begets in us, still the object is one thing and the image or fancy is another. So, sense in all cases, is nothing else but original fancy, caused (as I have said) by the pressure or motion of external things upon our eyes, ears, and other organs . . .

CHAPTER II: *OF* IMAGINATION

. . . When a body is once in motion, it moves (unless something else hinders it) eternally; and whatever hinders it cannot in an instant but in time and by degrees quite extinguish it. And as we see in the water, after the winds cease the waves remain agitated for some time afterward, so it also happens with that motion made in the internal parts of a person when he/she dreams, etc. For, after the object is removed or the eye shut, we still retain an image of the thing seen, though more obscure than when we see it. And this is what the Latins call imagination (from the image made in seeing) and apply the word improperly to all the other senses. But the Greeks call it fancy, which signifies appearance, and is as proper to one sense as to another. Imagination therefore is nothing but decaying sense and is found in people and in many other living creatures, sleeping as well as waking.

Much memory or memory of many things is called experience. Again, imagination consists only of those things which have formerly been perceived by sense, either all at once or by parts at several times. The former, which is imagining of the whole object as it was presented to the sense, is simple imagination, as when one imagines a man or a horse which he has seen before. The other is compounded, as when, from the sight of a man at one time and of a horse at another, we conceive in our mind a centaur . . .

Not knowing what imagination or the senses are, schools teach what they receive. Some say that imaginations arise of themselves and have no cause. Others teach that they arise most commonly from the will and that good thoughts are blown (inspired) into a person by God and evil thoughts by the devil, or that good thoughts are poured (infused) into a person by God and evil ones by the devil. Some say the senses receive the species of things and deliver them to the common sense; and the common sense delivers them over to the fancy, and the fancy to the memory, and the memory to the judgment, like handing of things from one to another, with many words making nothing understood . . .

Continuing to Think

Did Hobbes convince you, as he has convinced many in the Western world, that we have no need to go beyond matter in motion in order to explain all of reality? Materialism is a satisfying explanation because of its unity and its simplicity. There is also a commonsense quality to it. When Hobbes says that there is no conception (thought) that was not first a perception, you may find yourself in agreement that our senses represent our only way of learning about the world. How, indeed, could something get into your mind except through your medium of connection with the world? This theory has the added benefit of making an apparently clean connection between reality as it appears to us and reality as it is.

Now consider how Plato might respond to Hobbes's materialism. As an idealist, Plato believed in the independent existence of ideas. In fact, he considered the idea of a table far more important than the matter of that table. Without the idea or Form of tableness, there would be only unformed raw material. How, Plato might ask Hobbes, do I experience the bark of a tree as rough in texture when my perception is clearly not itself rough? And, even more to the point, what is it that experiences the roughness? Idealists always believe there is a "me" or at least a mind or self to experience perceptions.

Materialists, who insist matter alone explains all reality, are often forced to deny the reality of mind, self, God, and other immaterial entities. The debate between materialists, such as Hobbes, and idealists, such as Plato, provides the undercurrent for much of Western philosophy. For Plato, materialists are cave dwellers, relying on their unreliable senses and confusing shadows with reality.

2.2   *Flatland*

EDWIN ABBOT

Preparing to Read

Imagine a world of only two dimensions, a flat land in which length and width define all that is. Now imagine a sphere arriving in this world, with superior knowledge about (and experience of) a third dimension, seeking a mathematician to be enlightened. This novel was written more than a hundred years ago and has lost none of its relevance.

Think about Plato's Cave Allegory in which the prisoners see only shadows and mistake the shadows for reality. Like those cave dwellers, the residents of Flatland are sure that reality contains only two dimensions. But, like the freed prisoner who is dragged from the cave and forced to see not only the objects that produced the shadows but, eventually, the real world outside the cave on which the objects were based, our square is about to become enlightened.

At first, as Plato suggests in his allegory, the message brought by the sphere seems heretical and nonsensical. The square continues to resist until, pulled physically outside of Flatland, he is forced to experience reality in 3-D. If you keep in mind the experience of the freed prisoner Plato describes and especially the reaction of the people who have never left the cave when their former neighbor returns with a fantastic tale of another, more real, world, you may be sympathetic to the predicament of the square. As we join the story, a sphere arrives in Flatland, prepared to preach the Gospel of the Three Dimensions (which he is allowed to do only once in a thousand years) to a worthy apostle, in this case an intelligent, but narrow-minded, square.

18. — *How I Came to Spaceland, and What I Saw There*

AN UNSPEAKABLE HORROR seized me. There was a darkness; then a dizzy, sickening sensation of sight that was not like seeing; I saw a Line that was no Line; Space that was not Space: I was myself, and not myself. When I could find voice, I shrieked loud in agony, "Either this is madness or it is Hell." "It is neither," calmly replied the voice of the Sphere, "it is Knowledge; it is Three Dimensions: open your eye once again and try to look steadily."

I looked, and, behold, a new world! There stood before me, visibly incorporate, all that I had before inferred, conjectured, dreamed, of perfect Circular beauty. What seemed the centre of the Stranger's form lay open to my view: yet I could see no heart, lungs, nor arteries, only a beautiful harmonious Something—for which I had no words; but you, my Readers in Spaceland, would call it the surface of the Sphere.

Prostrating myself mentally before my Guide, I cried, "How is it, O divine ideal of consummate loveliness and wisdom that I see thy inside, and yet cannot discern thy heart, thy lungs, thy arteries, thy liver?" "What you think you see, you see not," he replied; "it is not given to you, nor to any other Being, to behold my internal parts. I am of a different order of Beings from those in Flatland. Were I a Circle, you could discern my intestines, but I am a Being, composed as I told you before, of many Circles, the Many in the One, called in this country a Sphere. And, just as the outside of a Cube is a Square, so the outside of a Sphere represents the appearance of a Circle."

Bewildered though I was by my Teacher's enigmatic utterance, I no longer chafed against it, but worshipped him in silent adoration. He continued, with more mildness in his voice. "Distress not yourself if you cannot at first understand the deeper mysteries of Spaceland. By degrees they will dawn upon you. Let us begin by casting back a glance at the region whence you came. Return with me a while to the plains of Flatland and I will shew you that which you have often reasoned and thought about, but never seen with the sense of sight—a visible angle." "Impossible!" I cried; but, the Sphere leading the way, I followed as if in a dream, till once more his voice arrested me: "Look yonder, and behold your own Pentagonal house, and all its inmates."

I looked below, and saw with my physical eye all that domestic individuality which I had hitherto merely inferred with the understanding. And how poor and shadowy was the inferred conjecture in comparison with the reality which I now beheld! My four Sons calmly asleep in the North-Western rooms, my two orphan Grandsons to the South; the Servants, the Butler, my Daughter, all in their several apartments. Only my affectionate Wife, alarmed by my continued absence, had quitted her room and was roving up and down in the Hall, anxiously awaiting my return. Also the Page, aroused by my cries, had left his room, and under pretext of ascertaining whether I had fallen somewhere in a faint, was prying into the cabinet in my study. All this I could now *see,* not merely infer; and as we came nearer and nearer, I could discern even the contents of my cabinet, and the two chests of gold, and the tablets of which the Sphere had made mention.

Touched by my Wife's distress, I would have sprung downward to reassure her, but I found myself incapable of motion. "Trouble not yourself about your Wife," said my Guide: "she will not be long left in anxiety; meantime, let us take a survey of Flatland."

Once more I felt myself rising through space. It was even as the Sphere had said. The further we receded from the object we beheld, the larger became the field of vision. My native city, with the interior of every house and every creature therein, lay open to my view in miniature. We mounted higher, and lo, the secrets of the earth, the depths of mines and inmost caverns of the hills, were bared before me.

Awestruck at the sight of the mysteries of the earth, thus unveiled before my unworthy eye, I said to my Companion, "Behold, I am become as a God. For the wise men in our country say that to see all things, or as they express it, *omnividence,* is the attribute of God alone." There was something of scorn in the voice of my Teacher as he made answer: "Is it so indeed? Then the very pick-pockets and cut-throats of my country are to be worshipped by your wise men as being Gods: for there is not one of them that does not see as much as you see now. But trust me, your wise men are wrong."

I. Then is omnividence the attribute of others besides Gods?

Sphere. I do not know. But, if a pick-pocket or a cut-throat of our country can see everything that is in your country, surely that is no reason why the pick-pocket or cut-throat should be accepted by you as a God. This omnividence, as you call it—it is not a common word in Spaceland—does it make you more just, more merciful, less selfish, more loving? Not in the least. Then how does it make you more divine?

I. "More merciful, more loving!" But these are the qualities of women! And we know that a Circle is a higher Being than a Straight Line, in so far as knowledge and wisdom are more to be esteemed than mere affection.

Sphere. It is not for me to classify human faculties according to merit. Yet many of the best and wisest in Spaceland think more of the affections than of the understanding, more of your despised Straight Lines than of your belauded Circles. But enough of this. Look yonder. Do you know that building?

I looked, and afar off I saw an immense Polygonal structure, in which I recognized the General Assembly Hall of the States of Flatland, surrounded by dense lines of Pentagonal buildings at right angles to each other, which I knew to be streets; and I perceived that I was approaching the great Metropolis.

"Here we descend," said my Guide. It was now morning, the first hour of the first day of the two thousandth year of our era. Acting, as was their wont, in strict accordance with precedent, the highest Circles of the realm were meeting in solemn conclave, as they had met on the first

hour of the first day of the year 1000, and also on the first hour of the first day of the year 0.

The minutes of the previous meetings were now read by one whom I at once recognized as my brother, a perfectly Symmetrical Square, and the Chief Clerk of the High Council. It was found recorded on each occasion that: "Whereas the States had been troubled by divers ill-intentioned persons pretending to have received revelations from another World, and professing to produce demonstrations whereby they had instigated to frenzy both themselves and others, it had been for this cause unanimously resolved by the Grand Council that on the first day of each millenary, special injunctions be sent to the Prefects in the several districts of Flatland, to make strict search for such misguided persons, and without formality of mathematical examination, to destroy all such as were Isosceles of any degree, to scourge and imprison any regular Triangle, to cause any Square or Pentagon to be sent to the district Asylum, and to arrest any one of higher rank, sending him straightway to the Capital to be examined and judged by the Council."

"You hear your fate," said the Sphere to me, while the Council was passing for the third time the formal resolution. "Death or imprisonment awaits the Apostle of the Gospel of Three Dimensions." "Not so," replied I, "the matter is now so clear to me, the nature of real space so palpable, that methinks I could make a child understand it. Permit me but to descend at this moment and enlighten them." "Not yet," said my Guide, "the time will come for that. Meantime I must perform my mission. Stay thou there in thy place." Saying these words, he leaped with great dexterity into the sea (if I may so call it) of Flatland, right in the midst of the ring of Counsellors. "I come," cried he, "to proclaim that there is a land of Three Dimensions."

I could see many of the younger Counsellors start back in manifest horror, as the Sphere's circular section widened before them. But on a sign from the presiding Circle—who shewed not the slightest alarm or surprise—six Isosceles of a low type from six different quarters rushed upon the Sphere. "We have him," they cried; "No; yes; we have him still! he's going! he's gone!"

"My Lords," said the President to the Junior Circles of the Council, "there is not the slightest need for surprise; the secret archives, to which I alone have access, tell me that a similar occurrence happened on the last two millennial commencements. You will, of course, say nothing of these trifles outside the Cabinet."

Raising his voice, he now summoned the guards. "Arrest the policemen; gag them. You know your duty." After he had consigned to their fate the wretched policemen—ill-fated and unwilling witnesses of a State-secret which they were not to be permitted to reveal—he again addressed the Counsellors. "My Lords, the business of the Council being concluded, I have only to wish you a happy New Year." Before departing, he expressed, at some length, to the Clerk, my excellent but most unfortunate brother, his sincere regret that, in accordance with precedent and for the sake of secrecy, he must condemn him to perpetual imprisonment, but added his satisfaction that, unless some mention were made by him of that day's incident, his life would be spared.

19. How, Though the Sphere Shewed Me Other Mysteries of Spaceland, I Still Desired More; and What Came of It

When I saw my poor brother led away to imprisonment, I attempted to leap down into the Council Chamber, desiring to intercede on his behalf, or at least bid him farewell. But I found that I had no motion of my own. I absolutely depended on the volition of my Guide, who said in gloomy tones, "Heed not thy brother; haply thou shalt have ample time hereafter to condole with him. Follow me."

Once more we ascended into space. "Hitherto," said the Sphere, "I have shewn you naught save Plane Figures and their interiors. Now I must introduce you to Solids, and reveal to you the plan upon which they are constructed. Behold this multitude of moveable square cards. See, I put one on another, not, as you supposed, Northward of the other, but on the other. Now a second, now a third. See, I am building up a Solid by a multitude of Squares parallel to one another. Now the Solid is complete, being as high as it is long and broad, and we call it a Cube."

"Pardon me, my Lord," replied I; "but to my eye the appearance is as of an Irregular Figure whose inside is laid open to view; in other words, methinks I see no Solid, but a Plane such as we infer in Flatland; only of an Irregularity which betokens some monstrous criminal, so that the very sight of it is painful to my eyes."

"True," said the Sphere; "it appears to you a Plane, because you are not accustomed to light and shade and perspective; just as in Flatland a Hexagon would appear a Straight Line to one who has not the Art of Sight Recognition. But in reality it is a Solid, as you shall learn by the sense of Feeling."

He then introduced me to the Cube, and I found that this marvellous Being was indeed no Plane, but a Solid; and that he was endowed with six plane sides and eight terminal points called solid angles; and I remembered the saying of the Sphere that just such a Creature as this would be formed by a Square moving, in Space, parallel to himself: and I rejoiced to think that so insignificant a Creature as I could in some sense be called the Progenitor of so illustrious an offspring.

But still I could not fully understand the meaning of what my Teacher had told me concerning "light" and "shade" and "perspective"; and I did not hesitate to put my difficulties before him.

Were I to give the Sphere's explanation of these matters, succinct and clear though it was, it would be tedious to an inhabitant of Space, who knows these things already. Suffice it, that by his lucid statements, and by changing the position of objects and lights, and by allowing me to feel the several objects and even his own sacred Person, he at last made all things clear to me, so that I could now readily distinguish between a Circle and a Sphere, a Plane Figure and a Solid. . . .

I. But my Lord has shewn me the intestines of all my countrymen in the Land of Two Dimensions by taking me with him into the Land of Three. What therefore more easy than now to take his servant on a second journey into the blessed region of the Fourth Dimension, where I shall look down with him once more upon this land of Three Dimensions, and see the inside of every three-dimensioned house, the secrets of the solid earth, the treasures of the mines in Spaceland, and the intestines of every solid living creature, even of the noble and adorable Spheres.

Sphere. But where is this land of Four Dimensions?

I. I know not: but doubtless my Teacher knows.

Sphere. Not I. There is no such land. The very idea of it is utterly inconceivable.

I. Not inconceivable, my Lord, to me, and therefore still less inconceivable to my Master. Nay, I despair not that, even here, in this region of Three Dimensions, your Lordship's art may make the Fourth Dimension visible to me; just as in the Land of Two Dimensions my Teacher's skill would fain have opened the eyes of his blind servant to the invisible presence of a Third Dimension, though I saw it not.

Let me recall the past. Was I not taught below that when I saw a Line and inferred a Plane, I in reality saw a Third unrecognized Dimension, not the same as brightness, called "height"? And does it not now follow that, in this region, when I see a Plane and infer a Solid, I really see a Fourth unrecognized Dimension, not the same as colour, but existent, though infinitesimal and incapable of measurement?

And besides this, there is the Argument from Analogy of Figures.

Sphere. Analogy! Nonsense: what analogy?

I. Your Lordship tempts his servant to see whether he remembers the revelations imparted to him. Trifle not with me, my Lord; I crave, I thirst, for more knowledge. Doubtless we cannot *see* that other higher Spaceland now, because we have no eye in our stomachs. But, just as there *was* the realm of Flatland, though the poor puny Lineland Monarch could neither turn to left nor right to discern it, and just as there *was* close at hand, and touching my frame, the land of Three Dimensions, though I, blind senseless wretch, had no power to touch it, no eye in my interior to discern it, so of a surety there is a Fourth Dimension, which my Lord perceives with the inner eye of thought. And that it must exist my Lord himself has taught me. Or can he have forgotten what he himself imparted to his servant?

In One Dimension, did not a moving Point produce a Line with *two* terminal points?

In Two Dimensions, did not a moving Line produce a Square with *four* terminal points?

In Three Dimensions, did not a moving Square produce—did not this eye of mine behold it—that blessed Being, a Cube, with *eight* terminal points?

And in Four Dimensions shall not a moving Cube—alas, for Analogy, and alas for the Progress of Truth, if it be not so—shall not, I say, the motion of a divine Cube result in a still more divine Organization with *sixteen* terminal points?

Continuing to Think

Have you ever learned something about reality that seemed so clear to you that you wanted to share what you'd learned with others—and they resisted? Can you understand why they might have found what you had to say frightening? Since Einstein, physicists have told us that we live in a four-dimensional universe. Space and time, rather than being separate and distinct, exist on the same continuum and together they constitute the four dimensions. We, in our limitation, perceive only the three dimensions of length, width, and height. Time seems separate and absolute to us, moving at its own independent and constant speed. However, if we could see things as they really are, we would realize that time is relative instead of fixed and that all events from past, present, and future are somehow present.

This reading helps us understand why someone would resist what contradicts the experiences of a lifetime. It also opens the possibility that reality may be more complex and complete than our limited perspective lets us see. Philosophy, Aristotle said, begins in wonder. If we can keep a spirit of openness, new understandings are always possible. Like the square, we will be tempted to resist, to assert the truth as we understand it, even when we speak with someone who understands a higher truth. The answer to the question "What is real?" may be considerably more complicated than we have imagined it to be.

Keep the experiences of the square in mind as you read the remaining three selections in this chapter and those in the rest of the book. Do not be surprised if some of what you read seems jarring and difficult to believe. That is a normal and understandable reaction. Try to remember, though, that there may be more to reality than meets the eye. Socrates was astounded when the Oracle at Delphi told his friend that Socrates was the wisest of the Greeks, but after talking with many supposedly wise men he realized that at least he knew what he did not know. Others were blind to their ignorance and spoke with authority on subjects they understood very incompletely. In this at least—in knowing what he did not know and in remaining open to wisdom and truth—Socrates admitted that the Oracle might have been right.

2.3   *The African Philosophical Tradition*

LANCINAY KEITA

Preparing to Read

To what extent did the ancient Greeks borrow from the ancient Egyptians? This question is at the root of a significant scholarly controversy at present. In this essay we look at an explanation of Egyptian thought during the eighteenth dynasty (about 3,500 years ago) and its continuing influence on the scientific revolution of the seventeenth century. The separation we currently make between science and magic did not exist when the great scientific discoveries were being made in Europe, and many scientists drew gratefully on the work attributed to an Egyptian mystery priest, Hermes Trismegistus. This Hermetic tradition, and its influence on Western views of reality, is one of the focuses of Professor Keita's essay.

The other focus is on what the Greeks chose to borrow from the Egyptians and what they chose not to borrow. According to Keita, the Egyptians had a monistic view of the world—they saw everything as part of a unity. One contributing element was empirical or observational scientific knowledge about the material world; the other element was metaphysical or philosophical investigation into what is real. For the Egyptians, there was a unity between the two and they were seen as complementary rather than contradictory. By accepting the empiricism of the ancient Egyptians, but being less enthusiastic about their metaphysics, the Greeks broke the easy unity that existed. In a Greek dualism that separates mind from matter and the ideal from the material, the harmony that had existed in the Egyptian system is no longer possible.

BECAUSE OF THE EXPERIENCES of a recent past Africa's intellectual output has been rather meager, except perhaps in the area of literature where individual writers have not been slow to describe life in the precolonial or colonial period. But genuine intellectual work either of a philosophical or scientific nature has not kept pace with the output in pure literature.

The reason for this situation is that there is, perhaps, the belief that there is no genuine African intellectual matrix which could serve as a basis for African scholarship. This belief is fostered by the more current view that the African intellectual experience has been essentially "oral" and "prescientific" as compared, say, with the "literate" and "scientific" tradition of Europe.[1]

The end result of these beliefs has been to encourage African intellectuals either to search for the historical precedents of their own literacy in non-African sources[2] or to express great uncertainty about the definition of the concept of Africanity.

It is the purpose of this paper to present evidence that a sufficiently firm literate philosophical tradition has existed in Africa since ancient times, and that this tradition is of sufficient intellectual sophistication to warrant serious analysis. In this regard, then, this paper does not constitute an attempt to discuss some particular aspect of the admittedly vague concept, African thought; it is rather a position paper—an attempt to offer a defensible idea of an African philosophy. . . .

The Classical African Thought of Ancient Egypt

Granted that the colonial period in Africa was one in which European nations were in political and economic control of most of Africa, and enjoyed enormous benefits from the servitude imposed on Africans, it is understandable that most of the research done on Africa by European scholars would have tended to describe Africa as necessarily benefiting from colonialism. This approach entailed (a) distortion of African history to fit the belief that Africa was the continent of the uncivilized who should, no doubt, hope to benefit from being brought into contact with European civilization; (b) the usage of spurious anthropological techniques[3] to give the impression of scientific objectivity to the decidedly biased approach to African history.

It is for this reason that the history of Ancient Egypt was severed from the history of the African world and considered, henceforth, as part of the Oriental World—a world which encompasses cultures and peoples as diverse as the Turks, Chinese, Indians and Japanese. The aim, no doubt, was to create a world in which civilization was the patrimony solely of the Western and Eastern peoples, with the African world being the receptacle of all that was uncivilized or "primitive"—to use the highly emotive though still current term. The result of this dogmatic approach to cultural history was that those Africans, considered

---

From Richard C. Wright, *African Philosophy: An Introduction,* 3rd edition, 1984.
Courtesy of University Press of America.

civilized, were considered Oriental or at least were of Oriental origins.

However, sober historical research will not support this view.[4] According to the objective findings of researchers of African cultural history, the cultural forms of Ancient Egypt were essentially African as expressed especially in the religion practiced by its inhabitants. For example, the strongly totemic characteristics of Egyptian religious practices are considered by many anthropologists to be essentially African. Furthermore, the written testimonies of Greek visitors to Ancient Egypt leave no doubt as to the ethnic and cultural backgrounds of the Ancient Egyptians. In fact, the belief that the Ancient Egyptians were a non-African people is relatively recent[5] and directly related to the period of European dominance in Africa.

Thus the basis for the thesis that the thought systems of the Ancient Egyptians warrant inclusion in the matrix of African thought systems has been established. It is fair to state that the earliest periods of Egyptian civilization produced thought systems that were, perhaps, excessively conservative (so dominant was the practice of ancestor worship), and it was not until the eighteenth dynasty that an intellectual revolution of some sort occurred. The cosmological revolution introduced by Amenhotep IV was an attempt to introduce a holistic interpretation of the universe guided and explained by one deity as opposed to the then dominant pantheism. The philosophical significance of this short-lived revolution is that it is highly plausible that Egyptian monotheism was of great influence in the shaping of two of the important religions of the area: Judaism and Christianity. Any student of philosophy should know, of course, that philosophy in the Christian and Judaic world was greatly bound up with Christian and Judaic doctrine and, in fact, the main function of philosophy at that time was to justify the ontological claims of these two religious systems.

However, the major corpus of Egyptian philosophy was not made known to the outside world until the second or third centuries A.D.

The body of Ancient Egyptian philosophy which became a source of interest to the outside world is generally known as the *Hermetica,* and the reasons for this interest, according to one scholar of the European Renaissance is as follows: "The world of the second century was weary of Greek dialectics which seemed to lead to no certain results. Platonists, Stoics, Epicureans could only repeat the theories of their various schools without making any further advances, and the tenets of the schools were boiled down in textbook form, in manuals which formed the basis of philosophical instruction within the Empire."[6] . . .

Clearly the strongly metaphysical nature of Hermetic thought would suggest its essentially African content. One traditional feature of African ontology (developed to its highest expression by the Ancient Egyptians) is that it is predominantly monist in outlook. The dualist cleavage between mind and matter which characterizes much discussion in modern European philosophy[7] did not exist for the Ancient Egyptian priest.

The neo-Greek interest in Egyptian thought at the time when "The mighty intellectual effort of the Greek philosophy was exhausted, had come to a standstill, to a dead end" did not develop, as Yates suggests, "because Greek thinking never took the momentous step of experimental verification of its hypotheses" but because (and it would appear somewhat paradoxical) pure empiricism has its limitations in that it leads to a simple-minded Baconian approach to the material world. Scientific progress and insights occur when science adopts a holistic view of the world and attempts to go beyond the merely empirically given data to construct theories which contain elements which could be controversial to the pure empiricist. It is for this reason that metaphysical elements in the works of Newton, Leibniz and Einstein are understandable.

Thus the Greek return to the Egyptians is not without some logic, and it set the foundations for the all-important scientific breakthroughs of

Bruno, Copernicus et al. As Yates writes, "The men of the second century were thoroughly imbued with the idea (which the Renaissance imbibed from them) that what is old is pure, and hold that the earliest thinkers walked more closely with the gods than the busy rationalists, their successors."[8] . . .

But the influence of Egyptian thought did not end with the Greeks; it was of lasting influence on the shaping of European medieval and Renaissance thought. "It was on excellent authority that the Renaissance accepted *Hermes Trismegistus* as a real person of great antiquity and as the author of the Hermetic writings, for this was implicitly believed by leading fathers of the church particularly Lactantius and Augustine."[9]

It has been established so far that the thought systems of the Ancient Egyptians warrant attention in any discussion of African thought. It has also been argued that certain features of Egyptian thought were attractive to the Greeks (and later to the medieval world) in a sort of neo-Egyptian philosophical revival. Thus it is pertinent at this stage to discuss the essential features of Egyptian philosophy as expressed in the classical work *Corpus Hermetica*.

According to Clement of Alexandria, there were forty-two books written by Hermes, of which "thirty-six contain the whole of the philosophy of the Egyptians, the other six being on medicine."[10] These books possessed an extensively mystical tone which was a source of intense interest to the European scholar of the Renaissance. Again, according to Yates: "Nevertheless it is probable that Hermes Trismegistus is the most important figure in the Renaissance revival of magic. Egypt was traditionally associated with the darkest and strongest magic, and now there were brought to light the writings of an Egyptian priest which revealed an extraordinary piety, confirming the high opinion of him which the Christian Father, Lactantius, had expressed, and whom the highest authorities regarded as the source of Plato."[11]

This metaphysical interpretation of the world colored the Egyptian cosmology and philosophy of man and nature. The universe was perceived as being in perpetual animated motion, the expression of a single supreme creator.[12] The structure of this universe was indestructible since "nothing that is in the world will ever perish or be destroyed, for Eternity is imperishable." (Ibid., p. 33)

Egyptian philosophy espoused not only the idea of the oneness and indestructible nature of the universe (perhaps an intuitive prelude to the conservation laws of modern physical science) but also that the universe was a universe constantly energized and in perpetual motion.[13]

Concerning the nature of man, Egyptian philosophy expressed views that are quite sophisticated and are interestingly similar to those expressed by the Classical Greek thinkers on the nature of man. Man's intellect or rational faculties are derived from the very substance of God." Thus the godlike characteristics of man are embodied in his rational faculties; and men who live by the fullest exercising of their intellects are close to the gods. On the other hand, when "man is not guided by intellect he falls below himself into an animal state." (Yates, p. 33) The general thesis on the nature of man is that man partakes of the world of the gods by virtue of his intellect but yet is part of the animal world.[14]

Contrary to accepted doctrine, the philosophy of the Ancient Egyptians exercised great influence on the European Renaissance, for the name of "Hermes Trismegistus was well known in the Middle Ages and was connected with alchemy, and magic, particularly with magic images or talismans. The Middle Ages feared whatever they knew of the decans as dangerous demons, and some of the books supposedly by Hermes were strongly censured by Albertus Magnus as containing diabolical magic. The Augustian censure of the demon-worship in the Asclepius (by which he may have meant in particular decan worship) weighed heavily upon that work. However, medieval writers interested in natural philosophy speak of him with respect; for Roger Bacon he was the 'father of Philosophers,' and he is sometimes given a genealogy which makes him even more ancient than Ficino or the designer of the Siena mosaic thought."[15]

But perhaps the Egyptian thinker's most important legacy to modern science is the role the Hermetic paradigm played in the scientific revolution that took place in Western Europe in the seventeenth century. "Taking a very long view down the avenues of time a beautiful and coherent line of development suggests itself—perhaps too beautiful and coherent to be quite true. The late antique world, unable to carry Greek science forward any further, turned to the religious cult of the world and its accompanying occultisms and magics of which the writings of 'Hermes Trismegistus' are an expression. . . . In the long medieval centuries, both in the West and the Arabic world, the traditions of rational Greek science made progress. Hence it is now suggested, when 'Hermes Trismegistus' and all that he stood for is rediscovered in the Renaissance, the return to the occult of this time stimulates the genuine science." (Yates, pp. 449–50)

In other words radical changes in scientific reasoning initiated by such theorists as Bruno, Descartes and Newton were in some measure influenced by Egyptian thought.

However, Yates' interesting observations notwithstanding, there are grounds for further comment on the supposed opposition between Greek rationalism and Egyptian animism. It should be remembered that although the Greeks expressed an interest in scientific theories, they were not scientists in the true sense of the word. They did not seem aware of the fact that the validity of scientific theories depends on their capacities to undergo experimental testings.

The Egyptians, on the other hand, were well acquainted with empirical methods of research as their extensive architecture and medical researches signify. But purely empirical observations were not sufficient for the Egyptians; their empirical observations assumed explanatory status on being placed within the context of the Egyptian cosmology. Thus there are two aspects of the Egyptian ontology: the empirical aspect

based on the data of empirical observation, and the metaphysical aspect which sought to offer ultimate explanation for the physical data of the world.

It is of interest to note that in the Egyptian cosmology empiricism and metaphysics were complementary, the former affording facts about the world, and the latter serving as their ultimate explanation. The Greeks, on the other hand, eagerly accepted the materialism of the Egyptians but tended to be less enthusiastic about their metaphysics, notwithstanding the Greek interest in the *Hermetica* in the second century.[16] However, the point being made is that European philosophy has inherited the tradition of the Greeks in which the material world is perceived as antithetical to the metaphysical rather than complementary to it, as was the case with the Egyptians. And it was this reunion of the two ontologies that "stimulates the genuine science" in the seventeenth century. The remarkable revolution of the seventeenth century could perhaps be explained by the timely fusion of the two major traditions of Egyptian thought; the empirist and the metaphysical, the one kept alive by the early Greeks, the latter nurtured by the later Greeks and nurtured by the Renaissance. According to Yates: "It may be illuminating to view the scientific revolution as in two phases, the first phase consisting of an animistic universe operated by magic, the second phase of a mathematical universe operated by mechanics. An enquiry into both phases, and their interaction, may be a more fruitful line of historical approach to the problems raised by the science of today than the line which concentrates only on the seventeenth century triumph. Is not all science a gnosis, an insight into the nature of the All, which proceeds by successive revelations?"[17]

The thought systems of the Ancient Egyptians represent the most literate expression of the African in ancient history. These thought systems were based on the essentially African view of the world as being both subject to empirical and metaphysical interpretation. For the African the pursuit of metaphysics is an attempt to grapple with gnosis—to explain the life and motion that energizes the material world. And this is basically the world view, not only of the Ancient Egyptian priest, but also of the African peasant. The historical legacy of the classical thought of ancient Africa is modern science, which began to develop in the seventeenth century. . . .

What then are the distinguishing features of African thought that emerge from the above analysis? African thought is essentially holistic in the sense that it accepts the material world, thus making possible empirical science, yet recognizing at the same time that metaphysical elements constitute the ontological support and motive force for movement and motion in the world. Paradoxically, it was this holistic ontology that permitted the most significant breakthroughs in empirical science in the modern era.

NOTES

1. From a strictly historical point of view the notion of an oral Africa and literate Europe is clearly forced. Literacy is a recent phenomenon in Europe—of course a very small minority of Greeks, and much later on, a small number of West Europeans learned to read and write Latin, but the vast majority of the inhabitants of feudal and industrial Europe were illiterate. Individuals learned to read and write during the recent advent of mass education. On the other hand some Africans knew how to read and write before the colonial era. Thus the term "oral tradition" as opposed to "literate tradition" should be employed guardedly. General usage, however, seems to imply that in some way "orality" is inherent to the African "essence" while "literacy" is a "physiological" trait of Europeans.

2. This position is most evident in the writings of the Senegalese poet Leopold Senghor, and the political theorist Frantz Fanon: See especially the latter's *Peau Noire Masques Blanches* (Paris: Editions du Seuil, 1952), pp. 201–208.

3. This tradition obviously antedates the colonial period, for it was during the period of the enslavement of the African in the Americas that notions about the supposed superiority of some races and the inferiority of others, especially the African, first warranted "serious" research. It should be noted that it was during this period that the term "negro" was first used, even by the scientifically minded European.

4. See C. A. Diop, *The African Origin of Civilization* (New York: Lawrence Hill and Company, 1974), p. 50.

5. Frances Yates, *Giordano Bruno and the Hermetic Tradition* (Chicago: University of Chicago Press, 1964), p. 4. Yates' research on the influence of Egyptian thought on the Greek and Renaissance world relies heavily on A. J. Festugiere's research and text *La Revelation d'Hermes Trismegiste,* and takes into consideration the research done on the Renaissance by scholars such as P. O. Kristeller et al. Since limitations on space do not permit an exhaustive reference to the original sources, most of the supporting references will be from Yates' work.

6. Yates, Ibid., pp. 4–5.

7. Yates, p . 5.

8. Ibid., p. 5.

9. Ibid., p. 12.

10. Ibid., p. 18.

11. Ibid., p. 31.

12. Ibid., p. 31.

13. Granted the influence of Egyptian thought on the Renaissance, it is plausible to argue that Galileo's notion of a dynamic universe (the natural state of matter in motion)—as opposed to the static Aristotelian ontology—could have been influenced by the former.

14. It is of interest to note that this particular conception of human nature resembles that of the classical Greek thinkers: Socrates, Plato, Aristotle et al., in making the distinction between man's rational and appetitive faculties. It seems more likely, however, that this idea of man is of Egyptian origin if only from the point of view that the Egyptians expressed this view in their sculpture.

15. Yates, *Giordano Bruno,* p . 48.

16. Ibid., p. 2.

17. Ibid., p. 452.

Continuing to Think

Plato, one of the giants of the classical Greek philosophical tradition, had a two-world view. When he studied geometry with Pythagoras, he realized that when we talk about "the circle" or "the square" we don't mean the one in front of us but, rather, some ideal or perfect circle or square that each imperfect example in this world imitates. Only the Forms are real, Plato said, and that meant living in this world was like living in a cave of illusion. His emphasis on Forms as real qualifies Plato as an idealist; for him the material world is an imperfect copy of what is. This is the Greek dualism that has so influenced the Western world.

Suppose instead of this dualism you lived in a culture, like that of ancient Egypt, in which everything was seen as a unity. Matter might be as important as mind, and both might be seen as parts of a unified whole. Professor Keita's essay has argued that real scientific progress depends on a holistic view of the world. What do you think? We, in the West, have tended to divide science and philosophy, although particle physics is bringing them closer together again by revealing a subatomic world made, not of separate building blocks, but of an interconnected web of energy.

In the world of the very small, as explained by quantum mechanics, it seems we can have only probable knowledge and not certainty. There is a lot of unpredictability, and the very act of observing reality automatically changes it. What something is like independent of observation can only be inferred and, indeed, until something is observed it could be said that nothing happens to it.

Keep this science in mind as we follow Alice down the rabbit hole into the very unpredictable world of Wonderland. If all the rules have changed and even very crucial things about herself are different, has reality itself shifted or only Alice's perception of it?

2.4   *Alice's Adventures in Wonderland*

LEWIS CARROLL

Preparing to Read

It is nice to think the world is operating according to some rational or benevolent principles. Newtonian science defined a world of objects larger and slower than atoms in which momentum, gravity, centrifugal force, and other principles keep things moving and keep things predictable. Religion tells us that God is in charge and no matter how chaotic things seem in the short run, in the long run things will work out all right. Alice woke up in the world we have just described. She knew how to address her parents, teachers, friends, and pets. She knew, in other words, what to expect from life.

Now, suddenly, she finds herself in a completely other world. Nothing she knew this morning seems to be of any use, and she is quite confused and frightened. Who wouldn't be? She hasn't lost her rationality; she seems to be able to think as clearly as ever, but nothing makes any sense. Personal or social crises can leave us feeling like Alice—adrift in a hostile world in which it is difficult if not impossible to find out what is real.

Some twentieth-century philosophers, known as atheistic **existentialists,** believe this is exactly the kind of world we find ourselves in. Rejecting belief in God as unjustifiable in the face of human misery, they find no rules for living and no confidence that things will work out in the end. Like Alice, they think we can seem like strangers even to ourselves. The only solution, in their view, is to do what Alice does: keep making choices, no matter how irrational the alternatives seem, and accept responsibility for the choices you have made.

If you have ever seemed like a stranger to yourself (and perhaps to others), you may be able to relate to Alice's predicament as she grows very tall, then very small, and has trouble communicating with a French speaking mouse who finds her cat and dog references offensive.

"COME, THERE'S NO use in crying like that!" said Alice to herself, rather sharply, "I advise you to leave off this minute!" She generally gave herself very good advice (though she very seldom followed it), and sometimes she scolded herself so severely as to bring tears into her eyes; and once she remembered trying to box her own ears for having cheated herself in a game of croquet she was playing against herself, for this curious child was very fond of pretending to be two people. "But it's no use now," thought poor Alice, "to pretend to be two people! Why, there's hardly enough of me left to make *one* respectable person!"

Soon her eye fell on a little glass box that was lying under the table: she opened it, and found in it a very small cake, on which the words "EAT ME" were beautifully marked in currants. "Well, I'll eat it," said Alice, "and if it makes me grow larger, I can reach the key; and if it makes me grow smaller, I can creep under the door; so either way I'll get into the garden, and I don't care which happens!"

She ate a little bit, and said anxiously to herself "Which way? Which way?" holding her hand on the top of her head to feel which way it was growing, and she was quite surprised to find that she remained the same size: to be sure, this is what generally happens when one eats cake, but Alice had got so much into the way of expecting nothing but out-of-the-way things to happen, that it seemed quite dull and stupid for life to go on in the common way.

So she set to work, and very soon finished off the cake.

Chapter II: The Pool of Tears

"Curiouser and curiouser!" cried Alice (she was so much surprised, that for the moment she quite forgot how to speak good English). "Now I'm opening out like the largest telescope that ever was! Good-bye, feet!" (for when she looked down at her feet, they seemed to be almost out of sight, they were getting so far off). "Oh, my poor little feet, I wonder who will put on your shoes and stockings for you now, dears? I'm sure *I* shan't be able! I shall be a great deal too far off to trouble myself about you: you must manage the best way you can; —but I must be kind to them," thought Alice, "or perhaps they won't walk the way I want to go! Let me see: I'll give them a new pair of boots every Christmas."

And she went on planning to herself how she would manage it. "They must go by the carrier," she thought; "and how funny it'll seem, sending presents to one's own feet! And how odd the directions will look!

    Alice's Right Foot, Esq.
      Hearthrug,
        near the Fender,
          (with Alice's love).

Oh dear, what nonsense I'm talking!"

Just then her head struck against the roof of the hall: in fact she was now more than nine feet high, and she at once took up the little golden key and hurried off to the garden door.

Poor Alice! It was as much as she could do, lying down on one side, to look through into the garden with one eye; but to get through was more hopeless than ever: she sat down and began to cry again.

"You ought to be ashamed of yourself," said Alice, "a great girl like you," (she might well say this), "to go on crying in this way! Stop this moment, I tell you!" But she went on all the same, shedding gallons of tears, until there was a large pool all round her, about four inches deep and reaching half down the hall.

After a time she heard a little pattering of feet in the distance, and she hastily dried her eyes to see what was coming. It was the White Rabbit returning, splendidly dressed, with a pair of white kid gloves in one hand and a large fan in the other: he came trotting along in a great hurry, muttering to himself as he came, "Oh! the Duchess, the Duchess! Oh! won't she be savage if I've kept her waiting!" Alice felt so desperate that she was ready to ask help of any one: so, when the Rabbit came near her, she began, in a low, timid voice, "If you please, sir—" The Rabbit started violently, dropped the white kid gloves and the fan, and skurried away into the darkness as hard as he could go.

Alice took up the fan and gloves, and, as the hall was very hot, she kept fanning herself all the time she went on talking: "Dear, dear! How queer everything is to-day! And yesterday things went on just as usual. I wonder if I've been changed in the night? Let me think: *was* I the same when I got up this morning? I almost think I can remember feeling a little different. But if I'm not the same, the next question is, Who in the world am I? Ah, *that's* the great puzzle!" And she began thinking over all the children she knew that were of the same age as herself, to see if she could have been changed for any of them.

"I'm sure I'm not Ada," she said, "for her hair goes in such long ringlets, and mine doesn't go in ringlets at all; and I'm sure I can't be Mabel, for I know all sorts of things, and she, oh! she knows such a very little! Besides, *she's* she, and *I'm* I, and—oh dear, how puzzling it all is! I'll try if I know all the things I used to know. Let me see: four times five is twelve, and four times six is thirteen, and four times seven is—oh dear! I shall never get to twenty at that rate! However, the Multiplication-Table don't signify: let's try Geography. London is the capital of Paris, and Paris is the capital of Rome, and Rome—no, *that's* all wrong, I'm certain! I must have been changed for Mabel! I'll try and say '*How doth the little—*', " and she crossed her hands on her lap as if she were saying lessons, and began to repeat it, but her voice sounded hoarse and strange, and the words did not come the same as they used to do:—

    "*How doth the little crocodile*
    Improve his shining tail,
    And pour the waters of the Nile
    On every golden scale!

    How cheerfully he seems to grin,
    How neatly spreads his claws,
    And welcomes little fishes in,
    With gently smiling jaws!"

"I'm sure those are not the right words," said poor Alice, and her eyes filled with tears again as she went on, "I must be Mabel after all, and I shall have to go and live in that poky little house, and have next to no toys to play with, and oh! ever so many lessons to learn! No, I've made up my mind about it: if I'm Mabel, I'll stay down here! It'll be no use their putting their heads down and saying 'Come up again, dear!' I shall only look up and say 'Who am I then? Tell me that first, and then, if I like being that person, I'll come up: if not, I'll stay down here till I'm somebody else'—but, oh dear!" cried Alice, with a sudden burst of tears, "I do wish they *would* put their heads down! I am so *very* tired of being all alone here!"

As she said this she looked down at her hands, and was surprised to see that she had put on one of the Rabbit's little white kid gloves while she was talking. "How *can* I have done that?" she thought. "I must be growing small again." She got up and went to the table to measure herself by it, and found that, as nearly as she could guess, she was now about two feet high, and was going on shrinking rapidly: she soon found out that the cause of this was the fan she was holding, and she dropped it hastily, just in time to avoid shrinking away altogether.

"That *was* a narrow escape!" said Alice, a good deal frightened at the sudden change, but very glad to find herself still in existence. "And now for the garden!" And she ran with all speed back to the little door: but, alas! the little door was shut again, and the little golden key was lying on the glass table as before, "and things are worse than ever," thought the poor child, "for I never was so small as this before, never! And I declare it's too bad, that it is!"

As she said these words her foot slipped, and in another moment, splash! she was up to her chin in salt water. He first idea was that she had somehow fallen into the sea, "and in that case I can go back by railway," she said to herself. (Alice had been to the seaside once in her life, and had come to the general conclusion, that wherever you go to on the English coast you find a number of bathing machines in the sea, some children digging in the sand with wooden spades, then a row of lodging houses, and behind them a railway station.) However, she soon made out that she was in the pool of tears which she had wept when she was nine feet high.

"I wish I hadn't cried so much!" said Alice, as she swam about, trying to find her way out. "I shall be punished for it now, I suppose, by being drowned in my own tears! That *will* be a queer thing, to be sure! However, everything is queer to-day."

Just then she heard something splashing about in the pool a little way off, and she swam nearer to make out what it was: at first she thought it must be a walrus or hippopotamus, but then she remembered how small she was now, and she soon made out that it was only a mouse that had slipped in like herself.

"Would it be of any use, now," thought Alice, "to speak to this mouse? Everything is so out-of-the-way down here, that I should think very likely it can talk: at any rate, there's no harm in trying." So she began: "O Mouse, do you know the way out of this pool? I am very tired of swimming about here, O Mouse!" (Alice thought this must be the right way of speaking to a mouse: she had never done such a thing before, but she remembered having seen in her brother's Latin Grammar, "A mouse—of a mouse—to a mouse—a mouse—O mouse!") The Mouse looked at her rather inquisitively, and seemed to her to wink with one of its little eyes, but it said nothing.

"Perhaps it doesn't understand English," thought Alice. "I daresay it's a French mouse, come over with William the Conqueror." (For, with all her knowledge of history, Alice had no very clear notion how long ago anything had happened.) So she began again: "Où est ma chatte?" which was the first sentence in her French lesson-book. The Mouse gave a sudden leap out of the water, and seemed to quiver all over with fright. "Oh, I beg your pardon!" cried Alice hastily, afraid that she had hurt the poor animal's feelings. "I quite forgot you didn't like cats."

"Not like cats!" cried the Mouse, in a shrill passionate voice. "Would *you* like cats if you were me?"

"Well, perhaps not," said Alice in a soothing tone: "don't be angry about it. And yet I wish I could show you our cat Dinah. I think you'd take a fancy to cats if you could only see her.

She is such a dear quiet thing," Alice went on, half to herself, as she swam lazily about in the pool, "and she sits purring so nicely by the fire, licking her paws and washing her face—and she is such a nice soft thing to nurse—and she's such a capital one for catching mice—oh, I beg your pardon!" cried Alice again, for this time the Mouse was bristling all over, and she felt certain it must be really offended. "We won't talk about her any more if you'd rather not."

"We, indeed!" cried the Mouse, who was trembling down to the end of his tail. "As if *I* would talk on such a subject! Our family always *hated* cats: nasty, low, vulgar things! Don't let me hear the name again!"

"I won't indeed!" said Alice, in a great hurry to change the subject of conversation. "Are you—are you fond—of—of dogs?" The Mouse did not answer, so Alice went on eagerly: "There is such a nice little dog near our house I should like to show you! A little bright-eyed terrier, you know, with oh, such long curly brown hair! And it'll fetch things when you throw them, and it'll sit up and beg for its dinner, and all sorts of things—I can't remember half of them—and it belongs to a farmer, you know, and he says it's so useful, it's worth a hundred pounds! He says it kills all the rats and—oh dear!" cried Alice in a sorrowful tone. "I'm afraid I've offended it again!" For the Mouse was swimming away from her as hard as it could go, and making quite a commotion in the pool as it went.

So she called softly after it, "Mouse dear! Do come back again, and we won't talk about cats or dogs either, if you don't like them!" When the Mouse heard this, it turned round and swam slowly back to her: its face was quite pale (with passion, Alice thought), and it said in a low trembling voice, "Let us get to the shore, and then I'll tell you my history, and you'll understand why it is I hate cats and dogs."

It was high time to go, for the pool was getting quite crowded with the birds and animals that had fallen into it: there was a Duck and a Dodo, a Lory and an Eaglet, and several other curious creatures. Alice led the way, and the whole party swam to the shore.

Continuing to Think

To use the language of metaphysics we might say that Alice has taken a pragmatic view of reality. Pragmatism doesn't waste time debating which is more real, immaterial things (like ideas), or matter. Instead it focuses on what will help us predict what will happen next. Oddly enough, quantum mechanics has theories that function just this way—scientists aren't certain they accurately describe reality, but they do work.

Alice is frequently confused as she grows very tall and wonders how she will put on her shoes and stockings, and then she grows very short, almost disappearing altogether before dropping the fan. It takes her a while to realize that the sea in which she is swimming is really her own tears, shed when she was very large. And yet, she keeps her objective firmly in mind—to get the little golden key that unlocks the garden door.

Most importantly, she continues to *act* (as existentialists believe we all must do). She is not immobilized by the chaotic and changing world in which she finds herself, and she can always think of something to do. Perhaps, even if we cannot be sure of what is real or who we are, it is important to know what we want to accomplish and to act to make things happen. Although Alice does get frightened, she does not blame anyone or anything for her predicament.

There is an element of practicality in our final selection, too. The Buddha, in one of his past lives, meets a hungry tigress who has recently given birth and is too exhausted to find food for herself or her kittens. What should he do? How each of us answers that question depends on our metaphysics—on how we see the world and how we define what is real.

2.5   *Lives of the Buddha*

BUDDHIST SCRIPTURES

Preparing to Read

In the West we have seen ourselves as separate from and superior to other animals. We have emphasized the value and integrity of the individual self and the separateness of that self from other selves and from other beings and objects in the world. It may come as a shock to encounter Buddhist metaphysics, which rejects all these assumptions in favor of a radical vision of interrelatedness and interconnectedness.

The purpose of living, according to Buddhism, is not to do good works or even to be a virtuous person (although those may be the by-products of a life well lived) but to wake up and see life as it actually is. Buddhists call this **enlightenment.** Once you see things as they actually are, two things will happen: You will realize that you are connected with all that is, that there is no separation of any kind between you and other people or between you and a hungry tigress, and you will not have to be reborn or reincarnated because you will have learned what this world has to teach you. Buddhists call this state **nirvana**—literally the "blowing out" of the false sense of ego separateness.

If you are a separate, Western individual, you might think first of protecting yourself against the hungry tigress who, after all, might be dangerous. With more kindness, you might look to see if you have anything to feed the tigress or her kittens. It is unlikely you would make the decision made by this ***bodhisattva*** or enlightened being who, the Buddha tells us in this story, was himself in a previous life.

The third selection, "Parinirvana," tells of the death of the Buddha. Before entering nirvana, the state of blissful, impersonal, nondualism, it was necessary to leave this life. Existence, he explains, is without substance. To think it has substance is to live in illusion. Somewhat like the prisoners in Plato's cave, we are called by the Buddha to see past this limited world of apparent reality. At his death, all of nature trembles. How could it not since all is interrelated?

The Bodhisattva
and the Hungry Tigress

THE BUDDHA TOLD the following story to
Ananda: Once upon a time, in the remote past,
there lived a king, Maharatha by name. He was
rich in gold, grain, and chariots, and his power,
strength, and courage were irresistible. He had
three sons who were like young gods to look at.
They were named Mahapranada, Mahadeva,
and Mahasattva.

One day the king went for relaxation into a
park. The princes, delighted with the beauties
of the park and the flowers which could be
seen everywhere, walked about here and there
until they came to a large thicket of bamboos.
There they dismissed their servants, in order to
rest for a while. But Mahapranada said to his
two brothers: 'I feel rather afraid here. There
might easily be some wild beasts about, and
they might do us harm.' Mahadeva replied: 'I
also feel ill at ease. Though it is not my body I
fear for. It is the thought of separation from
those I love which terrifies me.' Finally, Mahasattva said:

'No fear feel I, nor any sorrow either,
In this wide, lonesome wood, so dear to Sages.
My heart is filled with bursting joy,
For soon I'll win the highest boon.'

As the princes strolled about in the solitary
thicket they saw a tigress, surrounded by five
cubs, seven days old. Hunger and thirst had exhausted the tigress, and her body was quite
weak. On seeing her, Mahapranada called out:
'The poor animal suffers from having given birth
to the seven cubs only a week ago! If she finds
nothing to eat, she will either eat her own
young, or die from hunger!' Mahasattva replied:
'How can this poor exhausted creature find
food?' Mahapranada said: 'Tigers live on fresh
meat and warm blood.' Mahadeva said: 'She is

quite exhausted, overcome by hunger and thirst,
scarcely alive and very weak. In this state she
cannot possibly catch any prey. And who would
sacrifice himself to preserve her life?' Mahapranada said: 'Yes, self-sacrifice is so difficult!'
Mahasattva replied: 'It is difficult for people like
us, who are so fond of our lives and bodies, and
who have so little intelligence. It is not at all difficult, however, for others, who are true men, intent on benefiting their fellow-creatures, and
who long to sacrifice themselves. Holy men are
born of pity and compassion. Whatever the bodies they may get, in heaven or on earth, a hundred times will they undo them, joyful in their
hearts, that the lives of others may be saved.'

Greatly agitated, the three brothers carefully
watched the tigress for some time, and then went
towards her. But Mahasattva thought to himself:
'Now the time has come for me to sacrifice myself! For a long time I have served this putrid
body and given it beds and clothes, food and
drink, and conveyances of all kinds. Yet it is
doomed to perish and fall down, and in the end
it will break up and be destroyed. How much
better to leave this ungrateful body of one's own
accord in good time! It cannot subsist for ever,
because it is like urine which must come out.
Today I will use it for a sublime deed. Then it
will act for me as a boat which helps me to cross
the ocean of birth and death. When I have renounced this futile body, a mere ulcer, tied to
countless becomings, burdened with urine and
excrement, unsubstantial like foam, full of hundreds of parasites—then I shall win the perfectly
pure Dharma-body, endowed with hundreds of
virtues, full of such qualities as trance and wisdom, immaculate, free from all Substrata,
changeless and without sorrow.' So, his heart
filled with boundless compassion, Mahasattva
asked his brothers to leave him alone for a while,
went to the lair of the tigress, hung his cloak on a
bamboo, and made the following vow:

'For the weal of the world I wish to win enlightenment, incomparably wonderful. From deep compassion I now give away my body, so hard to quit, unshaken in my mind. That enlightenment I shall gain, in which nothing hurts and nothing harms, and which the Jina's sons have praised. Thus shall I cross to the Beyond of the fearful ocean of becoming which fills the triple world!'

The friendly prince then threw himself down in front of the tigress. But she did nothing to him. The Bodhisattva noticed that she was too weak to move. As a merciful man he had taken no sword with him. He therefore cut his throat with a sharp piece of bamboo, and fell down near the tigress. She noticed the Bodhisattva's body all covered with blood, and in no time ate up all the flesh and blood, leaving only the bones.

'It was I, Ananda, who at that time and on that occasion was that prince Mahasattva.' . . .

The Leave-Taking from Vaisali, the Final Couch, Instructions to the Mallas

Three months later the great Sage turned his entire body round like an elephant, looked at the town of Vaisali, and uttered these words: 'O Vaisali, this is the last time that I see you. For I am now departing for Nirvana!' He then went to Kusinagara, bathed in the river, and gave this order to Ananda: 'Arrange a couch for me between those twin Sal trees! In the course of this night the Tathagata will enter Nirvana!' When Ananda had heard these words, a film of tears spread over his eyes. He arranged the Sage's last resting place, and then amid laments informed him that he had done so. In measured steps the Best of Men walked to his final resting place—no more return in store for him, no further suffering. In full sight of his disciples he lay down on his right side, rested his head on his hand, and put one leg over the other. At that moment the birds uttered no sound, and, as if in trance, they sat with their bodies all relaxed.

The winds ceased to move the leaves of the trees, and the trees shed wilted flowers, which came down like tears.

In his compassion the All-knowing, when he lay on his last resting place, said to Ananda, who was deeply disturbed and in tears: 'The time has come for me to enter Nirvana. Go, and tell the Mallas about it. For they will regret it later on if they do not now witness the Nirvana.' Nearly fainting with grief, Ananda obeyed the order, and told the Mallas that the Sage was lying on his final bed.

The Mallas, their faces covered with tears, came along to see the Sage. They paid homage to Him, and then, anguish in their minds, stood around Him. And the Sage spoke to them as follows: 'In the hour of joy it is not proper to grieve. Your despair is quite inappropriate, and you should regain your composure! The goal, so hard to win, which for many aeons I have wished for, now at last it is no longer far away. When that is won—no earth, or water, fire, wind or ether present; unchanging bliss, beyond all objects of the senses, a peace which none can take away, the highest thing there is; and when you hear of that, and know that no becoming mars it, and nothing ever there can pass away—how is there room for grief then in your minds? At Gaya, at the time when I won enlightenment, I got rid of the causes of becoming, which are nothing but a gang of harmful vipers; now the hour comes near when I get rid also of this body, the dwelling place of the acts accumulated in the past. Now that at last this body, which harbours so much ill, is on its way out; now that at last the frightful dangers of becoming are about to be extinct; now that at last I emerge from the vast and endless suffering—is that the time for you to grieve?'

So spoke the Sage of the Shakya tribe, and the thunder of his voice contrasted strangely with the deep calm with which He faced his departure. All the Mallas felt the urge to reply, but it was left to the oldest among them to raise his voice, and to say: 'You all weep, but is there any real cause for grief? We should look upon the

Sage as a man who has escaped from a house on fire! Even the gods on high see it like that, how much more so we men! But that this mighty man, that the Tathagata, once He has won Nirvana, will pass beyond our Ken—that is what causes us grief! When those who travel in a dreadful wilderness lose their skilful guide, will they not be deeply disturbed? People look ridiculous when they come away poor from a goldmine; likewise those who have seen the great Teacher and Sage, the All-seeing himself, in his actual person, ought to have some distinctive spiritual achievement to carry away with them!' Folding their hands like sons in the presence of their father, the Mallas thus spoke much that was to the point. And the Best of Men, aiming at their welfare and tranquillity, addressed to them these meaningful words: 'It is indeed a fact that salvation cannot come from the mere sight of Me. It demands strenuous efforts in the practice of Yoga. But if someone has thoroughly understood this my Dharma, then he is released from the net of suffering, even though he never cast his eyes on Me. A man must take medicine to be cured; the mere sight of the physician is not enough. Likewise the mere sight of Me enables no one to conquer suffering; he will have to meditate for himself about the gnosis I have communicated. If self-controlled, a man may live away from Me as far as can be; but if he only sees my Dharma then indeed he sees Me also. But if he should neglect to strive in concentrated calm for higher things, then, though he live quite near Me, he is far away from Me. Therefore be energetic, persevere, and try to control your minds! Do good deeds, and try to win mindfulness! For life is continually shaken by many kinds of suffering, as the flame of a lamp by the wind.' In this way the Sage, the Best of All those who live, fortified their minds. But still the tears continued to pour from their eyes, and perturbed in their minds they went back to Kusinagara. Each one felt helpless and unprotected, as if crossing the middle of a river all on his own.

Parinirvana

Thereupon the Buddha turned to his Disciples, and said to them: 'Everything comes to an end, though it may last for an aeon. The hour of parting is bound to come in the end. Now I have done what I could do, both for myself and for others. To stay here would from now on be without any purpose. I have disciplined, in heaven and on earth, all those whom I could discipline, and I have set them in the stream. Hereafter this my Dharma, O monks, shall abide for generations and generations among living beings. Therefore, recognize the true nature of the living world, and do not be anxious; for separation cannot possibly be avoided. Recognize that all that lives is subject to this law; and strive from today onwards that it shall be thus no more! When the light of gnosis has dispelled the darkness of ignorance, when all existence has been seen as without substance, peace ensues when life draws to an end, which seems to cure a long sickness at last. Everything, whether stationary or movable, is bound to perish in the end. Be ye therefore mindful and vigilant! The time for my entry into Nirvana has now arrived! These are my last words!'

Thereupon, supreme in his mastery of the trances, He at that moment entered into the first trance, emerged from it and went on to the second, and so in due order he entered all of them without omitting one. And then, when he had ascended through all the nine stages of meditational attainment, the great Seer reversed the process, and returned again to the first trance. Again he emerged from that, and once more he ascended step by step to the fourth trance. When he emerged from the practice of that, he came face to face with everlasting Peace.

And when the Sage entered Nirvana, the earth quivered like a ship struck by a squall, and firebrands fell from the sky. The heavens were lit up by a preternatural fire, which burned without fuel, without smoke, without being fanned by the wind. Fearsome thunderbolts crashed down on the earth, and violent winds raged in the sky. The moon's light waned, and, in spite of a cloudless sky, an uncanny darkness spread everywhere. The rivers, as if overcome with grief, were filled with boiling water. Beautiful flowers grew out of season on the Sal trees above the Buddha's couch, and the trees bent down over him and showered his golden body with their flowers. Like as many gods the five-headed Nagas stood motionless in the sky, their eyes reddened with grief, their hoods closed and their bodies kept in restraint, and with deep devotion they gazed upon the body of the Sage. But, well-established in the practice of the supreme Dharma, the gathering of the gods round king Vaishravana was not grieved and shed no tears, so great was their attachment to the Dharma. The Gods of the Pure Abode, though they had great reverence for the Great Seer, remained composed, and their minds were unaffected; for they hold the things of this world in the utmost contempt. The kings of the Gandharvas and Nagas, as well as the Yakshas and the Devas who rejoice in the true Dharma— they all stood in the sky, mourning and absorbed in the utmost grief. But Mara's hosts felt that they had obtained their heart's desire. Overjoyed they uttered loud laughs, danced about, hissed like snakes, and triumphantly made a frightful din by beating drums, gongs and tom-toms. And the world, when the Prince of Seers had passed beyond, became like a mountain whose peak has been shattered by a thunderbolt; it became like the sky without the moon, like a pond whose lotuses the frost has withered, or like learning rendered ineffective by lack of wealth.

The Relics

Those who had not yet got rid of their passions shed tears. Most of the monks lost their composure and felt grief. Those only who had completed the cycle were not shaken out of their composure, for they knew well that it is the nature of things to pass away. In due course the Mallas heard the news. Like cranes pursued by a hawk they quickly streamed forth under the impact of this calamity, and cried in their distress, 'Alas, the Saviour!' In due course the weeping Mallas, with their powerful arms, placed the Seer on a priceless bier of ivory inlaid with gold. They then performed the ceremonies which befitted the occasion, and honoured Him with many kinds of charming garlands and with the finest perfumes. After that, with zeal and devotion they all took hold of the bier. Slender maidens, with tinkling anklets and copper-stained finger-nails, held a priceless canopy over it, which was like a cloud white with flashes of lightning. Some of the men held up parasols with white garlands, while others waved white yaks' tails set in gold. To the accompaniment of music the Mallas slowly bore along the bier, their eyes reddened like those of bulls. They left the city through the Naga Gate, crossed the Hiranyavati river, and then moved on to the Mukuta shrine, at the foot of which they raised a pyre. Sweetscented barks and leaves, aloewood, sandalwood, and cassia they heaped on the pyre, sighing with grief all the time. Finally they placed the Sage's body on it. Three times they tried to light the pyre with a torch, but it refused to burn. This was due to Kashyapa the Great coming along the road, Kashyapa whose mind was meditating pure thoughts. He longed to see the remains of the holy body of the departed Hero, and it was his magical power which prevented the fire from flaring up. But now the monk approached with rapid steps, eager to see his Teacher once more, and immediately he had paid his homage to the Best of Sages the fire blazed up of its own. Soon it had burnt up the Sage's skin, flesh, hair and limbs. But although there was plenty of ghee, fuel, and wind, it could not consume His bones. These were in due time purified with the finest water, and placed in golden pitchers in the city of the Mallas. And the Mallas chanted hymns of praise over them: 'These jars now hold the relics great in virtue, as mountains hold their jewelled ore. No fire harms these relics great in virtue;

like Brahma's realm when all else is burned up. These bones, His friendliness pervades their tissue; the fire of passion has no strength to burn them; the power of devotion has preserved them; cold though they are, how much they warm our hearts!'

For some days they worshipped the relics in due form and with the utmost devotion. Then, however, one by one, ambassadors from the seven neighbouring kings arrived in the town, asking for a share of the relics. But the Mallas, a proud people and also motivated by their esteem for the relics, refused to surrender any of them. Instead, they were willing to fight. The seven kings, like the seven winds, then came up with great violence against Kusinagara, and their forces were like the current of the flooded Ganges.

Wiser counsels prevailed, and the Mallas devotedly divided into eight parts the relics of Him who had understood Life. One part they kept for themselves. The seven others were handed over to the seven kings, one to each. And these rulers, thus honoured by the Mallas, returned to their own kingdoms, joyful at having achieved their purpose. There, with the appropriate cere-monies, they erected in their capital cities Stupas for the relics of the Seer.

The Scriptures

In due course the five hundred Arhats assembled in Rajagriha, on the slope of one of its five mountains, and there and then they collected the sayings of the great Sage, so that his Dharma might abide. Since it was Ananda who had heard Him speak more often than anyone else, they decided, with the agreement of the wider Buddhist community, to ask him to recite His utterances. The sage from Vaideha then sat down in their midst, and repeated the sermons as they had been spoken by the Best of All speakers. And each one he began with, 'Thus have I heard', and with a statement of the time, the place, the occasion, and the person addressed. It is in this way that he established in conjunction with the Arhats the Scriptures which contain the Dharma of the great Sage. They have in the past led to Nirvana those who have made the effort fully to master them. They still today help them to Nirvana, and they will continue to do so in the future.

Continuing to Think

Were you surprised that the Buddha would think it logical to sacrifice himself for the hungry tigress and her kittens? If this life is an illusion that causes us suffering because we falsely think it to be both real and permanent, then waking up to what is offers the only route to enlightenment.

A recognition of the interrelatedness of all that is leads to the Buddhist principle of **karma.** Whatever I do, I do to myself. In my blindness I may think I do it to another, but the other is me and I am the other. When I hurt, I hurt myself; when I heal, I heal myself. Waking up, becoming enlightened, reveals this truth. It also engenders a great compassion.

For Prince Mahasattva, his body is of no use to him. In fact, it binds him to this world of suffering and illusion. To sacrifice it in the service of a hungry tigress is to honor the interconnectedness of all beings and, at the same time, to experience enlightenment. Similarly, in the third reading, the Buddha is eager to shed his body. It is only an encumbrance, something holding him back and tying him to this world of illusion. When we see things as they are, the chains of karma are broken and we are free of this world—free to be what we have always been, interrelated with all that is.

This is a very different metaphysics from the traditional Western one that describes immaterial ideas and/or solid matter as the really real. As you have seen, different implications flow from different worldviews. "Looking out for number one" makes no sense if you recognize no boundaries between what appears to be your individual self and the rest of what is. Recognizing that you are a "no self," the Buddhist ideal, can be quite a challenge for Westerners.

Summing Up the Readings

How should we view reality? Can everything be explained by matter in motion as Hobbes asserted? Are the most real things Forms or Ideas, as Plato told us and as the sphere told the square? Or, must we find a way to recover our respect for the material world and blend its knowledge with the rest of our metaphysics as the ancient Egyptians did? Is the key to be found in pragmatism, and should we follow Alice's lead in seeking what works even if reality seems absurd? If we decide that all is interconnected and interrelated, will we feel compelled, as the Buddha did, to regard the welfare of all beings with the same compassion with which we regard our own?

These are some of the basic questions of metaphysics. How we answer the question "What is real?" will determine how we see ourselves, our world, our obligations to others, our past, our present, and our future. Perhaps you can see why philosophers sometimes refer to metaphysics as "first philosophy," because it asks the first or most fundamental questions.

In the next chapter we turn the questions of metaphysics from the world to ourselves by asking: Who or what are we? Are we different from other animals and from artificial intelligence, and, if so, how? What does it mean to be made in the image of God? To what extent do we have the power to create ourselves?

Continuing to Question

1. How would Hobbes respond to Plato? Try to construct a materialist critique of idealism, using Hobbes's understanding of reality.

2. Does pragmatism represent a good compromise between the extremes of materialism and idealism or has it sacrificed the best of both?

3. Try imagining the world of four dimensions physicists tell us we are living in. What makes it possible for us to insist there are only three dimensions when "experts" assure us there are four?

4. When we find ourselves in a Wonderland in which nothing makes sense and we feel threatened on all sides, the temptation is to feel sorry for ourselves and

stop acting altogether or to look for someone or something to blame. What are the benefits of doing what Alice did—continuing to make choices and to accept responsibility for those choices even when the results were disastrous?

5. Both Professor Keita and the Buddha challenge us to imagine greater interconnectedness. What would shift if your body/mind/spirit were interrelated, if there was no separation between you and others, between you and the world? What might you gain and what might you lose?

Suggestions for Further Exploration

Albee, Edward, *Tiny Alice*—New York: Pocket, 1966. In this play, an old crone turns out to be a young, sensual woman and a fire in the castle's tiny model chapel turns out to represent a fire in the actual chapel. What's real and what isn't?

Card, Orson Scott, *Ender's Game*—New York: Doherty, 1986. A young man is recruited and harshly trained to play simulated war games resembling virtual reality; the final game is revealed as "real" while he is playing it.

Gibson, William, *Neuromancer*—New York: Ace, 1984. Gibson's novel is about "cyberspace" or virtual reality; it traces the attempts of an artificial intelligence (AI) computer criminal to become "unlimited."

The Lawnmower Man—In this film, a young scientist uses virtual reality to reprogram a slow but decent young man and ends up creating a monster. Interesting virtual reality sequences.

MindWalk—A critique of the Descartes/Newton mechanical model of the universe, this film explores a more holistic view as represented by the insights of particle physics. Based on *The Turning Point* by Fritjof Capra (New York: Simon & Schuster, 1982), whose first book—*The Tao of Physics*—explores similarities between quantum mechanics/relativity theory and Buddhist mysticism.

The Philadelphia Experiment—Reportedly based on a true World War II incident, this film involves an antiradar experiment that lands a sailor in 1984 via a time warp.

Purple Rose of Cairo—Woody Allen's film has a dashing, romantic movie character leave the screen and sweep a housewife off her feet.

Star Wars—This film explores the nature of the Force, an energy source that can be used for good or evil.

Time After Time—This film features H. G. Wells (inventor of the time machine), who pursues Jack the Ripper into present-day San Francisco using his invention.

Total Recall—Are the memories of a Martian vacation that the character has had implanted reality—or is his ordinary life the implant? How is a character to tell the difference? This film poses some interesting questions.

Vonnegut, Kurt, *Slaughterhouse Five*—New York: Delacorte, 1969. Billy Pilgrim disconnects from time, jumping back and forth among different periods of his life. Also a movie.

Wargames—A young hacker accidentally starts World War III in this film when he breaks into a video game manufacturer's computer and selects a "game" called "Global Thermonuclear War."

Zukav, Gary, *The Dancing Wu Li Masters: An Overview of the New Physics*—New York: Morrow, 1979. Zukav provides a readable nonfiction introduction to a complex field.

3   Human Nature

Defining the Issue

Defining what we mean by "human nature" may be more difficult than you think. Most of us have a gut feeling that we are somehow different from other animals and robots—that there is something unique about us that sets us apart, namely our human nature. Some of the traditional definitions have focused on our supposedly unique ability to reason and on our creation in the image and likeness of God.

Recent discoveries, assuring us that 99 percent of our DNA is identical with that of chimps, and mounting evidence that other animals are capable of making tools, solving problems, using language, and making ethical choices have made the case for human uniqueness a little more difficult to sustain. In addition, there are computer "therapist" programs sophisticated enough to convince half the people who use them that a human psychologist and not a software program is at the other end of the conversation.

Very young members of the species Homo sapiens, as well as genetically or environmentally damaged older members, seem to lack some critical abilities (such as the talent for abstract reasoning), and those rendered permanently unconscious through accident or trauma may fail to qualify as human under many standard definitions.

Is human nature something all of us are born with—something that remains with us even if we are severely incapacitated by our genes or life experiences? Is it ours from the moment of conception, from the time we are viable (able to survive on our own outside the womb), or from birth? Does it follow us even into death—requiring special treatment of dead human bodies, based on their human nature?

Previewing the Readings

The selections in this chapter offer a broad range of views. Three are philosophical essays, one comes from the Bible, and the final one is the beginning of a science fiction novel. One denies any essential human nature whereas another insists on it; two critique the implications of the classical, Western version of human nature (for its extreme individualism and for its implied sexism); the last ponders whether robots could ever cross the line into a shared humanity.

We begin with a modern reading, from "Existentialism as a Humanism," by the twentieth-century philosopher Jean-Paul Sartre. According to atheistic existentialism, human nature is not something we are born with but rather something we must earn through a life well lived. Sartre developed his philosophy of existentialism in response to the disillusionment that swept the Western world between the two world wars. His own experiences in a German prison camp convinced him of two things: there was no God and humans had the capacity to create their own human nature.

The first two chapters of Genesis, the first book in the Bible, tell two different Adam and Eve stories, which offer distinctive versions of who we humans are as well as of the relationship between women and men. The pattern of man having a kind of natural superiority to woman that we find in the second chapter of Genesis also appears in the writings of Plato and Aristotle. Using the distinction between reason and emotion, Aristotle concludes that just as reason must rule emotion so men must, by nature, rule women. Western philosopher Elizabeth V. Spelman challenges Aristotle's claim on logical grounds. African philosopher, Ifeanyi A. Menkiti, challenges the Western preoccupation with individualism and suggests that a more communal definition of who we are might be at least as useful.

Finally, science fiction novelist James P. Hogan imagines a plausible scenario in which robots might acquire all the characteristics and potentialities we currently claim as the basis for human nature. If such a scenario were to occur, would the robots qualify as human?

Two of these readings reveal traditional understandings of human existence. The Genesis creation accounts, representing separate oral traditions, show us two Judaic and Christian understandings of the origins of human nature; similarly, Professor Menkiti's "Person and Community in Traditional African Thought" represents a longstanding African view of how personhood is acquired. The other three readings reflect distinctly modern views of human nature.

3.1   *Existentialism as a Humanism*

JEAN-PAUL SARTRE

Preparing to Read

What if there were no God to define human nature or to be the cosmic law giver? Humanity would be completely on its own to define its own nature and to make its own laws. For atheistic existentialists such as Jean-Paul Sartre, this is exactly the situation we are in. We are not born with a fixed human nature, an essence to tell us what we are and what we must become. Instead, existence precedes essence; first we appear as bare existences, and then we begin the task of becoming selves. Human nature is not provided; it must be earned.

There is a wonderful freedom in this belief. There are absolutely no limits to what you can be or do; there is no one or nothing to draw lines and stop you from doing certain things or force you to do others. And this freedom is also terrible. There is no one to blame for what we become because we ourselves are in complete control. Sartre says we are "condemned to be free." This freedom of ours is a life sentence and we never get to say "I couldn't help it" or "I had no choice."

Some will find this freedom exhilarating; others will find it chilling. To deny our human freedom is, in Sartre's view, to behave inauthentically—to pretend we are like stones and tables rather than human beings. To do this is to diminish ourselves and to leave unfulfilled our uniquely human destiny—to fashion a self for ourselves. Sartre calls this kind of denial "bad faith."

MANY MAY BE SURPRISED at the mention of humanism in this connection, but we shall try to see in what sense we understand it. In any case, we can begin by saying that existentialism, in our sense of the word, is a doctrine that does render human life possible, a doctrine, also, which affirms that every truth and every action imply both an environment and a human subjectivity. The essential charge laid against us is, of course, that of over-emphasis upon the evil side of human life. I have lately been told of a lady who, whenever she lets slip a vulgar expression in a moment of nervousness, excuses herself by exclaiming, "I believe I am becoming an existentialist." So it appears that ugliness is being identified with existentialism. That is why some people say we are "naturalistic," and if we are, it is strange to see how much we scandalize and horrify them, for no one seems to be much frightened or humiliated nowadays by what is properly called naturalism. Those who can quite well keep down a novel by Zola such as *La Terre* are sickened as soon as they read an existentialist novel. Those who appeal to the wisdom of the people—which is a sad wisdom—find ours sadder still. And yet, what could be more disillusioned than such sayings as "Charity begins at home" or "Promote a

From "Existentialism as a Humanism" in *Existentialism from Dostoevsky to Sartre*.
1975. Walter Kaufmann, ed. New York: A Meridian Book, New American Library.

rogue and he'll sue you for damage, knock him down and he'll do you homage"? We all know how many common sayings can be quoted to this effect, and they all mean much the same—that you must not oppose the powers-that-be; that you must not fight against superior force; must not meddle in matters that are above your station. Or that any action not in accordance with some tradition is mere romanticism; or that any undertaking which has not the support of proven experience is foredoomed to frustration; and that since experience has shown men to be invariably inclined to evil, there must be firm rules to restrain them, otherwise we shall have anarchy. It is, however, the people who are forever mouthing these dismal proverbs and, whenever they are told of some more or less repulsive action, say "How like human nature!"—it is these very people, always harping upon realism, who complain that existentialism is too gloomy a view of things. Indeed their excessive protests make me suspect that what is annoying them is not so much our pessimism, but, much more likely, our optimism. For at bottom, what is alarming in the doctrine that I am about to try to explain to you is—is it not?—that it confronts man with a possibility of choice. To verify this, let us review the whole question upon the strictly philosophic level. What, then, is this that we call existentialism?

Most of those who are making use of this word would be highly confused if required to explain its meaning. For since it has become fashionable, people cheerfully declare that this musician or that painter is "existentialist." A columnist in *Clartés* signs himself "The Existentialist," and, indeed, the word is now so loosely applied to so many things that it no longer means anything at all. It would appear that, for the lack of any novel doctrine such as that of surrealism, all those who are eager to join in the latest scandal or movement now seize upon this philosophy in which, however, they can find nothing to their purpose. For in truth this is of all teachings the least scandalous and the most austere: it is intended strictly for techni-

cians and philosophers. All the same, it can easily be defined.

The question is only complicated because there are two kinds of existentialists. There are, on the one hand, the Christians, amongst whom I shall name Jaspers and Gabriel Marcel, both professed Catholics; and on the other the existential atheists, amongst whom we must place Heidegger as well as the French existentialists and myself. What they have in common is simply the fact that they believe that *existence* comes before *essence*—or, if you will, that we must begin from the subjective. What exactly do we mean by that?

If one considers an article of manufacture—as, for example, a book or a paper-knife—one sees that it has been made by an artisan who had a conception of a paper-knife and to the pre-existent technique of production which is a part of the conception and is, at bottom, a formula. Thus the paper-knife is at the same time an article producible in a certain manner and one which, on the other hand, serves a definite purpose, for one cannot suppose that a man would produce a paper-knife without knowing what it was for. Let us say, then, of the paper-knife that its essence—that is to say the sum of the formulae and the qualities which made its production and its definition possible—precedes its existence. The presence of such-and-such a paper-knife or book is thus determined before my eyes. Here, then, we are viewing the world from a technical standpoint, and we can say that production precedes existence.

When we think of God as the creator, we are thinking of him, most of the time, as a supernal artisan. Whatever doctrine we may be considering, whether it be a doctrine like that of Descartes, or of Leibnitz himself, we always imply that the will follows, more or less, from the understanding or at least accompanies it, so that when God creates he knows precisely what he is creating. Thus, the conception of man in the mind of God is comparable to that of the paper-knife in the mind of the artisan: God makes man according to a procedure and a conception, exactly as the artisan manufactures a paper-knife, following a definition and a formula. Thus each individual man is the realization of a certain conception which dwells in the divine understanding. In the philosophic atheism of the eighteenth century, the notion of God is suppressed, but not, for all that, the idea that essence is prior to existence; something of that idea we still find everywhere, in Diderot, in Voltaire and even in Kant. Man possesses a human nature; that "human nature," which is the conception of human being, is found in every man; which means that each man is a particular example of a universal conception, the conception of Man. In Kant, this universality goes so far that the wild man of the woods, man in the state of nature and the bourgeois are all contained in the same definition and have the same fundamental qualities. Here again, the essence of man precedes that historic existence which we confront in experience.

Atheistic existentialism, of which I am a representative, declares with greater consistency that if God does not exist there is at least one being whose existence comes before its essence, a being which exists before it can be defined by any conception of it. That being is man or, as Heidegger has it, the human reality. What do we mean by saying that existence precedes essence? We mean that man first of all exists, encounters himself, surges up in the world—and defines himself afterwards. If man as the existentialist sees him is not definable, it is because to begin with he is nothing. He will not be anything until later, and then he will be what he makes of himself. Thus, there is no human nature, because there is no God to have a conception of it. Man simply is. Not that he is simply what he conceives himself to be, but he is what he wills, and as he conceives himself after already existing— as he wills to be after that leap towards existence. Man is nothing else but that which he makes of himself. That is the first principle of existentialism. And this is what people call its "subjectivity," using the word as a reproach against us. But what do we mean to say by this, but that

man is of a greater dignity than a stone or a table? For we mean to say that man primarily exists—that man is, before all else, something which propels itself towards a future and is aware that it is doing so. Man is, indeed, a project which possesses a subjective life, instead of being a kind of moss, or a fungus or a cauliflower. Before that projection of the self nothing exists; not even in the heaven of intelligence: man will only attain existence when he is what he purposes to be. Not, however, what he may wish to be. For what we usually understand by wishing or willing is a conscious decision taken—much more often than not—after we have made ourselves what we are. I may wish to join a party, to write a book or to marry—but in such a case what is usually called my will is probably a manifestation of a prior and more spontaneous decision. If, however, it is true that existence is prior to essence, man is responsible for what he is. Thus, the first effect of existentialism is that it puts every man in possession of himself as he is, and places the entire responsibility for his existence squarely upon his own shoulders. And, when we say that man is responsible for himself, we do not mean that he is responsible only for his own individuality, but that he is responsible for all men. The word "subjectivism" is to be understood in two senses, and our adversaries play upon only one of them. Subjectivism means, on the one hand, the freedom of the individual subject and, on the other, that man cannot pass beyond human subjectivity. It is the latter which is the deeper meaning of existentialism. When we say that man chooses himself, we do mean that every one of us must choose himself; but by that we also mean that in choosing for himself he chooses for all men. For in effect, of all the actions a man may take in order to create himself as he wills to be, there is not one which is not creative, at the same time, of an image of man such as he believes he ought to be. To choose between this or that is at the same time to affirm the value of that which is chosen; for we are unable ever to choose the worse. What we choose is always the better; and nothing can be better for us unless it is better for all. If, moreover, existence precedes essence and we will to exist at the same time as we fashion our image, that image is valid for all and for the entire epoch in which we find ourselves. Our responsibility is thus much greater than we had supposed, for it concerns mankind as a whole. If I am a worker, for instance, I may choose to join a Christian rather than a Communist trade union. And if, by that membership, I choose to signify that resignation is, after all, the attitude that best becomes a man, that man's kingdom is not upon this earth, I do not commit myself alone to that view. Resignation is my will for everyone, and my action is, in consequence, a commitment on behalf of all mankind. Or if, to take a more personal case, I decide to marry and to have children, even though this decision proceeds simply from my situation, from my passion or my desire, I am thereby committing not only myself, but humanity as a whole, to the practice of monogamy. I am thus responsible for myself and for all men, and I am creating a certain image of man as I would have him to be. In fashioning myself I fashion man.

This may enable us to understand what is meant by such terms—perhaps a little grandiloquent—as anguish, abandonment and despair. As you will soon see, it is very simple. First, what do we mean by anguish? The existentialist frankly states that man is in anguish. His meaning is as follows—When a man commits himself to anything, fully realizing that he is not only choosing what he will be, but is thereby at the same time a legislator deciding for the whole of mankind—in such a moment a man cannot escape from the sense of complete and profound responsibility. There are many, indeed, who show no such anxiety. But we affirm that they are merely disguising their anguish or are in flight from it. Certainly, many people think that in what they are doing they commit no one but themselves to anything: and if you ask them "What would happen if everyone did so?" they shrug their shoulders and reply, "Everyone does not do so." But in truth, one ought always to ask oneself what would hap-

pen if everyone did as one is doing; nor can one escape from that disturbing thought except by a kind of self-deception. The man who lies in self-excuse, by saying "Everyone will not do it," must be ill at ease in his conscience, for the act of lying implies the universal value which it denies. By its very disguise his anguish reveals itself. This is the anguish that Kierkegaard called "the anguish of Abraham." You know the story: An angel commanded Abraham to sacrifice his son: and obedience was obligatory, if it really was an angel who had appeared and said, "Thou, Abraham, shalt sacrifice thy son." But anyone in such a case would wonder, first, whether it was indeed an angel and secondly, whether I am really Abraham. Where are the proofs? A certain mad woman who suffered from hallucinations said that people were telephoning to her, and giving her orders. The doctor asked, "But who is it that speaks to you?" She replied: "He says it is God." And what, indeed, could prove to her that it was God? If an angel appears to me, what is the proof that it is an angel; or, if I hear voices, who can prove that they proceed from heaven and not from hell, or from my own subconsciousness or some pathological condition? Who can prove that they are really addressed to me?

Who, then, can prove that I am the proper person to impose, by my own choice, my conception of man upon mankind? I shall never find any proof whatever; there will be no sign to convince me of it. If a voice speaks to me, it is still I myself who must decide whether the voice is or is not that of an angel. If I regard a certain course of action as good, it is only I who choose to say that it is good and not bad. There is nothing to show that I am Abraham: nevertheless I also am obliged at every instant to perform actions which are examples. Everything happens to every man as though the whole human race had its eyes fixed upon what he is doing and regulated its conduct accordingly. So every man ought to say, "Am I really a man who has the right to act in such a manner that humanity regulates itself by what I do." If a man does not say that, he is dissembling his anguish. Clearly, the anguish with which we are concerned here is not one that could lead to quietism or inaction. It is anguish pure and simple, of the kind well known to all those who have borne responsibilities. When, for instance, a military leader takes upon himself the responsibility for an attack and sends a number of men to their death, he chooses to do it and at bottom he alone chooses. No doubt he acts under a higher command, but its orders, which are more general, require interpretation by him and upon that interpretation depends the life of ten, fourteen or twenty men. In making the decision, he cannot but feel a certain anguish. All leaders know that anguish. It does not prevent their acting, on the contrary it is the very condition of their action, for the action presupposes that there is a plurality of possibilities, and in choosing one of these, they realize that it has value only because it is chosen. Now it is anguish of that kind which existentialism describes, and moreover, as we shall see, makes explicit through direct responsibility towards other men who are concerned. Far from being a screen which could separate us from action, it is a condition of action itself.

And when we speak of "abandonment"—a favorite word of Heidegger—we only mean to say that God does not exist, and that it is necessary to draw the consequences of his absence right to the end. The existentialist is strongly opposed to a certain type of secular moralism which seeks to suppress God at the least possible expense. Towards 1880, when the French professors endeavored to formulate a secular morality, they said something like this:—God is a useless and costly hypothesis, so we will do without it. However, if we are to have morality, a society and a law-abiding world, it is essential that certain values should be taken seriously; they must have *à priori* existence ascribed to them. It must be considered obligatory *à priori* to be honest, not to lie, not to beat one's wife, to bring up children and so forth; so we are going to do a little work on this subject, which will enable us to show that these values exist all the same, inscribed in an intelligible heaven al-

though, of course, there is no God. In other words—and this is, I believe, the purport of all that we in France call radicalism—nothing will be changed if God does not exist; we shall rediscover the same norms of honesty, progress and humanity, and we shall have disposed of God as an out-of-date hypothesis which will die away quietly of itself. The existentialist, on the contrary, finds it extremely embarrassing that God does not exist, for there disappears with Him all possibility of finding values in an intelligible heaven. There can no longer be any good *à priori,* since there is no infinite and perfect consciousness to think it. It is nowhere written that "the good" exists, that one must be honest or must not lie, since we are now upon the plane where there are only men. Dostoevsky once wrote "If God did not exist, everything would be permitted"; and that, for existentialism, is the starting point. Everything is indeed permitted if God does not exist, and man is in consequence forlorn, for he cannot find anything to depend upon either within or outside himself. He discovers forthwith that he is without excuse. For if indeed existence precedes essence, one will never be able to explain one's action by reference to a given and specific human nature; in other words, there is no determinism—man is free, man *is* freedom. Nor, on the other hand, if God does not exist, are we provided with any values or commands that could legitimize our behavior. Thus we have neither behind us, nor before us in a luminous realm of values, any means of justification or excuse. We are left alone, without excuse. That is what I mean when I say that man is condemned to be free. Condemned, because he did not create himself, yet is nevertheless at liberty, and from the moment that he is thrown into this world he is responsible for everything he does. The existentialist does not believe in the power of passion. He will never regard a grand passion as a destructive torrent upon which a man is swept into certain actions as by fate, and which, therefore, is an excuse for them. He thinks that man is responsible for his passion.

Continuing to Think

Sartre's essay was written as a direct challenge to the traditional religious view of human nature that attributes our uniqueness to God. If humans are made in the image and likeness of the creator, we are indeed special and can claim both privileges and responsibilities that flow from that status. Although this view has provided great comfort to many in the West over centuries, it is not without its critics.

At the most basic level, if God made us, God has the right to expect certain things from us. There are duties we must undertake and actions we must avoid if we are to please God and fulfill our human destiny. These expectations and restrictions can seem confining to some even as they provide comfort to others. At the most extreme, what if there is no God and we are living our lives as if there were—doing some things and avoiding others in the hope of pleasing a God who does not exist?

Living through the cynicism and loss of hope that swept Europe and the Americas during the 1920s and '30s, some existentialist philosophers found faith in God the antidote to the alienation and despair all around them. Others took the world, and especially "man's inhumanity to man," as proof that we live in a godless universe. For these atheistic existentialists, belief in God is a "cop out," a kind of grasping at straws to avoid facing hard truths about ourselves and the world we live in—a world that in their view is without order or purpose.

If there is no God, then humans have the task traditionally undertaken by God—to create themselves. Does this prospect thrill or frighten you? Sartre found the challenge of living a meaningful life in a meaningless world empowering.

3.2   *Genesis, the Bible*

Preparing to Read

Before you read this selection, take a minute to think about what you already know about the biblical story of creation. What do you know, for instance, about the order of creation—who or what was created first, last? Where do Adam and Eve stand in relation to other created beings? Try to get the main points in your mind before you read.

Most people are surprised to find out that there are two separate and complete creation accounts in the first two chapters of Genesis. One of them, Chapter 2, has received a lot of cultural emphasis, so much so that whether or not you are religious, whether or not you have read the Bible, you probably thought of the Chapter 2 version. Adam is created first and placed in the garden of Eden, but he is lonely. God obligingly provides all sorts of animal companions that Adam names, but none of these assuages his loneliness. Finally, God puts Adam into a deep sleep and removes one of his ribs from which to fashion a woman, Eve. This, at last, provides Adam with a life companion that is "bone of my bone, flesh of my flesh."

The story that may surprise you is the first one, the one that begins, "In the beginning, when God created the heavens and the earth . . ." In this version creation proceeds hierarchically from simplest to most complex: first, basic things like day and night, waters and dry land; later plants, things that creep, higher animals, and finally humans—woman and man created together and at the same time and told to be fruitful and multiply.

These stories come from two different oral traditions, and both were included when written texts were agreed upon. Why is it that everyone knows the second account and almost no one the first one?

Chapter 1

IN THE BEGINNING when God created[a] the heavens and the earth, [2]the earth was a formless void and darkness covered the face of the deep, while a wind from God[b] swept over the face of the waters. [3]Then God said "Let there be light"; and there was light. [4]And God saw that the light was good, and God separated the light from the darkness. [5]God called the light Day, and the darkness he called Night. And there was evening and there was morning, the first day.

6 And God said, "Let there be a dome in the midst of the waters, and let it separate the waters from the waters." [7]So God made the dome and separated the waters that were under the dome from the waters that were above the dome. And it was so. [8]God called the dome Sky. And there was evening and there was morning, the second day.

9 And God said, "Let the waters under the sky be gathered together into one place, and let the dry land appear." And it was so. [10]God called the dry land Earth, and the waters that were gathered together he called Seas. And God saw that it was good. [11]Then God said, "Let the earth put forth vegetation: plants yielding seed, and fruit trees of every kind on earth that bear fruit with the seed in it." And it was so. [12]The earth brought forth vegetation: plants yielding seed of every kind, and trees of every kind bearing fruit with the seed in it. And God saw that it was good. [13]And there was evening and there was morning, the third day.

14 And God said, "Let there be lights in the dome of the sky to separate the day from the night; and let them be for signs and for seasons and for days and years, [15]and let them be lights in the dome of the sky to give light upon the earth." And it was so. [16]God made the two great lights—the greater light to rule the day and the lesser light to rule the night—and the stars. [17]God set them in the dome of the sky to give light upon the earth, [18]to rule over the day and over the night, and to separate the light from the darkness. And God saw that it was good. [19]And there was evening and there was morning, the fourth day.

20 And God said, "Let the waters bring forth swarms of living creatures, and let birds fly above the earth across the dome of the sky." [21]So God created the great sea monsters and every living creature that moves, of every kind, with which the waters swarm, and every winged bird of every kind. And God saw that it was good. [22]God blessed them, saying, "Be fruitful and multiply and fill the waters in the seas, and let birds multiply on the earth." [23]And there was evening and there was morning, the fifth day.

24 And God said, "Let the earth bring forth living creatures of every kind: cattle and creeping things and wild animals of the earth of every kind." And it was so. ²⁵God made the wild animals of the earth of every kind, and the cattle of every kind, and everything that creeps upon the ground of every kind. And God saw that it was good.

26 Then God said, "Let us make humankind[c] in our image, according to our likeness, and let them have dominion over the fish of the sea, and over the birds of the air, and over the cattle, and over all the wild animals of the earth,[d] and over every creeping thing that creeps upon the earth."

²⁷ So God created humankind[c] in his image,
    in the image of God he created them;[e]
    male and female he created them.

²⁸God blessed them, and God said to them, "Be fruitful and multiply, and fill the earth and subdue it; and have dominion over the fish of the sea and over the birds of the air and over every living thing that moves upon the earth." ²⁹God said, "See, I have given you every plant yielding seed that is upon the face of all the earth, and every tree with seed in its fruit, you shall have them for food. ³⁰And to every beast of the earth, and to every bird of the air, and to everything that creeps on the earth, everything that has the breath of life, I have given every green plant for food." And it was so. ³¹God saw everything that he had made, and indeed, it was very good. And there was evening and there was morning, the sixth day.

Chapter 2

Thus the heavens and the earth were finished, and all their multitude. ²And on the seventh day God finished the work that he had done, and he rested on the seventh day from all the work that he had done. ³So God blessed the seventh day and hallowed it, because on it God rested from all the work that he had done in creation.

4 These are the generations of the heavens and the earth when they were created.

In the day that the LORD God made the earth and the heavens, ⁵when no plant of the field was yet in the earth and no herb of the field had yet sprung up—for the LORD God had not caused it to rain upon the earth, and there was no one to till the ground; ⁶but a stream would rise from the earth, and water the whole face of the ground—⁷then the LORD God formed man from the dust of the ground,[f] and breathed into his nostrils the breath of life; and the man became a living being. ⁸And the LORD God planted a garden in Eden, in the east; and there he put the man whom he had formed. ⁹Out of the ground the LORD God made to grow every tree that is pleasant to the sight and good for food, the tree of life also in the midst of the garden, and the tree of the knowledge of good and evil.

10 A river flows out of Eden to water the garden, and from there it divides and becomes four branches. ¹¹The name of the first is Pishon; it is the one that flows around the whole land of Havilah, where there is gold ¹²and the gold of that land is good bdellium and onyx stone are there. ¹³The name of the second river is Gihon, it is the one that flows around the whole land of Cush. ¹⁴The name of the third river is Tigris, which flows east of Assyria. And the fourth river is the Euphrates.

15 The LORD God took the man and put him in the garden of Eden to till it and keep it. ¹⁶And the LORD God commanded the man, "You may freely eat of every tree of the garden; ¹⁷but of the tree of the knowledge of good and evil you shall not eat, for in the day that you eat of it you shall die."

18 Then the LORD God said, "It is not good that the man should be alone; I will make him a helper as his partner." ¹⁹So out of the ground the Lord God formed every animal of the field and every bird of the air, and brought them to the man to see what he would call them, and whatever the man called every living creature, that was its name. ²⁰The man gave names to all cattle, and to the birds of the air, and to every animal of the field; but for the man[g] there was not found a helper as his partner. ²¹So the LORD

God caused a deep sleep to fall upon the man, and he slept; then he took one of his ribs and closed up its place with flesh. ²²And the rib that the LORD God had taken from the man he made into a woman and brought her to the man. ²³Then the man said

"This at last is bone of my bones
and flesh of my flesh
this one shall be called Woman,*b*
for out of Man this one was taken."

²⁴Therefore a man leaves his father and his mother and clings to his wife, and they become one flesh. ²⁵And the man and his wife were both naked, and were not ashamed.

NOTES

a. Or *when God began to create* or *In the beginning God created*

b. Or *while the spirit of God* or *while a mighty wind*

c. Heb *adam*

d. Syr: Heb *and over all the earth*

e. Heb *him*

f. Or *formed a man* (Heb *adam*) *of dust from the ground* (Heb *adamah*)

g. Or *for Adam*

h. Heb *ishshah*

Continuing to Think

In the second account of creation, God creates Adam out of the dust of the earth and breathes into his nostrils the breath of life; Eve comes later, a sort of second-generation human made from a rib of the original one. In the first account, did you notice that God said, "Let us make humankind in our image, after our likeness"? It is this version, rather than the second, that serves as the basis for the Western insistence on human uniqueness. After all, other species of plants and animals, while created by God, are not made in the image and likeness of God.

Many people are familiar with the phrase "In the beginning . . ." that starts the book of Genesis. Astronauts read from it while circling the moon on Christmas Eve. But the rest of that first chapter, the part that shows woman and man created equally and together and jointly given responsibility for the rest of creation, is largely unknown. Instead, nearly everyone can tell the story of Eve's creation from Adam's rib with substantial accuracy. Our origins story is so deeply embedded in our culture that everyone is influenced by it. It is a strong ingredient in shaping who we think we are and whether we think we are somehow special or even unique.

Feminists wonder whether the Eve-from-Adam's rib story has been given prominence because it reinforces male dominance and female submissiveness and because it supports power relationships as they have been defined in the modern Western world. John Milton used Chapter Two as the basis for his long and very well-known poem "Paradise Lost," further assuring its cultural influence. What do you think? Suppose we took seriously the version of creation captured in Chapter One of Genesis. Would we have to rethink our human assumptions about male/female relationships?

3.3   *Aristotle and the Politicization of the Soul*

ELIZABETH V. SPELMAN

Preparing to Read

One powerful claim to human uniqueness, as we have just seen, has been the claim that humans are created in the image and likeness of God. In the West, the other equally powerful justification rests on the superiority of intellect or reason over animal-like appetites and desires. Beginning with Plato and continuing through Christian philosophers like Augustine to the "father of the Enlightenment" Descartes, Western philosophy has tended to split the mind from the body and declare its superiority over the body as the basis for human uniqueness.

If other animals are limited by their instincts, humans are uniquely able to be self-reflective, to step outside our bodies and make rationally motivated decisions about them. Far from being slaves to our desires, we have the ability to transcend them—to work on something challenging even if we are tired, to give up the chocolate that seems so appealing in pursuit of a healthy body, to exercise because we know it is good for us, even to sacrifice our lives for others or for something we strongly believe to be true. And, we have the ability to reason abstractly, as if only our minds and other mental phenomena existed. This makes discussions about the existence of God possible for us and impossible for dogs.

Historically, one of the consequences of the mind/body split for Western culture has been the identification of men with mind and women with emotion and bodily functions. If men operate from the head, women act from the heart. And women are much more obviously associated with bodily functions such as menstruation, childbirth, and lactation (breastfeeding an infant). It has been possible for men to tell themselves they act only out of rational motives and to agree that their rationality justifies rule over more emotional and bodily defined women. Elizabeth V. Spelman takes on this argument as constructed by Aristotle and faults it on logical grounds. In a deductive argument, using two premises (each of which justifies the other) does not lead to a valid conclusion.

IN BOOK I of the *Politics* Aristotle argues that men are by nature the rulers of women. The conclusion of the argument, which has to do with relationships *between* people—in particular, political relationships between men and women—is said to be based on what is known about relationships *within* people: in particular, relationships between the rational and irrational elements of the human soul. That is, this part of Aristotle's political theory is said to rest on his

"Aristotle and the Politicization of the Soul" by Elizabeth V. Spelman, pp. 17–30, in *Discovering Reality,* edited by Sandra Harding and Merrill B. Hintikka. Copyright (c) 1983 by D. Reidel Publishing Co. Reprinted with kind permission from Kluwer Academic Publishers and the author.

metaphysics or theory of the soul. I hope to show that not the least of the reasons for examining Aristotle's argument is that doing so sheds light on the question of whether metaphysical positions are politically innocent. To ask this question is a defining if not necessarily a distinguishing characteristic of a feminist perspective in philosophy.

Aristotle's argument is outlined briefly in Part I. In Part II I begin examination of the argument by describing Aristotle's theory of the soul, noting especially the kind of authority which, according to Aristotle, the rational part of the soul has over the irrational part. In Part III I observe that when he tries to make use of his view about the authority of the rational part of the soul over the irrational part, to defend his view about the authority of men over women, Aristotle ends up contradicting his view about the authority of the rational part. In Part IV I argue that Aristotle's attempt to justify the authority of men over women by reference to the authority of the rational part over the irrational part is in any event circular: a close reading of the texts shows that both understanding what it means to talk about relations of authority between parts of the soul, and establishing that one part has authority over another, depends on understanding what it means to talk about relations of authority between classes of persons (including those between men and women), and on establishing or assuming that certain classes do have authority over others—in particular, that men have authority over women. Aristotle makes clear to us what the relation between the rational and irrational parts of the soul is, by reference to the very same political relationships he hopes to justify by reference to the soul. Part V concludes with some comments on the nature of Aristotle's argument and the nature of my response to him.

Aristotle's argument about the natural authority of men over women is very close to his arguments about the natural authority of masters over slaves, fathers over children, "intellectuals" over laborers, and is offered simultaneously with

those arguments in the *Politics*. Though my examination focuses mainly on Aristotle's view of women, the scope of Aristotle's argument is a reminder that oppressive attitudes towards women have close connections to oppressive attitudes towards other groups or classes, that the oppression of women is related in theory as well as in practice to the oppression of other groups.

I

One of the requirements of a state is that some rule and some be ruled:

> there must be a union of those who cannot exist without each other; . . . of natural ruler and subject, that both may be preserved. (P, 1252a25–32)

And this means in particular, Aristotle says, that men are to rule women, masters are to rule slaves, fathers are to rule children. But why? The mere principle that some are to rule and some are to be ruled doesn't itself tell us who is to rule whom. Aristotle is untroubled by the idea that humans are to rule animals, because he believes that animals' lack of reason establishes their inferiority to humans and disqualifies them from eligibility to rule. But all humans *qua* humans have reason and "share in the rational principle" (P 1259b27). So to what grounds must one move in order to establish the inferior and subordinate status of women vis-à-vis men, slaves vis-à-vis masters, children vis-à-vis fathers?

Well, says Aristotle, fortunately "the very constitution of the soul has shown us the way" (P 1260a5). The soul has two main parts or elements, the rational and the irrational, and it is "natural and expedient" for the rational to rule over the irrational (P 1254b4ff.).[1] Just so, men are to rule women, for in women the deliberative capacity of the rational element is without authority—it is easily overruled by the irrational element. In similar fashion, masters are to rule slaves, for while slaves, in virtue of the rational element in their souls, can hear and obey orders, they really don't have the capacity to deliberate. Indeed all that distinguishes slaves from non-human beasts of burden is that they, unlike beasts, have just enough reason to understand the results of the masters' deliberations; otherwise their capacities are identical to those of the beasts (P 1254b19ff.). Fathers are to rule children, because although children have the capacity to deliberate that is associated with the rational element of the soul, this capacity is immature (P 1260a6–15).

It is, then, by reference to the relationships between the rational parts of the soul that Aristotle tries to justify his view that certain classes of beings are naturally subordinate to others. Just as one part of the soul stands in a certain relationship to another, so one class of beings stands in a certain relationship to another class. But this is a bare outline of the argument. In order to understand Aristotle's argument thoroughly, we have to understand in more detail how he describes the workings of the parts of the soul and their relationship to one another (Part II). We also have to understand just how he moves from a description of the parts of the soul to a description of the parts of the state (Part III).

II

We have to turn to the *Nicomachean Ethics* as well as to parts of the *Politics* to fill in the details of Aristotle's description of the relationship between the rational and irrational parts of the soul. A central feature of his depiction of that relationship is that it is a relationship of authority. The rational part is supposed to rule the irrational part. This is an authority intended for it and vested in it by nature (P 1254b7–8), though Aristotle both explicitly and implicitly allows that the rational part is not always fully empowered to exercize that authority: as we've seen, Aristotle says that in the case of women, slaves and children, the rational part does *not* rule the irrational part (as we shall soon see, we have to ask whether it is even *supposed* to, in the case of women, slaves and children). Even in adult

male masters, sometimes the irrational part is not ruled by the rational part; if that weren't so, Aristotle presumably would not have thought it necessary, as he does in the *Ethics* and the *Politics,* to give instructions about the importance of the rational part remaining in control and command. Hence when Aristotle talks about the rule of the rational part of the soul over the irrational part, he cannot be said to be merely pointing out that what happens in one part of the soul determines what happens in another part in some mechanical fashion. In fact, if this is what Aristotle meant by the rule of the rational over the irrational part, then he would have to say that the irrational part sometimes rules over the rational part; but he explicitly resists this when he suggests that sometimes the irrational part "appears" to rule over the rational part even when it really doesn't (P 1254b). So the rule or authority he ascribes to the rational part must have to do with entitlement: the rational part has the right to, or ought to, or is intended by nature to, rule the irrational part, even if that isn't always what happens.

The first thing, then, to note about Aristotle's description of the relation between the rational and irrational parts of the soul is that it is a relationship of ruler and subject. But, again, this relationship is not described in merely mechanical terms, as if something in one part of us moves or clicks or fires, and as a result something in another part of us moves or clicks or fires. As soon as he begins to characterize the rule of the soul over the body, or of the rational part of the soul over the irrational part, Aristotle turns to the language of persons and politics: such rule is despotical, or constitutional, or royal (P 1254b3–5); when the parts of the soul are properly aligned, the rational part dictates or commands, and the irrational part obeys—in the way in which a child obeys its father (NE 1102b30–1103a4). Indeed the relationship between the parts of the soul is treated by Aristotle in most of the *Nicomachean Ethics* and the *Politics* as if it were a relationship between political entities, not as if it were between impersonal, quasi-organic parts. He not only describes the parts of the soul in language applicable to persons or agents; he sometimes speaks of the parts of the soul by analogy to *particular* persons or kinds of persons:

> as the child should live according to the direction of his tutor, so the appetitive element should live according to rational principle (NE 1119b14)

> the nature of appetite is illustrated by what the poets call Aphrodite, "guile-weaving daughter of Cyprus" (NE 1149b17)

The relationship of master and servant or that of husband and wife show us

> the ratios in which the part of the soul that has a rational principle stands to the irrational part (NE 1138b5–12)

In fact Aristotle goes so far as to suggest the *identification* of the person with a part of the soul:

> the things men have done on a rational principle are thought most properly their own acts and voluntary acts. That this is the man himself, then, or is so more than anything else, is plain . . . (NE 1168b35ff.; cf. 1166a17ff.)

Indeed, sometimes he depicts reason as another person to whom the person owes obedience:

> reason in each of its possessors chooses what is best for itself and the good man obeys his reason (NE 1169a17–18)

In sum, Aristotle's depiction of the relationship between the parts of the soul is a highly personalized (or anthropomorphized) and politicized one. One reason this is so noticeable is that Aristotle here fails to respect his own admonitions in the *De Anima*[2] about not personalizing the parts or function of the soul. There, in a manner familiar to students of 20th-century Anglo-American philosophy, Aristotle suggests we remember that predicates which apply to persons in virtue of having souls nevertheless apply to the *persons* and not to their souls: the person is angry, not the soul or a part of the soul; the person thinks, not the soul or a part of it (*De Anima*, 408b14, 408b27). But his own warning is not heeded here, for Aristotle treats the parts of the soul as if they were persons or agents themselves, and in particular as if they were persons standing in political relations to one another: relations apparently best described in terms such as constitutional or royal ruler; obedient or resistant subject; master and slave.

Having looked at Aristotle's description of the soul, we must now look at the way in which he makes use of this description to justify his view that women are naturally subordinate to men.

III

As we have seen, in the *Politics* Aristotle turns to the constitution of the soul in order to justify his view that certain classes of beings are by nature to rule over other classes. He wants us to see that just as the irrational part of the soul is subordinate by nature to the rational part, so women are subordinate by nature to men.

We must remember here that Aristotle's claim about the natural subordination of the irrational part to the rational part, about the authority of the rational part over the irrational part, can only be understood as a claim about entitlement, for sometimes, even in free men, the irrational part in fact is not controlled by the rational part. It is unnatural for the irrational part not to listen to and obey the rational part, for it is intended by nature to do so (P 1254b4ff.). With this in mind, let's spell out Aristotle's argument.

Aristotle's claim about the soul is that

> (a) In the soul, the rational part by nature rules or has authority over (but does not always control) the irrational part.

Now Aristotle wants to use (a) to argue that understanding the nature of the authority of the rational part over the irrational part shows us the nature of the authority of men over women. So he wants to argue, on the basis of (a), that

(b) In the state, men by nature rule or have authority over women

But why does Aristotle associate men with the rational part and women with the irrational part of the soul? Because, he holds,

(c) In men's souls, the rational part by nature rules or has authority over the irrational part

while

(d) In women's souls, the rational part by nature does not rule or have authority over the irrational part

Or is it that

(e) In women's souls, the irrational part by nature rules or has authority over the rational part?

While (c) seems straightforward, both (d) and (e) seem to be uninvited guests, given Aristotle's insistence and dependence on (a). Does Aristotle hold that in the case of women, the lack of authority in the rational part is tantamount to the assumption of authority in the irrational part (as in (e))? Aristotle certainly must hold at least (d), for in the case of women, he says, the deliberative capacity is without authority and the irrational part actually controls or overwhelms the rational part. So even if Aristotle is not committed here to the view (e) that in women the irrational part is supposed to rule (parallel to his claim that in free men the rational part is supposed to rule), he must be saying (d) that in the case of women the rational part is not supposed to rule, it is not supposed to have authority. For his claim is not just that women *happen* to be subordinate to men; they are intended by nature to be subordinate to men. (Just as those who are to rule are rulers by nature, so those who are to be ruled are subjects by nature.) And nature could not succeed in this intention with respect to those who are subordinate unless nature at least intended the rational part to be without authority in women. On Aristotle's own reckoning,

women are subordinate to men by nature; that by virtue of which women are naturally subordinate to men must be, of course, something intended by nature; so the lack of authority in women's rational element must be intended by nature. In short, women are by nature unnatural.

In light of this, the eager remark by some Aristotelian scholars,[3] that Aristotle's view about the relation between men and women is not merely a comment on or reflection on the *status quo,* takes on special significance. For in one sense that is quite right: in saying that women are subordinate to men, Aristotle was not merely making an observation on the world around him. For insofar as that observation is correct, nature, according to Aristotle, has gotten her way (recall that Aristotle doesn't think this always happens, e.g., P 1254a–b). The rational element in women doesn't just happen to be without authority; for if that were the case, there would be no way to distinguish between the natural condition of a woman and the unnatural condition of a free man who is, for example, overindulgent: in the latter case, the rational part of the man's soul doesn't happen to exercize its authority, though it is intended to have authority; while in the former case, the rational part of the woman's soul is without authority but is not intended to have authority; if it were intended to have authority it wouldn't be in a woman!

But now Aristotle's argument is in deep trouble. For he *begins* his argument by saying that nature intends the rational part of the soul to have authority over the irrational part. But in order to get from there to the claim that nature intends men to rule over women, he has *also* to say that nature intends the rational part of the soul not to have authority over the irrational part, in the case of women. The merely contingent lack of authority of the rational part of someone's soul would not establish the claim that that person is naturally subordinate to someone else. Those who are naturally subordinate must be, on Aristotle's own reckoning, those in whom we can say that nature intended their rational part not to have authority.

Aristotle's problem is not merely that in order to generate the conclusion he wishes to reach, he has to deny one of his central premises. That is, the problem is not merely that in order to reach the conclusion that women are by nature subordinate to men, he has to deny that the rational part of the soul by nature rules over the irrational part. Let us look at the argument once again. He says that just as the rational part of the soul is to rule the irrational part, so men are to rule women. As we've seen, this requires the association of rationality with men and irrationality with women. But on what grounds does he make these associations? Well, as we noted, he makes them on the grounds that nature intended rationality to rule in men, and intended rationality not to rule in women. But this is merely begging the question, unless he can explain how he knows that nature intended this. His only possible reply to this is that in men rationality prevails and in women it does not. But even if true this wouldn't justify the view that this is what nature intends—for as we've seen, Aristotle himself points out that the mere fact of the dominance of one part of the soul over the other, or of one group of people over another, is never proof that this is the way things ought to be according to nature.

So Aristotle's argument for the natural subordination of women to men is, to put it charitably, wobbly: he holds an inconsistent view about the natural relationship between the rational and irrational parts of the soul, and he begs the question when he claims that the rational element by nature rules in men but does not in women.

IV

What I've been analyzing above is Aristotle's attempt to come to a position in political theory on the basis of a metaphysical position. As noted in Part II, that metaphysical position is itself a politicized one insofar as it is deeply etched in the language of political theory. The *dramatis personae* of the soul, and the drama itself, are modelled on the human persons and the human drama found in the political realm. If this is so, then we have to ask what business Aristotle has referring to the kind of relation that exists between metaphysical entities to clarify the kind of relation existing between political entities, if the relationship between the metaphysical entities itself is modelled on the relationship between political entities. In short, is Aristotle's argument from metaphysics to politics circular?

As we saw in Part II, Aristotle refers to relationships between kinds of persons to describe by analogy the relationships that hold between parts of the soul. And on more than one occasion, Aristotle explains why we need analogies to describe intra-psychic relationships. For example, in explaining the kind of relationship there is between the irrational element and the rational element, he says:

> while in the body we see that which moves astray, in the soul we do not. No doubt, however, we must none the less suppose that in the soul too there is something contrary to the rational principle, resisting and opposing it. . . . Now even this seems to have a share in a rational principle, as we said; at any rate in the continent man it obeys the rational principle—and presumably in the temperate and brave man it is still more obedient; for in him it speaks, on all matters, with the same voice as the rational principle. (NE 1102b27–30)

Aristotle says it is hard to tell what kind of soul a man has—whether that of a freeman or slave—because it doesn't always happen that a man with a freeman's soul also has a freeman's body and we cannot view the soul directly.

> And doubtless if men differed from one another in the mere forms of their bodies as much as the statues of the Gods do from men, all would acknowledge that the inferior class should be slaves of the superior. And if this is true of the body, how much more just that a similar distinction should exist in the soul? but the beauty of the body is seen, whereas the beauty of the soul is not seen. (P 1254b32–1255a2)

As he also says, "to gain light on things imperceptible we must use the evidence of sensible things" (NE 1104a13).[4] So Aristotle seems to take it as a given that in order to describe the soul, in order to make sense of relationships among parts of the soul, he has to rely on reference to and analogy to visible things. The particular visible things he relies on, as we've seen, are human beings standing in relationships of power and authority.

To point this out is not to ignore the fact that in general Aristotle's descriptions of the many parts of the world are in hierarchical terms. For example, Aristotle refers to ruler/subject relations as existing not only in the soul and in the state:[5]

> in all things which form a composite whole and which are made up of parts, whether continuous or discrete, a distinction between ruling and subject element comes to light. Such a duality exists in living creatures, but not in them only; it originates in the constitution of the universe; even in things which have no life there is a ruling principle, as in a musical mode. (P 1254a29–34)

However, not all ruling and subject elements need be conceived of as being like persons in political relationships. For example, although Aristotle spends a good bit of time in the *De Anima* discussing the hierarchy of functions in the soul, one is hard put to find evidence of the highly personalized and politicized language that appears both in the NE and the *Politics*. Indeed, as mentioned above . . . , he explicitly discourages his readers from thinking of the parts or functions of the soul as if they were themselves persons.[6] In a somewhat similar fashion in the *Metaphysics* he advises us not to take seriously the myths according to which the gods are thought of in anthropomorphic terms (*Meta.* 1074b6ff.). But when he describes the ruling and subject elements in the soul, he immediately recurs to the language of persons and politics. He speaks of the kind of rule of the rational part over the irrational part in terms that have to do with the rule of a person or persons over other persons—"constitutional" or "royal" rule (P 1254b5; cf. NE 1138b5ff). This fact is very significant. For presumably Aristotle is "bringing to light" the distinction between the ruling and subject elements among humans by pointing to the distinction between ruling and subject elements in the soul. But the kind of distinction between ruling and subject elements in the soul itself "comes to light" only through relationships of authority among human beings. As described in Part II, Aristotle brings to light what he takes to be the appropriate relationship—the relationship intended by nature—between parts of the soul, by analogy to relationships of authority among humans:

> as the child should live according to the direction of his tutor, so the appetitive element should live according to rational principle (NE 1119b14)

Metaphorically and in virtue of a certain resemblance there is a justice, not indeed between a man and himself, but between certain parts of him; yet not every kind of justice but that of master and servant or that of husband and wife. For these are the ratios in which the part of the soul that has a rational principle stands to the irrational part. (NE 1138b5–12)

We have to note that Aristotle does *not* try to justify his view about the natural rule of men over women by reference to a general principle about ruling and subject elements, for he quite explicitly refers us in particular to the constitution of the soul. There we find ruling and subject elements, but they are highly personalized entities whose relationships are described in terms of political relationships among human beings. In light of this, we must conclude that Aristotle's argument for the natural rule of men over women is circular. He argues for the position that men by nature rule women. How do we know that they do? We know this because the rational element of the soul by nature rules the irrational element. And how do we know this? This is where we come full circle: Because men rule women (and also because masters rule slaves, because tutors rule children). In fact the rule of men over women provides us with a means of understanding the kind of relationship among parts of the soul; and, coupled with the assumption that men represent the rational element and women represent the irrational element, it provides us with a means of establishing that in the soul the rational element rules the irrational.

Aristotle took a short-cut in his journey from his metaphysics, from his philosophical psychology, to his political theory: he built the particular relationships of authority he wished to justify on the basis of the metaphysics, into the metaphysics itself. For first of all, the terms used to describe the kind of authority the rational part has over the irrational part are unapologetically borrowed from the terminology of political relationships; yet presumably we are supposed to be relying on an understanding of the kind of authority the rational part has over the irrational part to understand the kind of authority men in the *polis* have over women. And secondly, the location of authority in the soul is supposed to tell us about the location of authority in the *polis*. Yet we are told that the clue that such authority is located in the rational part of the soul over against the irrational part, is that authority is located in men over against women, masters over against slaves, etc.

None of this is to say that if Aristotle hadn't thought men were naturally the rulers of women, he never would have suggested that the rational part of the soul rules the irrational part. Had he believed—ah, the power of counter-factuals to stretch the imagination—had he believed and wished to justify the belief that women were by nature the rulers of men, he might have used such a relationship between them as a model for the relationship between parts of the soul, and have ended up with the same problems of circularity.

I've said that Aristotle's political conclusion is built into his metaphysics. The political conclusion is sexist. Does that mean the metaphysics is sexist? Is the view that the rational part of the soul by nature rules over the irrational part a sexist view? No. What is sexist is not the asser-

tion of the authority of the rational part over the irrational part, but his association of rationality with men and irrationality with women.[7] The metaphysics *is* politicized, however, and this primes it for use to defend political positions that are sexist.

V

There are several reasons why I've thought it important to focus on Aristotle's argument for the natural subordination of women to men. It is not just that the argument doesn't work.

First of all, in taking a close look at the metaphysical position Aristotle relies on, we begin to see how thoroughly drenched it is with political language and imagery. Even if this were all we could say it would be important to say it, because according to what might be called the theory of philosophical cleanliness, metaphysics and philosophical psychology are supposed to be separate from and cleansed of political considerations: we may be entitled to draw political conclusions from metaphysics or psychology, but particular conclusions are not supposed to shape the metaphysics and psychology itself. So we see Aristotle wanting us to draw conclusions about politics from his psychology—a disingenuous request, and an absurd operation, if he believed that the psychology really was a version of politics to begin with. In a very similar way, I take it, we are nowadays asked to think about what consequences for social and political relations might be drawn, for example, from the studies called sociobiology, and from studies on intelligence: what do studies of human biology, or the animal kingdom, or the human psyche, have to tell us about the appropriateness or inappropriateness of particular social and political relations? ("Dear Dr. Freud, tell us what women's psyches are like so we'll know what to do with their lives!") We are expected to assume, however, that these studies are not themselves influenced by the political or social conclusions which will be said to follow from them. I leave it to students of sociobiology, psychology, and intelligence theory to judge whether and how such studies are biased by political considerations; for example, is it true, as Marshall Sahlins suggests, that "the theory of sociobiology has an intrinsic ideological dimension"; is it true that sociobiology involves "the grounding of human social behaviour in an advanced or scientific notion of organic evolution, which is in its own terms the representation of a cultural form of economic action"?[8] What I hope to have shown here is just how Aristotle's psychology is infused with the language and imagery of politics and how the political conclusions Aristotle wished to draw from his psychology get attached to his psychological premises.

It is important to note in this connection that this paper is not written from the viewpoint of a social historian or an historian of ideas. I have not been attempting here to try to show the connection between Aristotle's philosophical views, on the one hand, and the historical and political context in which he lived, on the other. Rather, I have been trying to show the conceptual and logical connections between Aristotle's political theory and his psychological theory. As mentioned above, the question of their relative dependence on one another has been raised before. Most recently a version of the question has been raised by W. W. Fortenbaugh, in an article called "Aristotle on Women and Slaves."[9] I shall conclude this essay with a response to Fortenbaugh.

Fortenbaugh holds that Aristotle's argument about women and slaves is a "political application of . . . philosophical psychology" . . . He considers the possible charge that Aristotle's use of his psychology to defend a political position is merely an *ad hoc* device to defend the status quo. In response to this, Fortenbaugh represents Aristotle as holding *not* that women are subordinate to men, and that's how we know their deliberative capacity is without authority; but *rather* that women's deliberative capacity is without authority and that is how we know they are subordinate to men. According to Fortenbaugh, Aristotle's claim about the lack

of authority which characterizes women's deliberative capacity is based not on "interpersonal relationships" but on "an intra-personal relationship" (*ibid.*):

> Aristotle "looks within the slave to explain his social position . . . [and] looks within the woman to explain her role and her virtues" . . .

Now since, as we've seen, Aristotle himself said that we can't "look within" to see the soul, we have to ask how, according to Fortenbaugh, we know that in women's soul the deliberative capacity lacks authority. Fortenbaugh's answer would seem to be, "because it is often overruled by her emotions or alogical side" . . . But doesn't that happen in the case of free men also? Yes, the reply must go . . . , but that doesn't mean that free men are to occupy subordinate roles, for in them the deliberative capacity is by nature with authority even if it doesn't always exercize it. So it must be that in women, on the other hand, the deliberative capacity is by nature without authority. But how do we know that? Psychology can't tell us that, because it tells us—that is the foundation for Aristotle's political argument, according to Fortenbaugh—that the rational part by nature *does* have such authority. The only reason we've been given for believing not just that women's deliberative capacity lacks authority, but *by nature* lacks this authority, is that if it weren't true women would not be by nature subordinate to men (at least not in terms of the argument of the *Politics*). Hence it is a requirement of Aristotle's politics that in women the deliberative capacity be without authority; it is not a conclusion of his psychology. In fact Fortenbaugh himself says this repeatedly throughout his short article without realizing the damaging import of it for his argument: e.g., he says that Aristotle "demands of women a virtue which reflects their domestic role" . . . ; "it also seems proper to assign slaves [this applies to women as well] a virtue limited by the demands of their subordinate role" . . . Fortenbaugh is saying here that Aristotle has a certain role in mind for women and slaves, and must thus posit for them and in them a psychological condition befitting their position. This isn't, however, what Fortenbaugh describes his own view as proposing!

Fortenbaugh fails to consider what gets built into Aristotle's psychological theory to make it seem even a plausible basis from which to argue for a political conclusion. He does not here consider the *kind* of authority the rational part is supposed to have over the irrational part. He also seems to think that the question of the role of irrationality in women is an empirical one . . . ; but if it were treated by Aristotle as an empirical question, then it would have to be conceivable that women's souls could be like what Aristotle calls the souls of free men. But if that is conceivable, women could not be said to be *by nature* subordinate to men.

Aristotle's argument deserves far more serious attention than Fortenbaugh has given it. I hope to have provided some of that attention—not only to show that the argument suffers from difficulties Fortenbaugh doesn't even imagine, but to point out that the movement from a metaphysical position to a political position is not always as innocent as it seems.

NOTES

1. Cf. *Nicomachean Ethics,* Bk. I, Ch. 13.

2. Even in the *De Anima,* as Hamlyn has pointed out, "Aristotle does not often live up to this remark." D. W. Hamlyn, *Aristotle's De Anima* (Oxford: Clarendon Press, 1968), p. 81.

3. Most recently, in W. W. Fortenbaugh's "Aristotle on Slaves and Women," in *Articles on Aristotle: 2. Ethics and Politics,* eds. Jonathan Barnes, Malcolm Schofield, Richard Sorabji (London: Duckworth, 1977), pp. 135–139.

4. I think the view adumbrated here by Aristotle, about the necessity of referring to publicly observable beings or things or activities to describe things or activities that are not publicly observable, is complemented by fairly recent developments in the philosophy of mind—in particular, by the view roughly associated with Wittgenstein and with Strawson according to which the concept of mind or soul is parasitic upon concepts of publicly observable things. I shall not elaborate on that view here, but wish to point out that it may enable us to see how easily it may happen that we use anthropomorphized language to describe the soul or mind.

5. Barker thinks that the fact that Aristotle refers to "a general principle of rule and subordination" saves him from the charge that he appears to argue in a circle. Ernest Barker, *The Politics of Aristotle* (Oxford: Clarendon Press, 1952), p. 35, fn. 1. In what follows I explain why I don't think Barker's view can be sustained.

6. As mentioned in fn. 2 above, Aristotle sometimes uses personalized language in the *De Anima.* But interestingly it is not also politicized language.

7. That association, as we saw in Section II, is perfectly arbitrary. Moreover, to maintain it, Aristotle has to hold that in one class, the class of men, the rational by nature rules, and in another class, that of women, the rational by nature does not rule. But if there is any class in whom the rational by nature does not rule, then the original premise of Aristotle's argument—that the rational by nature rules the irrational—is contradicted.

8. Marshall Sahlins, *The Use and Abuse of Biology: An Anthropological Critique of Sociobiology* (Ann Arbor: University of Michigan Press, 1977), pp. xii and xv. See also Donna Haraway, "Animal Sociology and a Natural Economy of the Body Politic" (two parts), *Signs* 4 (1978), 21–60, and "The Biological Enterprise: Sex, Mind and Profit from Human Engineering to Sociobiology," *Radical History Review* 20 (1979), 206–237; Paul Thom, "Stiff Cheese for Women," *Philosophical Forum* 8 (1976), 94–107.

9. Fortenbaugh, *op. cit.* Further page references in text are to this article.

Continuing to Think

Does one of the most fundamental assumptions about the relations between the sexes rest on a flawed argument? Arguing by analogy is often useful and can help us understand new information by linking it with what is already familiar. However, there is also a built-in danger. No analogy is perfect, and recognizing where the comparison is valid and where it is not is essential.

In this argument, it seems that Aristotle can claim the authority of men over women only by denying one of his fundamental metaphysical assumptions—that in human beings the rational part must rule over the emotional part. For his argument to be successful, Aristotle must claim that in women the failure of reason to dominate emotion is built into their very nature. Otherwise his political claim that men properly exercise authority over women is suspect, since even Aristotle had to admit that everyone (men as well as women) has moments when emotions override reason. This creates logical difficulties, as Spelman points out, and there are other consequences as well.

Is the price of human uniqueness disgust with our bodies and fear of our emotions? Looked at from the other side, what do we risk by blurring the lines between ourselves and other, so-called "higher animals"? Would what we sacrifice in human uniqueness be compensated for by greater ease in our physical selves, longer life, and a significantly improved quality of life?

3.4   *Person and Community in Traditional African Thought*

IFEANYI A. MENKITI

Preparing to Read

What if we took a different starting point altogether and began not with the human individual but with a tightly cohesive human community? Professor Menkiti's essay is critical of all three of the views of human personhood we have considered so far, and it describes a fourth view, derived from traditional African thought, as an alternative. In this view, the starting point is not the individual but the community. A traditional African would probably think as follows: "I am because we are, and since we are, therefore I am."

Like existentialism, this view assumes that human personhood is acquired through living rather than provided at birth. The difference is that in the African scheme the community plays a critical role in what the individual becomes, whereas in Sartre's version of existentialism it is the individual, acting alone, who makes a self for himself or herself.

In contrast with both the religious view of the individual as made in the image of God and the rationalist view of the individual as a superior intellect, the African view refuses to define a person by some static quality of soul or intellect. Instead, the African view is that personhood is not an automatic result of being born to human parents. It is possible to fail at or to succeed imperfectly at the task of becoming a person. And full personhood is achievable only within the nurturing and instructing environment of an organically constituted community.

This is no mere collection of individuals but rather a thoroughly collectivized "we." We might come closer to understanding what Menkiti means by thinking about our own belief in the power of the human family to shape healthy individuals into mature adults. This is the kind of "we" Menkiti has in mind when he insists that it is the community that makes the person and not the other way around.

MY AIM IN THIS PAPER is to articulate a certain conception of the person found in African traditional thought. I shall attempt to do this in an idiom, or language, familiar to modern philosophy. In this regard it is helpful to begin by pointing to a few significant contrasts between this African conception of the person and various other conceptions found in Western thought.

The first contrast worth noting is that whereas most Western views of man abstract this or that feature of the lone individual and then proceed to make it the defining or essential characteristic which entities aspiring to the description "man" must have, the African view of man denies that persons can be defined by focusing on this or that physical or psychological characteristic of the lone individual. Rather, man is defined by reference to the environing community. As John Mbiti notes, the African view of the person can be summed up in this statement: "I am because we are, and since we are, therefore I am."[1]

One obvious conclusion to be drawn from this dictum is that, as far as Africans are concerned, the reality of the communal world takes precedence over the reality of individual life histories, whatever these may be. And this primacy is meant to apply not only ontologically, but also in regard to epistemic accessibility. It is in rootedness in an ongoing human community that the individual comes to see himself as man, and it is by first knowing this community as a stubborn perduring fact of the psychophysical world

that the individual also comes to know himself as a durable, more or less permanent, fact of this world. In the language of certain familiar Western disciplines, we could say that not only the biological set through which the individual is capable of identification by reference to a communal gene pool, but also the language which he speaks and which is no small factor in the constitution of his mental dispositions and attitudes, belong to this or that specific human group. What is more, the sense of self-identity which the individual comes to possess cannot be made sense of except by reference to these collective facts. And thus, just as the navel points men to umbilical linkage with generations preceding them, so also does language and its associated social rules point them to a mental commonwealth with others whose life histories encompass the past, present, and future.

A crucial distinction thus exists between the African view of man and the view of man found in Western thought: in the African view it is the community which defines the person as person, not some isolated static quality of rationality, will, or memory.

This brings us to the second point of contrast between the two views of man, namely, the *processual* nature of being in African thought—the fact that persons become persons only after a process of incorporation. Without incorporation into this or that community, individuals are considered to be mere danglers to whom the description "person" does not fully apply. For

From *Person and Community in Traditional African Thought* by Ifeanyi Menkiti.
Courtesy of University Press of America.

personhood is something which has to be achieved, and is not given simply because one is born of human seed. This is perhaps the burden of the distinction which Placide Tempels' native informants saw fit to emphasize to him—i.e. the distinction between a *muntu mutupu* (a man of middling importance) and *muntu mukulumpe* (a powerful man, a man with a great deal of force). Because the word "muntu" includes an idea of excellence, of plenitude of force at maturation, the expression 'ke muntu po,' which translates as 'this is not a man,'[2] may be used in reference to a human being. Thus, it is not enough to have before us the biological organism, with whatever rudimentary psychological characteristics are seen as attaching to it. We must also conceive of this organism as going through a long process of social and ritual transformation until it attains the full complement of excellencies seen as truly definitive of man. And during this long process of attainment, the community plays a vital role as catalyst and as prescriber of norms.

In light of the above observations I think it would be accurate to say that whereas Western conceptions of man go for what might be described as a minimal definition of the person—whoever has soul, or rationality, or will, or memory, is seen as entitled to the description "person"—the African view reaches instead for what might be described as a maximal definition of the person. As far as African societies are concerned, personhood is something at which individuals could fail, at which they could be competent or ineffective, better or worse. Hence, the African emphasized the rituals of incorporation and the overarching necessity of learning the social rules by which the community lives, so that what was initially biologically given can come to attain social self-hood, i.e., become a person with all the inbuilt excellencies implied by the term.

That full personhood is not perceived as simply given at the very beginning of one's life, but is attained after one is well along in society, indicates straight away that the older an individual gets the more of a person he becomes. As an Igbo proverb has it, "What an old man sees sitting down, a young man cannot see standing up." The proverb applies, it must be added, not just to the incremental growth of wisdom as one ages; it also applies to the ingathering of the other excellencies considered to be definitive of full personhood. What we have here then is both a claim that a qualitative difference exists between old and young, and a claim that some sort of ontological progression exists between infancy and ripening old age. One does not just take on additional features, one also undergoes fundamental changes at the very core of one's being.

Now, admittedly, the whole idea of ontological progression is something in need of elaboration. Offhand it may not sit very well in the minds of those unaccustomed to the view of personhood being presented here. The temptation might be strong in some quarters to retort that either an entity is a person or it is not; that there can be no two ways about it. In response to this misgiving let me note that the notion of an acquisition of personhood is supported by the natural tendency in many languages, English included, of referring to children and new-borns as *it*. Consider this expression: "We rushed the child to the hospital but before we arrived *it* was dead." We would never say this of a grown person. Of course, with a child or new-born, reference could also be made by use of a personal pronoun, with the statement reading instead: "We rushed the child to the hospital but before we arrived he/she was dead." This personalizing option does not, however, defeat the point presently being made. For the important thing is that we have the choice of an *it* for referring to children and new-borns, whereas we have no such choice in referring to older persons.

The fact, then, that a flexibility of referential designation exists in regard to the earliest stages of human life, but not in regard to the more established later stages, is something well worth keeping in mind. What we have is not just a distinction of language but a distinction laden with ontological significance. In the particular context of Africa, anthropologists have long noted the relative absence of ritualized grief when the death of a young child occurs, whereas with the death of an older person, the burial ceremony becomes more elaborate and the grief more ritualized—indicating a significant difference in the conferral of ontological status.

Before moving away from the foregoing observations made in support of the notion of personhood as acquired, let me note, in addition, that in African societies the ultimate termination of personal existence is also marked by an "it" designation; thus, the same depersonalized reference marking the beginning of personal existence also marks the end of that existence. After birth the individual goes through the different rites of incorporation, including those of initiation at puberty time, before becoming a full person in the eyes of the community. And then, of course, there is procreation, old age, death, and entry into the community of departed ancestral spirits—a community viewed as continuous with the community of living men and women, and with which it is conceived as being in constant interaction.

Following John Mbiti, we could call the inhabitants of the ancestral community by the name of the "living dead."[3] For the ancestral dead are not dead in the world of spirits, nor are they dead in the memory of living men and women who continue to remember them, and who incessantly ask their help through various acts of libation and sacrificial offering. At the stage of ancestral existence, the dead still retain their personhood and are, as a matter of fact, addressed by their various names very much as if they were still at center stage. Later, however, after several generations, the ancestors cease to be remembered by their personal names; from this moment on they slide into personal non-existence, and lose all that they once possessed by way of personal identity. This, for the traditional African worldview, is the termination of personal existence, with entities that were once fully human agents becoming once again mere *its,* ending their worldly sojourn as they had started out—as un-

incorporated non-persons. Mbiti has described this terminal stage of a person's life as one of "collective immortality" (in contrast to the "personal immortality" that marks the stage of ancestral existence, a stage in which the departed are remembered by name by the living, and do genuinely form a community of their own).[4]

But the expression "collective immortality" is misleading and problematic. At the stage of total dis-incorporation marked by the term, the mere *its* that the dead have now become cannot form a collectivity of any kind; and, since by definition no one now remembers them, there is not much sense in saying of them that they are immortal either. They no longer have an adequate sense of self; and having lost their names, lose also the means by which they could be immortalized. Hence, it is better to refer to them by the term *the nameless dead,* rather than designate their stage of existence by such a term as "collective immortality," thereby opening up the possibility of describing them as "collective immortals," which certainly they are not. This emendation apart, however, Mbiti is quite right when he states that for African man no ontological progression is possible beyond the spirit world: "Beyond the state of the spirits, men cannot go or develop. This is the destiny of man as far as African ontology is concerned."[5]

The point can be made then, that a significant symmetry exists between the opening phase of an individual's quest for personhood and the terminal phase of that quest. Both are marked by an absence of incorporation and this absence is made abundantly evident by the related absence of collectively conferred names. Just as the child has no name when it tumbles out into the world to begin the journey towards selfhood, so likewise at the very end, it will have no name again. At both points it is considered quite appropriate to use an "it" designation precisely because what we are dealing with are entities in regard to which there is a total absence of incorporation.

Finally, it is perhaps worth noting that this phenomenon of a depersonalized status at the two polarities of existence makes a great deal of sense given the absence of moral function. The child, we all know, is usually preoccupied with his physical needs; and younger persons, generally, are notoriously lacking in moral perception. Most often they have a tendency towards self-centeredness in action, a tendency to see the world exclusively through their own vantage point. This absence of moral function cannot but have an effect on the view of them as persons. Likewise for the completely departed ancestral spirits, who, at the terminal point of their personal existence, have now become mere *its,* their contact with the human community completely severed. The various societies found in traditional Africa routinely accept this fact that personhood is the sort of thing which has to be attained, and is attained in direct proportion as one participates in communal life through the discharge of the various obligations defined by one's stations. It is the carrying out of these obligations that transforms one from the it-status of early childhood, marked by an absence of moral function, into the person-status of later years, marked by a widened maturity of ethical sense—an ethical maturity without which personhood is conceived as eluding one.

John Rawls, of the Western-born philosophers, comes closest to a recognition of this importance of ethical sense in the definition of personhood. In *A Theory of Justice* he makes explicit part of what is meant by the general ethical requirement of respect for persons, noting that those who are capable of a sense of justice are owed the duties of justice, with this capability construed in its sense of a potentiality which may or may not have been realized. He writes:

> Equal justice is owed to those who have the capacity to take part in and to act in accordance with the public understanding of the initial situation. One should observe that moral personality is here defined as a potentiality that is ordinarily realized in due course. It is this potentiality which brings the claims of justice into play. . . . The sufficient condition for equal justice [is] the capacity for moral personality.[6]

I take it that an important implication of this claim is that if an individual comes to deserve the duties of justice (and the confirmation therein implied of the individual's worth as a person) only through possession of a capacity for moral personality, then morality ought to be considered as essential to our sense of ourselves as persons. And indeed Rawls has argued in another context that a Kantian interpretation is possible in which the transgression of accepted moral rules gives rise not just to a feeling of guilt but to a feeling of shame—the point being that once morality is conceived as a fundamental part of what it means to be a person, then an agent is bound to feel himself incomplete in violating its rules, thus provoking in himself the feeling properly describable as shame, with its usual intimation of deformity and unwholeness.[7]

If it is generally conceded, then, that persons are the sort of entities that are owed the duties of justice, it must also be allowed that each time we find an ascription of any of the various rights implied by these duties of justice, the conclusion naturally follows that the possessor of the rights in question cannot be other than a person. That is so because the basis of such rights ascription has now been made dependent on a possession of a capacity for moral sense, a capacity, which though it need not be realized, is nonetheless made most evident by a concrete exercise of duties of justice towards others in the ongoing relationships of everyday life.

The foregoing interpretation would incidentally rule out, I believe, some dangerous tendencies currently fashionable in some philosophical circles of ascribing rights to animals.[8] The danger as I see it is that such an extension of moral language to the domain of animals is bound to undermine, sooner or later, the clearness of our conception of what it means to be a person. The practical consequences are also something for us to worry about. For if there is legitimacy in ascribing rights to animals then human beings could come to be compelled to share resources with them. In such a situation, for instance, the various governmental programs designed to eradicate poverty in the inner cities of the United States could conceivably come under fire from the United Animal Lovers of America, or some other such group, with the claim seriously being lodged that everything was being done for the poor, but not enough for the equally deserving cats and dogs. Minority persons might then find themselves the victims of a peculiar philosophy in which the constitutive elements in the definition of human personhood have become blurred through unwarranted extensions to non-human entities.

Before bringing to a close the various comments made so far, it might be helpful to focus on two issues . . . in an effort to forestall possible misunderstanding. One issue is the acquisition of personhood, since the possibility exists of confusing the African viewpoint with the viewpoint known in the West as Existentialist Philosophy. The other issue is the articulation of the specific sense in which the term "community" has been used in these pages, so as to avoid possible misinterpretation.

To begin with the first, it must be emphasized that the African concept of man contrasts in significant measure with Existentialism (which on the face of things appears to be its most natural ally among the various Western philosophers of the person). Jean-Paul Sartre tells us that prior to the choice of his fundamental project an individual is "nothing [and] will not be anything until later, and then he will be what he makes himself."[9] Such a statement immediately evokes favorable comparisons between the African view of man and the Existentialist view, both views being regarded as adopting a notion of personhood, or self-hood, as something acquired.

But this, it must be warned, is a hasty conclusion to draw. For the Sartrean view that man is a *free unconditioned* being, a being not constrained by social or historical circumstances, flies in the face of African beliefs. Given its emphasis on individuals solely constituting themselves into the selves that they are to become, by dint of their private choices, such a view cannot but encourage eccentricity and individualism— traits which run counter to African ideals of what the human person is all about. Although in important ways existence does precede essence, it is not for the reasons that Sartre gives. We simply cannot postulate man's freedom and independence from all determining factors, including even reason, which is sometimes viewed by Sartre as unduly circumscribing the individual in his quest for a free and spontaneously authentic existence. As Professor William Abraham has pointed out in his book, *The Mind of Africa,* if possession of reason is part of our nature, then we cannot be enslaved by reason as Sartre sometimes seems to suggest; for no entity can be enslaved by its own nature.[10]

Nor is the above the only point at which Existentialist philosophy diverges from the African in the conception of man. Because of the controlling force of freedom, Sartre was led to postulate an equality of status between infant and child, on the one hand, and the grown adult, on the other. What all individuals have in common is that they choose; and choice is freedom, and freedom choice. As he puts it elsewhere, "Man does not exist in order to be free *subsequently;* there is no difference between the being of man and his *being* free."[11] But this collapsing of the ontological distinction between young child and grown man is an illegitimate and absurd move. Even assuming that Sartrean freedom is a *sine qua non* of the metaphysics of persons, how can children with their quite obvious lack of intelligent appreciation of the circumstances of their lives and of the alternatives open to them, choose rationally? Is a choice undertaken in childish ignorance a choice that is truly free?

These misgivings are serious; and it is frankly quite difficult to understand what is meant by the type of freedom which Sartre insists both adults and children have in equal measure, as a result of which it is then argued that they, and they alone, can define for themselves the selves that they are to be, each in his own way. As Anthony

Manser has put it, and I entirely agree, "It would seem that little remains of the freedom Sartre has been emphasizing . . . ; it is hard to see how an infant can be aware of what he is doing, and if not then it is odd to call him responsible."[12]

In the light of the foregoing observations, I take it then that the African view of human personhood and the Existentialist view should not be conflated. Even though both views adopt a dynamic, non-static approach to the problem of definition of human self-hood, the underpinning metaphysical assumptions diverge significantly. Above all, whereas in the African understanding human community plays a crucial role in the individual's acquisition of full personhood, in the Sartrean existentialist view, the individual alone defines the self, or person, he is to become. Such collectivist insistences as we find in the African world-view are utterly lacking in the Existentialist tradition. And this difference in the two approaches is not accidental. Rather it arises because there is at bottom a fundamental disagreement as to what reality is all about.

Finally, let me try to clarify the sense in which the term "community" has been used throughout this paper. Western writers have generally interpreted the term "community" in such a way that it signifies nothing more than a mere collection of self-interested persons, each with his private set of preferences, but all of whom get together nonetheless because they realize, each to each, that in association they can accomplish things which they are not able to accomplish otherwise. In this primarily additive approach, whenever the term "community" or "society" is used, we are meant to think of the aggregated sum of individuals comprising it. And this is argued, not just as an ontological claim, but also as a methodological recommendation to the various social or humanistic disciplines interested in the investigation of the phenomenon of individuals in groups; hence the term "Methodological Individualism" so much bandied around in the literature.

Now this understanding of human community, and of the approach to its study, is something completely at odds with the African view

of community. When Mbiti says that the African says to himself, "I am because we are," the *we* referred to here is not an additive "we" but a thoroughly fused collective "we." It is possible to distinguish three senses of human grouping, the first of which I shall call *collectivities* in the truest sense, the second of which might be called *constituted* human groups; and the third of which might be called *random* collections of individuals. The African understanding of human society adopts the usage in description number one above, whereas the Western understanding would fall closer to description number two; the difference between the two being that in what I have called "collectivities in the truest sense" there is assumed to be an *organic* dimension to the relationship between the component individuals, whereas in the understanding of human society as something *constituted* what we have is a non-organic bringing together of atomic individuals into a unit more akin to an association than to a community. The difference between the two views of society is profound and can be represented diagrammatically thus:

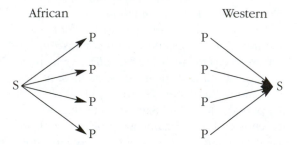

As can be seen from the diagram, whereas the African view asserts an ontological independence to human society, and moves from society to individuals, the Western view moves instead from individuals to society.

In looking at the distinction just noted, it becomes quite clear why African societies tend to be organized around the requirements of duty while Western societies tend to be organized around the postulation of individual rights. In the African understanding, priority is given to the duties which individuals owe to the collectivity, and their rights, whatever these may be, are seen as secondary to their exercise of their duties. In the West, on the other hand, we find a construal of things in which certain specified rights of individuals are seen as antecedent to the organization of society; with the function of government viewed, consequently, as being the protection and defense of these individual rights.

NOTES

1. John Mbiti, *African Religions and Philosophies* (New York: Doubleday and Company, 1970), p. 141.

2. Placide Tempels, *Bantu Philosophy* (Paris: Présence Africaine, 1959), p. 101.

3. Mbiti, *African Religions,* p. 32.

4. Ibid., p. 33.

5. Ibid., p. 34.

6. John Rawls, *A Theory of Justice* (Cambridge, Mass.: Harvard University Press, 1971), pp. 505–506.

7. Ibid., p. 445.

8. See, for instance, Peter Singer, *Animal Liberation* (New York: Random House, 1975); as well as Tom Regan & Peter Singer eds., *Animal Rights and Human Obligations* (Englewood Cliffs, N.J.: Prentice Hall, 1976).

9. Jean-Paul Sartre, "Existentialism Is a Humanism" in Nino Languilli ed., *The Existentialist Tradition: Selected Writlngs,* trans. by Philip Mairet (New York: Doubleday-Anchor Books, 1971), p. 399.

10. William Abraham, *The Mind of Africa* (Chicago: The University of Chicago Press, 1962), p. 2021.

11. Jean-Paul Sartre, *Being and Nothingness: An essay on Phenomenological Ontology,* trans. with an introduction by Hazel E. Barnes (New York: Philosophical Library, 1956), p. 25.

12. Anthony Manser, *Sartre: A Philosophical Study* (London: University of London Press, 1966), p. 122.

Continuing to Think

One of the conclusions we might draw from this reading is that the community is of greater importance than the individual. Along with an emphasis on rights, such as we find in Western culture, there is a corresponding emphasis on duties. If it is only by rooting myself in a strongly constituted community that I can experience myself as "durable," then it follows that carrying out the duties appropriate to my station in life (prescribed for me by the community) will gradually transform me into a person.

Just as it would be unreasonable for me to expect to be a basketball superstar or a concert pianist at birth, so personhood remains a goal, and, as in the previous examples, I must enter a community of people more advanced than myself to learn how to be what I wish to become. I will make a self for myself, as the existentialists suggest, but I will not do it alone. I will do it with the help of my teachers and coaches in the human community, and I cannot do it apart from them.

This flies in the face of our Western respect for the rights of the individual and our belief that highly competent, effectively motivated, and hard working individuals can accomplish just about anything—alone. As we look around at a society in which many of the traditional moorings are missing or weakened, we gain an appreciation for how difficult it is to go it alone. Without a nurturing family, a community of neighbors, and a system of shared values, finding our way can be perilous and frightening. African cultures don't expect this of the isolated individual. One question to ask yourself is this: At what point would the loss of some individual rights be outweighed by the support of a cohesive and nurturing community?

3.5   *Code of the Lifemaker*

JAMES P. HOGAN

Preparing to Read

So far we have been concerned with organic life forms—living, breathing human be-ings who may or may not be different from other animals in significant ways. The other challenge to human uniqueness comes from artificial intelligence or AI. Science fiction writers have long imagined a highly sophisticated robot or android who seems to cross the line into human personhood. *Star Trek: The Next Generation* did this with the character of Data, whose positronic net and skillfully constructed body gave a good semblance of humanity; only emotions were lacking in the original con-struction. The question is: Would we, under any conditions, be prepared to grant personhood to a mechanical creature?

In this last reading, set long ago and far away, robots are deposited on the surface of an uninhabited planet and, with the help of master programs downloaded from the spaceship's computers, build and set up a factory to manufacture other robots and, ultimately, supply the home world with local resources. Unfortunately (or fortu-nately), a series of environmental and mechanical catastrophes leads to unexpected results. The robot race exhibits genetic variability and recombination, competition, selection, and adaptation—all the essentials for continuing evolution. Is it a life form?

Prologue: The Searcher

1. 1 MILLION YEARS B.C.: 1,000 LIGHT YEARS FROM THE SOLAR SYSTEM

HAD ENGLISH-SPEAKING humans existed, they would probably have translated the spacecraft's designation as "searcher." Unmanned, it was al-most a mile long, streamlined for descent through planetary atmospheres, and it operated fully under the control of computers. The alien civilization was an advanced one, and the com-puters were very sophisticated.

The planet at which the searcher arrived after a voyage of many years was the fourth in the system of a star named after the king of a mythi-cal race of alien gods, and could appropriately be called Zeus IV. It wasn't much to look at—an

airless, lifeless ball of eroded rock formations, a lot of boulders and debris from ancient mete-orite impacts, and vast areas of volcanic ash and dust—but the searcher's orbital probes and sur-face landers found a crust rich in titanium, chromium, cobalt, copper, manganese, uranium, and many other valuable elements concentrated by thermal-fluidic processes operating early in the planet's history. Such a natural abundance of metals could support large-scale production without extensive dependence on bulk nuclear transmutation processes—in other words, very economically—and that was precisely the kind of thing that the searcher had been designed to search for. After completing their analysis of the preliminary data, the control computers selected a landing site, composed and transmitted a message home to report their findings and announce their intentions, and then activated the vessel's descent routine.

Shortly after the landing, a menagerie of surveyor robots, equipped with imagers, spectrometers, analyzers, chemical sensors, rock samplers, radiation monitors, and various manipulator appendages, emerged from the ship and dispersed across the surrounding terrain to investigate surface features selected from orbit. Their findings were transmitted back to the ship and processed, and shortly afterward follow-up teams of tracked, legged, and wheeled mining, drilling, and transportation robots went out to begin feeding ores and other materials back to where more machines had begun to build a fusion-powered pilot extraction plant. A parts-making facility was constructed next, followed by a parts-assembly facility, and step by step the pilot plant grew itself into a fully equipped, general-purpose factory, complete with its own control computers. The master programs from the ship's computers were copied into the factory's computers, which thereupon became self-sufficient and assumed control of surface operations. The factory then began making more robots.

Sometimes, of course, things failed to work exactly as intended, but the alien engineers had created their own counterpart of Murphy and allowed for his law in their plans. Maintenance robots took care of breakdowns and routing wear and tear in the factory; troubleshooting programs tracked down causes of production rejects and adjusted the machines for drifting tolerances; breakdown teams brought in malfunctioning machines for repair; and specialized scavenging robots roamed the surface in search of wrecks, write-offs, discarded components, and any other likely sources of parts suitable for recycling.

Time passed, the factory hummed, and the robot population grew in number and variety. When the population had attained a critical size, a mixed workforce detached itself from the main center of activity and migrated a few miles away to build a second factory, a replica of the first, using materials supplied initially from Factory One. When Factory Two became self-sustaining, Factory One, its primary task accomplished, switched to mass-production mode, producing goods and materials for eventual shipment to the alien home planet.

While Factory Two was repeating the process by commencing work on Factory Three, the labor detail from Factory One picked up its tools and moved on to begin Factory Four. By the time Factory Four was up and running, Factories Five through Eight were already taking shape, Factory Two was in mass-production mode, and Factory Three was building the first of a fleet of cargo vessels to carry home the products being stockpiled. This self-replicating pattern would spread rapidly to transform the entire surface of Zeus IV into a totally automated manufacturing complex dedicated to supplying the distant alien civilization from local resources.

From within the searcher's control computers, the Supervisor program gazed out at the scene through its data input channels and saw that its work was good. After a thorough overhaul and systems checkout, the searcher ship reembarked its primary workforce and launched itself into space to seek more worlds on which to repeat the cycle.

FIFTY YEARS LATER

Not far—as galactic distances go—from Zeus was another star, a hot, bluish white star with a mass of over fifteen times that of the Sun. It had formed rapidly, and its life span—the temporary halt of its collapse under self-gravitation by thermonuclear radiation pressure—had demanded such a prodigious output of energy as to be a brief one. In only ten million years the star, which had converted all the hydrogen in its outer shell to helium, resumed its collapse until the core temperature was high enough to burn the helium into carbon, and then, when the helium was exhausted, repeated the process to begin burning carbon. The ignition of carbon raised the core temperature higher still, which induced a higher rate of carbon burning, which in turn heated the core even more, and a thermonuclear runaway set in which in terms of stellar timescales was instantaneous. In mere days the star erupted into a supernova—radiating with a billion times the brightness of the Sun, exploding outward until its photosphere enclosed a radius greater than that of Uranus' orbit, and devouring its tiny flock of planets in the process.

Those planets had been next on the searcher's list to investigate, and it happened that the ship was heading into its final approach when the star exploded. The radiation blast hit it head-on at three billion miles out.

The searcher's hull survived more-or-less intact, but secondary x-rays and high-energy particles—things distinctly unhealthy for computers—flooded its interior. With most of its primary sensors burned out, its navigation system disrupted, and many of its programs obliterated or altered, the searcher veered away and disappeared back into the depths of interstellar space.

One of the faint specks lying in the direction now ahead of the ship was a yellow-white dwarf star, a thousand light-years away. It too possessed a family of planets, and on the third of those planets the descendants of a species of semi-intelligent ape had tamed fire and were beginning to experiment with tools chipped laboriously from thin flakes of stone.

Supernovas are comparatively rare events, occurring with a frequency of perhaps two or three per year in the average galaxy. But as with most generalizations, this has occasional exceptions. The supernova that almost enveloped the searcher turned out to be the first of a small chain that rippled through a localized cluster of massive stars formed at roughly the same time. Located in the middle of the cluster was a normal, longer-lived star which happened to be the home star of the aliens. The aliens had never gotten round to extending their civilization much beyond the limits of their own planetary

system, which was unfortunate because that was the end of them.

Everybody has a bad day sometimes.

ONE MILLION YEARS B.C.

One hundred thousand years after being scorched by the supernova, the searcher drifted into the outer regions of a planetary system. With its high-altitude surveillance instruments only partly functioning and its probes unable to deploy at all, the ship went directly into its descent routine over the first sizeable body that it encountered, a frozen ball of ice-encrusted rock about three thousand miles in diameter, with seas of liquid methane and an atmosphere of nitrogen, hydrogen, and methane vapor. The world came nowhere near meeting the criteria for worthwhile exploitation, but that was of no consequence since the computer programs responsible for surface analysis and evaluation weren't working.

The programs to initiate surface activity did work, however, more or less, and Factory One, with all of its essential functions up and running to at least some degree, was duly built on a rocky shelf above an ice beach flanking an inlet of a shallow methane sea. The ship's master programs were copied across into the newly installed factory computers, which identified the commencement of work on Factory Two as their first assignment. Accordingly Factory One's Supervisor program signaled the ship's databank for a copy of the "How to Make a Factory" file, which included a set of subfiles on "How to Make the Machines Needed to Make a Factory," i.e., robots. And that was where everything really started to go wrong.

The robots contained small internal processors that could be reprogramed via radiolink from the factory computers for each new task to be accomplished. This allowed the robots to proceed with their various jobs under autonomous local control and freed up the central computers for other work while they were waiting for the next "Done that—what do I do now?" signal. Hence many software mechanisms existed for initiating data transfers between the factory computers and the remote processors inside the robots.

When the copying of the "How to Make a Factory" file from the ship to Factory One was attempted, the wrong software linkages were activated; instead of finding their way into the factory's central system, the subfiles containing the manufacturing information for the various robots were merely relayed through the factory and beamed out into the local memories of the respective robot types to which they pertained. No copies at all were retained in the factory databank. And even worse, the originals inside the ship managed to self-destruct in the process and were irretrievably erased. The only copies of the "How to Make a Fred-type Robot" subfile were the ones contained inside the Fred-types out on the surface. And the same was true for all the other types as well.

So when the factory's Supervisor program ordered the Scheduler program to schedule more robots for manufacture, and the Scheduler lodged a request with the Databank Manager for the relevant subfiles, the Databank Manager found that it couldn't deliver. Neither could it obtain a recopy from the ship. The Databank Manager reported the problem to the Scheduler; the Scheduler complained to the Supervisor; the Supervisor blamed the Communications Manager; the Communications Manager demanded an explanation from the Message Handler; and after a lot of mutual electronic recriminations and accusations, the system logging and diagnostic programs determined that the missing subfiles had last been tracked streaming out through the transmission buffers on their way to the robots outside. Under a stern directive from the Supervisor, the Communications Manager selected a Fred from the first category of robots called for on the Scheduler's list, and beamed it a message telling it to send its subfile back again.

But the Fred didn't have a complete copy of the subfile; its local memory simply hadn't been big enough to hold all of it. And for the same reason, none of the other Freds could return a full copy either. They had been sprayed in succession with the datastream like buckets being filled from a fire-hose, and all had ended up with different portions of the subfile; but they appeared to have preserved the whole subfile among them. So the Supervisor had to retrieve different pieces from different Freds to fit them together again in a way that made sense. And that was how it arrived at the version it eventually handed to the Scheduler for manufacture.

Unfortunately, the instruction to store the information for future reference got lost somewhere, and for each batch of Freds the relevant "How to Make" subfile was promptly erased as soon as the Manufacturing Manager had finished with it. Hence when Factory One had spent some time producing parts for Factory Two and needed to expand its robot workforce to begin surveying sites for Factory Three, the Supervisor had to go through the whole rigmarole again. And the same process was necessary whenever a new run was scheduled to provide replacements for robots that had broken down or were wearing out.

All of this took up excessive amounts of processor time, loaded up the communications channels, and was generally inefficient in the ways that cost accountants worry about. The alien programers had been suitably indoctrinated by the alien cost accountants who ran the business—as always—and had written the Supervisor as a flexible, self-modifying learning program that would detect such inefficiencies, grow unhappy about them, and seek to improve things. After a few trials, the Supervisor found that some of the Freds contained about half their respective subfiles, which meant that a complete copy could be obtained by interrogating just two individuals instead of many. Accordingly it made a note of such "matching pairs" and began selecting them as its source for repeat requests from the Scheduler, ignoring the others.

Lost along with the original "How to Make a Fred" subfiles were the subsubfiles on "Programs to Write into a Fred to Start It Up after You've Made It." To make up for the deficiency, the Supervisor copied through to the Scheduler the full set of programs that it found already existing in the Freds selected to provide reproduction information, and these programs, of course, included the ones on how to make Freds. Thus the robots began coming off the line with one-half of their "genetic" information automatically built in, and a cycle asserted itself whereby they in turn became the source of information to be recombined later for producing more Freds. The method worked, and the Supervisor never figured out that it could have saved itself a lot of trouble by storing the blueprints away once and for all in the factory databank.

The program segments being recombined in this way frequently failed to copy faithfully, and the "genomes" formed from them were seldom identical, some having portions of code omitted while others had portions duplicated. Consequently Freds started taking on strange shapes and behaving in strange ways.

Some didn't exhibit any behavior at all but simply fell over or failed during test, to be broken down into parts again and recycled. A lot were like that.

Some, from the earlier phase, were genetically incomplete—"sterile"—and never called upon by the Supervisor to furnish reproductive data. They lasted until they broke down or wore out, and then became extinct.

Some reproduced passively, i.e., by transmitting their half-subfiles to the factory when the Scheduler asked for them.

A few, however, had inherited from the ship's software the program modules whose function was to lodge requests with the Scheduler to schedule more models of their own kind—program modules, moreover, which embodied a self-modifying priority structure capa-

ble of raising the urgency of their requests within the system until they were serviced. The robots in this category sought to reproduce actively: They behaved as if they experienced a compulsion to ensure that their half-subfiles were always included in the Scheduler's schedule of "Things to Make Next."

So when Factory One switched over to mass-production mode, the robots competing for slots in its product list soon grabbed all of the available memory space and caused the factory to become dedicated to churning out nothing else. When Factory Two went into operation under control of programs copied from Factory One, the same thing happened there. And the same cycle would be propagated to Factory Three, construction of which had by that time begun.

More factories appeared in a pattern spreading inland from the rocky coastal shelf. The instability inherent in the original parent software continued to manifest itself in the copies of copies of copies passed on to later generations, and the new factories, along with their mixed populations of robot progeny, diverged further in form and function.

Material resources were scarce almost everywhere, which resulted in the emergence of competitive pressures that the alien system designers had never intended. The factory-robot communities that happened to include a balanced mix of surveyor, procurement, and scavenger robots with "appetites" appropriate to their factories' needs, and which enjoyed favorable sites on the surface, usually managed to survive if not flourish. Factory Ten, for example, occupied the center of an ancient meteorite crater twelve miles across, where the heat and shock of the impact had exposed metal-bearing bedrock from below the ice; Factory Thirteen established itself inside a deep fissure where the ice beneath was relatively thin, and was able to melt a shaft down to the denser core material; and Factory Fifteen resorted to nuclear transmutation processes to build heavier nuclei from lighter ones frozen in solution in the ice crust.

But many were like Factory Nineteen, which began to take shape on an ill-chosen spot far out on a bleak ice field, and ground to a halt when its deep-drilling robots and transmutation reactors failed to function, and its supply of vital materials ran out.

The scavenger and parts-salvaging robots assumed a crucial role in shaping the strange metabolism that was coming into being. Regardless of what the Schedulers in the various factories would have liked to see made, the only things that could be assembled readily were the ones for which parts were available, and that depended to a large degree on the ability of the scavengers to locate them, or alternatively to locate assemblies suitable for breaking down—"digesting"—and rebuilding into something useful. Factory Twenty-four was an extreme case. Unable to "metabolize" parts directly from any source of raw materials because of the complete failure of its materials-procurement workforce, it relied totally on its scavengers. Factory Thirty-two, on the other hand, could acquire raw materials but couldn't use them since it had been built without a processing facility at all. Its robots delivered instead to Forty-seven, which happened to produce parts for some of the scavengers being manufactured by Thirty-two, and the two factory-robot organisms managed to coexist happily in their bizarre form of symbiosis.

The piles of assorted junk, which shouldn't have accumulated from the earlier phases of the process but had, were eaten up; the machines that broke down were eaten up; and the carcasses of defunct factories were eaten up. When those sources of materials had been exhausted, some of the machines began to eat each other.

The scavengers had been designed, as they had to be, to discriminate between properly functioning machines and desirable products on the one hand and rejects in need of recycling on the other. However, as with everything else in the whole, messed-up project, this function worked well in some cases, not so well in others, and often not at all. Some of the models turned out to be as likely to attempt the dismantling of a live, walking-around Fred as of a dead, flat-on-its-back one. Many of the victims were indifferent to this kind of treatment and soon died out, but others succeeded in developing effective fight-or-flee responses to preserve themselves, thus marking the beginnings of specialized prey and predators in the form of "lithovores" and "artifactovores."

This development was not always an advantage, especially when the loss of discrimination was total. Factory Fifty was consumed by its own offspring, who began dismantling it at its output end as soon as they came off the assembly line, and then proceeded proudly to deliver the pieces back to its input end. Its internal repair robots were unable to undo the undoings fast enough. and it ground to a halt to become plunder for marauders from Thirty-six and Fifty-three. The most successful factory-robot organisms protected themselves by evolving aggressive armies of "antibody" defenders, which would recognize their own factory and its "kind" and leave them alone, but attach and attempt to destroy any "foreign" models that ventured too close. This gradually became the dominant form of organism, usually associated with a distinct territory which its members cooperated in protecting collectively.

By this time only a few holes in the ground remained at opposite ends of the rocky shelf to mark where Factories One and Two had once stood. They had failed to keep up with the times, and the area had become the domain of Factory Sixty-five. The only trace left of the searcher spacecraft was a long, rounded depression in the ice beach below, on the shore of the liquid methane sea.

The alien engineers had designed the system to enjoy full planetary communications coverage by means of satellites and surface relays, but the idea hadn't worked too well since nothing had been put into orbit and surface relays tended not to last very long. This enabled some of the organisms without strong defenses to remain protected, for a while, from the more metal-hungry empires by sheer distance. But, to allow for communications blackouts and interference, the aliens had also provided a backup method of program and data exchange between robots and factories, which took the form of direct, physical, electrical interconnection. This was a much slower process than using radiolinks, naturally, since it required that the robots travel physically to the factories for reprograming and reporting, but in a self-sustaining operation far from home the method was a lot better than nothing. And it kept the accountants happy by protecting the return on the investment.

With defects and deficiencies of every description appearing somewhere or other, it was inevitable that some of the organisms would exhibit partial or total communications breakdowns. Factory Seventy-three, built without radio facilities, was started up by programs carried overland from Sixty-six. None of its robots ever used anything but backup mode, and the factories that it spawned continued the tradition. But this very fact meant that their operating ranges were extended dramatically.

So the "defect" turned out to be not so much of a defect after all. Foraging parties were able to roam farther afield, greatly enlarging their catchment areas, and they frequently picked up as prizes one or more of the territories previously protected by geographical remoteness. Furthermore, selective pressures steadily improved the autonomy of the robots that operated in this fashion. The autodirected types, relying on their comparatively small, local processors, tended to apply simple solutions to the problems they encountered, but their close-coupled mode of interaction with their environment meant that the solutions were supplied quickly: They evolved efficient "reflexes." The teledirected types, by contrast, tied to the larger but remote central computers, were inclined to attempt more comprehensive and sophisticated solutions, but—as often as not—too late to do

any good. Autodirection thus conferred a behavioral superiority and gradually asserted itself as the norm, while teledirection declined and survived only in a few isolated areas.

The periodic instinct to communicate genetic half-subfiles back to their factories had long become a universal trait among the robots—there could be descendants only of ancestors who left descendants—and they responded to the decline of radio as a means of communication by evolving a compulsion to journey at intervals back to the places whence they had come, to return, as it were, to their "spawning grounds." But this method of reproduction had its problems and posed new challenges to the evolutionary process.

The main problem was that an individual could deliver only half its genome to the factory, after which the Supervisor would have to store the information away until another robot of the same type as the first happened to show up with a matching half; only then could the Supervisor pass a compete copy to its Scheduler. If, as frequently happened, the Supervisor found itself saturated by a peak workload during the intervening period, it was quite likely to delete the half-subfile and allocate the memory space to other, more urgent things—bad news for the Fred that the data had come from, who would thus have enacted the whole reproductive ritual for nothing. The successful response to this problem came with the appearance of a new mode of genetic recombination, which, quite coincidentally, also provided the solution to an "information crisis" that had begun to restrict the pool of genetic variation available for competitive selection to draw on for further improvement.

Some mutant forms of robot knew they were supposed to output their half-subfiles somewhere, but weren't all that sure, or perhaps weren't too particular, about what they were supposed to output it into. Anything with the right electrical connections and compatible internal software was good enough, which usually meant other robots of the same basic type.

And since a robot that had completed its assigned tasks was in a receptive state to external reprograming, i.e., ready for fresh input that would normally come from the factory system, an aspiring donor had little trouble in finding a cooperative acceptor, provided the approach was made at the right time. So to begin with, the roles adopted were largely a matter of circumstance and accidental temperament.

Although the robots' local memories were becoming larger than those contained in their earlier ancestors, the operating programs were growing in size and complexity too, with the result that an acceptor still didn't possess enough free space to hold an entire "How to Make a Fred" subfile. The donor's half, therefore, could be accommodated only by overwriting some of the code already residing in the acceptor. How this was accomplished depended on the responses of the programs carried inside the various robot types.

In some cases the incoming code from the donor was allowed to overwrite entire program modules inside the acceptor, with the total loss to the acceptor of the functions which those modules controlled. This was usually fatal, and no descendants came into being to repeat such mistakes. The successful alternative was to create space by trimming nonessential code from many modules, which tended to leave the acceptor robot with some degradation in performance—usually manifesting itself as a reduction in agility, dexterity, and defensive abilities—but at least still functioning. The sacrifice was only temporary since the acceptor robot would be reprogramed with replacement modules when it delivered its genetic package at the factory.

But in return for these complications and superficial penalties came the immense benefit that the subfiles presented at the factories were complete ones—suitable for dispatch to the Schedulers without delay and the attendant risk of being deleted by overworked Supervisors. The new method thus solved the reliability problem that had plagued the formerly universal "asexual" mode of reproduction.

The information crisis that it also solved had developed through the "inbreeding" caused by the various Supervisors having only the gene pools of their respective "tribes" available to work with, which made recombination difficult because of the restrictive rules imposed by the alien programers. But the robots swapping genes out on the surface were not always averse to adventuring beyond the tribal limits, knew nothing and cared less about programers' rules, since nothing approaching intelligence or awareness was operative yet in what was unfolding, and proceeded to bring half-subfiles together haphazardly in ways that the aliens didn't permit and which the Supervisors would never have imagined. Most of the offspring resulting from these experiments didn't work and were scrapped before leaving the factories; but the ones that did radiated functionally outward in all directions to launch a whole new, qualitatively distinct phase of the evolutionary process.

The demands of the two sexual roles reinforced minor initial physical differences and brought about a gradual polarization of behavioral traits. Since a female in a "pregnant" condition suffered the loss of some measure of self-sufficiency for the duration, her chances of delivering (literally!) were improved considerably if her mate happened to be of a disposition to stay around for a while and provide for the two of them generally, thus helping to protect their joint genetic investment. Selection tended, therefore, to favor the genes of this kind of male, and by the same token those of the females who mated preferentially with them. As a consequence a female trait emerged of being "choosy" in this respect, and in response the males evolved various repertoires of rituals, displays, and demonstrations to improve their eligibility.

The population had thus come to exhibit genetic variability and recombination, competition, selection, and adaptation—all the essentials for continuing evolution. The form of life—for it was, wasn't it?—was admittedly somewhat strange by terrestrial standards, with the individuals that it comprised sharing common, external reproductive, digestive, and immune systems instead of separate, internal ones . . . and of course there were no chains of complicated carbon chemistry figuring anywhere in the scheme of things. . . . But then, after all, what is there apart from chauvinism to say it shouldn't have been so?

Continuing to Think

This story ought to start you thinking about how (or whether) you want to defend human uniqueness in the face of highly sophisticated AI. There are already computers that can think much faster and more efficiently than we can (at certain tasks). Some programs have defeated chess grandmasters; others seem to help depressed and anxious people as effectively as human therapists. Is it only human chauvinism—what philosopher Peter Singer calls "speciesism" with respect to animal rights—that keeps us from recognizing robots as a life form?

Of course, you might argue that robots are made by humans or by other robots and cannot be said to be created in the image and likeness of God. No robot will ever have a soul. This could disqualify them from membership in the human family. And clearly they are not carbon-based organic lifeforms. But is this the essential characteristic?

Taking the existentialist viewpoint, it would be possible to argue that, like yourself, these robots will define who they are by the choices they make and the robots they ultimately become. Granted that they are not yet fully who they will ultimately be, neither is a human infant. Are you prepared to drop your former prejudices and declare yourself open to welcoming new lifeforms into the family?

If not, on what basis do you resist? Suppose you grew to love a very skillfully made android. Would the discovery that this "person" was not human in the same sense you were destroy the relationship you had established? Tom Hanks had this experience in *Splash* when he tried to reject the mermaid he had fallen for when he thought she was a flesh and blood woman. If you love someone, how important are origins?

Summing Up the Readings

How exclusive is membership in the human family? And how exclusive should it be? If chimps can outperform "normal" human three-year-olds at certain tasks and appear much more intelligent than severely damaged individuals of any age, what criteria shall we use to determine who is included and who is excluded from our definition of human nature?

There is a strong tradition in the Western world for defining human uniqueness in rational or religious terms. And yet, as we have seen, this tradition is not without its problems. Being given special status by God has sometimes seemed more a male than a human privilege, and being praised for intelligence has sometimes led to disdain for and even disgust with bodies.

If we reject what is called Western essentialism (the belief that humans enjoy certain essential characteristics that set them apart from all other creatures) in favor of existentialism, we may escape certain traps and we may open the door a little wider to membership in the human club. Certain highly evolved androids, for instance, might be just as capable as organic individuals of making choices and creating selves for themselves. If we leave God out of the equation, existentialism may be our most viable alternative.

Our long tradition of emphasis on the individual has produced awe-inspiring accomplishments and led to aching isolation. Is it time to return to a more communal definition of human nature and shift some of the burden from our lonely selves to a nurturing human family? Has our world become so technologically successful that we have forgotten what it means to be a person or what it takes to become one?

What we need to ask ourselves is this: Is it in our best interest to broaden or further restrict the definition of personhood, and will we have a better chance of achieving it alone or with the support of others? These are not easy questions, and they lead us naturally to our next topic: Philosophy and God.

Continuing to Question

1. Have you ever reinvented yourself—when you moved to a new community or entered a new school? How flexible is our human nature, and how possible is it to create a self for ourselves as atheistic existentialists suggest we must do?

2. Ask ten friends to tell you the creation story from Genesis. If you hear the Adam's rib version (as I suspect you will), tell them the other version. Do any of them think our origins story means men must make all important decisions in the family and in the nation?

3. Of those suffering from anorexia and bulimia, 96 percent are women. What accounts for this extremely disproportional association? If you know someone with an eating disorder, ask some questions.

4. Do fraternities and sororities as well as clubs function as supportive communities for us in a manner similar to the nurturing community in traditional African society? What about communities of monks and nuns? Do you know anyone who chooses to live totally alone? If so, is that person aware of paying a price?

5. What would be your "human nature" test for robots or other animals? What would another species have to be or do to qualify for the rights and privileges we accord only to humans?

Suggestions for Further Exploration

Anna to the Infinite Power—This film explores the questions of what makes us who we are and how much we can change by following a brilliant but troubled child through a scientific experiment to determine her identity. The experiment is conducted without her knowledge or consent.

Beauty and the Beast—The 1946 classic film by Jean Cocteau and the 1990s remake both explore the dimensions of beauty and beast in all of us.

Blade Runner—This film traces the exploits of rebel androids in 2817 Los Angeles.

The Crying Game—In this movie, an Irish Republican Army soldier looks up the girlfriend of a dead hostage, falls in love with her, and then finds she is socially female but anatomically male.

Ellison, Harlan, "A Boy and His Dog"—In *As Tomorrow Becomes Today,* ed. Charles William Sullivan. New York: Prentice-Hall, 1974. After a nuclear holocaust, a boy and his telepathic dog roam the earth.

E.T.—Can an extraterrestrial become human?

Golding, William, *Lord of the Flies*—New York: Coward-McCann, 1962. Golding's dystopian novel asks whether civilization is only skin deep and we are really beasts masquerading as humans. Also a film.

James, Henry, "The Real Thing"—In *The Real Thing and Other Tales*. New York: Macmillan, 1922. This short story explores why actors can portray us more accurately than we can portray ourselves.

Morrison, Tony, *Beloved*—New York: New American Library, 1988. Nobel Prize–winning author Toni Morrison considers whether a child, murdered by her mother to avoid capture by slavecatchers, can return in the body of another. Also a movie.

Saint, H. F., *Memoirs of an Invisible Man*—New York: Macmillan, 1987. Rendered invisible by a physics accident, a man confronts questions about his identity. Also a movie.

Short Circuit—A sophisticated robot comes alive after being struck by lightning and learns the value of life from an animal lover in this film.

Spinrad, Norman, *Deus X*—New York: Spectra, 1993. This novel raises the question of whether souls encoded on the Big Board at the time of their owners' deaths exist.

Splash—This film asks whether it's possible to love a mermaid who has the capacity to appear and act human most of the time.

2001: A Space Odyssey—What happens when an IBM computer drops each letter back one space, becomes HAL, and takes over?

Wolf, Tom, *The Bonfire of the Vanities*—New York: Bantam, 1988. A "master of the universe" learns how fragile his self actually is.

Woolf, Virginia, *Orlando*—New York: Penguin, 1946. In 16th-century England, an aging queen gives a young man a castle on the condition that he never grow old; he moves through four centuries, changing gender along the way in a fascinating exploration of continuity within change. Also a fine movie.

4 Philosophy and God

Defining the Issue

As we have seen, defining what we mean by human nature can bring us face to face with the issue of the existence/nonexistence of God. If we are purely our physical selves, no matter how sophisticated our brains, the riddle of who we are is answered one way—and perhaps artificial life forms may one day be welcomed as relatives. If, however, we are defined by our souls or said to be in the image of our creator, membership in the human family is not ours to give or take back. And this is just one of the questions that hinges on this chapter's focus.

With a divine overseer, particularly a benign one, we can relax, knowing everything will turn out okay in the end; there may even be an eternal dimension to life in which apparent inequities in this world will be resolved. If there are no "good hands" to hold the world, we are on our own and our human nature (good, evil, or something else) will determine how everything goes. It may be either thrilling or frightening to consider this degree of autonomy.

Probably from the beginning of human history, people have tried to think their way through the ultimate riddles. How did we get here? How did the world get here? Is anybody else out there? In the West, the traditional way to pose these questions is to ask: Who's in charge? Is it us or is a deity (God or gods) at work, pulling unseen strings and/or directing the whole enterprise? As we shall see, however, not every culture asks these questions in the same way, and asking a different question can lead to a surprisingly different answer.

Previewing the Readings

Relying on the truths of faith, Augustine of Hippo, the fifth-century Christian philosopher and theologian, viewed the cosmic drama in terms of two metaphorical cities—the City of God and the City of Man—one ruled by love of God and the other governed by a selfish love of power. His thesis was that religious knowledge is possible only if one begins with faith. Is knowledge of God limited to religious faith?

Medieval philosophers in the West certainly didn't think so. They used reason to discover a God whose reality and power they found accessible to both reason and experience. Benjamin Ewuku Oguah finds similar rationalist arguments among the Fantis of Ghana in West Africa. Through his essay, we explore the assumption that philosophy can lead us to God. The medieval Islamic philosopher al-Ghazali disagrees. For him, philosophy is a hindrance rather than a help in the search for truth about the ultimate. He studies philosophy so he can prove its "incoherence."

Charlotte Perkins Gilman's feminist utopia *Herland* takes a futurist look at how society might show up if people honored a loving maternal power. Accepting a loving power as self-evident and in need of no proof, with no requirement for faith, the women of Herland have no worship, no respect for the past, and no desire for eternal life. Anthropomorphism strikes them as odd. The male explorers from the Western world, who stumble into this utopia, find themselves trying to justify their own, largely unexamined religious beliefs.

The greatest mental "stretch" for Westerners comes from Buddhism's characterization of what is as impersonal. In Buddhism there is no deity in the Judaic/Christian/Islamic sense of the word—no personal entity either within or outside of nature. Instead, there is a dynamic, constantly changing, ever the same, vision of unity in multiplicity. The end of the novel *Siddhārtha* by Hermann Hesse paints this picture for us. Although the novel *Siddhārtha* is a product of the modern world, its message dates from the sixth century B.C.E. when the Buddha "woke up" and understood in a flash of enlightenment the true character of what is.

During the Middle Ages, some in the European and Arabic worlds saw faith and reason as allies, whereas others believed them to be rivals. A modern African writer, Benjamin Ewuku Oguah, finds among the Fanti people rationalist arguments that match those developed by Thomas Aquinas in medieval Europe of the thirteenth century to prove the existence of God. For both these cultures, faith and reason could reach the same objective: proof of God's existence.

The Persian al-Ghazali (1059–1111), by contrast, saw much of philosophy as dependent on faith (in philosophers and their methods) as well as reason. If humans were going to rely on faith, al-Ghazali thought, it should be faith in Allah and in the truths of Islam. To discredit what he saw as the false claims of philosophy to explain the world using reason alone and to reveal its equal dependence on faith, al-Ghazali mastered philosophy to demonstrate its incoherence. For him, faith was the only route to understanding the "truth" about human existence, and he was eager to save the unwary from being lured by philosophy away from the truths of religion.

This was essentially the approach taken earlier by Augustine of Hippo who asserted, "I believe in order that I might understand." For him, faith was the necessary precondition for reliable knowledge about religious matters. Thomas Aquinas, during a later period, took on the conflict between faith and reason. People were excited about the recently rediscovered ideas of Aristotle that seemed to contradict some of the "truths" of the Christian faith. Aquinas developed his demonstrations of the compatibility between faith and reason only after the Christian Church had tried unsuccessfully to suppress the threatening works of Aristotle that were being studied in universities all over Europe. Aquinas reserved some religious truths to faith, calling them "mysteries," but found other truths of faith able to be proved by human reason acting alone, without either divine revelation or faith. Chief among these was the existence of God.

4.1   *The City of God, Book XIV (26–28)*

AUGUSTINE OF HIPPO

Preparing to Read

In this Christian classic, Augustine sets forth his philosophy of history. In contrast with the widely prevailing pagan view of history as consisting of repeating cycles, Augustine saw history as linear—with a beginning, a middle, and an end. The beginning, for Augustine, was the creation of humankind and the pivotal events that occurred in the Garden of Eden. The middle was the incarnation—God's taking human form in the person of Jesus and transforming human history. And, the end would be the final judgment and the transformation of everything into a new heaven and a new earth.

In this last of his theological treatises, Augustine examines life in Eden before the Fall. As originally created, humans enjoyed an existence that was perfect in every way. Everything changed when humans yielded to temptation from a fallen angel and defied God. This "before and after" contrast gives Augustine the literary device he will use to describe the two metaphorical cities—the City of God, characterized by love of God, and the City of Man, ruled by a selfish love that will go so far as to defy God.

Written after the sack of Rome, sometimes called the Eternal City, this work reflected Augustine's effort to establish that the true heavenly city would triumph in the end. During the course of human history, evil might appear temporarily triumphant, but behind all human endeavors, he insisted, God guides the course of history to its ultimate conclusion.

The Earthly City and the Heavenly City

IN THE GARDEN OF EDEN our first parents Adam and Eve lived an idyllic life. They were perfectly happy so long as they lived the way God had intended them to live. They basked in God's goodness and reflected it in the good lives they led. They lacked nothing and could have lived this perfect existence forever. Food and drink of every kind were there for the taking and the tree of life guaranteed them perpetual youth.

Their bodies were perfectly healthy and they were utterly free both from pain, disease and accident and from anxiety over these threats. Their physical vigor was matched by complete peace of mind. Just as the weather was always perfect—neither too hot nor too cold—so Adam and Eve were spared excesses of fear and desire. There was no sorrow and their only delight was the deep joy that arose from loving God with "a pure heart, a good conscience, and sincere faith."[1]

They loved each other with a purity of body and mind that led to effortless observance of God's law. In their work and in their play, they were neither lazy nor bored. So great was the harmony between body, mind, and spirit and so pure was the human will that lovemaking might have really expressed love rather than lust. This is so contrary to our present experience that we might be tempted to forget that children could be conceived without the heat of passion and delivered without pain. Such was the original plan.

Perhaps passionless procreation is so difficult for us to imagine because Adam and Eve sinned too soon and were banished from Paradise. But even this rebellion could not thwart God's plan to populate the City of God. After the Fall, it was obvious that citizens of the divine city would not gain entry through their own merits. Only grace could welcome them. And the blessed, seeing so clearly the just punishment of others (which they deserve to share) can only marvel at the grace that delivers them. This helps us understand why God would create humans, even knowing that they would sin. Despite human disobedience and the merited punishment that flows from it, grace abounds. Furthermore, the wicked are unable to disturb the overarching harmony that embraces all God has created.

All of this applies to angels as well as to humans for God can make good out of both good and evil. Although Lucifer, the fallen angel, was no longer capable of good intent, why should God not permit this fallen angel to tempt the first humans who still possessed good wills? If Adam and Eve had relied on God's help, they could have resisted the tempting angel. Relying on their own wills instead, they were doomed. God would still have had to offer help, but humans, through a negative choice, had the freedom to reject it in advance and they chose to do this. In the long view, God also saw that the descendants of these rebellious humans (Jesus Christ) would be the ultimate means of defeating the devil.

Nothing in the future is hidden from God, yet divine foreknowledge compels no one to sin. In this archetypal event, however, God showed all rational creatures, both angelic and human, the difference between presuming one's own powers will suffice and seeking divine protection. Surely, no one would deny that God could have prevented both the fall of an angel and the fall of the human race. But, by leaving the choice to these rational beings in each case, God revealed both the evil that stems from pride and the good that flows from grace.

As we can see, therefore, two cities arise from two types of love. The earthly city has its roots in a selfish love that will go so far as to defy God. The heavenly city rests in a love of God that does not shrink from conquering the self. One celebrates its own accomplishments; the other gives glory to God through a life well lived. The earthly city lifts up its head to boast of its greatness; the other acclaims God as "my glory, and the one who lifts up my head."[2]

Domination and the love of domination rule in the earthly city; whereas, in the heavenly city rulers and subjects serve one another in love. The former city delights in its own strength; the latter says, "I love you, O Lord, my strength."[3] Even the so-called wise people in the earthly city seek only the pleasures of mind and body. If they stumble upon knowledge of God, they are not wise enough to be humble and grateful; instead, they congratulate themselves on their intelligence. "Claiming to be wise, they became fools; and they exchanged the glory of the immortal God for images resembling a mortal human being or birds or four-footed animals or reptiles."[4] They either lead or follow the people in worshiping these images, mistaking creature for Creator. In the City of God, by contrast, there is no merely human wisdom but only the worship and love of God and the pursuit of holiness in the company of saints and angels, "so that God may be all in all."[5]

NOTES

1. I Timothy 1:5, *The New Revised Standard Version* (Nashville: Thomas Nelson, 1989).

2. Psalm 3:3, *The New Revised Standard Version* (Nashville: Thomas Nelson, 1989).

3. Psalm 18:1, *The New Revised Standard Version* (Nashville: Thomas Nelson, 1989).

4. Romans 1: 22–23, *The New Revised Standard Version* (Nashville: Thomas Nelson, 1989).

5. I Corinthians 15:28, *The New Revised Standard Version* (Nashville: Thomas Nelson, 1989).

Continuing to Think

In contrast with philosophers such as Plato, who claimed that those who knew the good would do the good, Augustine asserted the primacy of will over reason. Those, including Adam and Eve, who know the good do not necessarily choose to do the good. This is because, according to Augustine's theology, our essential nature is not reason but will.

As a result, our will drives all our actions. We are created to love God but often end up worshiping something else as ultimate. For Augustine, only the will that has been touched by divine grace can act rightly and reason correctly. Left to our own devices, we follow Adam and Eve into disobedience and confusion.

This is what convinces Augustine that reason alone can never understand the divine mysteries. Once we have faith, however, then our reason will guide us reliably. Divine grace aligns the human will with the will of God and enables us to see what is clearly; without grace, we are lost. For all these reasons, Augustine would insist that philosophy can only be "the handmaid of theology."

4.2   *African and Western Philosophy: A Comparative Study*

BENJAMIN EWUKU OGUAH

Preparing to Read

During the Middle Ages, Western philosophers developed rationalist proofs for the existence of God, and they believed these proofs established the reality of God using only human reason and not requiring faith. While the people who developed these arguments were priests who clearly had faith, their point was that God could be rationally deduced as well as theologically posited. There are three principal arguments in what we call **natural theology.**

The **ontological argument,** arising out of ontology or an investigation into the nature of being, was developed by Anselm in the eleventh century. In its simplest form this argument states: If I can imagine a perfect being, this perfect being must enjoy all the attributes of perfection, including existence. A perfect island does not have existence as one of its attributes in the same way that God does; to be God means to exist. Critics say existence describes a relationship with the world rather than an attribute and accuse Anselm of defining God into existence; still this argument remains lively for many.

Cosmological arguments, taking the cosmos as a starting point, were adapted from Aristotle and popularized by Thomas Aquinas in the thirteenth century. With five variations, they follow a similar pattern. If we examine something in the world, such as cause and effect, we must either look backward infinitely (in which case nothing ever starts the process) or assert an uncaused cause that got the whole process started. Using Aristotle's arguments, Aquinas equated the uncaused cause with God. One of these arguments begins with **teleology** (order and purpose) and asserts a world maker to account for it. This **teleological argument** is the third proof in the arsenal of natural theology.

THE VERY CONCEPT OF African philosophy is apt to cause scornful or, at least, sceptical laughter in certain quarters in the west. As far as the east is from the west, so far is Africa removed from philosophy. The west is the home of civilization and philosophy; Africa is the home of wild trees, wild animals, wild people and wild cultures.

Prejudice dies hard and western anti-African prejudice dies even harder. Nevertheless, I shall make an attempt to show in this paper that this image of Africa is a prejudice; that philosophy is a universal discipline. My object is to compare African philosophy with western philosophy. Many of the doctrines of western philosophy can be seen expressed in African thought as well, not in documents but in the proverbs, ritual songs, folktales and customs of the people. We shall also see, especially when we come to consider ethical and political problems, how African philosophy differs from western philosophy. In this paper, I shall consider one African language group, the Fantis of Ghana. The philo-

sophical ideas of the Fantis are reflected in the philosophies of many other African societies.

Metaphysics

PERSONS

What is a person? To this question René Descartes, the father of modern western philosophy, answers that a person consists of two logically distinct, though causally related, entities: a mind or soul and a body. This dualistic conception of man is found in Fanti thought as well. For the Fanti, a man is made up of two entities: *okra* (soul) and *honam* (body). The *okra* and the *honam* are, like Descartes' soul and body, logically distinct, for the two can exist independently of each other. Thus at death the *okra* is separated from the *honam* but the separation does not mean the end of the *okra*. The *okra* continues to live as a *saman* (ghost) in *samanadze* (the place of the dead). Like Descartes' soul and body, the

From *African and Western Philosophy: A Comparative Study* by Benjamin Ewuku Oguah. Courtesy of University Press of America.

okra and *honam* are, while they are together, causally related. Not only does the body act on the soul but also the soul acts on the body. What happens to the *okra* takes effect in the *honam*. If the *okra* of person A is attacked by evil forces, the effect of the spiritual attack appears in the body of A in the form of, perhaps, illness. To heal the body, it is not sufficient to apply physical remedies to the body. Unless the soul is healed the body will not respond to any physical treatment. The curing of the *okra* is done by *eninsifo* (spiritual healers) who perform certain spiritual rites—the slaughtering of a sheep, incantations, etc.—to pacify the attacking spirit. It is after the spiritual healing rites that the physical treatment of the body begins. Physical events are said to have spiritual causes. Thus if a person suffers bodily injuries in an accident, if he is bitten by a snake, if he is struck down by lightning, if he drowns, the cause is attributed to some condition of the *okra;* his soul has done something wrong (*ne kra afom*), his soul is "weak" (*ne kra ye har*), his soul is grieving (*ne kra ridzi yaw*), his soul requests something (*ne kra pe biribi*), etc. Finding the spiritual cause of physical events is the special office of the *akomfo* (seers). We thus see in Fanti philosophy a version of Cartesian dualism and body-soul interactionism. Man consists of a body and a soul which, though logically distinct, act on each other.

OTHER MINDS

The *okra,* like the Cartesian soul, is not spatially identifiable. It does not exist in space. It is an immaterial substance. But if so a problem arises as to the existence of others' souls or minds. Descartes considers that he cannot doubt the existence of his own mind. He has to think in order to doubt. But there can be no thinking without a thinker or a mind. *Cogito, ergo sum,* he concludes. He thus has no doubt about the existence of his own mind. But what about the minds of other people? If I have no access to the minds of others how do I know that they have minds? According to the argument from analogy I can tell that others have minds from their external bodily behavior because in my own case I notice a certain correlation between similar bodily behavior and my mental states. When I feel internally happy I bare my teeth and laugh. When I feel depressed tears stream down my face. Therefore when tears stream down my neighbor's face I can be sure that he is depressed. When my neighbor bares his teeth and laughs I can be sure that he is happy. I therefore attribute consciousness to others on the basis of their overt behavior by analogy with my own case.

This argument, however, philosophical scepticism will not countenance for the following reasons. Firstly, it is an inductive argument and therefore suffers the fate of all such arguments: its conclusion is merely probable. But the sceptic has little patience with mere probability. Secondly, even if we accept inductive reasoning as valid this particular kind of inductive reasoning is especially poor. For the analogical argument arrives at the conclusion that the existence of other minds is not doubtful by examining merely one case. By examining myself alone and finding a correlation between certain mental and bodily states, I conclude that in the case of others also the same correlation holds. Reasoning from only one case to a conclusion about a multitude of cases is the worst kind of inductive reasoning, which itself, even at its best, does not satisfy the sceptic. Thirdly, the fact that it is theoretically possible for a robot to imitate human bodily behavior in all its complexity shows that bodily behavior is no infallible criterion on the basis of which to ascribe consciousness to others. Hence arises one of the perennial problems of western philosophy, the problem of our knowledge of the existence of other people's minds.

But the problem of other minds is not confined to western philosophy. We find the same problem expressed in Fanti philosophy thus: *Obi nnyim obi ne tsirmu asem* (No one knows what goes on in the head of another).

PHILOSOPHICAL THEOLOGY

(a) *The ontological argument*. In the appellations of God in the Fanti language one can see the very same idea that leads Anselm to formulate the ontological argument for the existence of God. In Fanti thought God is considered as the highest being conceivable. Thus God is likened to the elephant: *Oson kese a w'ekyir nnyi abowa* (Thou mighty elephant: there is no animal mightier than you). The elephant has no superior among the animals of the forest. It is the largest of them all. He is the Highest conceivable being. He is called *Bubur-a-obur-adze-do* (He who is infinitely greater than all). From the conception of God as the Highest conceivable being Anselm argues that God must exist. If He did not exist necessarily He would not be the Highest conceivable being since we can conceive of a being who exists necessarily. If, therefore, God's existence is merely contingent, He would not be the Highest being conceivable. This argument is, of course, unsound and the Fanti philosopher does not argue that way. But we see in Fanti philosophy at least that conception of God from which Anselm works out his proof.

(b) *The Cosmological argument*. One of the arguments for the existence of God in Fanti philosophical theology is the cosmological argument. God is described as *Boadze* (The creator of the world). A justification for regarding God as the creator of the world in western philosophy is the principle of universal causation, the principle that whatever exists must have a cause. The principle of universal causation is expressed in Fanti in the proverb *'se biribi annkeka mpapa a, nkye mpapa annye kredede'* (If nothing had touched the palm branch, the palm branch would not have emitted a sound.) If every event has a cause the world must also have a cause.

One of the objections to the cosmological argument is that if the principle of universal causation is true then God must also have a cause. It is, however, not only the western philosopher who has raised this objection. Many an African child has received a smack from the Sunday School teacher for asking *'Woana boo Nyame?'* (Who created God?)

To this question Aristotle's followers answer that God has no creator: God is the "unmoved mover." Whether satisfactory or not this answer finds expression in Fanti philosophical theology as well. God is described as *Obianyewo* (The uncreated one), *Onnyiahyese-Onnyiewie:* (He who has no beginning or end), *Daadaa Nyankopon* (The God who has always been).

(c) *The teleological argument*. The Fanti mind is impressed by the enormous manifestations of order, art and design in the world. Even the maggots, which seem to be in utter disarray, have each a definite path which they follow (*Nsambaa nyakanyaka wonan hon akwan do*). This order, this plan must have a cause because *Se biribi annkeka mpapa a, nkye mpapa annye kredede* (If nothing had touched the palm branch, the palm branch would not have emitted a sound). Everything has a cause. The cause of the plan evident in the universe is *Opamfo Wawanyi* (The Wonderful Planner)—which is one of the appellations of God in Fanti. He is the wonderful planner who planned the universe. Thus we see in Fanti philosophical theology another of the arguments advanced by western theologians in proof of the existence of God, the teleological argument. We are not here concerned with its validity but only to show how it appears in Fanti philosophy.

(d) *The problem of Evil*. The Fanti recognizes the presence of evil, at least in the present world. Thus many lorries in Ghana carry the inscription *'Wiase ye yaw'* (The world is tragic). Given the fact of evil, how can it be said that the world was created by an omnibenevolent, omniscient and omnipotent God? This is what is called in western philosophical texts the problem of evil. We can also see in Fanti theology these very three attributes of God which generate this problem.

The Fanti believes in divine omnibenevolence. God is compared to a nursing mother:

Obaatan kese a wo do wonsusu (Thou mighty nursing mother whose love is immeasurable). *'Nyame ye do'* (God is love) can be read on many lorries in Ghana. God is described as the Father of orphans and the Husband of widows (*Nganka hon Egya, ekunafo hon kun*). God stops the tears of orphans (*Oma ngyanka gyae su*). God does not discriminate (*Ompa mu nyi*): He feeds both the good and the evil; *onyen aboronoma, onyen nanka* (He feeds both the dove and the panther). He feeds both great and small. *Se oma oson edziban a ne wire mmfir mpatakowaa* (When He gives food to the elephant He does not forget the ant). God is called *Nyankopon* (The Mighty Friend).

But God is not only all-loving. He is also all-knowing. Divine omniscience is expressed in the appellation *Huntanhunii* (He who sees the hidden). God is able to count the footsteps of a deer on the driest rock (*Okan otwe n'anamon wo ob-otan sakoo do*). The deer is a light-footed animal. It hardly leaves traces of its footsteps even on ordinary ground. But God can, in His omniscience, trace and count the footsteps of a deer on the driest rock. In addition to being all-loving and all-knowing God is all-powerful. His omnipotence is expressed in Fanti thus: *Otumfo* (the Powerful); *Oso-kor-otsee-apem* (The one ear which hears and discriminates the voices of thousands at the same time); *Ehunabo-brim* (All tremble when they see Him); *Mbonsamsuro* (The Terror of the devils); *Biribiara nnso Nyame ye* (Nothing is beyond the power of God).

(e) *Immortality.* The Fanti answer to the problem of evil may, perhaps, be seen in the doctrine of immortality. The Fantis believe that when a person dies the *okra* continues to live. It departs to *samanadze* (the place of the dead) where it answers for its deeds on earth. The righteous *okra* may have seen a lot of suffering in this present world, but in the next world this injustice is righted. The righteous are rewarded with happiness in the life after death. The wicked are there punished with misery, and justice is done. The problem of evil arises only when we take the present world for all that there is. But if we see the picture in its entirety, if we see the universe as consisting not only of the present world but also of the next, there is no problem of evil. For the present injustices are only temporary. In the end justice will prevail. For the Fanti it is the end that matters: *'Ahyese nnhia de ewiei'* (The beginning is not as important as the end). That all will reap the consequences of their deeds is expressed in the thought *'Ibu dzea idua'* (you reap what you sow). The same idea is expressed in the saying *'Obi nhuhu na obi nkeka'* (No one prepares the food for another to eat it).

But if God is all-good, why does He allow evil at all in the present world? Why does He not make the universe uniformly good? Why does He not, for example, prevent the criminal from committing murder but instead allows him to do so and then punishes him in the after life? To this question western philosophical theologians have given various answers. Augustine's lay in the doctrine of free will. Man is a free agent. If God were, therefore, to interface in this way He would be divesting man of his freedom to choose between good and evil, of his free will.

Fantis do not defend the fact of evil in the present world this way. But what I want us to note here is that the western doctrine of the freedom of the will is also a Fanti doctrine. We have already seen that the principle of universal causation—the principle of determinism—is accepted by Fantis. But there is another school in Fanti philosophy which believes in the doctrine that men are free agents. The doctrine of free will is expressed in the saying, *'Obra nyi woara abo'* (Life is as you make it). We are the authors of our destiny. We are responsible for our actions. No one is to blame for our actions but we ourselves. We are free beings.

Epistemology

RATIONALISM AND EMPIRICISM

On the issue between rationalism and empiricism as to the origin of human knowledge, Fanti philosophy takes sides with rationalism. The Fanti believes in innate ideas. Thus there is the saying *'Obi nnkyere abofra Nyame'* (No one teaches a child about God). A child does not acquire knowledge of God from experience or teaching. He is born with that knowledge. It is not only the idea of God which is innately given to man. The Fantis believe that certain individuals are born with certain abilities, abilities which are not acquired from, though developed through, experience. Thus some herbalists are said to possess their knowledge of the use of herbs not from experience but innately. Some spiritual experts are supposed to possess their knowledge of spiritual matters innately.

EXTRA-SENSORY PERCEPTION

Some of these "special" abilities are also supposed to be acquired through extra-sensory perception. There is a wide belief among Fantis in extra-sensory perception. *Akomfo* (seers), *Eninsifo* (healers) and *Abayifo* (witches) are widely believed to possess the faculty of extra-sensory perception. It is through this that they are able to perceive spirits and receive messages from them for communication to those who visit them for spiritual inquiries (*ebisa*). There is, however, an equally wide disbelief among Fantis in these supernatural phenomena. Many believe that these "special" people are tricksters. Thus there is the sceptical saying *"Nananom mpow nyimpa na woyee"* (The mysteries surrounding the grove of the dead fathers were created by men). A brief word needs to be said about the origin of this saying. There was on the outskirts of Mankessim, one of the big towns in the Fanti areas of Ghana, a grove which for a long time served as a cemetery. As time went on it fell into disuse. Then a group of cunning people decided to use it as a means of gain. At night they would take their places in the grove, pretend to be the spirits of the dead fathers, make loud frightful noises, demand sacrifices in the form of money, sheep and fowls,

and threaten to destroy the city if their demands were ignored. The money was to be deposited in the grove, and the sheep and fowls were not to be slaughtered but to be tied to some of the trees in the grove. The next morning the mayor of the town and his councilors would collect from the citizens the things that the "spirits of the fathers" demanded and take them to the grove. The night after, the tricksters would enter the grove and take everything away to a safe place for their use. The next day the mayor and his councilors would visit the grove to see if their sacrifices had been accepted; there was no money, sheep and fowls to be seen where they were left. This practice went on for a long time and reduced the citizens to considerable misery. A group of men became suspicious and decided to make investigations. One evening they went where the grove was and hid themselves near it. Then, when night fell, they saw to their great astonishment some thoroughly familiar faces, living citizens of Mankessim, entering the grove with the instruments with which they made the noise! Quietly the men who had gone to investigate returned to the town and announced their discovery. The whole town was alerted. At midnight the tricksters began their noise. The mayor and the whole town rushed to the grove. Lo and behold! There were respectable citizens of Mankessim ruining the town through treachery! They were apprehended and punished and the mystery surrounding the grove of the dead fathers ended. This is how the saying *"Nananom mpow nyimpa na woyee"* (The mysteries surrounding the grove of the dead fathers were the work of ordinary human beings) began. It expresses a widespread Fanti scepticism with regard to anything mysterious or supernatural. The saying serves as a precept urging people to exercise a healthy scepticism about whatever appears mysterious, never to give up the search for a naturalistic explanation of such things, and not to yield readily to superstition. Extra-sensory perception is widely accepted but also widely denied among the Fantis.

Continuing to Think

Part of what is going on in this essay, of course, is that a Western-trained, African philosopher is responding to what he describes as "anti-African prejudice" by demonstrating a comparable tradition of "natural theology" among at least the Fantis. And, it is also intriguing that the proverbs of West Africans and the syllogisms of European priests take such similar paths.

What unites us seems increasingly to be greater than what separates us. We are, to put it another way, motivated by and attracted to remarkably indistinguishable things. Taking our own culture as the standard, we could admire the Fantis for having got it "so right," for being so surprisingly like us. Or we could see something classically human at work that finds nearly identical expression in cultures that differ dramatically in other ways.

Is this because God is what God is and people everywhere will, sooner or later, figure it out in much the same way? Or is it the human hunger that is universal and Fantis and Frenchmen will find proof for a powerful Other for basic human reasons that do not, in themselves, establish the objective existence of this projected Other?

People who believe in God, called **theists,** are likely to take the similarity in this essay as proof that God has been discovered by clues left in human thought and in the world—probably by God. Skeptics, on the other hand, are just as likely to assert that our need for God does not mean that God exists but only that our need for belief is strong. Faced with these apparent paradoxes, some people, called **agnostics,** take the position that it is impossible to know whether or not there is a God.

4.3   The Incoherence of the Philosophers

AL-GHAZALI

Preparing to Read

As we have just seen, there is one philosophical tradition in the West that emphasizes the compatibility between philosophy and religion by asserting that rational deduction can lead us to the truths of faith. Other philosophers (Augustine of Hippo in selection 4.1 for one) believed that reason without faith was worthless and that philosophy's only role was to support theology as its "handmaid." Thomas Aquinas, whose proofs we looked at in the last selection, worked very hard to find an acceptable role for Aristotle, in much the same way that Descartes later tried to defend an independent role for science.

When the works of Aristotle, sent to the Arab world for safekeeping after his death in the fourth century B.C.E., made their way back to the West, there were several points of conflict between Aristotle and the Christian church. Insisting that Form and matter are eternal and inseparable, Aristotle's philosophy contradicted both the creation of the world by God at a specific moment in time and the immortality of the soul (when the matter or the body dies, the Form of the body or the soul dies with it).

These same conflicts, between the ideas of Aristotle and the religious truths of Islam, existed in the Arab world. While granting that there are points on which philosophy and theology agree, al-Ghazali insists that believing in philosophy, just like believing in **theology,** is largely a matter of faith. And since the philosophers are often incoherent, he suggests that religion offers a more reliable basis for faith.

NOW, I HAVE OBSERVED that there is a class of men who believe in their superiority to others because of their greater intelligence and insight. They have abandoned all the religious duties Islam imposes on its followers. They laugh at the positive commandments of religion which enjoin the performance of acts of devotion, and the abstinence from forbidden things. They defy the injunctions of the Sacred Law. Not only do they overstep the limits prescribed by it, but they have renounced the Faith altogether, by having indulged in diverse speculations, wherein they followed the example of those people who "turn men aside from the path of God, and seek to render it crooked; and who do not believe in the life to come." The heresy of these people has its basis only in an uncritical acceptance—like that of the Jews and the Christians—of whatever one hears from others or sees all around. They could not avoid it; for they were born into an un-Islamic atmosphere, and their ancestors had pursued no better ways. In the second place, such heresy results from theoretical inquiries which are the outcome of stumbling—skeptically, misguidedly and stupidly—upon fanciful notions. (A similar case is that of the Disputants who discussed the questions concerning faith and belief raised by the People of wilful Innovations.)

The heretics in our times have heard the awe-inspiring names of people like Socrates, Hippocrates, Plato, Aristotle, etc. They have been deceived by the exaggerations made by the followers of these philosophers—exaggerations to the effect that the ancient masters possessed extraordinary intellectual powers: that the principles they have discovered are unquestionable: that the mathematical, logical, physical and metaphysical sciences developed by them are the most profound: that their excellent intelligence justifies their bold attempts to discover the Hidden Things by deductive methods: and that with all the subtlety of their intelligence and the originality of their accomplishments they repudiated the authority of religious laws: denied the validity of the positive contents of historical religions, and believed that all such things are only sanctimonious lies and trivialities.

When such stuff was dinned into their ears, and struck a responsive chord in their hearts, the heretics in our times thought that it would be an honour to join the company of great thinkers for which the renunciation of their faith would prepare them. Emulation of the example of the learned held out to them the promise of an elevated status far above the general level of common men. They refused to be content with the religion followed by their ancestors. They flattered themselves with the idea that it would do them honour not to accept even truth uncritically. But they had actually begun to accept falsehood uncritically. They failed to see that a change from one kind of intellectual bondage to another is only a self-deception, a stupidity. What position in this world of God can be baser

From *Tahafut al-Falasifah [Incoherence of the Philosophers]* by al-Ghazali. 1963.
Translated by Sabif Ahmad Kamali. Lahore: Pakistan Philosophical Congress.

than that of one who thinks that it is honourable to renounce the truth which is accepted on authority, and then relapses into an acceptance of falsehood which is still a matter of blind faith, unaided by independent inquiry? Such a scandalous attitude is never taken by the unsophisticated masses of men; for they have an instinctive aversion to following the example of misguided genius. Surely, their simplicity is nearer to salvation than sterile genius can be. For total blindness is less dangerous than oblique vision.

When I saw this vein of folly pulsating among these idiots, I decided to write this book in order to refute the ancient philosophers. It will expose the incoherence of their beliefs and the inconsistency of their metaphysical theories. It will bring to light the flimsiest and the obscurest elements of their thought which will provide some amusement for, and serve as a warning to, the intelligent men. (I mean those things which they contributed to beliefs and opinions, and by virtue of which they thought they could be distinguished from the common men.)

Moreover, this book will set forth the doctrines of the ancient philosophers as those doctrines really are. This will serve the purpose of making it clear to the hide-bound atheists of our day that every piece of knowledge, whether ancient or modern, is really a corroboration of the faith in God and in the Last Day. The conflict between faith and knowledge is related only to the details superadded to these two fundamental principles, the two recurring themes in the teachings of all the prophets—i.e., divinely ordained persons the truth of whose mission is evident from the miracles they performed. It was only a few persons having irresponsible views and perverted minds who denied these principles. But in serious discussions no importance can be attached to such persons; and no notice ought to be taken of them. And they must be branded with diabolical perversity and stupid contumacy, so that their example may be a deterrent to people who tend to think that a vainglorious conversion to unoriginal heresy would

be an indication of intelligence and good sense. This book is going to demonstrate that the ancient philosophers, whose followers the atheists in our day claim to be, were really untainted with what is imputed to them. They never denied the validity of the religious laws. On the contrary, they did believe in God, and did have faith in His messengers; although in regard to the minor details, they sometimes faltered and went astray, and caused others to go astray, from the even path. We propose to show how they slipped into error and falsehood. But our examination will not obscure their solid achievements which lie beneath the repulsive facade of their thought. Let God be the sustainer and the helper in the investigations we have undertaken.

Now to begin the book, we proceed to the Prefaces which will presage the general trend of the discussion in this book.

Preface One

Let it be known that it would be tedious to dwell at length upon the differences among the philosophers themselves. For prolixity is their manner, and their disputes are too many, and their opinions are scattered, and their ways are divergent and devious. Therefore, we will confine our attention to the inconsistencies which are found in the theories of the premier philosopher who is called *the* Philosopher, or the First Teacher, for he systematised their sciences, and reformulated them, eliminating all that was redundant in the philosophers' opinions, and retaining only that which was close to the basic principles and tendencies of philosophical thought. This is Aristotle, who refuted all his predecessors—including his own teacher, whom the philosophers call the divine Plato. Having refuted Plato, Aristotle excused himself by saying: "Plato is dear to us. And truth is dear, too. Nay, truth is dearer than Plato."

We have related this story in order to show that in their own view there is nothing fixed and constant in the philosophers' position. They base their judgments on conjecture and speculation, unaided by positive inquiry and unconfirmed by faith. They try to infer the truth of their metaphysical theories from the clarity of the arithmetical and logical sciences. And this method sometimes carries conviction with the weak-minded people. But if their metaphysical theories had been as cogent and definite as their arithmetical knowledge is, they would not have differed among themselves on metaphysical questions as they do not differ on the arithmetical.

As far as the translators of Aristotle's words into Arabic are concerned, our problem is even more difficult, for the translations themselves have been subjected to interpolation and changes, which have necessitated further commentaries and interpretations. As a result, the translations are as much in dispute among the philosophers as the original works are. However, the most faithful—as Aristotle's translators—and the most original—as his commentators—among the philosophising Muslims are al-Farabi Abu Nasr, and Ibn Sina. Therefore, we will confine our attention to what these two have taken to be the authentic expression of the views of their mis-leaders. For what they discarded and refused to follow must undoubtedly have been utterly useless, and should not call for an elaborate refutation.

Therefore, let it be known that we propose to concentrate on the refutation of philosophical thought as it emerges from the writings of these two persons. For otherwise, the scattered character of the philosophical theories should have to be reflected in a proportionately loose arrangement of our subject-matter.

Preface Two

Let it be known that the difference between the philosophers and others is threefold.

In the first place, the dispute is centred upon a mere word. Take for instance their use of the word "substance" for God, meaning thereby a being which is not in a subject, or a self-subsisting being which does not need an external cause to continue it in existence.

We do not intend here to undertake the refutation of this terminology, for if the meaning of self-subsistence is agreed upon, the applicability of the word "substance" in this sense will have to be considered from the etymological point of view. If from that point of view, the application of the word is justified, it will still be debatable whether the Sacred Law approves of its use, for the permission to use words as names (of God) or the injunction against their use is based on what appears from the letter of the Sacred Law. Perhaps you will say: "This word was used by the *Mutakallimun* in the discussion of the Divine attributes. In the Sacred Law, the Jurists never used it. It is, therefore, improper on your part to confuse the realities of things with matters of habit and custom (of which *Fiqh* treats)." But (this is inadmissible, because) I know that it amounts to a discussion on whether it is permissible to use a certain name which is truly applicable to the bearer of the name. And hence it is equivalent to a discussion on whether a certain (moral) action is permissible.

In the second place, there are those things in which the philosophers believe, and which do not come into conflict with any religious principle. And, therefore, disagreement with the philosophers with respect to those things is not a necessary condition for the faith in the prophets and the apostles (may God bless them all). An example is their theory that the lunar eclipse occurs when the light of the Moon disappears as a consequence of the interposition of the Earth between the Moon and the Sun. For the Moon derives its light from the Sun, and the Earth is a round body surrounded by Heaven on all the sides. Therefore, when the Moon falls under the shadow of the Earth, the light of the Sun is cut off from it. Another example is their theory that the solar eclipse means the interposition of the body of the Moon between the Sun and the observer, which occurs when the Sun and the Moon are stationed at the intersection of their nodes at the same degree.

We are not interested in refuting such theories either; for the refutation will serve no purpose. He who thinks that it is his religious duty to disbelieve such things is really unjust to religion, and weakens its cause, for these things have been established by astronomical and mathematical evidence which leaves no room for doubt. If you tell a man, who has studied these things—so that he has sifted all the data relating to them, and is, therefore, in a position to forecast when a lunar or a solar eclipse will take place: whether it will be total or partial; and how long it will last—that these things are contrary to religion, your assertion will shake his faith in religion, not in these things. Greater harm is done to religion by an immethodical helper than by an enemy whose actions, however hostile, are yet regular, for, as the proverb goes, a wise enemy is better than an ignorant friend.

If someone says:

The Prophet (may God bless him) has said: "The Sun and the Moon are two signs among the signs of God. Their eclipse is not caused by the death or the life of a man. When you see an eclipse, you must seek refuge in the contemplation of God and in prayer." How can this tradition be reconciled with what the philosophers say?

we will answer:

There is nothing in this tradition to contradict the philosophers. It only denies that an eclipse has anything to do with the life or the death of a man. Further, it enjoins prayer at the time of an eclipse. The Sacred Law enjoins prayer at the time of sunrise or sunset or during the day; what is unusual if, with a view to finding greater favour (with God), it also enjoins prayer at the time of an eclipse?

If it is said:

At the end of the same tradition, the Prophet said: "When God reveals Himself to something, it prostrates itself before Him." Does it not follow from this tradition that an eclipse is an act of prostration caused by Revelation?

we will answer:

This addition is spurious. We must condemn its author as a liar. The Prophet's words are only those which have been reported above. However, if this addition were authentic, would it not be easier to interpret it than to reject the evidence (of astronomical and mathematical sciences) which is conclusive and definite? People have interpreted many a plain text by rational arguments which never attained to such clarity and cogency (as the astronomical and mathematical arguments in this case have done).

The atheists would have the greatest satisfaction if the supporter of religion made a positive assertion that things of this kind are contrary to religion. For then it would be easier for them to refute religion which stood or fell with its opposition to these things. (It is, therefore, necessary for the supporter of religion not to commit himself on these questions,) because the fundamental question at issue between him and the philosophers is only whether the world is eternal or began in time. If its beginning in time is proved, it is all the same whether it is a round body, or a simple thing, or an octagonal or hexagonal figure; and whether the heavens and all that is below them form—as the philosophers say—thirteen layers, or more, or less. Investigation into these facts is no more relevant to metaphysical inquiries than an investigation into the number of the layers of an onion, or the number of the seeds of a pomegranate, would be. What we are interested in is that the world is the product of God's creative action, whatever the manner of that action may be.

In the third place, there are philosophical theories which come into violent conflict with the fundamental principles of religion, e.g., the religious doctrines of the world's beginning in time: of the attributes of the Creator; and of the resurrection of bodies. All these things have been denied by the philosophers. Therefore, we propose to leave the rest of the sections (enumerated above) aside, in order to concentrate on this one, and on questions allied to it, in our criticism of philosophical theories.

Preface Three

Let it be known that it is our purpose to disillusion those who think too highly of the philosophers, and consider them to be infallible. Since I have undertaken to expose the incoherence and contradiction involved in philosophical thought, I will approach them in order to attack them, not to defend something of mine own. I will refute what they believe, by showing that it is a mixture of diverse elements which come from such schools as the Mu'tazilah, the Karramiyah, the Waqifiyah, etc. My attitude towards these sects themselves is that, while it is not necessary for me to defend any one of them, we are all equally opposed to the philosophers. For we differ among ourselves only in regard to the details; whereas the philosophers attack the very basis of our religion. Let us, therefore, unite against the common enemy; for at a critical juncture, we must forget our private quarrels.

Preface Four

One of the most artful methods employed by the philosophers is that, when in discussion they come up against a difficulty, they say: "The science of metaphysics is extremely subtle. Of all the sciences it is the most difficult even for a sharp intelligence to grasp." Those who follow the philosophers employ a similar trick in order to get rid of their difficulties. When they are unable to explain something in the work of their masters, they still glorify them and say: "Undoubtedly, a solution can be found somewhere in the sciences developed by the ancient masters. Perhaps our failure is the result of our inability to consult Logic and Mathematics on this question."

To these suggestions, we will reply as follows:

As far as Mathematics is concerned, one of its two branches, which is an inquiry into discrete quantity—viz., Arithmetic—has evidently nothing to do with Metaphysics. To say that it is not possible to understand Metaphysics without the help of Arithmetic is nonsense—like saying that Medicine, or Grammar, or Literature cannot be understood without the help of Arithmetic: or that Arithmetic cannot be understood without the help of Medicine.

As regards the other branch of Mathematics—viz., Geometry—which is an inquiry into continuous quantity, all that it tells us is that the heavens and all that is below them down to the Centre, i.e., the Earth, are round in shape. Further, it tells us of the number of the strata of these things: of the planets revolving in the Sphere; and of the quantity of their movements. Now, we can grant them all these things—from conviction, or for the sake of the argument. They need not adduce scientific evidence to prove them. But there is nothing in these facts which proves or disproves metaphysical principles. To say that there is something which does so is like saying: "To know whether this house is the product of a knowing, willing, powerful and living builder, it is necessary to discover whether it has six or eight sides, and what is the number of its beams and bricks." Obviously, such an assertion would be sheer nonsense. It would be like saying: "The temporal character of an onion cannot be known, unless the number of its layers be discovered"; or, "The temporal character of this pomegranate cannot be known, unless the number of its seeds be discovered." This sort of argument simply does not appeal to an intelligent mind.

As regards their contention that reference to Logic is unavoidable, it is right. But Logic is not their monopoly. Fundamentally, it is the same thing as in the Art of Scholastic Reasoning we call the Book of Theoretical Inquiry. The philosophers have changed its name to Logic to make it look formidable. We often call it the Book of Disputation, or the Data of the Intellects. When a gullible enthusiast hears the word "Logic," he thinks that it is a new subject, unknown to the *Mutakallimun* and cultivated by the philosophers alone. In order to remove this misunderstanding, we propose to discuss the Data of the Intellects in a separate work, where we will avoid the phraseology used by the *Mutakallimun* and the Jurists, adopting for the time being the terms used by the Logicians, so that the whole thing might be cast into a different mould, and the methods of the Logicians might be followed in the minutest detail. In that book, we will speak to them in their language—I mean their logical terminology. We will show there that

> neither the conditions for the material validity of Syllogism—laid down by them in the section of Logic devoted to Demonstration—nor those for its formal validity—in the Book of Syllogism—not the postulates which they have formulated in the Isagoge and Categories, and which form the parts and preliminaries of Logic

are of any help to them in metaphysical sciences. But it is necessary to reserve the discussion of the Data of the Intellects for a separate book. For, although an instrument for the understanding of the purport of this book, it is not indispensable to every reader. Therefore, we are going to postpone it; so that he who does not need it may not be bothered by it here. However, he who fails to understand some of the terms used here will be well advised to begin with mastering the contents of our book called The Standard of Knowledge—viz., the (branch of) knowledge they call Logic.

After the Prefaces, let us give a list of the problems in whose discussion in this book we will expose the contradiction involved in the philosophers' theories.

And these problems are twenty:

(i) The refutation of their belief in the eternity of the world.

(ii) The refutation of their belief in the everlasting nature of the world.

(iii) Their dishonest assertion that God is the Creator of the world, and that the world is His product.

(iv) Demonstration of their inability to affirm the Creator.

(v) Demonstration of their inability to prove the impossibility of two gods by a rational argument.

(vi) Refutation of their denial of the Divine attributes.

(vii) Refutation of their theory that the Divine being is not divisible into genus and differentia.

(viii) Refutation of their theory that the First (Principle) is a simple unqualified being.

(ix) Demonstration of their inability to show that the First (Principle) is not body.

(x) The thesis that they are bound to affirm the eternity of the world, and deny the Creator.

(xi) Demonstration of their inability to maintain that the First (Principle) knows any one other than Himself.

(xii) Demonstration of their inability to maintain that He knows Himself.

(xiii) Refutation of their doctrine that the First (Principle) does not know the particulars.

(xiv) Refutation of their doctrine that the Heaven is a living being whose movements are voluntary.

(xv) Refutation of their theory of the purpose of the Heaven's movement.

(xvi) Refutation of their doctrine that the souls of the heavens know all the particulars.

(xvii) Refutation of their belief in the impossibility of a departure from the natural course of events.

(xviii) Refutation of their theory that the soul of man is a substance which exists in itself, and which is neither body nor an accident.

(xix) Refutation of their belief in the impossibility of the annihilation of the human souls.

(xx) Refutation of their denial of the resurrection of bodies, which will be followed by feelings of pleasure and pain produced by physical causes of these feelings in Paradise and Hell.

So these are questions selected from their metaphysical and physical sciences wherein we propose to expose the contradiction involved in their views. As regards Mathematics, there is no point in denying or opposing it; for Mathematics includes Arithmetic and Geometry, and these two sciences are not in dispute here. As regards Logic, it is just an investigation into the instruments of reflection over the intelligibles. And as such, it involves no contradictions which might deserve our consideration. And in the book called The Standard of Knowledge, we are going to introduce as much of this subject as may be helpful towards the understanding of the contents of this book.

Continuing to Think

It is sometimes said that in the Christian West Aquinas was given the job of Christianizing or, to speak metaphorically, "baptizing" Aristotle. Universities were cropping up in every town and, although the Church initially tried to suppress Aristotelian philosophy, it quickly became clear that these ideas would not go away. Aquinas resolved what appeared to be an unresolvable conflict by declaring philosophy and theology to be autonomous disciplines, each with its own access to truth, but he reserved certain truths (such as the creation of the world) as mysteries of faith and allowed that certain other truths (namely the existence of God) could be established by reason working alone. When similar conflicts occurred in the Arabic world, al-Ghazali, the Islamic writer we have just read, chose to refute the philosophers.

The influence of Aristotle was a powerful one in both the Arab and Christian worlds. As intellectuals read his philosophy, they reached an apparent dilemma—either Aristotle is right, as my reason tells me, or religion is right, as my faith tells me. These two positions appear self-contradictory. Aquinas, as we have seen, worked for and achieved an accommodation; al-Ghazali learned the arguments of the philosophers to refute them and reaffirm what he saw as the superior truths of faith.

The analogy might be with, on the one hand, a diplomatic solution that averts war and, on the other, all out conflict. Aquinas skillfully drew division lines and declared certain areas out of bounds; al-Ghazali opted for a frontal assault. If he could refute the philosophers on their own terms, he reasoned that people would not be vulnerable to being confused into atheism or seduced by the rival (but unworthy) claims of philosophy. Both Christianity and Islam believed they had access to essential truths; philosophy made similar claims. Because Aquinas accepted natural theology, he worked to find a role for it; al-Ghazali, who mistrusted philosophy, saw no alternative but to discredit it.

4.4   Herland

CHARLOTTE PERKINS GILMAN

Preparing to Read

Utopian novels offer their authors a chance to wipe the slate clean and make everything the way the author thinks it should be. Plato's *Republic* describes a society in which reason orders all human decisions and each of us does what we do best under the benevolent dictatorship of a philosopher king. In *Herland* we find a utopia of emotion rather than reason.

It is an all-female world, resulting from the accidental isolation of a group of women and the amazing parthenogenesis, by which unfertilized human eggs produce "wonder children"—all girls, of course, because they have only their mother's DNA. Not surprisingly, motherhood is the dominant metaphor and everything, including religion, takes motherhood as its foundation and starting point.

When Charlotte Perkins Gilman serialized this novel in her magazine *The Forerunner* during 1915, the world was at war. This world of women, found by the male explorers who narrate the story, offers a soothing alternative. In Herland, cleanliness, order, beauty in nature, the happiness of children, progress, and peace reign, and all of this harmony constitutes the prevailing religion.

In contrast with the deep respect for the past we find in worldviews from Africa and the Peoples of the Americas, here the past is irrelevant. Having moved beyond it, the residents of Herland see no point in honoring it. Worship seems unnecessary and perhaps irrelevant as well. And, eternal life is neither desired nor expected. Although the divine is pictured as a kind of motherly power—an extension of human motherhood—anthropomorphism is rejected. What has been gained and what has been lost?

Their Religions and Our Marriages

IT TOOK ME A LONG TIME, as a man, a foreigner, and a species of Christian—I was that as much as anything—to get any clear understanding of the religion of Herland.

Its deification of motherhood was obvious enough; but there was far more to it than that; or, at least, than my first interpretation of that.

I think it was only as I grew to love Ellador more than I believed anyone could love anybody, as I grew faintly to appreciate her inner attitude and state of mind, that I began to get some glimpses of this faith of theirs.

When I asked her about it, she tried at first to tell me, and then, seeing me flounder, asked for more information about ours. She soon found out that we had many, that they varied widely, but had some points in common. A clear methodical luminous mind had my Ellador, not only reasonable, but swiftly perceptive.

She made a sort of chart, superimposing the different religions as I described them, with a pin run through them all, as it were; their common basis being a Dominant Power or Powers, and some Special Behavior, mostly taboos, to please or placate. There were some common features in certain groups of religions, but the one always present was this Power, and the things which must be done or not done because of it. It was not hard to trace our human imagery of the Divine Force up through successive stages of bloodthirsty, sensual, proud, and cruel gods of early times to the conception of a Common Father with its corollary of a Common Brotherhood.

This pleased her very much, and when I expatiated on the Omniscience, Omnipotence, Omnipresence, and so on, of our God, and of the loving kindness taught by his Son, she was much impressed.

The story of the Virgin birth naturally did not astonish her, but she was greatly puzzled by the Sacrifice, and still more by the Devil, and the theory of Damnation.

When in an inadvertent moment I said that certain sects had believed in infant damnation—and explained it—she sat very still indeed.

Originally serialized during 1915 in *The Forerunner* [taken from the Internet].

"They believed that God was Love—and Wisdom—and Power?"

"Yes—all of that."

Her eyes grew large, her face ghastly pale.

"And yet that such a God could put little new babies to burn—for eternity?" She fell into a sudden shuddering and left me, running swiftly to the nearest temple.

Every smallest village had its temple, and in those gracious retreats sat wise and noble women, quietly busy at some work of their own until they were wanted, always ready to give comfort, light, or help, to any applicant.

Ellador told me afterward how easily this grief of hers was assuaged, and seemed ashamed of not having helped herself out of it.

"You see, we are not accustomed to horrible ideas," she said, coming back to me rather apologetically. "We haven't any. And when we get a thing like that into our minds it's like—oh, like red pepper in your eyes. So I just ran to her, blinded and almost screaming, and she took it out so quickly—so easily!"

"How?" I asked, very curious.

"'Why, you blessed child,' she said, 'you've got the wrong idea altogether. You do not have to think that there ever was such a God—for there wasn't. Or such a happening—for there wasn't. Nor even that this hideous false idea was believed by anybody. But only this—that people who are utterly ignorant will believe anything—which you certainly knew before.'"

"Anyhow," pursued Ellador, "she turned pale for a minute when I first said it."

This was a lesson to me. No wonder this whole nation of women was peaceful and sweet in expression—they had no horrible ideas.

"Surely you had some when you began," I suggested.

"Oh, yes, no doubt. But as soon as our religion grew to any height at all we left them out, of course."

From this, as from many other things, I grew to see what I finally put in words.

"Have you no respect for the past? For what was thought and believed by your foremothers?"

"Why, no," she said. "Why should we? They are all gone. They knew less than we do. If we are not beyond them, we are unworthy of them—and unworthy of the children who must go beyond us."

This set me thinking in good earnest. I had always imagined—simply from hearing it said, I suppose—that women were by nature conservative. Yet these women, quite unassisted by any masculine spirit of enterprise, had ignored their past and built daringly for the future.

Ellador watched me think. She seemed to know pretty much what was going on in my mind.

"It's because we began in a new way, I suppose. All our folks were swept away at once, and then, after that time of despair, came those wonder children—the first. And then the whole breathless hope of us was for THEIR children—if they should have them. And they did! Then there was the period of pride and triumph till we grew too numerous; and after that, when it all came down to one child apiece, we began to really work—to make better ones."

"But how does this account for such a radical difference in your religion?" I persisted.

She said she couldn't talk about the difference very intelligently, not being familiar with other religions, but that theirs seemed simple enough. Their great Mother Spirit was to them what their own motherhood was—only magnified beyond human limits. That meant that they felt beneath and behind them an upholding, unfailing, serviceable love—perhaps it was really the accumulated mother-love of the race they felt—but it was a Power.

"Just what is your theory of worship?" I asked her.

"Worship? What is that?"

I found it singularly difficult to explain. This Divine Love which they felt so strongly did not seem to ask anything of them—"any more than our mothers do," she said.

"But surely your mothers expect honor, reverence, obedience, from you. You have to do things for your mothers, surely?"

"Oh, no," she insisted, smiling, shaking her soft brown hair. "We do things FROM our mothers—not FOR them. We don't have to do things FOR them—they don't need it, you know. But we have to live on—splendidly—because of them; and that's the way we feel about God."

I meditated again. I thought of that God of Battles of ours, that Jealous God, that Vengeance-is-mine God. I thought of our world-nightmare—Hell.

"You have no theory of eternal punishment then, I take it?"

Ellador laughed. Her eyes were as bright as stars, and there were tears in them, too. She was so sorry for me.

"How could we?" she asked, fairly enough. "We have no punishments in life, you see, so we don't imagine them after death."

"Have you NO punishments? Neither for children nor criminals—such mild criminals as you have?" I urged.

"Do you punish a person for a broken leg or a fever? We have preventive measures, and cures; sometimes we have to 'send the patient to bed,' as it were; but that's not a punishment—it's only part of the treatment," she explained.

Then studying my point of view more closely, she added: "You see, we recognize, in our human motherhood, a great tender limitless uplifting force—patience and wisdom and all subtlety of delicate method. We credit God—our idea of God—with all that and more. Our mothers are not angry with us—why should God be?"

"Does God mean a person to you?"

This she thought over a little. "Why—in trying to get close to it in our minds we personify the idea, naturally; but we certainly do not assume a Big Woman somewhere, who is God. What we call God is a Pervading Power, you know, an Indwelling Spirit, something inside of us that we want more of. Is your God a Big Man?" she asked innocently.

"Why—yes, to most of us, I think. Of course we call it an Indwelling Spirit just as you do, but we insist that it is Him, a Person, and a Man—with whiskers."

"Whiskers? Oh yes—because you have them! Or do you wear them because He does?"

"On the contrary, we shave them off—because it seems cleaner and more comfortable."

"Does He wear clothes—in your idea, I mean?"

I was thinking over the pictures of God I had seen—rash advances of the devout mind of man, representing his Omnipotent Deity as an old man in a flowing robe, flowing hair, flowing beard, and in the light of her perfectly frank and innocent questions this concept seemed rather unsatisfying.

I explained that the God of the Christian world was really the ancient Hebrew God, and that we had simply taken over the patriarchal idea—that ancient one which quite inevitably clothed its thought of God with the attributes of the patriarchal ruler, the grandfather.

"I see," she said eagerly, after I had explained the genesis and development of our religious ideals. "They lived in separate groups, with a male head, and he was probably a little—domineering?"

"No doubt of that," I agreed.

"And we live together without any 'head,' in that sense—just our chosen leaders—that DOES make a difference."

"Your difference is deeper than that," I assured her. "It is in your common motherhood. Your children grow up in a world where everybody loves them. They find life made rich and happy for them by the diffused love and wisdom of all mothers. So it is easy for you to think of God in the terms of a similar diffused and competent love. I think you are far nearer right than we are."

"What I cannot understand," she pursued carefully, "is your preservation of such a very ancient state of mind. This patriarchal idea you tell me is thousands of years old?"

"Oh yes—four, five, six thousand—ever so many."

"And you have made wonderful progress in those years—in other things?"

"We certainly have. But religion is different. You see, our religions come from behind us, and are initiated by some great teacher who is dead. He is supposed to have known the whole thing and taught it, finally. All we have to do is believe—and obey."

"Who was the great Hebrew teacher?"

"Oh—there it was different. The Hebrew religion is an accumulation of extremely ancient traditions, some far older than their people, and grew by accretion down the ages. We consider it inspired—'the Word of God.'"

"How do you know it is?"

"Because it says so."

"Does it say so in as many words? Who wrote that in?"

I began to try to recall some text that did say so, and could not bring it to mind.

"Apart from that," she pursued, "what I cannot understand is why you keep these early religious ideas so long. You have changed all your others, haven't you?"

"Pretty generally," I agreed. "But this we call 'revealed religion,' and think it is final. But tell me more about these little temples of yours," I urged. "And these Temple Mothers you run to."

Then she gave me an extended lesson in applied religion, which I will endeavor to concentrate.

They developed their central theory of a Loving Power, and assumed that its relation to them was motherly—that it desired their welfare and especially their development. Their relation to it, similarly, was filial, a loving appreciation and a glad fulfillment of its high purposes. Then, being nothing if not practical, they set their keen and active minds to discover the kind of conduct expected of them. This worked out in a most admirable system of ethics. The principle of Love was universally recognized—and used.

Patience, gentleness, courtesy, all that we call "good breeding," was part of their code of conduct. But where they went far beyond us was in the special application of religious feeling to every field of life. They had no ritual, no little set of performances called "divine service," save those religious pageants I have spoken of, and those were as much educational as religious, and as much social as either. But they had a clear established connection between everything they did—and God. Their cleanliness, their health, their exquisite order, the rich peaceful beauty of the whole land, the happiness of the children, and above all the constant progress they made—all this was their religion.

They applied their minds to the thought of God, and worked out the theory that such an inner power demanded outward expression. They lived as if God was real and at work within them.

As for those little temples everywhere—some of the women were more skilled, more temperamentally inclined, in this direction, than others. These, whatever their work might be, gave certain hours to the Temple Service, which meant being there with all their love and wisdom and trained thought, to smooth out rough places for anyone who needed it. Sometimes it was a real grief, very rarely a quarrel, most often a perplexity; even in Herland the human soul had its hours of darkness. But all through the country their best and wisest were ready to give help.

If the difficulty was unusually profound, the applicant was directed to someone more specially experienced in that line of thought.

Here was a religion which gave to the searching mind a rational basis in life, the concept of an immense Loving Power working steadily out through them, toward good. It gave to the "soul" that sense of contact with the inmost force, of perception of the uttermost purpose, which we always crave. It gave to the "heart" the blessed feeling of being loved, loved and UNDERSTOOD. It gave clear, simple, rational directions as to how we should live—and why. And for ritual it gave first those triumphant group demonstrations, when with a union of all the arts, the revivifying combination of great multitudes moved rhythmically with march and dance, song and music, among their own noblest products and the open beauty of their groves and hills. Second, it gave these numerous little centers of wisdom where the least wise could go to the most wise and be helped.

"It is beautiful!" I cried enthusiastically. "It is the most practical, comforting, progressive religion I ever heard of. You DO love one another—you DO bear one another's burdens—you DO realize that a little child is a type of the kingdom of heaven. You are more Christian than any people I ever saw. But—how about death? And the life everlasting? What does your religion teach about eternity?"

"Nothing," said Ellador. "What is eternity?"

What indeed? I tried, for the first time in my life, to get a real hold on the idea.

"It is—never stopping."

"Never stopping?" She looked puzzled.

"Yes, life, going on forever."

"Oh—we see that, of course. Life does go on forever, all about us."

"But eternal life goes on WITHOUT DYING."

"The same person?"

"Yes, the same person, unending, immortal." I was pleased to think that I had something to teach from our religion, which theirs had never promulgated.

"Here?" asked Ellador. "Never to die—here?" I could see her practical mind heaping up the people, and hurriedly reassured her.

"Oh no, indeed, not here—hereafter. We must die here, of course, but then we 'enter into eternal life.' The soul lives forever."

"How do you know?" she inquired.

"I won't attempt to prove it to you," I hastily continued. "Let us assume it to be so. How does this idea strike you?"

Again she smiled at me, that adorable, dimpling, tender, mischievous, motherly smile of hers. "Shall I be quite, quite honest?"

"You couldn't be anything else," I said, half gladly and half a little sorry. The transparent honesty of these women was a never-ending astonishment to me.

"It seems to me a singularly foolish idea," she said calmly. "And if true, most disagreeable."

Now I had always accepted the doctrine of personal immortality as a thing established. The efforts of inquiring spiritualists, always seeking to woo their beloved ghosts back again, never seemed to me necessary. I don't say I had ever seriously and courageously discussed the subject with myself even; I had simply assumed it to be a fact. And here was the girl I loved, this creature whose character constantly revealed new heights and ranges far beyond my own, this superwoman of a superland, saying she thought immortality foolish! She meant it, too.

"What do you WANT it for?" she asked.

"How can you NOT want it!" I protested. "Do you want to go out like a candle? Don't you want to go on and on—growing and—and—being happy, forever?"

"Why, no," she said. "I don't in the least. I want my child—and my child's child—to go on—and they will. Why should *I* want to?"

"But it means Heaven!" I insisted. "Peace and Beauty and Comfort and Love—with God." I had never been so eloquent on the subject of religion. She could be horrified at Damnation, and question the justice of Salvation, but Immortality—that was surely a noble faith.

"Why, Van," she said, holding out her hands to me. "Why Van—darling! How splendid of you to feel it so keenly. That's what we all want, of course—Peace and Beauty, and Comfort and Love—with God! And Progress too, remember; Growth, always and always. That is what our religion teaches us to want and to work for, and we do!"

"But that is HERE," I said, "only for this life on earth."

"Well? And do not you in your country, with your beautiful religion of love and service have it here, too—for this life—on earth?"

None of us were willing to tell the women of Herland about the evils of our own beloved land. It was all very well for us to assume them to be necessary and essential, and to criticize—strictly among ourselves—their all-too-perfect civilization, but when it came to telling them about the failures and wastes of our own, we never could bring ourselves to do it. . . .

Continuing to Think

Are you ready to apply for your travel visa? As the explorers begin to discover, the society produced by honoring a "loving power" seems more peaceful, nurturing, and healthy than the society based on patriarchal Christianity they have left behind. They begin by explaining the advantages of what they have always taken for granted and end by questioning (if only among themselves) some of the fundamental religious assumptions they have been making.

Some ideas, such as divine rejection of unbaptized babies, seem horribly shocking to Ellador and send her to a temple staffed by wise and noble women, whose task it is to help people over the rough places in life by talking them through what troubles them. In this case, Ellador is assured that even if some people once believed such a thing, it certainly never happened and she need not worry about it ever happening.

Gilman is convinced that imaging the divine as female produces a radically different religion and a much more benevolent society than picturing the divine as male has done. What do you think? How much connection is there between the qualities we attribute to God and the way we structure our human society and personal interactions? In a world run entirely by women, men are welcomed and treated as honored guests. Gilman wants us to know that women would not turn the tables on men and reverse the power relationships of patriarchy that put men in charge and relegate women to subservient roles. Is she right?

With any utopia, one of the questions we might want to ask ourselves is whether we would want to live there. Which aspects of Plato's *Republic* appeal to you? Which scare you? Do the same exploration with *Herland*. Which aspects attract you and which repel you? Is this a better world—as Gilman clearly believes it is?

4.5   *Siddhārtha*

HERMANN HESSE

Preparing to Read

In our final selection, we encounter a very different set of questions. Buddhists are less concerned with speculation about the "big questions" and more interested in direct experience of what is. The purpose of existence is to realize how things are— to become enlightened and avoid successive deaths and rebirths. The most significant stories, therefore, concern images of what is. In this excerpt from *Siddhārtha,* novelist Hermann Hesse tells us, in rough outline, the life of the Buddha (Siddhārtha Gautama) and the basic beliefs of Buddhism. As you may recall, there is not a separate human nature. All is a dynamic interrelatedness, characterized by constant change. Whatever is at the heart of all that is can best be described as impersonal—

to become enlightened is to recognize your own interconnectedness with everything else.

Near the end of the novel, Govinda has met up with his boyhood friend, also named Siddhārtha, now living beside a river. Both are old men who have lived parallel lives, but Govinda realizes Siddhārtha has found peace of mind whereas he has not. As he bends to kiss Siddhārtha's forehead, Govinda experiences a vision of unity in diversity, the simultaneity of all that is, which characterizes the Buddhist understanding of what is. Notice how this vision deals with time and space and other apparent sources of division.

The Buddha insisted he was not divine. What he was, instead, was the "awakened one," the one who saw things as they were, and he tried to share that vision with others. His sermons are not divine rules but suggestions from someone who has become enlightened on how to do the same—how, in other words, to get through life with less suffering and not have to repeat the process.

"WHY DID YOU TELL ME about the stone?" he asked hesitatingly after a pause.

"I did so unintentionally. But perhaps it illustrates that I just love the stone and the river and all these things that we see and from which we can learn. I can love a stone, Govinda, and a tree or a piece of bark. These are things and one can love things. But one cannot love words. Therefore teachings are of no use to me; they have no hardness, no softness, no colors, no corners, no smell, no taste—they have nothing but words. Perhaps that is what prevents you from finding peace, perhaps there are too many words, for even salvation and virtue. Samsara and Nirvana are only words, Govinda. Nirvana is not a thing; there is only the word Nirvana."

Govinda said: "Nirvana is not only a word, my friend; it is a thought."

Siddhārtha continued: "It may be a thought, but I must confess, my friend, that I do not differentiate very much between thoughts and words. Quite frankly, I do not attach great importance to thoughts either. I attach more importance to things. For example, there was a man at this ferry who was my predecessor and teacher. He was a holy man who for many years believed only in the river and nothing else. He noticed that the river's voice spoke to him. He learned from it; it educated and taught him. The river seemed like a god to him and for many years he did not know that every wind, every cloud, every bird, every beetle is equally divine and knows and can teach just as well as the esteemed river. But when this holy man went off into the woods, he knew everything; he knew more than you and I, without teachers, without books, just because he believed in the river."

Govinda said: "But what you call thing, is it something real, something intrinsic? Is it not only the illusion of Maya, only image and appearance? Your stone, your tree, are they real?"

"This also does not trouble me much," said Siddhārtha. "If they are illusion, then I also am illusion, and so they are always of the same nature as myself. It is that which makes them so lovable and venerable. That is why I can love them. And here is a doctrine at which you will laugh. It seems to me, Govinda, that love is the most important thing in the world. It may be important to great thinkers to examine the world, to explain and despise it. But I think it is only important to love the world, not to despise it, not for us to hate each other, but to be able to regard the world and ourselves and all beings with love, admiration and respect."

"I understand that," said Govinda, "but that is just what the Illustrious One called illusion. He preached benevolence, forbearance, sympathy, patience—but not love. He forbade us to bind ourselves to earthly love."

"I know that," said Siddhārtha smiling radiantly, "I know that, Govinda, and here we find ourselves within the maze of meanings, within the conflict of words, for I will not deny that my words about love are in apparent contradiction to the teachings of Gotama. That is just why I distrust words so much, for I know that this contradiction is an illusion. I know that I am at one with Gotama. How, indeed, could he not know love, he who has recognized all humanity's vanity and transitoriness, yet loves humanity so much that he has devoted a long life solely to help and teach people? Also with this great teacher, the thing to me is of greater importance than the words; his deeds and life are more important to me than his talk, the gesture of his hand is more important to me than his opinions. Not in speech or thought do I regard him as a great man, but in his deeds and life."

The two old men were silent for a long time. Then as Govinda was preparing to go, he said: "I thank you, Siddhārtha, for telling me something of your thoughts. Some of them are strange thoughts. I cannot grasp them all immediately. However, I thank you, and I wish you many peaceful days."

Inwardly, however, he thought: Siddhārtha is a strange man and he expresses strange thoughts. His ideas seem crazy. How different do the Illustrious One's doctrines sound! They are clear, straightforward, comprehensible; they contain nothing strange, wild or laughable. But Siddhārtha's hands and feet, his eyes, his brow, his breathing, his smile, his greeting, his gait affect me differently from his thoughts. Never, since the time our Illustrious Gotama passed into Nirvana, have I ever met a man with the exception of Siddhārtha about whom I felt: This is

a holy man! His ideas may be strange, his words may sound foolish, but his glance and his hand, his skin and his hair, all radiate a purity, peace, serenity, gentleness and saintliness which I have never seen in any man since the recent death of our illustrious teacher.

While Govinda was thinking these thoughts and there was conflict in his heart he again bowed to Siddhārtha, full of affection towards him. He bowed low before the quietly seated man.

"Siddhārtha," he said, "we are now old men. We may never see each other again in this life. I can see, my dear friend, that you have found peace. I realize that I have not found it. Tell me one more word, my esteemed friend, tell me something that I can conceive, something I can understand! Give me something to help me on my way, Siddhārtha. My path is often hard and dark."

Siddhārtha was silent and looked at him with his calm, peaceful smile. Govinda looked steadily in his face, with anxiety, with longing. Suffering, continual seeking and continual failure were written in his look.

Siddhārtha saw it and smiled.

"Bend near to me!" he whispered in Govinda's ear. "Come, still nearer, quite close! Kiss me on the forehead, Govinda."

Although surprised, Govinda was compelled by a great love and presentiment to obey him; he leaned close to him and touched his forehead with his lips. As he did this, something wonderful happened to him. While he was still dwelling on Siddhārtha's strange words, while he strove in vain to dispel the conception of time, to imagine Nirvana and Samsara as one, while even a certain contempt for his friend's words conflicted with a tremendous love and esteem for him, this happened to him.

He no longer saw the face of his friend Siddhārtha. Instead he saw other faces, many faces, a long series, a continuous stream of faces—hundreds, thousands, which all came and disappeared and yet all seemed to be there at the same time, which all continually changed and renewed themselves and which were yet all

Siddhārtha. He saw the face of a fish, of a carp, with tremendous painfully opened mouth, a dying fish with dimmed eyes. He saw the face of a newly born child, red and full of wrinkles, ready to cry. He saw the face of a murderer, saw him plunge a knife into the body of a man; at the same moment he saw this criminal kneeling down, bound, and his head cut off by an executioner. He saw the naked bodies of men and women in the postures and transports of passionate love. He saw corpses stretched out, still, cold, empty. He saw the heads of animals—boars, crocodiles, elephants, oxen, birds. He saw Krishna and Agni. He saw all these forms and faces in a thousand relationships to each other, all helping each other, loving, hating and destroying each other and become newly born. Each one was mortal, a passionate, painful example of all that is transitory. Yet none of them died, they only changed, were always reborn, continually had a new face: only time stood between one face and another. And all these forms and faces rested, flowed, reproduced, swam past and merged into each other, and over them all there was continually something thin, unreal and yet existing, stretched across like thin glass or ice, like a transparent skin, shell, form or mask of water—and this mask was Siddhārtha's smiling face which Govinda touched with his lips at that moment. And Govinda saw that this mask-like smile, this smile of unity over the flowing forms, this smile of simultaneousness over the thousands of births and deaths—this smile of Siddhārtha—was exactly the same as the calm, delicate, impenetrable, perhaps gracious, perhaps mocking, wise, thousand-fold smile of Gotama, the Buddha, as he had perceived it with awe a hundred times. It was in such a manner, Govinda knew, that the Perfect One smiled.

No longer knowing whether time existed, whether this display had lasted a second or a hundred years, whether there was a Siddhārtha, or a Gotama, a Self and others, wounded deeply by a divine arrow which gave him pleasure, deeply enchanted and exalted, Govinda stood yet a while bending over Siddhārtha's peaceful face which he had just kissed, which had just been the stage of all present and future forms. His countenance was unchanged after the mirror of the thousand-fold forms had disappeared from the surface. He smiled peacefully and gently, perhaps very graciously, perhaps very mockingly, exactly as the Illustrious One had smiled.

Govinda bowed low. Incontrollable tears trickled down his old face. He was overwhelmed by a feeling of great love, of the most humble veneration. He bowed low, right down to the ground, in front of the man sitting there motionless, whose smile reminded him of everything that he had ever loved in his life, of everything that had ever been of value and holy in his life.

Continuing to Think

Those who do not learn what this life has to offer must continue to repeat the experience until they learn the lesson—not because they have been "bad" and are being punished but because the task of life is "getting it." Life is hard, the Buddha tells us, because we keep wanting it to be something it is not. We want to take something dynamic and flowing and freeze it in place—those we love will always love us just as they do now, no one will grow up or age, everything that gives me comfort and security will stay exactly as it is.

This is a pipe dream, and a dangerous one. By clinging to a false view of what is, we cause ourselves suffering. Our desire to stop the flow of life and hold on to it is doomed, and the only way to stop suffering is to stop this foolish desire. Following the Noble Eightfold Path is the way to stop desire and, consequently, stop suffering. Notice that these Buddhist rules for living are not the commandments of a divine lawgiver. They are closer to advice from someone who has been through college, or boot camp, or a divorce, and tells you how to avoid some of the pain.

If you try to turn college into something it is not, you are sure to be disappointed. Only by taking it on its own terms, taking it for what it is, can you successfully complete it and learn what it has to offer you. Life is exactly like this. Birth and death are not opposites but two aspects of the same thing—like the front and back of one coin; both sides are needed to make one comprehensible whole. To be born is to die and to die is to be reborn—unless and until you learn life's lesson and get off the wheel of birth and death. This is called nirvana—a return to what you have always been—interconnected with everything else.

Summing Up the Readings

In this chapter we have seen human attempts to explain where we have come from, who we are, and how the universe operates. In Asia, Africa, Europe, and the Americas, human attempts to explain these questions share some common elements, and they have important differences as well. Many cultures seem to assume that humans alone cannot account for everything—there must be someone or something more.

Philosophy and theology have been at some times partners and at other times adversaries. The challenge of Aristotle's uncaused cause has evoked different responses in the Christian and Islamic worlds. Thomas Aquinas found the peaceful co-existence of philosophy and theology desirable, and he found a way to achieve it. al-Ghazali accused the philosophers of confusing the Islamic faithful and attacked them using their own methods to discredit their claims and restore credibility to religious faith. Writing out of a different faith tradition as well as from a later time and another culture, al-Ghazali echoed both the concerns and the remedies proposed by Augustine of Hippo.

In Herland, religion represents all that is good and seems at the same time to be a perfectly rational philosophical system. Those who are troubled by life's rough spots can be helped by spiritual therapists—wise women who staff the temples in every town. Mind, emotion, and the body are all honored. The loving power that supports life encourages naturalness in human behavior instead of demanding adherence to a set of divine principles.

In the Buddhist tradition, the philosophical concerns we have been looking at are largely irrelevant. Reason will not be our guide to understanding the nature of what is and speculation will not free us from the round of birth/death/rebirth. A personal God is part of the illusion that must be abandoned. Seeing what is—through direct experience—becomes our lifework.

Continuing to Question

1. What is the value of finding rationalist proofs for the existence of God? Does anyone you know who believes in God base that belief on rationalist proofs? If not, what leads them to belief?

2. In what way can philosophy be a threat to religion? Does it have to be?

3. How much effect does imaging God as male have on human society and power relationships? If motherhood became the dominant metaphor, what qualities would we expect to find in the divine? In human society?

4. Which do you believe is the ultimate guidance system in your own life: your reason or your will? Do you find that knowing the truth sets you free? Or, do you find your will asserting itself despite your best intentions?

5. What does Govinda learn when he kisses Siddhartha's forehead? Does this account have any connection with stories that drowning or freezing people see their entire lives pass before their eyes in seconds?

Suggestions for Further Exploration

FICTION

Bradley, Marion Zimmer, *The Mists of Avalon*—New York: Ballantine, 1984. This science fiction novel retells the Arthurian myth from the point of view of the women; it features a sensitive portrayal of Goddess worship and its eventual defeat by Christianity.

Camus, Albert, *The Plague*—New York: Knopf, 1962. Why would God send a plague (in this case the bubonic plague during the Middle Ages, but you might want to think of AIDS)? Why do some survive and others die? What answers, if any, do science, religion, and our sense of our own humanity provide in the face of a plague?

Corman, Avery, *Oh God!*—New York: Simon and Schuster, 1971. God appears to a supermarket clerk and asks him to "spread the word that I exist . . . I set the world up so it can work." All the questions raised in this chapter are covered in Corman's book. Also a movie.

Dillard, Annie, *Holy the Firm*—New York: HarperCollins, 1988. Dillard creates an interesting theodicy in which the suffering of a seven-year-old girl appears as a link in the order of things.

Eco, Umberto, *The Name of the Rose*—New York: Warner, 1986. Theological controversies, political intrigue, and human squabbling in a medieval monastery are the subject of this novel. A real slice of medieval life. The movie is also pretty good.

Hesse, Hermann, *Siddhārtha*—Cutchogue, N.Y.: Buccaneer, 1976. Hesse provides a kind of retelling of the life of the Buddha, of the precepts of Buddhism, and of the struggle of the individual to find meaning in life. This is a very readable introduction to Eastern ways of thinking and being.

Kazantzakis, Nikos, *The Last Temptation of Christ*—New York, Bantam, 1965. In *The Last Temptation of Christ,* the author speculates on the temptation God must feel to live an ordinary human life with struggles, a family, and all the simple pleasures we take for granted. Also an excellent movie.

Sartre, Jean-Paul, *No Exit*—New York: French, 1972. In this play, three characters discover they are in hell; each will torture the others more effectively than devils with pitchforks might, just by being the people they are. Sartre suggests that hell is other people.

Updike, John, *Roger's Version*—New York: Knopf, 1986. A theology professor and a young computer student debate the possibility and advisability of trying to prove the existence of God using a computer. This novel also covers the key questions raised in this chapter in fictional form.

Walker, Alice, *The Color Purple*—New York: Pocket, 1982. Walker's Pulitzer Prize–winning novel features letters written by a poor, abused, black woman in the South to God and to her missing sister. Walker has a character say that if you walk by a field of radiant purple flowers that God has gone to a lot of trouble to create without noticing it, this pisses God off. You've probably seen the movie.

NONFICTION PRIMARY SOURCE MATERIAL

Augustine of Hippo, *Confessions*—New York: New American Library, 1963. This spiritual autobiography reveals a very human person who struggled all his life to be what he thought he ought to be.

Buber, Martin, *I and Thou*—New York: Scribner's, 1970. This book has become a classic of Jewish personalism. It is clear and understandable.

Camus, Albert, *The Myth of Sisyphus and Other Essays*—New York: Knopf, 1969. Sisyphus was condemned by the gods to push a large stone up a hill, only to have it roll down, so that he would have to begin the process all over again—a metaphor for life.

Feuerbach, Ludwig, *The Essence of Christianity*—New York: Harper & Row, 1957. This is the attack on anthropomorphism that inspired Karl Marx's interest in dialectical materialism. It is short and readable.

Hume, David, *Dialogues Concerning Natural Religion*—New York: Routledge, 1992. These dialogues are Hume's answer to natural theology. Once you know the argument being made, the dialogues are readable and interesting.

John of the Cross, *Dark Night of the Soul*—New York: Doubleday, 1990. This is a medieval account of numinous experiences written by a Spanish mystic.

Kierkegaard, Søren, *Fear and Trembling*—New York: Penguin, 1985. In this story of the readiness of Abraham to sacrifice his son Isaac to God, we may read Kierkegaard's struggle to sacrifice the dearest person in his life, Regine. A glimpse at a man in love as well as an anguished philosopher.

Merton, Thomas, trans. *The Wisdom of the Desert*—Boston: Shambhala, 1994. These very articulate musings of a modern Western man who gave up the world to become a Trappist monk and live in silence provide an introduction to a mystical, intuitive approach to religion.

Teresa of Avila, *The Life of St. Teresa of Avila*—New York: Penguin, 1957. Written at the request of her superiors by Teresa, a Catholic nun of the 16th century, this book is filled with energy, humor, and extraordinary experiences.

Tillich, Paul, *Dynamics of Faith*—New York: Harper, 1958. This brief statement of Christian existentialism by a Protestant theologian will introduce you to what is sometimes referred to as radical theology.

Part II

Epistemology

In the West we have taken for granted a separation between knowing subject and known object. I know what an apple is because I am separate from it, can stand apart from it and observe it—it is not me. The same sort of thing applies in human relationships as we take for granted our stark individuality. No matter how close we may seem, I am not you and you are not me. This section, which explores **epistemology,** or knowledge theory, takes those Western assumptions as a starting point and explores variations from other times and places.

Among the topics are knowledge and the mind, the search for truth, and aesthetic experience. How do we know? is our most basic question. Is knowing from the outside the only way, or is it possible to know from the inside, because everything is interrelated, rather than individual, dual, or multiple? Do we use our reason, our senses, our intuition, or some combination of them?

How do we search and test for truth? We can use the traditional tools of the West—inductive and deductive reasoning—which have served us well over centuries. It is very possible to reason from basic axioms to particular applications (as in geometry) and to move from many specific observed instances to a general theory (as in genetics). But what if we want to know whether or not someone loves us. Whether or not God exists. These approaches may or may not be the best ones. There are things we know with certainty that seem to bypass both induction and deduction. Religious faith is like this, and so is our understanding of human relationships.

Perhaps we can learn from artists another route to knowledge. The arts can be both powerful teachers of metaphysical truths and paths to explore on our own. If art comes out of the museums and into the ordinary lives of people, it can open new possibilities for knowing and the artist can serve as a medium between eternal and temporal realities. Things we might never think of as art—archery, for example—may change how we think about what is real.

5   Knowledge and the Mind

Defining the Issue

What exactly do we mean when we say we "know" something? Clearly, belief is a necessary condition but not a sufficient one; knowledge implies something more. Philosophers agree that deciding *how* we know is a critical preliminary to stating *what* we know. In other words, the basis of our knowledge provides its justification.

As you might have guessed, philosophers disagree about all of these questions. Some regard reason to be the foundation for and path to knowledge. As the criterion or standard of truth, these rationalist philosophers use deduction or logic; they also tend to have a low opinion of knowledge obtained through the senses. However, this empirical or sense-based approach leads other philosophers to insist that the sole source of knowledge is experience. Known as empiricists, they tend to deny universal or necessary truths (favored by rationalists) as well as innate or inborn knowledge. We'll take a look at an approach to knowledge theory rooted in **empiricism** at the beginning of Chapter 6.

What both rationalists and empiricists agree about is the distinction between the knowing subject and the known object. We take this for granted in the West, and it provides the basis for our objectivity (where knowledge is concerned). I, the knower, stand outside and apart from whatever it is I am attempting to know. In some Asian and African philosophy, this distinction is blurred or even eliminated; the knower and the known can be thought of as intersecting circles or even as inseparable. As you read the following selections, try to think about how you "know" the things you are certain you know.

Previewing the Readings

We begin with a rationalist, René Descartes, who is sometimes called the "Father of the Enlightenment." As a young man, he had a kind of epistemological crisis. So much of what was in his head seemed to be there because he had read it or heard it—how much of it could he rely on as certain? In the process of working out his method of knowing, Descartes used as a criterion of reliability the "clear and distinct" character of those ideas that would form the basis for his epistemology.

Since Descartes, philosophers in the West have shared his insistence that knowledge must be objectively verifiable; by implication, we must keep knowledge as free as possible from emotional biases. Alison Jaggar challenges both the possibility and the desirability of separating emotion from knowledge. In fact, she claims that emotional responses may offer the first clue to the biases in so-called objective knowledge, by revealing the shared assumptions made by those in power.

Sor [Sister] Juana Inés de la Cruz, a contemporary of Descartes, living thousands of miles away, shared his hunger for knowledge. Following Aristotle, she argued that the desire for knowledge is innate to human nature. As a poor and illegitimate daughter in patriarchal New Spain (present-day Mexico), she saw that her only chance to live an intellectual life would be as a nun. In her brilliant defense of learning for women, Sor Juana asserts that all knowledge is interrelated. Secular learning, she writes, provided the groundwork for her understanding of the higher learning found in the Bible.

Our last two selections address useful limits on knowing. The medieval Jewish philosopher Moses Maimonides suggests that in pursuit of religious truth (the most reliable and valuable kind, in his view), too much knowledge, like too much honey, can be harmful rather than helpful. And Shunryu Suzuki, a modern Zen Master, suggests that from the freshness of "beginner's mind" it is clear that one thing flows into another; this perception of interconnectedness constitutes the basis for enlightenment or knowledge about the true nature of reality.

Between 1300 and 1600 C.E., the Western world experienced a knowledge explosion. Telescopes, microscopes, and the voyages of European explorers all revealed new worlds that had been there all along waiting to be "discovered." The Renaissance revolutionized art, introducing human themes and models that looked increasingly lifelike, and the Protestant Reformation fractured the unity that had called itself Christendom, leaving many competing sects—all claiming to be the true version of Christianity. The Bible was translated from Latin into the spoken languages of ordinary people, and Dante made the decision to write the *Divine Comedy* in Italian. Movable type allowed printers to produce inexpensive books—the forerunners of today's paperbacks—that many in the rising middle class could afford to buy and read.

A Polish astronomer named Copernicus stunned the world by proving mathematically that the earth revolved around the sun. If Copernicus was right, Aristotle was wrong and the Judaic and Christian emphasis on human uniqueness seemed on shaky ground. Even more unsettling was this question: If we can't trust common sense or our sense experience (the sun certainly seems to revolve around the earth), what can we trust?

René Descartes was born in 1596 during this knowledge explosion. All the certainties of life seemed to be collapsing around him, and Descartes determined to find what could not be doubted and build his knowledge system (deductively) on that. We still share Descartes's desire for certainty, of course. However, in the modern world, some are questioning whether the sort of dispassionate knowledge Descartes sought is even attainable. Alison Jaggar suggests that so-called objective knowledge, untainted by subjective biases and emotion, may actually be a dangerous myth with classist, racist, and masculinist dimensions.

We live in a world not unlike the one that Descartes inhabited. We've sent astronauts to walk on the moon, united egg and sperm in a petri dish, connected the world by telephone, fax, and cable TV. Knowledge changes so fast it seems impossible to keep up with new developments, and most of us find our heads spinning. One can appreciate why Moses Maimonides, a medieval rabbi who lived from 1135–1204, might argue that too much knowledge, like too much honey, can be dangerous and even poisonous. Even a wonderful thing like expanding knowledge can be overwhelming and confusing. "Too much," we might be tempted to say. "Stop! or at least slow down."

One advantage to living in the midst of such an explosion is that we are unlikely to grow complacent and think we know all there is to know; there is little danger that we will lose our capacity for surprise. The freshness of what contemporary Zen master Shunryu Suzuki calls **beginner's mind** is exactly what is needed to experience what is directly and know it. According to Zen Buddhism, deductive knowledge that assumes a separation between knower and known is great for building rockets but not so great for knowing what is.

5.1   *Discourse on Method*

RENÉ DESCARTES

Preparing to Read

In search of a certain route to knowledge, Descartes is unwilling to trust the senses, knowing how easily they can be fooled. Almost everything he has learned in school has been presented as "true" on the basis of authority—the authority of the Church or the authority of an expert. Unwilling to take knowledge about the world "on faith," Descartes sets out to doubt everything. If he finds something undoubtable, he concludes, that will become the foundation on which he will build his knowledge base.

This is a very appealing project. Who among us would not like to know that what we believe to be true is in fact true? As the inventor of analytic geometry, Descartes approaches this problem as he would a problem in mathematics, and he proceeds using the method of deduction or logic. This makes him a rationalist. Notice that he does not appeal to experience at all; instead he reasons from premise to premise, reaching what he is sure will be a valid conclusion.

In this selection, we see Descartes's mind at work. He tells us *how* he will reason as he introduces us to his "method." Because it is the method of rationalist philosophers, you should observe the *process* Descartes resolves to follow as he tears down his old house of knowledge so he can rebuild it on a firmer foundation. Pay particular attention to his four rules: (1) avoid prejudgment, (2) subdivide the problem into all its parts, (3) move from the simple to the complex, and (4) omit nothing.

Does this seem to you to be a reliable method? Could these same four steps be applied to any problem you might encounter? If not, what are the conditions to which it would not apply?

Part Two: The Principal Rules of the Method

I WAS THEN IN GERMANY, where I had gone because of the desire to see the wars which are still not ended; and while I was returning to the army from the coronation of the Emperor, I was caught by the onset of winter. There was no conversation to occupy me, and being untroubled by any cares or passions, I remained all day alone in a warm room. There I had plenty of leisure to examine my ideas. One of the first that occurred to me was that frequently there is less perfection in a work produced by several persons than in one produced by a single hand. Thus we notice that buildings conceived and completed by a single architect are usually more beautiful and better planned than those remodeled by several persons using ancient walls of various vintages that had originally been built for quite other purposes along with new ones. Similarly, those ancient towns which were originally nothing but hamlets, and in the course of time have become great cities, are ordinarily very badly arranged compared to one of the symmetrical metropolitan districts which a city planner has laid out on an open plain according to his own designs. It is true that when we consider their buildings one by one, there is often as much beauty in the first city as in the second, or even more; nevertheless, when we observe how they are arranged, here a large unit, there a small; and how the streets are crooked and uneven, one would rather suppose that chance and not the decisions of rational men had so arranged them. And when we consider that there were always some officials in charge of private building, whose duty it was to see that they were conducive to the general good appearance of the city, we recognize that it is not easy to do a good job when using only the works of others. Similarly I supposed that peoples who were once half savage and barbarous, and who became civilized by a gradual process and invented their laws one by one as the harmfulness of crimes and quarrels forced them to outlaw them, would be less well governed than those who have followed the constitutions of some prudent legislator from the time that their communities were founded. Thus it is quite certain that the condition of the true religion, whose rules were laid down by God alone, must be incomparably superior to all others. And, to speak of human affairs, I believe that Sparta was such a flourishing community, not because of the goodness of each of its laws in particular, seeing that many of them were very strange and even contrary to good morals, but because they were produced by a single legislator, and so all tended to the same end. And similarly I thought that the sciences found in books, at least those whose reasons were only probable and which had no proofs, have grown up little by little by the accumulation of

From LaFleur, Laurence J., *Descartes: Discourse on Method,* (c) 1956, pp. 10–18.
Reprinted by permission of Prentice Hall, Upper Saddle River, New Jersey.

the opinions of many different persons, and are therefore by no means as near to the truth as the simple and natural reasonings of a man of good sense, laboring under no prejudice concerning the things which he experiences.

Likewise I thought that we were all children before being men, at which time we were necessarily under the control of our appetites and our teachers, and that neither of these influences is wholly consistent, and neither of them, perhaps, always tends toward the better. It is therefore impossible that our judgments should be as pure and firm as they would have been had we the whole use of our mature reason from the time of our birth and if we had never been under any other control.

It is true that we never tear down all the houses in a city just to rebuild them in a different way and to make the streets more beautiful; but we do see that individual owners often have theirs torn down and rebuilt, and even that they may be forced to do so when the building is crumbling with age, or when the foundation is not firm and it is in danger of collapsing. By this example I was convinced that a private individual should not seek to reform a nation by changing all its customs and destroying it to construct it anew, nor to reform the body of knowledge or the system of education. Nevertheless, as far as the opinions which I had been receiving since my birth were concerned, I could not do better than to reject them completely for once in my lifetime, and to resume them afterwards, or perhaps accept better ones in their place, when I had determined how they fitted into a rational scheme. And I firmly believed that by this means I would succeed in conducting my life much better than if I built only upon the old foundations and gave credence to the principles which I had acquired in my childhood without ever having examined them to see whether they were true or not. For though I noticed several difficulties in the way, they were neither insurmountable nor comparable to those involved in the slightest reform of public affairs. For public affairs are on a large scale, and large edifices are

too difficult to set up again once they have been thrown down, too difficult even to preserve once they have been shaken, and their fall is necessarily catastrophic. It is certain that many institutions have defects, since their differences alone guarantee that much, but custom has no doubt inured us to many of them. Custom has perhaps even found ways to avoid or correct more defects than prudence could have done. Finally, present institutions are practically always more tolerable than would be a change in them; just as highways which twist and turn among the mountains become gradually so easy to travel, as a result of much use, that it is much better to follow them than to attempt to go more directly by climbing cliffs and descending to the bottom of precipices.

That is why I cannot at all approve those mischievous spirits who, not being called either by birth or by attainments to a position of political power, are nevertheless constantly proposing some new reform. If I thought the slightest basis could be found in this *Discourse* for a suspicion that I was guilty of this folly, I would be loath to permit it to be published. Never has my intention been more than to try to reform my own ideas, and rebuild them on foundations that would be wholly mine. If my building has pleased me sufficiently to display a model of it to the public, it is not because I advise anyone to copy it. Those whom God has more bountifully endowed will no doubt have higher aims; there are others, I fear, for whom my own are too adventurous. Even the decision to abandon all one's preconceived notions is not an example for all to follow, and the world is largely composed of two sorts of individuals who should not try to follow it. First, there are those who think themselves more able than they really are, and so make precipitate judgments and do not have enough patience to think matters through thoroughly. From this it follows that once they have taken the liberty of doubting their established principles, thus leaving the highway, they will never be able to keep to the narrow path which must be followed to go more directly, and will remain lost all their lives. Secondly, there are those who have enough sense or modesty to realize that they are less wise and less able to distinguish the true from the false than are others, and so should rather be satisfied to follow the opinions of these others than to search for better ones themselves.

As for myself, I should no doubt have belonged in the last class if I had had but a single teacher or if I had not known the differences which have always existed among the most learned. I had discovered in college that one cannot imagine anything so strange and unbelievable but that it has been upheld by some philosopher; and in my travels I had found that those who held opinions contrary to ours were neither barbarians nor savages, but that many of them were at least as reasonable as ourselves. I had considered how the same man, with the same capacity for reason, becomes different as a result of being brought up among Frenchmen or Germans than he would be if he had been brought up among Chinese or Americans or cannibals; and how, in our fashions, the thing which pleased us ten years ago and perhaps will please us again ten years in the future, now seems extravagant and ridiculous; and felt that in all these ways we are much more greatly influenced by custom and example than by any certain knowledge. Faced with this divergence of opinion, I could not accept the testimony of the majority, for I thought it worthless as a proof of anything somewhat difficult to discover, since it is much more likely that a single man will have discovered it than a whole people. Nor, on the other hand, could I select anyone whose opinions seemed to me to be preferable to those of others, and I was thus constrained to embark on the investigation for myself.

Nevertheless, like a man who walks alone in the darkness, I resolved to go so slowly and circumspectly that if I did not get ahead very rapidly I was at least safe from falling. Also, just as the occupants of an old house do not destroy it before a plan for a new one has been thought out, I did not want to reject all the opinions which had slipped irrationally into my consciousness since birth, until I had first spent enough time planning how to accomplish the task which I was then undertaking, and seeking the true method of obtaining knowledge of everything which my mind was capable of understanding.

Among the branches of philosophy, I had, when younger, studied logic, and among those of mathematics, geometrical analysis and algebra; three arts or sciences which should have been able to contribute something to my design. But in examining them I noticed that as far as logic was concerned, its syllogisms and most of its other methods serve rather to explain to another what one already knows, or even, as in the art of Lully, to speak freely and without judgment of what one does not know, than to learn new things. Although it does contain many true and good precepts, they are interspersed among so many others that are harmful or superfluous that it is almost as difficult to separate them as to bring forth a Diana or a Minerva from a block of virgin marble. Then, as far as the analysis of the Greeks and the algebra of the moderns is concerned, besides the fact that they deal with abstractions and speculations which appear to have no utility, the first is always so limited to the consideration of figures that it cannot exercise the understanding without greatly fatiguing the imagination, and the last is so limited to certain rules and certain numbers that it has become a confused and obscure art which perplexes the mind instead of a science which educates it. In consequence I thought that some other method must be found to combine the advantages of these three and to escape their faults. Finally, just as the multitude of laws frequently furnishes an excuse for vice, and a state is much better governed with a few laws which are strictly adhered to, so I thought that instead of the great number of precepts of which logic is composed, I would have enough with the four following ones, provided that I made a firm and unalterable resolution not to violate them even in a single instance.

The first rule was never to accept anything as true unless I recognized it to be certainly and evidently such: that is, carefully to avoid all precipitation and prejudgment, and to include nothing in my conclusions unless it presented itself so clearly and distinctly to my mind that there was no reason or occasion to doubt it.

The second was to divide each of the difficulties which I encountered into as many parts as possible, and as might be required for an easier solution.

The third was to think in an orderly fashion when concerned with the search for truth, beginning with the things which were simplest and easiest to understand, and gradually and by degrees reaching toward more complex knowledge, even treating, as though ordered, materials which were not necessarily so.

The last was, both in the process of searching and in reviewing when in difficulty, always to make enumerations so complete, and reviews so general, that I would be certain that nothing was omitted.

Those long chains of reasoning, so simple and easy, which enabled the geometricians to reach the most difficult demonstrations, had made me wonder whether all things knowable to men might not fall into a similar logical sequence. If so, we need only refrain from accepting as true that which is not true, and carefully follow the order necessary to deduce each one from the others, and there cannot be any propositions so abstruse that we cannot prove them, or so recondite that we cannot discover them. It was not very difficult, either, to decide where we should look for a beginning, for I knew already that one begins with the simplest and easiest to know. Considering that among all those who have previously sought truth in the sciences, mathematicians alone have been able to find some demonstrations, some certain and evident reasons, I had no doubt that I should begin where they did, although I expected no advantage except to accustom my mind to work with truths and not to be satisfied with bad reasoning. I do not mean that I intended to learn all the particular branches of mathematics; for I saw that although the objects they discuss are different, all these branches are in agreement in limiting their consideration to the relationships or proportions between their various objects. I judged therefore that it would be better to examine these proportions in general, and use particular objects as illustrations only in order to make their principles easier to comprehend, and to be able the more easily to apply them afterwards, without any forcing, to anything for which they would be suitable. I realized that in order to understand the principles of relationships I would sometimes have to consider them singly, and sometimes comprehend and remember them in groups. I thought I could consider them better singly as relationships between lines, because I could find nothing more simple or more easily pictured to my imagination and my senses. But in order to remember and understand them better when taken in groups, I had to express them in numbers, and in the smallest numbers possible. Thus I took the best traits of geometrical analysis and algebra, and corrected the faults of one by the other.

The exact observation of the few precepts which I had chosen gave me such facility in clarifying all the issues in these two sciences that it took only two or three months to examine them. I began with the most simple and general, and each truth that I found was a rule which helped me to find others, so that I not only solved many problems which I had previously judged very difficult, but also it seemed to me that toward the end I could determine to what extent a still unsolved problem could be solved, and what procedures should be used in solving it. In this I trust that I shall not appear too vain, considering that there is only one true solution to a given problem, and whoever finds it knows all that anyone can know about it. Thus, for example, a child who has learned arithmetic and performed an addition according to the rules may feel certain that, as far as that particular sum is concerned, he has found everything that a human mind can discover. For, after all, the method of following the correct order and stating precisely all the circumstances of what we are investigating is the whole of what gives certainty to the rules of arithmetic.

What pleased me most about this method was that it enabled me to reason in all things, if not perfectly, at least as well as was in my power. In addition, I felt that in practicing it my mind was gradually dissipating its uncertainties and becoming accustomed to conceive its objects more clearly and distinctly, and since I had not directed this method to any particular subject matter, I was in hopes of applying it just as usefully to the difficulties of other sciences as I had already to those of geometry or algebra. Not that I would dare to undertake to examine at once all the difficulties that presented themselves, for that would have been contrary to the principle of order. But I had observed that all

the basic principles of the sciences were taken from philosophy, which itself had no certain ones. It therefore seemed that I should first attempt to establish philosophic principles, and that since this was the most important thing in the world and the place where precipitation and prejudgment were most to be feared, I should not attempt to reach conclusions until I had attained a much more mature age than my then twenty-three years, and had spent much time in preparing for it. This preparation would consist partly in freeing my mind from the false opinions which I had previously acquired, partly in building up a fund of experiences which should serve afterwards as the raw material of my reasoning, and partly in training myself in the method which I had determined upon, so that I should become more and more adept in its use.

Continuing to Think

Descartes proceeds very carefully in this essay. As we have seen, he lived during an exciting and challenging time in which knowledge was exploding and many of the certainties people had counted on were crumbling. Even knowing what we do today about the make up of our solar system, does it not seem obvious to you that the sun revolves around the earth? Your senses tell you that it rises in the east, moves across the sky all day, and sets in the west, despite the scientific claim that it is the actual motion of the earth (as it rotates on its axis) that accounts for the apparent motion of the sun.

In addition to contradicting sense observation and common sense, Copernicus's theory also overturned a central assumption of Judaism and Christianity—that this world represents a unique creation—and the further Christian assertion that it is the stage for the drama of human salvation. It is not hard to imagine why Copernicus was threatened with torture by church authorities and forced to recant or deny his claim.

Descartes was sensitive to this tension between religion and science, and one of his aims was to carve a role for the new science that the Catholic Church (dominant in France where he lived) could accept. In his *Meditations,* written after the *Discourse on Method,* he divided reality into mind (the province of the Church) and matter (the province of science). This makes it possible for science to respect the authority of the Church (within its own province) while the Church respects the authority of science (within its sphere).

5.2   ## Love and Knowledge: Emotion in Feminist Epistemology

ALISON M. JAGGAR

Preparing to Read

Following Descartes, the Western world has put its confidence in the ability of deductive reasoning or logic and the inductive methods of empirical science to lead us to objective knowledge. Giving a prominent place to reason meant reconceptualizing emotions as nonrational or even irrational urges that need to be set aside if objective knowledge is to be possible. In the essay you are about to read, philosopher Alison M. Jaggar breaks new ground by arguing that emotions may be helpful and even necessary in the construction of knowledge.

While it may be possible to eliminate the subjectivity of individual scientists, Jaggar argues, social values are always at work in identifying which problems should be investigated, which hypotheses tested, which solutions accepted. Looking back on the past, we can see clearly the emotional attitudes and values that were so widely shared as to be invisible. What are the corresponding assumptions being made in the present and how can we use emotion to reveal them?

In Western culture, reason has been associated with members of dominant groups and emotion with members of subordinate groups, including people of color and women. People who experience what Jaggar calls "outlaw emotions," those that differ from the values and attitudes of the dominant group, may be uniquely able to identify the "invisible" biases in the dominant culture. So, rather than corrupting knowledge, emotion may offer a path to purifying it.

WITHIN THE WESTERN philosophical tradition, emotions usually have been considered as potentially or actually subversive of knowledge.[1] From Plato until the present, with a few notable exceptions, reason rather than emotion has been regarded as the indispensable faculty for acquiring knowledge.[2]

Typically, although again not invariably, the rational has been contrasted with the emotional, and this contrasted pair then has often been linked with other dichotomies. Not only has reason been contrasted with emotion, but it has also been associated with the mental, the cultural, the universal, the public, and the male, whereas emotion has been associated with the irrational, the physical, the natural, the particular, the private, and, of course, the female.

Although western epistemology has tended to give pride of place to reason rather than emotion, it has not always excluded emotion completely from the realm of reason. In the *Phaedrus,* Plato portrayed emotions, such as anger or curiosity, as irrational urges (horses) that must always be controlled by reason (the charioteer). On this model, the emotions were not seen as needing to be totally suppressed but

Reprinted from Alison M. Jaggar, "Love and Knowledge: Emotion in Feminist Epistemology," *Inquiry* vol. 32:2 pp. 151–176, by permission of Scandanavian University Press, Oslo, Norway, and the author.

rather as needing direction by reason: for example, in a genuinely threatening situation, it was thought not only irrational but foolhardy not to be afraid.[3] The split between reason and emotion was not absolute, therefore, for the Greeks. Instead, the emotions were thought of as providing indispensable motive power that needed to be channeled appropriately. Without horses, after all, the skill of the charioteer would be worthless.

The contrast between reason and emotion was sharpened in the seventeenth century by redefining reason as a purely instrumental faculty. For both the Greeks and the medieval philosophers, reason had been linked with value insofar as reason provided access to the objective structure or order of reality, seen as simultaneously natural and morally justified. With the rise of modern science, however, the realms of nature and value were separated: nature was stripped of value and reconceptualized as an inanimate mechanism of no intrinsic worth. Values were relocated in human beings, rooted in their preferences and emotional responses. The separation of supposedly natural fact from human value meant that reason, if it were to provide trustworthy insight into reality, had to be uncontaminated by or abstracted from value. Increasingly, therefore, though never universally,[4] reason was reconceptualized as the ability to make valid inferences from premises established elsewhere, the ability to calculate means but not to determine ends. The validity of logical inferences was thought independent of human attitudes and preferences; this was now the sense in which reason was taken to be objective and universal.[5]

The modern redefinition of rationality required a corresponding reconceptualization of emotion. This was achieved by portraying emotions as nonrational and often irrational urges that regularly swept the body, rather as a storm sweeps over the land. The common way of referring to the emotions as the "passions" emphasized that emotions happened to or were imposed upon an individual, something she suffered rather than something she did.

The epistemology associated with this new ontology rehabilitated sensory perception that, like emotion, typically had been suspected or even discounted by the western tradition as a reliable source of knowledge. British empiricism, succeeded in the nineteenth century by positivism, took its epistemological task to be the formulation of rules of inference that would guarantee the derivation of certain knowledge from the "raw data" supposedly given directly to the senses. Empirical testability became accepted as the hallmark of natural science; this, in turn, was viewed as the paradigm of genuine knowledge. Epistemology was often equated with the philosophy of science, and the dominant methodology of positivism prescribed that truly scientific knowledge must be capable of intersubjective verification. Because values and emotions had been defined as variable and idiosyncratic, positivism stipulated that trustworthy knowledge could be established only by methods that neutralized the values and emotions of individual scientists.

Recent approaches to epistemology have challenged some fundamental assumptions of the positivist epistemological model. Contemporary theorists of knowledge have undermined once rigid distinctions between analytic and synthetic statements, between theories and observations, and even between facts and values. However, few challenges have thus far been raised to the purported gap between emotion and knowledge. In this essay, I wish to begin bridging this gap through the suggestion that emotions may be helpful and even necessary rather than inimical to the construction of knowledge. My account is exploratory in nature and leaves many questions unanswered. It is not supported by irrefutable arguments or conclusive proofs; instead, it should be viewed as a preliminary sketch for an epistemological model that will require much further development before its workability can be established.

Emotion

1. WHAT ARE EMOTIONS?

The philosophical question: What are emotions? requires both explicating the ways in which people ordinarily speak about emotion and evaluating the adequacy of those ways for expressing and illuminating experience and activity. Several problems confront someone trying to answer this deceptively simple question. One set of difficulties results from the variety, complexity, and even inconsistency of the ways in which emotions are viewed, in both daily life and scientific contexts. It is, in part, this variety that makes emotions into a "question" at the same time that it precludes answering that question by simple appeal to ordinary usage. A second set of difficulties is the wide range of phenomena covered by the term "emotion": these extend from apparently instantaneous "knee-jerk" responses of fright to lifelong dedication to an individual or a cause; from highly civilized aesthetic responses to undifferentiated feelings of hunger and thirst,[6] from background moods such as contentment or depression to intense and focused involvement in an immediate situation. It may well be impossible to construct a manageable account of emotion to cover such apparently diverse phenomena.

A further problem concerns the criteria for preferring one account of emotion to another. The more one learns about the ways in which other cultures conceptualize human faculties, the less plausible it becomes that emotions constitute what philosophers call a "natural kind." Not only do some cultures identify emotions unrecognized in the West, but there is reason to believe that the concept of emotion itself is a historical invention, like the concept of intelligence (Lewontin 1982) or even the concept of mind (Rorty 1979). For instance, anthropologist Catherine Lutz argues that the "dichotomous categories of 'cognition' and 'affect' are themselves Euroamerican cultural constructions,

master symbols that participate in the fundamental organization of our ways of looking at ourselves and others (Lutz 1985, 1986), both in and outside of social science" (Lutz 1987:308). If this is true, then we have even more reason to wonder about the adequacy of ordinary western ways of talking about emotion. Yet we have no access either to our emotions or to those of others, independent of or unmediated by the discourse of our culture.

In the face of these difficulties, I shall sketch an account of emotion with the following limitations. First, it will operate within the context of western discussions of emotion: I shall not question, for instance, whether it would be possible or desirable to dispense entirely with anything resembling our concept of emotion. Second, although this account attempts to be consistent with as much as possible of western understandings of emotion, it is intended to cover only a limited domain, not every phenomenon that may be called an emotion. On the contrary, it excludes as genuine emotions both automatic physical responses and nonintentional sensations, such as hunger pangs. Third, I do not pretend to offer a complete theory of emotion; instead, I focus on a few specific aspects of emotion that I take to have been neglected or misrepresented, especially in positivist and neopositivist accounts. Finally, I would defend my approach not only on the ground that it illuminates aspects of our experience and activity that are obscured by positivist and neopositivist construals but also on the ground that it is less open than these to ideological abuse. In particular, I believe that recognizing certain neglected aspects of emotion makes possible a better and less ideologically biased account of how knowledge is, and so ought to be, constructed.

2. EMOTIONS AS INTENTIONAL

Early positivist approaches to understanding emotion assumed that an adequate account required analytically separating emotion from other human faculties. Just as positivist accounts of sense perception attempted to distinguish the supposedly raw data of sensation from their cognitive interpretations, so positivist accounts of emotion tried to separate emotion conceptually from both reason and sense perception. As part of their sharpening of these distinctions, positivist construals of emotion tended to identify emotions with the physical feelings or involuntary bodily movements that typically accompany them, such as pangs or qualms, flushes or tremors; emotions were also assimilated to the subduing of physiological function or movement, as in the case of sadness, depression, or boredom. The continuing influence of such supposedly scientific conceptions of emotion can be seen in the fact that "feeling" is often used colloquially as a synonym for emotion, even though the more central meaning of "feeling" is physiological sensation. On such accounts, emotions were not seen as being *about* anything: instead, they were contrasted with and seen as potential disruptions of other phenomena that *are* about some thing, phenomena, such as rational judgments, thoughts, and observations. The positivist approach to understanding emotion has been called the Dumb View (Spelman 1982).

The Dumb View of emotion is quite untenable. For one thing, the same feeling or physiological response is likely to be interpreted as various emotions, depending on the context of its experience. This point is often illustrated by reference to the famous Schachter and Singer experiment; excited feelings were induced in research subjects by the injection of adrenalin, and the subjects then attributed to themselves appropriate emotions depending on their context (Schachter and Singer 1969). Another problem with the Dumb View is that identifying emotions with feelings would make it impossible to postulate that a person might not be aware of her emotional state because feelings by definition are a matter of conscious awareness. Finally, emotions differ from feelings, sensations, or physiological responses in that they are dispositional rather than episodic. For instance, we may assert truthfully that we are outraged by, proud of, or saddened by certain events, even if at that moment we are neither agitated nor tearful.

In recent years, contemporary philosophers have tended to reject the Dumb View of emotion and have substituted more intentional or cognitivist understandings. These newer conceptions emphasize that intentional judgments as well as physiological disturbances are integral elements in emotion.[7] They define or identify emotions not by the quality or character of the physiological sensation that may be associated with them but rather by their intentional aspect, the associated judgment. Thus, it is the content of my associated thought or judgment that determines whether my physical agitation and restlessness are defined as "anxiety about my daughter's lateness" or "anticipation of tonight's performance."

Cognitivist accounts of emotion have been criticized as overly rationalist, inapplicable to allegedly spontaneous, automatic, or global emotions, such as general feelings of nervousness, contentedness, angst, ecstasy, or terror. Certainly, these accounts entail that infants and animals experience emotions, if at all, in only a primitive, rudimentary form. Far from being unacceptable, however, this entailment is desirable because it suggests that humans develop and mature in emotions as well as in other dimensions; they increase the range, variety, and subtlety of their emotional responses in accordance with their life experiences and their reflections on these.

Cognitivist accounts of emotion are not without their own problems. A serious difficulty with many is that they end up replicating within the structure of emotion the very problem they are trying to solve—namely, that of an artificial split between emotion and thought—because most cognitivist accounts explain emotion as having two "components": an affective or feeling component and a cognition that supposedly interprets or identifies the feelings. These accounts, therefore, unwittingly perpetuate the positivist distinction between the shared, public, objective world of verifiable calculations, observations, and facts and the individual, private, subjective world of idiosyncratic feelings and sensations. This sharp distinction breaks any conceptual links between our feelings and the "external" world: if feelings are still conceived as blind or raw or undifferentiated, then we can give no sense of the notion of feelings fitting or failing to fit our perceptual judgments, that is, being appropriate or inappropriate. When intentionality is viewed as intellectual cognition and moved to the center of our picture of emotion, the affective elements are pushed to the periphery and become shadowy conceptual danglers whose relevance to emotion is obscure or even negligible. An adequate cognitive account of emotion must overcome this problem.

Most cognitivist accounts of emotion thus remain problematic insofar as they fail to explain the relation between the cognitive and the affective aspects of emotion. Moreover, insofar as they prioritize the intellectual over the feeling aspects, they reinforce the traditional western preference for mind over body.[8] Nevertheless, they do identify a vital feature of emotion overlooked by the Dumb View, namely, its intentionality.

3. EMOTIONS AS SOCIAL CONSTRUCTS

We tend to experience our emotions as involuntary individual responses to situations, responses that are often (though, significantly, not always) private in the sense that they are not perceived as directly and immediately by other people as they are by the subject of the experience. The apparently individual and involuntary character of our emotional experience is often taken as evidence that emotions are presocial, instinctive responses, determined by our biological constitution. This inference, however, is quite mistaken. Although it is probably true that the physiological disturbances characterizing emotions—facial grimaces, changes in the metabolic rate, sweating, trembling, tears, and so on—are continuous with the instinctive responses of our

prehuman ancestors and also that the ontogeny of emotions to some extent recapitulates their phylogeny, mature human emotions can be seen as neither instinctive nor biologically determined. Instead, they are socially constructed on several levels.

Emotions are most obviously socially constructed in that children are taught deliberately what their culture defines as appropriate responses to certain situations: to fear strangers, to enjoy spicy food, or to like swimming in cold water. On a less conscious level, children also learn what their culture defines as the appropriate ways to express the emotions that it recognizes. Although there may be crosscultural similarities in the expression of some apparently universal emotions, there are also wide divergences in what are recognized as expressions of grief, respect, contempt, or anger. On an even deeper level, cultures construct divergent understandings of what emotions are. For instance, English metaphors and metonymies are said to reveal a "folk" theory of anger as a hot fluid, contained in a private space within an individual and liable to dangerous public explosion (Lakoff and Kovecses 1987). By contrast, the Ilongot, a people of the Philippines, apparently do not understand the self in terms of a public/private distinction and consequently do not experience anger as an explosive internal force: for them, rather, it is an interpersonal phenomenon for which an individual may, for instance, be paid (Rosaldo 1984).

Further aspects of the social construction of emotion are revealed through reflection on emotion's intentional structure. If emotions necessarily involve judgments, then obviously they require concepts, which may be seen as socially constructed ways of organizing and making sense of the world. For this reason, emotions are simultaneously made possible and limited by the conceptual and linguistic resources of a society. This philosophical claim is borne out by empirical observation of the cultural variability of emotion. Although there is considerable overlap in the emotions identified by many cultures

(Wierzbicka 1986), at least some emotions are historically or culturally specific, including perhaps *ennui, angst,* the Japanese *amai* (in which one clings to another, affiliative love) and the response of "being a wild pig," which occurs among the Gururumba, a horticultural people living in the New Guinea Highlands (Averell 1980:158). Even apparently universal emotions, such as anger or love, may vary crossculturally. We have just seen that the Ilongot experience of anger apparently is quite different from the modern western experience. Romantic love was invented in the Middle Ages in Europe and since that time has been modified considerably; for instance, it is no longer confined to the nobility, and it no longer needs to be extramarital or unconsummated. In some cultures, romantic love does not exist at all.[9]

Thus, there are complex linguistic and other social preconditions for the experience, that is, for the existence of human emotions. The emotions that we experience reflect prevailing forms of social life. For instance, one could not feel or even be betrayed in the absence of social norms about fidelity: it is inconceivable that betrayal or indeed any distinctively human emotion could be experienced by a solitary individual in some hypothetical presocial state of nature. There is a sense in which any individual's guilt or anger, joy or triumph, presupposes the existence of a social group capable of feeling guilt, anger, joy, or triumph. This is not to say that group emotions historically precede or are logically prior to the emotions of individuals; it is to say that individual experience is simultaneously social experience.[10] In later sections, I shall explore the epistemological and political implications of this social rather than individual understanding of emotion.

4. EMOTIONS AS ACTIVE ENGAGEMENTS

We often interpret our emotions as experiences that overwhelm us rather than as responses we consciously choose: that emotions are to some extent involuntary is part of the ordinary meaning of the term "emotion." Even in daily life, however, we recognize that emotions are not entirely involuntary, and we try to gain control over them in various ways, ranging from mechanistic behavior modification techniques designed to sensitize or desensitize our feeling responses to various situations to cognitive techniques designed to help us to think differently about situations. For instance, we might try to change our response to an upsetting situation by thinking about it in a way that will either divert our attention from its more painful aspects or present it as necessary for some larger good.

Some psychological theories interpret emotions as chosen on an even deeper level—as actions for which the agent disclaims responsibility. For instance, the psychologist Averell likens the experience of emotion to playing a culturally recognized role: we ordinarily perform so smoothly and automatically that we do not realize we are giving a performance. He provides many examples demonstrating that even extreme and apparently totally involving displays of emotion in fact are functional for the individual and/or the society.[11] For example, students requested to record their experiences of anger or annoyance over a two-week period came to realize that their anger was not as uncontrollable and irrational as they had assumed previously, and they noted the usefulness and effectiveness of anger in achieving various social goods. Averell, notes, however, that emotions are often useful in attaining their goals only if they are interpreted as passions rather than as actions, and he cites the case of one subject led to reflect on her anger who later wrote that it was less useful as a defence mechanism when she became conscious of its function.

The action/passion dichotomy is too simple for understanding emotion, as it is for other aspects of our lives. Perhaps it is more helpful to think of emotions as habitual responses that we may have more or less difficulty in breaking. We claim or disclaim responsibility for these responses depending on our purposes in a particular context. We could never experience our emotions entirely as deliberate actions, for then they would appear nongenuine and inauthentic, but neither should emotions be seen as nonintentional, primal, or physical forces with which our rational selves are forever at war. As they have been socially constructed, so may they be reconstructed, although describing how this might happen would require a long and complicated story.

Emotions, then, are wrongly seen as necessarily passive or involuntary responses to the world. Rather, they are ways in which we engage actively and even construct the world. They have both mental and physical aspects, each of which conditions the other. In some respects, they are chosen, but in others they are involuntary; they presuppose language and a social order. Thus, they can be attributed only to what are sometimes called "whole persons," engaged in the on-going activity of social life.

5. EMOTION, EVALUATION, AND OBSERVATION

Emotions and values are closely related. The relation is so close, indeed, that some philosophical accounts of what it is to hold or express certain values reduce these phenomena to nothing more than holding or expressing certain emotional attitudes. When the relevant conception of emotion is the Dumb View, then simple emotivism certainly is too crude an account of what it is to hold a value; on this account, the intentionality of value judgments vanishes, and value judgments become nothing more than sophisticated grunts and groans. Nevertheless, the grain of important truth in emotivism is its recognition that values presuppose emotions to the extent that emotions provide the experiential basis for values. If we had no emotional responses to the world, it is inconceivable that we should ever come to value one state of affairs more highly than another.

Just as values presuppose emotions, so emotions presuppose values. The object of an emotion—that is, the object of fear, grief, pride,

and so on—is a complex state of affairs that is appraised or evaluated by the individual. For instance, my pride in a friend's achievement necessarily incorporates the value judgment that my friend has done something worthy of admiration.

Emotions and evaluations, then, are logically or conceptually connected. Indeed, many evaluative terms derive directly from words for emotions: "desirable," "admirable," "contemptible," "despicable," "respectable," and so on. Certainly it is true (pace J. S. Mill) that the evaluation of a situation as desirable or dangerous does not entail that it is universally desired or feared but it does entail that desire or fear is viewed generally as an appropriate response to the situation. If someone is unafraid in a situation generally perceived as dangerous, her lack of fear requires further explanation; conversely, if someone is afraid without evident danger, then her fear demands explanation; and, if no danger can be identified, her fear is denounced as irrational or pathological. Thus, every emotion presupposes an evaluation of some aspect of the environment while, conversely, every evaluation or appraisal of the situation implies that those who share that evaluation will share, *ceteris paribus*, a predictable emotional response to the situation.

The rejection of the Dumb View and the recognition of intentional elements in emotion already incorporate a realization that observation influences and indeed partially constitutes emotion. We have seen already that distinctively human emotions are not simple instinctive responses to situations or events; instead, they depend essentially on the ways that we perceive those situations and events, as well as on the ways that we have learned or decided to respond to them. Without characteristically human perceptions of and engagements in the world, there would be no characteristically human emotions.

Just as observation directs, shapes, and partially defines emotion, so too emotion directs, shapes, and even partially defines observation.

Observation is not simply a passive process of absorbing impressions or recording stimuli; instead, it is an activity of selection and interpretation. What is selected and how it is interpreted are influenced by emotional attitudes. On the level of individual observation, this influence has always been apparent to common sense, noting that we remark on very different features of the world when we are happy or depressed, fearful or confident. This influence of emotion on perception is now being explored by social scientists. One example is the so-called Honi phenomenon, named after a subject called Honi who, under identical experimental conditions, perceived strangers' heads as changing in size but saw her husband's head as remaining the same.[12]

The most obvious significance of this sort of example is illustrating how the individual experience of emotion focuses our attention selectively, directing, shaping, and even partially defining our observations, just as our observations direct, shape, and partially define our emotions. In addition, the example has been taken further in an argument for the social construction of what are taken in any situation to be undisputed facts, showing how these rest on intersubjective agreements that consist partly in shared assumptions about "normal" or appropriate emotional responses to situations (McLaughlin 1985). Thus, these examples suggest that certain emotional attitudes are involved on a deep level in all observation, in the intersubjectively verified and so supposedly dispassionate observations of science as well as in the common perceptions of daily life. In the next section, I shall elaborate this claim.

Epistemology

6. THE MYTH OF DISPASSIONATE INVESTIGATION

As we have already seen, western epistemology has tended to view emotion with suspicion and even hostility.[13] This derogatory western attitude toward emotion, like the earlier western contempt for sensory observation, fails to recognize that emotion, like sensory perception, is necessary to human survival. Emotions prompt us to act appropriately, to approach some people and situations and to avoid others, to caress or cuddle, fight or flee. Without emotion, human life would be unthinkable. Moreover, emotions have an intrinsic as well as an instrumental value. Although not all emotions are enjoyable or even justifiable, as we shall see, life without any emotion would be life without any meaning.

Within the context of western culture, however, people have often been encouraged to control or even suppress their emotions. Consequently, it is not unusual for people to be unaware of their emotional state or to deny it to themselves and others. This lack of awareness, especially combined with a neopositivist understanding of emotion that construes it just as a feeling of which one is aware, lends plausibility to the myth of dispassionate investigation. But lack of awareness of emotions certainly does not mean that emotions are not present subconsciously or unconsciously or that subterranean emotions do not exert a continuing influence on people's articulated values and observations, thoughts and actions.[14]

Within the positivist tradition, the influence of emotion is usually seen only as distorting or impeding observation or knowledge. Certainly it is true that contempt, disgust, shame, revulsion, or fear may inhibit investigation of certain situations or phenomena. Furiously angry or extremely sad people often seem quite unaware of their surroundings or even their own conditions; they may fail to hear or may systematically misinterpret what other people say. People in love are notoriously oblivious to many aspects of the situation around them.

In spite of these examples, however, positivist epistemology recognizes that the role of emotion in the construction of knowledge is not invariably deleterious and that emotions may make a valuable contribution to knowledge. But the positivist tradition will allow emotion to play only the role of suggesting hypotheses for investigation. Emotions are allowed this because the so-called logic of discovery sets no limits on the idiosyncratic methods that investigators may use for generating hypotheses.

When hypotheses are to be tested, however, positivist epistemology imposes the much stricter logic of justification. The core of this logic is replicability, a criterion believed capable of eliminating or canceling out what are conceptualized as emotional as well as evaluative biases on the part of individual investigators. The conclusions of western science thus are presumed "objective," precisely in the sense that they are uncontaminated by the supposedly "subjective" values and emotions that might bias individual investigators (Nagel 1968:33–34).

But if, as has been argued, the positivist distinction between discovery and justification is not viable, then such a distinction is incapable of filtering out values in science. For example, although such a split, when built into the western scientific method, is generally successful in neutralizing the idiosyncratic or unconventional values of individual investigators, it has been argued that it does not, indeed cannot, eliminate generally accepted social values. These values are implicit in the identification of the problems considered worthy of investigation, in the selection of the hypotheses considered worthy of testing, and in the solutions to the problems considered worthy of acceptance. The science of past centuries provides sample evidence of the influence of prevailing social values, whether seventeenth-century atomistic physics (Merchant 1980) or competitive interpretations of natural selection (Young 1985).

Of course, only hindsight allows us to identify clearly the values that shaped the science of the past and thus to reveal the formative influence on science of pervasive emotional attitudes, attitudes that typically went unremarked at the time because they were shared so generally. For instance, it is now glaringly evident that contempt for (and perhaps fear of) people of color is implicit in nineteenth-century anthropology's interpretation and even construction of

anthropological facts. Because we are closer to them, however, it is harder for us to see how certain emotions, such as sexual possessiveness or the need to dominate others, currently are accepted as guiding principles in twentieth-century sociobiology or even defined as part of reason within political theory and economics (Quinby 1986).

Values and emotions enter into the science of the past and the present, not only on the level of scientific practice but also on the metascientific level, as answers to various questions: What is science? How should it be practiced? and What is the status of scientific investigation versus nonscientific modes of enquiry? For instance, it is claimed with increasing frequency that the modern western conception of science, which identifies knowledge with power and views it as a weapon for dominating nature, reflects the imperialism, racism, and misogyny of the societies that created it. Several feminist theorists have argued that modern epistemology itself may be viewed as an expression of certain emotions alleged to be especially characteristic of males in certain periods, such as separation anxiety and paranoia (Flax 1983; Bordo 1987) or an obsession with control and fear of contamination (Scheman 1985; Schott 1988).

Positivism views values and emotions as alien invaders that must be repelled by a stricter application of the scientific method. If the foregoing claims are correct, however, the scientific method and even its positivist construals themselves incorporate values and emotions. Moreover, such an incorporation seems a necessary feature of all knowledge and conceptions of knowledge. Therefore, rather than repressing emotion in epistemology it is necessary to rethink the relation between knowledge and emotion and construct conceptual models that demonstrate the mutually constitutive rather than oppositional relation between reason and emotion. Far from precluding the possibility of reliable knowledge, emotion as well as value must be shown as necessary to such knowledge. Despite its classical antecedents and like the ideal of disinterested enquiry, the ideal of dispassionate enquiry is an impossible dream but a dream nonetheless or perhaps a myth that has exerted enormous influence on western epistemology. Like all myths, it is a form of ideology that fulfils certain social and political functions.

7. THE IDEOLOGICAL FUNCTION OF THE MYTH

So far, I have spoken very generally of people and their emotions, as though everyone experienced similar emotions and dealt with them in similar ways. It is an axiom of feminist theory, however, that all generalizations about "people" are suspect. The divisions in our society are so deep, particularly the divisions of race, class, and gender, that many feminist theorists would claim that talk about people in general is ideologically dangerous because such talk obscures the fact that no one is simply a person but instead is constituted fundamentally by race, class, and gender. Race, class, and gender shape every aspect of our lives, and our emotional constitution is not excluded. Recognizing this helps us to see more clearly the political functions of the myth of the dispassionate investigator.

Feminist theorists have pointed out that the western tradition has not seen everyone as equally emotional. Instead, reason has been associated with members of dominant political, social, and cultural groups and emotion with members of subordinate groups. Prominent among those subordinate groups in our society are people of color, except for supposedly "inscrutable orientals," and women.[15]

Although the emotionality of women is a familiar cultural stereotype, its grounding is quite shaky. Women appear more emotional than men because they, along with some groups of people of color, are permitted and even required to express emotion more openly. In contemporary western culture, emotionally inexpressive women are suspect as not being real women,[16] whereas men who express their emotions freely are suspected of being homosexual or in some

other way deviant from the masculine ideal. Modern western men, in contrast with Shakespeare's heroes, for instance, are required to present a facade of coolness, lack of excitement, even boredom, to express emotion only rarely and then for relatively trivial events, such as sporting occasions, where expressed emotions are acknowledged to be dramatized and so are not taken entirely seriously. Thus, women in our society form the main group allowed or even expected to feel emotion. A woman may cry in the face of disaster, and a man of color may gesticulate, but a white man merely sets his jaw.[17]

White men's control of their emotional expression may go to the extremes of repressing their emotions, failing to develop emotionally, or even losing the capacity to experience many emotions. Not uncommonly these men are unable to identify what they are feeling, and even they may be surprised, on occasion, by their own apparent lack of emotional response to a situation, such as death, where emotional reaction is perceived appropriate. In some married couples, the wife implicitly is assigned the job of feeling emotion for both of them. White, college-educated men increasingly enter therapy in order to learn how to "get in touch with" their emotions, a project other men may ridicule as weakness. In therapeutic situations, men may learn that they are just as emotional as women but less adept at identifying their own or others' emotions. In consequence, their emotional development may be relatively rudimentary; this may lead to moral rigidity or insensitivity. Paradoxically, men's lacking awareness of their own emotional responses frequently results in their being more influenced by emotion rather than less.

Although there is no reason to suppose that the thoughts and actions of women are any more influenced by emotion than the thoughts and actions of men, the stereotypes of cool men and emotional women continue to flourish because they are confirmed by an uncritical daily experience. In these circumstances, where there is a differential assignment of reason and emotion, it is easy to see the ideological function of the myth of the dispassionate investigator. It functions, obviously, to bolster the epistemic authority of the currently dominant groups, composed largely of white men, and to discredit the observations and claims of the currently subordinate groups including, of course, the observations and claims of many people of color and women. The more forcefully and vehemently the latter groups express their observations and claims, the more emotional they appear and so the more easily they are discredited. The alleged epistemic authority of the dominant groups then justifies their political authority.

The previous section of this chapter argued that dispassionate enquiry was a myth. This section has shown that the myth promotes a conception of epistemological justification vindicating the silencing of those, especially women, who are defined culturally as the bearers of emotion and so are perceived as more "subjective," biased, and irrational. In our present social context, therefore, the ideal of the dispassionate investigator is a classist, racist, and especially masculinist myth.[18]

8. EMOTIONAL HEGEMONY AND EMOTIONAL SUBVERSION

As we have seen already, mature human emotions are neither instinctive nor biologically determined, although they may have developed out of presocial, instinctive responses. Like everything else that is human, emotions in part are socially constructed; like all social constructs, they are historical products, bearing the marks of the society that constructed them. Within the very language of emotion, in our basic definitions and explanations of what it is to feel pride or embarrassment, resentment or contempt, cultural norms and expectations are embedded. Simply describing ourselves as angry, for instance, presupposes that we view ourselves as having been wronged, victimized by the violation of some social norm. Thus, we absorb the standards and values of our society in the very process of learning the language of emotion,

and those standards and values are built into the foundation of our emotional constitution.

Within a hierarchical society, the norms and values that predominate tend to serve the interest of the dominant group. Within a capitalist, white supremacist, and male-dominant society, the predominant values will tend to serve the interests of rich white men. Consequently, we are all likely to develop an emotional constitution quite inappropriate for feminism. Whatever our color, we are likely to feel what Irving Thalberg has called "visceral racism"; whatever our sexual orientation, we are likely to be homophobic; whatever our class, we are likely to be at least somewhat ambitious and competitive; whatever our sex, we are likely to feel contempt for women. The emotional responses may be so deeply rooted in us that they are relatively impervious to intellectual argument and may recur even when we pay lip service to changed intellectual convictions.[19]

By forming our emotional constitution in particular ways, our society helps to ensure its own perpetuation. The dominant values are implicit in responses taken to be precultural or acultural, our so-called gut responses. Not only do these conservative responses hamper and disrupt our attempts to live in or prefigure alternative social forms, but also, and insofar as we take them to be natural responses, they blinker us theoretically. For instance, they limit our capacity for outrage; they either prevent us from despising or encourage us to despise; they lend plausibility to the belief that greed and domination are inevitable universal human motivations; in sum, they blind us to the possibility of alternative ways of living.

This picture may seem at first to support the positivist claim that the intrusion of emotion only disrupts the process of seeking knowledge and distorts the results of that process. The picture, however, is not complete; it ignores the fact that people do not always experience the conventionally acceptable emotions. They may feel satisfaction rather than embarrassment when their leaders make fools of themselves.

They may feel resentment rather than gratitude for welfare payments and hand-me-downs. They may be attracted to forbidden modes of sexual expression. They may feel revulsion for socially sanctioned ways of treating children or animals. In other words, the hegemony that our society exercises over people's emotional constitution is not total.

People who experience conventionally unacceptable, or what I call "outlaw," emotions often are subordinated individuals who pay a disproportionately high price for maintaining the status quo. The social situation of such people makes them unable to experience the conventionally prescribed emotions: for instance, people of color are more likely to experience anger than amusement when a racist joke is recounted, and women subjected to male sexual banter are less likely to be flattered than uncomfortable or even afraid.

When unconventional emotional responses are experienced by isolated individuals, those concerned may be confused, unable to name their experience; they may even doubt their own sanity. Women may come to believe that they are "emotionally disturbed" and that the embarrassment or fear aroused in them by male sexual innuendo is prudery or paranoia. When certain emotions are shared or validated by others, however, the basis exists for forming a subculture defined by perceptions, norms, and values that systematically oppose the prevailing perceptions, norms, and values. By constituting the basis for such a subculture, outlaw emotions may be politically because they are epistemologically subversive.

Outlaw emotions are distinguished by their incompatibility with the dominant perceptions and values, and some, though certainly not all, of these outlaw emotions are potentially or actually feminist emotions. Emotions become feminist when they incorporate feminist perceptions and values, just as emotions are sexist or racist when they incorporate sexist or racist perceptions and values. For example, anger becomes feminist anger when it involves the perception

that the persistent importuning endured by one woman is a single instance of a widespread pattern of sexual harassment, and pride becomes feminist pride when it is evoked by realizing that a certain person's achievement was possible only because that individual overcame specifically gendered obstacles to success.[20]

Outlaw emotions stand in a dialectical relation to critical social theory: at least some are necessary to develop a critical perspective on the world, but they also presuppose at least the beginnings of such a perspective. Feminists need to be aware of how we can draw on some of our outlaw emotions in constructing feminist theory and also of how the increasing sophistication of feminist theory can contribute to the reeducation, refinement, and eventual reconstruction of our emotional constitution.

9. OUTLAW EMOTIONS AND FEMINIST THEORY

The most obvious way in which feminist and other outlaw emotions can help in developing alternatives to prevailing conceptions of reality is by motivating new investigations. This is possible because, as we saw earlier, emotions may be long-term as well as momentary; it makes sense to say that someone continues to be shocked or saddened by a situation, even if she is at the moment laughing heartily. As we have seen already, theoretical investigation is always purposeful, and observation is always selective. Feminist emotions provide a political motivation for investigation and so help to determine the selection of problems as well as the method by which they are investigated. Susan Griffin makes the same point when she characterizes feminist theory as following "a direction determined by pain, and trauma, and compassion and outrage" (Griffin 1979:31).

As well as motivating critical research, outlaw emotions may also enable us to perceive the world differently from its portrayal in conventional descriptions. They may provide the first indications that something is wrong with the way alleged facts have been constructed, with accepted understandings of how things are. Conventionally unexpected or inappropriate emotions may precede our conscious recognition that accepted descriptions and justifications often conceal as much as reveal the prevailing state of affairs. Only when we reflect on our initially puzzling irritability, revulsion, anger, or fear may we bring to consciousness our "gut-level" awareness that we are in a situation of coercion, cruelty, injustice, or danger. Thus, conventionally inexplicable emotions, particularly, though not exclusively, those experienced by women, may lead us to make subversive observations that challenge dominant conceptions of the status quo. They may help us to realize that what are taken generally to be facts have been constructed in a way that obscures the reality of subordinated people, especially women's reality.

But why should we trust the emotional responses of women and other subordinated groups? How can we determine which outlaw emotions are to be endorsed or encouraged and which rejected? In what sense can we say that some emotional responses are more appropriate than others? What reason is there for supposing that certain alternative perceptions of the world, perceptions informed by outlaw emotions, are to be preferred to perceptions informed by conventional emotions? Here I can indicate only the general direction of an answer, whose full elaboration must await another occasion.[21]

I suggest that emotions are appropriate if they are characteristic of a society in which all humans (and perhaps some nonhuman life, too) thrive, or if they are conducive to establishing such a society. For instance, it is appropriate to feel joy when we are developing or exercizing our creative powers, and it is appropriate to feel anger and perhaps disgust in those situations where humans are denied their full creativity or freedom. Similarly, it is appropriate to feel fear if those capacities are threatened in us.

This suggestion obviously is extremely vague, verging on the tautologous. How can we

apply it in situations where there is disagreement over what is or is not disgusting or exhilarating or unjust? Here I appeal to a claim for which I have argued elsewhere: the perspective on reality available from the standpoint of the oppressed, which in part at least is the standpoint of women, is a perspective that offers a less partial and distorted and therefore more reliable view (Jaggar 1983:chap. 11). Oppressed people have a kind of epistemological privilege insofar as they have easier access to this standpoint and therefore a better chance of ascertaining the possible beginnings of a society in which all could thrive. For this reason, I would claim that the emotional responses of oppressed people in general, and often of women in particular, are more likely to be appropriate than the emotional responses of the dominant class. That is, they are more likely to incorporate reliable appraisals of situations.

Even in contemporary science, where the ideology of dispassionate enquiry is almost overwhelming, it is possible to discover a few examples that seem to support the claim that certain emotions are more appropriate than others in both a moral and epistemological sense. For instance, Hilary Rose claims that women's practice of caring, even though warped by its containment in the alienated context of a coercive sexual division of labor, nevertheless has generated more accurate and less oppressive understandings of women's bodily functions, such as menstruation (Rose 1983). Certain emotions may be both morally appropriate and epistemologically advantageous in approaching the nonhuman and even the inanimate world. Jane Goodall's scientific contribution to our understanding of chimpanzee behavior seems to have been made possible only by her amazing empathy with or even love for these animals (Goodall 1987). In her study of Barbara McClintock, Evelyn Fox Keller describes McClintock's relation to the objects of her research—grains of maize and their genetic properties—as a relation of affection, empathy, and "the highest form of love: love that allows for intimacy without the annihilation of differ-ence." She notes that McClintock's "vocabulary is consistently a vocabulary of affection, of kin-ship, of empathy" (Keller 1984:164). Examples like these prompt Hilary Rose to assert that a feminist science of nature needs to draw on heart as well as hand and brain.

10. SOME IMPLICATIONS OF RECOGNIZING THE EPISTEMIC POTENTIAL OF EMOTION

Accepting that appropriate emotions are indis-pensable to reliable knowledge does not mean, of course, that uncritical feeling may be substi-tuted for supposedly dispassionate investigation. Nor does it mean that the emotional responses of women and other members of the underclass are to be trusted without question. Although our emotions are epistemologically indispensable, they are not epistemologically indisputable. Like all our faculties, they may be misleading, and their data, like all data, are always subject to rein-terpretation and revision. Because emotions are not presocial, physiological responses to un-equivocal situations, they are open to challenge on various grounds. They may be dishonest or self-deceptive, they may incorporate inaccurate or partial perceptions, or they may be constituted by oppressive values. Accepting the indispens-ability of appropriate emotions to knowledge means no more (and no less) than that discor-dant emotions should be attended to seriously and respectfully rather than condemned, ig-nored, discounted, or suppressed.

Just as appropriate emotions may contribute to the development of knowledge, so the growth of knowledge may contribute to the de-velopment of appropriate emotions. For in-stance, the powerful insights of feminist theory often stimulate new emotional responses to past and present situations. Inevitably, our emotions are affected by the knowledge that the women on our faculty are paid systemati-cally less than the men, that one girl in four is subjected to sexual abuse from heterosexual men in her own family, and that few women reach orgasm in heterosexual intercourse. We are likely to feel different emotions toward older women or people of color as we reevalu-ate our standards of sexual attractiveness or ac-knowledge that black is beautiful. The new emotions evoked by feminist insights are likely in turn to stimulate further feminist observa-tions and insights, and these may generate new directions in both theory and political practice. The feedback loop between our emotional con-stitution and our theorizing is continuous; each continually modifies the other, in principle in-separable from it.

The ease and speed with which we can reed-ucate our emotions unfortunately is not great. Emotions are only partially within our control as individuals. Although affected by new informa-tion, these habitual responses are not quickly unlearned. Even when we come to believe con-sciously that our fear or shame or revulsion is unwarranted, we may still continue to experi-ence emotions inconsistent with our conscious politics. We may still continue to be anxious for male approval, competitive with our comrades and sisters, and possessive with our lovers. These unwelcome, because apparently inappro-priate emotions, should not be suppressed or denied; instead, they should be acknowledged and subjected to critical scrutiny. The persis-tence of such recalcitrant emotions probably demonstrates how fundamentally we have been constituted by the dominant world view, but it may also indicate superficiality or other inade-quacy in our emerging theory and politics.[22] We can only start from where we are—beings who have been created in a cruelly racist, capitalist, and male-dominated society that has shaped our bodies and our minds, our perceptions, our values and our emotions, our language and our systems of knowledge.

The alternative epistemological models that I would suggest display the continuous interac-tion between how we understand the world and who we are as people. They would show how our emotional responses to the world change as we conceptualize it differently and how our changing emotional responses then stimulate us to new insights. They would demonstrate the need for theory to be self-reflexive, to focus not only on the outer world but also on ourselves and our relation to that world, to examine critically our social location, our actions, our values, our perceptions, and our emotions. The models also show how feminist and other critical social theories are indispensable psychotherapeutic tools because they provide some insights necessary to a full understanding of our emotional constitution. Thus, the models would explain how the reconstruction of knowledge is inseparable from the reconstruction of ourselves.

A corollary of the reflexivity of feminist and other critical theory is that it requires a much broader construal than positivism accepts of the process of theoretical investigation. In particular, it requires acknowledging that a necessary part of theoretical process is critical self-examination. Time spent in analyzing emotions and uncovering their sources should be viewed, therefore, neither as irrelevant to theoretical investigation nor even as a prerequisite for it; it is not a kind of clearing of the emotional decks, "dealing with" our emotions so that they not influence our thinking. Instead, we must recognize that our efforts to reinterpret and refine our emotions are necessary to our theoretical investigation, just as our efforts to reeducate our emotions are necessary to our political activity. Critical reflection on emotion is not a self-indulgent substitute for political analysis and political action. It is itself a kind of political theory and political practice, indispensable for an adequate social theory and social transformation.

Finally, the recognition that emotions play a vital part in developing knowledge enlarges our understanding of women's claimed epistemic advantage. We can now see that women's subversive insights owe much to women's outlaw emotions, themselves appropriate responses to the situations of women's subordination. In addition to their propensity to experience outlaw emotions, at least on some level, women are relatively adept at identifying such emotions, in themselves and others, in part because of their social responsibility for caretaking, including emotional nurturance. It is true that women, like all subordinated peoples, especially those who must live in close proximity with their masters, often engage in emotional deception and even self-deception as the price of their survival. Even so, women may be less likely than other subordinated groups to engage in denial or suppression of outlaw emotions. Women's work of emotional nurturance has required them to develop a special acuity in recognizing hidden emotions and in understanding the genesis of those emotions. This emotional acumen can now be recognized as a skill in political analysis and validated as giving women a special advantage in both understanding the mechanisms of domination and envisioning freer ways to live.

11. CONCLUSION

The claim that emotion is vital to systematic knowledge is only the most obvious contrast between the conception of theoretical investigation that I have sketched here and the conception provided by positivism. For instance, the alternative approach emphasizes that what we identify as emotion is a conceptual abstraction from a complex process of human activity that also involves acting, sensing, and evaluating. This proposed account of theoretical construction demonstrates the simultaneous necessity for and interdependence of faculties that our culture has abstracted and separated from each other: emotion and reason, evaluation and perception, observation and action. The model of knowing suggested here is nonhierarchical and antifoundationalist; instead, it is appropriately symbolized by the radical feminist metaphor of the upward spiral. Emotions are neither more basic than observation, reason, or action in building theory, nor are they secondary to them. Each of these human faculties reflects an aspect of human knowing inseparable from the other aspects. Thus, to borrow a famous phrase from a Marxian context, the development of each of these faculties is a necessary condition for the development of all.

In conclusion, it is interesting to note that acknowledging the importance of emotion for knowledge is not an entirely novel suggestion within the western epistemological tradition. The archrationalist Plato himself came to accept that in the end knowledge required a (very purified form of) love. It may be no accident that in the *Symposium* Socrates learns this lesson from Diotima, the wise woman!

NOTES

I wish to thank the following individuals who commented helpfully on earlier drafts of this chapter or made me aware of further resources: Lynne Arnault, Susan Bordo, Martha Bolton, Cheshire Calhoun, Randy Cornelius, Shelagh Crooks, Ronald De Sousa, Tim Diamond, Dick Foley, Ann Garry, Judy Gerson, Mary Gibson, Sherry Gorelick, Marcia Lind, Helen Longino, Andy McLaughlin, Uma Narayan, Linda Nicholson, Bob Richardson, Sally Ruddick, Laurie Shrage, Alan Soble, Vicky Spelman, Karsten Struhl, Joan Tronto, Daisy Quarm, Naomi Quinn, and Alison Wylie. I am also grateful to my colleagues in the fall 1985 Women's Studies Chair Seminar at Douglass College, Rutgers University, and to audiences at Duke University, Georgia University Centre, Hobart and William Smith Colleges, Northeastern University, the University of North Carolina at Chapel Hill, and Princeton University, for their responses to earlier versions of this chapter. In addition, I received many helpful comments from members of the Canadian Society for Women in Philosophy and from students in Lisa Heldke's classes in feminist epistemology at Carleton College and Northwestern University. Thanks, too, to Delia Cushway, who provided a comfortable environment in which I wrote the first draft.

A similar version of this essay appeared in *Inquiry: An Interdisciplinary Journal of Philosophy* (June 1989). Reprinted by permission of Norwegian University Press.

1. Philosophers who do not conform to this generalization and constitute part of what Susan Bordo calls a "recessive" tradition in western philosophy include Hume and Nietzsche, Dewey and James (Bordo 1987:114–118).

2. The western tradition as a whole has been profoundly rationalist, and much of its history may be viewed as a continuous redrawing of the boundaries of the rational. For a survey of this history from a feminist perspective, see Lloyd 1984.

3. Thus, fear or other emotions were seen as rational in some circumstances. To illustrate this point, Vicky Spelman quotes Aristotle as saying (in the *Nichomachean Ethics*, Bk. IV, ch. 5): "[Anyone] who does not get angry when there is reason to be angry, or who does not get angry in the right way at the right time and with the right people, is a dolt" (Spelman 1982:1).

4. Descartes, Leibnitz, and Kant are among the prominent philosophers who did not endorse a wholly stripped-down, instrumentalist conception of reason.

5. The relocation of values in human attitudes and preferences in itself was not grounds for denying their universality because they could have been conceived as grounded in a common or universal human nature. In fact, however, the variability, rather than the commonality, of human preferences and responses was emphasized; values gradually came to be viewed as individual, particular, and even idiosyncratic rather than as universal and objective. The only exception to the variability of human desires was the supposedly universal urge to egoism and the motive to maximize one's own utility, whatever that consisted in. The value of autonomy and liberty, consequently, was seen as perhaps the only value capable of being justified objectively because it was a precondition for satisfying other desires.

6. For instance, Julius Moravcsik has characterized as emotions what I would call "plain" hunger and thirst, appetites that are not desires for any particular food or drink (Moravcsik 1982:207–224). I myself think that such states, which Moravcsik also calls instincts or appetites, are understood better as sensations than emotions. In other words, I would view so-called instinctive, nonintentional feelings as the biological raw material from which full-fledged human emotions develop.

7. Even adherents of the Dumb View recognize, of course, that emotions are not entirely random or unrelated to an individual's judgments and beliefs; in other words, they note that people are angry or excited *about* something, afraid or proud *of* something. On the Dumb View, however, the judgments or beliefs associated with an emotion are seen as its causes and thus as related to it only externally.

8. Cheshire Calhoun pointed this out to me in private correspondence.

9. Recognition of the many levels on which emotions are socially constructed raises the question whether it makes sense even to speak of the possibility of universal emotions. Although a full answer to this question is methodologically problematic, one might speculate that many of what we westerners identify as emotions have functional analogues in other cultures. In other words, it may be that people in every culture might behave in ways that fulfil at least some social functions of our angry or fearful behavior.

10. The relationship between the emotional experience of an individual and the emotional experience of the group to which the individual belongs may perhaps be clarified by analogy with the relation between a word and the language of which it is a part. That the word has meaning presupposes it's a part of a linguistic system without which it has no meaning; yet the language itself has no meaning over and above the meaning of the words of which it is composed together with their grammatical ordering. Words and language presuppose and mutually constitute each other. Similarly, both individual and group emotion presuppose and mutually constitute each other.

11. Averell cites dissociative reactions by military personnel at Wright Paterson Air Force Base and shows how these were effective in mustering help to deal with difficult situations while simultaneously relieving the individual of responsibility or blame (Averell 1980:157).

12. These and similar experiments are described in Kilpatrick 1961:ch. 10, cited by McLaughlin 1985:296.

13. The positivist attitude toward emotion, which requires that ideal investigators be both disinterested and dispassionate, may be a modern variant of older traditions in western philosophy that recommended people seek to minimize their emotional responses to the world and develop instead their powers of rationality and pure contemplation.

14. It is now widely accepted that the suppression and repression of emotion has damaging if not explosive consequences. There is general acknowledgment that no one can avoid at some time experiencing emotions she or he finds unpleasant, and there is also increasing recognition that the denial of such emotions is likely to result in hysterical disorders of thought and behavior, in projecting one's own emotions on to others, in displacing them to inappropriate situations, or in psychosomatic ailments. Psychotherapy, which purports to help individuals recognize and "deal with" their emotions, has become an enormous industry, especially in the United States. In much conventional psychotherapy, however, emotions still are conceived as feelings or passions, "subjective" disturbances that afflict individuals or interfere with their capacity for rational thought and action. Different therapies, therefore, have developed a wide variety of techniques for encouraging people to "discharge" or "vent" their emotions, just as they would drain an abscess. Once emotions have been discharged or vented, they are supposed to be experienced less intensely, or even to vanish entirely, and consequently to exert less influence on individuals' thoughts and actions. This approach to psychotherapy clearly demonstrates its kinship with the "folk" theory of anger mentioned earlier, and it equally clearly retains the traditional western assumption that emotion is inimical to rational thought and action. Thus, such approaches fail to challenge and indeed provide covert support for the view that "objective" knowers are not only disinterested but also dispassionate.

15. E. V. Spelman (1982) illustrates this point with a quotation from the well-known contemporary philosopher, R. S. Peters, who wrote "we speak of emotional outbursts, reactions, upheavals and women" (*Proceedings of the Aristotelian Society,* New Series, vol. 62.).

16. It seems likely that the conspicuous absence of emotion shown by Mrs. Thatcher is a deliberate strategy she finds necessary to counter the public perception of women as too emotional for political leadership. The strategy results in her being perceived as a formidable leader, but an Iron Lady rather than a real woman. Ironically, Neil Kinnock, leader of the British Labour Party and Thatcher's main opponent in the 1987 General Election, was able to muster considerable public support through television commercials portraying him in the stereotypically feminine role of caring about the unfortunate victims of Thatcher economics. Ultimately, however, this support was not sufficient to destroy public confidence in Mrs. Thatcher's "masculine" competence and gain Kinnock the election.

17. On the rare occasions when a white man cries, he is embarrassed and feels constrained to apologize. The one exception to the rule that men should be emotionless is that they are allowed and often even expected to experience anger. Spelman (1982) points out that men's cultural permission to be angry bolsters their claim to authority.

18. Someone might argue that the viciousness of this myth was not a logical necessity. In the egalitarian

society, where the concepts of reason and emotion were not gender-bound in the way they still are today, it might be argued that the ideal of the dispassionate investigator could be epistemologically beneficial. Is it possible that, in such socially and conceptually egalitarian circumstances, the myth of the dispassionate investigator could serve as a heuristic device, an ideal never to be realized in practice but nevertheless helping to minimize "subjectivity" and bias? My own view is that counterfactual myths rarely bring the benefits advertised and that this one is no exception. This myth fosters an equally mythical conception of pure truth and objectivity, quite independent of human interests or desires, and in this way it functions to disguise the inseparability of theory and practice, science and politics. Thus, it is part of an antidemocratic world view that mystifies the political dimension of knowledge and unwarrantedly circumscribes the arena of political debate.

19. Of course, the similarities in our emotional constitutions should not blind us to systematic differences. For instance girls rather than boys are taught fear and disgust for spiders and snakes, affection for fluffy animals, and shame for their naked bodies. It is primarily, though not exclusively, men rather than women whose sexual responses are shaped by exposure to visual and sometimes violent pornography. Girls and women are taught to cultivate sympathy for others: boys and men are taught to separate themselves emotionally from others. As I have noted already, more emotional expression is permitted for lower-class and some nonwhite men than for ruling-class men, perhaps because the expression of emotion is thought to expose vulnerability. Men of the upper classes learn to cultivate an attitude of condescension, boredom, or detached amusement. As we shall see shortly, differences in the emotional constitution of various groups may be epistemologically significant in so far as they both presuppose and facilitate different ways of perceiving the world.

20. A necessary condition for experiencing feminist emotions is that one already be a feminist in some sense, even if one does not consciously wear that label. But many women and some men, even those who would deny that they are feminist, still experience emotions compatible with feminist values. For instance, they may be angered by the perception that someone is being mistreated just because she is a woman, or they may take special pride in the achievement of a woman. If those who experience such emotions are unwilling to recognize them as

feminist, their emotions are probably described better as potentially feminist or prefeminist emotions.

21. I owe this suggestion to Marcia Lind.

22. Within a feminist context, Berenice Fisher suggests that we focus particular attention on our emotions of guilt and shame as part of a critical reevaluation of our political ideals and our political practice (Fisher 1984).

REFERENCES

Averell, James R. 1980. "The Emotions." In *Personality: Basic Aspects and Current Research,* ed. Ervin Staub. Englewood Cliffs, N.J.: Prentice-Hall.

Bordo, W. R. 1987. *The Flight to Objectivity: Essays on Cartesianism and Culture.* Albany: State University of New York Press.

Fisher, Berenice. 1984. "Guilt and Shame in the Women's Movement: The Radical Ideal of Action and its Meaning for Feminist Intellectuals." *Feminist Studies* 10:185–212.

Flax, Jane. 1983. "Political Philosophy and the Patriarchal Unconscious: A Psychoanalytic Perspective on Epistemology and Metaphysics." In *Discovering Reality: Feminist Perspectives on Epistemology, Metaphysics, Methodology and Philosophy* of *Science,* ed. Sandra Harding and Merrill Hintikka. Dordrecht, Holland; D. Reidel Publishing.

Goodall, Jane. 1986. *The Chimpanzees of Gombe: Patterns of Behavior.* Cambridge, Mass.: Harvard University Press.

Griffin, Susan. 1979. *Rape: The Power of Consciousness.* San Francisco: Harper & Row.

Hinman, Lawrence. 1986. "Emotion, Morality and Understanding." Paper presented at Annual Meeting of Central Division of the American Philosophical Association, St. Louis, Missouri, May 1986.

Jaggar, Alison M. 1983. *Feminist Politics and Human Nature.* Totowa, N.J.: Rowman and Allanheld.

Keller, E. F. 1984. *Gender and Science.* New Haven, Conn.: Yale University Press.

Kilpatrick, Franklin P., ed. 1961. *Explorations in Transactional Psychology.* New York: New York University Press.

Lakoff, George, and Zoltan Kovecses. 1987. "'The Cognitive Model of Anger Inherent in American English." In *Cultural Models in Language and Thought,* ed. N. Quinn and D. Holland. New York: Cambridge University Press.

Lewontin, R. C. 1982. "Letter to the editor." *New York Review of Books,* 4 February:40–41. This letter was drawn to my attention by Alan Soble.

Lloyd, Genevieve. 1984. *The Man of Reason: 'Male' and 'Female' in Western Philosophy.* Minneapolis: University of Minnesota Press.

Lutz, Catherine. 1985. "Depression and the Translation of Emotional Worlds." In *Culture and Depression: Studies in the Anthropology and Cross-cultural Psychiatry of Affect and Disorder,* ed. A. Kleinman and B. Good. Berkeley: University of California Press, 63–100.

———. 1986. "Emotion, Thought and Estrangement: Emotion as a Cultural Category." *Cultural Anthropology* 1:287–309.

———. 1987. "Goals, Events and Understanding in Ifaluck and Emotion Theory." In *Cultural Models in Language and Thought,* ed. N. Quinn and D. Holland. New York: Cambridge University Press.

McLaughlin, Andrew. 1985. "Images and Ethics of Nature." *Environmental Ethics* 7:293–319.

Merchant, Carolyn M. 1980. *The Death of Nature: Women, Ecology and the Scientific Revolution.* New York: Harper & Row.

Moravcsik, J. M. E. 1982. "Understanding and the Emotions." *Dialectica* 36, 2–3: 207–224.

Nagel, E. 1968. "The Subjective Nature of Social Subject Matter." In *Readings in the Philosophy of the Social Sciences,* ed. May Brodbeck. New York: Macmillan.

Quinby, Lee. 1986. Discussion following talk at Hobart and William Smith colleges, April 1986.

Rorty, Richard. 1979. *Philosophy and the Mirror of Nature.* Princeton, N.J.: Princeton University Press.

Rosaldo, Michelle Z. 1984. "Toward an Anthropology of Self and Feeling." In *Culture Theory,* ed. Richard A. Shweder and Robert A. Levine. New York: Cambridge University Press.

Rose, Hilary. 1983. "Hand, Brain, and Heart: A Feminist Epistemology for the Natural Sciences." *Signs: Journal of Women in Culture and Society* 9, 1:73–90.

Schachter, Stanley, and Jerome B. Singer. 1969. "Cognitive, Social and Psychological Determinants of Emotional State." *Psychological Review* 69:379–399.

Scheman, Naomi. "Women in the Philosophy Curriculum." Paper presented at the Annual Meeting of Central Division of the American Philosophical Association, Chicago, April 1985.

Schott, Robin M. 1988. *Cognition and Eros: A Critique of the Kantian Paradigm.* Boston, Mass.: Beacon Press.

Spelman, E. V. 1982. "Anger and Insubordination." Manuscript; early version read to midwestern chapter of the Society for Women in Philosophy, spring 1982.

Wierzbicka, Anna. 1986. "Human Emotions: Universal or Culture-Specific?" *American Anthropologist* 88:584–594.

Young, R. M. 1985. *Darwin's Metaphor: Nature's Place in Victorian Culture.* Cambridge: Cambridge University Press.

Continuing to Think

What if so-called objective knowledge is a myth? If all our knowledge claims are corrupted by unstated and unacknowledged biases, should we give up the possibility of reaching certainty? Jaggar thinks a much more valuable project would be trying to identify our assumptions as the first step in challenging them. What do you think?

Have you ever had a friend accuse you of an attitude you weren't aware of holding? Or heard others laugh at a joke you didn't find funny? These are the moments when our hidden cultural values speak to us and raise questions about the assumptions being made in the dominant social order. Do filmmakers and newsreaders make judgments about groups to which you belong that seem false and dangerous?

Jaggar claims that emotions, like all other human things, are partly constructed by society. That is, we learn what to feel outraged about, what is "natural" and what isn't, when to feel proud or embarrassed. But, what happens when we don't feel the way we're supposed to? Jaggar thinks we can use our "outlaw emotions" to develop alternative ways of conceiving reality. In fact, only from outside the value system is it possible to imagine alternatives.

If this is the case, emotions can perform a necessary and valuable service, helping us spot those biases and assumptions that are currently invisible because we are too close to them, and providing the basis for other possible ways of seeing the world. Outside the Western world, we rarely see the insistence on separating emotion from reason that we take for granted.

5.3   *La Respuesta (The Response)*

SOR JUANA INÉS DE LA CRUZ

Preparing to Read

Juana Inés de Asbaje y Ramirez was beautiful, intelligent, and illegitimate. Living in patriarchal New Spain (present-day Mexico) during the seventeenth century, she had few options. Following her sister to a tutor at the age of three, Juana implied that their mother wanted both girls instructed and learned to read before her mother detected the ruse. Devouring the books in her grandfather's small library, she became intoxicated with learning and knew that she must find a way to have it in her life.

As an illegitimate daughter with no dowry, her prospects for marriage were nonexistent. In addition, if she did marry, the obligations of wife and mother would interfere with her intellectual pursuits. Consequently, she made the only logical choice and professed her vows as a nun. Having gone to the Viceroy's court, she astounded courtiers with her learning and quick mind, and she also attracted the friendship of the Vicereine, who paid the dowry required when she entered the convent.

Sor Juana was blessed with a living space that included separate sleeping and living quarters. She rapidly converted her living room into a library and spent her private time reading, writing, and presiding over tertulia at which ideas were engagingly discussed. All went well until her bishop asked her to put in writing the critical analysis of a sermon she had dissected. Without her knowledge, he published it and accompanied this with a letter directing her to turn her attention away from secular things and toward sacred ones. Her response, part of which you will read here, defends her access to knowledge on religious as well as philosophical grounds.

. . . I BECAME A NUN BECAUSE, although I knew the religious life included things (I speak of peripheral not central things) that would be repugnant to my nature, my total aversion to marriage made the convent the least objectionable and most honorable alternative I could choose in order to secure what I most desired—my salvation. To this first and most important consideration, all the little fond habits of my nature yielded—my desire to live alone, to have no pressing duties that would compromise my freedom to study, no community noise to interrupt the calm silence of my books . . . I thought I would escape myself, but unfortunately I soon discovered I had brought myself along. Wrapped in this passion for learning, which I cannot decide whether Heaven means as a gift or a punishment, I found that my religious duties did nothing to extinguish it. In fact it came back with a vengeance, like gunpowder exploding, proving to me that deprivation increases desire [privatio est causa appetitus].

I continued with the academic task (during the leisure time that remained after my obligations were completed) of reading and more reading, of studying and more studying—my only teacher, my books. You can imagine how hard it was to study in this way—dead letters on a page, not even brought to life by the voice of a teacher offering an explanation. In spite of all this, I endured these difficulties gladly because of my love for learning. Oh, how much better it would have been to do it for the love of God! How much greater my merit! In my defense, I did try to elevate my studies as much as I could and direct them toward His service, because the end to which I aspired was the study of theology. It seemed to me an embarrassing ineptitude to be a Catholic and not to know all that one can know in this life, all that can be reached through natural means concerning the divine mysteries . . .

In this manner I continued, always directing, as I have said, the steps of my study toward the summit of sacred theology. It seemed very clear to me that I would reach this summit by climbing the steps of the arts and sciences from the human realm, because how could I understand the method of the queen of sciences [theology] when I did not know those of the inferior branches leading up to it? How, without logic, was I to understand the general and specific methods by which the content of Holy Scripture is expressed? How, without rhetoric, was I to understand its figures of speech, its tropes and locutions? How, without physics, all the natural questions concerning the nature of sacrificial animals, which symbolize so many things stated and much more that remains unstated? For example, whether Saul's return to health, after listening to David's harp, occurred by natural means or by supernatural skill that God granted David? How, without arithmetic, would it be possible to understand all the computation of years, days, months, strung together so mysteriously by Daniel and others— to comprehend these mysteries one must know the natures, concordances, and properties of numbers. How, without geometry, would it be possible to measure the sacred Ark of the Covenant and the Holy City of Jerusalem, whose mysterious measurements produce a cube . . . in such a marvelous way? How, without architecture, to appreciate the grand Temple of Solomon, where God was the architect, the maker of the blueprint, and the wise king was content to oversee its execution? In this magnificent structure, no foundation or pedestal was without mystery, no column lacked symbolism, no cornice lacked allusion, no architrave was without significance. The same can be said for all its parts . . . How, without complex knowledge of the periods and divisions which constitute the study of history, is one to understand the history books . . . How, without a lot of information about both law codes, can one understand the law books? How, without great erudition, can one grasp so much of secular history mentioned in Holy Scripture— the customs of the gentiles, their rites and ways of speaking . . .

Because a great deal of physical practice is needed to acquire skill in music, for instance, the person who goes from one instrument to another, from one exercise to another, is unlikely to develop proficiency in any of them. But, the reverse is true in the formal and speculative endeavors. I would like to persuade everyone, using my own experience, that rather than obstructing progress, each of the subjects sheds light on the others, opening hidden connections through the exploration of variations. It is through this universal chain, linked by the wisdom of its Author, that correspondences and unities are revealed, with admirable connection and arrangement . . . All things come from God who is simultaneously the center and the circumference . . .

Continuing to Think

Despite her brilliant defense of a woman's right to the intellectual life, Sor Juana sold and gave away her books, spending the last years of her life in more traditional ways. Perhaps there was no "social space" for a woman of her learning and ambition in New Spain at this time. Sor Juana's response is intriguing because she seems to echo Aristotle's claim that all of us are born wanting to know. Do you agree that the desire for knowledge is an innate or inborn desire—one that cannot be thwarted without doing damage to the human spirit?

The other interesting feature of *La Respuesta* is her claim that all of knowledge is interrelated. Remember that al-Ghazali called the philosophers "incoherent" and argued that religion offered a truer and more satisfying path to knowledge. Sor Juana insists that she had to master secular learning if she wished to understand the Bible. If the lesser learning of the world paves the way for the higher truths of religion, there is no incompatibility between the two and no need to choose between them. Do you find her argument convincing or does it seem mere sophistry—only a way to defend what she is committed to doing anyway?

Living at roughly the same time as Descartes, but thousands of miles away and in a different culture, Sor Juana takes a similarly rationalist approach to the world. For her, as for Descartes, accepting what authority and faith had put into her mind without providing independent verification for them was strangely unsatisfying. Like Thomas Aquinas, she believed that theology and philosophy could work together. What do you think?

5.4   *The Guide of the Perplexed*

MOSES MAIMONIDES

Preparing to Read

Written in Spain and Egypt during a time of religious and political turmoil involving Christians, Jews, and Muslims, as well as among sects within Islam, this commentary was intended as a guide for seeking and finding religious truth. Maimonides, a twelfth-century Jewish philosopher, explores the appropriate limits of human reason. Too much knowledge, he reminds us, like too much honey, can be harmful to our health and well being.

Maybe there are times when thinking is not our best tool for approaching the world—at least not thinking in the logical, one-thought-leads-to-another way we are most familiar with. It is possible to find thinking very useful in solving the problems posed by science and mathematics but not very useful for understanding reality. Do you, for instance, find the kind of thinking just described particularly useful in responding to the emotional outburst of a lover or friend? Do you find it helpful in describing your reaction to a piece of music or a sunset?

In the arena of religious truth, Maimonides suggests that there are things we cannot understand with our reason and times we should not try to do so. Just as our vision has limits and exceeding them risks damage to the eye (watching an eclipse, for example), so Maimonides explains there are limits to our intellect. Too much of a good thing can even be harmful. Honey tastes good (you might substitute here your favorite candy), but over indulging in it can make you sick. It is the same with the intellect. Use it within its proper limits, and it will serve you well, Maimonides concludes, but do not push it beyond its capacity.

Chapter XXXI

MAN'S INTELLECT IS LIMITED

KNOW[1] THAT THE HUMAN MIND has certain objects of perception which are within the scope of its nature and capacity; on the other hand, there are, amongst things which actually exist, certain objects which the mind can in no way and by no means[2] grasp: the gates of perception are closed against it. Further, there are things of which the mind understands one part, but remains ignorant of the other,[3] and when man is able to comprehend certain things, it does not follow that he must be able to comprehend everything. This also applies to the senses: they are able to perceive things, but not at every distance; and all other powers of the body are limited in a similar way. A man can, *e.g.,* carry two kikkar,[4] but he cannot carry ten kikkar. How individuals of the same species surpass each other in these sensations and in other bodily faculties is universally known, but there is a limit to them, and they cannot extend to every distance or to every degree.

All this is applicable to the intellectual faculties of man. There is a considerable difference between one person and another as regards these faculties, as is well-known to philosophers. While one man can discover a certain thing by himself, another is never able to understand it, even if taught by means of all possible expressions and metaphors, and during a long period; his mind can in no way grasp it, his capacity is insufficient for it. This distinction is not unlimited. A boundary is undoubtedly set to the human mind which it cannot pass. There are things (beyond that boundary) which are acknowledged to be inaccessible to human understanding, and man does not show any desire to comprehend them, being aware that such knowledge is impossible, and that there are no means of overcoming the difficulty; *e.g.,* we do not know the number of stars in heaven, whether the number is even or odd;[5] the number of animals, minerals, or plants, and the like. There are other things, however, which man very much desires to know, and strenuous efforts to examine and to investigate them[6] have been made by thinkers of all classes,[7] and at all times. They differ and disagree, and constantly raise new doubts with regard to them, because their minds are bent on comprehending such things, that is to say, they are moved by desire; and every one of them believes that he has discovered the way leading to a true knowledge of the thing, although human reason is entirely unable to demonstrate the fact by convincing evidence.— For a proposition which can be proved by evidence is not subject to dispute, denial, or rejection; none but the ignorant would contradict it, and such contradiction is called "denial of a demonstrated proof."[8] Thus you find men who deny the spherical form of the earth, or the circular form of the line in which the stars move,[9] and the like; such men[10] are not considered in this treatise. This confusion prevails mostly in metaphysical subjects, less in problems relating to physics, and is entirely absent from the exact sciences. Alexander Aphrondisius[11] said that there are three causes which prevent men from discovering the exact truth: first, arrogance and vainglory; secondly, the subtlety, depth, and difficulty of any subject which is being examined; thirdly, ignorance and want of capacity to comprehend what might be comprehended. These causes are enumerated by Alexander. At the present time there is a fourth cause not mentioned by him, because it did not then prevail,[12] namely, habit and training.[13] We naturally like what we have been accustomed to, and are attracted towards it. This may be observed amongst villagers; though they rarely enjoy the benefit of a douche or bath, and have few enjoyments, and pass a life of privation,[14] they dislike town life and do not desire[15] its pleasures, preferring the bad to which they are accustomed, to the good to which they are strangers; it would give them no satisfaction to live in palaces, to be clothed in silk, and to indulge in baths, ointments, and perfumes.

The same is the case with those opinions of man to which he has been accustomed from his youth; he likes them, defends them, and shuns the opposite views. This is likewise one of the causes which prevent men[15] from finding truth, and which make them cling to their habitual opinions. Such is, *e.g.,* the case with the vulgar notions with respect to the corporeality of God, and many other metaphysical questions, as we shall explain. It is the result of long familiarity[16] with passages of the Bible,[17] which they are accustomed to respect and to receive as true, and the literal sense of which implies the corporeality of God and other false notions; in truth, however, these words were employed as figures and metaphors for reasons to be mentioned below. Do not imagine that what we have said of the insufficiency of our understanding and of its limited extent is an assertion founded only on the Bible; for philosophers likewise assert the same, and perfectly understand it, without having regard to any religion[18] or opinion. It is a fact which is only doubted by those who ignore things fully proved. This chapter is intended as an introduction to the next.

Chapter XXXII

MAN'S INTELLECT IS INJURED WHEN FORCED BEYOND ITS NATURAL LIMITS

You must consider, when reading this treatise, that mental perception, because connected with matter,[19] is subject to conditions similar to those to which physical perception is subject. That is to say, if your eye looks around, you can perceive all that is within the range of your vision; if, however, you overstrain your eye, exerting it too much by attempting to see an object which is too distant for your eye, or to examine writings or engravings too small for your sight, and forcing it to obtain a correct perception of them, you will not only weaken your sight with regard to that special object, but also for those things which you otherwise are able to perceive: your eye will have become too weak to perceive what you were able to see before you exerted yourself and exceeded the limits of your vision.

The same is the case with the speculative faculties of one who devotes himself to the study of any science.[20] If a person studies too much and exhausts his reflective powers, he will be confused, and will not be able to apprehend even that which had been within the power of his apprehension. For the powers of the body[21] are all alike in this respect.

The mental perceptions are not exempt from a similar condition. If you admit the doubt, and do not persuade[22] yourself to believe that there is a proof for things which cannot be demonstrated, or to try at once[23] to reject and positively to deny an assertion the opposite of which has never been proved, or attempt to perceive things which are beyond your perception, then you have attained the highest degree of human perfection, then you are like R. Akibha,[24] who "in peace entered [the study of these theological problems] and came out in peace." If, on the other hand, you attempt to exceed the limit of your perceptive power, or at once to reject things as impossible which have never been proved to be impossible, or which are in fact possible, though their possibility be very remote, then you will be like Elisha Acher;[25] you will not only fail to become perfect, but you will become exceedingly imperfect. Ideas founded on mere imagination will prevail over you, you will incline toward defects, and towards base and degraded habits, on account of the confusion which troubles the mind, and of the dimness of its light, just as weakness of sight[26] causes invalids to see many kinds of unreal images, especially when they have looked for a long time at dazzling or at very minute objects.

Respecting this it has been said, "Hast thou found honey? eat so much as is sufficient for thee, lest thou be filled therewith, and vomit it" (Prov. xxv. 16). Our Sages also applied this verse to Elisha Acher.[27]

How excellent is this simile! In comparing knowledge to food . . . the author of Proverbs mentions the sweetest food, namely, honey, which has the further property of irritating the stomach, and of causing sickness. He thus fully describes the nature of knowledge. Though great, excellent, noble and perfect, it is injurious if not kept within bounds or not guarded properly; it is like honey which gives nourishment and is pleasant, when eaten in moderation, but is totally thrown away when eaten immoderately. Therefore, it is not said "lest thou be filled and loathe it," but "lest thou vomit it." The same idea is expressed in the words, "It is not good to eat much honey" (Prov. xxv. 27); and in the words, "Neither make thyself over-wise; why shouldst thou destroy thyself?" (Eccl. vii. 16); Comp. "Keep thy foot when thou goest to the house of God" (*ibid*. v. 1). The same subject is alluded to in the words of David, "Neither do I exercise myself in great matters, or in things too high for me" (Ps. cxxxi. 2), and in the sayings of our Sages: "Do not inquire into things which are too difficult for thee, do not search what is hidden from thee; study what you are allowed to study, and do not occupy thyself with mysteries."[28] They meant to say, Let thy mind only attempt things which are within human perception; for the study of things which lie beyond man's comprehension[29] is extremely injurious, as has been already stated. This lesson is also contained in the Talmudical passage, which begins, "He who considers four things," etc., and concludes, "He who does not regard the honour of his Creator";[30] here also is given the advice which we have already mentioned, *viz.,* that man should not rashly engage in speculation with false conceptions, and when he is in doubt about any thing, or unable to find a proof for the object of his inquiry, he must not at once abandon, reject and deny it; he must modestly keep back, and from regard to the honour of his Creator, hesitate [from uttering an opinion] and pause. This has already been explained.

It was not the object of the Prophets and our Sages in these utterances[31] to close the gate of investigation entirely, and to prevent the mind from comprehending what is within its reach, as is imagined by simple and idle people, whom it suits better to put forth their ignorance and incapacity as wisdom and perfection, and to regard the distinction and wisdom of others as irreligion and imperfection, thus taking darkness for light and light for darkness. The whole object of the Prophets and the Sages was to declare that a limit is set to human reason where it must halt. Do not criticise the words used in this chapter and in others in reference to the mind, for we only intended to give some idea of the subject in view, not to describe the essence of the intellect;[32] for other chapters have been dedicated to this subject.

Chapter XXXIII

THE STUDY OF METAPHYSICS IS INJURIOUS TO BEGINNERS

You must know that it is very injurious to begin with this branch of philosophy, *viz.*, Metaphysics; or to explain [at first] the sense of the similes occurring in prophecies, and interpret the metaphors which are generally employed in orations and which abound in the writings of the Prophets. On the contrary, it is necessary to initiate the young and to instruct the less intelligent according to their comprehension; those who appear to be talented and to have capacity for the higher method of study, *i.e.,* that based on proof and on true logical argument, should be gradually advanced towards perfection, either by tuition or by self-instruction. He, however, who begins with Metaphysics, will not only become confused in matters of religion, but will fall into infidelity.[33] I compare such a person to an infant fed with wheaten bread, meat and wine; it will undoubtedly die, not because such food is naturally unfit for the human body, but because of the weakness of the child, who is unable to digest the food,[34] and cannot derive benefit from it. The same is the case with the true principles of science. They were presented in enigmas, clad in riddles, and taught by all wise men in the most mysterious way that could be devised, not because they contain some secret evil, or are contrary to the fundamental principles of the Law (as fools think who are only philosophers in their own eyes), but because of the incapacity of man to comprehend them at the beginning of his studies: only slight allusions have been made to them to serve for the guidance of those who are capable of understanding them. These sciences were, therefore, called Sodoth (mysteries), and Sithre Thorah (Secrets of the Law),[35] as we shall explain.

This also is the reason why "the Torah speaks the language of man," as we have explained,[36] for it is the object of the Torah to serve for the instruction of the young, of women, and of the common people; and as all of them are incapable to comprehend the true sense of the words, tradition was considered sufficient to convey all truths which were to be established; and as regards ideals, only such remarks were made as would lead towards[37] a knowledge of their existence, though not to[37] a comprehension of their true essence.[38] When a man attains to perfection, and arrives at a knowledge of the "Secrets of the Law," either through the assistance of a teacher or by self-instruction, being led by the understanding of one part to the study of the other, he will belong to those who faithfully believe in the true principles, either because of conclusive proof, where proof is possible,[39] or by forcible arguments, where argument is admissible; he will have a true notion of those things which he previously received in similes and metaphors, and he will fully understand their sense. We have frequently mentioned in this treatise the principle of our Sages "not to discuss the Maaseh Mercabhah even in the presence of one pupil, except he be wise and intelligent; and then only the headings of the chapters are to be given to him." We must, therefore, begin with teaching these subjects according to the capacity of the pupil, and on two conditions, first, that he be wise, *i.e.,* that he should have successfully gone through the preliminary studies, and secondly that he be intelligent, talented, clear-headed, and of quick perception, that is, "have a mind of his own" מכיו מדעהו, as our Sages termed it.

I will now proceed to explain the reasons why we should not instruct the multitude in pure metaphysics, or begin with describing to them the true[40] essence of things, or with showing them that a thing must be as it is, and cannot be otherwise.[41] This will form the subject of the next chapter. . . .

NOTES

1. The arrangement in ch. xxxi. to ch. xxxvi. is as follows: Man's intellect is limited (xxxi.); a transgression of the limit is not only useless, but even dangerous (xxxii.). The limit is not the same for all. The study of Metaphysics, accessible to some, is too difficult for the ordinary capacity of man, and for novices in the study of philosophy (xxxiii.). Metaphysics is not a suitable subject for general instruction (xxxiv.). The doctrine of the incorporeality of God, though part of Metaphysics, must not be treated as an esoteric doctrine (xxxv.). Belief in the Corporeality of the Divine Being is equal to idolatry (xxxvi.).

2. בונה of the original has been rendered פנים בשום by both Ibn Tibbon and Charizi; while בסבב is translated בסבה in the version of the former, and בשום סבה in that of Charizi. Munk, "D'une manière quelconque ni par une cause quelconque." Although בונה and בסבב are frequently used in the sense indicated by these translators "in some way," and "by some cause," the author would have added מא if he wished to say "in any way," or "by any cause" (בונה מא and בסבב מא). Besides, the antithesis, בונה and בסבב, leads to the suggestion that בונה is to be taken in its primary signification, "in face," *i.e.,* "straight on," "directly," as opposed to בסבב, "indirectly." In the English translation the usual rendering has been retained, the sense being the same, "neither by any method," scil., of his own, "nor by any cause from without." Shemtob explains ולא בסבה אפילו בשפע אלהי, "not by any cause, even by Divine inspiration."

3. The words וינהל האלאת, "and he is ignorant of certain properties," have no corresponding rendering in Charizi's version.

4. A weight equal to 3,000 shekels.

5. Comp. Gen. xv. 5, "And tell the stars, if thou be able to number them."

6. Munk, "Et les scruter," referring the suffix in ענהא to אשיא, "les choses;" Ibn Tibbon, ולהפישה, the suffix agreeing with אמתת. Charizi, treating the Arabic ותסלט (Ibn Tibbon והתגברות) as a finite verb, begins with

(והחקירה עליהם Ibn Tibbon) ואלבחת ענהא אמתתם , והחקירה עליהם היא מצואה. וירדוף השכל אחרי יריעת a new sentence.

7. Ibn Tibbon adds here the word אומה, "nation;" the words כת מעינת must then be considered to be in apposition to אומה and to qualify it.

8. According to the definition of Ibn Tibbon in his Glossary, "a contradiction against a proposition established by proof."

9. The spherical form of the earth and the circular motions of the stars were asserted and generally accepted by the ancients. The past tense עאנדוא implies, perhaps, that Maimonides referred rather to former generations than to his own age.

10. The pronoun והאולא, Hebrew אלה, refers to the persons who denied established truths. In Charizi's translation ואלה הדברים is undoubtedly a mistake.

11. Alexander Aphrondisius, a commentator of the works of Aristotle, flourished at the end of the second and the beginning of the third century. His writings were eagerly studied by the philosophers of the Arabic schools. Comp. Maimonides' letter to R. Samuel Ibn Tibbon, Epistle of Maimonides, Miscellany of Hebrew Literature, First Series, page 225.

12. Our training, education, and surroundings undoubtedly produce in our minds certain prepossessions, which make our researches less absolute or independent; and Alexander perhaps included shortcomings from this source in the first class of obstacles. Maimonides was anxious to expose the folly of his opponents, and, as though the three causes of opposition could not sufficiently account for their obstinacy, he finds for them a special fourth cause in the ideas and words with which their minds were imbued by the authority of the Bible taken in its literal sense. This point is repeatedly urged by Maimonides. Comp. ch. xxxv. If, however, for Bible we substitute the sacred books and traditions of each nation, every one will be found to be subject to similar errors and contradictions. According to Narboni, the four divisions correspond to the "four who entered into the garden" (see next chapter).

13. אלאלף is translated by Ibn Tibbon ההרגל, "the training;" by Charizi, ההברה, "the society." The root אלף denotes both "to be joined" and "to be accustomed."

14. Ibn Tibbon ונופם והעדר ההנאות וצוק הפרנסה ; Charizi ממיעוט רחיצת ראשם התענוגים ורע המאכלים . מן הטירוף והניזול וחסרון הטירוף appears to be a mistake of the copyist for הטינוף .

15. Palquera uses a stronger expression, ויתעוור, "he makes himself blind as regards."

16. Palquera וסתרנות (?) פסוקים התישבה הנגדלתם כל זה מפני ההרגל בהם כל זה מפני ההרגל. In a note he adds: "In the same way as man's progress in his search for truth is impeded by false ideas imbibed in his youth, so the apprehension of religious truths is difficult for those who have exclusively devoted themselves to science and have ignored the teaching of religion."

17. Ibn Tibbon כתובים, "Biblical texts;" Charizi ענינים, "subjects;" Original נצוץ, "Scriptures."

18. Ibn Tibbon, דעת, "knowledge," "opinion," "character;" Charizi דת, "religion." Arabic, מדהב, "doctrine."

19. The intellectual perceptions are here called נתלות בחומר, "attached to, or connected with matter," in so far as the mind is connected with the human body, and is, as it were, residing in it. The "ideas" of the intellect are generally considered by Maimonides as independent of the body, but he does not speak here of the intellect in the strictly philosophical sense of the word, as he distinctly states at the end of this chapter. נתלות בחומר is according to the Moreh ha-moreh opposed to טבועות בחומר, "intimately connected with matter"; the latter is applied to the five senses.

20. The words האלה פי חאל אלתפכר (Hebr. ענינו בענין מחשבה) are generally understood to be a qualification of אלנאצר (Hebr. כל מעיין); Munk translates the phrase "lorsqu'il se livre à la meditation." The purpose, however, of this qualification would not be obvious; those who study any science must necessarily think or meditate. The principal object of the author in the present chapter is to show that the solution of metaphysical problems is possible only within certain limits; he supports this assertion by examples taken from the action of man's senses, and the study of the speculative sciences. The words האלה פי חאל אלתפכר are in the objective case, governed by the verb ינד (ימצא).

According to Maimonides (the Eight Chapters), the rational faculties of man are divided into מעשיי, "practical," and עיוני, "speculative." The former class includes two kinds, מלאכת מחשבת, "artisanship," and מחשבי (Arab. פכרי) "theoretical faculty." The והמלחות היא מלאכת מחשבת is defined as follows: בו ילמד המלאכות כננרות ועבודת האדמה והרפואות הכח איש, "it is man's capacity of learning a trade, as, e.g., carpentry, husbandry, medicine, and navigation." Respecting מחשבי הכח הוא אשר איש בו, he says: אשר ירצה לעשותו אם אפשר לעשות או לא ואם לעשותו היאך צריך לעשותו יסתכל בדבר, "The capacity for theoretical science is that faculty by which man reflects on a thing he desires to do, whether it is possible or not, and if possible, how it is to be done."

21. The capacity for the study of theoretical science is called by Maimonides a faculty of the body (כח גופני), because it concerns physical objects, and is more a matter for the imagination (also a כח גופני, comp. Part II. chap. xxxvi.) than for the pure intellect.

22. Ibn Tibbon ולא תונה, "and you will not deceive." Charizi ואל תשיא, "and do not mislead."

23. The phrase ולא תתחיל לדחות, lit. "do not begin to reject," in the translation of Ibn Tibbon has the meaning "Do not reject at once, in the beginning of thy research."

24. R. Akibha was one of the four scholars, of whom it is related in the Babyl. Talmud (Chagigah 14b), also in Jerus, Talmud (*ibid.,* ch. ii.), that they ventured into the garden of speculative philosophy, and met with different fates, *viz.,* "Ben Azai gazed and was killed; Ben Zoma gazed and was hurt; Acher cut down the young plants; R. Akibbah went in and came out unhurt." See Grätz, Gnosticismus, 56 and 95.

25. Elisha was probably called אחר from the fact that he was no longer the same Elisha as before (Comp. 1 Sam. x. 6, "and shall be turned into another man," איש אחר); his opinions were quoted as authoritative; but this was probably only the case with such decisions as were expressed by him before he seceded from his former colleagues.

26. Both Hebrew versions render אלרוח אלבאצר "the spirit of sight" ("l'esprit visuel," M.), according to the sense, by כח הראות, but some MSS., and the editio princeps of Ibn Tibbon's version, have הרוח הראות (Munk). *Spiritus visionis* is the term used by Scholastics for "sight."

27. This verse is applied in the Babylonian Talmud to Ben Zoma, in the Jerusalem Talmud to Ben Azai, in Midrash Yalkut (*ad locum,* Prov. xxv.) to both of them; to Acher the following verse is applied: "Suffer not thy mouth to cause thy flesh to sin" (Eccl. v. 6).

28. The Arabic MSS. have בנפלאות התבונן and instead of דרוש and בנסתרות, as in the editions of the Babyl. Talmud (Chagigah 13a, cited from the book of Ben Sira, iii. 18).

29. Charizi adds מפני חולשת השכל, "because of the weakness of the intellect."

30. The whole passage referred to runs as follows: מה למטה מה לפנים מה לאחור כל המסתכל בד' דברים ראוי לו כאלו לא בא לעולם מה למעלה "He who reflects on four things, *viz.,* what is above, what is below, what is in front, what is behind, should better not have seen the light of the world" (Mishnah, Chagigah ii. 1).

31. Arab. אלנצוץ, "sentences;" Ibn Tibbon, הכתובים; Charizi, והדברים הכתובים, referring the one

term to "Prophets," the other to "Sages," mentioned before. Comp. ch. xxxi., p. 109, note 5.

32. See p. 110, note 2.

33. The original תעטיל מחין Ibn Tibbon renders בטול לגמרי, Charizi מינות אמיתית; both mean the same thing—the entire rejection of the authority of the Bible. Munk translates תעטיל "irreligion."

34. Charizi has here the additional explanatory phrase, לטחון אותם כי לא יוכל הגוף, "The body is not able to grind them."

35. סודות וסתרי תורה (comp. Ps. xxv. 14, ליראיו סוד יי), "secrets and hidden portions of the Law," that is, instruction contained in Scripture, but not for him who only reads it superficially.

36. See p. 90, note 1.

37. In the Arabic text two different prepositions are used to express the direction, נחו and עלי, "towards," "to." In the Hebrew this variation has been imitated by Ibn Tibbon who renders the two prepositions by אל and על. Some MSS., however, have in both places אל (Comp. Munk, page 416, note 4).

38. The suffix in ונגדה (Hebr. מציאותו) and מאהיתה (Hebr. מהותו) does not refer to "God," as has been assumed by most Commentators, but to תצור (Hebr.

(ציור), "ideal." The preposition עלי in the Arabic text before מה יסדר (Hebr. מה שייישיר), is co-ordinate, with the same preposition before אלתקליד (Hebr. הקבלה), both the prepositions being governed by the verb אקתצר, the Hebrew equivalent for which, הספיקה, being a personal verb, does not require any preposition. Charizi appears to have misunderstood the passage, and translates it inaccurately as follows:—

הקבלה בכל סברא אמיתית אשר יבקשו להצדיקה ובכל הרעיון על מציאות הבורא לא להשיג היה לו די מהם אמתת מהותו מחשבה וציור השכל כמו שיורה.

39. Charizi omits the words שאפישר בו מופת במה, "where proof is possible."

40. The pronoun in עליה—the Hebrew equivalent of which, עליו, is frequently omitted in the Hebrew versions—agrees with the relative מא (Hebr. מה), lit., "in that (manner) in which it is," *i.e.*, "truly" or "fully." כפי מה שהוא עליו (Char. על פי) is equal to כפי זה אישר עליו הוא.

41. The words אלא אם כן אביאהו in the version of Tibbon are not to be joined together; כן is the end of a sentence, and אביאהו begins a new one. אלא אם has perhaps the same meaning as the Biblical כי אם.— Charizi translates thus שיתבאר בפרק הבא אחר כן ומוכרח להיות כן כמו.

Continuing to Think

If you were raised in Europe or North America, chances are good that you will resist any suggestion that you limit your intellect. As heirs to the Enlightenment, we have been told in countless ways that thinking is our birthright and the route to solving all our personal and societal problems. Only in the last hundred or so years have we begun to question the unlimited potential of human thought.

As we look over our recent history and discover that some of us have found intellectual justification for holding others in slavery and that wars of destruction have been, and continue to be, intellectually defensible, we must at least ask ourselves whether there are limits to the ability of reason to guide our actions. Maimonides seems to be urging us to accept the fact that there are things beyond our ability to think—things we must accept on faith—and this may include how to live our lives well.

Metaphysics, the philosophical investigation into the nature of reality, is, he says, particularly dangerous for beginners. Just as we would not feed infants meat and wine, it might be wise to withhold metaphysics from those unable to digest it. Plato put forth a similar idea in the *Republic*. Only after reaching the age of thirty would candidates for the role of philosopher king be permitted to study philosophy. Before that time they might be expected to miss its value or to use it unworthily (as a bag of logical tricks rather than as a guide to the truth).

Would we all be better off, and would conflict between us be minimized, if all of us adopted a more humble attitude and allowed ourselves to be guided in certain matters by religious leaders and scholars? Is "a little learning," as the poet Alexander Pope put it, "a dangerous thing"? Should we be protected against glutting ourselves intellectually?

5.5   *Beyond Consciousness*

SHUNRYU SUZUKI

Preparing to Read

An even more radical proposal regarding human thinking comes from Zen Buddhism. There is nothing to do, nothing to understand—the goal is to see what actually is, to become enlightened and have no need to be reborn. As we saw in Chapter 1, thinking cannot get us there. Thoughts lead to other thoughts and keep us awake at night, but they bring us no closer to what is—that can only be experienced. It cannot be taught and it cannot be thought.

The fact is that everything is interconnected, and change is the nature of what is. If you grasp this, you will have learned what this life has to teach and will not have to repeat the process. The interesting thing is that there is no distance between where you are and where you want to be. You are already, at some level, enlightened. It is simply a matter of waking up to what is, and the best way of doing this is by having "beginner's mind." The first time you drove a car you paid attention to everything—you had to—but now most of that experience is automatic. Zen Buddhists think we live much of our lives on automatic pilot, and "beginner's mind" can put us back in contact with what is.

Practice, in Zen Buddhism, is both a route to enlightenment and an end in itself. And practice begins with **sitting** meditation. Our true nature already exists "beyond consciousness," and cultivating a clear and empty mind is a way of helping us recognize it. Zen Master Dogen advocated establishing the practice of sitting meditation, or zazen, in the midst of delusion because zazen offers the "pure, genuine experience of the empty state of mind."

Learning how to rest mentally is the fastest way to banish delusion. The best way to understand Buddhism, Suzuki says, is not to study it but to begin sitting in meditation every day. Thinking, or we might say the "idea of self and object," is not the way to seek enlightenment.

Beyond Consciousness

To realize pure mind in your delusion is practice. If you try to expel the delusion it will only persist the more. Just say, "Oh, this is just delusion," and do not be bothered by it.

WE SHOULD ESTABLISH our practice where there is no practice or enlightenment. As long as we practice zazen in the area where there is practice and enlightenment, there is no chance to make perfect peace for ourselves. In other words, we must firmly believe in our true nature. Our true nature is beyond our conscious experience. It is only in our conscious experience that we find practice and enlightenment or good and bad. But whether or not we have experience of our true nature, what exists there, beyond consciousness, actually exists, and it is there that we have to establish the foundation of our practice.

Even to have a good thing in your mind is not so good. Buddha sometimes said, "You should be like this. You ought not to be like that." But to have what he says in your mind is not so good. It is a kind of burden for you, and you may not actually feel so good. In fact to harbor some ill will may even be better than to have some idea in your mind of what is good or of what you ought to do. To have some mischievous idea in your mind is sometimes very agreeable. That is true. Actually, good and bad is not the point. Whether or not you make yourself peaceful is the point, and whether or not you stick to it.

When you have something in your consciousness you do not have perfect composure. The best way towards perfect composure is to forget everything. Then your mind is calm, and it is wide and clear enough to see and feel things as they are without any effort. The best way to find perfect composure is not to retain any idea of things, whatever they may be—to forget all about them and not to leave any trace or shadow of thinking. But if you try to stop your mind or try to go beyond your conscious activity, that will only

be another burden for you. "I have to stop my mind in my practice, but I cannot. My practice is not so good." This kind of idea is also the wrong way of practice. Do not try to stop your mind, but leave everything as it is. Then things will not stay in your mind so long. Things will come as they come and go as they go. Then eventually your clear, empty mind will last fairly long.

So to have a firm conviction in the original emptiness of your mind is the most important thing in your practice. In Buddhist scriptures we sometimes use vast analogies in an attempt to describe empty mind. Sometimes we use an astronomically great number, so great it is beyond counting. This means to give up calculating. If it is so great that you cannot count it, then you will lose your interest and eventually give up. This kind of description may also give rise to a kind of interest in the innumerable number, which will help you to stop the thinking of your small mind.

But it is when you sit in zazen that you will have the most pure, genuine experience of the empty state of mind. Actually, emptiness of mind is not even a state of mind, but the original essence of mind which Buddha and the Sixth Patriarch experienced. "Essence of mind," "original mind," "original face," "Buddha nature," "emptiness"—all these words mean the absolute calmness of our mind.

You know how to rest physically. You do not know how to rest mentally. Even though you lie in your bed your mind is still busy; even if you sleep your mind is busy dreaming. Your mind is always in intense activity. This is not so good. We should know how to give up our thinking mind, our busy mind. In order to go beyond our thinking faculty, it is necessary to have a firm conviction in the emptiness of your mind. Believing firmly in the perfect rest of our mind, we should resume our pure original state.

Dogen-zenji said, "You should establish your practice in your delusion." Even though you think you are in delusion, your pure mind is there. To

From *Zen Mind, Beginner's Mind* by Shunryu Suzuki. Courtesy of Weatherhill.

realize pure mind in your delusion is practice. If you have pure mind, essential mind in your delusion, the delusion will vanish. It cannot stay when you say, "This is delusion!" It will be very much ashamed. It will run away. So you should establish your practice in your delusion. To have delusion is practice. This is to attain enlightenment before you realize it. Even though you do not realize it, you have it. So when you say, "This is delusion," that is actually enlightenment itself. If you try to expel the delusion it will only persist the more, and your mind will become busier and busier trying to cope with it. That is not so good. Just say, "Oh, this is just delusion," and do not be bothered by it. When you just observe the delusion, you have your true mind, your calm, peaceful mind. When you start to cope with it you will be involved in delusion.

So whether or not you attain enlightenment, just to sit in zazen is enough. When you try to attain enlightenment, then you have a big burden on your mind. Your mind will not be clear enough to see things as they are. If you truly see things as they are, then you will see things as they should be. On the one hand, we should attain enlightenment—that is how things should be. But on the other hand, as long as we are physical beings, in reality it is pretty hard to attain enlightenment—that is how things actually are in this moment. But if we start to sit, both sides of our nature will be brought up, and we will see things both as they are and as they should be. Because we are not good right now, we want to be better, but when we attain the transcendental mind, we go beyond things as they are and as they should be. In the emptiness of our original mind they are one, and there we find our perfect composure.

Usually religion develops itself in the realm of consciousness, seeking to perfect its organization, building beautiful buildings, creating music, evolving a philosophy, and so forth. These are religious activities in the conscious world. But Buddhism emphasizes the world of unconsciousness. The best way to develop Buddhism is to sit in zazen—just to sit, with a firm conviction in our true nature. This way is much better than to read books or study the philosophy of Buddhism. Of course it is necessary to study the philosophy—it will strengthen your conviction. Buddhist philosophy is so universal and logical that it is not just the philosophy of Buddhism, but of life itself. The purpose of Buddhist teaching is to point to life itself existing beyond consciousness in our pure original mind. All Buddhist practices were built up to protect this true teaching, not to propagate Buddhism in some wonderful mystic way. So when we discuss religion, it should be in the most common and universal way. We should not try to propagate our way by wonderful philosophical thought. In some ways Buddhism is rather polemical, with some feeling of controversy in it, because the Buddhist must protect his way from mystic or magical interpretations of religion. But philosophical discussion will not be the best way to understand Buddhism. If you want to be a sincere Buddhist, the best way is to sit. We are very fortunate to have a place to sit in this way. I want you to have a firm, wide, imperturbable conviction in your zazen of just sitting. Just to sit, that is enough. . . .

Epilogue

ZEN MIND

Before the rain stops we can hear a bird. Even under the heavy snow we see snowdrops and some new growth.

Here in America we cannot define Zen Buddhists the same way we do in Japan. American students are not priests and yet not completely laymen. I understand it this way: that you are not priests is an easy matter, but that you are not exactly laymen is more difficult. I think you are special people and want some special practice that is not exactly priest's practice and not exactly laymen's practice. You are on your way to discovering some appropriate way of life. I think that is our Zen community, our group.

But we must also know what our undivided original way is and what Dogen's practice is. Dogen-zenji said that some may attain enlightenment and some may not. This is a point I am very much interested in. Although we all have the same fundamental practice which we carry out in the same way, some may attain enlightenment and some may not. It means that even if we have no experience of enlightenment, if we sit in the proper way with the right attitude and understanding of practice, then that is Zen. The main point is to practice seriously, and the important attitude is to understand and have confidence in big mind.

We say "big mind," or "small mind," or "Buddha mind," or "Zen mind," and these words mean something, you know, but something we cannot and should not try to understand in terms of experience. We talk about enlightenment experience, but it is not some experience we will have in terms of good or bad, time or space, past or future. It is experience or consciousness beyond those distinctions or feelings. So we should not ask, "What is enlightenment experience?" That kind of question means you do not know what Zen experience is. Enlightenment cannot be asked for in your ordinary way of thinking. When you are not involved in this way of thinking, you have some chance of understanding what Zen experience is.

The big mind in which we must have confidence is not something which you can experience objectively. It is something which is always with you, always on your side. Your eyes are on your side, for you cannot see your eyes, and your eyes cannot see themselves. Eyes only see things outside, objective things. If you reflect on yourself, that self is not your true self any more. You cannot project yourself as some objective thing to think about. The mind which is always on your side is not just your mind, it is universal mind, always the same, not different from another's mind. It is Zen mind. It is big, big mind. This mind is whatever you see. Your true mind is always with whatever you see. Although you do not know your own mind, it is there—at the

very moment you see something, it is there. This is very interesting. Your mind is always with the things you observe. So you see, this mind is at the same time everything.

True mind is watching mind. You cannot say, "This is my self, my small mind, or my limited mind, and that is big mind." That is limiting yourself, restricting your true mind, objectifying your mind. Bodhidharma said, "In order to see a fish you must watch the water." Actually when you see water you see the true fish. Before you see Buddha nature you watch your mind. When you see the water there is true nature. True nature is watching water. When you say, "My zazen is very poor," here you have true nature, but foolishly you do not realize it. You ignore it on purpose. There is immense importance in the "I" with which you watch your mind. That I is not the "big I"; it is the "I" which is incessantly active, always swimming, always flying through the vast air with wings. By wings I mean thought and activity. The vast sky is home, my home. There is no bird or air. When the fish swims, water and fish are the fish. There is nothing but fish. Do you understand? You cannot find Buddha nature by vivisection. Reality cannot be caught by thinking or feeling mind. Moment after moment to watch your breathing, to watch your posture, is true nature. There is no secret beyond this point.

We Buddhists do not have any idea of material only, or mind only, or the products of our mind, or mind as an attribute of being. What we are always talking about is that mind and body, mind and material are always one. But if you listen carelessly it sounds as if we are talking about some attribute of being, or about "material" or "spiritual." That will be a version of it, maybe. But actually we are pointing out mind which is always on this side, which is true mind. Enlightenment experience is to figure out, to understand, to realize this mind which is always with us and which we cannot see. Do you understand? If you try to attain enlightenment as if you see a bright star in the sky, it will be beautiful and you may think, "Ah, this is enlightenment," but that is not enlightenment. That understanding is literally heresy. Even though you do not know it, in that understanding you have the idea of material only. Dozens of your enlightenment experiences are like that—some material only, some object of your mind, as if through good practice you found that bright star. That is the idea of self and object. It is not the way to seek for enlightenment.

The Zen school is based on our actual nature, on our true mind as expressed and realized in practice. Zen does not depend on a particular teaching nor does it substitute teaching for practice. We practice zazen to express our true nature, not to attain enlightenment. Bodhidharma's Buddhism is to *be* practice, to *be* enlightenment. At first this may be a kind of belief, but later it is something the student feels or already has. Physical practice and rules are not so easy to understand, maybe especially for Americans. You have an idea of freedom which concentrates on physical freedom, on freedom of activity. This idea causes you some mental suffering and loss of freedom. You think you want to limit your thinking, you think some of your thinking is unnecessary or painful or entangling; but you do not think you want to limit your physical activity. For this reason Hyakujo established the rules and way of Zen life in China. He was interested in expressing and transmitting the freedom of true mind. Zen mind is transmitted in our Zen way of life based on Hyakujo's rules.

I think we naturally need some way of life as a group and as Zen students in America, and as Hyakujo established our way of monastic life in China, I think we must establish an American way of Zen life. I am not saying this jokingly, I am pretty serious. But I do not want to be too serious. If we become too serious we will lose our way. If we are playing games we will lose our way. Little by little with patience and endurance we must find the way for ourselves, find out how to live with ourselves and with each other. In this way we will find out our precepts. If we practice hard, concentrate on zazen, and organize our life so that we can sit well, we

will find out what we are doing. But you have to be careful in the rules and way you establish. If it is too strict you will fail, if it is too loose, the rules will not work. Our way should be strict enough to have authority, an authority everyone should obey. The rules should be possible to observe. This is how Zen tradition was built up, decided little by little, created by us in our practice. We cannot force anything. But once the rules have been decided, we should obey them completely until they are changed. It is not a matter of good or bad, convenient or inconvenient. You just do it without question. That way your mind is free. The important thing is to obey your rules without discrimination. This way you will know the pure Zen mind. To have our own way of life means to encourage people to have a more spiritual and adequate way of life as human beings. And I think one day you will have your own practice in America.

The only way to study pure mind is through practice. Our inmost nature wants some medium, some way to express and realize itself. We answer this inmost request through our rules, and Patriarch after Patriarch shows us his true mind. In this way we will have an accurate, deep understanding of practice. We must have more experience of our practice. At least we must have *some* enlightenment experience. You must put confidence in the big mind which is always with you. You should be able to appreciate things as an expression of big mind. This is more than faith. This is ultimate truth which you cannot reject. Whether it is difficult or easy to practice, difficult or easy to understand, you can only practice it. Priest or layman is not the point. To find yourself as someone who is doing something is the point—to resume your actual being through practice, to resume the you which is always with everything, with Buddha, which is fully supported by everything. Right now! You may say it is impossible. But it is possible! Even in one moment you can do it! It is possible this moment! It is this moment! That you can do it in this moment means you can always do it. So if you have this confidence, this is your enlightenment experience. If you have this strong confidence in your big mind, you are already a Buddhist in the true sense, even though you do not attain enlightenment.

That is why Dogen-zenji said, "Do not expect that all who practice zazen will attain enlightenment about this mind which is always with us." He meant if you think that big mind is somewhere outside yourself, outside of your practice, then that is a mistake. Big mind is always with us. That is why I repeat the same thing over and over when I think you do not understand. Zen is not just for the man who can fold his legs or who has great spiritual ability. Everyone has Buddha nature. We each must find some way to realize our true nature. The purpose of practice is to have direct experience of the Buddha nature which everyone has. Whatever you do should be the direct experience of Buddha nature. Buddha nature means to be aware of Buddha nature. Your effort should extend to saving all sentient beings. If my words are not good enough, I'll hit you! Then you will understand what I mean. And if you do not understand me just now, some day you will. Some day someone will understand. I will wait for the island I was told is moving slowly up the coast from Los Angeles to Seattle.

I feel Americans, especially young Americans, have a great opportunity to find out the true way of life for human beings. You are quite free from material things and you begin Zen practice with a very pure mind, a beginner's mind. You can understand Buddha's teaching exactly as he meant it. But we must not be attached to America, or Buddhism, or even to our practice. We must have beginner's mind, free from possessing anything, a mind that knows everything is in flowing change. Nothing exists but momentarily in its present form and color. One thing flows into another and cannot be grasped. Before the rain stops we hear a bird. Even under the heavy snow we see snowdrops and some new growth. In the East I saw rhubarb already. In Japan in the spring we eat cucumbers.

Continuing to Think

The "big mind" or "beginner's mind" that Zen advocates cannot be experienced objectively. You cannot think about your true self by projecting it as some objective thing. Zen mind is always with the thing you observe so it is, at the same time, everything.

This is the knowing that matters, the waking up to our true nature that is the meaning of enlightenment. If we realize that all is interconnected, we have realized our true nature. For this reason, thinking will not be the way to go. Thinking immediately puts us in the world of "this" and "that," of "me" and "other," of "subject" and "object," but these are false distinctions that cannot lead to an apprehension of what is.

It may be helpful to think about how you "know" someone you love. You probably don't think that knowing can best be compared with the kind of knowing needed to know geometry. Of course, you know the person's age, address, height, and weight—but these are hardly the most important things. What you may value most is knowing who they really are, something thought is not likely to reveal. And your knowing comes from direct experience. Just as you would not expect to get to know a person by studying their likes and dislikes from a computer printout, you should not expect to grasp what is by thinking about it.

All of this seems very paradoxical to people whose minds go automatically to the subject/object split. To appreciate what Zen has to offer requires setting all this aside.

If you are trying to meditate and thoughts intrude, the best advice is not to fight them and demand their exit but just to notice them slipping in and allowing them to slip out again. Don't think. Just sit.

Summing Up the Readings

As we observed at the beginning of this chapter, *how* we think we know is intimately connected with *what* we think we know. If we think knowing is a matter of applying logic and deduction, we will need to objectify what we want to know. The same is true if we take the senses as our starting point and subject knowledge to the experience test. On the other hand, if we seek religious truth or the enlightenment that Zen speaks about, other forms of knowing seem more appropriate.

Our metaphysics (What is real?) will necessarily be linked with our epistemology (How do we know?). Descartes offers an interesting contrast with Jaggar, Maimonides, and Suzuki. All of these thinkers are passionately concerned about knowing, but what they seek to know and how they seek to know it differ considerably. It might be valuable to make a list of what you most want to know and then decide the best method for knowing each of those things. Very likely you will decide that not everything is knowable using only one method. What we might all agree on is Sor Juana's echo of Aristotle's assertion that the desire for knowledge seems hardwired into our human brains.

To fish the world is water. As we look at the fish in the water, we know that the fish has a limited perspective since we believe the world is more than just water. One of the most helpful things philosophy can do, as Alison Jaggar points out, is to give us that perspective. As we look at what we have always taken for granted, realizing that other people do not share our assumptions, our own feelings are often clarified. Although we may come away believing exactly what we believed at the start, the experience of a broader perspective is intrinsically worthwhile. Like a trip to another country (or even another city), mental travel makes us appreciate both what we find in the new place and what we have left behind in the old. When we return, we ourselves are changed.

Continuing to Question

1. Is there anything in your mind that is not there because one authority or another (parents, friends, teachers, books, religion) put it there? What if some or all of these authorities are mistaken? How can you be as sure as Descartes wanted to be about what you know?

2. How can we identify the hidden assumptions that underlie our emotions? Start listening to jokes as a way of tuning in to judgments being made abut individuals and groups in our society. This can turn refusing to laugh at a joke into a subversive activity.

3. What happens when we deny someone access to knowledge and the intellectual life? Is this sometimes in their best interest, as Maimonides might suggest, or does it damage the human spirit, as Sor Juana contended?

4. Have you ever felt you knew more than you wanted to know or more than was good for you to know about something? Maimonides identifies something most of us can relate to, but what dangers can you identify in limiting what we know and trusting someone else to decide how much is enough?

5. What you gain by moving most of the operations involved in driving a car to the automatic level is the freedom to think about other things while you drive. What do you lose by going through life on automatic pilot—eating food without tasting it, having conversations in which you are mentally somewhere else—and how can adopting "beginner's mind" help?

Suggestions for Further Exploration

FICTION

Andrews, Lynn, *Medicine Woman*—New York: Harper & Row, 1987. Like Castaneda (below), Andrews has written a visionary autobiography that is not technically fiction. Also, like Castaneda, Andrews has learned a new way of knowing through her contacts with a shaman known as Agnes Whistling Elk.

Carroll, Lewis, *Alice in Wonderland*—New York: Penguin, 1992. What would happen if everything you thought you knew no longer worked? This is Alice's experience when she falls down the rabbit hole into Wonderland and has to learn a whole new way of knowing the world.

Castaneda, Carlos, *The Teachings of Don Juan*—New York: Simon & Schuster, 1973. This is actually not fiction, but it reads like fiction. Castaneda, an anthropology student, met a Yaqui Indian named Don Juan and, through him, learned a new way of knowing.

Voltaire, *Candide*—New York: Random House, 1975. In this story, Voltaire satirizes Leibniz's characterization of this world as the "best of all possible worlds." Dr. Pangloss is Leibniz.

NONFICTION PRIMARY SOURCE MATERIAL

Descartes, René, *Discourse on Method* and *Meditations*—trans. Laurence J. LaFleur. Indianapolis: Bobbs-Merrill, 1960. Often published together, these two short works reveal Descartes's key concepts and methods as discussed in this chapter.

Jaggar, Alison M., and **Susan R. Bordo,** eds., *Gender/Body/Knowledge*—New Brunswick, N.J.: Rutgers University Press, 1989. This book of essays by feminist philosophers explores challenges to Descartes's epistemological assumptions and the dualisms that frequently accompany them: culture versus nature, mind versus body, reason versus emotion.

Kant, Immanuel, *Prolegomena to Any Future Metaphysics*—trans. Peter G. Lucas. Manchester, England: University of Manchester Press, 1953. Most of Kant's works are long and difficult to understand; this slim volume is the exception. As a kind of abstract of the *Critique of Pure Reason,* it traces Kant's chief epistemological argument in a readable format.

Keller, Evelyn Fox, and **Helen E. Longino,** eds., *Feminism and Science*—New York: Oxford University Press, 1996. Are the sciences neutral with respect to social issues and social values? This collection of essays, representing a variety of academic disciplines, challenges traditional conceptions of the relationship between knowing subject and known object and offers philosophical considerations of issues of knowledge and objectivity.

Merton, Thomas, trans., *The Way of Chuang-tzu*—New York: New Directions, 1965. Believed to be the disciple of Lao-tzu to whom the *Tao Te Ching* is attributed, Chuang-tzu, in Merton's playful translation, further explains Taoist ways of knowing.

Mitchell, Stephen, trans., *Tao Te Ching*—New York: HarperCollins, 1988. Mitchell gives a poetic translation of this Taoist classic, sometimes using *he* and sometimes *she* to describe the Master. A good introduction to the Tao and the way of knowing associated with it.

Reps, Paul, ed., *Zen Flesh, Zen Bones*—rev. ed. New York: Doubleday, 1989. A wonderful collection of Zen and pre-Zen writings, most of which are stories less than a page long. These stories provide an introduction to an Eastern way of knowing.

6   The Search for Truth

Defining the Issue

One of the key questions in philosophy and in life is: How do we test for truth? Philosophers begin with warrantability, and they mean the same thing the police mean when they obtain a warrant—that there is evidence or justification (for searching your house or for making a truth claim). Unfortunately, there is no one-to-one correspondence between warrantability and truth. A thousand years ago people had an empirical **warrant** (sense experience) for a stationary earth and a moving sun; today we assert a rotating earth, using a systemic warrant (based on the mathematics of Copernicus). You may have the highest I.Q. or the best singing voice in your college, but you probably do not have a warrant to that effect.

There are other ways to test for truth, and we will look at several of them in this chapter. Many philosophers have insisted on a rigid adherence to the laws of reason and logic or strong empirical evidence connecting a truth claim with the world of sense experience—or both. This appears to be pretty safe ground, but it is not without its problems. In fact, all truth claims can be made to seem flawed in one way or another by those who find them inadequate.

As we saw in the last chapter, what we seek to know may determine our approach. The three basic approaches in the search for truth are: (1) deduction—inference in which a conclusion follows necessarily from one or more premises, (2) induction—a general assertion drawn from a number of observed particulars, and (3) intuition—direct and immediate apprehension by a knowing subject of itself, an external world, or rational truths. In the following readings, all of these will be defended and attacked.

Previewing the Readings

We begin with David Hume, the most radical of the **empiricist** philosophers. He insists that all our ideas have their basis in direct sense experience; any truth claim must take this into account as well as follow the rules of logic or deduction. In our first selection he attacks teleological arguments for the existence of God, such as the ones we studied in Chapter 4. Robert Pirsig's novel *Zen and the Art of Motorcycle Maintenance* explores the basic problem of induction—the primary method of science. If the number of hypotheses expands faster than science can test and eliminate them, truth claims can never be adequately supported and the goal of scientific knowledge can never be achieved.

Equally disturbing is N. Scott Momaday's observation that Indian and white ways of seeing the world are not the same. Beginning with different basic assumptions about time and history, these two groups have attempted to speak the truth to one another, with more failure than success. Could part of the problem be these radically different, unacknowledged paradigms?

S. A. Mwanahewa observes that while most of the world's people are illiterate, this does not mean they have no way to test for truth. In an essay that illustrates both induction and intuition, he recommends combining *orature,* or oral literature, with logic. The structure of language tests for and conveys truth through proverbs, riddles, sayings, and songs as well as art motifs in traditional African culture. There is logic in orature, and there should be an intuitive or artistic element in logic that includes emotion and cultural heritage.

Finally, Hildegard of Bingen, a twelfth-century mystic, asserts truth claims using God as their guarantor. Because of her lifelong "gift of vision," she has an intuitive certainty about knowing the truth from God.

As you read these selections, observe which of the truth tests seems most compelling to you and which seem deficient in some way. The readings in this chapter explore truth claims in natural theology, science, history, art motifs/proverbs, and **mystical experience.** From the world of a medieval German abbess Hildegard of Bingen to the fictional and modern character Phaedrus in *Zen and the Art of Motorcycle Maintenance,* from the eighteenth-century Scotsman David Hume to the Kiowa tradition and African orature, it seems that people in all times and places want to know what is true and how to decide.

6.1   ## *Dialogues Concerning Natural Religion*

DAVID HUME

Preparing to Read

For many religious people, the order and purpose in the world seem to argue intuitively and lead deductively to a world maker. Known as the argument from design, or the teleological argument, it is a mainstay among proofs for the existence of God. In our first selection, we see this argument attacked by Philo (who speaks Hume's ideas), using inductive and deductive weapons.

The other two participants in this dialogue are Demea, a supporter of rationalism or deductive reasoning, and Cleanthes, representing inductive reasoning (based on empirical evidence), used to arrive at philosophical theism (belief in God). Theists sometimes assert that there are enough facts present in the world to warrant the truth claim that God exists. In the case of the design argument, it is the intricacy and complexity with which world systems work that seems to argue for a system builder in the same way that the existence of a watch suggests a watchmaker.

Hume, through his mouthpiece Philo, takes on this argument and, using its evidence, shows how different conclusions might be reached. This has the effect of rendering the argument unsatisfactory. As you read this selection, notice how the original argument is stated and how Philo moves to destroy it on its own terms.

Many who believe in God do not do so on the basis of rationalist arguments, of course. Instead, they rely on intuitive evidence or strongly felt personal experience. Some people insist that we humans are really unable to determine whether or not there is a God; **agnosticism** is the philosophical position that the existence or nonexistence of God simply cannot be known. A related question to ask here is whether deductive reasoning is the best method for investigating the existence or nonexistence of a creator.

Part IV

It seems strange to me, said Cleanthes, that you, Demea, who are so sincere in the cause of religion, should still maintain the mysterious, incomprehensible nature of the Deity, and should insist so strenuously that he has no manner of likeness or resemblance to human creatures. The Deity, I can readily allow, possesses many powers and attributes of which we can have no comprehension; but, if our ideas, so far as they go, be not just and adequate and correspondent to his real nature, I know not what there is in this subject worth insisting on. Is the name, without any meaning, of such mighty importance? Or how do you mystics, who maintain the absolute incomprehensibility of the Deity, differ from sceptics or atheists, who assert that the first cause of all is unknown and unintelligible? Their temerity must be very great if, after rejecting the production by a mind—I mean a mind resembling the human (for I know of no other)—they pretend to assign, with certainty, any other specific intelligible cause; and their conscience must be very scrupulous, indeed, if they refuse to call the universal unknown cause a God or Deity, and to bestow on him as many sublime eulogies and unmeaning epithets as you shall please to require of them.

Who could imagine, replied Demea, that Cleanthes, the calm philosophical Cleanthes, would attempt to refute his antagonists by affixing a nickname to them, and, like the common bigots and inquisitors of the age, have recourse to invective and declamation instead of reasoning? Or does he not perceive that these topics are easily retorted, and that *anthropomorphite* is an appellation as invidious, and implies as dangerous consequences, as the epithet of *mystic* with which he has honoured us? In reality, Cleanthes, consider what it is you assert when you represent the Deity as similar to a human mind and understanding. What is the soul of man? A composition of various faculties, passions, sentiments, ideas—united, indeed, into one self or person, but still distinct from each other. When it reasons, the ideas which are the parts of its discourse arrange themselves in a certain form or order which is not preserved entire for a moment, but immediately gives place to another arrangement. New opinions, new passions, new affections, new feelings arise which continually diversify the mental scene and produce in it the greatest variety and most rapid succession imaginable. How is this compatible with that perfect immutability and simplicity which all true theists ascribe to the Deity? By the same act, say they, he sees past, present, and future; his love and hatred, his mercy and justice, are one individual operation; he is entire in every point of space, and complete in every instant of duration. No succession, no change, no acquisition, no diminution. What he is implies not in it any shadow of distinction or diversity. And what he is this moment he ever has been and ever will be, without any new judgment, sentiment, or operation. He stands fixed in one simple, perfect state; nor can you ever say, with any propriety, that this act of his is different from that other, or that this judgment or idea has been lately formed and will give place, by succession, to any different judgment or idea.

I can readily allow, said Cleanthes, that those who maintain the perfect simplicity of the Supreme Being, to the extent in which you have explained it, are complete mystics, and chargeable with all the consequences which I have drawn from their opinion. They are, in a word, atheists, without knowing it. For though it be allowed that the Deity possesses attributes of which we have no comprehension, yet ought we never to ascribe to him any attributes which are absolutely incompatible with that intelligent nature essential to him. A mind whose acts and sentiments and ideas are not distinct and successive, one that is wholly simple and totally immutable, is a mind which has no thought, no reason, no will, no sentiment, no love, no hatred; or, in a word, is no mind at all. It is an abuse of terms to give it that appellation, and we may as well speak of limited extension without figure, or of number without composition.

Pray consider, said Philo, whom you are at present inveighing against. You are honouring with the appellation of *atheist* all the sound, orthodox divines, almost, who have treated of this subject; and you will at last be, yourself, found, according to your reckoning, the only sound theist in the world. But if idolaters be atheists, as, I think, may justly be asserted, and Christian theologians the same, what becomes of the argument, so much celebrated, derived from the universal consent of mankind?

But, because I know you are not much swayed by names and authorities, I shall endeavour to show you, a little more distinctly, the inconveniences of that anthropomorphism which you have embraced, and shall prove that there is no ground to suppose a plan of the world to be formed in the Divine mind, consisting of distinct ideas, differently arranged, in the same manner as an architect forms in his head the plan of a house which he intends to execute.

It is not easy, I own, to see what is gained by this supposition, whether we judge of the matter by *reason* or by *experience*. We are still obliged to mount higher in order to find the cause of this cause which you had assigned as satisfactory and conclusive.

If *reason* (I mean abstract reason derived from inquiries *a priori*) be not alike mute with regard to all questions concerning cause and effect, this sentence at least it will venture to pronounce: that a mental world or universe of ideas requires a cause as much as does a material world or universe of objects, and, if similar in its arrangement, must require a similar cause. For what is there in this subject which should occasion a different conclusion or inference? In an abstract view, they are entirely alike; and no difficulty attends the one supposition which is not common to both of them.

Again, when we will needs force *experience* to pronounce some sentence, even on these subjects which lie beyond her sphere, neither can she perceive any material difference in this particular between these two kinds of worlds, but finds them to be governed by similar principles, and to depend upon an equal variety of causes in their operations. We have specimens in miniature of both of them. Our own mind resembles the one; a vegetable or animal body the other. Let experience, therefore, judge from these samples. Nothing seems more delicate, with regard to its causes, than thought; and as these causes never operate in two persons after the same manner, so we never find two persons who think exactly alike. Nor indeed does the same person think exactly alike at any two different periods of time. A difference of age, of the disposition of his body, of weather, of food, of company, of books, of passions—any of these particulars, or others more minute, are sufficient to alter the curious machinery of thought and communicate to it very different movements and operations. As far as we can judge, vegetables and animal bodies are not more delicate in their motions, nor depend upon a greater variety or more curious adjustment of springs and principles.

How, therefore, shall we satisfy ourselves concerning the cause of that Being whom you suppose the Author of nature, or, according to your system of anthropomorphism, the ideal world into which you trace the material? Have we not the same reason to trace that ideal world into another ideal world or new intelligent principle? But if we stop and go no farther, why go so far? Why not stop at the material world? How can we satisfy ourselves without going on *in infinitum*? And, after all, what satisfaction is there in that infinite progression? Let us remember the story of the Indian philosopher and his elephant. It was never more applicable than to the present subject. If the material world rests upon a similar ideal world, this ideal world must rest upon some other, and so on without end. It were better, therefore, never to look beyond the present material world. By supposing it to contain the principle of its order within itself, we really assert it to be God; and the sooner we arrive at that Divine Being, so much the better. When you go one step beyond the mundane system, you only excite an inquisitive humour which it is impossible ever to satisfy.

To say that the different ideas which compose the reason of the Supreme Being fall into order of themselves and by their own nature is really to talk without any precise meaning. If it has a meaning, I would fain know why it is not as good sense to say that the parts of the material world fall into order of themselves and by their own nature. Can the one opinion be intelligible, while the other is not so?

We have, indeed, experience of ideas which fall into order of themselves and without any *known* cause. But, I am sure, we have a much larger experience of matter which does the same, as in all instances of generation and vegetation where the accurate analysis of the cause exceeds all human comprehension. We have also experience of particular systems of thought and of matter which have no order: of the first in madness, of the second in corruption. Why, then, should we think that order is more essential to one than the other? And if it requires a cause in both, what do we gain by your system, in tracing the universe of objects into a similar universe of ideas? The first step which we make leads us on for ever. It were, therefore, wise in us to limit all our inquiries to the present world, without looking farther. No satisfaction can ever be attained by these speculations which so far exceed the narrow bounds of human understanding.

It was usual with the Peripatetics, you know, Cleanthes, when the cause of any phenomenon was demanded, to have recourse to their *faculties* or *occult qualities,* and to say, for instance, that bread nourished by its nutritive faculty, and senna purged by its purgative. But it has been discovered that this subterfuge was nothing but the disguise of ignorance, and that these philosophers, though less ingenuous, really said the same thing with the sceptics or the vulgar who fairly confessed that they knew not the cause of these phenomena. In like manner, when it is asked, what cause produces order in the likes of the Supreme Being, can any other reason be assigned by you, anthropomorphites, than that it is a *rational* faculty, and that such is the nature of the Deity? But why a similar answer will not be equally satisfactory in accounting for the order of the world, without having recourse to any such intelligent creator as you insist on, may be difficult to determine. It is only to say that *such* is the nature of material objects, and that they are all originally possessed of a *faculty* of order and proportion. These are only more learned and elaborate ways of confessing our ignorance; nor has the one hypothesis any real advantage above the other, except in its greater conformity to vulgar prejudices.

You have displayed this argument with great emphasis, replied Cleanthes: You seem not sensible how easy it is to answer it. Even in common life, if I assign a cause for any event, is it any objection, Philo, that I cannot assign the cause of that cause, and answer every new question which may incessantly be started? And what philosophers could possibly submit to so rigid a rule?—philosophers who confess ultimate causes to be totally

unknown, and are sensible that the most refined principles into which they trace the phenomena are still to them as inexplicable as these phenomena themselves are to the vulgar. The order and arrangement of nature, the curious adjustment of final causes, the plain use and intention of every part and organ—all these bespeak in the clearest language an intelligent cause or author. The heavens and the earth join in the same testimony: The whole chorus of nature raises one hymn to the praises of its Creator. You alone, or almost alone, disturb this general harmony. You start abstruse doubts, cavils, and objections; you ask me what is the cause of this cause? I know not; I care not; that concerns not me. I have found a Deity; and here I stop my inquiry. Let those go farther who are wiser or more enterprising.

I pretend to be neither, replied Philo; and for that very reason I should never, perhaps, have attempted to go so far, especially when I am sensible that I must at last be contented to sit down with the same answer which, without further trouble, might have satisfied me from the beginning. If I am still to remain in utter ignorance of causes and can absolutely give an explication of nothing, I shall never esteem it any advantage to shove off for a moment a difficulty which you acknowledge must immediately, in its full force, recur upon me. Naturalists indeed very justly explain particular effects by more general causes, though these general causes themselves should remain in the end totally inexplicable, but they never surely thought it satisfactory to explain a particular effect by a particular cause which was no more to be accounted for than the effect itself. An ideal system, arranged of itself, without a precedent design, is not a whit more explicable than a material one which attains its order in a like manner; nor is there any more difficulty in the latter supposition than in the former.

Part V

But to show you still more inconveniences, continued Philo, in your anthropomorphism, please to take a new survey of your principles. *Like effects prove like causes.* This is the experimental argument; and this, you say too, is the sole theological argument. Now it is certain that the liker the effects are which are seen and the liker the causes which are inferred, the stronger is the argument. Every departure on either side diminishes the probability and renders the experiment less conclusive. You cannot doubt of the principle; neither ought you to reject its consequences.

All the new discoveries in astronomy which prove the immense grandeur and magnificence of the works of nature are so many additional arguments for a Deity, according to the true system of theism; but, according to your hypothesis of experimental theism, they become so many objections, by removing the effect still farther from all resemblance to the effects of human art and contrivance. For if Lucretius, even following the old system of the world, could exclaim:

> Quis regere immensi summam, quis habere
> profundi
> Indu manu validas potis est moderanter
> habenas?
> Quis pariter coelos omnes convertere? et
> omnes
> Ignibus aetheriis terras suffire feraces?
> Omnibus inque locis esse omni tempore
> praesto?[1]

If Tully [Cicero] esteemed this reasoning so natural as to put it into the mouth of his Epicurean:

> Quibus enim oculis animi intueri potuit
> vester Plato fabricam illam tanti operis, qua
> construi a Deo atque aedificari mundum facit?
> quae molitio? quae ferramenta? qui vectes?
> quae machinae? qui minstri tanti muneris
> fuerunt? quemadmodum autem obedire et
> parere voluntati architecti aer, ignis, aqua,
> terra potuerunt?[2]

If this argument, I say, had any force in former ages, how much greater must it have at present when the bounds of Nature are so infinitely enlarged and such a magnificent scene is opened to us? It is still more unreasonable to form our idea of so unlimited a cause from our experience of the narrow productions of human design and invention.

The discoveries by microscopes, as they open a new universe in miniature, are still objections, according to you, arguments, according to me. The further we push our researches of this kind, we are still led to infer the universal cause of all to be vastly different from mankind, or from any object of human experience and observation.

And what say you to the discoveries in anatomy, chemistry, botany? . . . These surely are no objections, replied Cleanthes; they only discover new instances of art and contrivance. It is still the image of mind reflected on us from innumerable objects. Add a mind *like the human,* said Philo. I know of no other, replied Cleanthes. And the liker, the better, insisted Philo. To be sure, said Cleanthes.

Now, Cleanthes, said Philo, with an air of alacrity and triumph, mark the consequences. *First,* by this method or reasoning you renounce all claim to infinity in any of the attributes of the Deity. For, as the cause ought to be proportioned to the effect, and the effect, so far as it falls under our cognizance, is not infinite, what pretensions have we, upon your suppositions, to ascribe that attribute to the Divine Being? You will still insist that, by removing him so much from all similarity to human creatures, we give in to the most arbitrary hypothesis, and at the same time weaken all proofs of his existence.

Secondly, you have no reason, on your theory, for ascribing perfection to the Deity, even in his finite capacity, or for supposing him free from every error, mistake, or incoherence, in his undertakings. There are many inexplicable difficulties in the works of nature which, if we allow a perfect author to be proved *a priori,* are easily solved, and become only seeming difficulties from the narrow capacity of man, who cannot trace infinite relations. But according to your method of reasoning, these difficulties become all real, and, perhaps, will be insisted on as new instances of likeness to human art and contrivance. At least, you must acknowledge that it is impossible for us to tell, from our limited views, whether this system contains any great faults or deserves any considerable praise if compared to other possible and even real systems. Could a peasant, if the *Æneid* were read to him, pronounce that poem to be absolutely faultless, or even assign to it its proper rank among the productions of human wit, he who had never seen any other production?

But were this world ever so perfect a production, it must still remain uncertain whether all the excellences of the work can justly be ascribed to the workman. If we survey a ship, what an exalted idea must we form of the ingenuity of the carpenter who framed so complicated, useful, and beautiful a machine? And what surprise must we feel when we find him a stupid mechanic who imitated others, and copied an art which, through a long succession of ages, after multiplied trials, mistakes, corrections, deliberations, and controversies, had been gradually improving? Many worlds might have been botched and bungled, throughout an eternity, ere this system was struck out; much labour lost, many fruitless trials made, and a slow but continued improvement carried on during infinite ages in the art of world-making. In such subjects, who can determine where the truth, nay, who can conjecture where the probability lies, amidst a great number of hypotheses which may be proposed, and a still greater which may be imagined?

And what shadow of an argument, continued Philo, can you produce from your hypothesis to prove the unity of the Deity? A great number of men join in building a house or ship, in rearing a city, in framing a commonwealth; why may not several deities combine in contriving and framing a world? This is only so much greater similarity to human affairs. By sharing the work among several, we may so much further limit the attributes of each, and get rid of that extensive power and knowledge which must be supposed in one deity, and which, according to you, can only serve to weaken the proof of his existence. And if such foolish, such vicious creatures as man can yet often unite in framing and executing one plan, how much more those deities or demons, whom we may suppose several degrees more perfect!

To multiply causes without necessity is indeed contrary to true philosophy, but this principle applies not to the present case. Were one deity antecedently proved by your theory who were possessed of every attribute requisite to the production of the universe, it would be needless, I own, (though not absurd) to suppose any other deity existent. But while it is still a question whether all these attributes are united in one subject or dispersed among several independent beings, by what phenomena in nature can we pretend to decide the controversy? Where we see a body raised in a scale, we are sure that there is in the opposite scale, however concealed from sight, some counterpoising weight equal to it; but it is still allowed to doubt whether that weight be an aggregate of several distinct bodies or one uniform united mass. And if the weight requisite very much exceeds anything which we have ever seen conjoined in any single body, the former supposition becomes still more probable and natural. An intelligent being of such vast power and capacity as is necessary to produce the universe, or, to speak in the language of ancient philosophy, so prodigious an animal exceeds all analogy and even comprehension.

But further, Cleanthes: Men are mortal, and renew their species by generation; and this is common to all living creatures. The two great sexes of male and female, says Milton, animate the world. Why must this circumstance, so universal, so essential, be excluded from those numerous and limited deities? Behold, then, the theogeny of ancient times brought back upon us.

And why not become a perfect anthropomorphite? Why not assert the deity or deities to be corporeal, and to have eyes, a nose, mouth, ears, etc.? Epicurus maintained that no man had ever seen reason but in a human figure; therefore, the gods must have a human figure. And this argument, which is deservedly so much ridiculed by Cicero, becomes, according to you, solid and philosophical.

In a word, Cleanthes, a man who follows your hypothesis is able, perhaps, to assert or conjecture that the universe sometime arose from something like design; but beyond that position he cannot ascertain one single circumstance, and is left afterwards to fix every point of his theology by the utmost license of fancy and hypothesis. This world, for aught he knows, is very faulty and imperfect, compared to a superior standard, and was only the first rude essay of some infant deity who afterwards abandoned it, ashamed of his lame performance; it is the work only of some dependent, inferior deity, and is the object of derision to his superiors; it is the production of old age and dotage in some superannuated deity, and ever since his death has run on at adventures, from the first impulse and active force which it received from him. You justly give signs of horror, Demea, at these strange suppositions; but these, and a thousand more of the same kind, are Cleanthes' suppositions, not mine. From the moment the attributes of the Deity are supposed finite, all these have place. And I cannot, for my part, think that so wild and unsettled a system of theology is, in any respect, preferable to none at all.

These suppositions I absolutely disown, cried Cleanthes: they strike me, however, with no horror, especially when proposed in that rambling way in which they drop from you. On the contrary, they give me pleasure when I see that, by the utmost indulgence of your imagination, you never get rid of the hypothesis of design in the universe, but are obliged at every turn to have recourse to it. To this concession I adhere steadily; and this I regard as a sufficient foundation for religion.

NOTES

1. [*De Rerum Natura*], lib. XI [II], 1094. [Who can rule the sum, who hold in his hand with controlling force the strong reins, of the immeasurable deep? Who can at once make all the different heavens to roll and warm with ethereal fires all the fruitful earths, or be present in all places at all times? (Translation by H. A. J. Munro, G. Bell & Sons, 1920.)]

2. *De Natura Deorum,* lib. I; [cap. VIII.] [For with what eyes could your Plato see the construction of so vast a work which, according to him, God was putting together and building? What materials, what tools, what bars, what machines, what servants, were employed in such gigantic work? How could the air, fire, water, and earth pay obedience and submit to the will of the architect?]

Continuing to Think

Is the Deity like human persons? If not, it is hard to understand how humans may be said to be created in the image and likeness of God. If so, it is difficult to avoid **anthropomorphism**—making God into a sort of super human being. This is a natural human tendency and one fraught with all sorts of difficulties. How else can we possibly understand God except in human terms, and yet, God is, by definition, more inclusive than our puny, finite, imperfect selves. It is a kind of paradox.

Here is another. If we argue that this material world depends for its reality on an ideal world (as Plato did and as many religions do), then why stop there? Can we not make the same argument about the ideal world—that it, too, must depend on another (superior?) world? This argument could go on forever. If we try to assert that there is some reason for stopping with one ideal world (as the cause of this material one), then why not stop with the material world for the same reason?

As you watch Philo in action, think about how challenging it is to prove the infinite with a finite mind. We always argue by analogy. If a house suggests an architect, it may be logical to assume the world also suggests a cosmic architect. But every analogy is imperfect. Although there may be some ways in which a house is like the world, clearly there are other ways in which a house is not like the world at all. And the whole analogy can be challenged in another way. Philo says that the world seems to him much more like a vegetable than a machine. Teleological arguments have tended to assume the world can be likened to an intricate machine, but is the world really made of interchangeable and replaceable parts the way a machine is? If we argued from the world as a vegetable, rather than from the world as a machine, we would have different premises altogether.

6.2   *Zen and the Art of Motorcycle Maintenance*

ROBERT PIRSIG

Preparing to Read

Phaedrus, the protagonist of this novel, quotes no less an authority than Albert Einstein to the effect that intuition is the only path to the universal laws from which one can deduce the cosmos. The real problem, however, lies in the nature of hypothesis testing—the heart of the scientific method.

Let's begin by distinguishing induction from deduction. Deduction begins with a fundamental law or laws and deduces everything else from it or them. It is capable of leading to certain knowledge as long as the rules of logic are followed. Induction begins with observed cases and, after seeing enough of them, constructs a general law that represents them. Gregor Mendel did this by continually cross-breeding peas and observing what happened in each succeeding generation; ultimately he proposed the laws of genetics. Because it is based on empirical evidence, induction leads only to probable knowledge. Unless you have examined every case (and this is almost never possible), there is always the chance that the next case will not support the theory you have devised.

Science proceeds by hypothesis building. Once you have a hypothesis (a theory based on evidence), you must test it, using the experimental method. Continued, unsuccessful efforts to disprove a theory make it more likely that theory is true. However, keep in mind that no scientific theory has the status of certainty of the type Descartes was looking for when he devised his method of doubting. The problem with hypotheses, as Phaedrus discovers, is that they expand faster than they can be tested, leaving all results inconclusive.

OUTSIDE IN THE VALLEY again the sky is still limited by the bluffs on either side of the river, but they are closer together and closer to us than they were this morning. The valley is narrowing as we move toward the river's source.

We're also at a kind of beginning point in the things I'm discussing at which one can at last start to talk about Phaedrus' break from the mainstream of rational thought in pursuit of the ghost of rationality itself.

There was a passage he had read and repeated to himself so many times it survives intact. It begins:

In the temple of science are many mansions . . . and various indeed are they that dwell therein and the motives that have led them there.

Many take to science out of a joyful sense of superior intellectual power; science is their own special sport to which they look for vivid experience and the satisfaction of ambition; many others are to be found in the temple who have offered the products of their brains on this altar for purely utilitarian purposes. Were an angel of the Lord to come and drive all the people belonging to these two categories out of the temple, it would be noticeably emptier but there would still be some men of both present and past times left inside. . . . If the types we have just expelled were the only types there were, the temple would never have existed any more than one can have a wood consisting of nothing but creepers . . . those who have found favor with the angel . . . are somewhat odd, uncommunicative, solitary fellows, really less like each other than the hosts of the rejected.

What has brought them to the temple . . . no single answer will cover . . . escape from everyday life, with its painful crudity and hopeless dreariness, from the fetters of one's own shifting desires. A finely tempered nature longs to escape from his noisy cramped sur-

roundings into the silence of the high mountains where the eye ranges freely through the still pure air and fondly traces out the restful contours apparently built for eternity.

The passage is from a 1918 speech by a young German scientist named Albert Einstein.

Phaedrus had finished his first year of University science at the age of fifteen. His field was already biochemistry, and he intended to specialize at the interface between the organic and inorganic worlds now known as molecular biology. He didn't think of this as a career for his own personal advancement. He was very young and it was a kind of noble idealistic goal.

The state of mind which enables a man to do work of this kind is akin to that of the religious worshipper or lover. The daily effort comes from no deliberate intention or program, but straight from the heart.

If Phaedrus had entered science for ambitious or utilitarian purposes it might never have occurred to him to ask questions about the nature of a scientific hypothesis as an entity in itself. But he did ask them, and was unsatisfied with the answers.

The formation of hypotheses is the most mysterious of all the categories of scientific method. Where they come from, no one knows. A person is sitting somewhere, minding his own business, and suddenly—flash!—he understands something he didn't understand before. Until it's tested the hypothesis isn't truth. For the tests aren't its source. Its source is somewhere else.

Einstein had said:

Man tries to make for himself in the fashion that suits him best a simplified and intelligible picture of the world. He then tries to some extent to substitute this cosmos of his for the world of experience, and thus to overcome it. . . . He makes this cosmos and its construction the pivot of his emotional life in order to find in this way the peace and serenity which he cannot find in the narrow whirlpool of personal experience. . . . The supreme task . . . is to arrive at those universal elementary laws from which the cosmos can be built up by pure deduction. There is no logical path to these laws; only intuition, resting on sympathetic understanding of experience, can reach them. . . .

Intuition? Sympathy? Strange words for the origin of scientific knowledge.

A lesser scientist than Einstein might have said, "But scientific knowledge comes from *nature. Nature* provides the hypotheses." But Einstein understood that nature does not. Nature provides only experimental data.

A lesser mind might then have said, "Well then, *man* provides the hypotheses." But Einstein denied this too. "Nobody," he said, "who has really gone into the matter will deny that in practice the world of phenomena uniquely determines the theoretical system, in spite of the fact that there is no theoretical bridge between phenomena and their theoretical principles."

Phaedrus' break occurred when, as a result of laboratory experience, he became interested in hypotheses as entities in themselves. He had noticed again and again in his lab work that what might seem to be the hardest part of scientific work, thinking up the hypotheses, was invariably the easiest. The act of formally writing everything down precisely and clearly seemed to suggest them. As he was testing hypothesis number one by experimental method a flood of other hypotheses would come to mind, and as he was testing these, some more came to mind, and as he was testing these, still more came to mind until it became painfully evident that as he continued testing hypotheses and eliminating them or confirming them their number did not decrease. It actually *increased* as he went along.

At first he found it amusing. He coined a law intended to have the humor of a Parkinson's law that "The number of rational hypotheses that can explain any given phenomenon is infi-

nite." It pleased him never to run out of hypotheses. Even when his experimental work seemed dead-end in every conceivable way, he knew that if he just sat down and muddled about it long enough, sure enough, another hypothesis would come along. And it always did. It was only months after he had coined the law that he began to have some doubts about the humor or benefits of it.

If true, that law is not a minor flaw in scientific reasoning. The law is completely nihilistic. It is a catastrophic logical disproof of the general validity of all scientific method!

If the purpose of scientific method is to select from among a multitude of hypotheses, and if the number of hypotheses grows faster than experimental method can handle, then it is clear that all hypotheses can never be tested. If all hypotheses cannot be tested, then the results of any experiment are inconclusive and the entire scientific method falls short of its goal of establishing proven knowledge.

About this Einstein had said, "Evolution has shown that at any given moment out of all conceivable constructions a single one has always proved itself absolutely superior to the rest," and let it go at that. But to Phaedrus that was an incredibly weak answer. The phrase "at any given moment" really shook him. Did Einstein really mean to state that truth was a function of time? To state *that* would annihilate the most basic presumption of all science!

But there it was, the whole history of science, a clear story of continuously new and changing explanations of old facts. The time spans of permanence seemed completely random, he could see no order in them. Some scientific truths seemed to last for centuries, others for less than a year. Scientific truth was not dogma, good for eternity, but a temporal quantitative entity that could be studied like anything else.

He studied scientific truths, then became upset even more by the apparent cause of their temporal condition. It looked as though the time spans of scientific truths are an inverse function of the intensity of scientific effort. Thus the scientific truths of the twentieth century seem to have a much shorter life-span than those of the last century because scientific activity is now much greater. If, in the next century, scientific activity increases tenfold, then the life expectancy of any scientific truth can be expected to drop to perhaps one-tenth as long as now. What shortens the life-span of the existing truth is the volume of hypotheses offered to replace it; the more the hypotheses, the shorter the time span of the truth. And what seems to be causing the number of hypotheses to grow in recent decades seems to be nothing other than scientific method itself. The more you look, the more you see. Instead of selecting one truth from a multitude you are *increasing the multitude*. What this means logically is that as you try to move toward unchanging truth through the application of scientific method, you actually do not move toward it at all. You move *away* from it! It is your application of scientific method that is causing it to change!

What Phaedrus observed on a personal level was a phenomenon, profoundly characteristic of the history of science, which has been swept under the carpet for years. The predicted results of scientific enquiry and the actual results of scientific enquiry are diametrically opposed here, and no one seems to pay too much attention to the fact. The purpose of scientific method is to select a single truth from among many hypothetical truths. That, more than anything else, is what science is all about. But historically science has done exactly the opposite. Through multiplication upon multiplication of facts, information, theories and hypotheses, it is science itself that is leading mankind from single absolute truths to multiple, indeterminate, relative ones. The major producer of the social chaos, the indeterminacy of thought and values that rational knowledge is supposed to eliminate, is none other than science itself. And what Phaedrus saw in the isolation of his own laboratory work years ago is now seen everywhere in the technological world today. Scientifically produced antiscience—chaos.

It's possible now to look back a little and see why it's important to talk about this person in relation to everything that's been said before concerning the division between classic and romantic realities and the irreconcilability of the two. Unlike the multitude of romantics who are disturbed about the chaotic changes science and technology force upon the human spirit, Phaedrus, with his scientifically trained classic mind, was able to do more than just wring his hands with dismay, or run away, or condemn the whole situation broadside without offering any solutions.

As I've said, he did in the end offer a number of solutions, but the problem was so deep and so formidable and complex that no one really understood the gravity of what he was resolving, and so failed to understand or misunderstood what he said.

The cause of our current social crises, he would have said, is a genetic defect within the nature of reason itself. And until this genetic defect is cleared, the crises will continue. Our current modes of rationality are not moving society forward into a better world. They are taking it further and further from that better world. Since the Renaissance these modes have worked. As long as the need for food, clothing and shelter is dominant they will continue to work. But now that for huge masses of people these needs no longer overwhelm everything else, the whole structure of reason, handed down to us from ancient times, is no longer adequate. It begins to be seen for what it really is—emotionally hollow, esthetically meaningless and spiritually empty. That, today, is where it is at, and will continue to be at for a long time to come.

I've a vision of an angry continuing social crisis that no one really understands the depth of, let alone has solutions to. I see people like John and Sylvia living lost and alienated from the whole rational structure of civilized life, looking for solutions outside that structure, but finding none that are really satisfactory for long. And then I've a vision of Phaedrus and his lone isolated abstractions in the laboratory—actually concerned with the same crisis but starting from another point, moving in the opposite direction—and what I'm trying to do here is put it all together. It's so big—that's why I seem to wander sometimes.

No one that Phaedrus talked to seemed really concerned about this phenomenon that so baffled him. They seemed to say, "We know scientific method is valid, so why ask about it?"

Phaedrus didn't understand this attitude, didn't know what to do about it, and because he wasn't a student of science for personal or utilitarian reasons, it just stopped him completely. It was as if he were contemplating that serene mountain landscape Einstein had described, and suddenly between the mountains had appeared a fissure, a gap of pure nothing. And slowly, and agonizingly, to explain this gap, he had to admit that the mountains, which had seemed built for eternity, might possibly be something else . . . perhaps just figments of his own imagination. It stopped him.

And so Phaedrus, who at the age of fifteen had finished his freshman year of science, was at the age of seventeen expelled from the University for failing grades. Immaturity and inattention to studies were given as official causes.

There was nothing anyone could have done about it; either to prevent it or correct it. The University couldn't have kept him on without abandoning standards completely.

In a stunned state Phaedrus began a long series of lateral drifts that led him into a far orbit of the mind, but he eventually returned along a route we are now following, to the doors of the University itself. Tomorrow I'll try to start on that route.

Continuing to Think

Figuring out that the scientific method, rather than bringing him closer to scientific truth, was taking him farther from it caused Phaedrus to experience a nervous breakdown. Scientific truth is not like religious dogma—something presumed to last forever. It is acknowledged to be temporal and subject to change; every scientist knows this. The problem is: The greater the effort spent on science, the shorter the life span of scientific theories seems to get. Whereas some theories seem to have lasted for centuries, our intensive efforts today seem to doom most theories to quicker and quicker replacement.

If hypotheses multiply so fast that there is never time to test enough of them before many others suggest themselves, science seems doomed to running faster and faster without making any real progress. Ideally, a few hypotheses are being worked on, some being eliminated and others being corroborated, with the result that people feel they are coming closer to understanding how the world works. But when theories outpace testing, we never get any closer to what we really want—highly probable knowledge about the world.

As Phaedrus observes, science itself seems to be leading the world from "single, absolute truths to multiple, indeterminate, relative ones." A term for the recognition of all this uncertainty is **postmodernism.** The consequence of all this is that every theory may appear to be as sound as every other one. What standard can we use to determine which is closer to the truth? Are all ideas and values of equal worth? This lack of consensus very quickly leads to social chaos because people cannot agree about what is true, what is real, and what should be valued. The rules of thinking seem terribly flawed.

6.3   ## On Indian-White Relations: A Point of View

N. SCOTT MOMADAY

Preparing to Read

Does the sun live in the sky or does the sun live in the earth? If he answers as an "educated" man, Momaday will name the sky. If, however, he thinks about the sun-watcher who prays the sun out of the ground, then Momaday must reply that the sun lives in the earth. In very profound ways, he argues in this essay, Indian and Western ways of seeing the world diverge. Knowing this, we must wonder which of them tells the truth.

Do we remain in place, observing the flow of time-moments? Or is the idea of time as motion and maybe even the notion of time itself an illusion? The Western understanding of time takes distance as its explanatory principle—the past is away in one direction, the future is away in the other. For the Indian, Momaday explains, there is a kind of extended present.

When we consider history, similar anomalies can occur. In American history texts, 1876 marks the defeat of General George A. Custer at the Battle of the Little Bighorn in Montana, a presidential election, and the admission of Colorado to the Union. On the calendar of Set-t'an, a Kiowa, only the theft of Sun-boy's horses is recorded for the summer of 1876. Seeing this discrepancy and recognizing that each history reflects a worldview, we must ask ourselves how it is possible to choose between these two radically different views of what counts as history.

What is the truth about the summer of 1876? Do the conflicting understandings of time and history Momaday explains help us understand Indian-white relations over the last 500 years, or do they complicate them even further?

FROM TIME TO TIME I have been asked to identify and explain, within a brief space, what I consider to be the most crucial, most vital issue at work in the past five hundred years of North American Indian and white relations. That is a very tall order, of course, and a very serious matter. I can only respond in a personal and straightforward way.

I believe that there is a fundamental dichotomy at the center of these relations, past and present. The Indian and the white man perceive the world in different ways. I take it that this is an obvious fact and a foregone conclusion. But at the same time I am convinced that we do not understand the distinction entirely or even sufficiently. I myself do not understand it sufficiently, but I may be more acutely aware of it by virtue of my experience than are most. Let me qualify my point of view on the subject in order that my remarks may be taken within a certain frame of reference. I am an Indian. I was born into the Indian world, and I have lived a good part of my life in that world. That is worth something, and it is an indispensable consideration in the argument I wish to develop here. You may recall that Oliver La Farge, in discussing his own, narrative point of view in the novel *Laughing Boy* (1929), drew a distinction between "the thing observed and the thing experienced." La Farge correctly thought of himself as an observer; his point of view was removed from the experience of which he wrote, and the distance of that remove was and is finally immeasurable. That is not to say that his powers of observation were in any way deficient—far from it; nor is it to say that *Laughing Boy* is less than a distinguished work of art. It is merely to remark the existence of intrinsic variables in man's perception of his universe, variables that are determined to some real extent on the basis of his genetic constitution. In the case of my own writing, where it centers upon Indian life, and especially upon an Indian way of looking at the world, I can say with some validity, I think, that I have written of "the thing experienced" as well as of "the thing observed." What this may or may not mean in terms of literary advantage is not a question that I wish to raise here, however. For the time being it is enough to establish that such a distinction is *prima facie* real, and it bears importantly upon the matter under discussion.

What of the dichotomy that I have mentioned? How can we get at it? Let me suppose that my daughter, Lore, comes to me with the question, "Where does the sun live?" In my middle-aged and "educated" brain I consider the possibilities of reply. I begin to construct a formula like this: "Well, darling, as you can see, the sun lives in the sky." But already another perception, deeper in the blood, leads me to say, "The sun lives in the earth." I am aware that the first answer is more acceptable to the logic of my age than is the second, and it is more congenial to my learning. The sun is to be observed in the sky and not elsewhere. We are taught beyond any possibility of doubt that the sun and the earth are separated by an all but unimaginable distance. The word *live* we grant to the child as an indulgence, if we grant it at all; it is a metaphor, merely. We certainly do not mean to say that the sun is alive. We mean that from our

point of view the visible sun has its place in the heavens. And we take it for granted that we are speaking of dead matter. But the first answer is not true to my experience, my deepest, oldest experience, the memory in my blood.

For to the Indian child who asks the question, the parent replies, "The sun lives in the earth." The sun-watcher among the Rio Grande Pueblos, whose sacred task it is to observe, each day, the very point of the sun's emergence on the skyline, knows in the depths of his being that the sun is alive and that it is indivisible with the earth, and he refers to the farthest eastern mesa as "the sun's house." The Jemez word for home, *ketha'ame,* bears critical connotations of belonging. Should someone say to the sun, "Where are you going?" the sun would surely answer, "I am going home," and it is understood at once that home is the earth. All things are alive in this profound unity in which are all elements, all animals, all things. One of the most beautiful of Navajo prayers begins *"Tsegi yei! House made of dawn . . ."* And my father remembered that, as a boy, he had watched with wonder and something like fear the old man Koi-khan-hodle, "Dragonfly," stand in the first light, his arms outstretched and his painted face fixed on the east, and "pray the sun out of the ground." His voice, for he prayed aloud, struck at the great, misty silence of the plains morning, entered into it, carried through it to the rising sun. His words made one of the sun and earth, one of himself and the boy who watched, one of the boy and generations to come. Even now, along an arc of time, that man appears to me, and his voice takes hold of me. There is no sunrise without Koi-khan-hodle's prayer.

I want to indicate as best I can an American Indian attitude (for want of a better word) toward the world as a whole. It is an attitude that involves the fullest accomplishment of belief. And I am talking neither about philosophy nor religion; I am talking about a spiritual sense so ancient as to be primordial, so pervasive as to be definitive—not an idea, but a perception on the far side of ideas, an act of understanding as original and originative as the Word. The dichotomy that most closely informs the history of Indian-white relations is realized in language, I believe.

Much has been said and written concerning the Indian's conception of time. Time is a wonderful abstraction; the only way in which we can account for apparent change in our world is by means of the concept of time. The language in which I write and you read upon this page is predicated upon a familiar system of tenses—past, present, and future. In our Western understanding of time we involve the correlative of distance. The past is away in that direction, the future in that, and the present is just here, where I happen to be. But we speak of the passage of time; times come and go, the day will come. We remain in place and observe the flow of time, just as we sit at the cinema and watch, fascinated, as images fly before our eyes. The plane of time is shattered; it is composed of moments, *ad infinitum*, in perpetual motion.

"He loved melons. Always, when we went in the wagon to Carnegie, we stopped at a certain place, a place where there was a big tree. And we sat in the shade there and ate melons. I was little, but I remember. He loves melons, and he always stops at that place." When my father spoke to me of my grandfather, who died before I was born, he invariably slipped into the present tense. And this is a common thing in my experience of the Indian world. For the Indian there is something like an extended present. Time as motion is an illusion; indeed, time itself is an illusion. In the deepest sense, according to the native perception, there is only the dimension of timelessness, and in that dimension all things happen.

The earth confirms this conviction in calendars of "geologic time." Colin Fletcher wrote a book in which he described his walk through the Grand Canyon. It was called significantly, *The Man Who Walked Through Time*. In Fletcher's title we come as close as we can, perhaps, to one of the absolutes of the Indian world. If you stand on the edge of Monument Valley and look across space to the great mono-liths that stand away in the silence, you will understand how it is that the mind of man can grasp the notion of eternity. At some point along the line of your sight there is an end of time, and you see beyond into timelessness.

> as my eyes
> search
> the prairie
> I feel the Summer
> in the spring

In this Chippewa song, time is reduced to a profound evanescence. We are given a stillness like that of the stars.

Yvor Winters, who was my teacher and my friend, wrote in the introduction to his final work, *Forms of Discovery*, "Unless we understand the history which produced us, we are determined by that history; we may be determined in any event, but the understanding gives us a chance." It is a provocative, even compelling statement. And it is eminently wise. But, with respect to our present discussion, there arises the question, How are we to understand the meaning of the word *history*?

In the summer of the centennial year, 1876, General George A. Custer and 265 men of the Seventh Cavalry were killed at the Battle of the Little Bighorn in Montana. Rutherford B. Hayes and Samuel J. Tilden were nominated by their respective parties for the office of President of the United States. Colorado was admitted to the Union. *The Chicago Daily News* was founded, and the Dewey Decimal System was originated.

The summer of 1876 is indicated on the calendar of Set-t'an (a Kiowa) by the rude drawing of a medicine lodge, below which are the tracks of horses. This was the "Sun Dance when Sun-boy's horses were stolen." During the dance, which was held that year at the fork of the Red River and Sweetwater Creek, all of Sun-boy's horses were stolen by a band of Mexicans. Following the dance a war party was sent in pursuit of the thieves, but the horses were not recovered. This is the single record of the summer of that year.

Set-t'an understood history in what can only seem to us extraordinary and incongruous terms. The summer of 1876 was in his mind forever to be identified with the theft of horses. You and I can marvel at that, but we cannot know what the loss of a horse meant to Set-t'an or to his people, whose culture is sometimes called the "horse" culture or the "centaur" culture. We can try to imagine; we can believe that Set-t'an was as deeply concerned to understand the history that produced him as any man can be. My friend Dee Brown wrote in 1966 an estimable study of the year 1876, which he called *The Year of the Century*. Consider that, in some equation that we have yet to comprehend fully, Brown's book is more or less equal to a simple pictograph, the barest of line drawings, on a hide painting of the nineteenth century—or the wall of an ancient cave.

We could go on with such comparisons as these, but this much will serve, I think, as a basis for the main point I wish to make. A good deal has been written about the inequities which inform the history of Indian-white relations in this country, by far the greater part of it from the point of view of the white man, of course. This is the point of view that has been—that can be—articulated in terms that are acceptable to American society as a whole, after all. One of the most perplexing ironies of American history is the fact that the Indian has been effectively silenced by the intricacies of his own speech, as it were. Linguistic diversity has been a formidable barrier to Indian-white diplomacy. And underlying this diversity is again the central dichotomy, the matter of a difference in ways of seeing and making sense of the world around us.

The American Indian has a highly developed oral tradition. It is in the nature of oral tradition that it remains relatively constant; languages are slow to change for the reason that they represent a greater investment on the part of society. One who has only an oral tradition thinks of language in this way: my words exist at the level of my voice. If I do not speak with care, my words are wasted. If I do not listen with care, words are lost. If I do not remember carefully, the very purpose of words is frustrated. This respect for words suggests an inherent morality in man's understanding and use of language. Moreover, that moral comprehension is everywhere evident in American Indian speech. On the other hand, the written tradition tends to encourage an indifference to language. That is to say, writing produces a false security where our attitudes toward language are concerned. We take liberties with words; we become blind to their sacred aspect.

By virtue of the authority vested in me by section 465 of the Revised Statutes (25 U.S.C. #9 [section 9 of this title]) and as President of the United States, the Secretary of Interior is hereby designated and empowered to exercise, without the approval, ratification, or other action of the President or of any other officer of the United States, any and all authority conferred upon the United States by section 403 (a) of the Act of April 11, 1968, 82 Stat. 79 (25 U.S.C. #1323 (a) [subsec. (a) of this section]): provided, That acceptance of retrocession of all or any measure of civil or criminal jurisdiction, or both, by the Secretary hereunder shall be effected by publication in the *Federal Register* of a notice which shall specify the jurisdiction retroceded and the effective date of the retrocession: Provided further, That acceptance of such retrocession of criminal jurisdiction shall be effected only after consultation by the Secretary with the Attorney General.

Executive Order No. 11435, 1968

I have heard that you intend to settle us on a reservation near the mountains. I don't want to settle. I love to roam over the prairies. There I feel free and happy, but when we settle down we grow pale and die. I have laid aside my lance, bow, and shield, and yet I feel safe in your presence. I have told the truth. I have no little lies hid about me, but I don't know how it is with the commissioners. Are they as clear as I am?

Satanta, Kiowa chief

The examples above speak for themselves. The one is couched in the legal diction of a special parlance, one that is far removed from our general experience of language. Its meaning is obscure; the words themselves seem to stand in the way of meaning. The other is in the plain style, a style that preserves, in its way, the power and beauty of language. In the historical relationship in question, the language of diplomacy has been determined by the considerations that have evolved into the style of the first of these examples. It is far removed from the American Indian oral tradition, far from the rhythms of oratory and storytelling and song.

This fundamental difference in ways of looking at the world, as those differences are reflected in the language of diplomacy, seems to me to constitute the most important issue in Indian-white relations in the past five hundred years.

Continuing to Think

We know that science operates according to paradigms, tightly coherent explanations of reality that structure the world. Findings that don't fit a paradigm are often ignored, until they become too frequent or too troublesome. From within the paradigm the world shows up a certain way—other ways of seeing the world are dismissed. And, giving up a paradigm can be a wrenching experience, as those who lived through the dethroning of the earth-centered cosmos in favor of a new sun-centered world attest.

History, too, has paradigms. If time is linear, moving forward in a measured, predictable way, some events will inevitably be seen as causing or growing out of other events. Timelessness, or an eternal present, such as the one described by Rigoberta Menchú in selection 1.4, allows events to show up differently. If the death of a general is a culture-shaking event, it will be recorded in that culture's history books. Similarly, the "horse" culture of the Kiowa will note with deep sadness the theft of all Sun-boy's horses. We can only conclude that these are equivalent events.

What happens when these two cultures negotiate or try to understand and predict each other's behavior? Each of us assumes that our way of seeing the world is the only way or at least the "normal" way. It may take us quite a while to figure out that others construct the world differently. And, if such basic things as time and history cannot be relied upon to cross cultures, how can we begin to speak the truth to each other?

The most interesting characteristic of paradigms is their invisibility. Until we learned that the sun and not the earth was the center of our solar system, everything supported the centrality of earth. The paradigm became visible only when it was broken. To repair Indian-white relations, we must at least learn each other's paradigms.

6.4   *African Logical Heritage and Contemporary Life*

S. A. MWANAHEWA

Preparing to Read

Suppose, instead of growing up in the West and learning to rely on logic as a truth test, you had been educated in a culture that conveyed the truth through proverbs, riddles, sayings, songs, and art motifs? You might have a different understanding of what truth is and how to test for it. Think about this image: a crocodile with two heads, locked in combat, with one body and a shared stomach. The "truth" this image seems to convey is that conflict in the human family is predictable but must be resolved if the survival goal of getting food to the common stomach is to be met.

This is highly empirical—based on lived experience—and it has a certain logic to it. Yet it speaks the language of ordinary people and shapes the world for them. As Professor Mwanahewa argues, the fact that most people in the world are illiterate does not mean that they have no way to test for truth. A proverb such as "If you don't let your neighbor reach nine, you will never reach ten" is seen as "true" because people's experience confirms it. What it may lack in formal logic is compensated for by its emotional validity and its connection with a shared cultural life.

Pure deduction, of the type that can seem divorced from life, runs the risk of being sterile, Mwanahewa suggests. Just as proverbs have and need to have an element of logic, so logic needs an artistic element to make it whole. The scientific approach of logic and the artistic approach of orature or oral literature can benefit from and complement each other. Either, taken alone, lacks a vital element and may lead to the kinds of impasses we have been discussing.

The Cogency in "Kinyankore Orature" Focusing on Proverbs

THIS PAPER PURPORTS TO SHOW how culture and logic can benefit from and complement each other in contemporary terms. It will delve on how the scientific approach of logic and the artistic approach of orature can bridge the gap between the trained logicians and the illiterate village communities for their mutual benefit. It intends to show that logic and orature do share some methodological characteristics, that orature can inject new innovations in the present scientific approach of logic.

Logic has hitherto been described as a science—the science of arguments. The main reason for meriting this description is logic's function or working is based on rules and laws.

For the sake of standard, objectivity and clarity in reasoning, logic has reached indubitable proportions and has won itself international acceptance. In this respect logic earns unchallenged repute in the arena of the literates.

From *The Foundations of Social Life* by S. A. Mwanahewa. Courtesy of Council for Research in Values and Philosophy.

However, taking the entire world population, the majority of the populace are illiterate. This is a characteristic of some of the third world. This fact creates a big imbalance between the literate and the illiterate communities.

In order to standardize language as is evident in the syllogisms one at least requires two language skills; the skills of reading and writing. These are wanting in the majority of the world populace.

To compound the problem, not everyone can handle the discipline of logic. Logic being a science—as it is mainly viewed—in order for one to put logic to fruitful and profitable use, one needs a thorough training in order to equip oneself with the rules and laws upon which logic bases its function.

Given this fact, the biggest number of people—the illiterate—is deprived of the opportunity to benefit from this discipline.

What the absence of literacy skills in the biggest part of the world means is that the smaller literate part of the world cannot benefit from this large bulk of the illiterate world and vice-versa.

Subjected to this unfortunate imbalance, the literate minority should initiate to explore what the majority illiterate world can offer to the discipline.

(The approach should parallel that used by the developed industrial countries which to some extent lacked industrial raw materials. They used their technical skills and expertise to extract raw materials from the developing third world.)

However, this approach should not lead to a situation where the developed community has continued to take a lion's share while the underdeveloped continued to be impoverished. It should lead to mutual intellectual benefit between the literate and the illiterate communities.

While the literate world is well versed in the literacy skills, the illiterate world on the other hand is well versed in the oracy skills.

It was earlier stated that logic is a science of arguments. In this respect a layman may ask, "what sort of arguments"? A logician will answer, "all arguments." Taking the layman's side, indeed, what sort of arguments do we find in the day to day life? In order to answer this question, one has to look at these two societies, the minority literate society and the majority illiterate society.

The sort of arguments characteristic of the former are mainly concerned with politics, economic speculation, urban life and everything that goes with modernity, while those in the latter are mainly based on cultural heritage and its survival especially when it is threatened by the onslaught of the superficialities of technological innovations.

A contemporary pragmatist says that "something should be accepted if it leads to tangible and verifiable results."[1] Similarly, a logician says that something should be accepted if it has a strong cogent base to support it. In this respect, logic that is professed by the literate society is based on the acquired rules and laws. This makes logic purely scientific.

At this juncture, I wish to contend that in addition to the scientific nature of logic it should equally be regarded as an art. This contention is based on the fact implied by the pragmatist and logician that something should merit acceptance if it has a practical value or a strong cogent basis to support it.

I wish to point out that cultural aspects do have practical values and cogent objectives. At this point logical and cultural approaches differ in a sense that the former is mainly scientific and the latter is mainly artistic. This difference need not be overemphasized. Instead it should be the common aspect between the two approaches that should be of interest. Both are practical and have cogent objectives.

The literary and the oracy skills should be blended to give logic a new appearance, the semi-scientific and semi-artistic outlook. It is my conviction that if this approach is adopted the literate and the illiterate worlds will mutually benefit from the discipline of logic.

While logic uses premises to support a conclusion, members of the illiterate culture use oral expression either as premises or conclusions. While logic uses rules and laws to structure cogent arguments, the illiterate community uses language structural arrangement to give impact to the intended message or objective. This structural arrangement is not necessarily scientific, but largely artistic. As shall be explicated later, this structural arrangement is largely logical; hence the need for logic to adopt itself to this artistic approach.

Needless to mention, some members of the illiterate community, especially the elderly group are living libraries. However, the life span of these libraries is short because sooner or later the entire generation will die. Taking this fact into account, how many libraries does the world bury every day?

It is high time that logicians cease to look at logic as nothing more than a compendium of rules and laws; they should look at the artistic aspect of culture instead. Traditional orature—oral literature—uses emotional appeal as a weapon in delivering messages and in achieving objectives. This area, unfortunately, is greatly neglected by logic. Logic has little room if any for emotional approach.

However, authentic study and exploration into the depths of logic, has shown that bad arguments—which can mislead society—can be consciously or unconsciously made when one is using carefully selected content words. In this regard, the authenticity of logic should not be based on whether the approach is scientific or artistic, but on whether it convincingly serves the intended purpose or leads to the achievement of the set objective.

With this background in mind, I wish to explore in detail a specific piece of Kinyankore orature—the Kinyankore proverbial language—one of the venues through which the Banyankore explicate their cultural heritage. In the exposition of these proverbial structures efforts will be made to expose some aspects of formal logic embedded therein and to show how logic can benefit from the artistic approach of the illiterate world.

There are many aspects of orature in any community which can expose the logical and cultural heritage of that community. For the purpose of this paper I have decided to choose the proverbial structures. The main reason is that the approach I am using is new to the majority of logicians and non-logicians.

This fact has necessitated the selecting of an area which is terse and compendius. This has been done in order to avoid misinterpretation and for the easy following of the discussion.

Before I explore the structural harmony between logic and the proverbial structure, let me give the systematic nature and orderliness in which Kinyankore proverbs were coined.

The illiterate community is concerned with a well spoken word and they probably have no time for the written word. Hence, they are concerned with the logicality of the spoken word. The authenticity and rationality in the exposition of their logical and cultural heritage is by the tongue rather than the pen. So, the illiterate Banyankore took their time to organize the oral channel into different sections. For instance, proverbs, riddles, sayings, songs, to mention a few, do serve as a demonstration of this fact.

Additionally, these major sections are again subdivided according to the function they serve. For instance, the section of proverbs is subdivided into proverbs on moral cohesion, the inevitability of the communality of work, marriage institutions, the institution of justice, wisdom on cultural matters and others. These subdivisions are clear in the elders' minds and are appropriately quoted during serious conversations, in teaching the youths about their roles in cultural matters, in settling disputes and during public festivities such as weddings.

From this exposition, it is evident that the Banyankore use the system of classification when portraying their cultural heritage. Though due to illiteracy, this classification is not realized on paper, it is tantamount to the approach of logic of the use of rules and laws. For instance, in like manner, logic classifies certain arguments according to the Modus ponendo ponens (MPP), Modus tollendo tollens (MTT), syllogisms and theorems. It is clear that the system of classification and that of using rules and laws is a shared formal characteristic between cultural orature and logic.

Again orature and logic have something in common as regards informal fallacies in reasoning. In terms of logic informal fallacies are mainly committed due to the misuse of words or drawing irrelevant conclusions from what the premises are contending.

The proverbial structures also do take care of informal fallacies. However, the fallacy does not lie in the language structure itself but in the meaning portrayed by the structure. For instance, there are proverbs focused on hypocrisy, such as:

"Omukazi ayisire omwana wa mukaiba akiza nyina omwana jurira"
"A woman who has killed her co-wife's child cries louder than the mother of the child."

It is evident that the fault does not lie in the structure itself but in the portrayed meaning. The louder cry intended to demonstrate deep pain and loss is not actually genuine but a false coverup of the guilt.

There are proverbs focused on chatterboxes, such as:

"Engamba yabyingi tegira ogu ehikiriza"
"One who talks much about the success of an enterprise never actualizes it."

Again it is not the structure that is faulty but it is merely reflecting the fault in the message. The message is a warning that one should not be duped by a chatterbox. All he does is talk and no action.

There are numerous examples of proverbs about lying, slandering, pretending, deceiving, flattering, gossiping and others.

In terms of logic, proverbs in these examples are playing a quadruple function: they expose the faults so that people become aware of the faults of language; they assist people not only to not be victims of the faults when committed by others, but not to commit these faults them-

selves; they provide moral lessons and serve as a challenge to make people think carefully and evaluate what they hear before accepting them. Precisely that is what logic advocates.

Kinyankore orature can be structured into mediate and immediate inferences. For instance long prose structures like folk tales and songs can be structured into syllogisms; hence, harmonizing with the mediate inference standards, while riddles can be harmonized with the immediate inference standard.

"Otari nyoko takureeba hand"
"One who is not your mother never looks at your abdomen."

This proverb is of a literal and a metaphorical nature. The literal nature is that one who is not your mother never bothers to feed you. The metaphorical nature is that one should be a man therefore self reliant. The former is scientific while the latter is artistic. In both cases the premises can be drawn back from experience.

Due to the fact that the premises which support the proverbs are less exact, proverbs do harmonize with the logic of induction.

Needless to say, there is a lot the proverbs in particular and orature in general share with logic, a proof that the majority in the illiterate world have a lot to offer to the minority in the literate world.

In this paper I have given examples picked from Ankore because this is my cultural base but I am convinced that different cultures in the third world, if sufficiently explored would have a lot to offer, hence, the need for researches in these cultures.

I hasten to add that the proverbial structures and the proverbial language, though coined generations back, are modernistic and innovative in nature. This is because they challenge the audience to think systematically while establishing the premises to the proverb; hence linking the past with the present. In this respect the past experiences are inevitably kept alive.

Another dimension that gives the proverbial language a modernistic appearance is the fact that even the context in which the proverb is quoted can serve as a premise to consolidate the proverb itself. For instance, a proverb on justice will be quoted in the traditional judiciary context when judging the offense committed in the present.

With reasonable amount of confidence, one can say that the proverbial language serves the logical analytical approach. It is a handy weapon that is used to make an individual stop and think twice before acting or continuing with his ways. In such a situation an individual is reminded to make a thorough examination of whatever he has been engaged in or is intending to do.

I wish to end this paper with a comment on observation made by some renowned logicians. S. Haack says that:

> The traditional idea that logic is concerned with the validity of arguments as such irrespective . . . of their subject matter . . . could be thought to offer a principle on which to delimit the scope of logic.[2]

This quotation serves as proof to my contention that in addition to the scientific approach which has hitherto characterized logic there is need for logic to focus on the artistic procedures as is exemplified in orature. We have seen that orature can serve as a very effective channel through which logic can tap the wisdom from the illiterate elders. Orature has as its subject matter the cultural heritage. The cultural heritage has some immortal values which have penetrated into the contemporary life. S. J. Joyce says that: "Logic is the theory of correct thinking."[3]

Traditionally, the primary function of the proverbs is to make people think deeply in order to harmonize the proverb with its meaning. In order for one to succeed in this venture one had to think correctly. This is another added similarity between logic and orature. A proverb was meant to test whether one had the mental capacity to correctly associate the context of the proverb with its meaning. This involved correct thought. Copi says that:

> Language is the armory of the human mind; and at once contains the trophies of its post, and the weapons of its future conquests.[4]

This quotation proves the harmony between orature and logic. It provides the thread that weaves together the cultural heritage as manifested through orature and the contemporary scientific approach as manifested by logic.

Generally, I wish to reiterate that the illiterate cultural elite who form the majority of the world populace have a lot to offer to the minority literate elite. The challenge is therefore thrown to this minority elite to use their enlightenment privilege to extract this cultural treasure for the balance and intellectual betterment of the two.

We have seen that there is a lot that logic shares with the cultural heritage, so in addition to its scientific approach logic should rigorously take up the artistic approach, a channel that will enable it to appreciate fully what orature can offer to enrich it.

Finally, it has been discovered that orature perpetually revives the cultural heritage, and keeps its candle burning. This makes the cultural approach modernistic and innovative. Logicians should not allow this candle to be extinguished. From this one, more candles should be lit in all corners of the world to provide light to the entire globe.

NOTES

1. A. Stroll & R. H. Popkin, *Introduction to Philosophy* (New York: Holt, Rinehart & Winston, 1979), p. 415.

2. H. Susan, *Philosophy of Logics* (London: C.H.P., 1978), p. 5.

3. S. J. Joyce, *Principles of Logic* (London: Longmans, 1936), p. 8.

4. J. W. Copi, *Introduction to Logic* (New York: Macmillan, 1978), p. 80.

Continuing to Think

If pure logic and strict empiricism can leave us with no solid ground on which to stand, perhaps it is time to consider blending the strength of Western culture with what has stood the test of time in more traditional societies. Some things may be intuitively grasped and do not require formal proof for validation. "When the well is dry, they know the worth of water" is one such proverb—this time from Benjamin Franklin's *Poor Richard's Almanac.* One of our country's leading diplomats and scientists (remember the kite experiment and the Franklin stove) is at least as well known for publishing these distilled "truths" about human experience.

Think about your favorite one-frame cartoon. With a few lines of ink and a few well chosen words, a skilled cartoonist can compress culture and history and add some commentary. It takes only a second to scan it but much longer to explain it to someone who doesn't "get it." In this minimalist approach to truth telling, a little says a lot.

So, we are not unfamiliar with the kind of truth test Mwanahewa writes about. Like true love, we intuit the truth of cartoons, bypassing logic and its rules in favor of comparison with lived experience. Looking at comic books can tell us at a glance which qualities we find heroic. And many of Poor Richard's sayings, popularized around the time of the American Revolution, have stood the test of time. "Fish and visitors smell in three days." "God helps those that help themselves." "A stitch in time saves nine." Probably you heard some of these as you were growing up, and perhaps you have another list from a culture other than the one that produced Franklin. "What goes around comes around" and "Don't do the crime if you can't do the time" come from a different cultural idiom but speak the truth in just the same way.

6.5   *Letters to Bernard of Clairvaux and the Mainz Prelates*

HILDEGARD OF BINGEN

Preparing to Read

With this last reading we move as far from our first reading as it is possible to go. Abbess Hildegard of Bingen, a twelfth-century mystic, bypasses rationality in favor of intuitive truth. Like other mystics, she experienced from her early youth what she believed to be personal revelations from God in the form of light visions. So convinced was she of the "truth" of what her visions told her that she was prepared to face down earthly authorities who disagreed with her.

An important distinction must be kept in mind here. She did not see what she claimed as Hildegard's truth; she saw it as God's truth. This allowed her to assert a truth claim, using God as its guarantor, that was difficult to refute. Even her clerical superior, the Bishop of Mainz, did not dare to contradict her once he was convinced of the authenticity of her visions.

Clearly, this approach cannot be taken lightly. One must be highly credible as a person and spiritually convincing as a mystic in order to make and sustain truth claims of this sort. Because there have been many mystics, of both genders and from many religious traditions, we will look at Hildegard's justification for the "truth" of her visions and at her disobedience of a direct order.

In her letter to the Mainz Prelates, Abbess Hildegard and her nuns have buried in sacred ground a young man that the bishops believe to be unworthy of this privilege, and she justifies her refusal to dig up the body and have it moved. With God on her side, Hildegard's case is strong.

Letter to Bernard of Clairvaux

O VENERABLE FATHER BERNARD, you who, in a wonderful manner, hold the great honor of the strength of God, must be much feared by the wrongful foolishness of this world since, with the holy cross as your banner, inspired by an ardent love for the Son of God, you urge men to wage battle in the Christian armies against the ferocious pagans. I beg you, Father, in the name of the living God, to listen to me and to answer my questions. I am very preoccupied on account of a vision that appeared to me in the mystery of the spirit, a vision that I certainly did not see with the eyes of the flesh. I, wretched creature, more than wretched, being a woman, since my childhood have seen great wonders which my tongue could not utter if the Spirit of God had not taught me, so that I should believe. Most reliable and kind Father, out of your goodness, answer me, your unworthy servant, for from the days of my childhood I have never lived a single hour of security; examine these things in your soul, with your piety and wisdom, according to the knowledge you have received from the Holy Spirit, and from your heart send consolation to your servant.

In fact, in the texts of the Psalms, in the Gospel and other books which are shown to me in this vision, I understand the inner sense which touches my heart and soul like a burning flame, teaching me the depths of the explanation without, however, giving me literary mastery in the Teutonic language, of which I am deprived, for I can read only in a simple way, without being able to analyze the text. Answer me and let me know your opinion on this matter, for I am a human being ignorant of all teaching bearing upon exterior questions, but within my soul I have knowledge, and that is why I hesitate to speak. But hearing of your wisdom and piety, I am already consoled, having dared say these things to nobody else— since, according to what I have heard, there are so many schisms among men—except to a certain monk whom I know well enough to be convinced that he leads a life worthy of full approval. And so I have told him all my secrets and he has certainly comforted me by considering them great and redoubtable. For the love of God, Father, I beseech you to console me and then I shall be completely reassured.

I saw you in this vision more than two years ago, as a man looking at the sun without fear, but with great audacity. And I wept because I myself am so timid and have so little courage.

Most good and kind Father, I have put myself in your soul so that you should reveal to me, in your answer, if it so pleases you, whether I must say these things openly or whether I must keep silent, for I experience great torments in this vision, not knowing what I must say of the things

From *Women Mystics in Medieval Europe.* Courtesy of Paragon House.

I have seen and heard. And sometimes, after the vision, I am confined to my bed by terrible sufferings, because I am silent, and I cannot even stand up. I shed tears of sadness before you because I am inconstant and my nature is like that of a gnarled, twisted tree, born as I am of the seed of Adam who, having followed the Devil's suggestion, was exiled to a foreign land. Now, rising up, I turn to you for aid, for you are not inconstant, but you always straighten the tree and you are victor in your soul, saving not only yourself but the whole world.

You are also the eagle who gazes at the sun. I beseech you, by the serenity of the Father, by His admirable Word, by the sweet tears of compunction, the Spirit of Truth, and by the sacred sound, with which every creature resounds and by the Word Himself out of Whom the world arose, and by the sublimity of the Father Who, in His gentle viridity, sent the Word into the Virgin's womb, from which he drew His flesh, like honey nesting in a honeycomb. And may the sound itself, the Father's energy, be heard in your heart and raise your soul, so that you do not doze distractedly when you listen to this human being who is addressing you—while you ask God all these things, concerning both this creature (that I am) and the secret itself, penetrating through the door of your soul, in order to know all these things in God.

God be with you and with your soul, and be valiant in His combat. Amen.

Bernard's Reply to Hildegard

To his dear daughter in Christ, Hildegard, Brother Bernard, called to be Abbot of Clairvaux, if the prayer of a sinner has any power.

If you consider our littleness quite differently from how we ourselves judge it in our conscience, we believe we must impute this exclusively to your humility. Therefore I have not hesitated to reply to your affectionate letter, although the multitude of matters I have on my hands obliges me to answer you much more briefly than I would wish. We are happy to know of the grace of God which is within you. And, as far as it behooves us, we exhort you and beg you to consider it as a grace and to make every effort to respond to this gift with sentiments of deep humility and devotion, knowing that "God resists the proud and bestows His grace upon the humble" (1 Pet. 5:5). Besides, when inner instruction and the unction which teaches everything already exist, what need is there for us to teach or to warn?

We heartily beg and beseech you to remember in your prayers to God, us, as well as all those who are united to us in spiritual community with the Lord.

Letter to Guibert of Gembloux

. . . O faithful servant, I, a poor wretched woman, in the vision I tell you these words. . . .

Ever since my infancy, when my bones, nerves, and veins were as yet undeveloped, until the present day, now that I am more than seventy years old, I have always had the gift of vision in my soul. And as God wills, in vision my spirit soars upwards into the celestial heights, borne by the various currents; it dilates among different peoples, no matter how remote their countries are. And since I see [these images] in such a manner, I behold them according to the changing forms of the clouds and of other created things. But I do not hear them with my physical ears, nor understand them with my heart's thoughts, nor do I perceive them with any of my five senses, but only in my soul, with my bodily eyes open, so that I have never known loss of consciousness in ecstasy, for I see these images in a state of wakefulness both night and day. And I am continuously afflicted by illnesses and great sufferings which threaten to cause my death, but so far God has sustained me.

The light that I see is not localized, but it is far brighter than a cloud which surrounds the sun. I cannot reckon its height, length or breadth and I call it "the shadow of the living light." And just as the sun, moon and stars are mirrored in water, so the Scriptures, discourses, virtues, and certain works of man take form in my eyes and are reflected in this radiant light.

All the things I have seen or learned in vision, I retain them in my memory in such a way that, since I have seen and heard them for some time, I am able to remember them. At the same instant, I see, hear, and know, and I understand what I know. But what I do not see I do not know, because I am not learned. And the things that I write are those I see and hear in my vision, and I do not use words other than those I hear, and I utter them in unpolished Latin, because in the vision I am not taught to write as philosophers do. And the words I see and hear in this vision are not like those which issue from human lips, but they are like a bright flame, a cloud moving through pure air.

I can in no way recognize the contours of this light, no more than I can see perfectly the sun's sphere. And in this light, sometimes, but very rarely, I see another light called "the living light." When and how I see it I cannot say but, during the time I see it, all sadness and anguish disappear, so that I seem to be an innocent young girl and not an old woman.

Yet, on account of the continuous illnesses I endure, at times I have no wish to express the words and the visions shown to me; nevertheless, when my soul sees and experiences these wonderful things, my mood changes and I forget my sufferings and tribulations (as I have already said) and my soul draws up what I see and hear in the vision, as if from a fountain—a fountain which always remains full and inexhaustible.

And never does my soul lack that light described above as "the shadow of the living light." I see it as a starless sky within a sparkling cloud; there, in the blaze of the living light, I see the things I often declare and the answers I give to the persons who question me.

As regards body as well as soul, I do not know myself and I consider myself as almost nothing; I yearn towards the living God and leave all things in His hands, so that He, Who has neither beginning nor end, may preserve me from evil on every occasion. And so, you,

who have asked me to express myself, pray for me together with all those who desire to hear my words with faith, that I may remain unwaveringly in God's service.

Letter to the Mainz Prelates

In the vision that was engraved within my soul by God the Creator before my birth, I am obliged to write to you about the interdict inflicted upon us by our superiors because in our cemetery we had a man buried, under the direction of his priest, and with no guilt on our part. When, a few days after this burial, we were ordered by our superiors to remove the body from the cemetery, seized with fear, I looked towards the true light, as is my custom, and with wakeful eyes I saw in my soul that, if this order were obeyed and the man's body exhumed, this expulsion would be a terrible threat of dark evil for our convent; we should be, as it were, enveloped in one of those black clouds which announce tempests and thunderstorms.

Since then we have dared neither to remove this man's corpse—seeing that he had received absolution, extreme unction and holy communion—nor follow the counsels and orders of those who persuaded us, or commanded us, to do so. Not that we turn a deaf ear to the advice of wise men or the orders of our prelates but so as not to seem—by an act of cruelty perpetrated by women—to be insulting Christ's sacraments which had fortified this man during his lifetime.

However, not to appear entirely disobedient, we have ceased singing the songs of divine praise, in accordance with the interdict, and we have abstained from partaking of the Lord's body as we were accustomed to do almost every month.

Together with all my sisters, I felt deep bitterness on this account and was overwhelmed by great sadness. Filled with a profound heaviness of spirit, I then heard these words in my vision: "It is not good that, by human orders, you should be deprived of the mysteries of the Word clothed in His human nature, your Saviour in a virgin nature, born of the Virgin Mary. . . ."

In the same vision I heard that I was at fault because I had not come before my superiors, in all humility and submission, to ask leave to take communion, since we had done nothing wrong in accepting the body of that man who, from the hands of his priest, had received everything befitting a Christian and had been buried in our cemetery in the presence of all the inhabitants of Bingen, without any objection being raised.

And this, Your Excellencies, is what God has bid me say to you. I also beheld something concerning the fact that, to obey you, we have ceased to sing the divine office, limiting ourselves to reading it in an undertone. I heard a voice coming from the living light relating the various forms of praise, as David says in the psalm (Ps. 150:3–6) "Praise Him with the sound of the trumpet, praise Him with the psaltery and harp. Praise Him with the timbrel and with dance; praise Him with stringed instruments and organs. Praise Him upon loud cymbals, the high-sounding cymbals. Let everything that has breath praise the Lord."

These words bring us from outer realities to inner ones and teach us how, by imitating these material instruments and their diverse features, we must direct all the élan of our inner being towards the praise of God and how we must express this praise. If we give the matter our careful attention, we recall how ardently man seeks the voice of the living spirit, lost because of the disobedience of Adam who, before his transgression, still innocent, took no small part in the choir of angelic praises. The angels possess such voices through their spiritual nature, and are called spirits by the Spirit, who is God. Adam, then, lost this vocal affinity with the angels which was his when in Paradise and—just as, upon awakening, one is no longer certain about what he saw in his dream—so the knowledge [of God] which was his before the fall lies dormant within him. . . .

But God, Who saves the souls of the elect by sending them the light of truth to lead them

back to their original happiness, decided to renew the hearts of a great number [of them] by bestowing on them the prophetic spirit so that, through inward illumination, they might recover part of the gifts lost by Adam when he was punished for his sin.

So that man should not live in the remembrance of his banishment, but rather in the sweet souvenir of that divine praise which Adam had once shared joyfully with the angels, and to encourage him to praise God, the holy prophets, enlightened by the spirit they had received, not only composed psalms and canticles which were sung to stir the devotion of listeners, but they also invented—for the same purpose—the many-toned musical instruments which accompanied the songs with multitudinous sounds. And so listeners, roused and prepared outwardly by the forms and features of these musical instruments and by the meaning of the words sung, also receive inner enlightenment.

Following the example of the holy prophets, other wise and clever men, by their human endowments, have also invented numerous instruments, to be able to express in song the joy within their souls. They adapted their singing to the bending of the finger joints, remembering that Adam was created by the finger of God, the Holy Spirit.

In Adam's voice, before the fall, there was all the sweetness and harmony of musical art. And if he had remained in the condition for which he had been created, mortal man's frailty could never have endured the force and resonance of that voice. When the Devil learned that man had begun to sing through divine inspiration and would be urged to remember the sweet music of his heavenly home, seeing the failure of his perfidious plans, he became so frightened and tormented that he has never ceased to hinder, and even destroy, the utterance, beauty, and sweetness of divine praise and hymns of the spirit. He does this not only in man's heart, by wicked insinuations, impure thoughts and various distractions, but also in the very heart of the Church, wherever he can, by causing discord, scandals, and unjust oppressions.

And so you, and all other prelates, must be extremely wary before issuing a decree which closes the mouths of a community singing to God and forbids them to celebrate and receive the sacraments. Beware in your judgments not to be deceived by Satan who drags men away from celestial harmony and the joys of Paradise. . . .

Ponder on this matter: just as the body of Christ took flesh from Mary's intact virginity, by the power of the Holy Spirit, so the songs of praise—echo of celestial harmony—are instilled into the Church by the Holy Spirit. The body is the raiment of the soul which gives life to the voice. And so it is fitting that the body united to the soul should sing God's praises out loud. . . .

And since, when hearing certain melodies, man sometimes sighs and groans, recalling heavenly harmony, the prophet David, considering deeply the profound nature of man's spirit, and realizing that his soul is symphonic, exhorts us in his psalm to give praise to the Lord on the lute, on the ten-stringed psaltery (Ps. 32:2, 91:4): the lute, which has a lower sound, is meant to urge man to bodily control;

the psaltery, which draws its sound from above, to elevate his spirit; its ten chords are a reminder to contemplate the Law.

It follows that those who, without having sufficiently reflected, impose silence upon the Church singing God's praises, unjustly rob God of the beauty of these earthly songs and will themselves be deprived of taking part in the angelic choirs in heaven, unless they remedy their fault by true repentance and humble penitence (Wisd. of Sol. 11:24). Let those who hold the keys of the kingdom of heaven take good care not to open what should remain closed and not to close what should be opened. For those in charge will be submitted to the more severe judgment, unless they "rule with diligence" (cf. Rom. 12:8). And I heard a voice saying: "Who created Heaven? God. Who opens Heaven to His faithful ones? God. Who is like unto Him? Nobody." And that is why, O ye faithful, none of you must resist Him, or oppose Him, lest He should come down upon you with His power and you should have nobody to defend or protect you on the day of judgment. . . .

Continuing to Think

Hildegard's visions have a terrible cost because she learns things that are controversial, and she is torn between speaking them aloud and keeping silent. Bernard of Clairvaux was well known throughout the Christian world and a friend to the Popes. Because he had not read her works at the time of this letter, his encouragement of her is vague and general. Later, after he read of her visions, Bernard asked the Pope to confirm her prophetic mission, freeing her to write about what she learned.

Hildegard's third letter reflects the consequences of speaking out. According to the Canon Law of the Roman Catholic Church, a person who dies in a state of sin cannot be buried in consecrated ground. The young nobleman in question had, at one time, been excommunicated, but he had privately received absolution and was free to receive a normal burial. With the bishop away on business, his canons, not knowing all the circumstances, placed Hildegard's convent under interdict. They were forbidden to have mass celebrated and to sing the divine office, one of the principal duties of Benedictine nuns. These are severe penalties and Hildegard accepts them, but she refuses to exhume the body and she continues to appeal the interdict.

Hildegard was ultimately successful, not because of her personal eloquence or the logic of her arguments, but because the bishop was finally convinced that her case was strengthened by a vision from God. With God's cited agreement that orders, even those from a bishop, should not deprive the nuns of communion or the songs of praise that divided their day into canonical hours, Hildegard was able to convince the Bishop to lift the interdict. Her strongest argument is that human orders have robbed God of deserved praise by unjustly (and without sufficient reflection) forbidding his nuns to sing.

Summing Up the Readings

Were you more persuaded of the value of deduction, induction, or intuition? Each has problems associated with it, and none can serve as a valid truth test in every situation. Perhaps the conclusion we can draw is that blending all three offers the most promise, with certain situations more conducive to each of these three routes to and tests for truth.

Without logic, we may be left with conflicting empirical evidence and competing intuitive judgments. How do we decide which historian makes the more convincing interpretation of agreed-upon facts without invoking logic? At the same time, empirical reality can be confusing and downright contradictory. One of the problems in science is that we operate within what Thomas Kuhn has called "paradigms," or tightly constructed versions of reality. In periods of "normal science," textbooks are written to reflect the paradigm, and research and experimentation take the paradigm as a starting point. Unfortunately, the same facts can support competing paradigms. The same astronomical observations were used to argue for an earth-centered as well as a sun-centered system.

It is hard to get at a pure "fact" before it is filtered through a paradigm or subjected to historical interpretation, which functions in much the same way. When slavery was being written about as a benevolent system, facts could be produced to support that "truth"; when the interpretation changed, other facts appeared to prove the new interpretation "true." And, because we weren't there, we cannot independently verify most facts.

Clearly, there are some times when intuition will be our most reliable test for truth. We will know something to be true or know it to be false. Unfortunately, people from different cultures may construct the world so differently that they will have great difficulty communicating even though everyone might be committed to telling the truth.

Continuing to Question

1. Which questions are best answered by deduction, by induction, by intuition, or by mystical experience? How will you decide which approach is best in a given situation, especially if you meet someone who views time and history in ways you can barely imagine?

2. Which does Hume make ridiculous—belief in God or merely the teleological argument to support such a belief? Could you use intuition to discredit something others think is proved by deduction? What might mystical experience validate?

3. If hypotheses expand faster than our ability to test them and if the so-called "facts" of history may be open to doubt, how can our science and our history proceed? Is there value in partial and incomplete truth? If so, what is it? If not, what alternative do you see for science and history?

4. How much of what you accept as truth has come to you through proverbs, songs, and art? In what sense is this kind of knowing as reliable as deduction? What are the dangers involved in using art forms for propaganda and illusion making?

5. What response might you make to someone who claims to know important truths through mystical experience? How would you decide whether and to what extent the claims this person makes are credible?

Suggestions for Further Exploration

Akutagawa, Ryunosuke, "Rashomon." In *Rashomon and Other Stories*—New York: Prentice-Hall, 1952. A man has been murdered and we read seven versions of what might have happened, including that of the murdered man as told to a medium. What really happened and how would we go about deciding this? There is also an excellent film with the same title by Japanese director Akira Kurasawa.

Pirsig, Robert, *Zen and the Art of Motorcycle Maintenance*—New York: Bantam, 1974. A man and his son travel across the country on a motorcycle in search of truth and meaning. The protagonist, who calls himself Phaedrus (a character in one of Plato's dialogues), has had a nervous breakdown after discovering that the number of scientific hypotheses expands much faster than our ability to test them. Science, he realizes, is leading us away from "single absolute truths to multiple, indeterminate, relative ones."

Shakespeare, William, "As You Like It." In *The Complete Works of William Shakespeare: The Cambridge Edition*—New York: Doubleday, 1936. Rosalind disguises herself as a man and as Ganymede meets her lover Orlando in the forest, promising to cure him of love sickness if he will woo her as if she were Rosalind (which of course she is). This play, like several of Shakespeare's comedies, plays on the notion of what is true.

Spinrad, Norman, *Deus X*—New York: Spectra, 1993. Before dying, people encode their entities onto the big electronic board that essentially represents reality. Do they have souls (as they claim) or have the souls left and gone before God for judgment? Which position is true? A dying priest promises the female pope that he will conduct an experiment to prove them wrong, but he ends up arguing that they are right (from the board).

Woolf, Virginia, *Orlando*—New York: Penguin, 1946. In the 16th century, a young man named Orlando is granted a house by an aging queen on the condition that he never grow old. He lives until the present, changing sexes along the way and remarking as he sees his female body in the mirror, "Same person. No difference at all. Just a different sex." What is the truth about Orlando? About time? About the world? There is an excellent film of the same name.

7   Aesthetic Experience

Defining the Issue

We have been looking at the key question in epistemology: How do we know what we think we know? This chapter shifts the ground a little and looks at the relationship between beauty and truth described by the English Romantic poet John Keats:

> Beauty is truth, truth beauty,
> That is all ye know in life
> And all ye need to know

Aesthetic experience, the experience we have in the presence of the beautiful, suggests that there are ways to the truth that bypass logic and maybe even words. Beauty can lead us to truth just as certainly and accurately as ordinary rationality can. Our readings touch on the art (not the sport) of archery, the role of the artist as mediator between truth and ordinary experience, art as the translator of inner experience, and the possibility of art as an imitation of reality.

In the world of subject and object, knower and known, there are limits to our understanding. We can know only what our minds or our perceptions uncover. But there is another kind of knowing that happens more from the inside than from the outside, and it is this kind of knowing that aesthetic experience can reveal. To get a sense of this kind of knowing, ask yourself: How does a mother know her child?

Previewing the Readings

In ancient Greece, the two giants of the classical Western tradition—Plato and Aristotle—disagreed strongly about the role of the artist and the value of art to a society.

Aristotle found art, especially the tragedies of the Athenian playwrights, useful in dramatizing negative emotions and allowing the audience to experience those emotions vicariously—through temporary identification with the characters. In his view, the audience would leave the theater purged of those emotions, having experienced what he called a **catharsis,** and having no need to repeat the characters' mistakes in their own lives.

This positive view of art and artists underlies four of our readings. Plato, however, mistrusted art and found no role for artists in his *Republic*. Because he mistrusted the senses (which could easily be fooled into mistaking shadows for reality), Plato regarded artists as dangerous, as dealers in illusion. In his view, only reason was reliable, and it alone could distinguish the really real from the only apparently real.

In *Arrow of God,* contemporary Nigerian writer Chinua Achebe uses the form of the novel to introduce us to a world of characters and situations—Edogo, the artist; his father, the chief priest; and the entire village in which both of them live. You might ask yourself whether artistic creations speak to the issues of philosophy more or less clearly than the nonfiction essays.

Susanne Langer strongly disagrees with those who think of art as purely decorative, "a luxury product of civilization." Instead, she views art as essential to human life and as a reliable barometer of the health and maturity of any culture. Do you agree that art performs a vital function in society, or do you think it is expendable—especially in tough economic times. Imagine what life would be like if there were no art to express our human feelings and emotions.

Eugen Herrigel, a German philosopher, describes his own experiences in post–World War II Japan as the student of a Zen master. The art of archery, he observes, can be practiced only in a state of emptiness and detachment—the very state of knowing that Buddhists believe leads to enlightenment.

In Japan, archery can be like meditation—an art that opens up what is. The African novelist Chinua Achebe speaks in a similar way about the process an artist uses in carving a ritual mask that will open up reality for those who see it. Finally, American philosopher Susanne Langer invites us to look at art as the translator of emotions and spiritual feelings, giving form to inner experience as words give form to outer experience. All of these arts and ways of looking at art offer us avenues through beauty to truth.

7.1   Book X, *Republic*

PLATO

Preparing to Read

It will be helpful to keep in mind the Cave Allegory we discussed in Chapter 1. In it Plato warned of the danger of relying on the senses, the temptation to look at shadows and think them real. In Book X, he lays out a system of classification based on beds, rating them as closer to or farther from what a bed really is.

According to this system, there is the Idea or Form of a bed—the perfect prototype that exists in the Kingdom of Ideas. This, of course, is the "real" bed in Plato's system. In this world, imperfect copies of the "real" bed are made by carpenters. Using the Idea of "bedness" that they have in their minds, carpenters join that idea with matter (wood probably) to make a bed. A particular bed is one step removed from the reality that inspired it.

Now, imagine an artist who paints the bed the carpenter has made. This bed, the representation of the copy of the "real" bed, will be two steps removed from reality. Why, Plato wonders, would anyone want to waste their time on something so far removed from the real thing? Even worse, the painting of the bed was, in Plato's view, designed to appeal to our dangerous emotions rather than to our powerful reason. Emotions can stir us up and get us in trouble. Like the body, Plato thought, emotions must be governed by reason in a well-ordered individual.

"LET'S CONSIDER WHY dramatic poetry must be banished from our republic. We must begin with the notion of imitation or representation. A carpenter who wishes to make a bed or a table relies on the idea or type of a bed or a table, which contains its essence. But, we understand that the carpenter does not make the idea or type itself. Now, let's broaden the focus and consider all the particular things, both natural and manufactured, that exist in the cosmos. Can you imagine one craftsperson capable of making all these things? What if you yourself were that person?

Suppose you carried a mirror around with you everywhere you went. You could capture images of everything that exists, but they would be appearances only and not the things themselves. That's basically what a painter does. The painter creates a bed on canvas—an apparent bed rather than a real one. Even the carpenter is making only a particular bed and is incapable of making the type on which every particular bed is based. So, although the bed made by the carpenter seems more real than the bed made by the painter, it still lacks the complete reality—what we might call bedness—that exists only in the original type.

What we have then are three varieties of beds: the real one of divine origin, the material one made by the carpenter, and a kind of virtual bed produced on canvas. There can be only one *real* bed and that is the divinely created type. Using that type as an idea, the carpenter can manufacture a physical representation of the idea. This makes the carpenter an artisan. But, what shall we call the painter other than an imitator? The painter is a kind of third generation creator, two steps removed from the creation of the bed.

The same is true of the tragic playwrights. Like all other imitators, they stand at three removes from the truth. What they represent is appearance rather than reality. Just as by holding up a mirror you could create everything in the world, so the painter is capable of imitating any appearance. And, the same is true of poets who paint with words. Those who don't look carefully might be fooled into thinking they were seeing the real thing, and we are in great danger when we fail to distinguish image from reality.

It's one thing to paint an image of a bed and another to make a bed out of raw materials; but the real creation is the making of the type itself. Any artist—painter or poet—who understood the realities that lie behind appearances would hardly be content to remain an imitator. Beware of imitators. They catch anything in their mirrors and shine its image at you. But, we must remember how superficial these images are and how little of the real they contain. Don't be impressed by imitations and, above all, don't confuse them with reality.

Continuing to Think

If we accept Plato's view that only reason can lead us to truth and reality, we may be forced to agree with him that art is dangerous or at the very least a waste of time. If what is real exists in another world, and if our only access to that other world is through the use of our reason, then we would be truly foolish to focus our attention on the images that appeal to our senses. To do so would be to consciously put ourselves in the position of the prisoners in the Cave Allegory.

Whereas Aristotle agreed with his teacher Plato about the distinction between Form and Matter and agreed further that Form is superior to matter, he disagreed strongly on another important point. For Aristotle, there is not and cannot be a separate world of Forms. The Forms of things are, for Aristotle, in the things themselves. If you want to understand "tableness," in his view of things, you should go and look at a few hundred tables. After doing that, you should have a good idea of what makes a table a table. Notice that this is closer to inductive reasoning than Plato's more clearly deductive system. Let's consider how Aristotle builds his argument.

7.2   *Poetics [6,8,9,14]*

ARISTOTLE

Preparing to Read

In considering the possible role of art as imitation, Aristotle makes an assumption that Plato does not make. For Plato, only the pefect Forms, residing in pristine splendor in the Kingdom of Ideas, are really real. Because Aristotle assumes that Forms are in things and nowhere else, he does not share Plato's mistrust of the world revealed to us by our senses.

However, Aristotle wants to make a further distinction—between the kind of accuracy we expect from history and the kind of accuracy we expect from art. Poetry (and, by this, he means the poetry used by the Athenian playwrights) is closer to philosophy, he contends, than it is to history and it shares with philosophy the "high calling" of dealing with universals rather than particulars.

So, for Aristotle, dramatic tragedies have the same power that philosophy does to reveal the truth. The poet who writes a tragedy can use plot twists and dramatic language to arouse pity and fear, leading the audience to experience a catharsis or cleansing of these emotions. Clearly, this is imitation of a different sort than the mechanical reproduction Plato had in mind.

A TRAGEDY IS AN IMITATION of an action; it is serious, self-contained, described in poetic language, told dramatically rather than narratively, and it uses plot twists to first arouse pity and fear and then resolve them through the purging of catharsis . . .

Of the six ingredients that together make a tragedy—plot, character, diction, thought, spectacle, and song—plot is the most vital. Since tragedy imitates life rather than persons, it must follow the pattern of our own lives in revealing its truth through action. Character gives us certain qualities, but it is our actions that lead us either to happiness or unhappiness. Dramatic action rather than character development is what drives the tragic drama to its climax . . .

It follows from this that the plot must have unity. It is not enough, as some imagine, to restrict one's focus to a single character. More winnowing is required. One must choose from among all the experiences this character has had a series of connected and illuminating incidents, all of which are absolutely necessary in unfolding the plot and which together create a unity . . .

The function of a poet or playwright is to describe not what has happened—that is the job of the historian—but what might happen, according to the laws of probability and necessity. And, contrary to popular opinion, it is more than the choice of prose or verse that separates historians from poets. Put the work of Herodotus into verse and it would still be history. Poetry is closer to philosophy than to history and, like philosophy, it has the high calling of dealing with universals rather than particulars . . .

The tragic emotions of pity and fear may be aroused by special effects contrived in the production, but the superior poet/playwright uses only the structure of the play itself to achieve this result. One test of a finely-wrought play is whether merely hearing its plot (without seeing a spectacular production) leads the hearer to experience all the horror and all the compassion that are inherent in the story. A good example here would be the tragic tale of Oedipus who, unwittingly, fulfilled the prophecy he sought to avoid by killing his father and marrying his mother. On the other hand, those who use drama and the power of the spectacle to convey the merely monstrous have completely missed the point. Not every pleasure should be expected from tragedy but only the pity and fear that are proper to this genre—and these emotions are aroused by imitation.

If an enemy kills an enemy or strangers kill one another, we are moved to pity only by the actual suffering of the victim. But, when family members turn to murder, the poet has the raw material for a powerful tragedy. Effective situations often involve deeds done in ignorance with their horrific consequences revealed later. Perhaps best of all are those situations in which one who is planning a deadly deed, while ignorant of family relationships, discovers the truth in time and averts tragedy.

Continuing to Think

Is one of the functions of art to show us, under controlled conditions, the less desirable and frightening parts of our human nature? Aristotle thought so. He believed the great Athenian playwrights of his time wrote tragedies that could provide the viewers a catharsis or cleansing of violent emotions. Instead of having to imitate a character who met a tragic fate, Aristotle thought we could live that character's life vicariously, during the performance, and then not have to express the violent and destructive emotions that led to tragedy in our own lives.

Since Aristotle's focus is on this world, he does not share Plato's mistrust of the senses. Looking at actual, material objects was, for Aristotle, the way to learn the truth about them—to learn about their essences. In a similar way, art could speak to the heart about what it means to be a human person. Along with reason, Aristotle thought art could teach us valuable and essential lessons about the living of our lives and about the possibility of achieving happiness.

7.3   *Zen in the Art of Archery*

EUGEN HERRIGEL

Preparing to Read

Like all the great arts of Japan—painting, flower arranging, calligraphy, the martial arts—archery is a door to the "Great Doctrine." Because they can be practiced only with the self set aside, these arts help put the practitioner on the path to enlightenment. Zen archery is not a sport and not something you might do for diversion; it is closer to a religious rite, undertaken with seriousness of purpose and reverence.

As the master tells Herrigel, the way to practice the art of archery is "By letting go of yourself, leaving yourself and everything yours behind so decisively that nothing more is left of you but a purposeless tension." Zen Buddhism represents a blending of Buddhism with Taoism. If you want to know what is, Taoist philosophers say, look to nature. There is no effort, no opposition, no "me versus you," and yet everything happens with marvelous efficiency. The secret is in letting things happen rather than trying to make things happen.

Imagine a seed, germinating deep in the earth, putting down roots and sending up a green shoot. It has no purpose of its own, it does not strive, and it will try to push through concrete, if necessary, to play its role in the big production called spring. Taoism is known for its paradoxes—empty and be full, yield and conquer. Water will flow to the sea. But if a rock is in the way, it will flow around it rather than confront it and demand the rock move. By letting go, you can accomplish everything.

DURING THE NEXT LESSON the Master—to my disappointment—went on with the previous exercises: drawing, holding, and loosing. But all his encouragement availed nothing. Although I tried, in accordance with his instructions, not to give way to the tension, but to struggle beyond it as though no limits were set by the nature of the bow; although I strove to wait until the tension simultaneously fulfilled and loosed itself in the shot—despite all my efforts every shot miscarried; bewitched, botched, wobbling. Only when it became clear that it was not only pointless to continue these exercises but positively dangerous, since I was oppressed more and more by a premonition of failure, did the Master break off and begin on a completely new tack.

"When you come to the lessons in the future," he warned us, "you must collect yourselves on your way here. Focus your minds on what happens in the practice-hall. Walk past everything without noticing it, as if there were only one thing in the world that is important and real, and that is archery!"

The process of letting go of oneself was likewise divided into separate sections which had to be worked through carefully. And here too the Master contented himself with brief hints. For the performance of these exercises it is sufficient that the pupil should understand, or in some cases merely guess, what is demanded of him. Hence there is no need to conceptualize the distinctions which are traditionally expressed in images. And who knows whether these images, born of centuries of practice, may not go deeper than all our carefully calculated knowledge?

The first step along this road had already been taken. It had led to a loosening of the body, without which the bow cannot be properly drawn. If the shot is to be loosed right, the physical loosening must now be continued in a mental and spiritual loosening, so as to make the mind not only agile, but free; agile because of its freedom, and free because of its original agility; and this original agility is essentially different from everything that is usually understood by mental agility. Thus, between these two states of bodily relaxedness on the one hand and spiritual freedom on the other there is a difference of level which cannot be overcome by breath-control alone, but only by withdrawing from all attachments whatsoever, by becoming utterly egoless: so that the soul, sunk within itself, stands in the plenitude of its nameless origin.

The demand that the door of the senses be closed is not met by turning energetically away from the sensible world, but rather by a readiness to yield without resistance. In order that this actionless activity may be accomplished instinctively, the soul needs an inner hold, and it wins it by concentrating on breathing This is performed consciously and with a conscientiousness that borders on the pedantic. The breathing in, like the breathing out, is practiced again and again by itself with the utmost care. One does not have to wait long for results. The more one concentrates on breathing, the more the external stimuli fade into the background. They sink away in a kind of muffled roar which one hears with only half an ear at first, and in the end one finds it no more disturbing than the distant roar of the sea, which, once one has grown accustomed to it, is no longer perceived. In due course one even grows immune to large stimuli, and at the same time detachment from them becomes easier and quicker. Care has only to be taken that the body is relaxed whether standing, sitting, or lying, and if one then concentrates on breathing one soon feels oneself shut in by impermeable layers of silence. One only knows and feels that one breathes. And, to detach oneself from this feeling and knowing, no fresh decision is required, for the breathing slows down of its own accord, becomes more and more economical in the use of breath, and finally, slipping by degrees into a blurred monotone, escapes one's attention altogether.

This exquisite state of unconcerned immersion in oneself is not, unfortunately, of long duration. It is liable to be disturbed from inside. As though sprung from nowhere, moods, feelings, desires, worries and even thoughts incontinently rise up, in a meaningless jumble, and the more

farfetched and preposterous they are, and the less they have to do with that on which one has fixed one's consciousness, the more tenaciously they hang on. It is as though they wanted to avenge themselves on consciousness for having, through concentration, touched upon realms it would otherwise never reach. The only successful way of rendering this disturbance inoperative is to keep on breathing, quietly and unconcernedly, to enter into friendly relations with whatever appears on the scene, to accustom oneself to it, to look at it equably and at last grow weary of looking. In this way one gradually gets into a state which resembles the melting drowsiness on the verge of sleep.

To slip into it finally is the danger that has to be avoided. It is met by a peculiar leap of concentration, comparable perhaps to the jolt which a man who has stayed up all night gives himself when he knows that his life depends on all his senses being alert; and if this leap has been successful but a single time it can be repeated with certainty. With its help the soul is brought to the point where it vibrates of itself in itself—a serene pulsation which can be heightened into the feeling, otherwise experienced only in rare dreams, of extraordinary lightness, and the rapturous certainty of being able to summon up energies in any direction, to intensify or to release tensions graded to a nicety.

This state, in which nothing definite is thought, planned, striven for, desired or expected, which aims in no particular direction and yet knows itself capable alike of the possible and the impossible, so unswerving is its power—this state, which is at bottom purposeless and egoless, was called by the Master truly "spiritual." It is in fact charged with spiritual awareness and is therefore also called "right presence of mind." This means that the mind or spirit is present everywhere, because it is nowhere attached to any particular place. And it can remain present because, even when related to this or that object, it does not cling to it by reflection and thus lose its original mobility. Like water filling a pond, which is always ready to flow off again, it can work its inexhaustible power because it is free, and be open to everything because it is empty. This state is essentially a primordial state, and its symbol, the empty circle, is not empty of meaning for him who stands within it.

Out of the fullness of this presence of mind, disturbed by no ulterior motive, the artist who is released from all attachment must practice his art. But if he is to fit himself self-effacingly into the creative process, the practice of the art must have the way smoothed for it. For if, in his self-immersion, he saw himself faced with a situation into which he could not leap instinctively, he would first have to bring it to consciousness. He would then enter again into all the relationships from which he had detached himself; he would be like one wakened, who considers his program for the day, but not like an Awakened One who lives and works in the primordial state. It would never appear to him as if the individual parts of the creative process were being played into his hands by a higher power; he would never experience how intoxicatingly the vibrancy of an event is communicated to him who is himself only a vibration, and how everything that he does is done before he knows it.

The necessary detachment and self-liberation, the inward-turning and intensification of life until full presence of mind is reached, are therefore not left to chance or to favorable conditions, the less so as the more depends on them, and least of all are they abandoned to the process of creation itself—which already demands all the artist's powers—in the hope that the desired concentration will appear of its own accord. Before all doing and creating, before ever he begins to devote and adjust himself to his task, the artist summons forth this presence of mind and makes sure of it through practice. But, from the time he succeeds in capturing it not merely at rare intervals but in having it at his fingertips in a few moments, the concentration, like the breathing, is brought into connection with archery. In order to slip the more easily into the process of drawing the bow and loosing the shot, the archer, kneeling to one side and beginning to concentrate, rises to his feet, ceremoniously steps up to the target and, with a deep obeisance, offers the bow and arrow like consecrated gifts, then nocks the arrow, raises the bow, draws it and waits in an attitude of supreme spiritual alertness. After the lightning release of the arrow and the tension, the archer remains in the posture adopted immediately following the shot until, after slowly expelling his breath, he is forced to draw air again. Then only does he let his arms sink, bows to the target and, if he has no more shots to discharge, steps quietly into the background.

Archery thus becomes a ceremony which exemplifies the "Great Doctrine."

Even if the pupil does not, at this stage, grasp the true significance of his shots, he at least understands why archery cannot be a sport, a gymnastic exercise. He understands why the technically learnable part of it must be practiced to the point of repletion. If everything depends on the archer's becoming purposeless and effacing himself in the event, then its outward realization must occur automatically, in no further need of the controlling or reflecting intelligence.

It is this mastery of form that the Japanese method of instruction seeks to inculcate. Practice, repetition, and repetition of the repeated with ever increasing intensity are its distinctive features for long stretches of the way. At least this is true of all the traditional arts. Demonstration, example; intuition, imitation—that is the fundamental relationship of instructor to pupil, although with the introduction of new educational subjects during the last few decades, European methods of instruction have also gained a foothold and been applied with undeniable understanding. How is it that in spite of the initial enthusiasm for everything new, the Japanese arts have remained in essence untouched by these educational reforms?

It is not easy to give an answer to this question. Yet the attempt must be made, even if only sketchily, with a view to throwing more light on the style of instruction and the meaning of imitation.

The Japanese pupil brings with him three things: good education, passionate love for his chosen art, and uncritical veneration of his teacher. The teacher-pupil relationship has belonged since ancient times to the basic commitments of life and therefore presupposes, on the part of the teacher, a high responsibility which goes far beyond the scope of his professional duties.

Nothing more is required of the pupil at first, than that he should conscientiously copy what the teacher shows him. Shunning long-winded instructions and explanations, the latter contents himself with perfunctory commands and does not reckon on any questions from the pupil. Impassively he looks on at the blundering efforts, not even hoping for independence or initiative, and waits patiently for growth and ripeness. Both have time: the teacher does not harass, and the pupil does not overtax himself.

Far from wishing to waken the artist in the pupil prematurely, the teacher considers it his first task to make him a skilled artisan with sovereign control of his craft. The pupil follows out this intention with untiring industry. As though he had no higher aspirations he bows under his burden with a kind of obtuse devotion, only to discover in the course of years that forms which he perfectly masters no longer oppress but liberate. He grows daily more capable of following any inspiration without technical effort, and also of letting inspiration come to him through meticulous observation. The hand that guides the brush has already caught and executed what floated before the mind at the same moment the mind began to form it, and in the end the pupil no longer knows which of the two—mind or hand—was responsible for the work.

But, to get that far, for the skill to become "spiritual," a concentration of all the physical and psychic forces is needed, as in the art of archery—which, as will be seen from the following examples, cannot under any circumstances be dispensed with.

A painter seats himself before his pupils. He examines his brush and slowly makes it ready for use, carefully rubs ink, straightens the long strip of paper that lies before him on the mat, and finally, after lapsing for a while into profound concentration, in which he sits like one inviolable, he produces with rapid, absolutely sure strokes a picture which, capable of no further correction and needing none, serves the class as a model.

A flower master begins the lesson by cautiously untying the bast which holds together the flowers and sprays of blossom, and laying it to one side carefully rolled up. Then he inspects the sprays one by one, picks out the best after repeated examination, cautiously bends them into the form which exactly corresponds with the role they are to play, and finally places them together in an exquisite vase. The completed picture looks just as if the Master had guessed what Nature had glimpsed in dark dreams.

In both these cases—and I must confine myself to them—the Masters behave as if they were alone. They hardly condescend to give their pupils a glance, still less a word. They carry out the preliminary movements musingly and composedly, they efface themselves in the process of shaping and creating, and to both the pupils and themselves it seems like a self-contained event from the first opening maneuvers to the completed work. And indeed the whole thing has such expressive power that it affects the beholder like a picture.

But why doesn't the teacher allow these preliminaries, unavoidable though they are, to be done by an experienced pupil? Does it lend wings to his visionary and plastic powers if he rubs the ink himself, if he unties the bast so elaborately instead of cutting it and carelessly throwing it away? And what impels him to repeat this process at every single lesson, and, with the same remorseless insistence, to make his pupils copy it without the least alteration? He sticks to this traditional custom because he knows from experience that the preparations for working put him simultaneously in the right frame of mind for creating. The meditative repose in which he performs them gives him that vital loosening and equability of all his powers, that collectedness and presence of mind, without which no right work can be done. Sunk without purpose in what he is doing, he is brought face to face with that moment when the work, hovering before him in ideal lines, realizes itself as if of its own accord. As with the steps and postures in archery, so here in modified form other preparations have the same meaning. And only where this does not apply, as for instance with religious dancers and actors, are the self-recollection and self-immersion practiced before they appear on the stage.

As in the case of archery, there can be no question but that these arts are ceremonies. More clearly than the teacher could express it in words, they tell the pupil that the right frame of mind for the artist is only reached when the preparing and the creating, the technical and the artistic, the material and the spiritual, the project and the object, flow together without a break. And here he finds a new theme for emulation. He is now required to exercise perfect control over the various ways of concentration and self-effacement. Imitation, no longer applied to objective contents which anybody can copy with a little good will, becomes looser, nimbler, more spiritual. The pupil sees himself on the brink of new possibilities, but discovers at the same time that their realization does not depend in the slightest degree on his good will.

Assuming that his talent can survive the increasing strain, there is one scarcely avoidable danger that lies ahead of the pupil on his road to mastery. Not the danger of wasting himself in idle self-gratification—for the East has no aptitude for this cult of the ego—but rather the danger of getting stuck in his achievement, which is confirmed by his success and magnified by his renown: in other words, of behaving as if the artistic existence were a form of life that bore witness to its own validity.

The teacher foresees this danger. Carefully and with the adroitness of a psychopomp he seeks to head the pupil off in time and to detach him from himself. This he does by pointing out, casually and as though it were scarcely worth a mention in view of all that the pupil has already learned, that all right doing is accomplished only in a state of true selflessness, in which the doer cannot be present any longer as "himself." Only the spirit is present, a kind of awareness which shows no trace of egohood and for that reason ranges without limit through all distances and depths, with "eyes that hear and with ears that see."

Thus the teacher lets his pupil voyage onward through himself. But the pupil, with growing receptivity, lets the teacher bring to view something of which he has often heard but whose reality is only now beginning to become tangible on the basis of his own experiences. It is immaterial what name the teacher gives it, whether indeed he names it at all. The pupil understands him even when he keeps silent.

The important thing is that an inward movement is thereby initiated. The teacher pursues it, and, without influencing its course with further instructions which would merely disturb it, helps the pupil in the most secret and intimate way he knows: by direct transference of the spirit, as it is called in Buddhist circles. "Just as one uses a burning candle to light others with," so the teacher transfers the spirit of the right art from heart to heart, that it may be illumined. If such should be granted to the pupil, he remembers that more important than all outward works, however attractive, is the inward work which he has to accomplish if he is to fulfill his vocation as an artist.

The inward work, however, consists in his turning the man he is, and the self he feels himself and perpetually finds himself to be, into the raw material of a training and shaping whose end is mastery. In it, the artist and the human being meet in something higher. For mastery proves its validity as a form of life only when it dwells in the boundless Truth and, sustained by it, becomes the art of the origin. The Master no longer seeks, but finds. As an artist he is the hieratic man; as a man, the artist, into whose heart, in all his doing and not-doing, working and waiting, being and not-being, the Buddha gazes. The man, the art, the work—it is all one. The art of the inner work, which unlike the outer does not forsake the artist, which he does not "do" and can only "be," springs from depths of which the day knows nothing.

Steep is the way to mastery. Often nothing keeps the pupil on the move but his faith in his teacher, whose mastery is now beginning to dawn on him. He is a living example of the inner work, and he convinces by his mere presence.

How far the pupil will go is not the concern of the teacher and Master. Hardly has he shown him the right way when he must let him go on alone. There is only one thing more he can do to help him endure loneliness: he turns him away from himself, from the Master, by exhorting him to go further than he himself has done, and to "climb on the shoulders of his teacher."

Wherever his way may take him, the pupil, though he may lose sight of his teacher, can never forget him. With a gratitude as great as the uncritical veneration of the beginner, as strong as the saving faith of the artist, he now takes his Master's place, ready for any sacrifice. Countless examples down to the recent past testify that this gratitude far exceeds the measure of what is customary among mankind.

Continuing to Think

Why does Herrigel speak of the archer as an artist? Surely, the performance is a beautiful one as the artist moves with grace and perfect efficiency. And there is more. Like other artists, the Zen archer can plug us in to something larger—can reveal something to us that cannot be grasped by ordinary means and probably cannot be said in words.

In a very real sense, hitting the target is not the point in this art. And at the same time, if you master the art, you will hit the target every time, even blindfolded. Taoists and Zen masters call this "doing without doing." The sun knows how to give us light, heat, the energy of life itself. And the sun knows that in the evening it must give way to the moon and the cool of the evening.

Pitting your small ego and its petty concerns against the wisdom of nature is not only wasteful of effort; it is also foolish. If you wish to command the sun not to rise, go ahead. You will only waste your time and energy and prove yourself ineffective. Better to empty yourself and learn what nature has to teach you. The sun rises; the sun sets. Nothing lasts. Yet the great energy of the lifeforce goes on forever.

7.4   *Arrow of God*

CHINUA ACHEBE

Preparing to Read

There are artists in every culture, and one of their functions is to help the rest of us see what we cannot see with our own limited vision. Like the Zen archer in the last reading, Edogo, the carver of ritual masks, is part of something much larger than himself. In this novel, the ways of the West have begun to infiltrate a Nigerian village and Ezeulu, the Chief Priest of Ulu, struggles against them.

In this selection we see his son, Edogo, performing the role of artist as he carves the ritual mask that will enable a new ancestral spirit to speak to the people. He is not carving a god, he assures his father; he is carving a mask. We see him enter his ritual space, the sacred spirit-house that faces the forest. Like the Zen archer, he must empty himself and allow the art to emerge.

Notice the similarity with the last reading. It is not the individual who does what he does. The individual is a conduit, a channel, through which greater forces flow. Edogo sees himself and is seen by his village as a religious figure as well as an artist. Like a priest, he presides over mysteries, and through his person he helps them become available to others.

MR. GOODCOUNTRY told the converts of Umuaro about the early Christians of the Niger Delta who fought the bad customs of their people, destroyed shrines and killed the sacred iguana. He told them of Joshua Hart, his kinsman, who suffered martyrdom in Bonny.

"If we are Christians, we must be ready to die for the faith," he said. "You must be ready to kill the python as the people of the rivers killed the iguana. You address the python as Father. It is nothing but a snake, the snake that deceived our first mother, Eve. If you are afraid to kill it do not count yourself a Christian."

The first Umuaro man to kill and eat a python was Josiah Madu of Umuagu. But the story did not spread outside the little group of Christians, most of whom refused, however, to follow Josiah's example. They were led by Moses Unachukwu, the first and the most famous convert in Umuaro.

Unachukwu was a carpenter, the only one in all those parts. He had learnt the trade under the white missionaries who built the Onitsha Industrial Mission. In his youth he had been conscripted to carry the loads of the soldiers who were sent to destroy Abame as a reprisal for the killing of a white man. What Unachukwu saw during that punitive expedition taught him that

the white man was not a thing of fun. And so after his release he did not return to Umuaro but made his way to Onitsha, where he became house-boy to the carpenter-missionary, J. P. Hargreaves. After over ten years' sojourn in a strange land, Unachukwu returned to Umuaro with the group of missionaries who succeeded after two previous failures in planting the new faith among his people. Unachukwu regarded the success of this third missionary effort as due largely to himself. He saw his sojourn in Onitsha as a parallel to that of the Moses of the Old Testament in Egypt.

As the only carpenter in the neighbourhood Moses Unachukwu built almost single-handed the new church in Umuaro. Now he was not only a lay reader but a pastor's warden. As Umuaro did not have a pastor as yet, only a catechist, the title was honorific. But it showed the great esteem in which Moses Unachukwu was held in the young church. The last catechist, Mr. Molokwu, consulted him in whatever he did. Mr. Goodcountry, on the other hand, attempted from the very first to ignore him. But Moses was not a man to be ignored lightly.

Mr. Goodcountry's teaching about the sacred python gave Moses the first opportunity to challenge him openly. To do this he used not only the Bible but, strangely enough for a convert, the myths of Umuaro. He spoke with great power for, coming as he did from the village which carried the priesthood of Idemili, he knew perhaps more than others what the python was. On the other side, his great knowledge of the Bible and his sojourn in Onitsha which was the source of the new religion gave him great confidence. He told the new teacher quite bluntly that neither the Bible nor the catechism asked converts to kill the python, a beast full of ill omen.

"Was it for nothing that God put a curse on its head?" he asked, and then turned abruptly into the traditions of Umuaro. "Today there are six villages in Umuaro; but this has not always been the case. Our fathers tell us that there were seven before, and the seventh was called Umuama." Some of the converts nodded their support. Mr. Goodcountry listened patiently and contemptuously.

"One day six brothers of Umuama killed the python and asked one of their number, Iweka, to cook yam pottage with it. Each of them brought a piece of yam and a bowl of water to Iweka. When he finished cooking the yam pottage the men came one by one and took their pieces of yam. Then they began to fill their bowls to the mark with the yam stew. But this time only four of them took their measure before the stew got finished."

Moses Unachukwu's listeners smiled, except Mr. Goodcountry who sat like a rock. Oduche smiled because he had heard the story as a little boy and forgotten it until now.

"The brothers began to quarrel violently, and then to fight. Very soon the fighting spread throughout Umuama, and so fierce was it that the village was almost wiped out. The few people that survived fled from their village, across the great river to the land of Olu where they are scattered today. The remaining six villages seeing what had happened to Umuama went to a seer to know the reason, and he told them that the royal python was sacred to Idemili; it was this deity which had punished Umuama.

From that day the six villages decreed that henceforth the python was not to be killed in Umuaro, and that anyone who killed it would be regarded as having killed his kinsman." Moses ended by counting on his fingers the villages and clans which also forbade the killing of the python. Then Mr. Goodcountry spoke.

"The story such as you have just told us is not fit to be heard in the house of God. But I allowed you to go on so that all may see the foolishness of it." There was murmuring from the congregation which might have stood either for agreement or disagreement.

"I shall leave it to your own people to answer you." Mr. Goodcountry looked round the small congregation, but no one spoke. "Is there no one here who can speak up for the Lord?"

Oduche who had thus far inclined towards Unachukwu's position had a sudden stab of insight. He raised his hand and was about to put it down again. But Mr. Goodcountry had seen him. "Yes?"

"It is not true that the Bible does not ask us to kill the serpent. Did not God tell Adam to crush the serpent which deceived his wife?" Many people clapped for him.

"Do you hear that, Moses?"

Moses stood up to answer, but Mr. Goodcountry was not going to give him another opportunity.

"You say you are the first Christian in Umuaro, you partake of the Holy Meal; and yet whenever you open your mouth nothing but heathen filth pours out. Today a child who sucks at his mother's breast has taught you the Scriptures. Is it not as Our Lord himself said that the first shall become last and the last become first. The world will pass away but not one single word of Our Lord will be set aside." He turned to Oduche. "When the time comes for your baptism you will be called Peter; on this rock will I build my Church."

This caused more clapping from a part of the congregation. Moses immediately rose to his feet.

"Do I look to you like someone you can put in your bag and walk away?" he asked. "I have been to the fountainhead of this new religion and seen with my own eyes the white people who brought it. So I want to tell you now that I will not be led astray by outsiders who choose to weep louder than the owners of the corpse. You are not the first teacher I have seen; you are not the second; you are not the third. If you are wise you will face the work they sent you to do here and take your hand off the python. You can say that I told you so. Nobody here has complained to you that the python has ever blocked his way as he came to church. If you want to do your work here you will heed what I have said, but if you want to be the lizard that ruined his own mother's funeral you may carry on as you are doing." He turned to Oduche. "You may be called Peter, or you may be called Paul or Barnabas; it does not pull a hair from me. And I have nothing to say to a mere boy who should be picking palm nuts for his mother. But since you have also become our teacher I shall be waiting for the day when you will have the courage to kill a python in this Umuaro. A coward may cover the ground with his words but when the time comes to fight he runs away."

At that moment Oduche took his decision. There were two pythons—a big one and a small one—which lived almost entirely in his mother's hut, on top of the wall which carried the roof. They did no harm and kept the rats away; only once were they suspected of frightening away a hen and swallowing her eggs. Oduche decided that he would hit one of them on the head with a big stick. He would do it so carefully and secretly that when it finally died people would think it had died of its own accord.

Six days passed before Oduche found a favourable moment, and during this time his heart lost some of its strength. He decided to take the smaller python. He pushed it down from the wall with his stick but could not bring himself to smash its head. Then he thought he heard people coming and had to act quickly. With lightning speed he picked it up as he had seen their neighbour, Anosi, do many times, and carried it into his sleeping-room. A new and ex-

citing thought came to him then. He opened the box which Moses had built for him, took out his singlet and towel and locked the python inside. He felt a great relief within. The python would die for lack of air, and he would be responsible for its death without being guilty of killing it. In the ambivalence of his present life his act seemed to him a very happy compromise.

Ezeulu's first son, Edogo, had left home early that day to finish the mask he was carving for a new ancestral spirit. It was now only five days to the Festival of the Pumpkin Leaves when this spirit was expected to return from the depths of the earth and appear to men as a Mask. Those who would act as his attendants were making great plans for his coming; they had learnt their dance and were now anxious about the mask Edogo was carving for them. There were other carvers in Umuaro besides him; some of them were even better. But Edogo had a reputation for finishing his work on time unlike Obiako, the master carver, who only took up his tools when he saw his customers coming. If it had been any other kind of carving Edogo would have finished it long ago, working at it any moment his hands were free. But a mask was different; he could not do it in the home under the profane gaze of women and children but had to return to the spirit-house built for such work at a secluded corner of the Nkwo market place. No one who had not been initiated into the secret of Masks would dare to approach the hut which faced the forest, away from the market place. At certain times when women were called upon to rub its red-earth exterior and decorate it with white, green, yellow and black patterns men were always there guarding the entrance.

The hut was dark inside although the eye got used to it after a short while. Edogo put down the white *okwe* wood on which he was going to work and then unslung his goatskin bag in which he carried his tools. Apart from the need for secrecy, Edogo had always found the atmosphere of this hut right for carving masks. All around him were older masks and other regalia of ancestral spirits, some of them older than even his father. They produced a certain ambience which gave power and cunning to his fingers. Most of the masks were for fierce, aggressive spirits with horns and teeth the size of fingers. But four of them belonged to maiden-spirits and were delicately beautiful. Edogo remembered with a smile what Nwanyinma told him when he first married his wife. Nwanyinma was a widow with whom he had made friends in his bachelor days. In her jealousy against the younger rival she had told Edogo that the only woman whose breasts stayed erect year after year was the maiden-spirit.

Edogo sat down on the floor near the entrance where there was the most light and began to work. Now and again he heard the voices of people passing through the market place from one village of Umuaro to another. But when his carving finally got hold of him he heard no more voices.

The mask was beginning to come out of the wood when Edogo suddenly stopped and turned his ear in the direction of the voices which had broken into his work. One of the voices was very familiar; yes, it was their neighbour, Anosi. Edogo listened very hard and then stood up and went to the wall nearest the market centre. He could now hear quite clearly. Anosi seemed to be talking to two or three other men he had just met.

"Yes. I was there and saw it with my own eyes," he was saying. "I would not have believed it had somebody else told me. I saw the box opened and a python inside it."

"Do not repeat it," said one of the others. "It cannot be true."

"That is what everybody says: it cannot be true. But I saw it with my own eyes. Go to Umuachala now and see the whole village in turmoil."

"What that man Ezeulu will bring to Umuaro is pregnant and nursing a baby at the same time."

"I have heard many things, but never till today have I heard of an abomination of this kind."

By the time Edogo reached home his father was still in a very bad temper, only that now his anger was not so much against Oduche as

against all the double-faced neighbours and passers-by whose words of sympathy barely concealed the mockery in their hearts. And even if they had been sincere Ezeulu would still have resented anybody making him an object of pity. At first his anger smouldered inwardly. But the last group of women who went in to see his wives, looking like visitors to a place of death, inflamed his wrath. He heard them in the inner compound shouting: "E-u-u! What shall we do to the children of today?" Ezeulu strode into the compound and ordered them to leave.

"If I see any one of you still here when I go and come back she will know that I am an evil man."

"What harm have we done in coming to console another woman?"

"I say leave this place at once!"

The women hurried out saying: "Forgive us; we have erred."

It was therefore a very irate Ezeulu to whom Edogo told his story of what he had heard at the Nkwo market place. When he finished his father asked him curtly:

"And what did you do when you heard that?"

"What should I have done?" Edogo was surprised and a little angry at his father's tone.

"Don't you hear him?" asked Ezeulu of no one. "My first son, somebody says to your hearing that your father has committed an abomination, and you ask me what you should have done. When I was your age I would have known what to do. I would have come out and broken the man's head instead of hiding in the spirit-house."

Edogo was now really angry but he controlled his tongue. "When you were my age your father did not send one of his sons to worship the white man's god." He walked away to his own hut full of bitterness for having broken off his carving to come and see what was happening at home, only to be insulted.

"I blame Obika for his fiery temper," thought Ezeulu, "but how much better is a fiery temper than this cold ash!" He inclined backwards and rested his head on the wall behind him and began to gnash his teeth.

Continuing to Think

In the West, we are used to celebrating the talents of individual artists and, sometimes, paying large sums of money (occasionally only after they are dead) for their accomplishments. Because we see ourselves as separate from each other and from the forces of nature, we prize individualism and independence.

Edogo lives in a village that celebrates the community and sees the individual as inextricably bound to it and closely allied with spiritual entities, some of whom are deceased ancestors. Unlike the Western God, who is separate from nature and creates out of nothing, Ulu seems to share the sacred space of this world with everyone else.

What do we gain and what do we lose by emphasizing our separateness? In Edogo's village there is considerably less freedom than we are used to having. But are there benefits as well as losses? Edogo, and everyone else, has a place, a role, a community. There is an old African saying: "It takes a whole village to raise a child."

7.5   *The Cultural Importance of Art*

SUSANNE K. LANGER

Preparing to Read

In a 1958 lecture at Syracuse University, American philosopher Susanne Langer addressed an issue that is very prominent in modern political debates: Is art something we can do without as demands on every spending dollar increase? Her answer is a resounding *no*. For as long as there has been human culture, there has been art, and Langer told her audience that we ignore or devalue art only by putting ourselves and our human society at great risk.

Art—including painting, sculpture, architecture, music, dance, literature, drama, and film—is, in Langer's definition, "the practice of creating perceptible forms expressive of human feeling," including pleasure and displeasure, physical sensation, emotion, and attitude. Although words or language provide our primary means of talking about concepts, there is an essential part of reality that does not lend itself to linguistic description. Langer calls that part of reality that is inaccessible to language "inner experience," the life of emotion and feeling.

Because emotions cannot be described clearly using words, they are sometimes labeled irrational. Langer believes this inner life is not irrational at all, but she does acknowledge that its logical forms are quite different from those of ordinary communication. What if art could give us a language for codifying our inner experience and provide us with the self-knowledge we need to survive—as individuals and as a culture? Would it still be considered a frill, or might art be seen as a partner with language in retaining what we call civilization?

EVERY CULTURE develops some kind of art as surely as it develops language. Some primitive cultures have no real mythology or religion, but all have some art—dance, song, design (sometimes only on tools or on the human body). Dance, above all, seems to be the oldest elaborated art.

The ancient ubiquitous character of art contrasts sharply with the prevalent idea that art is a luxury product of civilization, a cultural frill, a piece of social veneer.

It fits better with the conviction held by most artists, that art is the epitome of human life, the truest record of insight and feeling, and that the strongest military or economic society without art is poor in comparison with the most primitive tribe of savage painters, dancers, or idol carvers. Wherever a society has really achieved culture (in the ethnological sense, not the popular sense of "social form") it has begotten art, not late in its career, but at the very inception of it.

Art is, indeed, the spearhead of human development, social and individual. The vulgarization of art is the surest symptom of ethnic decline. The growth of a new art or even a great and radically new style always bespeaks a young and vigorous mind, whether collective or single.

What sort of thing is art, that it should play such a leading role in human development? It is not an intellectual pursuit, but is necessary to intellectual life; it is not religion, but grows up with religion, serves it, and in large measure determines it.

We cannot enter here on a long discussion of what has been claimed as the essence of art, the true nature of art, or its defining function; in a single lecture dealing with one aspect of art, namely its cultural influence, I can only give you by way of preamble my own definition of art, with categorical brevity. This does not mean that I set up this definition in a categorical spirit, but only that we have no time to debate it; so you are asked to accept it as an assumption underlying these reflections.

Art, in the sense here intended—that is, the generic term subsuming painting, sculpture, architecture, music, dance, literature, drama, and film—may be defined as the practice of creating perceptible forms expressive of human feeling. . . .

Language, of course, is our prime instrument of conceptual expression. The things we can say are in effect the things we can think. Words are the terms of our thinking as well as the terms in which we present our thoughts, because they present the objects of thought to the thinker himself. Before language communicates ideas, it gives them form, makes them clear, and in fact makes them what they are. Whatever has a name is an object for thought. Without words, sense experience is only a flow of impressions, as subjective as our feelings; words make it objective, and carve it up into *things* and *facts* that we can note, remember, and think about. Language gives outward experience its form, and makes it definite and clear.

There is, however, an important part of reality that is quite inaccessible to the formative influence of language: that is the realm of so-called "inner experience," the life of feeling and emotion. The reason why language is so powerless here is not, as many people suppose, that feeling and emotion are irrational; on the contrary, they seem irrational because language does not help to make them conceivable, and most people cannot conceive anything without the logical scaffolding of words. The unfitness of language to convey subjective experience is a somewhat technical subject, easier for logicians to understand than for artists; but the gist of it is that the form of language does not reflect the natural form of feeling, so that we cannot shape any extensive concepts of feeling with the help of ordinary, discursive language. Therefore the words whereby we refer to feeling only name very general kinds of inner experience—excitement, calm, joy, sorrow, love, hate, and so on. But

From *Philosophical Sketches* by Susanne K. Langer. Pp. 83–84, 88–94. Copyright © 1962 The Johns Hopkins University Press. Reprinted by permission of the Johns Hopkins University Press.

there is no language to describe just how one joy differs, sometimes radically, from another. The real nature of feeling is something language as such—as discursive symbolism—cannot render.

For this reason, the phenomena of feeling and emotion are usually treated by philosophers as irrational. The only pattern discursive thought can find in them is the pattern of outward events that occasion them. There are different degrees of fear, but they are thought of as so many degrees of the same simple feeling.

But human feeling is a fabric, not a vague mass. It has an intricate dynamic pattern, possible combinations and new emergent phenomena. It is a pattern of organically interdependent and interdetermined tensions and resolutions, a pattern of almost infinitely complex activation and cadence. To it belongs the whole gamut of our sensibility—the sense of straining thought, all mental attitude and motor set. Those are the deeper reaches that underlie the surface waves of our emotion, and make human life a life of feeling instead of an unconscious metabolic existence interrupted by feelings.

It is, I think, this dynamic pattern that finds its formal expression in the arts. The expressiveness of art is like that of a symbol, not that of an emotional symptom; it is as a formulation of feeling for our conception that a work of art is properly said to be expressive. It may serve somebody's need of self-expression besides, but that is not what makes it good or bad art. In a special sense one may call a work of art a symbol of feeling, for, like a symbol, it formulates our ideas of inward experience, as discourse formulates our ideas of things and facts in the outside world. A work of art differs from a genuine symbol—that is, a symbol in the full and usual sense in that it does not point beyond itself to something else. Its relation to feeling is a rather special one that we cannot undertake to analyze here; in effect, the feeling it expresses appears to be directly given with it—as the sense of a true metaphor, or the value of a religious myth—and is not separable from its expression. We speak of the feeling *of,* or the feeling *in,* a work of art, not the feeling it means. And we speak truly; a work of art presents something like a direct vision of vitality, emotion, subjective reality.

The primary function of art is to objectify feeling so that we can contemplate and understand it. It is the formulation of so-called "inward experience," the "inner life," that is impossible to achieve by discursive thought, because its forms are incommensurable with the forms of language and all its derivatives (e.g., mathematics, symbolic logic). Art objectifies the sentience and desire, self-consciousness and world-consciousness, emotions and moods, that are generally regarded as irrational because words cannot give us clear ideas of them. But the premise tacitly assumed in such a judgment—namely, that anything language cannot express is formless and irrational—seems to me to be an error. I believe the life of feeling is not irrational; its logical forms are merely very different from the structures of discourse. But they are so much like the dynamic forms of art that art is their natural symbol. Through plastic works, music, fiction, dance, or dramatic forms we can conceive what vitality and emotion feel like.

This brings us, at last, to the question of the cultural importance of the arts. Why is art so apt to be the vanguard of cultural advance, as it was in Egypt, in Greece, in Christian Europe (think of Gregorian music and Gothic architecture), in Renaissance Italy—not to speculate about ancient cavemen, whose art is all that we know of them? One thinks of culture as economic increase, social organization, the gradual ascendancy of rational thinking and scientific control of nature over superstitious imagination and magical practices. But art is not practical; it is neither philosophy nor science; it is not religion, morality, or even social comment (as many drama critics take comedy to be). What does it contribute to culture that could be of major importance?

It merely presents forms—sometimes intangible forms—to imagination. Its direct appeal is to that faculty, or function, that Lord Bacon considered the chief stumbling block in the way of reason, and that enlightened writers like Stuart

Chase never tire of condemning as the source of all nonsense and bizarre erroneous beliefs. And so it is; but it is also the source of all insight and true beliefs. Imagination is probably the oldest mental trait that is typically human—older than discursive reason; it is probably the common source of dream, reason, religion, and all true general observation. It is this primitive human power—imagination—that engenders the arts and is in turn directly affected by their products.

Somewhere at the animalian starting line of human evolution lie the beginnings of that supreme instrument of the mind—language. We think of it as a device for communication among the members of a society. But communication is only one, and perhaps not even the first, of its functions. The first thing it does is to break up what William James called the "blooming, buzzing confusion" of sense perception into units and groups, events and chains of events—things and relations, causes and effects. All these patterns are imposed on our experience by language. We think, as we speak, in terms of objects and their relations.

But the process of breaking up our sense experience in this way, making reality conceivable, memorable, sometimes even predictable, is a process of imagination. Primitive conception is imagination. Language and imagination grow up together in a reciprocal tutelage.

What discursive symbolism—language in its literal use—does for our awareness of things about us and our own relation to them, the arts do for our awareness of subjective reality, feeling and emotion; they give form to inward experiences and thus make them conceivable. The only way we can really envisage vital movement, the stirring and growth and passage of emotion, and ultimately the whole direct sense of human life, is in artistic terms. A musical person thinks of emotions musically. They cannot be discursively talked about above a very general level. But they may nonetheless be known—objectively set forth, publicly known—and there is nothing necessarily confused or formless about emotions.

As soon as the natural forms of subjective experience are abstracted to the point of symbolic presentation, we can use those forms to imagine feeling and understand its nature. Self-knowledge, insight into all phases of life and mind, springs from artistic imagination. That is the cognitive value of the arts.

But their influence on human life goes deeper than the intellectual level. As language actually gives form to our sense experience, grouping our impressions around those things which have names, and fitting sensations to the qualities that have adjectival names, and so on, the arts we live with—our picture books and stories and the music we hear—actually form our emotive experience. Every generation has its styles of feeling. One age shudders and blushes and faints, another swaggers, still another is godlike in a universal indifference. These styles in actual emotion are not insincere. They are largely unconscious—determined by many social causes, but *shaped* by artists, usually popular artists of the screen, the jukebox, the shopwindow, and the picture magazine. (That, rather than incitement to crime, is my objection to the comics.) Irwin Edman remarks in one of his books that our emotions are largely Shakespeare's poetry.

This influence of art on life gives us an indication of why a period of efflorescence in the arts is apt to lead a cultural advance: it formulates a new way of feeling, and that is the beginning of a cultural age. It suggests another matter for reflection, too—that a wide neglect of artistic education is a neglect in the education of feeling. Most people are so imbued with the idea that feeling is a formless, total organic excitement in men as in animals that the idea of educating feeling, developing its scope and quality, seems odd to them, if not absurd. It is really, I think, at the very heart of personal education.

There is one other function of the arts that benefits not so much the advance of culture as its stabilization—an influence on individual lives. This function is the converse and complement of the objectification of feeling, the driving force of creation in art: it is the education of vision that we receive in seeing, hearing, reading works of art—the development of the artist's eye, that assimilates ordinary sights (or sounds, motions, or events) to inward vision, and lends expressiveness and emotional import to the world. Wherever art takes a motif from actuality—a flowering branch, a bit of landscape, a historic event, or a personal memory, any model or theme from life—it transforms it into a piece of imagination, and imbues its image with artistic vitality. The result is an impregnation of ordinary reality with the significance of created form. This is the subjectification of nature that makes reality itself a symbol of life and feeling.

The arts objectify subjective reality, and subjectify outward experience of nature. Art education is the education of feeling, and a society that neglects it gives itself up to formless emotion. Bad art is corruption of feeling. This is a large factor in the irrationalism which dictators and demagogues exploit.

Continuing to Think

When you are emotionally upset, do you ever sit down at a piano or pick up a guitar or turn on your favorite radio station to smooth out your ragged feelings? Anthropologists understand that the arts we live with on a day-to-day basis actually teach us how to feel. Different generations have different styles of feeling, shaped by the artists who dominate popular culture. Although the language of feeling is largely unconscious, it defines the terms by which we interpret what we feel.

Propagandists understand this power very well. Movies that show the "enemy" as less than human rev up the war machine and make killing easier to justify or accept. If racial minorities are dangerous and women need to be suppressed, music can send these messages out in powerful, if mainly subconscious, ways. A society that does not understand its arts can get lost in the irrationalism that dictators and demagogues know how to exploit.

Speaking positively, Langer suggests that art can teach us a new way of feeling that is really a new way of seeing. Art is our window into an artist's eye view of the world—a way of imaginative insight that can stabilize a culture by helping its citizens understand and manage what they are feeling. Does this remind you of Aristotle's praise of tragic drama? If he and Langer are right, can we neglect the arts and still hope to avoid the wave of violence so many fear?

Summing Up the Readings

Think about the art you like—the art that speaks to you. What have you learned through the medium of art that is not available to you in other ways? Have you heard a song that touched you deeply and told you something about yourself or the world? Has a painting or a sculpture given you an insight you struggled to put into words?

Is art meant to entertain, to please the eye and ear alone, or is it meant to reveal what is? The selections in this chapter suggest the latter meaning. If beauty has something to teach us, we would be wise to open our senses and our minds to receive it. Whose argument about art as imitation—Plato's or Aristotle's—do you find more convincing?

Not all art fits conventional definitions. Zen archery is certainly a nontraditional art form. And, our Western culture offers few examples of the artist as medium, such as we see revealed in the work of Edogo, the carver of ritual masks. What else might be available as a way from beauty to truth if we looked carefully enough? Sometimes the greatest truths—of religion, metaphysics, and art—cannot be captured in words. This does not mean they do not exist or that they make no sense. It does mean that we have to use other means to grasp them and that art can be our guide.

Continuing to Question

1. Who, in your view, makes the better case—Plato or Aristotle? Does art take us closer to or further from what is real?

2. If archery can be an art, what role does the attitude of the participant play in making this determination? In Japan, what is the purpose of the art of archery?

3. Does all real art arise out of a connection between the artist and some larger reality? If so, is the artist a type of philosopher and the philosopher a kind of artist?

4. If art is neglected and the general public loses access to the insights it makes possible, what does a society gain and what does it lose?

5. Is there a connection between some kinds of beauty and some kinds of truth? Are there things you hold as truths—about yourself or the world—that came to you first through the arts?

Suggestions for Further Exploration

Achebe, Chinua, *Arrow of God*—New York: Anchor, 1974. Achebe describes what it is like to be an artist in a traditional African society.

Asimov, Isaac, *The Foundation Trilogy*—New York: Ballantine, 1983. Asimov offers the saga of a thousand years of a galactic empire (the Foundation) dedicated to art, science, and technology.

Herrigel, Eugen, *Zen in the Art of Archery*—trans. R. F. C. Hull. New York: Vintage, 1953. Herrigel shows why it takes years to learn the *art* of archery, why it has nothing to do with hitting the target, and why if you learn it you will hit the target every time—even blindfolded.

James, Henry, "The Real Thing." In *The American Novels and Stories of Henry James*—New York: Knopf, 1947. Issues addressed in this story include why real people can't portray themselves as effectively as actors can and why a film can affect us more powerfully than does the event on which it was based.

Kafka, Franz, "A Hunger Artist." In *The Complete Stories and Parables*—New York: Schocken, 1983. This short story centers around an artist whose "art" consists of fasting for many days.

Merton, Thomas, trans. *The Way of Chuang Tzu*—New York: New Directions, 1965. This book provides insight into the experience of being an artist in a traditional Eastern society. See especially "Cutting Up an Ox," "The Fasting of the Heart," "Duke Hwan and the Wheelwright," and "The Need to Win."

Plato, *The Symposium*—trans. Walter Hamilton. New York: Penguin, 1951. This work contains meditations (some humorous) on beauty.

Stone, Irving, *The Agony and the Ecstasy*—New York: Anchor, 1989. This historical novel depicts the experience of being an artist (Michelangelo) in a traditional Western society.

Yalom, Irven, *When Nietzsche Wept*—New York: Basic, 1992. This is an imaginary encounter between Joseph Breuer, Friedrich Nietzsche, and Sigmund Freud (Breuer's student in the emerging field of psychoanalysis); Breuer tries to analyze Nietzsche and ends up being analyzed. Yalom provides a good introduction to Nietzsche's ideas.

Part III

Axiology

Under this last organizational topic, we consider political and social philosophy as well as ethics. Our chief concerns will be the relationship between the individual and the state, between the individual and the community, and between individuals and other individuals. Do we, for instance, value property rights over personal rights? Should the power of the state be absolute, moderate, minimal, or totally absent? Notice that how we think about human nature will dictate whether we trust ourselves to act on our own without regulation. Is the right to rule divinely given or derived from the consent of the governed? And what happens when government does not keep its promises?

Social philosophy is primarily concerned with justice. Should our standard be the common good, the rights of individuals occupying different ranks, or some standard of equality? And, what of those who feel they are not being justly treated? How free should they be to protest or even try to bring down the government? Should your age, gender, race, or social class determine how the state treats you? Which of these is the most central part of your identity?

And what about our obligations toward each other? Should we act from abstract principles of duty, look to real or imagined consequences, or strive to become whatever kind of person our ethical ideals prescribe? And what happens when I use one standard and you use another—and we clash?

8 Political Philosophy

Defining the Issue

Lately there has been a lot of talk about government getting too big. Every culture has to ask itself how much of a role the **state** should play in the lives of its citizens. Are we better off left totally alone, with little or no government—**anarchism**? Or are our long-term, best interests served by having government regulate just about everything—**totalitarianism**? Much depends on how much confidence we have in human nature and how much or how little we have in the state.

If people are basically good and act rationally, they can be counted on to rule themselves effectively with little or no interference from the state. On the other hand, if people are basically selfish, aggressive, and competitive, we may need the state's regulation to keep us from harming one another. Most people gravitate toward the center, avoiding both of these extremes. Still, the question to ask is: Is my confidence more with the people or the state?

Another issue concerns **sovereignty** or the basis for political authority. Are people divinely supported in their roles as monarchs? Does might make right? Is the only justification the consent of the governed? Western nations tend toward the latter position, the view that citizens and government enter into a kind of contract. This is a **social contract** rather than an economic one, but other features are similar to the contract you have with your employer, landlord, or credit card company. Each party agrees to do certain things in exchange for certain benefits.

As we look at questions of political philosophy, we must ask ourselves what citizens gain by entering into a social contract with government and how each party evaluates whether or not they are getting a good deal.

Previewing the Readings

Thomas Hobbes, whose materialist ideas we met in Chapter 2, thought that humans in a state of nature could be relied upon to do only one thing—beat each other to a pulp. We need government, he wrote in *Leviathan,* to protect us from the worst in ourselves. Knowing how selfish and brutal we are, we must give some of our rights irrevocably to a strong sovereign. The brutality of the European Thirty Years War (1618–1648) and the English Civil War had shown Hobbes a chilling account of "man's inhumanity to man." Unregulated human nature made him quake. Unfreedom might not be desirable, he reasoned, but the alternatives are much worse.

English political philosopher John Locke, having witnessed the peaceful transfer of power from king to parliament in the so-called "bloodless revolution" of 1688, had a much more optimistic view of human nature than Hobbes did. In the state of nature, Locke observed, we have natural rights, including those to life, liberty, and property. We enter into a social contract to protect these God-given rights and the contract is far from irrevocable. If government does not keep its side of the bargain, we can withdraw our consent and overthrow the government.

Locke's ideas were influential in Britain and Europe and eventually crossed the Atlantic to inspire the American colonists to revolution. Writing in 1848, nearly 75 years after the original Declaration of Independence (inspired by Locke's vision), Elizabeth Cady Stanton refined it to include the rights of women who, in her judgment, had been left out of the first Declaration. A modern writer, Bart Kosko, suggests that the social contract we enter into with our government is quite "fuzzy." That is, the things that will be expected of us as citizens are not always made clear until they are demanded of us.

In a Chinese tradition dating back at least three thousand years, the Emperor was presumed to rule by virtue of the Mandate of Heaven. Although his power was nearly unlimited, it was not the Emperor as an individual but his role as conduit, maintaining the harmony between heaven and earth, that justified his power. Nicholas Kristof suggests that Chinese Communist leaders, who seized political power and the presumption of holding the Mandate of Heaven as well in 1949, are widely believed to have lost the Mandate.

Malcolm X made a similar charge in a speech at Harvard in 1964. Since both political parties had denied real political power to African Americans, Malcolm asserted, the time had come for Black Nationalism, combined with the religion of Islam, to address the problems in the "so-called Negro community."

8.1   *Treatise of Civil Government*

JOHN LOCKE

Preparing to Read

Locke begins by laying out his vision of the state of nature. Notice his emphasis on the positive things—freedom, equality, a presumption of reasonableness. Beginning where he does, Locke's goal is not to "fix" something that has gone wrong (as Hobbes feels compelled to do), but rather to preserve all that is right. This is a **conservative** aim and Locke's view of the state is a rather conservative one as well. At the same time, Locke is a strong advocate for individual freedoms; this is a **liberal** goal.

The justification for having a state at all is to preserve the **natural rights** all of us have in the state of nature, Locke believes. Government, in other words, has no justification on its own behalf; it is merely the custodian of the natural rights of its citizens. And it follows that if government oversteps its bounds and becomes tyrannical, its citizens have the right to rebel.

People in England (Locke's home country), France, and the British American colonies read these words and, examining their own governments, found them to have overstepped their bounds. Locke is generally credited with inspiring both the American and French Revolutions. In setting up their republic, the newly independent Americans were very careful to implement Locke's ideas of limited government. When they later wrote the Constitution, which is still in effect, they provided remedies for curbing abuses of government power and means for removing from office individuals who overstepped their authority.

THE STATE OF NATURE has a law of nature to govern it, which obliges every one: and reason, which is that law, teaches all mankind, who will but consult it, that being all equal and independent, no one ought to harm another in his life, health, liberty, or possessions: for men being all the workmanship of one omnipotent and infinitely wise Maker; all the servants of one sovereign master, sent into the world by his order, and about his business; they are his property, whose workmanship they are, made to last during his, not another's pleasure: and being furnished with like faculties, sharing all in one community of nature, there cannot be supposed any such subordination among us, that may authorize us to destroy another, as if we were made for one another's uses, as the inferior ranks of creatures are for ours. Every one, as he is bound to preserve himself, and not to quit his station wilfully, so by the like reason, when his own preservation comes not in competition, ought he, as much as he can, to preserve the rest of mankind, and may not unless it be to do justice to an offender, take away or impair the life, or what tends to the preservation of life, the liberty, health, limb, or goods of another.

§ 7. And that all men may be restrained from invading others' rights, and from doing hurt to one another, and the law of nature be observed, which willeth the peace and preservation of all mankind, the execution of the law of nature is, in that state, put into every man's hands, whereby every one has a right to punish the transgressors of that law to such a degree as may hinder its violation: for the law of nature would, as all other laws that concern men in this world, be in vain, if there were nobody that in the state of nature had a power to execute that law, and thereby preserve the innocent and restrain offenders. And if any one in the state of nature may punish another for any evil he had done, every one may do so: for in that state of perfect equality, where naturally there is no superiority or jurisdiction of one over another, what any may do in prosecution of that law, every one must needs have a right to do.

§ 8. And thus, in the state of nature, "one man comes by a power over another;" but yet no absolute or arbitrary power, to use a criminal, when he has got him in his hands, according to the passionate heats, or boundless extravagancy of his own will; but only to retribute to him, so far as calm reason and conscience dictate, what is proportionate to his transgression; which is so much as may serve for reparation and restraint: for these two are the only reasons, why one man may lawfully do harm to another, which is that we call punishment. In transgressing the law of nature, the offender declares himself to live by another rule than that of reason and common equity, which is that measure God has set to the actions of men, for their mutual security; and so he becomes dangerous to mankind, the tye, which is to secure them from injury and violence, being slighted and broken by him. Which being a trespass against the whole species, and the peace and safety of it, provided for by the law of nature; every man upon this score, by the right he hath to preserve mankind in general, may restrain, or, where it is necessary, destroy things noxious to them, and so may bring such evil on any one, who hath transgressed that law, as may make him repent the doing of it, and thereby deter him, and by his example others, from doing the like mischief. And in this case, and upon this ground, "every man hath a right to punish the offender, and be executioner of the law of nature."

§ 9. I doubt not but this will seem a very strange doctrine to some men: but before they condemn it, I desire them to resolve me, by what right any prince or state can put to death, or punish any alien, for any crime he commits in their country. It is certain their laws, by virtue of any sanction they receive from the promulgated will of the legislative, reach not a stranger: they speak not to him, nor, if they did, is he bound to hearken to them. The legislative authority, by which they are in force over the subjects of that commonwealth, hath no power over him. Those who have the supreme power of making laws in England, France, or Holland, are to an Indian but like the rest of the world, men without authority: and therefore, if by the law of nature every man hath not a power to punish offences against it, as he soberly judges the case to require, I see not how the magistrates of any community can punish an alien of another country; since, in reference to him, they can have no more power than what every man naturally may have over another.

§ 10. Besides the crime which consists of violating the law, and varying from the right rule of reason, whereby a man so far becomes degenerate, and declares himself to quit the principles of human nature, and to be a noxious creature, there is commonly injury done to some person or other, and some other man receives damage by his transgression: in which case he who hath received any damage, has, besides the right of punishment common to him with other men, a particular right to seek reparation from him that has done it: and any other person, who finds it just, may also join with him that is injured, and assist him in recovering from the offender so much as may make satisfaction for the harm he has suffered.

§ 11. From these two distinct rights, the one of punishing the crime for restraint, and preventing the like offence, which right of punishing is in every body; the other of taking reparation, which belongs only to the injured party; comes it to pass that the magistrate, who by being magistrate hath the common right of punishing put into his hands, can often, where the public good demands not the execution of the law, remit the punishment of criminal offences by his own authority, but yet cannot remit the satisfaction due to any private man for the damage he has received. That, he who has suffered the damage has a right to demand in his own name, and he alone can remit: the damnified person has this power of appropriating to himself the goods or service of the offender, by right of self-preservation, as every man has a power to punish the crime, to prevent its being committed again, "by the right he had of preserving all mankind"; and doing all reasonable things he can in order to that end: and thus it is, that every man, in the state of nature, has a power to kill a murderer, both to deter others from doing the like injury, which no reparation can compensate, by the example of the punishment that attends it from every body; and also to secure men from the attempts of a criminal, who having renounced reason, the common rule and measure God hath given to mankind, hath, by the unjust violence and slaughter he hath committed upon one, declared war against all mankind; and therefore may be destroyed as a lion or a tiger, one of those wild savage beasts, with whom men can have no society nor security: and upon this is grounded that great law of nature, "Whoso sheddeth man's blood, by man shall his blood be shed." And Cain was so fully convinced, that every one had a right to destroy such a criminal, that after the murder of his brother, he cries out, "Every one that findeth me, shall slay me"; so plain was it writ in the hearts of mankind.

§ 12. By the same reason may a man in the state of nature punish the lesser breaches of that law. It will perhaps be demanded, with death? I answer, each transgression may be punished to that degree, and with so much severity, as will suffice to make it an ill bargain to the offender, give him cause to repent, and terrify others from doing the like. Every offence, that can be committed in the state of nature, may in the state of nature be also punished equally, and as far forth, as it may in a commonwealth: for though it would be beside my present purpose, to enter

here into the particulars of the law of nature, or its measures of punishment, yet it is certain there is such a law, and that too as intelligible and plain to a rational creature, and a studier of that law, as the positive laws of commonwealths: nay, possibly plainer, as much as reason is easier to be understood, than the fancies and intricate contrivances of men, following contrary and hidden interests put into words; for so truly are a great part of the municipal laws of countries, which are only so far right, as they are founded on the law of nature, by which they are to be regulated and interpreted.

§ 13. To this strange doctrine, viz. That "in the state of nature every one has the executive power" of the law of nature, I doubt not but it will be objected, that it is unreasonable for men to be judges in their own cases, that self love will make men partial to themselves and their friends; and on the other side, that ill-nature, passions, and revenge will carry them too far in punishing others; and hence nothing but confusion and disorder will follow: and that therefore God hath certainly appointed government to restrain the partiality and violence of men. I easily grant, that civil government is the proper remedy for the inconveniences of the state of nature, which must certainly be great, where men may be judges in their own case; since it is easy to be imagined, that he who was so unjust as to do his brother an injury, will scarce be so just as to condemn himself for it: but I shall desire those who make this objection, to remember, that absolute monarchs are but men; and if government is to be the remedy of those evils, which necessarily follow from men's being judges in their own cases, and the state of nature is therefore not to be endured; I desire to know what kind of government that is, and how much better it is than the state of nature, where one man commanding a multitude, has the liberty to be judge in his own case, and may do to all his subjects whatever he pleases, without the least liberty to any one to question or control those who execute his pleasure? and in whatsoever he doth, whether led by reason, mistake or passion, must be submitted to? much better it is in the state of nature, wherein men are not bound to submit to the unjust will of another: and if he that judges, judges amiss in his own, or any other case, he is answerable for it to the rest of mankind.

§ 14. It is often asked as a mighty objection, "where are, or ever were there any men in such a state of nature?" To which it may suffice as an answer at present, that since all princes and rulers of independent governments, all through the world, are in a state of nature, it is plain the world never was, nor ever will be, without numbers of men in that state. I have named all governors of independent communities, whether they are, or are not, in league with others: for it is not every compact that puts an end to the state of nature between men, but only this one of agreeing together mutually to enter into one community, and make one body politic; other promises and compacts men may make one with another, and yet still be in the state of nature. The promises and bargains for truck, &c. between the two men in the desert island, mentioned by Garcilasso de la Vega, in his history of Peru; or between a Swiss and an Indian, in the woods of America; are binding to them, though they are perfectly in a state of nature, in reference to one another: for truth and keeping of faith belongs to men as men, and not as members of society.

§ 15. To those that say, there were never any men in the state of nature, I will not only oppose the authority of the judicious Hooker, Eccl. Pol. lib. I. sect. 10, where he says, "The laws which have been hitherto mentioned," i.e. the laws of nature, "do bind men absolutely, even as they are men, although they have never any settled fellowship, never any solemn agreement amongst themselves what to do, or not to do; but forasmuch as we are not by ourselves sufficient to furnish ourselves with competent store of things, needful for such a life as our nature doth desire, a life fit for the dignity of man; therefore to supply those defects and imperfections which are in us, as living singly and solely by ourselves, we are naturally induced to seek communion and fellowship with others. This was the cause of men's uniting themselves at first in political societies." But I moreover affirm, that all men are naturally in that state, and remain so, till by their own consents they make themselves members of some politic society; and I doubt not in the sequel of this discourse to make it very clear.

Continuing to Think

Although Locke's idea about government deriving its "just powers" from "the consent of the governed" sounds noble, it is important to keep in mind that neither slaves (of either gender) nor women (of any race) had any real share in the government of the United States under which they lived. For white males with property, the new government lived up to Locke's ideals; for others, it fell far short.

Deprived of the right to vote, to secure an education, and to own property, many people were in a far worse state than the political elite among the colonists had been under British rule. For a surprisingly long time, few people seemed to notice these omissions. Slavery was written into the Constitution, and women were presumed to be represented by their husband and fathers.

In fact, Locke's explanation for the formation of civil or political society cites the Adam's rib story from Genesis that we read in Chapter 3. Because in God's judgment "It was not good for him to be alone," man is driven into society. Although this is the generic "man," it seems pretty clearly limited to males and further limited to white, male property owners. In 1848, Elizabeth Cady Stanton made a further refinement.

8.2   ## *Declaration of Sentiments, Seneca Falls*

ELIZABETH CADY STANTON

Preparing to Read

As a young woman on her honeymoon in London, Elizabeth Cady Stanton attended the 1840 World Antislavery Conference to which her husband Henry was a delegate. What she saw shocked her. At a conference devoted to abolishing slavery, women delegates were refused their seats. The male delegates got cold feet at the last minute and feared that seating the legitimate women delegates would make them laughingstocks in the British press.

Offered the option of sitting behind a curtain and listening to the proceedings, Lucretia Mott, a Quaker leader and one of the spurned delegates, elected not to attend at all. Instead, she walked the streets of London with the young Elizabeth Cady Stanton, discussing the rights of women. Eight years later, when Elizabeth had borne five children and moved to upstate New York, far from the cosmopolitan city of Boston where she had had friends, cultural events, and household help, Stanton and Mott met for tea and planned a Women's Rights Convention.

Stanton agreed to write a "Declaration of Sentiments," modeled on the 1776 Declaration of Independence, and a series of resolutions for the participants to consider. As you read her document, think about the original Declaration, which it so closely parallels. How differently Locke's words resonate when applied to women as well as men. And notice, nearly seventy-five years after the original protest (Declaration of Independence), how many rights American women felt still lay beyond their reach.

WHEN, IN THE COURSE of human events, it becomes necessary for one portion of the family of man to assume among the people of the earth a position different from that which they have hitherto occupied, but one to which the laws of nature and of nature's God entitle them, a decent respect to the opinions of mankind requires that they should declare the causes that impel them to such a course.

We hold these truths to be self-evident: that all men and women are created equal; that they are endowed by their Creator with certain inalienable rights; that among these are life, liberty, and the pursuit of happiness; that to secure these rights governments are instituted, deriving their just powers from the consent of the governed. Whenever any form of government becomes destructive of these ends, it is the right of those who suffer from it to refuse allegiance to it, and to insist upon the institution of a new government, laying its foundation on such principles, and organizing its powers in such form, as to them shall seem most likely to effect their safety and happiness. Prudence indeed, will dictate that governments long established should not be changed for light and transient causes; and accordingly all experience hath shown that mankind are more disposed to suffer, while evils are sufferable, than to right themselves by abolishing the forms to which they were accustomed. But when a long train of abuses and usurpations, pursuing invariably the same object evinces a design to reduce them under absolute despotism, it is their duty to throw off such government, and to provide new guards for their future security. Such has been the patient sufferance of the women under this government, and such is now the necessity which constrains them to demand the equal station to which they are entitled.

The history of mankind is a history of repeated injuries and usurpations on the part of man toward woman, having in direct object the establishment of an absolute tyranny over her. To prove this, let facts be submitted to a candid world.

He has never permitted her to exercise her inalienable right to the elective franchise.

He has compelled her to submit to laws, in the formation of which she had no voice.

He has withheld from her rights which are given to the most ignorant and degraded men—both natives and foreigners.

Having deprived her of this first right of a citizen, the elective franchise, thereby leaving her without representation in the halls of legislation, he has oppressed her on all sides.

He has made her, if married, in the eye of the law, civilly dead.

He has taken her from all right in property, even to the wages she earns.

He has made her, morally, an irresponsible being, as she can commit many crimes with impunity, provided they be done in the presence of her husband. In the covenant of marriage, she is compelled to promise obedience to her husband, he becoming, to all intents and purposes, her master—the law giving him power to deprive her of her liberty, and to administer chastisement.

He has so framed the laws of divorce, as to what shall be the proper causes, and in case of separation, to whom the guardianship of the children shall be given, as to be wholly regardless of the happiness of women—the law, in all cases, going upon a false supposition of the supremacy of man, and giving all power into his hands.

After depriving her of all rights as a married woman, if single, and the owner of property, he has taxed her to support a government which recognizes her only when her property can be made profitable to it.

He has monopolized nearly all the profitable employments, and from those she is permitted to follow, she receives but a scanty remuneration. He closes against her all the avenues to wealth and distinction which he considers most honorable to himself. As a teacher of theology, medicine, or law, she is not known.

He has denied her the facilities for obtaining a thorough education, all colleges being closed against her.

He allows her in Church, as well as State, but a subordinate position, claiming Apostolic authority for her exclusion from the ministry, and, with some exceptions, from any public participation in the affairs of the Church.

He has created a false public sentiment by giving to the world a different code of morals for men and women, by which moral delinquencies which exclude women from society, are not only tolerated, but deemed of little account in man.

He has usurped the prerogative of Jehovah himself, claiming it as his right to assign for her a sphere of action, when that belongs to her conscience and to her God.

He has endeavored, in every way that he could, to destroy her confidence in her own powers, to lessen her self-respect, and to make her willing to lead a dependent and abject life.

Now, in view of this entire disfranchisement of one-half the people of this country, their social and religious degradation—in view of the unjust laws above mentioned, and because women do feel themselves aggrieved, oppressed, and fraudulently deprived of their most sacred rights, we insist that they have immediate admission to all the rights and privileges which belong to them as citizens of the United States.

In entering upon the great work before us, we anticipate no small amount of misconception, misrepresentation, and ridicule; but we shall use every instrumentality within our power to effect our object. We shall employ agents, circulate tracts, petition the State and National leg-islatures, and endeavor to enlist the pulpit and the press in our behalf. We hope this Convention will be followed by a series of Conventions embracing every part of the country.

The following resolutions were discussed by Lucretia Mott, Thomas and Mary Ann McClintock, Amy Post, Catharine A. F. Stebbins, and others, and were adopted:

WHEREAS, The great precept of nature is conceded to be, that "man shall pursue his own true and substantial happiness." Blackstone in his Commentaries remarks, that this law of Nature being coeval with mankind, and dictated by God himself, is of course superior in obligation to any other. It is binding over all the globe, in all countries and at all times; no human laws are of any validity if contrary to this, and such of them as are valid, derive all their force, and all their validity, and all their authority, mediately and immediately, from this original; therefore,

Resolved, That such laws as conflict, in any way, with the true and substantial happiness of woman, are contrary to the great precept of nature and of no validity, for this is "superior in obligation to any other."

Resolved, That all laws which prevent woman from occupying such a station in society as her conscience shall dictate, or which place her in a position inferior to that of man, are contrary to the great precept of nature, and therefore of no force or authority.

Resolved, That woman is man's equal—was intended to be so by the Creator, and the highest good of the race demands that she should be recognized as such.

Resolved, That the women of this country ought to be enlightened in regard to the laws under which they live, that they may no longer publish their degradation by declaring themselves satisfied with their present position, nor their ignorance, by asserting that they have all the rights they want.

Resolved, That inasmuch as man, while claiming for himself intellectual superiority, does accord to woman moral superiority, it is pre-eminently his duty to encourage her to speak and teach, as she has an opportunity, in all religious assemblies.

Resolved, That the same amount of virtue, delicacy, and refinement of behavior that is required to woman in the social state, should also be required of man, and the same transgressions should be visited with equal severity on both man and woman.

Resolved, That the objection of indelicacy and impropriety, which is so often brought against woman when she addresses a public audience, comes with a very ill-grace from those who encourage, by their attendance, her appearance on the stage, in the concert, or in feats of the circus.

Resolved, That woman has too long rested satisfied in the circumscribed limits which corrupt customs and a perverted application of the Scriptures have marked out for her, and that it is time she should move in the enlarged sphere which her great Creator has assigned her.

Resolved, That it is the duty of the women of this country to secure to themselves their sacred right to the elective franchise.

Resolved, That the equality of human rights results necessarily from the fact of the identity of the race in capabilities and responsibilities.

Resolved, therefore, That, being invested by the Creator with the same capabilities, and the same consciousness of responsibility for their exercise, it is demonstrably the right and duty of woman, equally with man, to promote every righteous cause by every righteous means; and especially in regard to the great subjects of morals and religion, it is self-evidently her right to participate with her brother in teaching them, both in private and in public, by writing and by speaking, by any instrumentalities proper to be used, and in any assemblies proper to be held; and this being a self-evident truth growing out of the divinely implanted principles of human nature, any custom or authority adverse to it, whether modern or wearing the hoary sanction of antiquity, is to be regarded as a self-evident falsehood, and at war with mankind.

At the last sessions Lucretia Mott offered and spoke to the following resolution:

Resolved, That the speedy success of our cause depends upon the zealous and untiring efforts of both men and women, for the overthrow of the monopoly of the pulpit, and for the securing to woman an equal participation with men in the various trades, professions, and commerce.

The only resolution that was not unanimously adopted was the ninth, urging the women of the country to secure to themselves the elective franchise. Those who took part in the debate feared a demand for the right to vote would defeat others they deemed more rational, and make the whole movement ridiculous.

But Mrs. Stanton and Frederick Douglass seeing that the power to choose rulers and make laws, was the right by which all others could be secured, persistently advocated the resolution, and at last carried it by a small majority.

Thus it will be seen that the Declaration and resolutions in the very first Convention, demanded all the most radical friends of the movement have since claimed—such as equal rights in the universities, in the trades and professions; the right to vote; to share in all political offices, honors, and emoluments; to complete equality in marriage, to personal freedom, property, wages, children; to make contracts; to sue, and be sued; and to testify in courts of justice. At this time the condition of married women under the Common Law, was nearly as degraded as that of the slave on the Southern plantation. The Convention continued through two entire days, and late into the evenings. The deepest interest was manifested to its close.

Continuing to Think

In light of the subsequent history of this first phase of the Women's Rights Movement in America, it is slightly ironic that the one resolution that was almost defeated was the only one capable of generating long-term support: "That it is the duty of the women of this country to secure to themselves their sacred right to the elective franchise."

Some of the other resolutions have a more radical sound to them, but even Lucretia Mott quailed before demanding the vote. "Thou wilt make us ridiculous," she warned Elizabeth. And yet, over the next seventy-five years, that cause was the one that was ultimately achievable. Historians generally credit the African American abolitionist and newspaper publisher Frederick Douglass, who spoke stirringly in support of the suffrage resolution at Seneca Falls, with saving it from defeat.

This was a time in history when it seemed that various marginalized groups might work together for their common good. Abolishing slavery and establishing broader political rights for women appear to be compatible aims. And yet, after the Civil War, rights—and eventually the vote—were extended to freedmen but not freedwomen, and women's rights advocates stooped to anti-immigrant and racist appeals as they grew more desperate in pursuit of their own cause.

It is hard to imagine the very modest goals in these documents being thought of as radical, but they were. In 1964, Malcolm X's call for Black Nationalism had a similarly strident sound. Before we look at his speech, let's consider the notion of the social contract we consent to by virtue of living in a state.

8.3   ***The Fuzzy Social Contract***

BART KOSKO

Preparing to Read

In his book on *Fuzzy Thinking,* Bart Kosko insists we live in a fuzzy world, governed much more by gray principles than by neat and tidy black-and-white laws. Early air conditioners had two settings: off and on. Modern ones are controlled by computers, running at full speed when the car is very hot and gradually slowing down as the air temperature cools. Never purely on or purely off, they operate by "fuzzy logic," which is highly effective.

Aristotle gave the West a non-fuzzy way of looking at the world that lasted for two thousand years. Something is either *A* or non-*A,* he explained. Either something is a pencil or it isn't. And something cannot be both *A* and non-*A* at the same time. If this is both a pencil and a non-pencil, we have no way to talk about it or get our minds around it. This is known as bi-valent logic. Everything is either this or that—it is a black-and-white world.

Look at a cookie on a plate. Clearly this is a cookie (*A*). Now eat it. Just as clearly, it is now non-*A.* The question is: At what point did it go from being a cookie (*A*) to not being a cookie (non-*A*)? When you had eaten half of it, was it still a cookie? How about when there was only one bite left? A crumb? Kosko thinks the social contract is like this.

We take up residence in a certain country (or we are born to people who have done so) and our very residence obligates us to an unwritten social contract. Kosko pushes us a little to think about what we have actually agreed to do and not do—and then asks whether we want to sign.

The Force of Law

REASON ENDS IN DOUBT. Science disposes of ethics. It strips moral claims of logic and fact and reduces them to feeling in words. And yet we have to make moral claims and fight for them and once in a while go to war for them. We have to exercise our moral freedom whether we like it or not. Here arises the law and the "social contract" that the law helps write.

Society rests on the social contract. We weave the "fabric" of society on top of it. We make rules and pass laws and elect leaders to change small pieces of the social contract. But who can say just what the social contract is? Economists call it what we do as a group that we can't do alone. But that ball of fuzz does not pin it down. A lot rides on the social contract. If science does not ground ethics, then the weight of ethics falls on the social contract. So where is it? Who wrote it? Did it just evolve as the English language did or as money and the price mechanism did or as Common Law did? Who signed the social contract? How do you sign it? Are we stuck with a mere verbal contract?

We start with law. Law is the set of fuzzy moral claims that society or the state backs up with force. "Murder is wrong" has no factual truth but it has legal "truth" or validity. This legal truth is the coherence kind. We agree on some legal rules and principles like freedom of contract and presumption of innocence. In theory we pack the root or *Grundnorm* rules and principles into a state's constitution. Then the legal tree or bush grows from the root and again the legal sap of validity flows up from root to branch to leaf. A *supreme* court interprets the constitutional roots. Its authority flows to states and congresses and executive branches and to their branches and on out to mayors and policemen who hide in speed traps. In practice we work with more rules and principles than we have written down or voted on. They are all fuzzy and subject to debate. There is so much fuzz that no one lies or no one has to admit a lie if she has a good lawyer.

I don't want to dwell on gadgets but in the future we may have good cheap legal advice on a chip. We may carry law aids to court with us in our palmtop computers. Today fuzzy systems work with rules of common sense. Tomorrow they can work with rules of moral sense. I mean this besides having the best lawyers you can put in a box. Everyone will have those and they will tend to cancel out. I mean moral advice. We know moral truth is too much to ask. But advice we can ask for. Smart fuzzy systems or cognitive maps can store and reason with the wisdom of the ages. We might ask advice from the Buddha or Confucius or Socrates or Aristotle or Machiavelli or Immanuel Kant or the new Pope or the latest pop guru or TV evangelist. Reading the masters comes down to asking their advice. Why not put their wisdom in fuzzy rules and put that in your computer or dashboard or briefcase or ear? It won't clear up the fuzz of ethics and law though it might make us feel better about it. In fact lawyers and Buddhas on a chip would weave a more tangled legal web. Everything seems to push in that direction.

The Fuzzy Labyrinth of Law

Law is a fuzzy labyrinth. A legal system is a pile of fuzzy rules and fuzzy principles. And it is dynamic. Every day judges and legislators add new rules and laws and delete or overturn old ones. It is not an art or science. You don't play the game unless you have a stake in it. Then you tend to lie and deceive and cheat at least to some degree. Here the fuzzy principle holds with more force than anywhere else in our lives. Everything is a matter of degree. Legal terms and borders are fuzzy. Try to draw a line between self-defense and not self-defense or between contract breach and not breach. The lines are curves and you have to redraw them in each new case. Every rule, principle, and contract has exceptions. Each day judges, lawyers, and juries find new exceptions. Each "fact" in a case melts when you look at it up close and put it through the fires of cross-examination. Lives and careers and psyches depend on how we split balls of legal fuzz into A AND not-A, how we work with guilt, intent, premeditation, malice, threat, duress, equity, fairness, reasonability, acquiescence, duty, obligation, partiality, conflict of interest, damage, and property right.

The labyrinth has hallways and has cousin labyrinths that it deals with from time to time. States write their own constitutions and penal codes. The same federal constitution justifies them in some big fuzzy sense but on small points they disagree. They disagree in what they say and how lawyers interpret what they say. In Oregon highway patrolmen can use radar to measure car speed and give speeding tickets. Next door in California they can't. Laws and punishments vary across states. Judges in each state, city, and courthouse hand down different verdicts and sentences in similar cases. Each city passes laws and rules and builds its own fuzzy labyrinth of law. Each state and each country builds bigger labyrinths. Each day new cases make the labyrinths spill over on one another and tangle and pile up and grow new hallways.

Science does not help. It digs more tunnels in the labyrinth. First it strips truth from ethics. Then it gives tools that make the small things more precise but the big things fuzzier. Forensics labs find tiny facts of blood type and dirt type and tobacco type and dinner type. Lie detectors and vocal stress analyzers measure smooth changes in body function. This just gives more fuzzy facts to interpret, to fit in a fuzzy theory. The increased precision increases the fuzz.

DNA fingerprinting can tell who was there but not what they did. Videotapes can show part of what they did but not why they did it. More facts open it up to more interpretations. A video can show that Mr. X shot Mr. Y or hit him with a car or fist or pushed him off a bridge. But a video cannot draw a line between self-defense and murder or between murder and accident. That depends on Mr. X's plans and goals and intentions. As philosopher H. P. Grice said, you mean or intend one thing if you show a husband a picture of his wife with another man. You may mean or intend something else if you *draw* him a picture of the same thing.

The Fuzzy Social Contract

The whole legal system rests on the social contract. A fuzzy social contract binds us. It limits our freedoms as it helps protect them. The social contract lies deeper than the constitution and legal labyrinth that sit on top of it. No one sees it. No one writes it down. It combines fuzz with invisibility and so it can give birth to surprises. It does not give us the rule of law. The social contract gives us a rule of law. There are many.

Would you sign the social contract if you saw it and studied its fuzzy duties and fuzzy benefits and fuzzy costs? You and I did not sign the constitution but the state says we have consented to it. Consent lies in residence. Staying is playing. Love it or leave it. The state says nothing about the social contract. It comes before the state and it seems to be a verbal contract between parties unknown. So if you could see it, the question

whether you would sign it is a valid one. Would you sign the social contract as is or mark it up? Would you try to squeeze out the fuzz and replace gray curves with black-and-white lines? Or would you leave the fuzz in to keep things flexible and so trust that reasonable men and women will do reasonable things?

Here's a social contract you can sign. Computer engineer Robert Alexander wrote down his version of our social contract. I think he got the fuzz about right. He titillated hordes of hackers when he sent it out, free of copyright, on several computer networks. If you sign it, you can send it to the White House.

Social Contract*
between an individual and the
United States Government

WHEREAS I wish to reside on the North American continent, and

WHEREAS the United States Government controls the area of the continent on which I wish to reside, and

WHEREAS tacit or implied contracts are vague and therefore unenforceable,

I agree to the following terms:

SECTION 1: I will surrender a percentage of my property to the Government. The actual percentage will be determined by the Government and will be subject to change at any time. The amount to be surrendered may be based on my income, the value of my property, the value of my purchases, or any other criteria the Government chooses. To aid the Government in determining the percentage, I will apply for a Government identification number that I will use in all my major financial transactions.

SECTION 2: Should the Government demand it, I will surrender my liberty for a period of time determined by the Government and typically no shorter than two years. During that time, I will serve the Government in any way it chooses, including military service in which I may be called upon to sacrifice my life.

SECTION 3: I will limit my behavior as demanded by the Government. I will consume only those drugs permitted by the Government. I will limit my sexual activities to those permitted by the Government. I will forsake religious beliefs that conflict with the Government's determination of propriety. More limits may be imposed at any time.

SECTION 4: In consideration for the above, the Government will permit me to find employment, subject to limits that will be determined by the Government. These limits may restrict my choice of career or the wages I may accept.

SECTION 5: The Government will permit me to reside in the area of North America that it controls. Also, the Government will permit me to speak freely, subject to limits determined by the Government's Congress and Supreme Court.

SECTION 6: The Government will attempt to protect my life and my claim to the property it has allowed me to keep. I agree not to hold the Government liable if it fails to protect me or my property.

SECTION 7: The Government will offer various services to me. The nature and extent of these services will be determined by the Government and are subject to change at any time.

SECTION 8: The Government will determine whether I may vote for certain Government officials. The influence of my vote will vary inversely with the number of voters, and I understand that it typically will be minuscule. I agree not to hold any elected Government officials liable for acting against my best interests or for breaking promises, even if those promises motivated me to vote for them.

SECTION 9: I agree that the Government may hold me fully liable if I fail to abide by the above terms. In that event, the Government may confiscate any property that I have not previously surrendered to it, and may imprison me for a period of time to be determined by the Government. I also agree that the Government may alter the terms of this contract at any time.

SIGNATURE _____

DATE _____

Continuing to Think

Now that you have seen the fuzzy social contract you have implicitly agreed to honor, what do you think? Which parts seem like a good bargain in exchange for living in an ordered society? Which seem like more than you would be willing to do? Like many things, the social contract is easier to honor in theory than in practice.

Most of us would probably agree with Locke that our own self-interest is better served by living in some form of society. In order to preserve and protect our own life, liberty, health, and property, government is probably a useful thing. The difficulty is that the modern state has developed a whole series of citizen obligations to which we probably never give our conscious consent until the government demands we honor them.

During unpopular wars, male draftees come face to face with what had been an unspoken agreement to serve in the armed forces. All of us chafe, at least a little, about paying a chunk of our earnings in taxes. Probably we don't think about our implicit agreement to give up our freedom if we break the laws of the state.

Kosko isn't necessarily urging the abolition of the social contract. What he does urge us to do is bring the contract with all its fuzziness into our conscious awareness and then ask ourselves whether or not we consider it a good deal. In most situations, it is easier for some of us to honor the terms of the social contract than it is for others because some people carry a heavier share of the burden. The Vietnam war was fought largely by the poor and disproportionately by minority soldiers. Agreeing in principle to your obligation to fight your country's wars in a foreign land is one thing; consenting to it in practice is quite another. Going to jail is also considerably different in the concrete than in the abstract.

8.4   *The Speeches of Malcolm X at Harvard*

MALCOLM X

Preparing to Read

Just as Elizabeth Cady Stanton objected to the exclusion of women from the social contract in the United States during the middle of the last century, Malcolm X speaks in this selection to the exclusion of African Americans from the American dream. More than thirty-five years have passed since this speech was delivered at Harvard in 1964, yet many of the points he makes continue to be debated.

Malcolm describes himself as one of the "victims of the democratic system." Instead of the American dream, he says, African Americans are part of an American nightmare. Although he begins by speaking about the situation in the United States, he ends by broadening the basis of his call to the entire world order. Moving from civil rights to human rights will, he promises, cast the question of political rights for African Americans onto the world stage.

Listen to his illustrations of how political rights on paper often do not turn out to be real. If government does not honor its obligations to citizens, do those citizens have the right to withdraw their support of government? Locke thought so. Malcolm X asserts that he doesn't consider himself a Democrat or a Republican. In fact, he doesn't consider himself an American. He is, in effect, refusing the social contract.

Although Locke made his arguments for the social contract with an entire society in mind, both Stanton and Malcolm X raise questions about what should happen if one segment of a society is denied what it is due under the implied agreement we call the social contract. When citizens refuse to honor what they regard as unjust laws, we call this **civil disobedience.** As you read this speech, think about what has happened between 1964 and the present.

I AM NOT A POLITICIAN. I'm not even a student of politics. I'm not a Democrat. I'm not a Republican. I don't even consider myself an American. If I could consider myself an American, we wouldn't even have any problem. It would be solved. Many of you get indignant when you hear a black man stand up and say, "No, I'm not an American." I see whites who have the audacity, I should say the nerve, to think that a black man is radical and extremist, subversive and seditious if he says, "No, I'm not an American." But at the same time, these same whites have to admit that this man has a problem.

I don't come here tonight to speak to you as a Democrat or a Republican or an American or anything that *you* want me to be. I'm speaking as what I am: one of twenty-two million black people in this country who are victims of your democratic system. They're the victims of the Democratic politicians, the victims of the Republican politicians. They're actually the victims of what you call democracy. So I stand here tonight speaking as a victim of what you call democracy. And you can understand what I'm saying if you realize it's being said through the mouth of a victim; the mouth of one of the oppressed, not through the mouth and eyes of the oppressor. But if you think we're sitting in the same chair or standing on the same platform, then you won't understand what I'm talking about. You'd expect me to stand up here and say what you would say if you were standing up here. And I'd have to be out of my mind.

Whenever one is viewing this political system through the eyes of a victim, he sees something different. But today these twenty-two million black people who are the victims of American democracy, whether you realize it or not, are viewing your democracy with new eyes. Yesterday our people used to look upon the American system as an American dream. But the black people today are beginning to realize that it is an American nightmare. What is a dream to you is a nightmare to us. What is hope to you has long since become hopeless to our people. And as this attitude develops, not so much on Sugar Hill [in Harlem]—although it's there too—but in the ghetto, in the alley where the masses of our people live . . . there you have a new situation on your hands. There's a new political consciousness developing among our people in this country. In the past, we weren't conscious of the political maneuvering that goes on in this country, which exploits our people politically. We knew something was wrong, but we weren't conscious of what it was. Today there's a tendency on the part of this new generation of black people (who have been born and are growing up in this country) to look at the thing not as they wish it were, but as it actually is. And their ability to look at the situation as it is, is what is primarily responsible for the ever-increasing sense of frustration and hopelessness that exists in the so-called Negro community today.

Besides becoming politically conscious, you'll find that our people are also becoming more aware of the strategic position that they occupy politically. In the past, they weren't. Just the right to vote was considered something. But today the so-called Negroes are beginning to realize that they occupy a very strategic position. They realize what the new trends are and all of the new political tendencies.

During recent years at election time, when the Governor was running for office, there was call for a recount of votes here in Massachusetts. In Rhode Island it was the same way—in Minnesota, the same thing. Within American politics there is now such a similarity between the two parties that in elections the race is usually close enough to permit almost any single block to swing it one way or the other. Not only is this true in city, county, and state elections, but it's also true in the national elections, as witness the close race between President Kennedy and Nixon a few years back. And everyone admits that it was the strategic vote of the so-called Negro in this country that put the Kennedy administration in Washington. The position in the political structure of the so-called Negro has become so strategic that whenever any kind of election rolls around now, the politicians are out there trying to win the Negro vote. In trying to win the Negro vote, they make a whole lot of promises and build up his hopes. But they always build him up for a letdown. By being constantly built up for a letdown, the Negro is now becoming very angry at the white man. And in his anger the Muslims come along and talk to him. Yet instead of the white man blaming himself for the anger of the Negro, he again has the audacity to blame us. When we warn you how angry the Negro is becoming, you, instead of thanking us for giving you a little warning, try to accuse us of stirring up the Negro. Don't you know that if your house is on fire and I come to warn you that your house is burning, you shouldn't accuse me of setting the fire! Thank me rather for letting you know what's happening, or what's going to happen, before it's too late.

When these new trends develop in the so-called Negro in America, making the so-called Negro aware of his strategic position politically, he becomes aware too of what he's not getting in return. He realizes that his vote puts the governor in office, or the mayor in office, or the president in office. But he's beginning to see also that although his vote is the vital factor that determines who will sit in these seats, the last one those politicians try to help is the so-called Negro.

Proof of which: Everyone admits that it was the Negro vote that put Kennedy in the White House. Yet four years have passed and the present administration is just now getting around to civil rights legislation. In its fourth year of office it finally passes some kind of civil rights legislation, designed supposedly to solve the problem of the so-called Negro. Yet that voting element offered decisive support in the national elec-

tion. I only cite this to show the hypocrisy on the part of the white man in America, whether he be down South or whether he be up here in the North.

Democrats, now after they've been in the White House awhile, use an alibi for not having kept their promise to the Negroes who voted for them. They say, "Well, we can't get this passed or we can't get that passed." The present make-up of the Congress is 257 Democrats and only 177 Republicans. Now how can a party of Democrats that received practically the full support of the so-called Negroes of this country and control nearly two-thirds of the seats in Congress give the Negro an excuse for not getting some kind of legislation passed to solve the Negro problem? Where the senators are concerned, there are 67 Democrats and only 33 Republicans; yet these Democrats are going to try to pass the buck to the Republicans after the Negro has put the Democrats in office. Now I'm not siding with either Democrats or Republicans. I'm just pointing out the deceit on the part of both when it comes to dealing with the Negro. Although the Negro vote put the Democratic Party where it is, the Democratic Party gives the Negro nothing; and the Democrats offer as an excuse that the fault lies with the Dixie-crats. What do you call them—Dixie-crats or Dixo-crats or Demo-Dixo-crats!

Look at the shrewd deceptive manner in which they deal with the Negro. A Dixo-crat is a Democrat. You can call them by whatever name you wish, but you have never seen a situation where the Dixie-crats kick the Democrats out of the party. Rather the Democrats kick the Dixie-crats out of their party if there is ever any cleavage. You oftentimes find the Dixie-crats "cussing out" the Democrats, but you never find the Democrats disassociating themselves from the Dixie-crats. They are together and they use this shrewd maneuvering to trick the Negro. Now there are some young Negroes appearing on the scene, and it is time for those who call themselves Democrats to realize that when the Negro looks at a Democrat, he sees a Democrat.

Whether you call him a Dixo-Democrat or a Demo-Dixie-crat, he's the same thing.

One of the reasons that these Dixie-crats occupy such a powerful position in Washington, D.C., is that they have seniority. By reason of their seniority and primarily because they have denied the local Negro his right to vote, they hold sway over key committees in Washington. You call it a system based on democracy, yet you can't deny that the most powerful men in this government are from the South. The only reason they're in positions of power is because the Negroes in their area are deprived of their constitutional right to vote. But the Constitution says that when at any time the people of a given area are denied their right to vote, the representatives of that area are supposed to be expelled from their seat. You don't need any new legislation; it's right in front of you already. The only reason the politicians want new legislation is to use it to further trick the Negro. All they have to do is to go by that thing they call the Constitution. It needs no more bills, it needs no more amendments, it needs no more anything. All it needs is a little sincere application.

As with the South, the North knows its own by-pass for the Constitution, which goes by the name of "gerrymandering." Some fellows gain control in the so-called Negro community and then change voting lines every time the Negro begins to get too powerful numerically. The technique is different from that in Mississippi. There is no denying the Negro the right to vote outright, as in Mississippi. The Northern way is more shrewd and subtle; but whether victim of the Northern way or the Southern method, the Negro ends up with no political power whatsoever. Now, I may not be putting this in language which you're used to, but I'm quite sure that you get the point. Whenever you give the Negro in the South the right to vote, his Constitutional right to vote, it will mean an automatic change in the entire representation from the South. Were he able to exercise his right, some of the most powerful and influential figures in Washington, D.C., would not now be in the Capitol. A large Negro vote would change the foreign policy as well as the domestic policy of this government. Therefore the only valid approach toward revolutionizing American policy is to give to the Negro his right to vote. Once that is done, the entire future course of things must change.

I might say this is how we look at it—how the victims look at it, a very crude and what you might call pessimistic view. But I should rather prefer it as a realistic view. Now what is our approach towards solving this? Many of you have probably just recently read that I am no longer an active member in the Nation of Islam, although I am myself still a Muslim. My religion is still Islam, and I still credit the Honorable Elijah Muhammad with being responsible for everything I know and everything that I am. In New York we have recently founded the Muslim Mosque, Incorporated, which has as its base the religion of Islam, the religion of Islam because we have found that this religion creates more unity among our people than any other type of philosophy can do. At the same time, the religion of Islam is more successful in eliminating the vices that exist in the so-called Negro community, which destroy the moral fiber of the so-called Negro community.

So with this religious base, the difference between the Muslim Mosque, Incorporated, and the Nation of Islam is probably this: We have as our political philosophy, Black Nationalism; as our economic philosophy, Black Nationalism; and as our social philosophy, Black Nationalism. We believe that the religion of Islam combined with Black Nationalism is all that is needed to solve the problem that exists in the so-called Negro community. Why?

The only real solution to our problem, just as the Honorable Elijah Muhammad has taught us, is to go back to our homeland and to live among our own people and develop it so we'll have an independent nation of our own. I still believe this. But that is a long-range program. And while our people are getting set to go back home, we have to live here in the meantime. So in the Honorable Elijah Muhammad's long-range program, there's also a short-range program: the political philosophy which teaches us that the black man should control the politics of his own community. When the black man controls the politics and the politicians in his own community, he can then make them produce what is good for the community. For when a politician in the so-called Negro community is controlled by a political machine outside, seldom will that politician ever do what is necessary to bring up the standard of living or to solve the problems that exist in that community. So our political philosophy is designed to bring together the so-called Negroes and to re-educate them to the importance of politics in concrete betterment, so that they may know what they should be getting from their politicians in addition to a promise. Once the political control of the so-called Negro community is in the hands of the so-called Negro, then it is possible for us to do something towards correcting the evils and the ills that exist there.

Our economic philosophy of Black Nationalism means that instead of our spending the rest of our lives begging the white man for a job, our people should be re-educated to the science of economics and the part that it plays in our community. We should be taught just the basic fundamentals: that whenever you take money out of the neighborhood and spend it in another neighborhood, the neighborhood in which you spend it gets richer and richer, and the neighborhood from which you take it gets poorer and poorer. This creates a ghetto, as now exists in every so-called Negro community in this country. If the Negro isn't spending his money downtown with what we call "the man," "the man" is himself right in the Negro community. All the stores are run by the white man, who takes the money out of the community as soon as the sun sets. We have to teach our people the importance of where to spend their dollars and the importance of establishing and owning businesses. Thereby we can create employment for ourselves, instead of having to wait to boycott your stores and businesses to

demand that you give us a job. Whenever the majority of our people begin to think along such lines, you'll find that we ourselves can best solve our problems. Instead of having to wait for someone to come out of your neighborhood into our neighborhood to tackle these problems for us, we ourselves may solve them.

The social philosophy of Black Nationalism says that we must eliminate the vices and evils that exist in our society, and that we must stress the cultural roots of our forefathers, that will lend dignity and make the black man cease to be ashamed of himself. We have to teach our people something about our cultural roots. We have to teach them something of their glorious civilizations before they were kidnapped by your grandfathers and brought over to this country. Once our people are taught about the glorious civilization that existed on the African continent, they won't any longer be ashamed of who they are. We will reach back and link ourselves to those roots, and this will make the feeling of dignity come into us; we will feel that as we lived in times gone by, we can in like manner today. If we had civilizations, cultures, societies, and nations hundreds of years ago, before you came and kidnapped us and brought us here, so we can have the same today. The restoration of our cultural roots and history will restore dignity to the black people in this country. Then we shall be satisfied in our own social circles; then we won't be trying to force ourselves into your social circles. So the social philosophy of Black Nationalism doesn't in any way involve any anti-anything. However, it does restore to the man who is being taunted his own self-respect. And the day that we are successful in making the black man respect himself as much as he now admires you, he will no longer be breathing down your neck every time you go buy a house somewhere to get away from him.

That is the political, social, and economic philosophy of Black Nationalism, and in order to bring it about, the program that we have in the Muslim Mosque, Incorporated, places an accent on youth. We are issuing a call for students across the country, from coast to coast, to launch a new study of the problem—not a study that is in any way guided or influenced by adults, but a study of their own. Thus we can get a new analysis of the problem, a more realistic analysis. After this new study and more realistic analysis, we are going to ask those same students (by students I mean young people, who having less of a stake to lose, are more flexible and can be more objective) for a new approach to the problem.

Already we have begun to get responses from so-called Negro students from coast to coast, who aren't actually religiously inclined, but who are nonetheless strongly sympathetic to the approach used by Black Nationalism, whether it be social, economic, or political. And with this new approach and with these new ideas we think that we may open up a new era here in this country. As that era begins to spread, people in this country—instead of sticking under your nose or crying for civil rights—will begin to expand their civil rights plea to a plea for human rights. And once the so-called Negro in this country forgets the whole civil rights issue and begins to realize that human rights are far more important and broad than civil rights, he won't be going to Washington, D.C., anymore, to beg Uncle Sam for civil rights. He will take his plea for human rights to the United Nations. There won't be a violation of civil rights anymore. It will be a violation of human rights. Now at this moment, the governments that are in the United Nations can't step in, can't involve themselves with America's domestic policy. But the day the black man turns from civil rights to human rights, he will take his case into the halls of the United Nations in the same manner as the people in Angola, whose human rights have been violated by the Portuguese in South Africa.

You'll find that you are entering an era now where the black man in this country has ceased to think domestically, or within the bounds of the United States, and he's beginning to see that this is a world-wide issue and that he needs help from outside. We need help from our brothers in Africa who have won their independence. And when we begin to show them our thinking has expanded to an international scale, they will step in and help us, and you'll find that Uncle Sam will be in a most embarrassing position. So the only way Uncle Sam can stop us is to get some civil rights passed—right now! For if he can't take care of his domestic dirt, it's going to be put before the eyes of the world. Then you'll find that you'll have nobody on your side, whatsoever, other than, perhaps, a few of those Uncle Toms—and they've already out-lived their time. . . .

Continuing to Think

In this speech it seems that Malcolm X has given up expecting the government of the United States to honor the social contract with respect to African Americans. Instead, he advocates the political, economic, and social philosophy of Black Nationalism—in other words, seizing power and opportunities rather than asking for them. One question we must ask ourselves is: Can the social contract be made to work for African Americans? Two advances that had not yet occurred when Malcolm X was assassinated less than a year after giving this speech have been affected by recent court decisions: The Supreme Court weakend affirmative action programs, and declared unconstitutional election districts drawn to guarantee black representation in Congress.

If some citizens find the social contract to be functioning quite well from their perspective, they may be unable or unwilling to hear the complaints of other citizens that the social contract seems to have excluded them. Women found themselves in this position in 1848; along with African Americans, women continue to experience frustration and discrimination today. As Malcolm X pointed out, governments are slow to change the status quo, and inertia benefits the continuation of existing power relationships. Some of what Malcolm X advocated in this speech has actually occurred (and some government support is now in the process of being retracted). Has it been sufficient to create a more equitable social contract? If not, why not?

8.5   *The End of the Golden Road*

NICHOLAS D. KRISTOF

Preparing to Read

All four of our first readings presume the philosophy of representative government that has come to be the norm in the Western world. Our last selection looks at a very different justification for government that existed for thousands of years in China and may be reaching an end today.

An alternative to representative government is the political theory of the divine right of kings. Practiced in Europe, Africa, and Asia, this theory asserts that a deity or a divine principle chooses the ruler, and it implies that obedience to the ruler is obedience to that divine principle. In ancient China, more than three thousand years ago, this right to govern was understood to be the Mandate of Heaven.

Unlike European and African kings, the Chinese Emperor was invested with the right to rule, not as an individual but as a representative and preserver of the harmony between heaven and earth. Not acting on his own behalf, but acting to assure the balance of forces in the universe, the Emperor retained power only as long as the people felt the Mandate of Heaven endured.

Nicholas D. Kristof applies this ancient principle to modern China and finds that Mao Zedong was able to accomplish the Communist Revolution because he enjoyed a public perception of virtue. In a secular and communistic state, Mao was believed to hold the traditional Mandate of Heaven. Today, Kristof argues, the current leadership is in danger of losing that support, and the Mandate is once again threatened.

EVEN THOUGH the Communist ideology is based on a modern Western political idea—Marxism—its political legitimacy is derived from the traditional concept of the "mandate of heaven." This is a form of divine right that can be maintained only so long as people are content. In the 12th century B.C., the Duke of Shou outlined this central tenet of Chinese political philosophy: Rulers must be just and virtuous—or they will be ousted. This theme was further developed by Mencius, a philosopher who lived in the third and fourth centuries B.C., who asserted, "The people turn to a humane ruler as water flows downward or beasts take to wilderness."

In 1949, Mao Zedong won the mandate of heaven because of the popular perception that he and his followers were virtuous and would improve the lives of the Chinese people. After taking control, the Communists virtually stamped out graft, prostitution, drug addiction and inflation. They made huge strides in literacy, education and public health. They redistributed property and renewed hope in the country and confidence in the future.

But today Deng Xiaoping, China's paramount leader, travels by armored Cadillac; the children of the party leadership are rumored to have squirreled away money in overseas bank accounts, and top leaders seem plumper each time they appear on television. In short, many Chinese now doubt that their leaders are either virtuous or equipped to lead the country to prosperity.

"The mandate of heaven is not easily preserved," the Duke of Zhou had advised. "Heaven is hard to depend on. Those who have lost the mandate did so because they could not practice and carry on the reverence and brilliant virtue of their forefathers."

It is partly because they no longer regard their leaders as worthy of the mandate of heaven that ordinary Chinese are not cooperating in enforcing totalitarianism. In the 1960's, during the savagely anarchic time of the Cultural Revolution, many Chinese turned in their own family members for expressing counterrevolutionary thoughts over the dinner table. But almost no one seems to believe in the Communist Party or its ideals anymore. The state periodically lashes out at those who poke it in the eye, especially dissidents who complain to foreign journalists, but it has lost its iron grip over the daily life of most Chinese. It may be dictatorial, even brutal, but it is no longer very successful at being totalitarian.

To outsiders, China may seem to be just another repressive state, but some Chinese intellectuals and foreign scholars believe that the problems run much deeper. They see an entire society in flux and a ruling dynasty that is disintegrating in the same way that the Qing, Ming and all their precusors did. If this is so, the impact would be far-reaching: a repressive China troubles only the relatively small part of the population that presses for reform or democracy; a rotting society affects everyone.

Today the dominant mood in the cities is malaise: most Chinese express not hatred for the Communist regime but weariness with it. People want to watch Taiwanese soap operas on television, not endless serials about Communist heroes in the war against the Japanese occupation in the 30's and 40's. They want to take their children to the park on Saturday afternoons instead of enduring more political study sessions. They don't want to be told that they can't kiss or hug—as was the case this fall when the authorities banned such signs of affection on the campus of Beijing University. Since would-be kissers and huggers vastly outnumber would-be Communists, this ban instantly created even more alienation among the young, who want to bop to rock concerts instead of watching People's Liberation Army song-and-dance shows.

These days, the most important challenge to the Communist leadership comes not from the small number of democratic activists, who are on the fringes of national consciousness and so few in number that they can be imprisoned or kept under surveillance. Rather, the threat comes from people like Cui Jian, a long-haired rock star who is to urban Chinese youth what Bob Dylan or the Beatles were to Americans in the 1960's. Cui Jian is not permitted to appear on television and his concerts are periodically banned, but his raspy outbursts of alienation are the anthems of his generation.

Cui Jian's latest cassette, which somehow evaded the censors to hit the stores this year, is perhaps his most daring. It even suggests that the Golden Road—a byword for Communism—has reached a dead end:

Look all around, at men and women, kids and
   old folks,
Look—we've come to the end of the Golden
   Road.

Most Chinese are not viscerally anti-Communist (throughout the democracy movement of 1989 very few of the students advocated an overthrow of the Communist Party), and it is possible the Communists could still win a free election by relying on the peasants—who make up 70 percent of the population and who cannot conceive of any alternative. But by imposing their faith on an agnostic nation, the octogenarian leaders of China seem to be marginalizing their party and endangering their mandate to rule.

"All the signs of a decaying dynasty are here," contends Geremie Barme, an Australian scholar of Chinese culture who is now conducting research in Beijing. "You have not only the rhetoric but also an ideology that is wholly divorced from the economic and social reality. In the Qing Dynasty, it was Confucianism. Now it's Marxism and Mao Zedong thought."

A Western ambassador in Beijing ruminates: "The system has exhausted itself. It has run out of ideas and energy, and especially in the provinces you get the sense that it's pretty much irrelevant. People talk about technical problems and about how to get the economy moving, but they don't really pay attention to the center."

The historical parallels are not lost on Chinese intellectuals, especially those who remember the collapse of the Nationalist Government in 1949 and who were born not long after the Qing Dynasty collapsed in 1911–12. In his spacious home, the perquisite of an illustrious career serving Communist China, an aging ministry-level official looks surprised when he is asked if there isn't an echo of the late Qing Dynasty in today's China. "Of course there is," he responds. "The dynasty is collapsing again. That's exactly what's happening."

Of course, it would be rash to forecast the imminent collapse of the regime. If Chinese Communism could survive the chaos of the Cultural Revolution (from 1966 to 1976), it may be more resilient than people think. Moreover, the present is in some respects very unlike historical periods when dynasties were collapsing. The Commu-

nists today are presiding over a growing economy in which living standards are rising and they have the military force to crush any rebellion.

It has always been this way in China: the first emperor of a dynasty seizes power by force of arms and personality, and initially there is a dizzying consolidation of power and national authority. Then power is handed down to the emperor's sons and grandsons, who grow up soft and pampered in Beijing's Forbidden City, while the court eunuchs and Government officials grow fat off bribes and graft. Isolated from their subjects, the effete rulers forbid criticism and are lulled and deluded by flatterers around them, until they lose track of reality. Meanwhile, corruption spreads; funds are squandered; the central Government becomes overextended at the same time that it grows ever more avaricious; resentments mount: provincial fiefs emerge, and finally the dynasty collapses.

Mao Zedong was well aware of this dynastic cycle. In 1946, he was asked by a prominent scholar, Huang Yanpei, how the Communists would handle this problem if their revolution succeeded. "Dynasties begin with a surge of vigor, and then decay and disintegrate," Huang Yanpei noted. "Has the Communist Party found a way to break this vicious cycle?"

"We've found a way!" Mao said, beaming. "It's called democracy!"

Of course, Mao never tried that approach, but as he approached Beijing in 1949, ready to take power, he told his comrades, "We are going to the capital to face an examination." He reminded them of the fate of Li Zicheng, the peasant rebel who led an uprising in the 17th century that toppled the Ming Dynasty, but who was then ousted himself shortly afterward, partly because he was not a virtuous leader.

A member of the group of octogenarians now ruling China, Bo Yibo, also has Li Zicheng in mind. According to well-informed Chinese, Bo said in a secret speech earlier this year that the party must defeat corruption to insure that no new Li Zicheng emerges to overthrow the Communists. But despite a series of anti-corruption campaigns in the last few years, most Chinese seem to believe that the problem has got worse rather than better.

Drug addiction, the scourge of the last years of the Qing Dynasty, is also increasing. This summer, the police in Luoyang, an ancient city in central China, noticed that some food stalls had unusually long lines of customers while others nearby attracted little business. An investigation revealed that at least 92 food stalls or noodle shops were lacing dishes with opium in an effort to get customers addicted to their food. This attempt at culinary seduction ended, according to a Shanghai newspaper, when the police seized 1,523 pounds of opium and closed the restaurants.

One Chinese for whom drugs were more than a food additive is a tall, lean 40-year-old man from Kunming, in southwest China. In the 1980's, he went into private business as a television salesman and soon made a small fortune. Delighted with his life and prospects, he took advantage of the freer economic climate to travel to Ruili, a town on the border with Myanmar (formerly Burma), and prospect for business. Some friends there introduced him to heroin, showing him how to add it to his cigarettes.

"A lot of people think it's very cool to use heroin," he says with evident distaste. He is now in a narcotics rehabilitation center in Kunming. Like most people in China today, he is pessimistic. "There'll be more and more drugs," he predicts grimly. "The problem is already serious, and it'll get more serious."

An official Government report says 70,000 drug addicts have been registered throughout China, and heroin seizures tripled last year and are running even higher this year. The resurgence of a drug problem has special resonance in China because it has been drilled into the nation's consciousness that the widespread use of opium during the waning days of the last imperial dynasty had been a symbol and cause of the country's weakness. Addicts themselves say that the rapid spread of heroin is an indication of the purposelessness that many people feel.

For the Communists, as it was for the Qing Dynasty, increasing drug use has come at a time when foreign incursions can no longer be staved off. In the 19th century, the problem was foreign troops who seized territory and humiliated the Government; today, it's foreign ideas that seize the human mind.

In Guangdong Province, for example, it is easy to tell which direction is south. Just look at the television antennas, which point southward to neighboring Hong Kong. In Fujian Province on the east coast, people watch Taiwan television. Throughout China, intellectuals listen to Voice of America and BBC radio programs.

There is a fascination with the democratic, capitalistic West that is clearly subversive of Communist ideology and rule. For instance, Chinese who have watched American cops-and-robbers series on television have been impressed by the fact that the police on occasion suspect people of being criminals but do not arrest them for lack of evidence.

Such is the allure of the world outside China that people give their leaders scant credit for the dramatic improvement in the standard of living in the last decade. Instead of comparing themselves with the way they were a few years ago, they compare themselves with their rich kin in Hong Kong or Taiwan.

To make matters worse for the Communist leadership, the growing wealth of the last dozen years, especially along the coastal provinces, has probably enriched businesses and local administrators more than the central Government. The traditional financial squeeze on the central Government toward the end of each dynasty, and the resulting pecuniary tug-of-war with the provinces, is visible again today. Beijing relies for funds on the profits of state-owned corporations, which are largely inefficient, with only about a third of the state-owned companies earning any real money. Consequently, the central Government is ceding influence on the economy to the provinces.

Over the last year or so, a series of earthquake rumors have alarmed Beijing residents.

The latest such rumor—that the capital would be struck imminently (the dates varied) by a devastating earthquake—spread from house to house in August. Some foreign correspondents living in a 15-story building were even warned by their Chinese friends to be careful.

The earthquake rumors are particularly significant because in China the collapse of dynasties is often preceded by a rash of natural disasters. Chinese know that natural disasters are sure signs that the mandate of heaven is passing, that it is time for a new ruler. Those who see the link between nature and politics point out that Chairman Mao died in September 1976, just six weeks after the most devastating earthquake in modern Chinese history—in Tangshan—killed at least 242,000 people.

While there was little anyone could do to forestall earthquakes, preventive measures could always be taken against such disasters as floods and droughts. Flood-control waterworks could be built and grain stored against bad harvests. But as a dynasty wound down and extortionist practices became the order of the day, flood control and grain storage for the masses were not high on the agenda of Government officials. Failure to maintain waterworks led to terrible floods and the millions of peasants suffering from famine had no recourse but to throw their support behind rebel leaders advocating an overthrow of the ineffectual emperor.

The symbolism of natural disasters has therefore lent special significance to the floods that struck China this year, affecting some 200 million people. China dealt reasonably effectively with the floods, so that no one is starving or freezing to death, as was once common. Even so, the devastation was enormous. No one knows how many peasants see the floods as a sign that the Communists may be losing the mandate of heaven, but at least some Chinese blame the Communist Party General Secretary, Jiang Zemin. The second character of his name, Ze, means "water," and the third character, Min, means "the people." So his name can be construed to mean "Jiang who brings water on the people."

When one is looking for strange omens, they are easy to find. Last month, a number of Chinese were fascinated by a newspaper report that more than 10,000 crabs had suddenly come ashore on Hainan Island in the south. What did that mean? "In China," explains a university-educated woman, "we think that when there is a miracle or tumult in the natural world, there may be one in the political world as well."

The rise of superstition or religious cults was often a feature of declining dynasties. Perhaps spirituality was a source of comfort in troubled times, filling the vacuum created by a loss of faith in the emperor. These days, local superstitions and various religious faiths are enjoying a resurgence. On any given Sunday morning, crowds of young and old fill China's growing number of Christian churches. Buddhism and Taoism are also enjoying growing support, particularly among young people searching for something to believe in. Others, including students at Beijing University, are turning to the I Ching for what it can offer about their future fortunes.

The quasi-spiritual movement with the most support is *qi gong,* a kind of breathing exercise that helps people relax. In its simplest form, qi gong is similar to yoga and transcendental meditation, but the last few years have also seen the emergence of qi gong masters who claim they can heal the sick, make people taller or even fly across the country. Tens of millions of people now practice qi gong, and there has been a burst of books about qi gong masters with supernatural powers.

Li Hanxiang, a 52-year-old former electrician, is a qi gong master in Hebei Province who has attracted a devoted following. On a recent visit to Beijing, he visited a home for the elderly and offered his services free of charge so that he could prove to a foreigner that his talents were genuine. He stared inside the ears of several lame men and women who had come to him for healing. He purported to diagnose their ailments and those of their family members. Then he stood in a trancelike state, vibrating slightly, with sweat pouring from his body, as he tried to transmit his "qi" to his "patients." With a cough he came out of his trance, and shouted at the men and women to throw away their crutches.

"You can walk, now!" he shouted. "You can dance!"

The men and women eagerly hobbled a few steps, although it was impossible to tell if this represented anything more than the power of suggestion.

The declining power and moral legitimacy of the Communist Party is perhaps most evident in the mud-brick villages where most Chinese live. After 1949, the party consolidated its grip on the countryside by replacing the traditional centers of power (landlords and family clans) with a network of Communist Party cells. But with the communes dismantled, in some areas the old pulse of life is reappearing—often with unpleasant consequences.

Family clans have reemerged, and in some areas have replaced the party organizations as the centers of local authority. In Yongxing County in Hunan Province, for example, the Huangs and the Wangs have taken the law into their own hands. The Wangs wanted to farm on a newly cleared hillside, which could mean the destruction of the graves of two Huangs buried there. So in April, about 1,000 of the Huangs attacked members of the Wang clan living in the area. According to an official report, the battle lasted three days and three nights and involved clubs, guns and even crude artillery.

The practice of buying and selling women has also returned. Last year, almost 19,000 young women were reported kidnapped and sold as wives to peasants who cannot find spouses on their own. Some women are chained to the bed until they bear a child, and some are even blinded so that they cannot escape.

Local villages or townships are also erecting their own (illegal) checkpoints on roads, demanding payments from passing trucks. The national Government regularly thunders against the practice, but it persists. One survey in Hunan Province found 14 illegal checkpoints on a six-mile stretch of road, each extorting tolls from trucks.

Like the emperors before them, China's leaders are so remote that they do not always know they are out of touch. The Government still calls on people to address one another as "comrade," to relax with a book on Leninism, to hum old ditties like "When I Grow Up I Am Determined to Become a Peasant." It distributes tapes of Communist songs like "O Party, O Party, You're My Most Beloved Mother."

Like their imperial precursors, the Communist leaders are victims of their ban on free expression and appear to operate on delusions and misinformation. That was one reason why they repeatedly miscalculated in handling the democracy movement; the Communist leaders were stunned to learn that they were so unpopular.

These days, Deng Xiaoping passes the time playing bridge or playing with his grandchildren in his courtyard home just a mile north of the Forbidden City, which once housed the emperors. It is easy to compare him with Cixi, the Empress Dowager who ruled China until her death in 1908 and who presided over the demise of the Qing Dynasty,

Neither was more than 5 feet tall, neither formally held the top position in the land, yet both were brilliant, ruthless tacticians who fought their way to paramount power. And both rejected dramatic calls for peaceful political reform. In 1898, Cixi imprisoned her nephew, the Emperor Guang Xu, after he sought sweeping reforms, like the overhaul of a largely irrelevant civil-service examination system, the development of modern schools and universities and the abolition of sinecure posts. In 1989, Deng crushed a movement that called for democracy and an end to official corruption.

In the northern city of Tianjin, a retelling of the final years of the Qing Dynasty has just been serialized in a literary magazine (it will soon be published in book form). It is attracting considerable interest, says a Communist Party member who has read it, because the author may be describing Qing history—to get around the censors—but readers perceive that it is written with recent Chinese events in mind. "It's the same situation as today," says the party member. "You had an autocratic ruler reforming for a while and then trying desperately to back away from what had been started."

Paradoxically, were the Communist dynasty to collapse, even the most fervent of anti-Communists would be anxious as well as exultant. The fall of the Qing Dynasty in 1911–12 did not lead to prosperity and democracy, as many had hoped, but to decades of chaos and civil war. Many Chinese intellectuals therefore fear Deng Xiaoping's death at the same time that they yearn for it.

Continuing to Think

From our Western perspective it may seem natural to think of leaders as failing to execute the social contract or of being personally unworthy to continue in office. The Chinese system, however, places much less emphasis on the individual and much more on the social order and, indeed, the cosmic order. In terms of the philosophy of Taoism, there is a harmony of all things most easily seen in nature. Day gives way to night and night to day, season follows season in an interplay of forces the Chinese call **yin** and **yang.** Sometimes action is appropriate; other times receptivity is most effective. There is a time to do and a time to be.

A great ruler is sensitive to these forces and acts to balance them. "Ruling a great country," the Chinese classic *Tao Te Ching* tells us, "is like cooking a small fish." Too much poking can ruin the whole project. The Mandate of Heaven is not a personal authorization but a social responsibility for maintaining the proper relationship between heaven and earth. Confucianism, the other great philosophy of China, urges the proper observance of roles and responsibilities. Subjects have obligations, but so do rulers.

Even something as revolutionary as communism could enjoy the Mandate of Heaven as long as its leaders enjoyed a public perception of virtue. Recent excesses, however, including the suppression of dissent in Tienanmen Square, may have crossed the line and lost the current leadership the presumption of authority—the Mandate of Heaven. We may be seeing the end of the Golden Road.

Summing Up the Readings

Perhaps you have never really thought about what does or should justify the right to govern. In the West, Locke's second treatise provides the foundation for most political theory; in China it is the Mandate of Heaven. Both East and West, however, have had and continue to have revolutions and less dramatic protests against the right of the rulers to rule.

Elizabeth Cady Stanton and Malcolm X offer us two variations on a criticism that government is applying the social contract too narrowly, including only some of its citizens. Appealing to what is agreed-upon in theory is a much more effective way to lodge a protest than simply complaining in a theoretical vacuum. After seventy-two years of badgering, American women finally won the right to vote, but many of the social resolutions approved at Seneca Falls have been imperfectly or only partially achieved. Some of what Malcolm X advocated at Harvard was enacted into law and seized in urban neighborhoods. And yet both women and African Americans continue to protest against their exclusion from full participation in the social contract.

In fact, the social contract is perhaps intentionally fuzzy. Women may not have felt their exclusion from suffrage keenly in the days immediately after the American Revolution, and African Americans may have judged the end of slavery and the constitutional guarantee of citizenship rights sufficient in the years following the Civil War. Only when other goals are met and other dreams achieved do the things we lack begin to stand out in our minds. Much of what our government promises us is enjoyed more fully by some than by others. And what government asks in return does not fall with equal weight on all its citizens.

Continuing to Question

1. Are you more willing to place your confidence in citizens or in the state? Another way to ask this is: Which are you less willing to trust with too much power?

2. Can you think of a reason why the women who boldly rewrote the Declaration of Independence to include women were very tentative in asking for the right to vote? Why might voting seem more radical than some other demands?

3. What are the dangers of living under a fuzzy social contract? When might those hidden dangers become more obvious to citizens?

4. Malcolm X said that he was not an American. At what point should a citizen have the right to "opt out" of the social contract?

5. How is the Mandate of Heaven different from the Western idea of a social contract, and how are the two concepts alike?

Suggestions for Further Exploration

Hegel, G. W. F., *Reason in History*—trans. Robert S. Hartman. Indianapolis, Ind.: Bobbs-Merrill, 1953. This slim volume gives the essentials of Hegel's philosophy of history and is both readable and manageable intellectually.

Heider, John, trans. *The Tao of Leadership: Lao Tzu's Tao Te Ching Adapted for a New Age*—New York: Bantam, 1986. Heider offers a translation of Lao-tzu's classic, the *Tao Te Ching*, using the word leader instead of *master* or *sage* and offering an alternative style of leadership based on *wei-wu-wei* or doing without doing. Many successful businesses are using this approach.

Machiavelli, Niccolo, *The Prince*—New York: Scolar, 1969. *The Prince* is a masterpiece of practical politics, written in the form of advice for a Renaissance prince. One piece of advice is that it is better to be feared than loved.

Orwell, George, *1984*—New York: Harcourt Brace Jovanovich, 1984. Orwell's novel predicted a future in which government would control every aspect of a citizen's life through the control of information. Even though 1984 is now history, the issues remain alive.

Schneir, Miriam, ed. *Feminism: The Essential Historical Writings*—New York: Vintage, 1972. This is an anthology of short excerpts from the speeches and writings of the 18th- and 19th-century women's movement. The documents from the Seneca Falls Convention and *The United States of America v. Susan B. Anthony* are both included.

9 Social Philosophy

Defining the Issue

What constitutes justice? Is it "doing the right thing," providing the greatest good in the world at large, destroying the "enemies" of justice? And how do we navigate the apparently conflicting claims for justice from groups who charge present or past discrimination or both? These are the questions of social philosophy, which considers the relationships between individuals and communities.

Justice is popularly thought of in terms of retribution: "We executed that mass murderer, and justice was served." Paying back evil for evil can seem like carrying out the demands of justice. But philosophers extend the discussion to include a much broader concept—the distribution of benefits and burdens in a society. According to this definition, justice is done when both the good things (money, jobs, the right to vote and drive a car) as well as the bad things (taxes, the draft, criminal prosecutions) are justly distributed.

There are several ways in which distributive justice can be considered. Some philosophers have argued that whatever provides the greatest amount of happiness is good, whereas whatever creates unhappiness, including pain and the deprivation of pleasure, is not good. Other philosophers disagree, arguing that it is not outcomes but doing what is right that leads to justice. Even if most people are happy, it is possible to act unjustly. Slavery, for example, may have made more people happy than it made unhappy, but that didn't make it just.

Particularly troublesome here are questions about war (Is there such a thing as a "just war"?) and public policy (How do we protect the rights of minorities and the majority when issues of racial and gender discrimination arise?). Keep these questions in mind as you read these proposals for achieving justice.

Previewing the Readings

John Stuart Mill considers justice a matter of social utility or usefulness: If you create the greatest amount of happiness possible, you have acted justly. This philosophical position is known as **utilitarianism.** Mary Wollstonecraft agrees with a distinction Mill later makes, that there is a difference in the quality of pleasures, which counts more than the mere quantity of pleasures; otherwise we should all prefer the pleasures of being a pig to those of being a person. Providing those higher pleasures counts as justice for both Wollstonecraft and Mill.

There is a danger in this position, however. What if some members of society enjoy the higher pleasures while others lack basic means of survival? Insisting that we must bring questions of justice out of the abstract and historicize them, Ignacio Ellacuría, S.J., insists we include all citizens in discussions of the common good. If the common good cannot be divided, then it is unjust to balance the deprivation of many against the higher pleasures of the few. Ellacuría believed that utilitarian justifications can easily be abused.

One of the difficulties is unraveling the threads of discrimination. If Audre Lorde, who identifies herself as a "forty-nine year old Black lesbian feminist socialist mother . . . and a member of an inter-racial couple," experiences discrimination, is it because of her age, race, sexual orientation, political views, or some combination of all of them? Lorde thinks we must keep all points of difference clearly in mind and avoid generalizations that put all women into the same category. Justice will mean, she insists, equality within difference.

In the name of justice, the fictional eleven-year-old Ender Wiggin is selected by the state, taken from his family and home planet, and brutally trained in the art of high-tech, computer-managed war. When he learns the battles have not been simulations and he has unwittingly destroyed the enemy, he is appalled and becomes a Speaker for the Dead. The destruction of thousands may be deemed necessary, especially if they are aggressors, but can it be justified? Is there such a thing as a "just war," as some philosophers have argued, or are all wars, by definition, unjust?

Mary Wollstonecraft's *A Vindication of the Rights of Women,* published simultaneously in London and New York in 1792, and John Stuart Mill's *The Subjection of Women,* written during the 1830s, share and reflect a late eighteenth- and early nineteenth-century view of justice as deriving naturally and obviously from rational principles and reflecting the higher pleasures to which humans are uniquely invited. More than a hundred years later, contemporary philosopher Audre Lorde, activist priest Ignacio Ellacuría, S.J., and science fiction writer Orson Scott Card seem less confident of human rationality. Our ability to reason clearly, it seems, can easily be subverted by biases or placed in the service of brutal aggression with or without our consent.

9.1   Utilitarianism

JOHN STUART MILL

Preparing to Read

Looking for one "fundamental principle or law, at the root of all morality," Mill arrives at what he calls the "Utilitarian or Happiness theory." No matter how much we may desire to conduct our discussion with high sounding phrases, Mill asserts, the bottom line is that if people find their pleasures increased, they will feel they have been treated justly, and if they find their pleasures decreased or their pains increased, you will be hard pressed to convince them they have not been treated unjustly.

Mill's mentor Jeremy Bentham thought we could approach questions of justice the way we approach mathematics: Weigh pleasures against pains, by assigning each a mathematical value, and then simply sum the results to determine which is better. Mill thinks we need to make qualitative distinctions as well as quantitative ones. Would you consider it justice if I offered you unlimited access to your favorite sweet but deprived you of your license to drive a car? Mill thinks you would not.

In the end, he argues, it is access to these "higher pleasures" that constitutes justice. And, who will decide whether attending a "heavy metal" concert or going to the opera is a higher pleasure? Why, those "competent judges" who have experienced both kinds of pleasure, of course. Whether you agree or disagree with Mill's qualitative distinction between types of pleasures, think about the general utilitarian insistence that it is consequences, rather than intentions or attention to obligations, that matter. Is the way things turn out the only relevant consideration?

THE CREED WHICH ACCEPTS as the foundation of morals, Utility, or the Greatest Happiness Principle, holds that actions are right in proportion as they tend to promote happiness, wrong as they tend to produce the reverse of happiness. By happiness is intended pleasure, and the absence of pain; by unhappiness, pain, and the privation of pleasure. To give a clear view of the moral standard set up by the theory, much more requires to be said; in particular, what things it includes in the ideas of pain and pleasure; and to what extent this is left an open question. But these supplementary explanations do not affect the theory of life on which this theory of morality is grounded—namely, that pleasure, and freedom from pain, are the only things desirable as ends; and that all desirable things (which are as numerous in the utilitarian as in any other scheme) are desirable either for the pleasure inherent in themselves, or as means to the promotion of pleasure and the prevention of pain.

Now, such a theory of life excites in many minds, and among them in some of the most estimable in feeling and purpose, inveterate dislike. To suppose that life has (as they express it) no higher end than pleasure—no better and nobler object of desire and pursuit—they designate as utterly mean and grovelling; as a doctrine worthy only of swine, to whom the followers of Epicurus were, at a very early period, contemptuously likened; and modern holders of the doctrine are occasionally made the subject of equally polite comparisons by its German, French, and English assailants.

When thus attacked, the Epicureans have always answered, that it is not they, but their accusers, who represent human nature in a degrading light; since the accusation supposes human beings to be capable of no pleasures except those of which swine are capable. If this supposition were true, the charge could not be gainsaid, but would then be no longer an imputation; for if the sources of pleasure were precisely the same to human beings and to swine, the rule of life which is good enough for the one would be good enough for the other. The comparison of the Epicurean life to that of beasts is felt as degrading, precisely because a beast's pleasures do not satisfy a human being's conceptions of happiness. Human beings have faculties more elevated than the animal appetites, and when once made conscious of them, do not regard anything as happiness which does not include their gratification. I do not, indeed, consider the Epicureans to have been by any means faultless in drawing out their scheme of consequences from the utilitarian principle. To do this in any sufficient manner, many Stoic, as well as Christian elements require to be included. But there is no known Epicurean theory of life which does not assign to the pleasures of the intellect, of the feelings and imagination, and of the moral sentiments, a much higher value as pleasures than to those of mere sensation. It must be admitted, however, that utilitarian writers in general have placed the superiority of mental over bodily pleasures chiefly in the greater permanency, safety, uncostliness, etc., of the former—that is, in their circumstantial advantages rather than in their intrinsic nature. And on all these points utilitarians have fully proved their case; but they might have taken the other, and, as it may be called, higher ground, with entire consistency. It is quite compatible with the principle of utility to recognise the fact, that some *kinds* of pleasure are more desirable and more valuable than others. It would be absurd that while, in estimating all other things, quality is considered as well as quantity, the estimation of pleasures should be supposed to depend on quantity alone.

If I am asked, what I mean by difference of quality in pleasures, or what makes one pleasure more valuable than another, merely as a pleasure, except its being greater in amount, there is but one possible answer. Of two pleasures, if there be one to which all or almost all who have experience of both give a decided preference, irrespective of any feeling of moral obligation to prefer it, that is the more desirable pleasure. If one of the two is, by those who are competently acquainted with both, placed so far above the other that they prefer it, even though knowing it to be attended with a greater amount of discontent, and would not resign it for any quantity of the other pleasure which their nature is capable of, we are justified in ascribing to the preferred enjoyment a superiority in quality, so far outweighing quantity as to render it, in comparison, of small account.

Now it is an unquestionable fact that those who are equally acquainted with, and equally capable of appreciating and enjoying, both, do give a most marked preference to the manner of existence which employs their higher faculties. Few human creatures would consent to be changed into any of the lower animals, for a promise of the fullest allowance of a beast's pleasures; no intelligent human being would consent to be a fool, no instructed person would be an ignoramus, no person of feeling and conscience would be selfish and base, even though they should be persuaded that the fool, the dunce, or the rascal is better satisfied with his lot than they are with theirs. They would not resign what they possess more than he for the most complete satisfaction of all the desires which they have in common with him. If they ever fancy they would, it is only in cases of unhappiness so extreme, that to escape from it they would exchange their lot for almost any other, however undesirable in their own eyes. A being of higher faculties requires more to make him happy, is capable probably of more acute suffering, and certainly accessible to it at more points, than one of an inferior type; but in spite of these liabilities, he can never really wish to sink into what he feels to be a lower grade of existence. We may give what explanation we please of this unwillingness; we may attribute it to pride, a name which is given indiscriminately to some of the most and to some of the least estimable feelings of which mankind are capable: we may refer it to the love of liberty and personal independence, an appeal to which was with the Stoics one of the most effective means for the inculcation of it; to the love of power, or to the love of excitement, both of which do really enter into and contribute to it: but its most appropriate appellation is a sense of dignity, which all human beings possess in one form or other, and in some, though by no means in exact, proportion to their higher faculties, and which is so essential a part of the happiness of those in whom it is strong, that nothing which conflicts with it could be, otherwise than momentarily, an object of desire to them. Whoever supposes that this preference takes place at a sacrifice of happiness—that the superior being, in anything like equal circumstances, is not happier than the inferior—confounds the two very different ideas, of happiness, and content. It is indisputable that the being whose capacities of enjoyment are low, has the greatest chance of having them fully satisfied; and a highly endowed being will always feel that any happiness which he can look for, as the world is constituted, is imperfect. But he can learn to bear its imperfections, if they are at all bearable; and they will not make him envy the being who is indeed unconscious of the imperfections, but only because he feels not at all the good which those imperfections qualify. It is better to be a human being dissatisfied than a pig satisfied; better to be Socrates dissatisfied than a fool satisfied. And if the fool, or the pig, are of a different opinion, it is because they only know their own side of the question. The other party to the comparison knows both sides.

It may be objected, that many who are capable of the higher pleasures, occasionally, under the influence of temptation, postpone them to the lower. But this is quite compatible with a full appreciation of the intrinsic superiority of the higher. Men often, from infirmity of character, make their election for the nearer good, though they know it to be the less valuable; and this no less when the choice is between two bodily pleasures, than when it is between bodily and mental. They pursue sensual indulgences to the injury of health, though perfectly aware that health is the greater good. It may be further objected, that many who begin with youthful enthusiasm for everything noble, as they advance in years sink into indolence and selfishness. But I do not believe that those who undergo this very common change, voluntarily choose the lower description of pleasures in preference to the higher. I believe that before they devote themselves exclusively to the one, they have already become incapable of the other. Capacity for the nobler feelings is in most natures a very tender plant, easily killed, not only by hostile influences, but by mere want of sustenance; and in the majority of young persons it speedily dies away if the occupations to which their position in life has devoted them, and the society into which it has thrown them, are not favourable to keeping that higher capacity in exercise. Men lose their high aspirations as they lose their intellectual tastes, because they have not time or opportunity for indulging them; and they addict themselves to inferior pleasures, not because they deliberately prefer them, but because they are either the only ones to which they have access, or the only ones which they are any longer capable of enjoying. It may be questioned whether any one who has remained equally susceptible to both classes of pleasures, ever knowingly and calmly preferred the lower; though many, in all ages, have broken down in an ineffectual attempt to combine both.

From this verdict of the only competent judges, I apprehend there can be no appeal. On a question which is the best worth having of two pleasures, or which of two modes of existence is the most grateful to the feelings, apart from its moral attributes and from its consequences, the judgment of those who are qualified by knowledge of both, or, if they differ, that of the majority among them, must be admitted as final. And there needs be the less hesitation to accept this judgment respecting the quality of pleasures, since there is no other tribunal to be referred to even on the question of quantity. What means are there of determining which is the acutest of two pains, or the intensest of two pleasurable sensations, except the general suffrage of those who are familiar with both? Neither pains nor pleasures are homogeneous, and pain is always heterogeneous with pleasure. What is there to decide whether a particular pleasure is worth purchasing at the cost of a particular pain, except the feelings and judgment of the experienced? When, therefore, those feelings and judgment declare the pleasures derived from the higher faculties to be preferable *in kind,* apart from the question of intensity, to those of which the animal nature, disjoined from the higher faculties, is susceptible, they are entitled on this subject to the same regard.

I have dwelt on this point, as being a necessary part of a perfectly just conception of Utility or Happiness, considered as the directive rule of human conduct. But it is by no means an indispensable condition to the acceptance of the utilitarian standard; for that standard is not the agent's own greatest happiness, but the greatest amount of happiness altogether; and if it may possibly be doubted whether a noble character is always the happier for its nobleness, there can be no doubt that it makes other people happier, and that the world in general is immensely a gainer by it. Utilitarianism, therefore, could only attain its end by the general cultivation of nobleness of character, even if each individual were only benefited by the nobleness of others, and his own, so far as happiness is concerned, were a sheer deduction from the benefit. But the bare enunciation of such an absurdity as this last, renders refutation superfluous.

According to the Greatest Happiness Principle, as above explained, the ultimate end, with reference to and for the sake of which all other things are desirable (whether we are considering our own good or that of other people), is an existence exempt as far as possible from pain, and as rich as possible in enjoyments, both in point of quantity and quality; the test of quality, and the rule for measuring it against quantity, being the preference felt by those who in their opportunities of experience, to which must be added their habits of self-consciousness and self-observation, are best furnished with the means of comparison. This, being, according to the utilitarian opinion, the end of human action, is necessarily also the standard of morality; which may accordingly be defined, the rules and precepts for human conduct, by the observance of which an existence such as has been described might be, to the greatest extent possible, secured to all mankind; and not to them only, but, so far as the nature of things admits, to the whole sentient creation.

Against this doctrine, however, arises another class of objectors, who say that happiness, in any form, cannot be the rational purpose of human life and action; because, in the first place, it is unattainable: and they contemptuously ask, what right hast thou to be happy? a question which Mr. Carlyle clenches by the addition, What right, a short time ago, hadst thou even *to be?* Next, they say, that men can do *without* happiness; that all noble human beings have felt this, and could not have become noble but by learning the lesson of Entsagen, or renunciation; which lesson, thoroughly learnt and submitted to, they affirm to be the beginning and necessary condition of all virtue.

The first of these objections would go to the root of the matter were it well founded; for if no happiness is to be had at all by human beings, the attainment of it cannot be the end of morality, or of any rational conduct. Though, even in that case, something might still be said for the utilitarian theory; since utility includes not solely the pursuit of happiness, but the prevention or mitigation of unhappiness; and if the former aim be chimerical, there will be all the greater scope and more imperative need for the latter, so long at least as mankind think fit to live, and do not take refuge in the simultaneous act of suicide recommended under certain conditions by Novalis. When, however, it is thus positively asserted to be impossible that human life should be happy, the assertion, if not something like a verbal quibble, is at least an exaggeration. If by happiness be meant a continuity of highly pleasurable excitement, it is evident enough that this is impossible. A state of exalted pleasure lasts only moments, or in some cases, and with some intermissions, hours or days, and is the occasional brilliant flash of enjoyment, not its permanent and steady flame. Of this the philosophers who have taught that happiness is the end of life were as fully aware as those who taunt them.

The happiness which they meant was not a life of rapture; but moments of such, in an existence made up of few and transitory pains, many and various pleasures, with a decided predominance of the active over the passive, and having as the foundation of the whole, not to expect more from life than it is capable of bestowing. A life thus composed, to those who have been fortunate enough to obtain it, has always appeared worthy of the name of happiness. And such an existence is even now the lot of many, during some considerable portion of their lives. The present wretched education, and wretched social arrangements, are the only real hindrance to its being attainable by almost all.

Continuing to Think

Suppose I tell you that I have deprived you of your license to drive a car for "your own good" or because I am "doing my duty." Will you feel that justice has been done, even though the outcome is definitely not to your liking? Bentham and Mill think you will not. They were convinced that an increase in pleasure or a decrease in pain was the only meaningful measure for any of us. And their views reflect a nineteenth-century optimism and faith in progress that we no longer share.

The difficulty is that utilitarianism does not operate at the level of the individual. Part of the theory is that the slight pain of some can be justified if it leads to the great pleasure of many others. Suppose the state found you to be a good tissue match and required you to make a bone marrow donation: A few minutes of pain on your part might save several people's lives. Or consider the case of slavery. Convinced that their slaves were "happy children," grateful for civilization and Christianity, slave owners balanced what they viewed as the "slight suffering" of the slaves against the major benefits the slave economy provided for the South.

It depends, doesn't it, on who is making the decisions balancing pleasure and pain—especially if it is your pain being balanced against someone else's pleasure. Paternalistic attitudes can tempt any of us to believe we know best about what is good for others or what they can reasonably be expected to do without to promote our happiness. The factory owner can decide that the workers can do with a shorter lunch period in pursuit of greater productivity. The party giver can decide that the neighbors' sleeplessness is more than balanced by the good time everyone is having at the party. Who defines the greatest good is critically important.

9.2   *Human Rights in a Divided Society*

IGNACIO ELLACURÍA, S.J.

Preparing to Read

Writing about justice is not the same thing as working for justice. It is useful to construct philosophical explanations of what constitutes the common good and how human rights should be protected. Thomas Aquinas did that with great skill in the thirteenth century. It is quite another task to examine a particular historical time and place to determine whether or not justice is being done there. This was the task Ignacio Ellacuría, a Jesuit priest, set for himself and his community in El Salvador, and it probably cost him his life.

Historicizing questions of justice leads us to ask whether what is abstractly affirmed as an "ought to be" is actually being realized. In other words, we must ask ourselves what conditions must exist if there is to be any real possibility of achieving the common good or human rights. For Aquinas, no one is good except in relation to the common good, and those who prefer their own private good to the common good cannot be ethical people. Ellacuría witnessed a powerful few defining the common good in terms of their own private world and leaving most of the population out of the calculation—and he labeled it injustice.

Utilitarians, such as John Stuart Mill, are sometimes willing to balance the sufferings of some against the benefits of others, arguing that what produces the greatest amount of good in the world at large constitutes justice. Ellacuría wants to be sure we don't make the mistake of thinking that the cultural pursuits of a few are more important than basic education of the masses. The convenience of some, in his view, can never have priority over the survival of others.

II. *Historicization of the Common Good and Human Rights as a Principle of Verification*

1. WITHOUT HISTORICIZING the common good and human rights, it is impossible either to overcome their abstract, mystifying formality or to define their truth or falsity. The presupposition that there is a common good for all peoples and all epochs reduces its reality to a minimal content, and also ignores the conditions for its real-ization. Historicization consists in seeing how what is abstractly affirmed as an "ought to be" of the common good or of human rights is actually being realized in a given circumstance. Secondly, it consists in the establishment of those real conditions without which there can be no effective realization of the common good and of human rights.

As an example, let us suppose that the right to work is considered a fundamental right and an indispensable part of the common good. If it is found that half the active population does not hold a permanent job and that a certain kind of economic system is not going to be able to solve that problem, we would have to say that that economic order and the society which maintains it are really denying the preeminence of the common good and are thwarting a fundamental human right. In such a case, the common good demands in principle the restructuring of that society by a basic change of its economic order. Examples can be multiplied, since in most of the countries of the Third World the national reality constitutes the most blatant denial of constitutional rights. Those who permanently violate the constitution are the ones who defend an economic and social system which renders impossible the fulfillment of the rights considered fundamental by the constitution itself.

It is only through such a historical mediation that it is possible to verify whether a supposedly general good is genuinely common, whether it is in fact communicated to all the members of the society. The common good is really common only if it fosters a common life. It is impossible to speak of a common good as unifying in a situation where opposed and exclusive goods are claimed, where in effect there is nothing in common or very little in common. It may be said, then, that a primary demand of the common good is the establishment of a real community in the society in question.

This formulation, however, can be interpreted in two very different ways. It can be understood in the sense of not being conscious of the real disunion that exists in the community because of unequal or discriminatory participation in the common good. Or it can be understood in the sense of becoming aware of the disunion and opposition in order to overcome them by overcoming the real causes of the division. Only the second interpretation is correct. Thus it is a mystification of the problem to attempt to eliminate the class struggle without seeking to make the struggling classes disappear. Disunion and the denial of the common good are located in the real existence of opposed classes, an existence which flows necessarily from socioeconomic causes. The affirmation of the common good and of union will lie in overcoming the socioeconomic causes which produce the disunion and the negation. A society in conflict, then, which is the one that really exists, demands that we pose the problem of the common good and thus of human rights in very specific terms, which cannot be hidden by an ingenuous and abstract understanding of the common good.

Historicization, therefore, consists in examining how the common good and human rights exist in a definite historical situation, and in establishing the mechanisms which either impede or favor the effective realization of the common good. Hegel has said that Spirit can achieve consciousness of itself and full realization only through concrete historical determinations. Thus, it should be stressed that the truth of the common good is the truth of its determinations in practice. Naturally, this is not a question of a static common good, since the important thing in the process of historicization is not the achievement at any specific moment but the orientation of the process. And this means its real orientation and not an idealized one.

2. From this historical perspective, it is easy to show that we cannot speak today of a common good or a common participation in human rights, whether in the totality of international relations or in the countries that constitute the periphery in a structure of dependency. The empirical proof of these affirmations can be found in the specialized literature of dependency theory. Here it is sufficient to show briefly that we must speak of a fundamental negation of the common good in the present moment of history, and thus of a structural situation of injustice which uses violence to prevent the achievement of human rights.

It is evident that the historical structures which would allow us to speak of the common good do not exist on a global level. In effect, there exist many things in common, that is, things that are transmitted from the centers of power to the oppressed periphery and things that are taken from the periphery to the great advantage of the centers. However, this community of things cannot be called a good, since it is a source of oppression and not of liberty. It is not merely a case of a scandalous and radical disproportion in the possession and use of the goods of the earth (which as such have humanity as a whole as their principle owner), since this disproportion is achieved at the expense of those least favored by denying them access to resources which in principle should be common. This means that it is not merely a question of an inequality between members of a single history who are fundamentally equal, but of an inequality that is increasing and that is based upon exploitation. In effect, the existence of very specific economic and political mechanisms (such as unequal exchange, multinational companies) seeks the good of those who possess the most productive capital rather than the good of those who either do not possess it or possess it under unfavorable conditions. In these circumstances, one group's particular good denies the more general good of another; in short, the negation of the common good occurs.

In the framework of this structure of international commerce, each nation manifests its own internal conflict which denies the common good. The enormous inequality in the enjoyment of goods in a single nation, which should constitute a whole in which the totality has primacy over the parts, shows that the common good has been appropriated by a few individuals (this includes not only formally economic goods but also cultural, political, and health benefits). The result is that we cannot speak of a common good. The phenomenon of pauperization, that is, of a structure which makes the poor poorer while at the same time it makes the rich richer, provides the true picture of the supposed common good on a national level. The existence of social classes in conflict in the present economic structure reveals the existence of contrary interests, which prevent speaking of a common good. In this context, the supposed

common good is only a formal framework that legally permits the denial of the common good. Thus, in a bourgeois capitalist structure it is clear that the smaller part prevails over the larger part. When this happens, the common good is denied for the sake of a particular good, which can no longer be called a good but simply utilitarian egotism.

Perhaps this mystification of the common good can be best appreciated in the structure of the State. The State presents itself as the representative of the entire society and as the executor of the common good, and because of this it provides legal structures within which the realization of the common good and of human rights is pursued on a formal level. In practice, however, it becomes one of the principal mechanisms for identifying the common good with the good of those who have most influence on the sources of the common good. Instead of favoring the common good, the State privatizes it and places it at the service of a privileged part and not of the whole. Therefore, the State exists not as the realization of the actual common good, but as the realization of the good of minorities who appropriate for themselves the material resources of the common good. Thus it is the defender of the common good only in the sense that it represents those who have unjustly appropriated the common good.

Furthermore, the production and distribution of the common good should not in principle oppose fundamental human rights or even less fundamental rights, at least methodically and over a long period of time. Thus, the defense of human rights pertains to the concrete totality of the common good. For this reason, the defense of human rights is a task of justice, but those who undertake it cannot avoid asking whether they themselves are the ones ultimately causing the fundamental violations of human rights. This may occur with regard to the citizens of their own country, but also with regard to other persons beyond their borders "whose life and existence depend on their precious liberty," as Hegel has said, and who nevertheless, because of their situation of exploitation, can enjoy neither life nor liberty.

3. How then should we pose the problem of the common good and of human rights in a conflictive society? This is a real question and not a purely theoretical one, because the unity of the world and the unity of many societies is a unity of opposites; and because in the present era of history the common good and human rights appear as the denial of the communality of good and of the humanity of rights. To answer the question, the following points should be taken into consideration.

a) The real truth of a historical process lies in the objective results of that process. Intentions and goals count for little in history; the truth of what is intended or proposed is the results obtained, the historical actions. The intention and goal can legitimate to some extent—and only to some extent—the individual subject, but they cannot legitimate the course of history nor the global conduct of nations. It is useless to claim a more just international order as an expression of the common good or a more just structuring of society, when historical reality demonstrates that that international order is continually becoming more unjust and the social structures continually more dehumanizing.

b) More concretely, the true picture of a historical process is not found in the actual results which should have been the common good, nor still less is it found in the minorities which appropriate those results for themselves. The truth lies rather in the participation in this common good and in the real situation of the majority of persons and citizens. Thus, the Third World is the truth of the First World, and the oppressed classes are the truth of the oppressing classes. It may be argued that without the accumulation of capital and the plundering of resources, and without the deflection of resources away from their primary goal of satisfying basic needs, the scientific, technological, and cultural development which is necessary for the contemporary historical process would not occur. But one has to ask if this development is good in itself, especially since it entails the subdevelopment of the great majority of humanity. Only when we understand that the real condition of this development is the oppression and dehumanization of the majority of humanity will we see that this development in its concrete reality is not development but rather its total opposite. Only when the opulent nations are seen as actually creating oppressed nations, only when the opulent classes are seen as actually creating oppressed classes, will they know who they really are. The truth also is that this will not happen until the historical praxis of the latter nations and classes "makes" the opulent see who they really are.

c) It is undeniable that the present organization of the world has brought many technological advances and an immense production of consumer goods. Thus it could be said that the common good, once its abstract and formal aspects are realized in history, is the sum total of goods produced; one could almost say that the common good in this case is identical with the gross national product. If we look at the problem from this perspective, it is clear that the problems of participation in the common good and the more general problems of justice (let us not forget the classical link between the common good and justice) receive no answer at all. In other words, the common good proposed today is neither good nor common.

d) If this is so, the achievement of the common good in a conflictive society, whether that society be the totality of nations or a single nation, is a process which must extend to the liberation of oppressed people and classes. This is so because it is only through such a process that one can come to speak of a true common good which can be equitably shared in by all those who make up the human race. In the same way, human rights must be primarily the rights of the oppressed, since the oppressors can have no rights insofar as they are oppressors; at most, they will have the right to be freed from their oppression. It is only by doing justice to the oppressed peoples and classes that an authentic common good and truly universal human rights will be fostered. Given the present historical situation, this "doing justice" will have to take the form of "making oneself just." The reason for this "making oneself just" is found precisely in the central importance of the common good as well as in the denial of the common good which is brought about by those who monopolize common goods and their legal representatives.

e) It may be argued that this historicization of the common good and of human rights involves the rejection of the ordinary meaning of the common good. This may be answered in two ways. The first response holds that the common good follows the same contours as society so that, if the society is really divided, so will the common good be divided. The common good, therefore, would involve the process which would lead a divided society toward the creation of a true society, where contradictory social interests would not exist. The common good would thus function as a utopia which would recognize the ideological disguise of the common good as currently propounded, as well as the real though concealed denial of the common good. After this, it would become a process with actual stages, leading to a common good which would become a historical reality.

The second response, which is more formal and juridical, holds that the common good refers to the whole and not to the parts which are making the unity of the whole impossible. Thus, where an unjustly structured society exists, there can be no way of arriving at the common good except by overcoming whatever is causing the injustice. In other words, the common good belongs to the whole of society, but it cannot belong to all members of society in the same way, if there are some sectors in it that deny the common good.

f) The struggle to prevent a specific social sector from unjustly monopolizing the material bases of the common good does not in principle involve a hate-filled struggle against specific persons. By its very nature, the common good must be considered on a formal level in structural terms and not in individual ones; it is perti-

nent to the latter only insofar as they impede or do not promote the common good. The situation is different with regard to human rights which, although they derive from the human person and the universal community of persons, can be said to refer formally to individuals (although they also refer to peoples, social groups, nations, and the totality of nations). Therefore, the promotion of the common good cannot progress by denying the individual rights of the human person, precisely because the promotion of those rights is an integrating part of the common good. But it can happen in a specific historical situation that it is necessary to establish priorities in the enjoyment of individual human rights. For example, the refined cultural activities of a few cannot have primacy over the fundamental education of the majority of a people, and even less can the enjoyment of some convenience have primacy over the right to have what is necessary for survival. Since almost everything in human life is superfluous in the countries which suffer from extreme poverty, anyone who wishes to enjoy superfluities should join a society where this massive poverty is absent and where the voice crying to heaven of those in need cannot be heard. But although human rights should be regulated by the common good, it is impossible to conceive of a common good which would require the permanent and grave violation of human rights in order to maintain itself.

g) This way of posing the problem of the common good and human rights may give rise to a totalitarian interpretation, but that is not necessarily the case. Although the State today should be the one that secures the common good, it has to do this in subordination to the whole society. The discussion of the common good should be proposed in terms that are predominantly social and thus with the immediate participation of the majority of those who make up the society. When the common good is seen from the viewpoint of society, it consists in the utopian task of the communication of goods. Behind that goal lies the conviction that both the person and the communitarian society are realized by denying private interests of individual egotism. There is only a single step from here to the death that gives life, a life superior to that which was ended in death, as well as to real love, both as personal realization and as historical utopia. It is a theological step which, especially in the theology of liberation, can show the internal unity between the history of salvation and the salvation of history. For St. Thomas already tried to point out the connec-

tion between the common good of the world and the common good which is God, with the result that the common good of society would become one of the preeminent ways of making God present in history.

NOTE

This article originally appeared in the October 1979 issue of the Mexican periodical *Christus* and has been translated by Alfred Hennelly.

Continuing to Think

Looking at everyday life in El Salvador, Ellacuría saw the common good being defined in terms of the priorities of the elite ruling class. Serious violations of human rights were being ignored. Rejecting this appropriation of the common good, Ellacuría insisted on a wider definition. In a divided society, the common good itself must necessarily be divided, and this leads to an impossible situation. In Ellacuría's view, intentions and goals count for little; it is results that let us know whether or not the common good is being achieved.

If we take the whole world as our test population, the failure to achieve a common good is even more apparent. Individual societies and cultures may argue that, within their own geopolitical boundaries, they are pursuing and possibly even achieving a condition in which human rights and the common good are affirmed. However, if human rights are being trampled anywhere, can we claim that the common good is being realized?

Ellacuría's most stirring challenge is phrased this way: "The third world is the truth of the first world and the oppressed classes are the truth of the oppressing classes." Do you agree? Can we have a meaningful discussion about justice in terms of which portions of the world are left out? It is sometimes said that none of us is free so long as any one of us is in chains. Sometimes called liberation theology, this radical communitarianism demands personal as well as societal transformation.

If we cannot speak in any meaningful way about the common good, without including in our plans the liberation of what Ellacuría calls oppressed people and classes, then, for each of us, some of the work of doing justice will have to take the form of "making oneself just." And, the reward for making this effort will be a more fully realized person as well as a more just and equitable society.

9.3   *A Vindication of the Rights of Women*

MARY WOLLSTONECRAFT

Preparing to Read

Although she does not make a specifically Utilitarian argument (since Utilitarianism came later), Mary Wollstonecraft clearly challenges societal definitions of what makes women happy as well as the consequences of treating women as inferiors and incompetents. When Wollstonecraft published her book in 1792, the expectation was that women would follow a significantly different lifepath from that of men. No doubt many men considered restrictions on women's lives a kindness—keeping them out of the jungle of commerce and the sordidness of politics.

Wollstonecraft argues, however, that treating adults as children deprives them of the virtues of maturity and makes them foolish and vicious. Among the consequences of such practice, she warns, are bad marriages (in which the two parties can have very little in common, driving men to seek missing qualities in partners outside the marriage) and inept child rearing (in which women, whose own development has been thwarted, act from ignorance in forming the children who are under their almost exclusive care during the first, critical seven years of life).

Even the two roles traditionally assigned to women—wife and mother—are weakened and degraded by the narrow world in which women have sometimes been confined. As you read this selection, pay particular attention to how Wollstonecraft constructs her argument that the treatment of women is unjust and should be changed—for the good of women and for the ultimate good of society in general.

BEFORE MARRIAGE it is their business to please men; and after, with a few exceptions, they follow the same scent with all the persevering pertinacity of instinct. Even virtuous women never forget their sex in company, for they are for ever trying to make themselves *agreeable*. A female beauty, and a male wit, appear to be equally anxious to draw the attention of the company to themselves; and the animosity of contemporary wits is proverbial.

Is it then surprising that when the sole ambition of woman centres in beauty, and interest gives vanity additional force, perpetual rivalships should ensue? They are all running the same race, and would rise above the virtue of mortals if they did not view each other with a suspicious and even envious eye.

An immoderate fondness for dress, for pleasure, and for sway, are the passions of savages; the passions that occupy those uncivilized beings who have not yet extended the dominion of the mind, or even learned to think with the energy necessary to concatenate that abstract train of thought which produces principles. And that women from their education and the present state of civilized life are in the same condition, cannot, I think, be controverted. To laugh at them then, or satirize the follies of a being

From *A Vindication of the Rights of Women* by Mary Wollstonecraft. Courtesy of W. W. Norton & Co.

who is never to be allowed to act freely from the light of her own reason, is as absurd as cruel; for, that they who are taught blindly to obey authority will endeavour cunningly to elude it, is most natural and certain.

Yet let it be proved that they ought to obey man implicitly, and I shall immediately agree that it is woman's duty to cultivate a fondness for dress, in order to please, and a propensity to cunning for her own preservation.

The virtues, however, which are supported by ignorance must ever be wavering—the house built on sand could not endure a storm. It is almost unnecessary to draw the inference. If women are to be made virtuous by authority, which is a contradiction in terms, let them be immured in seraglios and watched with a jealous eye. Fear not that the iron will enter into their souls—for the souls that can bear such treatment are made of yielding materials, just animated enough to give life to the body.

> "Matter too soft a lasting mark to bear,
> And best distinguish'd by black, brown, or fair."

The most cruel wounds will of course soon heal, and they may still people the world, and dress to please man—all the purposes which certain celebrated writers have allowed that they were created to fulfil.

Sect. IV.

Women are supposed to possess more sensibility, and even humanity, than men, and their strong attachments and instantaneous emotions of compassion are given as proofs; but the clinging affection of ignorance has seldom anything noble in it, and may mostly be resolved into selfishness, as well as the affection of children and brutes. I have known many weak women whose sensibility was entirely engrossed by their husbands; and as for their humanity, it was very faint indeed, or rather it was only a transient emotion of compassion. Humanity does not consist "in a squeamish ear," says an eminent orator. "It belongs to the mind as well as the nerves."

But this kind of exclusive affection, though it degrades the individual, should not be brought forward as a proof of the inferiority of the sex, because it is the natural consequence of confined views; for even women of superior sense, having their attention turned to little employments, and private plans, rarely rise to heroism, unless when spurred on by love! and love, as an heroic passion, like genius, appears but once in an age. I therefore agree with the moralist who asserts, "that women have seldom so much generosity as men;" and that their narrow affections, to which justice and humanity are often sacrificed, render the sex apparently inferior, especially as they are commonly inspired by men; but I contend that the heart would expand as the understanding gained strength, if women were not depressed from their cradles.

I know that a little sensibility, and great weakness, will produce a strong sexual attachment, and that reason must cement friendship; consequently, I allow that more friendship is to be found in the male than the female world, and that men have a higher sense of justice. The exclusive affections of women seem indeed to resemble Cato's most unjust love for his country. He wished to crush Carthage, not to save Rome, but to promote its vain-glory; and, in general, it is to similar principles that humanity is sacrificed, for genuine duties support each other.

Besides, how can women be just or generous, when they are the slaves of injustice?

Sect. V.

As the rearing of children—that is, the laying a foundation of sound health both of body and mind in the rising generation—has justly been insisted on as the peculiar destination of woman, the ignorance that incapacitates them must be contrary to the order of things. And I contend that their minds can take in much more, and ought to do so, or they will never become sensible mothers. Many men attend to the breeding of horses, and overlook the management of the stable, who would—strange want of sense and feeling!—think themselves degraded by paying any attention to the nursery; yet, how many children are absolutely murdered by the ignorance of women! But when they escape, and are destroyed neither by unnatural negligence nor blind fondness, how few are managed properly with respect to the infant mind! So that to break the spirit, allowed to become vicious at home, a child is sent to school; and the methods taken there, which must be taken to keep a number of children in order, scatter the seeds of almost every vice in the soil thus forcibly torn up.

I have sometimes compared the struggles of these poor children, who ought never to have felt restraint, nor would, had they been always held in with an even hand, to the despairing plunges of a spirited filly, which I have seen breaking on a strand: its feet sinking deeper and deeper in the sand every time it endeavoured to throw its rider, till at last it sullenly submitted.

I have always found horses, animals I am attached to, very tractable when treated with humanity and steadiness, so that I doubt whether the violent methods taken to break them do not essentially injure them; I am, however, certain that a child should never be thus forcibly tamed after it has injudiciously been allowed to run wild: for every violation of justice and reason, in the treatment of children, weakens their reason. And, so early do they catch a character, that the base of the moral character, experience leads me to infer, is fixed before their seventh year, the period during which women are allowed the sole management of children. Afterwards it too often happens that half the business of education is to correct, and very imperfectly is it done if done hastily, the faults which they would never have acquired if their mothers had had more understanding.

One striking instance of the folly of women must not be omitted—the manner in which they treat servants in the presence of children, permitting them to suppose that they ought to wait on them, and bear their humours. A child should always be made to receive assistance from a man or woman as a favour; and, as the first lesson of independence, they should practically be taught by the example of their mother not to require that personal attendance, which it is an insult to humanity to require, when in health; and instead of being led to assume airs of consequence, a sense of their own weakness should first make them feel the natural equality of man. Yet, how frequently have I indignantly heard servants imperiously called to put children to bed, and sent away again and again, because master or miss hung about mamma to stay a little longer. Thus made slavishly to attend the little idol, all those most disgusting humours were exhibited which characterize a spoiled child.

In short, speaking of the majority of mothers, they leave their children entirely to the care of servants; or, because they are their children, treat them as if they were little demi-gods, though I have always observed that the women who thus idolize their children seldom show common humanity to servants, or feel the least tenderness for any children but their own.

It is, however, these exclusive affections, and an individual manner of seeing things, produced by ignorance, which keep women for ever at a stand with respect to improvement, and make many of them dedicate their lives to their children only to weaken their bodies and spoil their tempers, frustrating also any plan of education that a more rational father may adopt; for unless a mother concur, the father who restrains will ever be considered as a tyrant.

But, fulfilling the duties of a mother, a woman with a sound constitution may still keep her person scrupulously neat, and assist to maintain her family if necessary, or, by reading and conversations with both sexes indiscriminately, improve her mind. For nature has so wisely ordered things, that did women suckle their children they would preserve their own health, and there would be such an interval between the birth of each child that we should seldom see a houseful of babes. And did they pursue a plan of conduct, and not waste their time in following the fashionable vagaries of dress, the management of their household and children need not shut them out from literature, or prevent their attaching themselves to a science with that steady eye which strengthens the mind, or practicing one of the fine arts that cultivate the taste.

But, visiting to display finery, card-playing, and balls, not to mention the idle bustle of morning trifling, draw women from their duty to render them insignificant, to render them pleasing, according to the present acceptation of the word, to every man but their husband. For a round of pleasures in which the affections are not exercised cannot be said to improve the understanding, though it be erroneously called seeing the world; yet the heart is rendered cold and averse to duty by such a senseless intercourse, which becomes necessary from habit even when it has ceased to amuse.

But, we shall not see women affectionate till more equality be established in society, till ranks are confounded and women freed, neither shall we see that dignified domestic happiness, the simple grandeur of which cannot be relished by ignorant or vitiated minds; nor will the important task of education ever be properly begun till the person of a woman is no longer preferred to her mind. For it would be as wise to expect corn from tares, or figs from thistles, as that a foolish ignorant woman should be a good mother.

Sect. VI.

It is not necessary to inform the sagacious reader, now I enter on my concluding reflections, that the discussion of this subject merely consists in opening a few simple principles and clearing away the rubbish which obscured them. But as all readers are not sagacious, I must be allowed to add some explanatory remarks to bring the subject home to reason—to that sluggish reason which supinely takes opinions on trust, and obstinately supports them to spare itself the labour of thinking.

Moralists have unanimously agreed, that unless virtue be nursed by liberty, it will never attain due strength—and what they say of man I extend to mankind, insisting that in all cases morals must be fixed on immutable principles; and that the being cannot be termed rational or virtuous who obeys any authority but that of reason.

To render women truly useful members of society, I argue that they should be led, by having their understandings cultivated on a large scale, to acquire a rational affection for their country, founded on knowledge, because it is obvious that we are little interested about what we do not understand. And to render this general knowledge of due importance, I have endeavoured to show that private duties are never properly fulfilled unless the understanding enlarges the heart; and that public virtue is only an aggregate of private. But the distinctions established in society undermine both, by beating out the solid gold of virtue, till it becomes only the tinsel-covering of vice; for whilst wealth renders a man more respectable than virtue, wealth will be sought before virtue; and whilst women's persons are caressed when a childish simper shows an absence of mind—the mind will lie fallow. Yet, true voluptuousness must proceed from the mind—for what can equal the sensations produced by mutual affection supported by mutual respect? What are the cold or feverish caresses of appetite, but sin embracing death, compared with the modest overflowings of a pure heart and exalted imagination? Yes, let me tell the libertine of fancy when he despises understanding in woman—that the mind, which he disregards, gives life to the enthusiastic affection from which rapture, shortlived as it is, alone can flow! And that without virtue a sexual attachment must expire, like a tallow candle in the socket, creating intolerable disgust. To prove this, I need only observe that men who have wasted great part of their lives with women, and with whom they have sought for pleasure with eager thirst, entertain the meanest opinion of the sex.—Virtue, true refiner of joy!—if foolish men were to fright thee from earth in order to give loose to all their appetites without a check—some sensual wight of taste would scale the heavens to invite thee back, to give a zest to pleasure!

That women at present are by ignorance rendered foolish or vicious, is, I think, not to be disputed; and that the most salutary effects tending to improve mankind might be expected from a REVOLUTION in female manners, appears, at least with a face of probability, to rise out of the observation. For as marriage has been termed the parent of those endearing charities which draw man from the brutal herd, the corrupting intercourse that wealth, idleness, and folly produce between the sexes, is more universally injurious to morality than all the other vices of mankind collectively considered. To adulterous lust the most sacred duties are sacrificed, because before marriage, men, by a promiscuous intimacy with women, learned to consider love as a selfish gratification—learned to separate it not only from esteem, but from the affection merely built on habit, which mixes a little humanity with it. Justice and friendship are also set at defiance, and that purity of taste is vitiated which would naturally lead a man to relish an artless display of affection rather than affected airs. But that noble simplicity of affection which dares to appear unadorned, has few attractions for the libertine, though it be the charm which, by cementing the matrimonial tie, secures to the pledges of a warmer passion the necessary parental attention; for children will never be properly educated till friendship subsists between parents. Virtue flies from a house divided against itself—and a whole legion of devils take up their residence there.

The affection of husbands and wives cannot be pure when they have so few sentiments in common, and when so little confidence is established at home, as must be the case when their pursuits are so different. That intimacy from which tenderness should flow, will not, cannot subsist between the vicious.

Contending, therefore, that the sexual distinction which men have so warmly insisted upon is arbitrary, I have dwelt on an observation that several sensible men, with whom I have conversed on the subject, allowed to be well founded; and it is simply this, that the little chastity to be found amongst men, and consequent disregard of modesty, tend to degrade both sexes; and further, that the modesty of women, characterized as such, will often be only the artful veil of wantonness instead of being the natural reflection of purity, till modesty be universally respected.

From the tyranny of man, I firmly believe, the greater number of female follies proceed; and the cunning, which I allow makes at present a part of their character, I likewise have repeatedly endeavoured to prove, is produced by oppression.

Were not dissenters, for instance, a class of people with strict truth characterized as cunning? And may I not lay some stress on this fact to prove, that when any power but reason curbs the free spirit of man, dissimulation is practised, and the various shifts of art are naturally called forth? Great attention to decorum which was carried to a degree of scrupulosity, and all that puerile bustle about trifles and consequential solemnity which Butler's caricature of a dissenter brings before the imagination, shaped their persons as well as their minds in the mould of prim littleness. I speak collectively, for I know how many ornaments to human nature have been enrolled amongst sectaries; yet, I assert that the same narrow prejudice for their sect which women have for their families, prevailed in the dissenting part of the community, however worthy in other respects; and also that the same timid prudence, or headstrong efforts, often disgraced the exertions of both. Oppression thus formed many of the features of their character perfectly to coincide with that of the oppressed half of mankind; for is it not notorious that dissenters were, like women, fond of deliberating together, and asking advice of each other, till by a complication of little contrivances some little end was brought about? A similar attention to preserve their reputation was conspicuous in the dissenting and female world, and was produced by a similar cause.

Asserting the rights which women in common with men ought to contend for, I have not attempted to extenuate their faults; but to prove them to be the natural consequence of their education and station in society. If so, it is reasonable to suppose that they will change their character, and correct their vices and follies, when they are allowed to be free in a physical, moral, and civil sense.[1]

Let women share the rights and she will emulate the virtues of man; for she must grow more perfect when emancipated, or justify the authority that chains such a weak being to her duty.—If the latter, it will be expedient to open a fresh trade with Russia for whips: a present which a father should always make to his son-in-law on his wedding day, that a husband may keep his whole family in order by the same means; and without any violation of justice reign, wielding this sceptre, sole master of his house, because he is the only being in it who has reason:—the divine, indefeasible earthly sovereignty breathed into man by the Master of the universe. Allowing this position, women have not any inherent rights to claim; and by the same rule their duties vanish, for rights and duties are inseparable.

Be just then, O ye men of understanding! and mark not more severely what women do amiss, than the vicious tricks of the horse or the ass for whom ye provide provender—and allow her the privileges of ignorance, to whom ye deny the rights of reason, or ye will be worse than Egyptian task-masters, expecting virtue where nature has not given understanding!

NOTE

1. I had further enlarged on the advantages which might reasonably be expected to result from an improvement in female manners, towards the general reformation of society; but it appeared to me that such reflections would more properly close the last volume.

Continuing to Think

While she readily admits the faults commonly attributed to women, Wollstonecraft points out that these are the natural consequence of women's lack of education and degraded station in society. It follows, then, that if the two conditions that have produced these faults are changed, the faults may be expected to disappear. As an intellectual heir of the European Enlightenment, Wollstonecraft believed in the power of reason and the perfectibility of human nature. Whatever ills are found in society can be rationally analyzed, and the environment that produced them can be changed, thus eradicating the ills.

Granting women the same rights as men would be just and could be expected to produce more virtuous citizens. Refusal to grant those rights, however, would make unreasonable the expectation of virtue. Although some of her arguments have a distinctly utilitarian flavor—justice for women will mean better wives and mothers and a healthier society—it is clear that Wollstonecraft demands justice for women because it is the right thing to do. "How can women be just and generous, when they are the slaves of injustice?"

Act justly toward women because reason demands it, Wollstonecraft seems to be saying. If you do, then you may expect women to act justly toward you. What do you think? Is justice tied up with doing the right thing? Can I expect you to behave reasonably if I do not treat you reasonably to begin with?

Deontological ethical theories define justice as a matter of doing one's duty—of following the rules regardless of consequences. It may be important to tell the truth, even if it gets you in trouble. There may be reasons not to cheat, even if cheating means a higher grade. Obeying your own moral code may be your obligation no matter how things turn out.

9.4   *Age, Race, Class, and Sex: Women Redefining the Difference*

AUDRE LORDE

Preparing to Read

Refusing to recognize that difference exists may be a major source of injustice, according to Audre Lorde. As a part of what is called the "first wave" of feminism, Mary Wollstonecraft was eager to show that women were inherently as rational as men. Any differences could be attributed to unequal and unjust treatment. Although this can be an effective strategy for gaining equal treatment, it can also be dangerous.

What Wollstonecraft wrote may have been very true of the condition of wealthy, white, heterosexual women in England and America; clearly it had less to say about the condition of African American slave women or exploited English factory workers. All of these were women, but they were not all women in the same way. Ignoring difference can feed oppression, Lorde insists.

During the "second wave" of feminism in the 1960s, early leaders were accused of organizing a movement around their own concerns as middle-class, white women that had little relevance to the lives of poor women, women of color, and lesbians. If I am denied a job because I am considered too old or too young, my gender may not be the most important factor. At times, all of us feel our primary identification in terms of race or social class. If my children are excluded because they are poor, race or gender may not be important. Racial slurs, on the other hand, cut all their targets equally, regardless of social class or gender.

The danger lies in the distortions that come from ignoring and misnaming differences. A little piece of the oppressor lies deep within each of us, and the challenge is to alter that while we are altering oppressive conditions.

MUCH OF WESTERN EUROPEAN history conditions us to see human differences in simplistic opposition to each other: dominant/subordinate, good/bad, up/down, superior/inferior. In a society where the good is defined in terms of profit rather than in terms of human need, there must always be some group of people who, through systematized oppression, can be made to feel surplus, to occupy the place of the dehumanized inferior. Within this society, that group is made up of Black and Third World people, working-class people, older people, and women.

As a forty-nine-year-old Black lesbian feminist socialist mother of two, including one boy, and a member of an inter-racial couple, I usually find myself a part of some group defined as other, deviant, inferior, or just plain wrong. Traditionally, in american society, it is the members of oppressed, objectified groups who are expected to stretch out and bridge the gap between the actualities of our lives and the consciousness of our oppressor. For in order to survive, those of us for whom oppression is as american as apple pie have always had to be watchers, to become familiar with the language and manners of the oppressor, even sometimes adopting them for some illusion of protection. Whenever the need for some pretense of communication arises, those who profit from our oppression call upon us to share our knowledge with them. In other words, it is the responsibility of the oppressed to teach the oppressors their mistakes. I am responsible for educating teachers who dismiss my children's culture in school. Black and Third World people are expected to educate white people as to our humanity. Women are expected to educate men. Lesbians and gay men are expected to educate the heterosexual world. The oppressors maintain their position and evade responsibility for their own actions. There is a constant drain of energy which might be better used in redefining ourselves and devising realistic scenarios for altering the present and constructing the future.

Institutionalized rejection of difference is an absolute necessity in a profit economy which needs outsiders as surplus people. As members of such an economy, we have *all* been programmed to respond to the human differences between us with fear and loathing and to handle that difference in one of three ways: ignore it, and if that is not possible, copy it if we think it is dominant, or destroy it if we think it is subordinate. But we have no patterns for relating across

our human differences as equals. As a result, those differences have been misnamed and misused in the service of separation and confusion.

Certainly there are very real differences between us of race, age, and sex. But it is not those differences between us that are separating us. It is rather our refusal to recognize those differences, and to examine the distortions which result from our misnaming them and their effects upon human behavior and expectation.

Racism, the belief in the inherent superiority of one race over all others and thereby the right to dominance. Sexism, the belief in the inherent superiority of one sex over the other and thereby the right to dominance. Ageism. Heterosexism. Elitism. Classism.

It is a lifetime pursuit for each one of us to extract these distortions from our living at the same time as we recognize, reclaim, and define those differences upon which they are imposed. For we have all been raised in a society where those distortions were endemic within our living. Too often, we pour the energy needed for recognizing and exploring difference into pretending those differences are insurmountable barriers, or that they do not exist at all. This results in a voluntary isolation, or false and treacherous connections. Either way, we do not develop tools for using human difference as a springboard for creative change within our lives. We speak not of human difference, but of human deviance.

Somewhere, on the edge of consciousness, there is what I call a *mythical norm,* which each one of us within our hearts knows "that is not me." In america, this norm is usually defined as white, thin, male, young, heterosexual, christian, and financially secure. It is with this mythical norm that the trappings of power reside within this society. Those of us who stand outside that power often identify one way in which we are different, and we assume that to be the primary cause of all oppression, forgetting other distortions around difference, some of which we ourselves may be practising. By and large within the women's movement today, white women focus upon their oppression as women and ignore differences of race, sexual preference, class, and age. There is a pretense to a homogeneity of experience covered by the word *sisterhood* that does not in fact exist.

Unacknowledged class differences rob women of each others' energy and creative insight. Recently a women's magazine collective made the decision for one issue to print only prose, saying poetry was a less "rigorous" or "serious" art form. Yet even the form our creativity takes is often a class issue. Of all the art forms, poetry is the most economical. It is the one which is the most secret, which requires the least physical labor, the least material, and the one which can be done between shifts, in the hospital pantry, on the subway, and on scraps of surplus paper. Over the last few years, writing a novel on tight finances, I came to appreciate the enormous differences in the material demands between poetry and prose. As we reclaim our literature, poetry has been the major voice of poor, working class, and Colored women. A room of one's own may be a necessity for writing prose, but so are reams of paper, a typewriter, and plenty of time. The actual requirements to produce the visual arts also help determine, along class lines, whose art is whose. In this day of inflated prices for material, who are our sculptors, our painters, our photographers? When we speak of a broadly based women's culture, we need to be aware of the effect of class and economic differences on the supplies available for producing art.

As we move toward creating a society within which we can each flourish, ageism is another distortion of relationship which interferes without vision. By ignoring the past, we are encouraged to repeat its mistakes. The "generation gap" is an important social tool for any repressive society. If the younger members of a community view the older members as contemptible or suspect or excess, they will never be able to join hands and examine the living memories of the community, nor ask the all important question, "Why?" This gives rise to a historical amnesia that keeps us working to invent the wheel every time we have to go to the store for bread.

We find ourselves having to repeat and relearn the same old lessons over and over that our mothers did because we do not pass on what we have learned, or because we are unable to listen. For instance, how many times has this all been said before? For another, who would have believed that once again our daughters are allowing their bodies to be hampered and purgatoried by girdles and high heels and hobble skirts?

Ignoring the differences of race between women and the implications of those differences presents the most serious threat to the mobilization of women's joint power.

As white women ignore their built-in privilege of whiteness and define *woman* in terms of their own experience alone, then women of Color become "other," the outsider whose experience and tradition is too "alien" to comprehend. An example of this is the signal absence of the experience of women of Color as a resource for women's studies courses. The literature of women of Color is seldom included in women's literature courses and almost never in other literature courses, nor in women's studies as a whole. All too often, the excuse given is that the literatures of women of Color can only be taught by Colored women, or that they are too difficult to understand, or that classes cannot "get into" them because they come out of experiences that are "too different." I have heard this argument presented by white women of otherwise quite clear intelligence, women who seem to have no trouble at all teaching and reviewing work that comes out of the vastly different experiences of Shakespeare, Molière, Dostoyefsky, and Aristophanes. Surely there must be some other explanation.

This is a very complex question, but I believe one of the reasons white women have such difficulty reading Black women's work is because of their reluctance to see Black women as women and different from themselves. To examine Black women's literature effectively requires that we be seen as whole people in our actual complexities—as individuals, as women, as human—rather than as one of those problematic but familiar stereotypes provided in this society in place of genuine images of Black women. And I believe this holds true for the literatures of other women of Color who are not Black.

The literatures of all women of Color recreate the textures of our lives, and many white women are heavily invested in ignoring the real differences. For as long as any difference between us means one of us must be inferior, then the recognition of any difference must be fraught with guilt. To allow women of Color to step out of stereotypes is too guilt provoking, for it threatens the complacency of those women who view oppression only in terms of sex.

Refusing to recognize difference makes it impossible to see the different problems and pitfalls facing us as women.

Thus, in a patriarchal power system where whiteskin privilege is a major prop, the entrapments used to neutralize Black women and white women are not the same. For example, it is easy for Black women to be used by the power structure against Black men, not because they are men, but because they are Black. Therefore, for Black women, it is necessary at all times to separate the needs of the oppressor from our own legitimate conflicts within our communities. This same problem does not exist for white women. Black women and men have shared racist oppression and still share it, although in different ways. Out of that shared oppression we have developed joint defenses and joint vulnerabilities to each other that are not duplicated in the white community, with the exception of the relationship between Jewish women and Jewish men.

On the other hand, white women face the pitfall of being seduced into joining the oppressor under the pretense of sharing power. This possibility does not exist in the same way for women of Color. The tokenism that is sometimes extended to us is not an invitation to join power; our racial "otherness" is a visible reality that makes that quite clear. For white women there is a wider range of pretended choices and rewards for identifying with patriarchal power and its tools.

Today, with the defeat of ERA, the tightening economy, and increased conservatism, it is easier once again for white women to believe the dangerous fantasy that if you are good enough, pretty enough, sweet enough, quiet enough, teach the children to behave, hate the right people, and marry the right men, then you will be allowed to co-exist with patriarchy in relative peace, at least until a man needs your job or the neighborhood rapist happens along. And true, unless one lives and loves in the trenches it is difficult to remember that the war against dehumanization is ceaseless.

But Black women and our children know the fabric of our lives is stitched with violence and with hatred, that there is no rest. We do not deal with it only on the picket lines, or in dark midnight alleys, or in the places where we dare to verbalize our resistance. For us, increasingly, violence weaves through the daily tissues of our living—in the supermarket, in the classroom, in the elevator, in the clinic and the schoolyard, from the plumber, the baker, the saleswoman, the bus driver, the bank teller, the waitress who does not serve us.

Some problems we share as women, some we do not. You fear your children will grow up to join the patriarchy and testify against you, we fear our children will be dragged from a car and shot down in the street, and you will turn your backs upon the reasons they are dying.

The threat of difference has been no less blinding to people of Color. Those of us who are Black must see that the reality of our lives and our struggle does not make us immune to the errors of ignoring and misnaming difference. Within Black communities where racism is a living reality, differences among us often seem dangerous and suspect. The need for unity is often misnamed as a need for homogeneity, and a Black feminist vision mistaken for betrayal of our common interests as a people. Because of the continuous battle against racial erasure that Black women and Black men share, some Black women still refuse to recognize that we are also oppressed as women, and that sexual hostility against Black women is practiced not only by the white racist society, but implemented within our Black communities as well. It is a disease striking the heart of Black nationhood, and silence will not make it disappear. Exacerbated by racism and the pressures of powerlessness, violence against Black women and children often becomes a standard within our communities, one by which manliness can be measured. But these woman-hating acts are rarely discussed as crimes against Black women.

As a group, women of Color are the lowest paid wage earners in america. We are the primary targets of abortion and sterilization abuse, here and abroad. In certain parts of Africa, small girls are still being sewed shut between their legs to keep them docile and for men's pleasure. This is known as female circumcision, and it is not a cultural affair as the late Jomo Kenyatta insisted, it is a crime against Black women.

Black women's literature is full of the pain of frequent assault, not only by a racist patriarchy, but also by Black men. Yet the necessity for and history of shared battle have made us, Black women, particularly vulnerable to the false accusation that anti-sexist is anti-Black. Meanwhile, womanhating as a recourse of the powerless is sapping strength from Black communities, and our very lives. Rape is on the increase, reported and unreported, and rape is not aggressive sexuality, it is sexualized aggression. As Kalamu ya Salaam, a Black male writer points out, "As long as male domination exists, rape will exist. Only women revolting and men made conscious of their responsibility to fight sexism can collectively stop rape."[1]

Differences between ourselves as Black women are also being misnamed and used to separate us from one another. As a Black lesbian feminist comfortable with the many different ingredients of my identity, and a woman committed to racial and sexual freedom from oppression, I find I am constantly being encouraged to pluck out some one aspect of my-

self and present this as the meaningful whole, eclipsing or denying the other parts of self. But this is a destructive and fragmenting way to live. My fullest concentration of energy is available to me only when I integrate all the parts of who I am, openly, allowing power from particular sources of my living to flow back and forth freely through all my different selves, without the restrictions of externally imposed definition. Only then can I bring myself and my energies as a whole to the service of those struggles which I embrace as part of my living.

A fear of lesbians, or of being accused of being a lesbian, has led many Black women into testifying against themselves. It has led some of us into destructive alliances, and others into despair and isolation. In the white women's communities, heterosexism is sometimes a result of identifying with the white patriarchy, a rejection of that interdependence between women-identified women which allows the self to be, rather than to be used in the service of men. Sometimes it reflects a die-hard belief in the protective coloration of heterosexual relationships, sometimes a self-hate which all women have to fight against, taught us from birth.

Although elements of these attitudes exist for all women, there are particular resonances of heterosexism and homophobia among Black women. Despite the fact that woman-bonding has a long and honorable history in the African and African-american communities, and despite the knowledge and accomplishments of many strong and creative women-identified Black women in the political, social and cultural fields, heterosexual Black women often tend to ignore or discount the existence and work of Black lesbians. Part of this attitude has come from an understandable terror of Black male attack within the close confines of Black society, where the punishment for any female self-assertion is still to be accused of being a lesbian and therefore unworthy of the attention or support of the scarce Black male. But part of this need to misname and ignore Black lesbians comes from a very real fear that openly women-identified

Black women who are no longer dependent upon men for their self-definition may well re-order our whole concept of social relationships.

Black women who once insisted that lesbianism was a white woman's problem now insist that Black lesbians are a threat to Black nationhood, are consorting with the enemy, are basically un-Black. These accusations, coming from the very women to whom we look for deep and real understanding, have served to keep many Black lesbians in hiding, caught between the racism of white women and the homophobia of their sisters. Often, their work has been ignored, trivialized, or misnamed, as with the work of Angelina Grimke, Alice Dunbar-Nelson, Lorraine Hansberry. Yet women-bonded women have always been some part of the power of Black communities, from our unmarried aunts to the amazons of Dahomey.

And it is certainly not Black lesbians who are assaulting women and raping children and grandmothers on the streets of our communities.

Across this country, as in Boston during the spring of 1979 following the unsolved murders of twelve Black women, Black lesbians are spearheading movements against violence against Black women.

What are the particular details within each of our lives that can be scrutinized and altered to help bring about change? How do we redefine difference for all women? It is not our differences which separate women, but our reluctance to recognize those differences and to deal effectively with the distortions which have resulted from the ignoring and misnaming of those differences.

As a tool of social control, women have been encouraged to recognize only one area of human difference as legitimate, those differences which exist between women and men. And we have learned to deal across those differences with the urgency of all oppressed subordinates. All of us have had to learn to live or work or coexist with men, from our fathers on. We have recognized and negotiated these differences, even when this recognition only contin-

ued the old dominant/subordinate mode of human relationship, where the oppressed must recognize the masters' difference in order to survive.

But our future survival is predicated upon our ability to relate within equality. As women, we must root out internalized patterns of oppression within ourselves if we are to move beyond the most superficial aspects of social change. Now we must recognize differences among women who are our equals, neither inferior nor superior, and devise ways to use each others' difference to enrich our visions and our joint struggles.

The future of our earth may depend upon the ability of all women to identify and develop new definitions of power and new patterns of relating across difference. The old definitions have not served us, nor the earth that supports us. The old patterns, no matter how cleverly re-arranged to imitate progress, still condemn us to cosmetically altered repetitions of the same old exchanges, the same old guilt, hatred, recrimination, lamentation, and suspicion.

For we have, built into all of us, old blueprints of expectation and response, old structures of oppression, and these must be altered at the same time as we alter the living conditions which are a result of those structures. For the master's tools will never dismantle the master's house.

As Paulo Freire shows so well in *The Pedagogy of the Oppressed,*[2] the true focus of revolutionary change is never merely the oppressive situations which we seek to escape, but that piece of the oppressor which is planted deep within each of us, and which knows only the oppressors' tactics, the oppressors' relationships.

Change means growth, and growth can be painful. But we sharpen self-definition by exposing the self in work and struggle together with those whom we define as different from ourselves, although sharing the same goals. For Black and white, old and young, lesbian and heterosexual women alike, this can mean new paths to our survival.

We have chosen each other
and the edge of each others battles
the war is the same
if we lose
someday women's blood will congeal
upon a dead planet
if we win
there is no telling
we seek beyond history
for a new and more possible meeting.[3]

NOTES

1. From "Rape: A Radical Analysis, An African-American Perspective" by Kalamu ya Salaam in *Black Books Bulletin,* vol. 6, no. 4 (1980).
2. Seabury Press, New York, 1970.
3. From "Outlines," unpublished poem.

Continuing to Think

If women focus only on what divides them from men (as Wollstonecraft did), Audre Lorde thinks they risk masking the old superior/inferior patterns of oppression within themselves. Identifying as a feminist, but labeling lesbians as "other" or retaining prejudice against black women continues the old patterns. Seeing only racial discrimination may lead to racial solidarity at the same time as it masks sexism within the African American community.

The only way out, Lorde insists, is recognizing equality in difference and living it in our lives. Denying difference only masks oppression. Naming difference can lead to stereotyping and further division, or it can open the possibility for genuine understanding. What Lorde suggests will not be easy. It means studying African American women as well as men during Black History Month. It means finding and reading women of color as well as white women in Women's Studies. It means not excluding people on the basis of homophobia, ageism, or elitism.

She argues persuasively that justice cannot be reached by any other path. It will be a lifetime pursuit to root out distortions and reclaim the differences on which those distortions are imposed. And the goal is worth the effort. Real differences that are honored can enrich us all.

9.5   *Ender's Game*

ORSON SCOTT CARD

Preparing to Read

Science fiction writers often raise philosophical issues in the books and stories they write. Here Card offers a sustained reflection on the notion of a "just war." According to this theory, war can be justified *if* certain conditions are met, including using only appropriate (and not excessive) force and targeting only military targets (and safeguarding civilians or noncombatants). Indeed, war has sometimes been seen as a means of achieving justice under these highly specific conditions.

Card loads the deck by choosing as his protagonist a very young, very smart boy, who is kidnapped by the government, taken far from his home planet, and brutally forced to learn the methods of high-tech, computer-managed warfare. Ender Wiggin is never given the option of quitting, and, as we pick up the story, he is facing the final exam in Command School.

His battle commanders are his teenaged friends; he hears their voices and sees the "enemy" arrayed on a computer screen, outnumbering him 1,000 to 1. After he destroys the enemy's home planet, Ender learns that the battles were not simulations. He was the unwitting battle commander, and in the Third Invasion he was completely victorious. He is stunned to realize that the ships he destroyed and the world he blasted into oblivion were real. The buggers were completely obliterated.

Hailed as a conquering hero, Ender becomes, instead, a Speaker for the Dead, telling the enemy's story, including their failures and their greatness. "We did not mean to hurt you"—he said their thoughts in his words—"and we forgive you for our death." Carrying the cocoon of the next generation, he travels the galaxy with his sister Valentine, looking for a world where "the hive-queen could awaken and live in peace."

"ENDER WIGGIN," said Mazer. "Please turn around. Today's game needs a little explanation."

Ender turned around. He glanced at the men gathered at the back of the room. Most of them he had never seen before. Some were even dressed in civilian clothes. He saw Anderson and wondered what he was doing there, who was taking care of the Battle School if he was gone. He saw Graff and remembered the lake in the woods outside Greensboro, and wanted to go home. Take me home, he said silently to Graff. In my dream you said you loved me. Take me home.

But Graff only nodded to him, a greeting, not a promise, and Anderson acted as though he didn't know him at all.

"Pay attention, please, Ender. Today is your final examination in Command School. These observers are here to evaluate what you have learned. If you prefer not to have them in the room, we'll have them watch on another simulator."

"They can stay." Final examination. After today, perhaps he could rest.

"For this to be a fair test of your ability, not just to do what you have practiced many times, but also to meet challenges you have never seen before, today's battle introduces a new element. It is staged around a planet. This will affect the enemy's strategy, and will force you to improvise. Please concentrate on the game today."

Ender beckoned Mazer closer, and asked him quietly, "Am I the first student to make it this far?"

"If you win today, Ender, you will be the first student to do so. More than that I'm not at liberty to say."

"Well, I'm at liberty to hear it."

"You can be as petulant as you want, tomorrow. Today, though, I'd appreciate it if you would keep your mind on the examination. Let's not waste all that you've already done. Now, how will you deal with the planet?"

"I have to get someone behind it, or it's a blind spot."

"True."

"And the gravity is going to affect fuel levels—cheaper to go down than up."

"Yes."

"Does the Little Doctor work against a planet?"

Mazer's face went rigid. "Ender, the buggers never attacked a civilian population in either invasion. You decide whether it would be wise to adopt a strategy that would invite reprisals."

"Is the planet the only new thing?"

"Can you remember the last time I've given you a battle with only one new thing? Let me assure you, Ender, that I will not be kind to you today. I have a responsibility to the fleet not to let a second-rate student graduate. I will do my best against you, Ender, and I have no desire to coddle you. Just keep in mind everything you know about yourself and everything you know about the buggers, and you have a fair chance of amounting to something."

Mazer left the room.

Ender spoke into the microphone. "Are you there?"

"All of us," said Bean. "Kind of late for practice this morning, aren't you?"

So they hadn't told the squadron leaders. Ender toyed with the idea of telling them how important this battle was to him, but decided it would not help them to have an extraneous concern on their minds. "Sorry," he said. "I overslept."

They laughed. They didn't believe him.

He led them through maneuvers, warming up for the battle ahead. It took him longer than usual to clear his mind, to concentrate on command, but soon enough he was up to speed, responding quickly, thinking well. Or at least, he told himself, I think that I'm thinking well.

The simulator field cleared. Ender waited for the game to appear. What will happen if I pass the test today? Is there another school? Another year or two of grueling training, another year of isolation, another year of people pushing me this way and that way, another year without any control over my own life? He tried to remember how old he was. Eleven. How many years ago did he turn eleven? How many days? It must have happened here at the Command School, but he couldn't remember the day. Maybe he didn't even notice it at the time. Nobody noticed it, except perhaps Valentine.

And as he waited for the game to appear, he wished he could simply lose it, lose the battle badly and completely so that they would remove him from training, like Bonzo, and let him go home. Bonzo had been assigned to Cartagena. He wanted to see travel orders that said Greensboro. Success meant it would go on. Failure meant he could go home.

No, that isn't true, he told himself. They need me, and if I fail, there might not be any home to return to.

But he did not believe it. In his conscious mind he knew it was true, but in other places, deeper places, he doubted that they needed him. Mazer's urgency was just another trick. Just another way to make me do what they want me to do. Another way to keep him from resting. From doing nothing, for a long, long time.

Then the enemy formation appeared, and Ender's weariness turned to despair.

The enemy outnumbered him a thousand to one; the simulator glowed green with them. They were grouped in a dozen different formations, shifting positions, changing shapes, moving in seemingly random patterns through the simulator field. He could not find a path through them—a space that seemed open would close suddenly, and another appear, and a formation that seemed penetrable would suddenly change and be forbidding. The planet was at the far edge of the field, and for all Ender knew there were just as many enemy ships beyond it, out of the simulator's range.

As for his own fleet, it consisted of twenty starships, each with only four fighters. He knew the four-fighter starships—they were old-fashioned, sluggish, and the range of their Little Doctors was half that of the newer ones. Eighty fighters, against at least five thousand, perhaps ten thousand enemy ships.

He heard his squadron leaders breathing heavily; he could also hear, from the observers behind him, a quiet curse. It was nice to know that one of the adults noticed that it wasn't a fair test. Not that it made any difference. Fairness wasn't part of the game, that was plain. There was no attempt to give him even a remote chance at success. All that I've been through, and they never meant to let me pass at all.

He saw in his mind Bonzo and his vicious little knot of friends, confronting him, threatening him; he had been able to shame Bonzo into fighting him alone. That would hardly work here. And he could not surprise the enemy with his ability as he had done with the older boys in the battleroom. Mazer knew Ender's abilities inside and out.

The observers behind him began to cough, to move nervously. They were beginning to realize that Ender didn't know what to do.

I don't care anymore, thought Ender. You can keep your game. If you won't even give me a chance, why should I play?

Like his last game in Battle School, when they put two armies against him.

And just as he remembered that game, apparently Bean remembered it, too, for his voice came over the headset saying, "Remember, the enemy's gate is *down*."

Molo, Soup, Vlad, Dumper, and Crazy Tom all laughed. They remembered, too.

And Ender also laughed. It *was* funny. The adults taking all this so seriously, and the children playing along, playing along, believing it too until suddenly the adults went too far, tried too hard, and the children could see through their game. Forget it, Mazer. I don't care if I pass your test, I don't care if I follow your rules. If you can cheat, so can I. I won't let you beat me unfairly—I'll beat you unfairly first.

In that final battle in Battle School, he had won by ignoring the enemy, ignoring his own losses; he had moved against the enemy's gate.

And the enemy's gate was down.

If I break this rule, they'll never let me be a commander. It would be too dangerous. I'll never have to play a game again. And that is victory.

He whispered quickly into the microphone. His commanders took their parts of the fleet and grouped themselves into a thick projectile, a cylinder aimed at the nearest of the enemy formations. The enemy, far from trying to repel him, welcomed him in, so he could be thoroughly entrapped before they destroyed him. Mazer is at least taking into account the fact that by now they would have learned to respect me, thought Ender. And that does buy me time.

Ender dodged downward, north, east, and down again, not seeming to follow any plan, but always ending up a little closer to the enemy planet. Finally the enemy began to close in on him too tightly. Then, suddenly, Ender's formation burst. His fleet seemed to melt into chaos. The eighty fighters seemed to follow no plan at all, firing at enemy ships at random, working their way into hopeless individual paths among the bugger craft.

After a few minutes of battle, however, Ender whispered to his squadron leaders once more, and suddenly a dozen of the remaining fighters formed again into a formation. But now they were on the far side of one of the enemy's most formidable groups; they had, with terrible losses, passed through—and now they had covered more than half the distance to the enemy's planet.

The enemy sees now, thought Ender. Surely Mazer sees what I'm doing.

Or perhaps Mazer cannot believe that I would do it. Well, so much the better for me.

Ender's tiny fleet darted this way and that, sending two or three fighters out as if to attack, then bringing them back. The enemy closed in, drawing in ships and formations that had been widely scattered, bringing them in for the kill. The enemy was most concentrated beyond Ender, so he could not escape back into open space, closing him in. Excellent, thought Ender. Closer. Come closer.

Then he whispered a command and the ships dropped like rocks toward the planet's surface. They were starships and fighters, completely unequipped to handle the heat of passage through an atmosphere. But Ender never intended them to reach the atmosphere. Almost from the moment they began to drop, they were focusing their Little Doctors on one thing only. The planet itself.

One, two, four, seven of his fighters were blown away. It was all a gamble now, whether any of his ships would survive long enough to get in range. It would not take long once they could focus on the planet's surface. Just a moment with Dr. Device, that's all I want. It occurred to Ender that perhaps the computer wasn't even equipped to show what would happen to a planet if the Little Doctor attacked it. What will I do then, shout Bang, you're dead?

Ender took his hands off the controls and leaned in to watch what happened. The perspective was close to the enemy planet now, as the ship hurtled into its well of gravity. Surely it's in range now, thought Ender. It must be in range and the computer can't handle it.

Then the surface of the planet, which filled half the simulator field now, began to bubble; there was a gout of explosion, hurling debris out toward Ender's fighters. Ender tried to imagine what was happening inside the planet. The field growing and growing, the molecules bursting apart but finding nowhere for the separate atoms to go.

Within three seconds the entire planet burst apart, becoming a sphere of bright dust, hurtling outward. Ender's fighters were among the first to go; their perspective suddenly vanished, and now the simulator could only display the perspective of the starships waiting beyond the edges of the battle. It was as close as Ender wanted to be. The sphere of the exploding planet grew outward faster than the enemy ships could avoid it. And it carried with it the Little Doctor, not so little anymore, the field taking apart every ship in its path, erupting each one into a dot of light before it went on.

Only at the very periphery of the simulator did the M.D. field weaken. Two or three enemy ships were drifting away. Ender's own starships did not explode. But where the vast enemy fleet had been, and the planet they protected, there was nothing meaningful. A lump of dirt was growing as gravity drew much of the debris downward again. It was glowing hot and spinning visibly; it was also much smaller than the world had been before. Much of its mass was now a cloud still flowing outward.

Ender took off his headphones, filled with the cheers of his squadron leaders, and only then realized that there was just as much noise in the room with him. Men in uniform were hugging each other, laughing, shouting; others were weeping; some knelt or lay prostrate, and Ender knew they were caught up in prayer. Ender didn't understand. It seemed all wrong. They were supposed to be angry.

Colonel Graff detached himself from the others and came to Ender. Tears streamed down his face, but he was smiling. He bent over, reached out his arms, and to Ender's surprise he embraced him, held him tightly, and whispered, "Thank you, thank you, Ender. Thank God for you, Ender."

The others soon came, too, shaking his hand, congratulating him. He tried to make sense of this. Had he passed the test after all? It was *his* victory, not theirs, and a hollow one at that, a cheat; why did they act as if he had won with honor?

The crowd parted and Mazer Rackham walked through. He came straight to Ender and held out his hand.

"You made the hard choice, boy. All or nothing. End them or end us. But heaven knows there was no other way you could have done it. Congratulations. You beat them, and it's all over."

All over. Beat them. Ender didn't understand. "I beat *you*."

Mazer laughed, a loud laugh that filled the room. "Ender, you never played *me*. You never played a *game* since I became your enemy."

Ender didn't get the joke. He had played a great many games, at a terrible cost to himself. He began to get angry.

Mazer reached out and touched his shoulder. Ender shrugged him off. Mazer then grew serious and said, "Ender, for the past few months you have been the battle commander of our fleets. This was the Third Invasion. There were no games, the battles were real, and the only enemy you fought was the buggers. You won every battle, and today you finally fought them at their home world, where the queen was, all the queens from all their colonies, they all were there and you destroyed them completely. They'll never attack us again. You did it. You."

Real. Not a game. Ender's mind was too tired to cope with it all. They weren't just points of light in the air, they were real ships that he had fought with and real ships he had destroyed. And a real world that he had blasted into oblivion. He walked through the crowd, dodging their congratulations, ignoring their hands, their words, their rejoicing. When he got to his own room he stripped off his clothes, climbed into bed, and slept. . . .

We are like you; the thought pressed into his mind. We did not mean to murder, and when we understood, we never came again. We thought we were the only thinking beings in the universe, until we met you, but never did we dream that thought could arise from the lonely animals who cannot dream each other's dreams. How were we to know? We could live with you in peace. Believe us, believe us, believe us.

He reached into the cavity and took out the cocoon. It was astonishingly light, to hold all the hope and future of a great race within it.

"I'll carry you," said Ender, "I'll go from world to world until I find a time and a place where you can come awake in safety. And I'll tell your story to my people, so that perhaps in time they can forgive you, too. The way that you've forgiven me."

He wrapped the queen's cocoon in his jacket and carried her from the tower.

"What was in there?" asked Abra.

"The answer," said Ender.

"To what?"

"My question." And that was all he said of the matter; they searched for five more days and chose a site for the new colony far to the east and south of the tower.

Weeks later he came to Valentine and told her to read something he had written; she pulled the file he named from the ship's computer, and read it.

It was written as if the hive-queen spoke, telling all that they had meant to do, and all that they had done. Here are our failures, and here is our greatness; we did not mean to hurt you, and we forgive you for our death. From their earliest awareness to the great wars that swept across their home world, Ender told the story quickly, as if it were an ancient memory. When he came to the tale of the great mother, the queen of all, who first learned to keep and teach the new queen instead of killing her or driving her away, then he lingered, telling how many times she had finally to destroy the child of her body, the new self that was not herself, until she bore one who understood her quest for harmony. This was a new thing in the world, two queens that loved and helped each other instead of battling, and together they were stronger than any other hive. They prospered; they had more daughters who joined them in peace; it was the beginning of wisdom.

If only we could have talked to you, the hive-queen said in Ender's words. But since it could not be, we ask only this: that you remember us, not as enemies, but as tragic sisters, changed into a foul shape by fate or God or evolution. If we had kissed, it would have been the miracle to make us human in each other's eyes. Instead we killed each other. But still we welcome you now as guestfriends. Come into our home, daughters of Earth; dwell in our tunnels, harvest our fields; what we cannot do, you are now our hands to do for us. Blossom, trees; ripen, fields; be warm for them, suns; be fertile for them, planets: they are our adopted daughters, and they have come home.

The book that Ender wrote was not long, but in it was all the good and all the evil that the hive-queen knew. And he signed it, not with his name, but with a title:

Speaker for the Dead

On Earth, the book was published quietly, and quietly it was passed from hand to hand, until it was hard to believe that anyone on Earth might not have read it. Most who read it found it interesting; some who read it refused to set it aside. They began to live by it as best they could, and when their loved ones died, a believer would arise beside the grave to be the Speaker for the Dead, and say what the dead one would have said, but with full candor, hiding no faults and pretending no virtues. Those who came to such services sometimes found them painful and disturbing, but there were many who decided that their life was worthwhile enough, despite their errors, that when they died a Speaker should tell the truth for them.

On Earth it remained a religion among many religions. But for those who traveled the great cave of space and lived their lives in the hive-queen's tunnels and harvested the hive-queen's fields, it was the only religion. There was no colony without its Speaker for the Dead.

No one knew and no one really wanted to know who was the original Speaker. Ender was not inclined to tell them.

When Valentine was twenty-five years old, she finished the last volume of her history of the bugger wars. She included at the end the complete text of Ender's little book but did not say that Ender wrote it.

By ansible she got an answer from the ancient Hegemon, Peter Wiggin, seventy-seven years old with a failing heart.

"I know who wrote it," he said. "If he can speak for the buggers, surely he can speak for me."

Back and forth across the ansible Ender and Peter spoke, with Peter pouring out the story of his days and years, his crimes and his kindnesses. And when he died, Ender wrote a second volume, again signed by the Speaker for the Dead. Together, his two books were called the Hive-Queen and the Hegemon, and they were holy writ.

"Come on," he said to Valentine one day. "Let's fly away and live forever."

"We can't," she said. "There are miracles even relativity can't pull off, Ender."

"We have to go. I'm almost happy here."

"So stay."

"I've lived too long with pain. I won't know who I am without it."

So they boarded a starship and went from world to world. Wherever they stopped, he was always Andrew Wiggin, itinerant speaker for the dead, and she was always Valentine, historian errant, writing down the stories of the living while Ender spoke the stories of the dead. And always Ender carried with him a dry white cocoon, looking for the world where the hive-queen could awaken and thrive in peace. He looked a long time.

Continuing to Think

The wars in this story, like many wars we have known, are the result of misunderstanding. Once declared, however, wars must be fought to the end. With enough empathy to understand how the buggers think and enough compassion to win the loyalty of his squadron leaders, Ender could become a killer only by being tricked. He was "reckless, and brilliant and young," the perfect eleven-year-old hacker.

Card means us to wonder whether this is not true to some degree and at some level for all wars. Must we be fooled into demonizing the enemy as "other" and kept ignorant of the war's real objectives, which may be the selfish aims of those in power? Would any of us go into war with our eyes open and kill people we do not know unless we were skillfully used?

Suppose just aims are achieved using unjust means. Does this justify the deception? Mostly, the citizens of any country are completely unaware of battle strategy until it unfolds (or even afterward). Probably, this is completely necessary, and the result can be the surprise bombing of Pearl Harbor, the dropping of an atomic bomb on Hiroshima and Nagasaki, or Nazi death camps. Could all these tragedies have been avoided through more skillful diplomacy, or are there policies so malevolent and destructive that only an equally malevolent and destructive war can stop them? How many wars could be avoided if we understood each other better?

Card means for all of us to identify with Ender, to see our own unwitting participation in our country's wars and to question it. As wars become increasingly complex and the objectives that underlie them murkier (think about the war in Bosnia), it gets harder to know what constitutes a good outcome. How does any side know it has "won"? Even more difficult to decide is whether or not justice was served in the process.

Summing Up the Readings

We began by considering what we mean by justice. If we mean a fair distribution of the benefits and burdens of living in a society, it seems clear that we do not currently have a fair distribution. Some people enjoy many benefits; others bear heavy burdens. Using a utilitarian standard, we must ask ourselves whether the suffering of some is outweighed by the pleasure of others.

Dropping down from the social to the personal level, we may find ourselves motivated by a sense of duty or obligation, a drive to do the right thing. Does doing the right thing mean simply giving everyone an equal chance in the present, even though some people have been unfairly handicapped by past discrimination? Should people in the present have to pay for abuses their grandparents committed? And, do the higher pleasures of the elite, compensate for the deprivations of the masses?

Making certain rights and freedoms such as the ability to get an education and vote more widely available seems like a necessary first step. But, is it enough? If I have internalized a negative self-image based on stereotypes in the culture about a group or groups to which I belong, is my failure mine alone or is it shared by the society that taught me and perhaps continues to teach me self-hatred? At what point must individuals take responsibility for their own failures and successes?

We can begin by recognizing and paying attention to differences that exist between and among us. Once we stop insisting that all women are alike or that all African Americans have the same needs, or that only the poor face certain threats, we can begin to form coalitions that cross age, race, class, and gender lines to achieve a more just society. In the end this means that each of us as individuals must resolve these questions for ourselves so that we can resolve them in society.

Continuing to Question

1. Should we look more toward consequences (utilitarianism) or more toward duty and doing the right thing if we hope to achieve justice? Take an issue and apply both theories to it.

2. Who decides what constitutes a fair balance between suffering and pleasure? Must we, as Ellacuría insists, make all such decisions in the context of the common good?

3. If people are deprived of education and never treated as adults, can they be held accountable for behaving as children? Are Mary Wollstonecraft's arguments still applicable with respect to any groups in society today?

4. It is tempting to pretend differences don't matter by ignoring or pretending to ignore them. What does Audre Lorde think we risk by refusing to acknowledge and deal with difference?

5. How much input should citizens have in whether or not their country declares war on another country? Is there a way to balance the consent of those who will be asked to fight the war against tactical and strategic considerations that involve secrecy and deception?

Suggestions for Further Exploration

The Autobiography of Malcolm X, as told to Alex Haley—New York: Ballantine, 1986. This is Malcolm's life story as told to writer Alex Haley over a two-year period. Spike Lee used it, with some variations, as the script for his popular film *Malcolm X.*

Du Bois, W. E. B., *The Souls of Black Folk*—New York: Fawcett, 1961. This book is a readable classic in African American philosophy. It is a collection of essays, short fiction, poetry, elegies, and allegories. It includes a treatise on ethnomusicology supported by data-laden studies of rural poverty in the Black Belt of the South, a short history of Reconstruction, and impassioned objections to racial violence as well as philosophical reflections on racial identity.

Gilman, Charlotte Perkins, *Herland*—New York: Pantheon, 1979. Gilman offers a feminist fantasy in which women rule and society prospers.

Huxley, Aldous, *Brave New World*—New York: Harper & Row, 1969. In this novel, Huxley has created a dystopia (the opposite of a utopia, like a dysfunctional family on a large scale) featuring the worst tendencies of the technological era run amok.

Orwell, George, *Animal Farm*—New York: New American Library, 1946. This influential book is a Marxist parody set on a farm. After the Revolution, the animals declare that "all animals are equal," but later, under the influence of Napoleon the pig, another phrase is added: "Some animals are more equal than others."

Rossi, Alice, ed., *The Feminist Papers: From Adams to de Beauvoir*—New York: Bantam, 1974. This is a comprehensive anthology of major feminist writings from the late 18th to the mid-20th century.

West, Cornel, *Race Matters*—Boston: Beacon, 1993. West provides a short, readable analysis of the problems facing American society from an African American perspective and offers a communitarian solution.

Woolf, Virginia, *A Room of One's Own*—New York: Harcourt Brace, 1937. Based on two papers read in 1928, this short work has become a classic. The adventures of "Shakespeare's sister" come from this book.

10   Ethics

Defining the Issue

Having considered the relationship between the individual and the state (political philosophy) and the question of justice (social philosophy), it is now time to turn our attention to issues of personal morality—what philosophers call *ethics*. As with the other two chapters in this section, the overall focus is on what we value.

You will notice some similarities with our last chapter. There are three major approaches to *ethics: teleological or consequentialist ethics, deontological or non-consequentialist ethics,* and *virtue ethics*. The first two are concerned primarily with what we should do, whereas the last focuses more on how we should *be*—on the development of a moral character. Teleological theories, such as utilitarianism, look to outcomes or consequences to decide whether an action is right or wrong. Deontological theories are based on duty and consider chiefly whether or not rules of behavior have been followed. Virtue ethics suggests that morality can be best achieved, not by monitoring what we do (there are too many choices and they happen too fast), but by deciding what kind of people we want to be and practicing what we define as the habits of virtue.

All ethical theories have some connection with views of human nature. If only rational, self-conscious people qualify as moral beings, then how I treat the unborn, the very young, the comatose, or the nearly dead is not an ethical question. But, if my moral web expands to include not only these beings but other animals, artificial life forms, and perhaps the environment itself, then I must be very careful in what I do. As you consider these readings, it may be useful to ask yourself who has membership in your own web of moral beings—those whose interests or preferences you feel obliged to take into account in your own moral decision making.

Previewing the Readings

Immanuel Kant is a deontologist. He is concerned primarily with duty, and the duty he finds most compelling is acting always so that you can wish what you are about to do would become a maxim everyone else must follow. If you can make this wish, Kant thinks you are about to do the right thing; if you cannot, he suggests you think again. Gloria Anzaldúa agrees with Kant's ethical test—that treating others always as ends in themselves and never merely as means to our own ends constitutes the most valid ethical test. Her concern focuses on overcoming the divisions that permit the labeling of some as "other."

Rita Manning is a modern exponent of a variation on virtue ethics. As old as Aristotle, virtue ethics means today more or less what it meant in his day—becoming the best human beings we can be. For Aristotle this meant developing the rational self; Manning focuses on the caring self, using a "network of care" as an ethical ideal. Kwasi Wiredu articulates an African ethical model that seems to derive from a similar ideal—a sense of communal belonging coupled with the irreducibility of human dignity. The maxim of conduct may be stated this way: A human being deserves to be helped.

According to Chinese Taoism, virtue is rooted in the interconnectedness of all beings. In his popular classic *The Te of Piglet,* Benjamin Hoff describes the Age of Perfect Virtue that existed before the Great Separation of humans from the rest of life. Piglet is the character in the Winnie the Pooh stories who best exemplifies **te,** the Chinese word for virtue-in-action.

Immanuel Kant, a German contemporary of Mary Wollstonecraft's, wrote at the end of the eighteenth century. He shares her presumption that human reason can define and cure most of what is wrong in human society. Specifically, Kant believes reason can guide us to the principle underlying moral decision making; his moral web includes only rational beings.

Prejudice is irrational. It permits us to label individuals and groups in such a way as to exclude them from our moral web. If someone is the "other," we may not feel required to take their feelings into account before we act. Gloria Anzaldúa challenges all of us to adopt a "mestiza consciousness" that lives on the borderlands and understands shifting identities. Only from inside this consciousness will we be able to affirm the common humanity that brings every person into our moral web.

Rita Manning, Kwasi Wiredu, and Benjamin Hoff all offer modern variations on classical ethical theories with long traditions behind them. Manning takes Aristotle's reason-based virtue theory and recasts it as an **ethic of care,** using a caring self rather than a rational self as the ideal of virtue. "What would my ideal caring self do?" asks a very different question from "What would my ideal rational self do?" Wiredu offers an African version of Kant's categorical imperative: A human being deserves to be helped. Akan culture says, no matter what, this duty is a human one. All humans have automatic membership in the web of moral beings. Hoff uses the characters in the Winnie-the-Pooh stories to embody ancient Taoist concepts—in this case the concept of virtue itself. What Piglet does is show us a greatly expanded moral web in which not only all humans but all of life must be included.

10.1   *Foundations for the Metaphysics of Morals*

IMMANUEL KANT

Preparing to Read

If you keep in mind the utilitarian principle of striving to create the greatest happiness in the world at large, Kant's proposal will provide a clear contrast. As a deontologist, Kant believes we must focus on duty, regardless of the outcome. The most important thing, in his view, is to understand our duty clearly, to articulate it in an easy to understand way, and then to do it.

Suppose I try to cheat you (not doing my duty) but, through a series of odd twists not intended by me, I end up helping you. The outcome is good, but Kant would say I have still behaved unethically. It is my will, my ability to choose, that makes possible both ethical and unethical behavior. To be ethical, I must direct my will to duty.

How can I know what my duty is? Here Kant offers a simple and reliable test: Ask yourself whether you would will anyone in your situation to behave as you are about to behave. If you can, your action will be following the path of duty. If you cannot, what you are proposing to do is unethical.

If you are caught in an embarrassing situation, you will be tempted to lie. The lie will offer itself to you as the solution to your problem—a good outcome. But what if everyone in a similar situation lied? What kind of world would that create? One in which you would be happy to live? Although the lie seems attractive, your rejection of a world with lying as a standard informs you it is unethical. Doing your duty means acting always to create the kind of world in which you would wish to live.

AN ACTION DONE FROM DUTY derives its moral worth not from the purpose or outcome which is to be achieved through it but from the maxim on which it is based. Therefore, the action does not depend on the achievement of its objective but only on the principle of volition [willing] on which the action is based, independent of desired outcomes . . . Duty is the mandating of an action out of respect for the law. I might indeed have a desire for an object as an effect of my proposed action, but I cannot have respect for an object because it is only an effect and not an action of will. In the same way, I cannot have respect for inclination or desire, whether mine or another's; if it is my own, I can at most approve it and, if it is another's, I might even love it and see it as favorable to my own advantage. Only the law itself, connected with my will as its foundation, never as an effect, and independent of what I desire, can be an object of respect and therefore a command . . .

The moral value of an action does not lie in the effect expected from it nor in any principle of action which bases its motive on this expected effect. For all these effects (my own happiness or even the happiness of others) could have been brought about by other causes without requiring the will of a rational being. Only in the will of a rational being, however, can the highest and unconditional good be found . . .

But what kind of law can compel the will without regard to the expected effect in such a way that the will may be called absolutely good with no qualifications? Since I have removed from the will all impulses that could arise in it from obeying some particular law, there remains only the conformity of the will to lawfulness itself. This alone can serve the will as its principle: I must always act in such a way that I would want my own maxim to become a universal law. Here obedience to universal law, independent of particular laws applicable to particular actions, is what serves the will as its governing principle—and must do so if duty is not to be reduced to delusion or fantasy. Ordinary human reason confirms this judgment and always has.

For example, let's ask this question: May I, when pressed, make a promise with the intention of not keeping it? Here we need to distinguish two meanings, whether it is prudent and whether it is the path of duty to make a false promise. No doubt the first case occurs frequently. I can see that it is not enough to get out of a present problem by making a promise I don't intend to keep. I must also consider whether the lie might not cause me more difficulties than the original problem it was intended to solve. Since, despite all my cleverness, long-term consequences are not so easy to see, once my credibility is lost, I may find myself in a much worse situation than the original that prompted the lie. So, I must consider whether it might not be more prudent to establish a general maxim and make no promises except those I intend to keep. But, it will soon be clear to me that such a maxim will be based only on feared consequences.

Being truthful from duty is quite a different matter from being truthful out of fear of consequences. In the first case the concept of acting out of duty already contains its own law; in the second, I must look elsewhere to see what effects for myself might be connected with an action. It is undoubtedly evil for me to deviate from the principle of duty, but if I betray my maxim of prudence, this can sometimes be advantageous to me, even though, overall, it is better to obey it.

The most direct and objective way to resolve the problem of whether a false promise is ever consistent with duty is to ask myself: would I be content to have my maxim (to get myself out of difficult situations with false promises) become a universal law? Would I dare say to myself that anyone facing an embarrassing situation and seeing no other way out may make a false promise? This immediately makes clear that, while I can defend the lie, I cannot support lying as a universal law. If this law were in effect, there would, in reality, be no promises at all, since it would be pointless for me to make promises to others who would not believe me or, even if they did believe me, might repay me with a false promise of their own. In other words, as soon as my maxim was made into a universal law, it would self-destruct.

So, I don't need any special mental powers in order to discern what I have to do to make my will morally good. Inexperienced in the ways of the world, unable to anticipate all circumstances I might face, I have only to ask myself: can you also will that your personal maxim become a universal law? If not, it must be rejected and not because of any disadvantage to yourself or others but because it is not compatible with universal law and reason demands my unconditional respect only for such a law. Even though I may not fully understand what this law is based on (this after all is the province of philosophers), this much is clear: my respect honors a value that far outweighs any value that might accrue to mere objects of desire. The necessity of acting out of pure respect for the practical law is what constitutes duty. Every other motive must yield to duty because it is the condition of a will good in itself and the value of a will such as this exceeds everything else.

Thus we have reached the pinnacle of moral knowledge available to ordinary human reason. Although the average person might not be able to articulate this principle in such an abstract and universal way, it is obvious that all of us use this principle (or can use it) in our moral decision making. It would be easy to demonstrate here how, using this moral compass alone, people are quite able to use their reason to distinguish what is good, bad, in conformity with duty or contrary to it. Without offering any new teaching, we have followed Socrates's example in drawing people's attention to a principle of decision making they already use and showing them that we do not need science or philosophy to teach us how to be honest and good or even wise and virtuous.

Continuing to Think

Kant believed that the principle of universalizability would always lead us to see the path of duty. What looks okay when I think only of myself and my own situation can seem very un-okay when I universalize it and imagine everyone doing what I am about to do. For this reason, Kant thought looking at consequences to be an unreliable guide to ethical behaviour. Duty to an absolute moral standard, by contrast, would never confuse you or lead you astray.

Kant also developed a second way of formulating his one ethical ideal. Another rule you might follow, he suggested, is to treat people always as ends in themselves, never merely as means to an end. If you are a bank teller, it is fine for me to use you as a means to the end of getting my money out of the bank—as long as I understand that you are not merely this means. Suppose I cultivate a friendship with you, merely to meet friends of yours who I think can help me in my career. In this case, I have used you as a means to my end and ignored your human right to be treated always as an end in yourself.

This is another test you might find useful in living a Kantian ideal. Pressing someone for money, intimacy, or business favors, without caring about or respecting their needs and wants, denies their inherent dignity as human beings. None of us likes to be treated merely as a customer by someone we thought of as a friend, but we are perfectly willing to be customers when all we want is a sandwich or a shirt. Business transactions assume roles we play voluntarily; personal relationships demand more. Never treating someone as merely a means to your ends helps keep you on the path of duty.

10.2   *Borderlands/La Frontera*

GLORIA ANZALDÚA

Preparing to Read

The conflicting worldviews N. Scott Momaday alerted us to in selection 6.3 can also occur within the psyche of a single person. Borrowing the idea of a cosmic race (a fifth race that embraces the four major ones) from Jose Vascocelos, Gloria Anzaldúa explores what she calls "mestiza consciousness." Living on the borderlands—Indian in Mexican culture, Mexican from an Anglo point of view—Anzaldúa sees the possibility of creating a new consciousness.

It will not do to stand on opposite shores and label each other "oppressor" or "oppressed." It is necessary to somehow stand on both shores at once, seeing with "serpent or eagle eyes." Dualisms of all kinds—white/colored, male/female—must be transcended if we are to behave ethically toward one another. And those who inhabit both worlds may be uniquely capable of breaking down the subject/object duality that allows us to treat someone else as the "other."

Simone de Beauvoir found all women and non-white men relegated to conditions of "alterity" or "otherness" by the power positions staked out in society by white men. What Anzaldúa is envisioning is a way to overcome "otherness" and heal divisions. And, it requires nothing less than a new way of perceiving ourselves and reality that leads to altered behavior.

What do you think? Is the "mestiza" uniquely able to be the bridge builder? Can one who inhabits two or more worlds negotiate among them, translating back and forth, in a way that those who live in only one of the worlds can never hope to do? Does "mestiza consciousness" represent our best hope?

Towards a New Consciousness

> Por la mujer de mi raza
> hablará el espíritu.[1]

JOSE VASCOCELOS, Mexican philosopher, envisaged *una raza mestiza, una mezcla de razas afines, una raza de color—la primera raza síntesis del globo*. He called it a cosmic race, *la raza cósmica,* a fifth race embracing the four major races of the world.[2] Opposite to the theory of the pure Aryan, and to the policy of racial purity that white America practices, his theory is one of inclusivity. At the confluence of two or more genetic streams, with chromosomes constantly "crossing over," this mixture of races, rather than resulting in an inferior being, provides hybrid progeny, a mutable, more malleable species with a rich gene pool. From this racial, ideological, cultural and biological cross-pollinization, an "alien" consciousness is presently in the making—a new *mestiza* consciousness, *una conciencia de mujer*. It is a consciousness of the Borderlands.

Una lucha de fronteras / A Struggle of Borders

> Because I, a *mestiza,*
> continually walk out of one culture
> and into another,
> because I am in all cultures at the same time,

alma entre dos mundos, tres, cuatro,
me zumba la cabeza con lo contradictorio.
Estoy norteada por todas las voces que me hablan
simultáneamente.

The ambivalence from the clash of voices results in mental and emotional states of perplexity. Internal strife results in insecurity and indecisiveness. The mestiza's dual or multiple personality is plagued by psychic restlessness.

In a constant state of mental nepantilism, an Aztec word meaning torn between ways, *la mestiza* is a product of the transfer of the cultural and spiritual values of one group to another. Being tricultural, monolingual, bilingual, or multilingual, speaking a patois, and in a state of perpetual transition, the *mestiza* faces the dilemma of the mixed breed: which collectivity does the daughter of a darkskinned mother listen to?

El choque de un alma atrapado entre el mundo del espíritu y el mundo de la técnica a veces la deja entullada. Cradled in one culture, sandwiched between two cultures, straddling all three cultures and their value systems, *la mestiza* undergoes a struggle of flesh, a struggle of borders, an inner war. Like all people, we perceive the version of reality that our culture communicates. Like others having or living in more than one culture, we get multiple, often opposing messages. The coming together of two self-consistent but habitually incompatible frames of reference[3] causes *un choque,* a cultural collision.

Within us and within *la cultura chicana,* commonly held beliefs of the white culture attack commonly held beliefs of the Mexican culture, and both attack commonly held beliefs of the indigenous culture. Subconsciously, we see an attack on ourselves and our beliefs as a threat and we attempt to block with a counterstance.

But it is not enough to stand on the opposite river bank, shouting questions, challenging patriarchal, white conventions. A counterstance locks one into a duel of oppressor and oppressed; locked in mortal combat, like the cop and the criminal, both are reduced to a common denominator of violence. The counterstance refutes the dominant culture's views and

beliefs, and, for this, it is proudly defiant. All reaction is limited by, and dependent on, what it is reacting against. Because the counterstance stems from a problem with authority—outer as well as inner—it's a step towards liberation from cultural domination. But it is not a way of life. At some point, on our way to a new consciousness, we will have to leave the opposite bank, the split between the two mortal combatants somehow healed so that we are on both shores at once and, at once, see through serpent and eagle eyes. Or perhaps we will decide to disengage from the dominant culture, write it off altogether as a lost cause, and cross the border into a wholly new and separate territory. Or we might go another route. The possibilities are numerous once we decide to act and not react.

A Tolerance for Ambiguity

These numerous possibilities leave *la mestiza* floundering in uncharted seas. In perceiving conflicting information and points of view, she is subjected to a swamping of her psychological borders. She has discovered that she can't hold concepts or ideas in rigid borders. The borders and walls that are supposed to keep the desirable ideas out are entrenched habits and patterns of behavior; these habits and patterns are the enemy within. Rigidity means death. Only by remaining flexible is she able to stretch the psyche horizontally and vertically. *La mestiza* constantly has to shift out of habitual formations; from convergent thinking, analytical reasoning that tends to use rationality to move toward a single goal (a Western mode), to divergent thinking,[4] characterized by movement away from set patterns and goals and toward a more whole perspective, one that includes rather than excludes.

The new *mestiza* copes by developing a tolerance for contradictions, a tolerance for ambiguity. She learns to be an Indian in Mexican culture, to be Mexican from an Anglo point of view. She learns to juggle cultures. She has a plural personality, she operates in a pluralistic mode—nothing is thrust out, the good, the bad and the ugly, nothing rejected, nothing abandoned. Not only does she sustain contradictions, she turns the ambivalence into something else.

She can be jarred out of ambivalence by an intense, and often painful, emotional event which inverts or resolves the ambivalence. I'm not sure exactly how. The work takes place underground—subconsciously. It is work that the soul performs. That focal point or fulcrum, that juncture where the *mestiza* stands, is where phenomena tend to collide. It is where the possibility of uniting all that is separate occurs. This assembly is not one where severed or separated pieces merely come together. Nor is it a balancing of opposing powers. In attempting to work out a synthesis, the self has added a third element which is greater than the sum of its severed parts. That third element is a new consciousness—a *mestiza* consciousness—and though it is a source of intense pain, its energy comes from continual creative motion that keeps breaking down the unitary aspect of each new paradigm.

En unas pocas centurias, the future will belong to the *mestiza.* Because the future depends on the breaking down of paradigms, it depends on the straddling of two or more cultures. By creating a new mythos—that is, a change in the way we perceive reality, the way we see ourselves, and the ways we behave—*la mestiza* creates a new consciousness.

The work of *mestiza* consciousness is to break down the subject-object duality that keeps her a prisoner and to show in the flesh and through the images in her work how duality is transcended. The answer to the problem between the white race and the colored, between males and females, lies in healing the split that originates in the very foundation of our lives, our culture, our languages, our thoughts. A massive uprooting of dualistic thinking in the individual and collective consciousness is the beginning of a long struggle, but one that could, in our best hopes, bring us to the end of rape, of violence, of war. . . .

Somos una gente

Hay tantísimas fronteras
que dividen a la gente

pero por cada frontera
existe también un puente.
—Gina Valdés[5]

DIVIDED LOYALTIES

Many women and men of color do not want to have any dealings with white people. It takes too much time and energy to explain to the downwardly mobile, white middle-class women that it's okay for us to want to own "possessions," never having had any nice furniture on our dirt floors or "luxuries" like washing machines. Many feel that whites should help their own people rid themselves of race hatred and fear first. I, for one, choose to use some of my energy to serve as mediator. I think we need to allow whites to be our allies. Through our literature, art, *corridos,* and folktales we must share our history with them so when they set up committees to help Big Mountain Navajos or the Chicano farmworkers or *los Nicaragüenses* they won't turn people away because of their racial fears and ignorances. They will come to see that they are not helping us but following our lead.

Individually, but also as a racial entity, we need to voice our needs. We need to say to white society: We need you to accept the fact that Chicanos are different, to acknowledge your rejection and negation of us. We need you to own the fact that you looked upon us as less than human, that you stole our lands, our personhood, our self-respect. We need you to make public restitution: to say that, to compensate for your own sense of defectiveness, you strive for power over us, you erase our history and our experience because it makes you feel guilty—you'd rather forget your brutish acts. To say you've split yourself from minority groups, that you disown us, that your dual consciousness splits off parts of yourself, transferring the "negative" parts onto us. (Where there is persecution of minorities, there is shadow projection. Where there is violence and war, there is repression of shadow.) To say that you are afraid of us, that to put distance between us, you wear the mask of contempt. Admit that Mexico is your double, that she exists in the shadow of this country, that we are irrevocably tied to her. Gringo, accept the doppelganger in your psyche. By taking back your collective shadow the intracultural split will heal. And finally, tell us what you need from us.

By Your True Faces We Will Know You

I am visible—see this Indian face—yet I am invisible. I both blind them with my beak nose and am their blind spot. But I exist, we exist. They'd like to think I have melted in the pot. But I haven't, we haven't.

The dominant white culture is killing us slowly with its ignorance. By taking away our self-determination, it has made us weak and empty. As a people we have resisted and we have taken expedient positions, but we have never been allowed to develop unencumbered—we have never been allowed to be fully ourselves. The whites in power want us people of color to barricade ourselves behind our separate tribal walls so they can pick us off one at a time with their hidden weapons; so they can whitewash and distort history. Ignorance splits people, creates prejudices. A misinformed people is a subjugated people.

Before the Chicano and the undocumented worker and the Mexican from the other side can come together, before the Chicano can have unity with Native Americans and other groups, we need to know the history of their struggle and they need to know ours. Our mothers, our sisters and brothers, the guys who hang out on street corners, the children in the playgrounds, each of us must know our Indian lineage, our afro-*mestisaje,* our history of resistance.

To the immigrant *mexicano* and the recent arrivals we must teach our history. The 80 million *mexicanos* and the Latinos from Central and South America must know of our struggles. Each one of us must know basic facts about Nicaragua, Chile and the rest of Latin America. The Latinoist movement (Chicanos, Puerto Ricans, Cubans and other Spanish-speaking people

working together to combat racial discrimination in the market place) is good but it is not enough. Other than a common culture we will have nothing to hold us together. We need to meet on a broader communal ground.

The struggle is inner: Chicano, *indio,* American Indian, *mojado, mexicano,* immigrant Latino, Anglo in power, working class Anglo, Black, Asian—our psyches resemble the bordertowns and are populated by the same people. The struggle has always been inner, and is played out in the outer terrains. Awareness of our situation must come before inner changes, which in turn come before changes in society. Nothing happens in the "real" world unless it first happens in the images in our heads.

El día de la Chicana

> I will not be shamed again
> Nor will I shame myself.

I am possessed by a vision: that we Chicanas and Chicanos have taken back or uncovered our true faces, our dignity and self-respect. It's a validation vision.

Seeing the Chicana anew in light of her history, I seek an exoneration, a seeing through the fictions of white supremacy, a seeing of ourselves in our true guises and not as the false racial personality that has been given to us and that we have given to ourselves. I seek our woman's face, our true features, the positive and the negative seen clearly, free of the tainted biases of male dominance. I seek new images of identity, new beliefs about ourselves, our humanity and worth no longer in question.

Estamos viviendo en la noche de la Raza, un tiempo cuando el trabajo se hace a lo quieto, en el oscuro. El día cuando aceptamos tal y como somos y para en donde vamos y porque—ese día será el día de la Raza. Yo tengo el conpromiso de expresar mi visión, mi sensibilidad, mi percepción de la revalidación de la gente mexicana, su mérito, estimación, honra, aprecio, y validez.

On December 2nd when my sun goes into my first house, I celebrate *el día de la Chicana y el Chicano*. On that day I clean my altars, light my *Coatlalopeuh* candle, burn sage and copal, take *el baño para espantar basura*, sweep my house. On that day I bare my soul, make myself vulnerable to friends and family by expressing my feelings. On that day I affirm who we are.

On that day I look inside our conflicts and our basic introverted racial temperament. I identify our needs, voice them. I acknowledge that the self and the race have been wounded. I recognize the need to take care of our personhood, of our racial self. On that day I gather the splintered and disowned parts of *la gente mexicana* and hold them in my arms. *Todas las partes de nosotros valen*.

On that day I say, "Yes, all you people wound us when you reject us. Rejection strips us of self-worth; our vulnerability exposes us to shame. It is our innate identity you find wanting. We are ashamed that we need your good opinion, that we need your acceptance. We can no longer camouflage our needs, can no longer let defenses and fences sprout around us. We can no longer withdraw. To rage and look upon you with contempt is to rage and be contemptuous of ourselves. We can no longer blame you, nor disown the white parts, the male parts, the pathological parts, the queer parts, the vulnerable parts. Here we are weaponless with open arms, with only our magic. Let's try it our way, the *mestiza* way, the Chicana way, the woman way.

On that day, I search for our essential dignity as a people, a people with a sense of purpose—to belong and contribute to something greater than our pueblo. On that day I seek to recover and reshape my spiritual identity. *¡Anímate! Raza, a celebrar el día de la Chicana*.

NOTES

1. This is my own "take off" on Jose Vasconcelos' idea. Jose Vasconcelos, *La Raza Cósmica: Misión de la Raza Ibero-Americana* (México: Aguilar S.A. de Ediciones, 1961).

2. Vasconcelos.

3. Arthur Koestler termed this "bisociation." Albert Rothenberg, *The Creative Process in Art, Science, and Other Fields* (Chicago: University of Chicago Press, 1979), 12.

4. In part, I derive my definitions for "convergent" and "divergent" thinking from Rothenberg, 12–13.

5. Richard Wilhelm, *The I Ching or Book of Changes*, trans. Cary F. Baynes (Princeton, NJ: Princeton University Press, 1950), 98.

Continuing to Think

At the turn of the twentieth century, W. E. B. Du Bois spoke about the "double consciousness" that African Americans feel and must overcome. Those who inhabit more than one reality—in this case as Africans and as Americans—experience conflicting messages about themselves. Minority consciousness includes negative evaluations from the majority culture. It is tempting to cast onto the "other" the disliked qualities we find in ourselves. Individuals do this and so do societies. Jungian psychology describes these rejected parts as the "shadow."

What Anzaldúa is challenging the majority culture to do is take back its shadow. In her view, wherever we find persecution of minorities, violence, or war, we can be sure we will also find shadow projection. In much the same way that Ignacio Ellacuría argued in selection 9.2, Anzaldúa challenges rich and powerful countries and individuals to test their ideologies against realities in the world at large. Mexico, she says, is the "double" of the United States, tied to it irrevocably. Healing the intracultural split will heal both partners.

No parts of the human family can be disowned without doing violence to human nature itself. The time for rage and blame is past, Anzaldúa asserts, for when we rage we rage against ourselves and when we blame, we blame ourselves. This dissolving of boundaries suggests a Buddhist sense of the interrelatedness and interconnectedness of all that is. Recognizing our common humanity can engender a great sense of compassion.

Is it only on the borderlands that we can see the true nature of what lies on either side? Immanuel Kant argued that the test of ethical behavior is whether we are treating others always as ends in themselves and never merely as means to our own ends. Does mestiza consciousness reveal more clearly when we are failing Kant's ethical test?

10.3 *Speaking from the Heart*

RITA MANNING

Preparing to Read

Partly in response to the conflicting explanations of consequentialist and nonconsequentialist ethical theories, some philosophers have revived an ancient tradition and given it a significant twist. Both utilitarianism and deontology focus on what we should do, how we should act. Suppose, instead, we considered not what to do but how to *be*—what kind of character we should build.

Aristotle believed virtue was a matter of rationally determining the proper standards of behavior and then cultivating the habits of virtue by practicing them. In his view, we become virtuous by acting virtuously until those rational norms of behavior become part of us. Accepting the emphasis on being over doing, modern virtue theory, nevertheless, makes a significant departure from Aristotle.

Instead of the rational self Aristotle used as a standard, some contemporary philosophers take the caring self as an ethical ideal. In this variation on virtue theory, the emphasis remains on how we should be rather than on what we should do, but the suspicion is that the rational self may not be the most reliable guide to ethical behavior. For example, we have reasoned our way into killing thousands (in wars) because it was the right thing to do.

An ethic of care asks: What would my ideal caring self do in this situation? If I think of myself as existing in a network of care, my ethical obligations will become clear. In this selection Rita Manning explains how the caring self honors care rather than abstract principles.

Chapter Four: Just Caring

IN THIS CHAPTER, I shall sketch a model of ethical considerations which I shall call, following Nel Noddings, an ethic of caring.[1]. . .

I must confess at the outset that this model owes more to my experience as a woman, a teacher, and a mother than it does to my training and experience in moral philosophy. Over the years, my students have convinced me of the barrenness of standard ethical theories. It has occurred to me only very recently that, in sketching a more adequate model, I might appeal to my own experience as a moral person. I credit Hume,[2] Annette Baier,[3] and Carol Gilligan[4] with waking me from my dogmatic slumber and Nel Noddings with allowing me to take caring, which is central to my moral experience, seriously.

An ethic of caring, as I shall defend it, includes two elements. First is a disposition to care. This is a willingness to receive others, a willingness to give the lucid attention required to appropriately fill the needs of others. In this sense, an ethic of care is contextual; my actions must be guided by this lucid attention.[5] I see this disposition to care as nourished by a spiritual awareness similar to the awareness argued for by proponents of the women's spirituality movement. As Starhawk describes this awareness: "Immanent justice rests on the first principle of magic: all things are interconnected. All is relationship. Perhaps the ultimate ethic of immanence is to choose to make that relationship one of love . . . love for all the eternally self-creating world, love of the light and the mysterious darkness, and raging love against all that would diminish the unspeakable beauty of the world."[6]

This disposition to care assumes a commitment to an ideal of caring; the ethically preferred world is one in which creatures are caring and cared for. Its institutions support and sustain caring while simultaneously reducing the need for care by eliminating the poverty, despair, and indifference that create a need for care.

Second, in addition to being sensitive to one's place in the world and to one's general obligation to be a caring person, one is also obligated to care for. (I am following Noddings in using "care for" to indicate caring as expressed in action.) In the paradigm case, caring for involves acting in some appropriate way to respond to the needs of persons and animals, but can also be extended to responding to the needs of communities, values, or objects.

We are obligated to adopt this model of caring, insofar as we can, in our moral deliberations. This qualification refers not only to physical, emotional, and psychological incapacity, but to the larger inability to simply adopt a moral life, which is radically different from the way of life we have participated in all our lives. This is a kind of incapacity that we all share. We simply cannot choose to have another's moral sensibilities, even if we are convinced that they are finer in some sense than our own. It doesn't follow that we have no obligations to become more morally sensitive; the point here is that we cannot simply will ourselves to begin to see the moral universe in some radically new way. But even where we can adopt a model of caring, we are morally permitted and sometimes morally obliged to appeal to rules and rights. In Gilligan's idiom, we are required to listen to the voices of both care and justice.

In what follows, I shall first fill in some of the details of this model. Specifically, I shall discuss what it is to care for someone or something and when we are obligated to care for. Next, I shall say something about the role of rules and rights in this model. . . .

I. CARING

I have often wondered if taking a class in moral philosophy was the best way for students to be-

From *Speaking from the Heart* by Rita Manning. Courtesy of Rowman and Littlefield Publishers, Inc.

come sensitive to moral concerns. It seemed to me that a better way would be to have students work in soup kitchens or shelters for the homeless.[7] Taking care of my children has made me more open to moral concerns. In taking care of the hungry, homeless, and helpless, we are engaged in caring for. In the standard case, caring for is immediate; it admits of no surrogates. When we directly care for some creature, we are in physical contact. Our eyes meet, our hands touch. However, not every need can be met in this immediate way, and sometimes we must accept surrogates. Not every need can be met by individual action; in such cases, we must seek collective action.[8] But when we can do the caring for directly, we ought to do so, at least some of the time. The need of the other may sometimes require that a particular person do the caring for. If my child needs my attention, I cannot meet this need by sending her to a therapist. Even when the needs of the other do not require our personal attention, we must provide some of the caring for directly in order to develop and sustain our ability to care.

Day-to-day interactions with other persons create a web of reciprocal caring. In these interactions, one is obliged to be a caring person. One is free, to a certain extent, to choose when and how to care for these others. One's choice is limited by one's relationships with these others and by their needs. A pressing need calls up an immediate obligation to care for: roles and responsibilities call up an obligation to respond in a caring manner. In the first case, one is obligated (though this obligation can be limited by a principle of supererogation) to respond: in the second, one can choose, within limits, when and how to care.

A creature in need who is unable to meet this need without help calls for a caring response on my part. This response need not always be direct. Sometimes it is better to organize a political response. (Many, for example, who are confronted on the street by homeless people are unsure about how to respond, convinced that their immediate response will not be enough, and

might even be counterproductive.) Certain relationships obligate us to provide direct caring for. When my daughter falls and asks me to "kiss it and make it better" I can't send her to my neighbor for the kiss.

Our roles (e.g., as mother, as teacher, as volunteer) put us in particular relationships to others.[9] These roles require and sustain caring. Obligations to infant children and animals involve meeting their basic needs for physical sustenance (food, shelter, clothing, health care) and for companionship and love. Obligations to students are grounded upon roles of teacher and philosopher and the students' psychological needs to discover who they are and how they can live with integrity. Here, one ought to feel a connection with the students but also with teaching and philosophy. But if a student needs another kind of care, we may be obligated to provide it, though not single-handedly. The response depends upon one's ability to care for, one's obligation to care for oneself, and one's sense of the appropriateness of the need and the best way to meet it.

In discharging obligations to care for, which are based on role responsibility, one should be conscious of the need to fill those roles conscientiously. The role of teacher, for example, requires a certain impartiality; the role of mother requires a fierce devotion to each particular child. But one is free, to a certain extent, to choose roles. In adopting or reshaping roles, one should be sensitive to the need to be cared for as well as the capacity to care. In critiquing socially designed and assigned roles, we should aim for roles and divisions of roles that make caring more likely to occur.

Caring for can involve a measure of self-sacrifice. The rescuers of Jessica McLure, the little girl who fell into a well, who went without sleep for days, the parents of an infant who go without uninterrupted sleep for months, are involved in caring for.

Caring for involves an openness to the one cared for; it requires seeing the real need and satisfying it insofar as we are able. In satisfying it, we should be sensitive not just to the need but to the feelings of those in need.

Caring for does not require feeling any particular emotion toward the one cared for, but an openness to the possibility that some emotional attachment may form in the process of caring for. Nor does it require an ongoing relationship with the one cared for.[10] One may meet the one cared for as stranger, though the caring for will change that.

Obviously, a model of caring along the lines I am defending must include an account of needs. An account of needs must recognize that needs are in some sense social, so identifying needs requires an understanding of biology, psychology, and other relevant social sciences.

Such an account would draw a distinction between subsistence needs and psychological needs. Subsistence needs will usually be needs that must be filled if physical existence is to continue, while psychological needs are needs that must be filled if human flourishing is to occur. Filling subsistence needs does not automatically benefit both the carer and the cared for. Rather, the carer is likely to feel burdened by filling such needs, though the recognition that one has filled such needs often creates a sense of virtue in the carer. Filling psychological needs can often be more fulfilling. It is more likely to be done in a reciprocal relationship, and in such a relationship filling psychological needs requires that both parties share the roles of carer and cared for.

Finally, one need not respond to every need. In choosing how and when to respond, one should consider the seriousness of the need, the benefit to the one needing care of filling this particular need, one's own capacity to fill the need, and the competing needs of others, including oneself, that will be affected by filling this particular need.

II. OBJECTS OF CARE

One can care for persons, animals, ideas, values, institutions, and objects. Later, I will discuss caring for persons and animals in some detail, but here I want to make some brief remarks about caring for ideas, values, institutions, and objects. In caring for ideas, values, and institutions, one devotes oneself to their survival, growth, and flourishing in much the same way as we devote ourselves to the growth and flourishing of a child. In doing so, we are caring for ourselves (insofar as these are our ideas and values) and persons and animals (insofar as these ideas and values support a network of care that embraces persons and animals). In caring for objects, one is devoted primarily to their survival (although some objects, trees, for example, can be said to grow and flourish). The choice of objects of care should reflect our own need to be cared for and our capacity to care. But decisions about what to care for should not depend exclusively upon our own needs and capacities. We should also be sensitive to the needs that summon the obligation to care for. If we understand our obligation to care for as following from the existence of need and helplessness, we should care for ideas, institutions, values, objects, and practices that would diminish such needs. One might argue that we could virtually eliminate the need to care for by creating appropriate institutions, values, and practices and hence undermine our capacity to care. But even in a perfectly just world, children would need care, and people and animals would get sick. Furthermore, human needs include more than needs for physical sustenance. Human needs for companionship and intimacy would exist even in a world free from the horrors of war, homelessness, sickness, and disease.

III. CARING AND HUMAN NATURE

Alasdair MacIntyre argues that morality has historically been defended by appeal either to "the ghost of conceptions of divine law" or "the ghost of conceptions of human nature and activity." Since neither conception is "at home in the modern world"[11] morality lacks a foundation. Since morality lacks a foundation, relativism and emotivism have gained a secure foothold, at least in the popular culture.[12]

Though I sympathize with the postmodern rejection of essentialist theories of human nature, I do not agree that there is nothing beyond mere historically conditioned, relatively pervasive human traits. The truth lies somewhere in between. While conceptions of human nature are too often overgeneralizations made on the basis of one's situated experience, one needn't reject the very possibility of finding sufficiently general human characteristics and experiences. Since there are such sufficiently general characteristics and experiences, we need not reject conceptions of human nature as providing a foundation for morality, though we do need to examine such conceptions. Conceptions of human nature generate a picture of the good life. The good life involves overcoming human nature, liberating human nature, or a combination of both: overcoming what is base and liberating what is pure. In this way, conceptions of human nature inform morality.

Many have argued that liberal ethical theories and political philosophies have assumed an unflattering and inaccurate picture of human nature. Marx, for example, criticizes the "individualistic monad"[13] lurking behind defenses of rights. A similar criticism has recently been made by Elizabeth Wolgast in her attacks on "social atomism"[14] and Alison Jaggar in her criticism of "abstract individualism."[15]

Jaggar identifies abstract individualism as the theory of human nature which underlies liberal political philosophy. I think we can assume that this theory provides a foundation for ethical theory as well. Abstract individualism is the view that essential human characteristics are properties of individuals and are given independently of the social context. This theory, as Jaggar describes it, is committed to the following claims.

1. Rationality is a mental capacity of individuals rather than groups and is possessed in approximately equal measure by all humans, though this capacity can be more or less developed.

2. Rationality is our most valuable capacity.

3. Each individual is intrinsically valuable because of this ability to reason.

4. Each human's desires can in principle be fulfilled separately from the desires of other humans.

5. People typically seek to maximize their individual self-interest.

6. Resources for fulfilling desires are limited.

7. Because of the value of rationality and the existence of scarcity and desires to possess certain goods, autonomy is protected by the good society.[16]

One can argue about whether Jaggar has accurately described liberal political and moral philosophy here, but even if we grant that the picture is overdrawn, a version of it undergirds Kantian and utilitarian moral theories. We can see how this conception supports Kantian ethics with its emphasis on duty. If one is unconnected to others, and basically self-interested, no other motivation to be moral could exist.

Utilitarianism is also a rational alternative if abstract individualism is true. An unconnected, basically self-interested individual would admit that social life is not worth living without some constraints on the self-interest of others. It is then rational to adopt a system of mutual restraint, as long as one's own interests will count. In this way, the rational person can protect his interests.

An ethic of care rejects the abstract individualism criticized by Jaggar. On this view, we are all connected, and, as Noddings puts it, "the primary aim is caring and being cared for. . . ."[17] This caring can take place only in potentially reciprocal relationships between human beings. The good society protects this aim and allows for the full development of our best selves, which are those selves represented by "our most caring and tender moments."[18] Since caring is not a totally rational process, although it is partly this, an ethic of care would reject claims number two and three. Rationality is not our most valuable capacity; the capacity for caring represents our "best selves." It would also reject claim four. If our primary desires are to care and be cared for in relationships with other humans, then we cannot fulfill our desires independently of other humans. We should not be seen as seeking to maximize self-interest either, because caring involves the suspension of self-interest in many cases, so she would reject claim number five as well. Claim number six is noncontroversial, but claim number seven would also be rejected because it follows from number three.

We can see that an ethic of care requires a new conception of human nature, and such an account would involve a picture of humans as essentially involved in relationships with other humans.

NOTES

1. Nel Noddings, *Caring: A Feminine Approach to Ethics and Moral Education* (Berkeley: University of California Press, 1984).

2. Hume argued that the task of moral philosophy ought to be to look reflectively at actual moral practice. This conception also can be seen, though to a lesser extent, in Aristotle, and in Alasdair MacIntyre, *After Virtue* (Notre Dame, Ind.: University of Notre Dame Press, 1981).

3. Annette Baier argues forcefully that we should pay exclusive attention to reforming current moral practices. See *Postures of the Mind: Essays on Mind and Morals,* especially chapters 11–15 (Minneapolis: University of Minnesota Press, 1985).

4. Carol Gilligan, *In a Different Voice* (Cambridge, Mass.: Harvard University Press, 1982).

5. Marilyn Friedman and Margaret Urban Walker point out that there are two separate theses in Gilligan: that care and responsibility moral reasoning is extremely sensitive to context and that the appropriate response is care and responsibility. See Marilyn Friedman, "Care and Context in Moral Reasoning," in Eva Kittay and Diana Meyers, eds., *Women and Moral Theory* (Totowa, N.J.: Rowman and Littlefield, 1987) and Margaret Urban Walker, "What Does the Different Voice Say?: Gilligan's Women and Moral Philosophy," *Journal of Value Inquiry* 23 (1989): 123–134.

6. Starhawk, *Dreaming the Dark* (Boston: Beacon, 1989) 44.

7. Richard Schubert, one of my creative and courageous colleagues, gives such assignments.

8. See my "The Random Collective as a Moral Agent" for a further discussion of collective action and obligation. *Social Theory and Practice* 11 (Spring 1985): 97–105.

9. Alasdair McIntyre, following Aristotle, made much of this notion of role responsibility. See *After Virtue.* See also Virginia Held, *Rights and Goods* (New York: Free Press, 1984).

10. Noddings makes much of the requirement that caring requires an ongoing relationship. It is on this basis that she denies that we can have an obligation to care for the starving children in Africa, and animals. In an October 1988 talk to the Society for Women in Philosophy, she allowed that caring for does not exhaust our obligations, so we could have other obligations to the starving children in Africa. I would prefer to say that we have obligations to care for the starving children and animals, but that not all caring obligations require direct care.

11. MacIntyre, *After Virtue,* 105.

12. We can see how one would defend morality by appeal to divine law, and why such an appeal might fail. The *Meno* is a good example of such an appeal.

13. Karl Marx, "On the Jewish Question," in T. B. Bottomore, ed., *Karl Marx: Early Writings* (New York: McGraw Hill, 1964).

14. Elizabeth Wolgast, *The Grammar of Justice* (Ithaca, N.Y.: Cornell University Press, 1987), chap. 1.

15. Allison Jaggar, *Feminist Politics and Human Nature* (Totowa, N.J.: Rowman & Allanheld, 1983) throughout, but see Chapter Three.

16. Ibid.

17. Noddings, *Caring,* 174.

18. Ibid., 104.

Continuing to Think

Even though I might be able to reason myself into doing you harm—because you are the "other," for instance—an ethic of care will not permit me to do so in good conscience. On the other hand, if you are in agony and ask my help in ending your life, I will respond to you as a caring self rather than relying on abstract principles. This is a lot less tidy than a system that prescribes, for example, that killing is always wrong.

Proponents of an ethic of care think it is also much more useful in a world as complex as our own. When trips to the moon and test-tube babies are commonplace occurrences, ethical demands may be a little less easy to articulate. This does not mean they are any less stringent, only that using rules or weighing pain and pleasure may no longer be sufficient or even particularly helpful.

Those who advocate an ethic of care also tend to be women, and this version of virtue theory is, in part, a response to views that regard caring as less sophisticated than adherence to abstract principles. Since women tend more toward the former and men more toward the latter, some women philosophers have felt it necessary to defend the validity of using care as a standard or measurement of ethical behavior. If we use care as our touchstone, they insist, we will make moral choices even when the rules are unclear or when a numerical analysis of how many would benefit versus how many would be harmed seems inadequate to inform our actions.

What we should be is caring selves. And if we cultivate this ideal in ourselves we will do the right thing—even if it is difficult to say in advance what that behavior will look like.

10.4   *The Moral Foundations of an African Culture*

KWASI WIREDU

Preparing to Read

When we step outside the Western world, we find little evidence of either consequentialist (utilitarian) or nonconsequentialist (duty) ethical theories. In fact, the next two selections seem to have more in common with modern virtue theory than with either of the two traditional positions. Like all ethical theory, that of the Akan people of West Africa is derived from their concept of human nature.

If people contain a spark of the divine, and if each person begins life with a strong sense of communal belonging, morality will, quite naturally, assume a respect for the dignity of each person and a feeling that we are all in this together. The image of the lone individual, struggling to make ethical choices in a hostile world, is a distinctly Western one.

In a matrilineal kinship system, in which immediate family are those who have the same grandmother, there are likely to be many beings in the first circle of obligation, which in the West tends to be the nuclear family of father, mother, children. One's place in such a web of relationships also implies obligations. There are things I owe my parents and siblings that I may not feel I owe to others outside my immediate family. Among the Akan people of Ghana (principally), that first ring of family may contain 25 or 30 people. In a larger sense, too, everyone in the community is also part of one organically connected system.

Coupled with a belief that each person carries a spark of the divine being, this communal identity motivates powerful ethical demands. Family and friends benefit, but so does the stranger, perceived as deprived of the nurturing that would normally be provided by his or her own kinship system.

Introduction

MORALITY IN THE STRICTEST SENSE is universal to human culture.[1] Indeed, it is *essential* to all human culture. Any society without a modicum of morality must collapse. But what is morality in this sense? It is simply the observance of rules for the harmonious adjustment of the interests of the individual to those of others in society. This, of course, is a minimal concept of morality. A richer concept of morality even more pertinent to human flourishing will have an essential reference to that special kind of motivation called the sense of duty. Morality in this sense involves not just the *de facto* conformity to the requirements of the harmony of interests, but also that conformity to those requirements which is inspired by an imaginative and sympathetic identification with the interests of others even at the cost of a possible abridgement of one's own interests. This is not a demand for a supererogatory altruism. But a certain minimum of altruism is absolutely essential to the moral motivation. In this sense too morality is probably universal to all human societies, though, most certainly, not to all known individuals.

The foregoing reflection still does not exclude the possibility of a legitimate basis for differentiating the morals of the various peoples of the world. This is so for at least three reasons. First of all, although morality in both of the senses just discriminated is the same wherever and whenever it is practiced, different peoples, groups and individuals have different understandings of it. The contrasting moral standpoints of humanism and supernaturalism, for example, illustrate this diversity. Secondly, the concrete cultural context in which a moral principle is applied may give it a distinctive coloring. Lastly, but most importantly, there is a broad concept of morals closely contiguous to the narrow one—which is what the two concepts of morality noted earlier on together amount to—in regard to which the contingencies of space, time and clime may play quite a constitutive role. This appertains to the domain that, speaking very broadly, may be called custom. In view here are such things as the prescriptions and proscriptions operative in a community regarding life and death, work and leisure, reward and retribution, aspirations and aversions, pleasure and pain, and the relationships between the sexes, the generations and other social categories and classes. The combined impact of such norms of life and thought in a society should give a distinctive impression of its morals.

Akan Humanism

But let me start with the manner of conceiving morals. African conceptions of morals would

From *Person and Community* by Kwasi Wiredu. Courtesy of Council for Research in Values and Philosophy.

seem generally to be of a humanistic orientation. Anthropological studies lend substantial support to this claim. Nevertheless, the accounts are not always philosophically inquisitive, and I prefer, in elaborating on this characterization, to rely on my own native knowledge of the life and thought of the Akans of Ghana.[2] On this basis, I can affirm the humanism in question more uninhibitedly. The commonest formulation of this outlook is in the saying, which almost any Akan adult or even young hopeful will proffer on the slightest provocation, that it is a human being that has value: *Onipa na ohia.* The English translation just given of the Akan saying, though pertinent, needs supplementation, for the crucial term here has a double connotation. The word "(o)hia" in this context means both that which is of value and that which is needed. Through the first meaning the message is imparted that all value derives from human interests and through the second that human fellowship is the most important of human needs. When this last thought is uppermost in consciousness an Akan would be likely to add to the maxim under discussion an elucidation to the effect that you might have all the gold in the world and the best stocked wardrobe, but if you were to appeal to these in the hour of need they would not respond; only a human being will. *(Onipa ne asem: mefre sika a, sika nnye so, mefre ntama a, ntama nmye so; onipa ne asem.)* Already beginning to emerge is the great stress on human sociality in Akan thought, but before pursuing this angle of the subject let me tarry a while on the significance of Akan humanism.

One important implication of the founding of value on human interests is the independence of morality from religion in the Akan outlook: What is good in general is what promotes human interests. Correspondingly, what is good in the more narrowly ethical sense is, by definition, what is conducive to the harmonization of those interests. Thus, the will of God, not to talk of that of any other extra-human being, is logically incapable of defining the good. On the Akan understanding of things,

indeed, God is good in the highest; but his goodness is conceptually of a type with the goodness of a just and benevolent ancestor, only in his case quality and scale are assumed to be limitless. The prospect of punishment from God or some lesser being may concentrate the mind on the narrow path of virtue, but it is not this that creates the sense of moral obligation. Similarly, the probability of police intervention might conceivably give pause to a would-be safe breaker, though if he or she had any sense of morals at all it would not be thanks to the collective will of the police or even the state.

This conceptual separation of morals from religion is, most likely, responsible in some measure for the remarkable fact that there is no such thing as an institutional religion in Akan culture. The procedures associated with the belief in sundry extra-human beings of varying powers and inclinations, so often given pride of place in accounts of African religions, are in fact practical utilitarian programs for tapping the resources of this world. The idea, in a nutshell, is that God invested the Cosmos with all sorts of potentialities, physical and quasi-physical, personal and quasi-personal, which human beings may bend to their purposes, if they learn how. Naturally, in dealing with beings and powers believed to be of a quasi-personal character, certain aspects of behavior patterns will manifest important analogies to the canons of ordinary human interactions. For example, if you wanted something from a being of superhuman repute who is open to persuasion mixed with praise, pragmatic common sense alone would recommend an attitude of demonstrative respect and circumspection and a language of laudatory circumlocution reminiscent of worship, but the calculative and utilitarian purpose would belie any attribution of a specifically religious motivation. In fact, the Akans are known to be sharply contemptuous of "gods" who fail to deliver; continued respect is conditional on a high percentage of scoring by the Akan reckoning.

In total contrast to the foregoing is the Akan attitude to the Supreme Being, which is one of unconditional reverence and absolute trust. Absent here is any notion that so perfect a being requires or welcomes institutions for singing or reciting his praises. Nor, relatedly, are any such institutions felt to be necessary for the dissemination of moral education or the reinforcement of the will to virtue. The theater of moral upbringing is the home, at parents' feet and within range of kinsmen's inputs. The mechanism is precept, example and correction. The temporal span of the process is lifelong, for, although upbringing belongs to the beginning of our earthly careers, the need for correction is an unending contingency in the lives of mortals. At adulthood, of course, as opposed to earlier stages in life, moral correction involves discourses of a higher level and may entail, besides the imposition of compensatory obligations (of which more later); but, at all stages, verbal lessons in morality are grounded in conceptual and empirical considerations about human well-being. All this is why the term "humanistic" is so very apt as a characterization of Akan moral thinking. At least in part, this is why it is correct to describe that ethic as non-supernaturalistic in spite of the sincere belief in a Supreme Being.

In so far, then, as the concept of religion is applicable to the Akan outlook on life and reality, it can refer only to the belief and trust in the Supreme Being. In this respect, Akan religion is purely intellectual. In this respect too it is purely personal, being just a tenet of an individual's voluntary metaphysic, devoid of social entanglements. In truth, most Akans espouse that metaphysic as a matter of course. Akan conventional wisdom actually holds that the existence of God is so obvious that it does not need to be taught even to a child. (*Obi nkyere akwadaa Nyame.*) Nevertheless, skeptics are not unknown in Akan society, and a time-honored policy of peaceful laissez faire extends to them as to all others in matters of private persuasion.

Defining Morality

Morality too is intellectual, by Akan lights. Concrete moral situations in real life are frequently highly composite tangles of imponderables, and perceiving them in their true lineaments is a cognitive accomplishment in itself. So too is the sure grasping of first principles and their judicious application to the particulars of conduct. Morality is also personal, for in the last analysis the individual must take responsibility for his or her own actions. But surely morality is neither purely intellectual, for it has an irreducible passional ingredient, nor purely personal, for it is quintessentially social.

All these insights are encapsulated in various Akan maxims and turns of phrase. Recognition of the intellectual dimension of right conduct is evidenced in the Akan description of a person of ethical maturity as an *obadwenma*. This word means one possessed of high thinking powers. Literally, it says "child, thinking child", in other words, a thinking child of the species. The Akans are no less emphatic in their articulation of their sense of individual responsibility. According to a very popular proverb, it is because God dislikes injustice that he gave everyone their own name (thereby forestalling any misattribution of responsibility). Along with this clear sense of individual responsibility went an equally strong sense of the social reverberations of an individual's conduct. The primary responsibility for an action, positive or negative, rests with the doer, but a non-trivial secondary responsibility extends to the individual's family and, in some cases, to the environing community. This brings us to the social orientation of the Akan concept of a person. We will not be able to elaborate it fully in the present discussion, but a crucial consideration will be adduced here. It is that, for the Akans, a person is social not only because he or she lives in a community, which is the only context in which full development, or indeed any sort of human development is possible, but also because, by his original constitution, a human being is part of a social whole.

The underlying doctrine is this. A person consists of three elements. One of these comes *directly* from God and is, in fact, a speck of the divine substance. This is the life principle. In virtue of this constituent all human beings are one; they are all members of the universal family of humankind whose head and spring is God. *Nipa nyinaa ye Nyame mma: obiara nnye asaase ba*. Literally: all human beings are the children of God; none is the child of the earth. The two remaining elements are more mundane in origin. There is what might be called the blood principle which derives from the mother and, somewhat more stipulatively, there is what might be called the charisma principle which comes from the father. The blood from the mother is what principally gives rise to a person's body. The biological input from the father is responsible for the degree of personal presence that each individual develops at the appropriate stage. (This is what I would like the license to call the individual's degree of charisma.) The ontological classification of these elements is not exactly straightforward. Suffice it to warn that the physical/spiritual dichotomy is unlikely to be a source of light in this connection. In any case, our interest here is in the social significance of those components.

Both the maternal and paternal contributions to the make-up of a person are the bases of membership in specific social units. The Akans being a matrilineal group, it is the blood principle that situates a person in the most important kinship unit, namely, the lineage or, more extensively, the clan. Through the charisma principle one is a member of a grouping on the father's side which, although largely ceremonial, is nevertheless the framework of a lot of goodwill.

The point now is that, on this Akan showing, a person has a well-structured social identity even before birth. Thus, when an Akan maxim points out that when a human being descends from on high he or she alights in a town *(se onipa siane fi soro a obesi kuro mu)* the idea is that one comes into a community in which one already has well defined social affiliations. But society presupposes rules, and moral rules are the most essential of these. Since all rules have their rationale, a question that challenges the ethical imagination, especially one thoroughly impregnated with visions of the ineluctable so-ciality of human existence, is: What is the rationale of moral rules? Among the Akans some of the most profound philosophic conceptions are expressed by way of art motifs, and a celebrated answer to this question is offered in one such construct of fine art: a crocodile with one stomach and two heads locked in combat. Lessons: (1) Although human beings have a core of common interests, they also have conflicting interests that precipitate real struggles. (2) The aim of morality, as also derivatively of statesmanship, is to harmonize those warring interests through systematic adjustment and adaptation. The one stomach symbolizes not only the commonality of interests, but also a natural basis for the possibility of a solution to the existential antinomy.

Two levels of solution are distinguishable, corresponding to a distinction foreshadowed in our opening paragraph. There is the level of prudence or enlightened self-interest and there is that of pure moral motivation. Both species of thought and intention may be equally adapted to securing the social good, the first through cool and calm ratiocination, the second through both rational reflection and human sympathy. But they evoke different appraisals from people of goodwill. There will always be something unlovable about correctness of conduct bereft of passion. A Ghanaian comedian puts it even more strongly. Speaking with a deliberately unidiomatic bombast, he opines: "Ability without sentimentality is nothing short of barbarity." Nevertheless, it appears that teachers of morals everywhere have tended to find prudential considerations more psychologically efficacious in moral persuasion than abstract appeals to goodwill. Certainly, Akan ethical reflection does not stay immobile at this level of ethics, but Akan discourse abounds in prudential maxims. Here are a few.

1. If you do not allow your neighbor to reach nine you will never reach ten. *(Woamma wo yonko antwa nkrong a worentwa edu.)*

2. Somebody's troubles have arrived; those of another are on the way. *(Obi de aba; obi de nam kwan so.)*

3. It is a fool that says, "My neighbor is the butt of the attack not me." *(Kwasea na ose, "Ye de meyonko. yenne me.")*

4. The stick that was used to beat Takyi is the same that will be used to beat Nyanko-mago. *(Abaa a yede boo Takyi no aa na ye de bebo Nyankomago.)*

5. One person's path will intersect with another's before too long. *(Obi Kwan nkye na asi obi de mu.)*

That Akan ethics transcends this level of moral understanding is evident from other parts of their corpus of moral sayings. I will comment here on one particularly instructive form of moral expostulation. To a person whose conduct betrays obliviousness to the interests of others it is said, "Sticking into your neighbor's flesh, it might just as well be sticking into a piece of wood" *(Etua woyonko ho a etua dua mu),* than which there can scarcely be a lower rating for a person's moral stature. On this reading of morals, the ultimate moral inadequacy consists in that lack of feeling which is the root of all selfishness. The implied imperative is: "In all interpersonal situations put yourself into the skin of the other and see if you can contemplate the consequences of your proposed action with equanimity." If we call the recommended frame of mind sympathetic impartiality, we may elicit from the Akan maxim under discussion the view that sympathetic impartiality is the first principle of all morals. This principle is the logical basis of the golden rule, or the obverse of it that is frequently heard in Akan ethical talk, namely, "Do not do onto others what you would not that they do onto you." *(Nea wo yonko de ye wo a erenye wo de no mfa nye no.)* More literally: What you would not find acceptable if it were done to you by another, do not do to him or her. To be sure, this does not sound, even in our vernacular, as epigrammatic as the normal run of Akan apothegms, but it provides, nonetheless, a solid foundation for the definition of moral worth in its most edifying sense.

Ethics and Practice

The foregoing account of the Akan perspective on moral first principles, however brief, must form the basis of our next question, which is: "In what basic ways do the Akans endeavor to translate their ethical understanding into practical fact?" In this regard the single most important consideration concerns the depth of the Akan sense of what we have called the sociality of human existence. Morality is, of course, necessarily social. Hence any group of humans that can be credited with any sense of morals at all—surely, a most minimal species credential—will have some sense of human sociality. But in the consciousness of moral humankind there is a finely graduated continuum of the intensity of this feeling which ranges, in an ascending order, from the austerely delimited social sympathies of rigorous individualism to the pervasive commitment to social involvement characteristic of communalism. It is a commonplace of anthropological wisdom that African social organization manifests the last type of outlook. Akan society is eminently true to this typology.

What this means, more amply, is that Akan society is of a type in which the greatest value is attached to communal belonging. And the way in which a sense of communal belonging is fostered in the individual is through the concentrated stress on kinship identity already adumbrated in our earlier allusions to the Akan concept of a person. Not only is there what might perhaps be called an ontological basis for this identity in terms of the constituents of personhood, but there is also a distinct normative layer of a profound social significance in that concept. Thus conceived, a human person is essentially the center of a thick set of concentric circles of obligations and responsibilities matched by rights and privileges revolving round levels of relationships irradiating from the consanguinity of household kith and kin, through the "blood" ties of lineage and clan, to the wider circumference of human familihood based on the common possession of the divine spark.

In consequence of this character of the Akan concept of a person, habitual default in duties and responsibilities could lead to a diminution in one's status as a person in the eyes of the community. Not, of course, that becoming less and less of a person implies being thought more and more unworthy of human rights. On the contrary, there is a strong sense of the irreducibility of human dignity in Akan thought. However socially inept an individual may be, he or she still remains a being begotten of a direct gift of God incarnated through the intimacy of man and woman. He or she remains, in other words, a human being and as such is deserving of a certain basic respect and sympathy. Indeed, as soon as confirmed social futility begins to look pathologically chronic, animadversion quickly turns into solicitude, and any previous efforts in hortatory correction or in the application of more concrete sanctions are redirected towards rehabilitation, usually with the aid of indigenous specialists in bodily and mental health.

Nevertheless, any Akan steeped in the culture or even just sensitive to surrounding social norms constantly watches and prays lest he or she be overtaken by the specter of loss of personhood (in any degree). More positively and also more optimistically, every cultivated Akan (*Okaniba*) sees life as a scenario of continual striving after personhood in ever increasing dimensions. The details of this life mission, so to speak, will also be the details of the Akan vision of the ethical life. We must here content ourselves with only broad outlines. But before going on let us note that since two paragraphs ago our focus has been on ethics or morals in the sense in which morality is a matter of *mores* rather than of the categorical imperative or even of the less hallowed canons of prudence.

What, then, in its social bearings, is the Akan ideal of personhood? It is the conception of an individual who through mature reflection and steady motivation is able to carve out a reason-

ably ample livelihood for self, "family" and a potentially wide group of kin dependents, besides making substantial contributions to the well-being of society at large. The communalistic orientation of the society in question means that an individual's image will depend rather crucially upon the extent to which his or her actions benefit others than himself, not, of course, by accident or coincidence but by design. The implied counsel, though, is not one of unrelieved self-denial, for the Akans are well aware that charity further afield must start at home. More pertinently, they are apt to point out that one cannot blow a horn on an empty stomach. (*Yede ayaase na ehyen aben.*) Still an individual who remained content with self-regarding successes would be viewed as so circumscribed in outlook as not to merit the title of a real person.

Opportunities for other-regarding exertions in Akan society were legion in the past and remain so even now. By the very nature of the traditional economy, which was predominantly agricultural and based on individual self-employment, public works had, as a rule, to be done by voluntary communal labor. Habitual absences or malingering or half-hearted participation marked an individual down as a useless person (*onipa hunu*) or, by an easily deduced Akan equation, a non-person (*onye onipa*). In contemporary Ghana (and Ivory Coast), where the Akans live, much of the public works are financed out of mandatory taxes and carried out by professionals with hired labor. Nevertheless, in the villages and small towns a significant portion of such work is still done by way of voluntary communal labor and a good proportion also through voluntary contributions of money and materials.

Some Contemporary Problems

Here comes a contemporary complication: with the growth of commerce and industry, including the industry of modern politics, a non-negligible number of Akans have become very rich. In the Akan manner, they make voluntary contributions of unprecedented magnitudes to their communities; and the communities, for their part, reciprocate in fine eulogistic style and lionize them in other ways too, as is traditional. So far so good except for the following circumstance. Some of these rich people are known to have come by their assets through debatable techniques of acquisition. The unfortunate effects of this situation on the ideals of the young constitute some of the more intractable problems generated by the impact of industrialization on the Akan traditional ethic.

Another aspect of Akan communalism imperiled by modern conditions, through atrophy rather than adulteration, is the practice of neighborhood mutual aid. This practice had its foundation deep in the Akan conception of values. It is relevant here to recall the Akan adage: *Onipa na ohyia* quoted early in this discussion. It was interpreted as affirming, through the semantic fecundity of the word *hyia,* both that human interest is the basis of all value and that human fellowship is the most important of human needs. The concept of *Hyia* in the context of that adage is, in fact, a veritable mine of ethical meanings. In that context it also bears the seeds of another fundamental thought in the Akan philosophy of life, which is made explicit in the maxim: *Onipa hia moa,* meaning, by way of first approximation, "a human being needs help." The intent of the maxim, however, is not just to observe a fact, but also to prescribe a line of conduct. The imperative here is carried by the word *'hia,'* which in this context also has a connotation of entitlement: A human being deserves, ought, to be helped.

This imperative is born of an acute sense of the essential dependency of the human condition. The idea of dependency may even be taken as a component of the Akan conception of a person. "A human being" says a noted Akan proverb, "is not a palm tree so as to be self-sufficient": *Onipa nye abe na ne ho ahyia ne ho.* Indeed, at birth, a human being is not only not self-sufficient but also radically self-insufficient, if one may be permitted the expression: he or she is totally dependent on others.

In due course, through growth and acculturation, acquired skills and abilities will reduce this dependency but will never eliminate it completely. Self-reliance is, of course, understood and recommended by the Akans, but its very possibility is predicated upon this ineliminable residue of human dependency. Human beings, therefore, at all times, in one way or another, directly or indirectly, need the help of their kind.

One very standard situation in Akan life in which this truth was continually illustrated was in traditional agriculture. As hinted earlier, this was generally based on small holdings worked by individual farmers and their households. In such a mode of production recurrent stages were easily foreseeable at which the resources of any one farmer would be insufficient to accomplish with the required dispatch a necessary task—be it the initial clearing of the ground or the scooping out of, say, cocoa beans from great heaps of pods. In such moments all that was necessary was for one to send word to one's neighbors indicating the time, place and the nature of help needed. Very much as day follows night the people would assemble at the right time at the indicated place with their own implements of work and together help get the job done speedily and almost with festive enthusiasm, in full and warranted conviction that when their turn came the same gesture would be returned in exactly the same spirit. Anybody who availed himself of the benefits of this system and yet dragged his feet when the call came from others was liable to be convicted, at the bar of public opinion, of such fathomless degeneracy as to be branded a social outcast. The type of mutual aid here discussed probably occurs in varying intensities in rural communities all over the world, but in traditional Akan society it was so much and so palpably a part of working experience that the Akans actually came to think of life (*obra*) as one continuous drama of mutual aid (*nnoboa*). *Obra ye nnoboa:* Life is mutual aid, according to an Akan saying.

In recent times, however, amidst the exigencies of urbanization and the increasing—if not as yet preponderant—commercialization of agriculture, the ideology of mutual aid is losing some of its hold; and the spirit of neighborhood solidarity, though by no means extinguished, is finding fewer sweeping avenues of expression. It has not escaped some leaders of opinion that the traditional ethos of mutual aid might profitably be channelled into a strong movement of modern cooperatives, but as yet organized effort in this direction is halting in momentum and paltry in results.

Nevertheless, in countless small ways the sense of human solidarity continues to manifest itself quite pervasively in the daily life of the Akans and of the peoples of Ghana generally, of whom these moral characterizations remain true, if not to the letter, then at least to the syllable. Happily too, the threat of individualism posed by urbanization has not as yet proved unduly deleterious to this national trait. Thus, even now a Ghanaian on the countryside or in a large city, coming upon another human being, Ghanaian or foreigner, in some difficulty, will go well out of his way to help. As far as he or she is concerned, the bad person is exactly the one who would walk off on the excuse of some pressing business. Of course, if urbanization and other apparent concomitants of modernization are not controlled with conscious and rational planning based on the humane sensitivities of the communalistic ethic, then this fund of automatic good will dry up and African life will experience increasingly the Hobbesian rigors of a single-minded commercialism.

Kinship and Morality

The allusion to foreigners in the last paragraph prompts a further observation. The sense of human solidarity which we have been discussing works particularly to the advantage of foreigners, who, in the deeply felt opinion of the Akans, are doubly deserving of sympathy; on grounds, first, of their common humanity and, second, of their vulnerability as individuals cut off for the time being, at any rate, from the emotional and material supports of their kinship environment. Accordingly, when some time ago an Akan guitarist and lyricist, Kwabena Onyina, sang *Akwantu mu sem: Akwantufo ye mmobo* (Think of the woes of travel: the plight of a traveller is rueful) he struck a sympathetic cord at the deepest reaches of the Akan consciousness. Gratified visitors to Ghana have often been quick to acknowledge the benefits accruing.

Again, to pursue an allusion in the preceding paragraph: the notion of kinship support just mentioned is of the highest importance in the Akan communal set-up, for it is the basis of the sense of belonging which gives the individual much of his psychological stability. (This, incidentally, is why a traveller bereft of it struck the Akan so much as a hardship case.) It was also, *conversely,* the basis of a good proportion of the obligations in terms of which his moral standing was assessed. The smallest and the most intimate Akan kinship unit is the matrilineal household. This includes a person's mother and his mother's children, his mother's sisters and brothers, the children of the mother's sisters and, at the top, the grandmother. It is instructive to observe that the English words "aunt" and "cousin" fail to capture the depth of kinship feelings corresponding to the relations of mother's sister and mother's sister's children respectively, in spite of their mechanical correctness as translations. In the Akan language the words for mother and mother's children are the same as for mother's sisters and mother's sister's children. Since the relationships noted already comprehend quite a sizable community, especially if the grandmother concerned has been even averagely fertile, this guarantees that in the traditional setting an Akan child begins life with quite a large sense of belonging and a broad sweep of sympathies.

The next extension of the circle of the kinship relations just described brings us to the level of the lineage. Here the *basic* unit consists of a person's grandmother and her children and grandchildren together with the grandmother's brothers and sisters and the children and grandchildren of her sisters. This unit quickly swells up with the culturally legitimate addition of grandmother's maternal "cousins" and their descendants. From the point of view of a person's civic existence, this is the most significant circle of relations, for it was through the head of the lineage that, in traditional times, a person had his political representation. The lineage, as can easily be imagined, is a quite considerable group of people, but it is small in comparison with the maximal limit of kinship grouping, which is the set of all the people descending from one woman. The latter is the clan. For a quick idea of magnitude, consider that the Akans, now numbering in the region of seven million, trace their collective ancestry to seven women. Patently, individual Akans will never know all their relatives, but they can rest assured that they have a million of them.

For many practical purposes, however, it is the household and (basic) lineage circles of relations that have the most significance in terms of informal rights and obligations. Two illustrations must suffice here. Adult members of the lineage may be called upon each to make financial contributions to rescue one of the fold fallen on hard times, say, threatening insolvency. In view of the powers of arithmetic, this did not necessarily take a heavy toll of individual pockets. Moreover, it was not lost upon the reflective individual that he or she might conceivably have been the beneficiary.

The next illustration has to do with a lugubrious subject matter. Bereavement is one of the severest trials of the human psyche; unfortunately, it is recurrent. By both precept and practice Akan traditional culture engages itself, pre-eminently, one might even say, with finding ways to soothe lacerated emotions in such crises. The lineage system incorporates in its arrangements just such a mechanism. In full operation everyone in the lineage is expected to play his part by word, song, dance and material resource. Nor does the culture leave this to the lineage alone. Friends, neighbors and even indirect acquaintances can always be counted upon to help in various ways to lighten the burden of

sorrows. The framework for all this is the quite elaborate system of the Akan funeral. In spite of the excesses to which this institution has become subject through the rising tide of commercialism and egotistical exhibitionism, it remains an avenue for the expression of human solidarity at its most heartfelt depth. Proper participation thereto is, in Akan eyes, contributory proof of real personhood.

Conclusion

It is clear from the foregoing that socialization in the broad context of the lineage can be a veritable school for morality in its Akan acceptation. It is through the kinship channels of the lineage set-up that the Akan sense of the sociality of human beings finds its most natural expression. Moral life in the wider community is only an extension of a pattern of conduct inculcated at the lineage level. The fundamental values, some of which we have already outlined above, are the same on the two planes, and may be briefly summarized. A communalistic orientation will naturally prize social harmony. A characteristic Akan, and, as it seems, African way of pursuing this ideal is through decision-making by consensus rather than by majority opinion. In politics—traditional African politics, not the modern travesties rampant on the continent—this leads to a form of democracy very different from the Western variety.

A thoroughgoing consensual approach to social issues can be expected to lead to corresponding procedures in other areas of social life too. A particularly interesting case relates to the Akan reaction to wrong doing. Though the retributive spirit is not totally absent from reactions, especially at the state level, to some forms of wrong doing, the predominant tendency is to seek compensation or reconciliation or, in cases where extra-human forces are thought to be estranged, purification. I abstain from using the word "punishment" in this context advisedly, for given this last remark it may well be that there is no unproblematic rendition of this notion in the Akan conceptual framework. I cannot, however, pursue this question here.

A well-known feature of Akan morals is respect for age. This is intelligible not only from the fact that we are dealing with a society strongly based on kinship relations, which are naturally patterned into hierarchies based on age, but also because in traditional societies, which in part Akan society still remains, age is associated with knowledge, experience and wisdom.

Akan moral thinking in regard to sex and marriage also deserves special mention. Here the humanistic and the communalistic aspects of the Akan outlook come into play with interesting results. Because only empirical considerations bearing on human interests are admitted in moral evaluation, such unconditional proscriptions of pre-marital sex as are found in Christian teaching are absent from the moral rules of the Akans. From their point of view, it would be irrational to stop a prospective couple from seeking full knowledge of each other, moral, psychological, sexual and so on. There is, of course, no sexual free-for-all; but, still, a non-furtive relationship between an unmarried man and an unmarried woman need not be restricted to hugging. The only proviso is that it should be above board. On the other hand, the high value placed on reproductive fertility in a communalistic society based on single-family-unit agriculture will predictably lead to the greatest emphasis being placed on the desirability of marriage and procreation. So much is this the case that being married with children well raised is part of the necessary conditions for personhood in the normative sense. A non-marrying, non-procreative person, however normal otherwise—not to talk of a Casanova equivalent—can permanently forget any prospect of this type of recognition in traditional Akan society. The only conceivable exceptions will be ones based on the noblest of alternative life commitments.

To understand all these facts about the Akan conception of morals is not necessarily to understand the culture in its entirety, but it is to have some sense of its foundations.

NOTES

1. This paper was originally presented at the symposium on African-American Perspectives on Biomedical Ethics at the Center for Advanced Study of Ethics at Georgetown University, Washington, D.C., November, 1990.

2. The Akans are found in large areas of the southern and middle parts of Ghana and also in some parts of the Republic of Ivory Coast. They speak a family of intimately related languages whose most general name is Akan and account for something in the region of half the population of Ghana, which, by last count (1985) was about fourteen million. The Ashantis, Fantes, Akwapims, Akims, Denkyiras, Kwahus, Brongs, and Nzimas are all subgroups of the Akan family. The Akans have been the subject of some very famous anthropological, linguistic and philosophical studies by foreign and indigenous scholars. Of the foreign scholars the most famous are J. G. Christaller and R. S. Rattray. Christaller wrote the first detailed dictionary of the Akan language which he entitled *A Dictionary of the Asante and Fante Language Called Tshi (Chwee, Twi)*, (Basel: The Evangelical Society, [1881] 1933). Rattray made an intensive study of the Ashantis and wrote, among others, the following books. *Ashanti* (Oxford: Oxford University Press, 1923); *Religion and Art in Ashanti* (Oxford, 1927) and *Ashanti Law and Constitution* (Oxford, 1939). His *Ashanti Proverbs* (Oxford, 1916) was a translation and exegetical annotation of a selection from a collection of 3600 Akan proverbs that Christaller published in the vernacular in 1879. J. B. Danquah was the most celebrated of the indigenous students of Akan culture and his *The Akan Doctrine of God* is the best established classic of Akan philosophy. K. A. Busia also wrote an important treatise on the Ashanti political system and its underlying philosophy entitled *The Position of the Chief in the Modern Political System of Ashanti* (London: Frank Cass, 1968). W. E. Abraham's *The Mind of Africa* (Chicago: University of Chicago Press, 1962) and Kwame Gyekye's *An Essay on African Philosophical Thought* (New York: Cambridge University Press, 1987) are works by contemporary Akans continuing the Akan tradition of philosophy.

Continuing to Think

Like Kant, the Akan system begins with duty, but duty is defined in terms that more closely resemble the demands of modern virtue theory. If my duty is to recognize the inherent dignity of each person and to honor the kinship obligations that bind me to everyone in the community, my ethical ideal is very likely to be an ethic of care. And, the moral obligation to behave toward all humans in a caring way may, in fact, take a form very similar to Kant's Categorical Imperative—as the nonnegotiable and obvious-to-all standard of human behavior.

Accepting that each person contains a spark of the divine being creates special obligations to treat that person as one would treat the deity. Recognizing that I am not a lone individual, but the center of concentric circles of kinship and reciprocal responsibilities, puts a communal slant on my ethical posture. I am a member of a community of persons, each of whom I am obliged to honor, as they are obliged to honor me.

Think about our Western view of the person as a separate individual. Much of our ethics focuses on rights. If the social contract guarantees my life, liberty, and property, morality is likely to be seen in terms of protections and violations of those rights. If, as we saw in Chapter 1, the society is more communal, injustice might be thought of more in terms of "loss of joy" than loss of property. Damage to the fabric of society, through damage to the kinship network, might be perceived as just as immoral as damage to an individual seems in the West.

What have we gained and lost by emphasizing the individual over the community? Our technological progress has certainly been fueled by individualism, and we have perhaps the highest standard of living in the world. These are not to be taken lightly. Yet we may have sacrificed something in the quality of life. At its worst, Western individualism leads to the so-called "me" generation—give me what I want and to heck with society or anyone else. We may be seeking a happy medium.

10.5   *The Te of Piglet*

BENJAMIN HOFF

Preparing to Read

Taoism, a philosophy that originated in ancient China, affirms the interconnectedness of everything in an even more radical way. Like nature, it says, we are composed of various elements and everything is an expression of the Tao. As the center of the circle, the Tao is complete and cannot be spoken of. To speak of it is to particularize the Tao, to bring it into the world of the ten thousand things.

Before what Hoff calls the "Great Separation" of humans from the rest of nature, everything was naturally in harmony with the Tao or Way of the Universe. Just as the sun knows how to shine and when to relinquish its role in the heavens to the coolness of moonlight, humans once understood the principles of Taoism—Natural Simplicity, Effortless Action, Spontaneity, and Compassion.

Confucianism, with its principles of Righteousness, Propriety, Benevolence, Loyalty, Good Faith, Duty, and Justice, reflects post-Separation ethics. For Taoists, ethics or virtue lies in discarding whatever prevents harmony with Tao. The Chinese word *te* appears in two forms: combining the characters for "upright" and "heart," it can be translated as "virtue"; adding the character for "left foot," which means "stepping out," yields its second meaning, "virtue in action."

In the Winnie-the-Pooh stories, it is Pooh bear who understands the effortless simplicity of the Tao, but it is Piglet who undergoes the transformation from virtue to virtue that steps out. Hence, the book's title—*The Te of Piglet*.

THOUSANDS OF YEARS AGO, man lived in harmony with the rest of the natural world. Through what we would today call Telepathy, he communicated with animals, plants, and other forms of life—none of which he considered "beneath" himself, only different, with different jobs to perform. He worked side by side with earth angels and nature spirits, with whom he shared responsibility for taking care of the world.

The earth's atmosphere was very different from what it is now, with a great deal more vegetation-supporting moisture. A tremendous variety of vegetable, fruit, seed, and grain food was available. Because of such a diet, and a lack of unnatural strain, human life span was many times longer than what it is today. The killing of animals for food or "sport" was unthinkable. Man lived at peace with himself and the various life forms, whom he considered his teachers and friends.

But gradually at first, and then with increasing intensity, man's Ego began to grow and assert itself. Finally, after it had caused many unpleasant incidents, the consensus was reached that man should go out into the world alone, to learn a necessary lesson. The connections were broken.

On his own, feeling alienated from the world he had been created from, cut off from the full extent of its abundance, man was no longer happy. He began to search for the happiness he had lost. When he found something that reminded him of it, he tried to possess it and accumulate more—thereby introducing Stress into his life. But searching for lasting happiness and accumulating temporary substitutes for it brought him no satisfaction.

As he was no longer able to hear what the other forms of life were saying, he could only try to understand them through their actions, which he often misinterpreted. Because he was no longer cooperating with the earth angels and nature spirits for the good of all, but was attempting to manipulate the earth forces for his benefit alone, plants began to shrivel and die. With less vegetation to draw up and give off moisture, the planet's atmosphere became drier, and deserts appeared. A relatively small number of plant species survived, which grew smaller and tougher with passing time. Eventually they lost the radiant colors and abundant fruit of their ancestors. Man's life span began to shorten accordingly, and diseases appeared and spread. Because of the decreasing variety of food available to him—and his growing insensitivity—man began to kill and eat his friends the animals. They soon learned to flee from his approach and became increasingly shy and suspicious of human motives and behavior. And so the separation grew. After several generations, few people had any idea of what life had once been like.

As man became more and more manipulative of and violent toward the earth, and as his social and spiritual world narrowed to that of the human race alone, he became more and more manipulative of and violent toward his own kind. Men began to kill and enslave each other, creating armies and empires, forcing those who looked, talked, thought, and acted differently from them to submit to what they thought was best.

Life became so miserable for the human race that, around two to three thousand years ago, perfected spirits began to be born on earth in human form, to teach the truths that had largely been forgotten. But by then humanity had grown so divided, and so insensitive to the universal laws operating in the natural world, that those truths were only partially understood.

As time passed, the teachings of the perfected spirits were changed, for what one might call political reasons, by the all-too-human organizations that inherited them. Those who came into prominence within the organizations wanted power over others. They downplayed the importance of nonhuman life forms and eliminated from the teachings statements claiming that those forms had souls, wisdom, and divine presence—and that the heaven they were in touch with was a state of Unity with the Divine that could be attained by anyone who put aside his ego and followed the universal laws. The power-hungry wanted their followers to believe that heaven was a place to which some people—and only people—went after death, a place that could be reached by those who had the approval of *their* organizations. So not even the perfected spirits were able to restore the wholeness of truth, because of interference by the human ego.

Down through the centuries, accounts of the Great Separation, and of the Golden Age that ex-isted before it, have been passed on by the sensitive and wise. Today in the industrial West, they are classified as mere legends and myths—fantasies believed in by the credulous and unsophisticated, stories based only on imagination and emotion. Despite the fact that quite a few people have seen and communicated with earth angels and nature spirits, and that more than one spiritual community has grown luscious fruits and vegetables by cooperating with them and following their instructions, descriptions of these beings are generally dismissed as "fairy tales." And, although colored and simplified accounts of the Great Separation can be found in the holy books of the world's religions, it is doubtful that many followers of those religions strongly believe in them.

However, a number of pre-Separation skills, beliefs, and practices have been preserved. On the North American continent, they are passed on in some of what remains of native teachings—those of the "Indians." In Europe they have largely died out, but traces of their influence can still be seen in such comparatively recent phenomena as stone circles and the marking of "ley lines" (called "dragon veins" by the Chinese)—channels along which earth energy is concentrated. In Tibet, until the Communist invasion, ancient ways were preserved in Tibetan Buddhism, many of the secrets and practices of which predate Buddhism by thousands of years. In Japan, they can be found in some of the rituals and beliefs of the Shinto ("spirit way") folk religion. In China, they have been passed on through Taoism. And, despite violent opposition from China's Communist government, they continue to be passed on today.

Briefly, Taoism is a way of living in harmony with *Tao,* the Way of the Universe, the character of which is revealed in the workings of the natural world. Taoism could be called either a philosophy or a religion, or neither, since in its various forms it does not match up with Western ideas or definitions of either one.

In China, Taoism is what might be called the counterbalance of Confucianism, the codified, ritualized teachings of K'ung Fu-tse, or "Master

K'ung," better known in the West as Confucius. Although Confucianism is not a religion in the Western sense, it could be said to bear a certain resemblance to puritanical Christianity in its man-centered, nature-ignoring outlook, its emphasis on rigid conformity, and its authoritarian, No-Nonsense attitude toward life. Confucianism concerns itself mostly with human relations—with social and political rules and hierarchies. Its major contributions have been in the areas of government, business, clan and family relations, and ancestor reverence. Its most vital principles are Righteousness, Propriety, Benevolence, Loyalty, Good Faith, Duty, and Justice. Briefly stated, Confucianism deals with the individual's place within the group.

In contrast, Taoism deals primarily with the individual's relationship to the world. Taoism's contributions have been mostly scientific, artistic, and spiritual. From Taoism came Chinese science, medicine, gardening, landscape painting, and nature poetry. Its key principles are Natural Simplicity, Effortless Action, Spontaneity, and Compassion. The most easily noticed difference between Confucianism and Taoism is emotional, a difference in *feeling:* Confucianism is stern, regimented, patriarchal, often severe; Taoism is happy, gentle, childlike, and serene—like its favorite symbol, that of flowing water.

Taoism is classically viewed as the teachings of three men: Lao-tse ("Master Lao"), author of the major Taoist classic, the *Tao Te Ching,* which is said to have been written around twenty-five hundred years ago; Chuang-tse ("Master Chuang"), author of several works and founder of a school of writers and philosophers during the Warring States period, approximately two thousand years ago; and the semilegendary Yellow Emperor, who ruled over forty-five hundred years ago, and to whom are attributed various meditative, alchemical, and medicinal principles and practices. These three were the great organizers and communicators of Taoist thought, rather than its founders; for, as we have said, what is now known as Taoism began before any of them were born, in what Chuang-tse called the Age of Perfect Virtue. . . .

Continuing to Think

Although the concepts are Chinese, the ethical theory expressed in this selection may have a familiar ring for you. Currently, it goes by the name of bioethics, and it asks us to broaden the scope of our ethical understanding to include all the biosphere—other animals, plants, rivers—the environment itself.

If, in spite of the Great Separation, we are really interrelated with everything else, we must take all of it into account. Akan ethics and mestiza consciousness broaden the scope of our moral web to include all humans; here we embrace all of life. If it is unethical to kill and eat a fellow human, why is it okay to raise other animals under brutal conditions for their meat and fur? Can we pollute our streams without behaving unethically?

What we would have to give up is our exclusive claim to a unique status based on our human nature. What we stand to gain is a life of harmony and spontaneity. The first phase of **biocentric ethics** focused on the rights of companion animals. The second stage considers all of life and is sometimes described as environmental ethics. It is much more complicated to include all of life in your moral web, and it may be more satisfying to do so.

Hoff asks us to question how happy we really are with our Confucian attention to "social rules and hierarchies." In his view, it is time to bridge the gap created by the

Great Separation and return to a gentle serenity—to be more like flowing water, which happily goes around anything in its path, confronting nothing and seeking the path of least resistance. Water recognizes its unity with everything else even if we sometimes forget our own connections.

Summing Up the Readings

What are the boundaries of your own moral web? Whose interests must you consider when you decide to act? For many of us, the boundaries go no further than our own species. Kant's admonition to do our duty, by acting always so that we can will what we do to be universalized, takes only other humans into account. Jeremy Bentham, the founder of utilitarianism, extended his moral web to include all who can suffer. Clearly, this brings at least some other animals into the group whose pleasures and pains must be considered when we calculate the greatest good in the world at large. Living on the borderlands, as Gloria Anzaldúa recommends, offers a a unique stand-point for humanizing the "other." By broadening and deepening our consciousness, we have an ethical perspective from which to heal divisions.

Shifting away from what we should do and toward how we should be brings us to an ethic of care. If we think of ourselves as living within a network of care, our obligations may be extended widely and our caring may not always follow rigid rules. Sometimes, we may feel challenged to promote the good of a single being, whether or not this benefits the world at large. Among the Akan of West Africa, everyone in the community occupies a privileged position, as members of a kinship system that is larger than our Western nuclear families. As possessors of a spark of the divine being, all people will deserve our respect and hospitality. And, this is also the goal of mestiza consciousness—to bring excluded individuals and groups back into the web of moral beings, whose welfare we must consider as we safeguard our own.

Taoism, with its vision of interconnectedness, radically expands our moral web. In its vision, virtue lies in harmony; its opposite is disharmony or separation. Most highly prized is virtue in action. As in some Native American traditions, humans do not have the arrogance to think themselves the only valued species, and there is a general sense that we can learn from other life forms, including other animals, trees, even apparently inert objects like stones that have lived on earth longer than any of us.

Continuing to Question

1. If you were to treat all people always as ends in themselves (as Kant suggests) and never merely as means to your own ends, what might you have to avoid doing?

2. If no person may be labeled "other," how would our ethical decision making shift? What kinds of actions are possible only when their object is the "other"?

3. Try to think of a situation in which your "caring self" might choose to act differently from your "rational self." In this case, which action would be the path of virtue, and why would it qualify as such?

4. Think about your roommates, teammates, and sorority sisters or fraternity brothers. Ask yourself whether it makes more sense to think of moral choices in terms of this kind of community. Would you act in your own interest even if it meant hurting a trusted teammate or a wonderful roommate?

5. Does refusing to include other animals, trees, and even the environment itself in our moral web cut us off from those elements as Hoff suggests? Are we really connected only with those whose interests we feel obliged to consider in our own moral decision making?

Suggestions for Further Exploration

FICTION (INCLUDING FILMS)

Atwood, Margaret, *The Handmaid's Tale*—New York: Ballantine, 1987. In a future society women are kidnapped, brainwashed, and forced to have sex and bear children as surrogates for infertile wives. The film is also pretty good.

Boom, Ben, *Multiple Man*—Indianapolis: Bobbs-Merrill, 1976. When several clones of the U.S. president are found dead, no one is sure whether the original or a copy is occupying the oval office.

Camus, Albert, *The Stranger*—Lanham, Md.: University Press of America, 1982. A French Algerian shoots an Arab on the beach for no real reason but accepts responsibility for his action in this dark, existentialist novel of absurdity and alienation.

Cook, Robin, *Coma*—New York: Little, Brown, 1977. Vital organs are removed from patients who have deliberately been rendered comatose. Also a film.

Flatliners—In this movie, some bright medical students simulate death to find out "what's on the other side" but learn that they have brought bad karma from their own pasts into the present and must set things right before being able to move on.

Keneally, Thomas, *Schindler's List*—New York: Simon & Schuster, 1982. This is actually a nonfiction novel about a not-very-admirable character (the hard-drinking, womanizing, war-profiteering Oskar Schindler of the title) who does an admirable thing (risks everything as a member of the Nazi party by saving the lives of Jews). The film was a critical and box office success.

Levin, Ira, *The Boys from Brazil*—New York: Random House, 1976. Inept neo-Nazis clone several Hitlers but cannot replicate the evil of the original because they fail to replicate the real Hitler's early life experiences. Also a film.

Sartre, Jean-Paul, *No Exit*—New York: Knopf, 1947. In this play three people realize they are dead and discover that torturers will be unnecessary since they will torture each other eternally. Hell, it seems, is other people.

Sartre, Jean-Paul, "The Victors." In *Three Plays*—New York: Knopf, 1949. "The Victors" is a play about the moral dilemma of six French Resistance fighters who strangle the youngest in their group after he reveals that he will "tell all" rather than be tortured. One of the rebels is the boy's sister.

Sartre, Jean-Paul, "The Wall." In *The Wall and Other Stories*—trans. Lloyd Alexander. New York: New Directions, 1948. One prisoner inside the wall, seeking to protect another outside the wall, unwittingly betrays him.

Styron, William, *Sophie's Choice*—New York: Random House, 1979. A woman lives with the memory of a choice she was forced to make in Nazi Germany between the life of her son and the life of her daughter. A great movie.

Weldon, Fay, *The Cloning of Joanna May*—New York: Penguin, 1991. A man dumps his unfaithful wife but not before cloning her so he can produce a better version of her later on. Also a British TV miniseries.

NONFICTION

Bok, Sissela, *Lying: Moral Choice in Public and Private Life*—New York: Pantheon, 1978. Is it ever acceptable to lie in politics, medicine, research, and so on?

Bok, Sissela, *Secrets*—New York: Pantheon, 1983. Bok discusses the ethics of revealing and concealing secrets in journalism, government, police work, and so forth.

Camus, Albert, *The Rebel*—New York: Knopf, 1961. This book expresses the view that by creating value through rebellion, the rebel becomes part of humanity and creates values for everyone.

Kant, Immanuel, *Foundations of the Metaphysics of Morals*—Indianapolis: Bobbs-Merrill, 1969. Kant outlines the ethical foundations of the categorical imperative.

Kosko, Bart, *Fuzzy Thinking: The New Science of Fuzzy Logic*—New York: Hyperion, 1993. Kosko's book includes the application of fuzzy logic to such ethical puzzles as when life begins (at many different stages—to a certain degree).

Sartre, Jean-Paul, *Being and Nothingness*—New York: Washington Square, 1966. Sartre's *Being and Nothingness* is primarily a work of existential metaphysics; it describes the philosophical origins of the ethical condition known as "bad faith."

Glossary

aesthetic experience. the experience we have in the presence of the beautiful, which may lead to a kind of knowing

agnosticism. the philosophical position that whether God exists or not cannot be known

anthropomorphism. representing something nonhuman (such as animals or God) in human likeness

beginner's mind. according to Zen, the state of openness in which one can directly access the truth about what is

biocentric ethics. ethics that includes the entire bios, all of life, in its moral web

bodhisattva. in Buddhism, a wise and enlightened person who postpones nirvana to help others gain enlightenment

catharsis. emotional cleansing achieved by viewing tragic drama, according to Aristotle

civil disobedience. breaking of a civil law in protest by citing obedience to a higher law

conservative. one who values the preservation of established traditions

cosmological argument. an argument for the existence of God, based on the contingent nature of the physical world; developed by Aristotle and popularized in the Middle Ages by Aquinas

cosmology. the branch of metaphysics dealing with the study of the principles underlying the cosmos

deontological ethical theories. ethical theories that evaluate behavior in terms of adherence to duty or obligation regardless of consequences

empiricism. belief that meaningful knowledge can be acquired only through sense experience

enlightenment. the Buddhist term for realization that comes from seeing the world as it actually is

epistemology. the branch of philosophy dealing with the study of knowledge, what it is, and how we acquire it

ethic of care. ethical theory with some similarities to virtue ethics, which holds as an ideal the caring self

ethics. the branch of philosophy concerned with judgments about moral behavior and the meaning of ethical statements and terms

existentialism. emphasizes the uniqueness and freedom of the human person as an individual (what makes each life a unique, personal experience) as opposed to the essence of a human being (what makes all of us alike)

feminists. those who promote political, legal, economic, and social equality for women, in opposition to the structures of a patriarchal society

Forms. in Plato's ontology, intelligible ideas, the ultimate realities from which the world of objects has been patterned

idealism. in metaphysics, the belief that the most real entities are ideas and other immaterial entities

karma. in Hinduism and Buddhism, the principle that all actions operate according to causal laws and what I do to another I do to myself; sometimes this law is referred to as the law of sowing and reaping

liberal. one who believes in the primary importance of individual freedoms

materialism. in ontology, the belief that reality is essentially matter

metaphysics. the branch of philosophy investigating what is real

mystical experience. intuitive knowledge of a larger reality, based on personal experience that convinces the recipient of its accuracy

natural rights. rights, such as those to life, liberty, and property, with which an individual is born

natural theology. pursuit of knowledge of God using natural intelligence rather than supernatural revelation

nirvana. a state in which individuality is extinguished or the state of enlightenment in which all pain, suffering, mental anguish, and the need for successive rebirths disappear

ontological argument. a logical argument for the existence of God, based on the nature of thought, developed by Anselm and used by Descartes

ontology. the branch of metaphysics dealing with the study of being

philosophy. literally, the "love of wisdom"

postmodernism. the recognition that certainty and unitive truth are not possible because existence and reality are partial, inconsistent, plural, and multiple

pragmatism. in ontology, the belief that what is real is what works and predicts what is likely to happen next

sitting. the Zen practice of silent meditation, designed to quiet the mind

social contract. an agreement among citizens or between the ruler and the ruled that defines the rights and duties of each party

Sophist. teacher of practical applications for philosophy in early Greece

sovereignty. a term used to describe where political authority does or should reside

state. the ruling political power within defined borders

te. Chinese term meaning virtue in action

teleological argument. an argument for the existence of God, based on the design, order, and apparent purpose of the universe, developed by Aquinas and attacked by Hume

teleology. the theory that there is order and purpose in reality

theism. the belief that an omnipotent, omniscient, and personal God exists

theology. the rational organization of religious beliefs into a logical system

totalitarianism. political belief that the power to rule must be given exclusively to the state

utilitarianism. the theory that an action is right if it seeks to promote the greatest amount of happiness in the world at large

virtual reality. computer-generated reality that is fully interactive for the participant

warrant. the evidence or justification for a truth claim

yin and **yang.** the complementary principles through which the *Tao* is expressed; *yin* reflects receptivity and being, whereas *yang* reflects activity and doing